Lecture Notes in Artificial Intel

Edited by J. G. Carbonell and J. Siekmann

T0238166

Subseries of Lecture Notes in Computer Science

Springer
Berlin
Heidelberg
New York
Barcelona
Hong Kong
London
Milan
Paris
Tokyo

Petra Perner   Azriel Rosenfeld (Eds.)

Machine Learning and Data Mining in Pattern Recognition

Third International Conference, MLDM 2003
Leipzig, Germany, July 5-7, 2003
Proceedings

 Springer

Series Editors

Jaime G. Carbonell, Carnegie Mellon University, Pittsburgh, PA, USA
Jörg Siekmann, University of Saarland, Saarbrücken, Germany

Volume Editors

Petra Perner
Institute of Computer Vision and Applied Computer Sciences
Arndtstr. 4, 04275 Leipzig, Germany
E-mail: ibaiperner@aol.com

Azriel Rosenfeld
University of Maryland, Center for Automation Research
College Park, Maryland 20742-3275, USA
E-mail: ar@cfar.umd.edu

Cataloging-in-Publication Data applied for

A catalog record for this book is available from the Library of Congress.

Bibliographic information published by Die Deutsche Bibliothek.
Die Deutsche Bibliothek lists this publication in the Deutsche Nationalbibliografie;
detailed bibliographic data is available in the Internet at <http://dnb.ddb.de>.

CR Subject Classification (1998): I.2, I.5, I.4, F.4,1, H.3

ISSN 0302-9743
ISBN 3-540-40504-6 Springer-Verlag Berlin Heidelberg New York

Springer-Verlag Berlin Heidelberg New York,
a member of BertelsmannSpringer Science+Business Media GmbH

http://www.springer.de

© Springer-Verlag Berlin Heidelberg 2003
Printed in Germany

Typesetting: Camera-ready by author, data conversion by DA-TeX, PTP-Berlin GmbH
Printed on acid-free paper   SPIN: 10929124   06/3142   5 4 3 2 1 0

Preface

The International Conference on Machine Learning and Data Mining (MLDM) is the third meeting in a series of biennial events, which started in 1999, organized by the Institute of Computer Vision and Applied Computer Sciences (IBaI) in Leipzig. MLDM began as a workshop and is now a conference, and has brought the topic of machine learning and data mining to the attention of the research community.

Seventy-five papers were submitted to the conference this year. The program committee worked hard to select the most progressive research in a fair and competent review process which led to the acceptance of 33 papers for presentation at the conference.

The 33 papers in these proceedings cover a wide variety of topics related to machine learning and data mining. The two invited talks deal with learning in case-based reasoning and with mining for structural data. The contributed papers can be grouped into nine areas: support vector machines; pattern discovery; decision trees; clustering; classification and retrieval; case-based reasoning; Bayesian models and methods; association rules; and applications.

We would like to express our appreciation to the reviewers for their precise and highly professional work. We are grateful to the German Science Foundation for its support of the Eastern European researchers. We appreciate the help and understanding of the editorial staff at Springer Verlag, and in particular Alfred Hofmann, who supported the publication of these proceedings in the LNAI series.

Last, but not least, we wish to thank all the speakers and participants who contributed to the success of the conference.

July 2003   Petra Perner and Azriel Rosenfeld

Co-chairs

Petra Perner — Institute of Computer Vision and Applied Computer Sciences IBaI Leipzig / Germany

Azriel Rosenfeld — University of Maryland / USA

Program Committee

Agnar Aamodt	NTNU / Norway
Horst Bunke	University of Bern / Switzerland
Terri Caelli	University of Alberta / Canada
Krzysztof Cios	University of Colorado / USA
Susan Craw	The Robert Gordon University / UK
Dragan Gamberger	Rudjer Boskovic Institute / Croatia
Lothar Gierl	University of Rostock /Germany
Howard J. Hamilton	University of Regina / Canada
Thomas S. Huang	University of Illinois / USA
Atsushi Imiya	Chiba University /Japan
Horace Ip	City University / Hong Kong
Brian Lovell	University of Queensland /Australia
Herbert Jahn	Aero Space Center / Germany
Donato Malerba	University of Bari / Italy
Ryszard Michalski	George Mason University / USA
Sethuraman Panch	Arizona State University / USA
Maria Petrou	University of Surrey / UK
Gabriella Sanniti di Baja	Istituto di Cibernetica / Italy
Fabio Roli	University of Cagliari / Italy
Michele Sebag	École Polytechnique / France
Arnold Smeulders	University of Amsterdam/ The Netherlands
Minerva Yeung	Intel Corporation / USA
Ari Visa	Tampere University / Finland
Patrick Wang	Northeastern University / USA
Harry Wechsler	George Mason University / USA
Sholom Weiss	IBM Yorktown Heights / USA

Additional Reviewers

Annalisa Appice
Margherita Berardi
Michelangelo Ceci
Mehmet Donderler
Liqiang Geng
Giorgio Giancinto
Giorgio Fumera
Frank Herrmann
Kamran Karimi
Wacek Kusnierczyk

John Langford
Francesca Alessandra Lisi
Daniel Oblinger
Thang Pham
Ricardo Vilalta
Xin Wang
Dietrich Wettschereck
Nirmalie Wiratunga
H.S. Wong
Hong Yao

Table of Contents

Case-Based Reasoning

Classification, Retrieval, and Feature Learning

Discovery of Frequently or Sequential Patterns

Bayesian Models and Methods

Association Rules Mining

Applications

Introspective Learning to Build Case-Based Reasoning (CBR) Knowledge Containers

Susan Craw

School of Computing, The Robert Gordon University
Aberdeen, Scotland, UK
S.Craw@comp.rgu.ac.uk
http://www.comp.rgu.ac.uk

Abstract. Case Based Reasoning systems rely on competent case knowledge for effective problem-solving. However, for many problem solving tasks, notably design, simple retrieval from the case-base in not sufficient. Further knowledge is required to help effective retrieval and to undertake adaptation of the retrieved solution to suit the new problem better. This paper proposes methods to learn knowledge for the retrieval and adaptation knowledge containers exploiting the knowledge already captured in the case knowledge.

1 Introduction

Case Based Reasoning (CBR) systems solve new problems by re-using the solutions to similar, previously solved problems. The main knowledge source for a CBR system is a database of previously solved problems and their solutions; the case knowledge. This retrieve-only approach is often suitable for classification problems where all solutions have been applied in the past, and where a sufficient sample of different problems with a given solution are easily available. But even with retrieve-only systems more detailed knowledge of the relevance of certain cases and the similarity of two problems may be needed. Retrieval knowledge may be needed to identify which features should be considered when determining relevance, what relative importances among features should be used when determining similarity. Furthermore, retrieval may not be sufficient, and the retrieved solution may need to be revised to reflect differences between the new and retrieved problems. This is particularly necessary for design problems where the database cannot contain all possible designs, and the re-used design is only an initial draft, which should be adapted to suit the new specification. Adaptation knowledge is required to capture the adaptations that should be applied and the circumstances in which they are needed. Case, retrieval and adaptation knowledge are three CBR knowledge containers proposed by Richter [10].

This paper describes an introspective approach to learning where the retrieval and adaptation knowledge is learned from the cases in the case knowledge. Such learning is knowledge-light since it does not demand further training data [12]. Implicit knowledge captured in the cases is exploited by utilising the

P. Perner and A. Rosenfeld (Eds.): MLDM 2003, LNAI 2734, pp. 1–6, 2003.

case knowledge as a source of training data, assuming that the case knowledge is a representative sample of the problem-solving domain. Smyth & McKenna [11] apply a similar approach when estimating the competence of a CBR system; competence is calculated from the individual cases in the case knowledge.

The following section briefly outlines relevant machine learning methods and related work in CBR. Section 3 summarises the retrieval and adaptation knowledge for case-based design and introduces our tablet formulation domain. Section 4 describes our GA method to optimise the decision tree index and k-NN retrieval by applying "leave-one-out" retrieval on the case knowledge data. This introspective approach is re-developed in Sect. 5 to create adaptation training data from which to learn various types of adaptation knowledge. Our findings are summarised in Sect. 6.

2   Related Work

Feature selection and weighting are important aspects of retrieval knowledge. These have been extensively studied in machine learning, with research for instance based learning being most relevant for CBR (e.g. [13]). Both Oatley et al. [9] and Bento & Gomez [4] use GAs to learn feature weighting for a CBR system. Each faces the problem that training data must be provided by the domain expert. We also use a GA but avoid the training data problem by generating it from the case knowledge.

Acquiring adaptation knowledge is a challenging problem tackled by several CBR researchers. Leake et al. [8] acquires adaptation cases from monitoring manual adaptation or the use of a rule-based repair theory. Case-based adaptation is applied where adaptation cases are retrieved and applied if possible, but when this fails a new adaptation case is learned from the expert's manual adaptation. This motivates our choice of CBR as one adaptation method. Hanney & Keane [5] apply a knowledge light approach similar to ours in which adaptation rules are induced from training data built from the case knowledge.

3   Learning Knowledge for Case-Based Design

Our knowledge acquisition tools are designed for a standard CBR model: a C4.5 decision tree index retrieves relevant cases from the case knowledge, a weighted average of feature value differences determines the similarity for a k-nearest neighbour retrieval, and some adaptation model seeks to recognise significant differences. Figure 1 illustrates the knowledge needed to form a fully-fledged CBR system and indicates that this is learned from the database of case knowledge.

Many of our experiments are based on the Tablet Formulation problem [1]. Given the physical and chemical properties of a drug and the dose to be delivered in a tablet, the task is to identify (from sets of inert excipients) a filler, binder, disintegrant, lubricant and surfactant, and the quantity of each, to enable the manufacture of a viable tablet. Formulation is a difficult design task since the

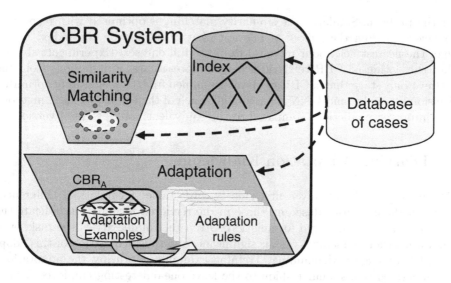

Fig. 1. From database to fully-fledged CBR system

excipients must balance the properties of the drug and are also constrained to provide a stable mixture.

4   Learning Retrieval Knowledge

Our model of CBR retrieval applies a C4.5 decision tree initially to select relevant cases. A leaf node does not predict the solution, but instead returns the training data (case knowledge) that was assigned to this node for subsequent similarity matching. The retrieval knowledge associated with indexing is the feature selection offered to C4.5, the feature weightings used to calculate information content, and the two pruning parameters for C4.5. The similarity knowledge is the feature weightings and k used by k-NN.

A simple GA wrapper is applied which searches the space of possible feature selections/weightings and parameter settings. Binary-valued genes represent feature selections and real-valued genes are used for feature weightings and parameter settings. The population of feature and parameter genes go through a standard cycle of mutation, reproduction and selection. For selection, we require a fitness function that estimates the retrieval quality of the CBR system with the particular feature selections/weightings and parameter settings. This is achieved using an exhaustive "leave-one-out" testing, where the selected case becomes the test problem and its desired solution, and the remaining cases form the case knowledge for a reduced CBR system. The average retrieval accuracy over all the case knowledge provides the fitness.

The advantage of this wrapper approach is that CBR retrieval as a whole is optimised. Thus the index is implicitly evaluated on its ability to retrieve relevant cases for the k-NN step, rather than its effectiveness in predicting a solution for the problem. Similarly, the similarity matching is optimised with respect to its selection from the subset of relevant cases identified by the index, rather than the nearest neighbour retrieval from the full dataset. Experiments showed that the optimised CBR retrieval achieved more accurate predictions from the retrieve-only stage than a CBR retrieval assembled from the separately optimised decision tree index and k-NN algorithm [6]. Each of the three optimised methods had improved predictions compared to the equivalent non-optimised version.

5   Learning Adaptation Knowledge

Retrieve-only CBR is only a first step towards tablet formulation. Differences between the new drug/dose and those in the retrieved formulation indicate the need to refine the retrieved formulation. Given the complexity of the task, even the formulation refinement task is significant, and thus acquisition of this adaptation knowledge is demanding. Training examples capturing the adaptations are generated in a similar fashion to the leave-one-out testing employed for the GA fitness function. Rather than simply calculating accuracy, an adaptation example is constructed from the differences between the problem part and solution of the test case and the retrieved case, together with the test problem. This adaptation example captures the solution adaptation that is required, and the differences from the retrieved case that triggered this refinement. Several adaptation examples can be generated for a selected leave-one-out test case, because several retrieved cases can each be the basis for an adaptation case.

The knowledge captured in adaptation cases can be exploited in several ways to generate useful adaptation knowledge. One approach in Fig. 1 is to build an adaptation CBR system CBR_A where CBR retrieval is applied to the adaptation training examples as case knowledge. Tablet formulation experiments showed that, for some components in the formulation task, CBR_A improved the predictions of retrieve-only formulation [7]. However, one of the important components (filler) continued to be difficult, whilst other components achieved good prediction with an optimised retrieve-only approach.

In a different approach in Fig. 1, CBR_A's retrieval was generalised by inducing rules from the adaptation examples. In addition to C4.5 rule induction we also applied an algorithm that combines induction and instance-based learning RISE [2]. We extended both basic algorithms to incorporate boosting, a technique that improves learning in tasks that exhibit varying degrees of difficulty [3]. The adaptation training examples were expanded by considering different adaptation actions to replace the labels in adaptation examples. Boosted C4.5 and RISE were applied to each subset of adaptation examples, thereby generating a set of adaptation "experts" each concentrating on a different type of adaptation. These adaptation experts were applied as a committee where the predicted adaptations entered a vote, and the winning adaptation was applied [14].

Tablet formulation has several problem-solving subtasks and each has slightly different adaptation requirements. We found that a committee of experts works well in general, but that some formulation subtasks are best adapted using boosted C4.5 experts, whilst RISE's instance-based approach is better for others. Nevertheless, the committee based approach was found to overcome the shortcomings of the case-based adaptation for the demanding formulation tasks.

6   Conclusions

The importance of case knowledge is obvious, and part of the popularity of CBR is that case knowledge is often reasonably straightforward to acquire. But for some types of problem-solving, in particular design, effective retrieval and adaptation knowledge is also essential. Knowledge acquisition is a hard, time-consuming task in general. Therefore there is a need to provide tools to assist with the acquisition for these other two CBR knowledge containers. This paper has applied various techniques to learn additional knowledge, without further training data, by utilising the knowledge already captured in the cases.

A standard GA-based feature selection and weighting and parameter setting approach is used. Its novelty is in the use of the case knowledge to provide the fitness. Its main contribution is that the full CBR retrieval is optimised, rather than optimising the decision tree induction and nearest-neighbour retrieval separately.

Acquiring adaptation knowledge is a challenging task. Retrieved solutions may be refined in many ways, and individual adaptations may interact. The case knowledge again offers learning opportunities where similar cases can be adapted to solve each other. A simple case-based adaptation suggested that this was promising, but a committee-based approach offers the variety of adaptation and provides the negotiated refinement that adaptation seems to need. Further work is needed to recognise the circumstances in which particular experts (expertise or learning) are more reliable.

Despite the apparent autonomy of our tools, the domain expert has a valuable role to play in providing feedback on the contents of the various knowledge containers. It is important that the knowledge learned is comprehensible and allows manual refinement.

Acknowledgments.   This research was supported by EPSRC grant GR/L98015. I acknowledge the valuable work of Jacek Jarmulak and Nirmalie Wiratunga who provided significant help in designing and developing the system and in its evaluation. I also thank Ray Rowe, AstraZeneca for giving useful feedback for the tablet formulation domain and for providing the formulation data.

References

1. S. Craw, N. Wiratunga, and R. Rowe. Case-based design for tablet formulation. In *Advances in Case-Based Reasoning, Proceedings of the 4th European Workshop on Case Based Reasoning*, LNCS 1488, pages 358–369, Dublin, Eire, 1998. Springer.

2. P. Domingos. Unifying instance-based and rule-based induction. *Machine Learning*, 24:141–168, 1996.
3. Y. Freund and R. Schapire. Experiments with a new boosting algorithm. In *Machine Learning: Proceedings of the 13th International Conference*, pages 148–156, 1996.
4. P. Gomes and C. Bento. Learning user preferences in case-based software reuse. In *Advances in Case-Based Reasoning: Proceedings of the 5th European Workshop on Case Based Reasoning*, LNAI 1898, pages 112–123, Trento, Italy, 2000. Springer.
5. K. Hanney and M.T. Keane. The adaptation knowledge bottleneck: How to ease it by learning from cases. In *Proceedings of the 2nd International Conference on Case Based Reasoning*, LNAI 1226, pages 359–370, Providence, RI, 1997. Springer.
6. J. Jarmulak, S. Craw, and R. Rowe. Genetic algorithms to optimise CBR retrieval. In *Proceedings of the 5th European Workshop on Case Based Reasoning*, LNAI 1898, pages 136–147, Trento, Italy, 2000. Springer.
7. J. Jarmulak, S. Craw, and R. Rowe. Using case-base data to learn adaptation knowledge for design. In *Proceedings of the 17th International Joint Conference on Artificial Intelligence*, pages 1011–1016, Seattle, WA, 2001. Morgan Kaufmann.
8. D.B. Leake, A. Kinley, and D. Wilson. Acquiring case adaptation knowledge: A hybrid approach. In *Proceedings of the 13th National Conference on Artificial Intelligence*. AAAI Press, 1996.
9. G. Oatley, J. Tait, and J. MacIntyre. A case-based reasoning tool for vibration analysis. In *Proceedings of the 18th SGES International Conference on KBS and Applied AI – Applications Stream*, pages 132–146, Cambridge, UK, 1998. Springer.
10. M.M. Richter. Introduction. In *Case-Based Reasoning Technology: From Foundations to Applications*, LNAI 1400. Springer, 1998.
11. B. Smyth and E. McKenna. Competence models and the maintenance problem. *Computational Intelligence*, 17(2):235–249, 2001.
12. W. Wilke, I. Vollrath, K.-D. Althoff, and R. Bergmann. A framework for learning adaptation knowledge based on knowledge light approaches. In *Proceedings of the 5th German Workshop on Case-Based Reasoning*, 1997.
13. D.R. Wilson and T.R. Martinez. Instance-based learning with genetically derived attribute weights. In *Proceedings of the International Conference on Artificial Intelligence, Expert Systems and Neural Networks*, pages 11–14, 1996.
14. N. Wiratunga, S. Craw, and R. Rowe. Learning to adapt for case-based design. In *Proceedings of the 6th European Conference on Case-Based Reasoning*, LNAI 2416, pages 423–437, Aberdeen, UK, 2002. Springer.

Graph-Based Tools for Data Mining and Machine Learning

Horst Bunke

Institut für Informatik und angewandte Mathematik
Universität Bern, Neubrückstrasse 10
CH-3012 Bern (Switzerland)
bunke@iam.unibe.ch

Abstract. Many powerful methods for intelligent data analysis have become available in the fields of machine learning and data mining. However, almost all of these methods are based on the assumption that the objects under consideration are represented in terms of feature vectors, or collections of attribute values. In the present paper we argue that symbolic representations, such as strings, trees or graphs, have a representational power that is significantly higher than the representational power of feature vectors. On the other hand, operations on these data structure that are typically needed in data mining and machine learning are more involved than their counterparts on feature vectors. However, recent progress in graph matching and related areas has led to many new practical methods that seem to be very promising for a wide range of applications.

Keywords: graph matching, graph edit distance, graph clustering, unique node labels, edit cost learning

1 Introduction

As data sets are continuously growing in size and number, there is a need to extract useful information from collections of data. The disciplines of data mining and machine learning are concerned with the application of methods such as clustering, classification, rule induction, and others to potentially large data repositories in order to extract relevant information and eventually convert data and information into knowledge [1,2,3]. A large number of algorithms have become available meanwhile that are suitable to solve these tasks. These methods come from various disciplines, such as statistical decision theory, neural nets, soft computing, and others. One serious limitation of almost all algorithms used in data mining and machine learning is that they only deal with feature vectors or lists of attribute-value pairs. That is, the objects subject to the data mining or machine learning process are represented through a list of values, either numeric or symbolic, of a certain number of predefined features.

In the discipline of structural pattern recognition, object representations in terms of symbolic data structures, such as strings, trees and graphs have been

P. Perner and A. Rosenfeld (Eds.): MLDM 2003, LNAI 2734, pp. 7–19, 2003.

proposed [4,5]. By means of such a representation, most of the limitations inherent to feature vectors can be overcome. For example, the number of constituents, such as symbols in a string, or nodes and edges in a graph, doesn't need to be predefined in a particular application domain and can vary from one object to another. This is in contrast with feature vector representations, where the dimensionality of the feature space is usually the same for all objects under consideration. Moreover, symbolic data structures, in particular trees and graphs, are able to explicitly model structural relationships that exist between parts or components of the objects under consideration, while a feature vector captures only a set of unary measurements.

On the other hand there exist some potential problems with the structural approach. First, many operations on symbolic data structures, though conceptually simple, are computationally expensive. As an example, consider the computation of the distance of a pair of objects, which is linear in the number of data items in case of feature vectors [3], quadratic in case of strings [6], and exponential for graphs [7]. Second, the repository of algorithmic procedures in the symbolic domain is quite limited when compared to the tools available for feature representations. Traditionally only procedures for measuring the similarity or, equivalently, the distance of two data structures have been available in the symbolic domain, restricting the repository of algorithmic tools to nearest neighbor classification and simple clustering procedures that only need pair-wise distances of the given objects. Obviously, there is no straightforward way to generalize more elaborate concepts from statistical decision theory, neural networks and similar fields from the n-dimensional real space to the symbolic domain. A third potential problem is distance computation in the symbolic domain itself. In fact, some distance measures for strings, trees and graphs have been proposed in the literature [5]. However, the most flexible and universally applicable distance measure, which is edit distance [6,8], suffers from the lack of suitable inference procedures to learn the costs of elementary edit operations from a set of samples.

In the current paper we address the three aforementioned problems and discuss potential solutions that have been proposed in the literature recently. The remainder of the paper is organized as follows. In the next section we introduce our basic notation and terminology. Then, in Sect. 3, recent work in graph clustering that uses the novel concepts of median and weighted mean of a set of graphs will be reviewed. A special class of graphs will be introduced in Sect. 4. This class of graphs is distinguished by the fact that some of the operations commonly used in data mining and machine learning have a very low computational complexity when compared to general graphs. We'll give two examples to demonstrate that this class of graphs has enough representational power to deal with real world applications. The problem of automatically learning the costs of the edit operations for graph similarity computation will be addressed in Sect. 5. Finally a summary and conclusions will be provided in Sect. 6.

2   Basic Concepts in Graph Matching

In this paper we will assume that the objects under consideration are represented by symbolic data structures rather than feature vectors. The most common symbolic data structures for object representation are strings, trees, and graphs. As both strings and trees is a special case of graphs, we'll exclusively focus on graphs in the remainder of this paper. In fact, even feature vectors can be regarded as a special case of graphs.

In a graph, the nodes typically represent objects or parts of objects, while the edges describe relations between objects or object parts. Formally, a graph is a 4-tuple, $g = (V, E, \mu, \nu)$, where V is the set of nodes, $E \subseteq V \times V$ is the set of edges, $\mu : V \to L_V$ is a function assigning labels to the nodes, and $\nu : E \to L_E$ is a function assigning labels to the edges. In this definition, L_V and L_E is the set of node and edge labels, respectively. These labels can be vectors of any dimension, including numeric, symbolic, or mixed numeric/symbolic entities.

If we delete some nodes from a graph g, together with their incident edges, we obtain a subgraph $g' \subseteq g$. A graph isomorphism from a graph g to a graph g' is a bijective mapping from the nodes of g to the nodes of g' that preserves all labels and the structure of the edges [7]. Similarly, a subgraph isomorphism from g' to g is an isomorphism from g' to a subgraph of g [7]. Another important concept in graph matching is maximum common subgraph [9,10]. A maximum common subgraph of two graphs, g and g', is a graph g'' that is a subgraph of both g and g' and has, among all possible subgraphs of g and g', the maximum number of nodes. Notice that the maximum common subgraph of two graphs is usually not unique. Graph isomorphism is a useful concept to find out if two objects are the same, up to invariance properties inherent to the underlying graph representation. Similarly, subgraph isomorphism can be used to find out if one object is part of another object, or if one object is present in a group of objects. Maximum common subgraph can be used to measure the similarity of objects even if there exists no graph or subgraph isomorphism between the corresponding graphs. Clearly, the larger the maximum common subgraph of two graphs is, the greater is their similarity [11,12,13].

Real world objects are usually affected by noise such that the graph representation of identical objects may not exactly match. Therefore it is necessary to integrate some degree of error tolerance into the graph matching process. A powerful alternative to maximum common subgraph computation is error-tolerant graph matching using graph edit distance. In its most general form, a graph edit operation is either a deletion, insertion, or substitution (i.e. label change). Edit operations can be applied to nodes as well as to edges. By means of edit operations differences between two graphs are modeled. In order to enhance the modeling capabilities, often a cost is assigned to each edit operation. The costs are real numbers greater than or equal to zero. They are application dependent. Typically, the more likely a certain distortion is to occur the lower is its costs. Some theoretical considerations about the influence of the costs on graph edit distance can be found in [14]. The edit distance, $d(g_1, g_2)$, of two graphs is equal to the minimum cost taken over all sequences of edit operations that transform graph g_1 into g_2. Formally,

$$d(g_1, g_2) = \min_S \{c(S) \mid S \text{ is a sequence of edit operations} \atop \text{that transform } g_1 \text{into } g_2\} \ . \tag{1}$$

Clearly, if $g_1 = g_2$ then no edit operation is needed and $d(g_1, g_2) = 0$. On the other hand, the more g_1 and g_2 differ from each other, the more edit operations are needed, and the larger is $d(g_1, g_2)$.

Notice that the definitions given above don't lend themselves directly to algorithmic procedures for the computation of graph isomorphism, subgraph isomorphism, maximum common subgraph, and graph edit distance. A large variety of computational paradigms has been proposed and can be found in the literature. Rather than listing theses approaches explicitly here, we refer to a recent review that covers most computational procedures as well as applications of graph matching in pattern recognition [15].

3   Recent Advances in Graph Clustering

Clustering plays a key role in data mining and machine learning. It is an instance of unsupervised learning that aims at splitting a set of unlabeled data items into groups, or clusters, such that similar objects become part of the same cluster, while dissimilar objects are put into different clusters. A huge number of clustering algorithms for object representation in terms of feature vectors have been proposed in the literature. For a survey see [16]. But surprisingly little work has been reported on graph clustering [17,18,19].[1] In this section we review two algorithmic concepts, viz. median of a set of graphs and weighted mean of a pair of graphs, that have been proposed recently [21,22]. These concepts are potentially useful to transfer some well known clustering-related algorithms from the domain of feature vectors to the graph domain.

In median graph computation we are given a set of graphs, $G = \{g_1, \ldots g_n\}$, and a distance function $d(g_1, g_2)$, and aim at deriving a single graph $\bar{g}$ that captures the essential information in set G well. In other words, we want to find a representative of set G that is optimal in some sense. A straightforward approach to capturing the essential information in set G is to find a graph $\bar{g}$ that minimizes the average distance to all graphs in G, i.e.

$$\bar{g} = \arg \min_g \frac{1}{n} \sum_{i=1}^{n} d(g, g_i) \ . \tag{2}$$

---

[1] There are some well-established algorithms that use graph theoretical concepts, for example, minimum spanning tree, to organize the clustering process [20]. However, these algorithms are not to be confused with the graph clustering procedures considered in this paper, which are characterized by the fact that graphs, rather than feature vectors, are the objects to be clustered, regardless of how the clustering process is internally organized.

Let's call graph $\bar{g}$ the m edian of G. If we constrain g to be a member of the given set G, then the resultant graph

$$\hat{g} = \arg\min_{g \in G} \frac{1}{n} \sum_{i=1}^{n} d(g, g_i) \; . \tag{3}$$

is called the set m edian of G.

Given set G, the computation of the set median is a straightforward task. It requires just $O(n^2)$ distance computations. (Notice, however, that each of these distance computations has a high computational complexity, in general.) But the set median is restricted in the sense that it can't really generalize from the given patterns represented by set G. Therefore, median is the more powerful and interesting concept. However, the actual computational procedure for finding a median of a given set of graphs is no longer obvious.

It was theoretically shown that for particular costs of the edit operations and the case where G consists of only two elements, any maximum common subgraph of the two graphs under consideration is a median [23]. Further theoretical properties of the median have been derived in [21]. These properties are useful to restrict the search space for median graph computation, which is known to be exponential in the number of graphs in set G and their size.

In [21], also a practical procedure for median graph computation using a genetic search algorithm was proposed. An interesting feature of this algorithm is the chromosome representation. This representation encodes both, a generalized median graph candidate, and the optimal mapping of the nodes of this candidate to the nodes of the given graphs. Hence, the computationally expensive step of computing the optimal mapping for each candidate arising during the genetic search is avoided. Nevertheless, it has to be mentioned that because of the high computational complexity inherent to the problem, the applicability of this procedure is still limited to graphs with a moderate number of nodes and edges, and sets with a moderate number of graphs.

Median graph computation can be understood, from the abstract point of view, as a procedure that synthesizes a graph that has some desired property. A similar task is the computation of a weighted mean of a pair of graphs. A weighted mean, g, of a pair of graphs, g_1 and g_2, is a graph that has given degrees of similarity to both g_1 and g_2. Formally, we call graph g a weighted mean of g_1 and g_2 if, for some real number α with $0 \leq \alpha \leq d(g_1, g_2)$, the following two conditions hold:

$$d(g_1, g) = \alpha, \tag{4}$$
$$d(g_1, g_2) = \alpha + d(g, g_2) \; . \tag{5}$$

Clearly, if g_1 and g_2 are represented in terms of feature vectors, then weighted mean computation can be easily solved by means of vector addition. In [22], a procedure for the computation of weighted mean in the domain of graphs has been proposed. This procedure can be derived, in a quite straightforward manner, from classical graph edit distance computation using a tree search procedure. In other words, a weighted mean, g, of g_1 and g_2 can be obtained as a by-product of computing $d(g_1, g_2)$.

With the concepts of median graph and weighted mean graph at our disposal it becomes possible to develop versions of the k-means clustering algorithm and self-organizing map that work in the graph domain [24]. Moreover cluster validation indices can be used to find the optimal number of clusters automatically [25].

4   A Class of Graphs with Linear Matching Complexity

Symbolic representations, especially graphs, are attractive because of their flexibility and powerful modeling capabilities. On the other hand, they suffer from a high computational complexity when compared to vector representations. There are two principal ways to overcome the computational complexity problem in symbolic matching. First, one can resort to suboptimal algorithms. As a matter of fact, a large number of such methods have been proposed in the literature. They are based on various computational paradigms. For an overview see [15]. Alternatively, one can restrict the representation to special classes of graphs with a lower inherent computational complexity. A well known example is the class of planar graphs [26]. Other examples can be found in [27]. In this section we will introduce a novel class of graphs for which many of the commonly used matching algorithms, such as isomorphism, subgraph isomorphism, maximum common subgraph and graph edit distance, have a complexity that is only quadratic in the number of nodes of the larger of the two graphs involved in the matching problem. Furthermore, in case of bounded valence graphs (i.e. graphs with an upper bound on the number of incident edges for each node) the complexity reduces to linear. This class of graphs has been analyzed in [28]. In the following we briefly outline the main results presented in [28].

The class of graphs considered in this section is characterized by the existence of unique node labels. Formally, we require that for any graph g and any pair $x, y \in V$ the condition $\mu(x) \neq \mu(y)$ holds if $x \neq y$. Furthermore, we assume that the underlying alphabet of node labels is an ordered set, for example, the integers, i.e. $L_V = \{1, 2, 3, \ldots\}$. The uniqueness condition implies that, whenever two graphs are being matched with each other, each node has at most one candidate for possible assignment in the other graph. This candidate is uniquely defined through its node label. Consequently, the most costly step in graph matching, which is the exploration of all possible mappings between the nodes of the two graphs under consideration, is no longer needed. Formally, because of the uniqueness property, we may drop set V from the definition of a graph and just maintain its ordered label set, L. Thus each node, x, can be represented through its label $\mu(x)$. Now it is easy to show that in order to check two graphs, g_1 and g_2, for isomorphism it is sufficient to test their node label, edge, and edge label sets for identity. These operations can be performed in quadratic time with respect to the number of nodes. In case of bounded valence graphs, the complexity reduces to linear. Similarly to testing two graphs for isomorphism, the test for subgraph isomorphism as well as the computation of maximum common subgraph and edit distance can be accomplished by means of elementary set operations, all of which have the same complexity as the test for isomorphism.

If constraints are imposed on a class of graphs, we usually loose some representational power. The class of graphs considered in this paper is restricted by the requirement of each node label being unique. Despite of this restriction, there exist some interesting applications for this class of graphs. From the general point of view, graphs with unique node labels seem to be appropriate whenever the objects from the problem domain, which are modeled through nodes, possess properties that can be used to uniquely identify them. In the following we briefly review two particular applications of this class of graphs.

The first application is computer network monitoring [29,30]. The considered task consists in detecting abnormal behavior of a computer network. For this purpose, the network under consideration is formally represented through a graph where the nodes correspond to the clients and servers in the network and the edges represent physical connections between them. Snapshots of the network are taken at regular points in time $t = 1, 2, \ldots$. Thus we get a sequence of graphs, $g_1, g_2, \ldots$. The distance between two consecutive graphs in this sequence, $d(g_i, g_{i+1})$, is computed for $i = 1, 2, \ldots$. and the change from time $t = i$ to $t = i + 1$ is considered abnormal if the distance $d(g_i, g_{i+1})$ exceeds a certain user defined threshold. This application fulfills, in a very natural way, the condition of all nodes in the graph being uniquely labeled, because all servers and clients in the network have unique names. Consequently the fast algorithms mentioned above can be applied to this problem. On the other hand, it must be mentioned that the monitoring of computer networks can be a quite demanding task, because in the near future the need will arise to monitor networks consisting of hundreds of thousands of nodes, or even more. Thus the availability of fast graph matching algorithms is an essential requirement.

The second application involving graphs with unique node labels is document classification and clustering [31,32]. With an increasing number of documents, particularly documents on the World Wide Web, being produced every day intelligent document retrieval and analysis has become an important issue. Traditionally document information processing is based on vector representations, where each term that can appear in a document becomes a feature (i.e. a dimension). The value assigned to each dimension indicates the number of occurrences of that particular term in the considered document [33]. However, document representation through feature vectors suffers from some drawbacks. First, it always assumes the same number of terms being used (i.e. the dimension of the feature space is fixed). Secondly, a vector representation is not able to capture any relational information, for example, information about the co-occurrence of certain terms in a document. To overcome these drawbacks, a graph model for document representation has been proposed in [31,32]. In the graph model, the n most frequent terms in a document are represented through graph nodes, and term adjacency is represented by means of the edges of the graph. Some variations of this scheme have been analyzed in [34]. The crucial observation is that this representation lends itself to graphs with unique node labels, because the

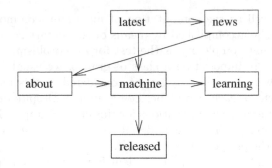

Fig. 1. Example of graph representation of a document

different terms occurring in a document are unique. As an example, consider the document

```
Latest news.
News about machine learning:
Latest machine released.
```

The corresponding graph representation is shown in Fig. 1.

Based on a graph representation such as the one shown in Fig. 1, graph clustering as discussed in Sect. 3, and nearest neighbor classification become available. In [31,32,34] the traditional vector model has been compared to the proposed graph model. The superiority of the graph over the vector model in terms of classification and clustering accuracy was demonstrated in a number of experiments. Thanks to the efficiency of the graph matching operations, which is due to the unique node label property, the graph model was even faster than the vector model in some instances. Although only documents from the World Wide Web have been considered in [31,32,34], the methods are not restricted to this kind of documents.

5   Learning Edit Costs for Graph Matching

One of the most powerful and flexible graph distance measures is edit distance. It is based on the idea of editing one of the two given graphs so as to make it identical (i.e. isomorphic) to the other graph, using elementary operations, such as deletion, insertion, and substitution of nodes and edges. As mentioned in Sect. 2, the edit distance, $d(g_1, g_2)$, of two graphs, g_1 and g_2, is defined as the cost of the cheapest sequence of edit operations that transform g_1 into g_2. It is easy to see that the costs of the edit operations have a crucial impact on $d(g_1, g_2)$. For an example, see Fig. 2 where three graphs, g_1, g_2, and g_3, are shown. If we allow only one type of edit operation, namely node substitution, and define the cost of substituting symbol a by b being smaller than substituting a by c, then $d(g_1, g_2) < d(g_1, g_3)$. Consequently, under a nearest neighbor classifier we

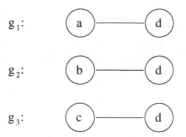

Fig. 2. Illustration of the influence of the edit costs

would assign the unknown graph g_1 to prototype g_2 rather than to g_3. However, if the substitution of a by b has a cost larger than the substitution of a by c then $d(g_1, g_2) > d(g_1, g_3)$ and the unknown graph g_1 gets assigned to prototype g_3. Despite the paramount importance of the costs of the edit operations, and the increasing popularity of graph edit distance, the automatic inference of the edit costs from a set of samples is still an open problem. While some potential solutions have been proposed for the case of string edit distance [35,36,37], the edit costs in graph matching are still manually set in a heuristic trial and error procedure, exploiting problem specific knowledge as much as possible; for an example see [38]. In this section we briefly outline a novel procedure for the automatic learning of the costs of graph edit operations from a set of sample graphs [39,40].

As one of the basic assumptions of the learning scheme proposed in [39,40], graphs with labels from the n-dimensional real space are considered. That is, each node label is a vector of fixed dimension consisting of n real numbers. Similarly, edge labels consist of a vector of m real numbers. (Notice, however, that there are no constraints imposed on the number of nodes and edges that may appear in a graph.) The proposed scheme takes a sample set of graphs as input and tries to minimize the average edit distance between a pair of graphs from the sample set by suitably adjusting the costs of the underlying edit operations. This is equivalent to minimizing the average intra-class distance of a given set of graphs that all belong to the same class. The proposed scheme is based on self-organizing map, SOM [41]. There is one SOM for each type of edit operation, i.e. for node deletion, node insertion, node substitution, edge deletion, edge insertion, and edge substitution. For example, the map for node substitution is an n-dimensional grid representing the space of node labels (i.e. n-dimensional real vectors). The cost of a node label substitution is proportional to the Euclidean distance between the two corresponding locations in the grid. The SOM learning procedure starts with a non-deformed n-dimensional grid. It computes the edit distance of a pair of graphs and moves each pair of grid points that correspond to a substitution closer to each other. In this way, the Euclidean distance of a pair of labels that are often substituted one by another, is iteratively minimized, which leads to a smaller overall graph edit distance between the two involved graphs. An example is shown in Fig. 3. Here we assume that a node

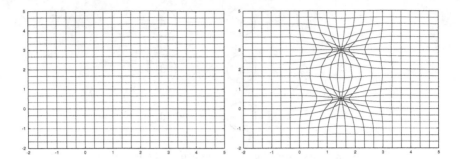

Fig. 3. *SOM*-based learning of substitution costs

label corresponds to a location in the 2-dimensional plane. Originally the SO M is not deformed and reflects the standard Euclidean distance (Fig. 3, left). In the course of the iterative learning procedure two areas have been identified where node substitutions occur often. Consequently, these areas have been contracted, and any two points within any of these contracted areas will have a smaller substitution cost after the learning process (Fig. 3, right). Hence the edit distance of any pair of graphs involving substitutions from one of those two areas will become smaller.

The proposed learning scheme has been successfully applied in a recognition experiment involving synthetically generated characters. In addition the SO M -based learning method has been used for the identification of diatoms. Here graphs derived from real images of diatoms were involved and with the automatically derived costs a higher recognition accuracy than with manually chosen costs was achieved [39].

6   Summary and Conclusions

Most of the algorithms commonly used in intelligent data analysis are based on object representations in terms of feature vectors. This representation formalism is advantageous in the sense that a rich repository of algorithmic tools is available, including subspace projection techniques, methods for clustering and classification, neural networks, and others. On the other hand feature vectors are limited because they can represent only unary properties and usually assume that the same number of attribute values being measured on each object. Symbolic data structures, including strings, trees, and graphs, are very suitable to overcome these limitations. However using such kind of object representation, we are facing the problem of an often increased computational complexity and the lack of suitable mathematical tools for a number of tasks. Yet recent work, mainly in the field of structural pattern recognition, has led to a number of novel algorithmic tools in the domain of graphs. These tools include a number of graph distance measures, graph clustering algorithms, and learning procedures for the parameters of graph distance based classifiers. Furthermore, if the underlying graphs fulfill some constraints very efficient algorithms exist.

There is no doubt that graph matching methodology and applications of graph matching have significantly progressed during recent years. Nevertheless there are many open questions. From the general point of view, in intelligent data analysis there is still a wide gap between tools based on feature vectors and tools based on structural representations. Bridging this gap, or making it smaller at least, is surely a major challenge for future research. This includes in particular the transfer, or adaptation, of many more tools from the n-dimensional real space to the graph domain.

Another issue is the filtering of large databases of graphs. In many applications we are faced with the task of retrieving graphs from a database that are similar to a given query graph. As the computation of graph isomorphism, subgraph isomorphism, maximum common subgraph and graph edit distance is computationally expensive in the general case, one cannot afford to match each graph in the database sequentially with the query graph. In [42,43] first attempts towards filtering procedures for graph retrieval from large databases have been proposed. The aim of these filtering procedures is to use some characteristic features of the given graphs, which can be quickly computed, in order to rule out as many graphs as possible from the graph database from being feasible match candidates. In [42,43] decision tree induction and traversal procedures have been proposed for this kind of database filtering. However many more indexing mechanisms seem possible and there is a definite need for further research.

From the practical point of view, there are many powerful software packages available for data mining using feature vectors. There is no doubt that the availability of these tools promoted the application of the underlying methods. However, for structural representations, no comparable software tools are available yet. But it can be expected that such tools could significantly contribute towards the acceptance and proliferation of structural matching techniques. Hence the development of such tools may be a worthwhile activity.

Acknowledgment. The author gratefully acknowledges contributions of his colleagues and students, in particular P. Dickinson, S. Günter, Ch. Irniger, X. Jiang, A. Kandel, M. Kraetzl, M. Last, M. Neuhaus, and A. Schenker. Financial support from the Swiss National Science Foundation under grant 2100-066700-01/1 is gratefully acknowledged.

References

1. Hand, D., Mannila, H., Smyth, P.: Principles of Data Mining. The MIT Press (2001)
2. Kantardzic, M.: Data Mining-Concepts, Models, Methods, and Algorithms. Wiley-Interscience (2003)
3. Mitchell, T.: Machine Learning. McGraw Hill (1997)

4. Fu, K.-S.: Syntactic Pattern Recognition and Applications. Prentice Hall (1982)
5. Bunke, H., Sanfeliu, A. (eds.): Syntactic and Structural Pattern Recognition-Theory and Applications. World Scientific (1990)
6. Wagner, R.A., Fischer, M.J.: The string-to-string correction problem. Journal of the Association for Computing Machinery 21(1) (1974) 168–173
7. Ullman, J.R.: An algorithm for subgraph isomorphism. Journal of the ACM 23(1) (1976) 31–42
8. Messmer, B.T., Bunke, H.: A new algorithm for error-tolerant subgraph isomorphism detection. IEEE Trans. PAMI 20(5) (1998) 493–507
9. McGregor, J.: Backtrack search algorithms and the maximal common subgraph problem. Software-Practice and Experience 12 (1982) 23–13
10. Levi, G.: A note on the derivation of maximal common subgraphs of two directed or undirected graphs. Calcolo 9 (1972) 341–354
11. Bunke, H., Shearer, K.: A graph distance metric based on the maximal common subgraph. Pattern Recognition Letters 19 (1998) 255–259
12. Wallis, W.D., Shoubridge, P., Kraetzl, M., Ray, D.: Graph distances using graph union Pattern Recognition Letters 22 (2001) 701–704
13. Fernandez, M.L, Valiente, G.: A graph distance metric combining maximum common subgraph and minimum common supergraph. Pattern Recognition Letters 22 (2001) 753–758
14. Bunke, H.: Error correcting graph matching: on the influence of the underlying cost function. IEEE Trans. PAMI 21 (1999) 917–922
15. Conte, D., Foggia, P., Sansone, C., Vento, M.: Thirty years of graph matching in pattern recognition. Int. Journal of Pattern Recognition and Art. Intelligence, Special issue on Graph Matching in Computer Vision and Pattern Recognition (to appear)
16. Jain, A., Murty, M., Flynn, P.: Data clustering: a review. ACM Computing Surveys 31 (1999) 264–323
17. Seong, D., Kim, H., Park, K.: Incremental clustering of attributed graphs. IEEE Trans. SMC (1993) 1399–1411
18. Luo, B., Wilson, R.E., Hancock, E.: Spectral feature vectors for graph clustering. In: Caelli, T. et al. (eds.): Structural, Syntactic and Statistical Pattern Recognition. Lecture Notes in Computer Science, Vol. 2396. Springer (2002) 83–93
19. Sanfeliu, A., Serratosa, F., Alquezar, R.: Synthesis of function-described graphs and clustering of attributed graph. Int. Journal of Pattern Recognition and Art. Intell. 16 (2002) 621–655
20. Zahn, C.T.: Graph-theoretical methods for detecting and describing Gestalt structures. IEEE Trans. Computers C-20 (1971) 68–86
21. Jiang, X., Münger, A., Bunke, H.: On median graphs: properties, algorithms, and applications. IEEE Trans. Pattern Analysis and Machine Intell. 23(10) (2001) 1144–1151
22. Bunke, H., Günter, S.: Weighted mean of a pair of graphs. Computing 67 (2001) 209–224
23. Bunke, H., Kandel, A.: Mean and maximal common subgraph of two graphs. Pattern Recognition Letters 21 (2000) 163–168
24. Günter, S., Bunke, H.: Self-organizing map for clustering in the graph domain. Pattern Recognition Letters 23 (2002) 401–417
25. Günter, S., Bunke, H.: Validation indices for graph clustering. Pattern Recognition Letters 24 (2003) 1107–1113
26. Hopcroft, J., Wong, J.: Linear time algorithm for isomorphism of planar graphs. Proc. 6th Annual Symposium on Theory of Computing (1974) 172–184

27. Jiang, X., Bunke, H.: Marked subgraph isomorphism of ordered graphs. In: Amin, A., Dori, D., Pudil, P., Freeman, H. (eds.): Advances in Pattern Recognition. Lecture Notes in Computer Science, Vol. 1451. Springer Verlag (1998) 122–131

28. Dickinson, P., Bunke, H., Dadej, A., Kraetzl, M.: On graphs with unique node labels. Proc. 4th IAPR Workshop on Graph based Representations, York (2003)

29. Bunke, H., Kraetzl, M., Shoubridge, P., Wallis, W.: Detection of abnormal change in time series of graphs. Journal of Interconnection Networks **3** (2002) 85–101

30. Bunke, H., Kraetzl, M.: Classification and detection of abnormal events in time series of graphs. In: Last, M., Kandel, A., Bunke, H. (eds.): Data Mining in Time Series Databases. World Scientific (2003)

31. Schenker, A., Last, M., Bunke, H., Kandel, A.: Clustering of documents using a graph model. In: Antonacopoulos, A., Hu, J. (eds.): Web Document Analysis: Challenges and Opportunities. World Scientific (2003)

32. Schenker, A., Last, M., Bunke, H., Kandel, A.: Classification of web documents using graph matching. Int. Journal of Pattern Recognition and Art. Intelligence (to appear)

33. Salton, G.: Automatic Text Processing: the Transformation, Analysis, and Retrieval of Information by Computer. Addison Wesley (1989)

34. Schenker, A., Last, M., Bunke, H., Kandel, A.: Graph representations for web document clustering. Proc. 1st Iberian Conf. on Pattern Recognition and Image Analysis (2003)

35. Ristad, E., Yianilos, P.: Learning string edit distance. IEEE Trans. PAMI **20** (1998) 522–532

36. Parizeau, M., Ghazzali, N., Hebert, J.-F.: Optimizing the cost matrix for approximate string matching using genetic algorithms. Pattern Recognition **31** (1998) 431–440

37. Gomez-Ballester, M., Forcada, M., Mico, M.: A gradient-ascent method to adapt the edit distance to a classification task. In: Torres, M.I., Sanfeliu, A. (eds.): Pattern Recognition and Applications. IOS Press (2000) 13–18

38. Ambauen, R., Fischer, S., Bunke, H.: Graph edit distance with node splitting and merging and its application to diatom identification. Proc. 4th IAPR Workshop on Graph based Representations, York (2003)

39. Neuhaus, M., Bunke, H.: Self-organizing graph edit distance. Proc. 4th IAPR Workshop on Graph based Representations, York (2003)

40. Neuhaus, M.: Learning Graph Edit Distance. Diploma Thesis, University of Bern (2003)

41. Kohonen, T.: Self-Organizing Maps. Springer Verlag (1995)

42. Irniger, Ch., Bunke, H.: Graph Matching: Filtering large databases of graphs using decision trees. In: Jolion, J.-M., Kropatsch, W., Vento, M. (eds.): Proc. 3rd IAPR-TC15 Workshop on Graph-based Representations in Pattern Recognition. (2001) 239–249

43. Irniger, Ch., Bunke, H.: Theoretical analysis and experimental comparison of graph matching algorithms for database filtering. Proc. 4th IAPR Workshop on Graph based Representations, York (2003)

Simplification Methods for Model Trees with Regression and Splitting Nodes

Michelangelo Ceci, Annalisa Apice, and Donato Malerba

Dipartimento di Informatica, Università degli Studi
via Orabona, 4, 70126 Bari, Italy
{ceci,appice,malerba}@di.uniba.it

Abstract. Model trees are tree-based regression models that associate leaves with linear regression models. A new method for the stepwise induction of model trees (SMOTI) has been developed. Its main characteristic is the construction of trees with two types of nodes: regression nodes, which perform only straight-line regression, and splitting nodes, which partition the feature space. In this way, internal regression nodes contribute to the definition of multiple linear models and have a "global" effect, while straight-line regressions at leaves have only "local" effects. In this paper the problem of simplifying model trees with both regression and splitting nodes is faced. In particular two methods, named Reduced Error Pruning (REP) and Reduced Error Grafting (REG), are proposed. They are characterized by the use of an independent pruning set. The effect of the simplification on model trees induced with SMOTI is empirically investigated. Results are in favour of simplified trees in most cases.

1 Introduction

In the classical regression setting, data is generated IID from an unknown distribution P on some domain $\mathbf{X}$ and labeled according to an unknown function g with range Y. The domain $\mathbf{X}$ is spanned by m independent (or predictor) random variables x_i (both numerical and categorical), while Y is a subset of $\Re$, that is, the dependent (or response) variable y is continuous. A learning algorithm receives a training sample $S=\{(\mathbf{x}, y) \in \mathbf{X} \times Y \mid y=g(\mathbf{x}) \}$ and attempts to return a function f close to g on the domain $\mathbf{X}$. Closeness of f to g can be measured in many ways, for instance, by means of the expected square error.

Statisticians have traditionally approached this problem by means of standard (non-) linear regression techniques. More recently, trees have begun to play an important role in statistical model building, especially in the context of regression problems. Methods for inducing or learning *regression trees* have been proposed by Breiman *et al.* [1]. A regression tree approximates the function g by means of a piecewise *constant* function, that is it associates a constant to each leaf. A generalization of regression trees is represented by *model trees* which approximate the function g by a piecewise *linear* function, that is they associate leaves with multiple linear models.

Some of the model tree induction systems developed are: M5 [12], RETIS [5], M5' [17], TSIR [6], and HTL [15,16]. Almost all these systems perform a *top-down* induction of models trees (TDIMT) in two stages: the first builds the tree structure through recursive partitioning of the training set, while the second associates leaves with models. This dichotomy has an intrinsic weakness, since partitioning strategy does not consider the models that can be associated to the leaves [7]. RETIS, which operate differently, suffers from problems of efficiency and collinearity. SMOTI (Stepwise Model Tree Induction) is a new TDIMT method that constructs model trees *stepwise*, by adding, at each step, either a *regression node* or a *splitting node*. In this way, a multiple linear model can be associated to each node during tree-building, thus preventing problems related to two-staged induction algorithms. The stepwise construction of the multiple linear models provides a solution to problems of efficiency and collinearity by selecting only a subset of variables [18]. Moreover, SMOTI potentially solves the problem of modeling phenomena where some variables have a global effect while others have only a local effect [8].

Similarly to other TDIMT approaches, SMOTI may generate model trees that overfit training data. Almost all TDIMT systems use some simplifying techniques to determine which nodes of the tree should be taken as leaves. These techniques are generally derived from those developed for decision trees [3]. In particular, RETIS bases its pruning algorithm on Niblett and Bratko's method [9], extended later by Cestnik & Bratko [2]. M5 uses a pessimistic-error-pruning-like strategy since it compares the error estimates obtained by pruning a node or not. The error estimates are based on the training cases and corrected in order to take into account the complexity of the model in the node. Similarly, in M5' the pruning procedure makes use of an estimate, at each node, of the expected error for the test data. The estimate is the resubstitution error compensated by a factor that takes into account the number of training examples and the number of parameters in the linear model associated to the node [17]. A method *à la* error-based-pruning is adopted in HTL, where the upper level of a confidence interval of the resubstitution error estimate is taken as the most pessimistic estimate of the error node [16].

In this paper, the a posteriori simplification (or pruning) of model trees induced by SMOTI has been investigated. In particular, after a brief introduction to SMOTI (next section), a framework for simplifying model trees with regression and splitting nodes is described. This framework is helpful to define two simplification methods and to investigate their theoretical properties (Secs. 4 and 5). Finally, experimental results are reported and discussed in Sect. 6.

2   Stepwise Construction of Model Trees

In SMOTI the top-down induction of models trees is performed by considering *regression steps* and *splitting tests* at the same level. This means that there are two types of nodes in the tree: regression nodes and splitting nodes (Fig. 1). The former compute straight-line regression, while the latter partition the feature space. They pass down observations to their children in two different ways. For a splitting node t, only a subgroup of the $N(t)$ observations in t is passed to each child (left or right). No change is made on training cases. For a regression node t, all the observations are passed down to its only child, but the values of both the dependent and independent numeric variables not included in the multiple linear model associated to t are transformed in order to remove the linear effect of those variables already included. Thus,

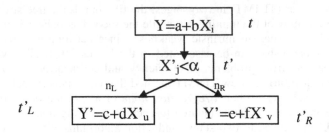

Fig. 1. A model tree with both a regression node (t) and a splitting note (t')

descendants of a regression node will operate on a modified training set. Indeed, according to the statistical theory of linear regression, the incremental construction of a multiple linear model is made by removing the linear effect of introduced variables each time a new independent variable is added to the model. For instance, let us consider the problem of building a multiple regression model with two independent variables through a sequence of straight-line regressions:

$$\hat{Y} = a + bX_1 + cX_2$$

We start regressing Y on X_1, so that the model:

$$\hat{Y} = a_1 + b_1X_1$$

is built. This fitted equation does not predict Y exactly. By adding the new variable X_2, the prediction might improve. Instead of starting from scratch and building a model with both X_1 and X_2, we can build a linear model for X_2 given X_1:

$$\hat{X}_2 = a_2 + b_2X_1$$

then compute the residuals on X_2 and Y:

$$X'_2 = X_2 - (a_2 + b_2X_1)$$
$$Y' = Y - (a_1 + b_1X_1)$$

and finally regress Y' on X'_2 alone:

$$\hat{Y}' = a_3 + b_3X'_2$$

By substituting the equations of X'_2 and Y' in the last equation we have:

$$\overline{Y - (a_1 + b_1X_1)} = a_3 + b_3(X_2 - (a_2 + b_2X_1))$$

Since $\overline{Y - (a_1 + b_1X_1)} = \hat{Y} - (a_1 + b_1X_1)$ we have :

$$\hat{Y} = (a_3 + a_1 - a_2b_3) + (b_1 - b_2b_3)X_1 + b_3X_2.$$

It can be proven that this last model coincides with the first model built, that is $a = a_3 + a_1 - a_2b_3$, $b = b_1 - b_2b_3$ and $c = b_3$. Therefore, when the first regression line of Y on X_1 is built we pass down both the residuals of Y and *the residuals of the regression of* X_2 *on* X_1. This means we remove the linear effect of the variables already included in the model (X_1) from both the response variable (Y) and those variables to be selected for the next regression step (X_2).

A more detailed explanation of SMOTI and a comparison with other TDIMT methods are reported in [7].

3   A Unifying Framework for Describing Simplification Methods

Pruning methods have been initially proposed to solve the overfitting problem of induced decision trees. A unifying framework for their descriptions is reported in [4]. In this paper we follow the same idea and develop two methods for the simplification of model trees with both regression nodes and splitting nodes.[1] The first method uses the classical pruning operator extended to regression nodes as well. The second method is based on a new grafting operator that replaces a splitting node with a sub-tree. To formally define these simplification methods, some notations are introduced. We start with the formal definition of a SMOTI tree, that is a tree with regression and splitting nodes, then we define the pruning and grafting relations, the search spaces, and finally the operators.

A *(rooted)* tree can be formally defined as a finite set of nodes, $N_T = \{t_0, t_1, ..., t_n\}$ and an associated relation $B_T \subseteq N_T \times N_T$ for which the following properties hold:

1. There exists exactly one node t_0 in N_T, named *root*, such that $\forall <t_i,t_j> \in B_T$: $t_j \neq t_0$;

2. $\forall t_j \in N_T$, $t_j \neq t_0$ there exists only one node $t_i \in N_T$ such that $<t_i,t_j> \in B_T$.

The set N_T can be partitioned into the set of internal nodes and the set of leaves $\tilde{T}$. Given a set O of N observations O_i, each of which is described by $m+1$- dimensional feature vector, $<X_1,...,X_m,Y>$ it is possible to build a tree-structured model named *SMOTI tree*. This is a particular tree T in which:

1. each node t is associated with a subset of O, $O(t)$, possibly modified by re-moving the linear effect of the variables added to the model;
2. the root t_0 is associated with O itself;
3. every edge $<t_i,t_j> \in B_T$ is labelled with $L_T(<t_i,t_j>)$;

$L_T(<t_i,t_j>)$ can be:

a)   a straight-line regression function $Y=a+bX_k$ *(regression label)*[2];
b)   a test on a numeric variable like $X_k \leq \alpha$ ($X_k > \alpha$) *(continuous split label)*;
c)   a test on a discrete variable like $X_k \in \{x_{k1}, ..., x_{kl}\}$ ($X_k \notin \{x_{k1}, ..., x_{kl}\}$) *(discrete split label)*.

An internal node $t_i \in N_T - \tilde{T}$ is called *regression (splitting) node* iff there exists an edge $<t_i,t_j> \in B_T$ such that $L_T(<t_i,t_j>)$ is a regression (continuous/discrete split) label.

---

[1] No simplification method was proposed in TSIR, the only other system that induces trees with two types of nodes.

[2] For the sake of simplicity, only original variables are reported in straight-line regression functions and in continuous splits.

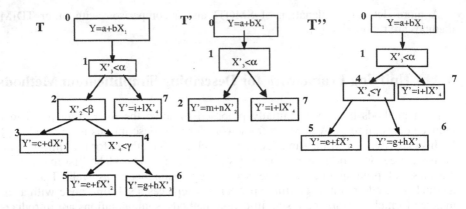

Fig. 2. The model tree T' is obtained by pruning T in node 2, while T" is obtained by grafting the subtree rooted in node 4 onto the place of node 2

If p is a path from the root t_0 of a tree T to a leaf t_i of T,
$$p = <t_0,t_1>,<t_1,t_2>,\ldots,<t_{i-1},t_i>$$
then the label associated to p, $L_T(p)$, is the sequence of labels:
$$L_T(p)=L_T(<t_0,t_1>), L_T(<t_1,t_2>),\ldots, L_T(<t_{i-1},t_i>).$$

Let T denote the set of all possible model trees that SMOTI can build from $\mathcal{O}$. It is possible to define two distinct partial order relations on T, denoted $\leq_P$ and $\leq_G$, which satisfy the properties of reflexivity, antisymmetry and transitivity. Let T and T' be two model trees in T. Then T' $\leq_P$ T iff for each path p' from the root of T' to a leaf in T', there exists a path p from the root of T to a leaf of T such that $L_{T'}(p')$ is a prefix of $L_T(p)$. Moreover, T' $\leq_G$ T, iff for each path p' from the root of T' to a leaf in T', there exists a path p from the root of T to a leaf of T, such that $L_{T'}(p')$ is obtained from $L_T(p)$ by dropping some continuous/discrete split labels in the sequence.

With reference to Figure 2, T' $\leq_P$ T and T" $\leq_G$ T, while the relations T" $\leq_P$ T and T' $\leq_G$ T do not hold.

Hence, given a SMOTI tree T, it is possible to define two sets of trees, namely:
$$S_P(T) =\{T' \in T \mid T' \leq_P T\}$$
$$S_G(T) =\{T' \in T \mid T' \leq_G T\}$$

We observe that $S_P(T) \not\subset S_G(T)$ and $S_G(T) \not\subset S_P(T)$, since T' $\leq_P$ T does not imply T' $\leq_G$ T and viceversa.

The *pruning operator* is defined as the function:
$$\pi_T: R_T \cup S_T \to T$$
where R_T and S_T denote the sets of regression and splitting nodes, respectively. The operator associates each internal node t with the tree $\pi_T(t)$, which has all the nodes of T except the descendants of t.

Analogously, the *grafting operator* is defined as the function:
$$\gamma_T: S_T \times N_T \to T$$
that associates each couple of internal nodes $<t,t'> \in S_T \times N_T$, with the tree $\gamma_T(<t,t'>)$, which has all nodes of T except those in the branch between t and t'. Intuitively, the

pruning operator applied to a node of a tree T returns a tree T' $\leq_p$ T while the grafting operator returns a tree T' $\leq_G$ T (see Figure 2).

The problem of simplifying a model tree can be cast as a search in a state space, where states are trees in either $S_P(T)$ or $S_G(T)$, and pruning and grafting are the only operators that can be applied to move from one state to another.

In order to give a precise definition of a simplification method the goal of the search in the state space has to be defined. For this reason, a function f that estimates the goodness of a tree is introduced. It associates each tree in the space S(T) with a numerical value, namely:

$$f : S(T) \to \Re$$

where $\Re$ is the set of real values. The goal of the search is to find the state in S(T) with the highest f value, so that pruning can be cast as a problem of function optimization.

Finally, the way in which the state space is explored also characterizes different simplification methods, which can be formally described by a 4-tuple:

(Space, Operators, Evaluation function, Search strategy)

where the *Space* represents the search space of pruning methods, *Operators* is a set of simplification (pruning or grafting) operators, *Evaluation function* associates each tree in the search space with a numerical value and the *search strategy* is the way in which the state space is explored in order to find the optimal state. This framework is used in the next sections to explain the two simplification methods.

4   Reduced Error Pruning

This method is based on the Reduced Error Pruning (REP) proposed by Quinlan for decision trees [11]. It uses a pruning set to evaluate the goodness of the subtrees of a model tree T. The pruning set is independent of the set of observations used to build the tree T, therefore, the training set must be partitioned into a *growing* set used to build the tree and a *pruning* set used to simplify T (Figure 3).

Search is accomplished in the pruning state space, $(S_P(T), \{\pi_T\})$ by means of the first-better strategy, according to which we move from one state T to a state T' just generated if T' is better than T with respect to the evaluation function f. Differently from the hill-climbing search, there is no generation of all states directly reachable from T in order to select the best one. Moreover, the first better strategy differs from the well-known best first strategy in the storing of only one generated state. Obviously, in this search strategy, the order in which states are generated is of crucial importance. It depends on:

1.   The traversal order: pre-order or post-order.
2.   The direction of pruning: bottom-up or top-down.

In REP, the traversal is post-order and the direction is bottom-up. The evaluation function f is defined as follows:

$$f(T) = \sum_{t \in \tilde{T}} R(t)$$

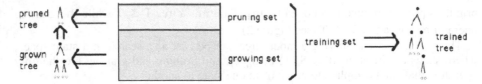

Fig. 3. The original data set can be split into two subsets: the growing set and the pruning set. The union of the growing and pruning set is called the training set. Trees learned from the growing/training set are called grown/trained trees, respectively. Pruning trees can be obtained by pruning either grown trees or trained trees. In the former case, a pruning set is used

where R(t) is the mean square error at leaf t. The search in the space moves from a state T_1 to a state $T_2 \in \pi_{T_1}(S_{T_1} \cup R_{T_1})$ if $f(T_1) \geq f(T_2)$. More precisely the algorithm analyzes the complete tree T and, for each internal node t, it compares the mean square error made on the pruning set when the subtree T_t is kept, with the mean square error made when T_t is pruned and the best regression function is associated to the leaf t. If the simplified tree has a better performance than the original one, it is advisable to prune T_t. This pruning operation is repeated on the simplified tree until further pruning increases the resubstitution error.

As already observed in [14], Quinlan's description of REP for decision trees does not specify how to choose the class associated to the pruned nodes. Following the majority class criterion, three alternatives are possible: the class is determined on the basis of the growing set, the pruning set or the training set. Analogously, in the case of model trees, the straight-line regression to be associated to a pruned node can be determined on the basis of one of the three sets: growing, pruning or training.

The following optimality theorem can be proven:

Theorem. Given a model tree T constructed on a set of observations $\mathcal{O}$ and a pruning set $\mathcal{O}'$, the REP version that determines the regression model on $\mathcal{O}$ returns the smallest tree in $S_p(T)$ with the lowest error with respect to $\mathcal{O}$.

The specification "the REP version that determines the regression model on $\mathcal{O}$" refers to the fact that once a node t has been pruned, the model associated to t is determined on the basis of the same growing set $\mathcal{O}$. Alternatively, it could be determined on the basis of either the pruning set or the whole training set.

Proof . We prove the theorem by induction on the depth of T.

Base Case. Let T be a root tree $\{t_0\}$. Then T is the only tree in $S_p(T)$ and REP returns T, since no pruning operation is possible.

Inductive Step: The proof is based on the additive property of the resubstitution error for model trees, according to which a local optimization on each branch T_{t_i} of t_0 leads to a global optimization on T. We assume the inductive hypothesis to be true for all model trees T' of depth d and we prove the theorem for the tree T of depth $d+1$, $d \geq 0$. Since T has a depth greater than 0, there are two possibilities:

    a.   T is the tree rooted in t_0, a regression node with a child t_1, and the subtree T_{t_1} has depth d.

    b.   T is the tree rooted in t_0, a splitting node with two children t_1 and t_2, and both subtrees T_{t_1}, T_{t_2} have maximum depth d.

Case a. REP, which follows the bottom-up direction when pruning, first prunes T_{t_1} and then checks whether T should be pruned in t_0. For the inductive hypothesis, REP finds the optimally pruned tree $T_{t_1}^*$ for the tree rooted in t_1. Let T' be the tree rooted in t_0, whose subtree is $T_{t_1}^*$. Then according to the definition of f, $f(T') = f(T_{t_1}^*)$, since T' and $T_{t_1}^*$ have the same leaves. Moreover, for any tree $T'' \in S_p(T)$ of depth greater than 0 we have $f(T') \le f(T'')$, since $f(T') = \sum_{t \in \tilde{T}_{t_1}^*} R(t) : \sum_{t \in \tilde{T}_{t_1}''} R(t) = f(T'')$.

Therefore, if $f(\{t_0\}) \le f(T')$ then REP prunes T in t_0, and the returned tree is the best subtree of T, since $R(t_0) = f(\{t_0\}) \le f(T') \le f(T'')$ for any tree $T'' \in S_p(T)$ of depth greater than 0. On the contrary, if $f(\{t_0\}) > f(T')$ then REP does not prune T in t_0 and the returned tree is T', which is the smallest tree in $S_p(T)$ with the lowest error with respect to $\mathcal{O}$.

Case b. Analogously, in the case of the splitting node, REP follows the bottom-up direction so that it first prunes T_{t_1} and T_{t_2} and then checks whether T should be pruned in t_0. For the inductive hypothesis REP finds the optimally pruned tree $T_{t_1}^*$ for the tree rooted in t_1 and $T_{t_2}^*$ for the tree rooted in t_2. Let T' be the tree rooted in t_0, whose subtrees are $T_{t_1}^*$ and $T_{t_2}^*$. Then $f(T') = f(T_{t_1}^*) + f(T_{t_2}^*)$, since the leaves of T' are leaves of either $T_{t_1}^*$ or $T_{t_2}^*$. Moreover, for any tree $T'' \in S_p(T)$ of depth greater than 0, we have $f(T') \le f(T'')$ since $f(T') = \sum_{t \in \tilde{T}_{t_1}^*} R(t) + \sum_{t \in \tilde{T}_{t_2}^*} R(t) : \sum_{t \in \tilde{T}_{t_1}''} R(t) + \sum_{t \in \tilde{T}_{t_2}''} R(t) = f(T'')$.

Therefore, if $f(\{t_0\}) \le f(T')$ then REP prunes T in t_0, and the returned tree is the best subtree of T, since $R(t_0) = f(\{t_0\}) \le f(T') \le f(T'')$ for any tree $T'' \in S_p(T)$ of depth greater than 0. On the contrary, if $f(\{t_0\}) > f(T')$ then REP does not prune T in t_0 and the returned tree is T', which is the smallest tree in $S_p(T)$ with the lowest error with respect to $\mathcal{O}$.

∎

Finally, the computational complexity of REP is linear in the number of internal nodes, since each node is visited only once to evaluate the opportunity of pruning it.

5   Reduced Error Grafting

The Reduced Error Grafting (REG) is conceptually similar to REP and uses a pruning set to evaluate the goodness of T', a subtree of T. However, the search is performed in the grafting state space, $(S_G(T), \{\gamma_T\})$, according to a first-better strategy with bottom-up post-order traversal. The evaluation function is the same defined for REP.

The search in $S_G(T)$ moves from a state T_1 to a state $T_2 \in \gamma_{T_1}(S_{T_1}, S_{T_1})$ if the inequality $f(T_1) \ge f(T_2)$ holds. More precisely the algorithm operates recursively. It analyzes the complete tree T and, for each split node t, it compares the resubstitution error made on the pruning set when the subtree T_t is kept, with the resubstitution error made on the pruning set when T_t is turned into REG(T_{t_1}) or REG(T_{t_2}), where t_1 and t_2 are children of t. Sometimes, the simplified tree has a better performance than the original one. In this case, it appears convenient to replace t with its best simplified subtree (left of right). This grafting operation is repeated on the simplified tree until the resubstitution error increases.

```
REG(tree,pruningSet)
begin
      if |pruningSet|=0 then return 0

      if the tree is a leaf then return ResubstitutionError(tree,pruningSet)
      if the root is a splitting node then
                partition pruningSet into pruningSet1 and pruningSet2
                newLeftBranch= leftBranch
                newRightBranch= rightBranch
                sxError=REG(leftBranch, pruningSet1)
                dxError=REG(rightBranch, pruningSet2)
                sxErrorGrafted=REG(newLeftBranch, pruningSet)
                dxErrorGrafted=REG (newRightBranch, pruningSet)
                if sxError+dxError<sxErrorGrafted AND
                      sxError+dxError<dxErrorGrafted then
                                   return sxError+dxError
                if sxErrorGrafted>dxErrorGrafted then
                                   tree= newRightBranch
                                   return dxErrorGrafted
                      else
                                   tree= newLeftBranch
                                   return sxErrorGrafted
      if the root is a Regression Node then
                remove the effect of the regression from pruningSet into pruningSet1
                sxError=REG (leftBranch, pruningSet1)
                return sxError
end
```

Fig. 4. Reduced error grafting algorithm

This method (see Fig. 4) is theoretically favored with respect to REP, since it allows the replacement of a subtree by one of its branches. In this way, it is possible to overcome a limit of those simplification strategies that make use of the pruning operator alone. Indeed, if t is a node that should be pruned according to some criterion, while t' is a child of t that should not be pruned according the same criterion, such simplification strategy either prunes and loses the accurate branch $T_{t'}$ or does not prune at all and keeps the inaccurate branch T_t. On the contrary, REG acts by grafting $T_{t'}$ onto the place of t, so saving the good sub-branch and deleting the useless node t.

Similarly to REP, a theorem on the optimality of the tree returned by REG can be proven.

Theorem. Given a model tree T constructed on a set of observations $\mathcal{O}$ and a pruning set $\mathcal{O}$, the REG version that determines the regression model on $\mathcal{O}$ returns the smallest tree in $S_G(T)$ with the lowest error with respect to $\mathcal{O}$.

Proof. We prove the theorem by induction on the depth of T.

Base Case. Let T be a root tree $\{t_0\}$. Then T is the only tree in $S_G(T)$ and REG returns, T since no grafting operation is possible.

Inductive Step: we assume the inductive hypothesis to be true for all model trees T' of depth d and we prove the theorem for the tree T of depth $d+1$, $d \geq 0$. Since T has a depth greater than 0, there are two possibilities:

   a.   T is the tree rooted in t_0, a regression node with a child t_1, and the subtree T_{t_1} has depth d.

   b.   T is the tree rooted in t_0, a splitting node with two children, t_1 and t_2, and both subtrees T_{t_1} and T_{t_2} have maximum depth d.

Case a. REG, which follows the bottom-up direction first simplifies T_{t_1}. For the inductive hypothesis REG finds the optimally simplified tree $T_{t_1}^*$ for the tree T_{t_1}.[3]

Let T' be the tree rooted in t_0, whose subtree is $T_{t_1}^*$. Then, according to the definition of f, $f(T') = f(T_{t_1}^*)$, since T' and $T_{t_1}^*$ have the same leaves. Moreover, for any tree $T'' \in S_G(T)$ of depth greater than 0 and rooted in t_0 with child t'', we have $f(T') \leq f(T'')$, since $f(T') = \sum_{t \in \tilde{T}_{t_1}^*} R(t) : \sum_{t \in \tilde{T}_{t''}''} R(t) = f(T'')$.

Therefore, REG returns T', which is the smallest tree in $S_G(T)$ with the lowest error with respect to $\mathcal{O}$.

Case b. In the case of a splitting node, REG follows the bottom-up direction, simplifies T_{t_1} and T_{t_2} with respect to $\mathcal{O}$ and then checks whether one of the simplified subtrees should be grafted in t_0. We denote the set of examples which fall in T_{t_1} (T_{t_2}) as $\mathcal{O}_1'$ ($\mathcal{O}_2'$). Let $T_{t_1}^*$ ($T_{t_2}^*$) be the subtree rooted in t_1 (t_2), returned by REG when pruned with respect to $\mathcal{O}_1'$ ($\mathcal{O}_2'$). For the inductive hypothesis, $T_{t_1}^*$ ($T_{t_2}^*$) is the optimally grafted subtree rooted in t_1 (t_2) with respect to $\mathcal{O}_1'$ ($\mathcal{O}_2'$), respectively, since the depth of $T_{t_1}^*$ ($T_{t_2}^*$) is not greater than d. Analogously, let $T_{t_1}^*$ ($T_{t_2}^*$) be the subtree rooted in t_1 (t_2), returned by REG when pruned with respect to $\mathcal{O}$. For the inductive hypothesis, $T_{t_1}^*$ ($T_{t_2}^*$) is the optimally grafted subtree rooted in t_1 (t_2) with respect to $\mathcal{O}'$.

---

[3] Note that the grafting operation applied to the tree T_{t_1} may not produce a tree rooted in t_1, so we denote it as $T_{t_1}^*$.

Let T' be the tree rooted in t_0 whose subtrees are $T^*_{t_1}$ and $T^*_{t_2}$. Then, for any tree $T'' \in S_G(T)$ of depth greater than 0 and rooted in t_0 with children t'_1 and t'_2, we have $f(T') \leq f(T'')$, since $f(T') = \sum_{t \in \widetilde{T}_{t_1}^*} R(t) + \sum_{t \in \widetilde{T}_{t_2}^*} R(t) : \sum_{t \in \widetilde{T}_{t_1'}} R(t) + \sum_{t \in \widetilde{T}_{t_2'}} R(t) = f(T'')$.

Therefore, if $f(T^*_{\hat{t}_1}) \leq f(T')$ and $f(T^*_{\hat{t}_1}) \leq f(T^*_{\hat{t}_2})$, where $f(T^*_{\hat{t}_1})$ and $f(T^*_{\hat{t}_2})$ are computed with respect to $\mathcal{O}'$, then REG replaces T' with $T^*_{\hat{t}_1}$, which is the best subtree of T, since

- $R(T^*_{\hat{t}_1}) = f(T^*_{\hat{t}_1}) \leq f(T') \leq f(T'')$ for any tree $T'' \in S_G(T)$ rooted in t_0 with depth greater than 0.

- $R(T^*_{\hat{t}_1}) = f(T^*_{\hat{t}_1}) \leq f(T'')$ for any tree $T'' \in S_G(T)$ not rooted in t_0 (both $T^*_{\hat{t}_1}$ and

    T'' have maximum depth d and the inductive hypothesis holds on $\mathcal{O}$).

Otherwise, if $f(T^*_{\hat{t}_2}) \leq f(T')$ and $f(T^*_{\hat{t}_2}) \leq f(T^*_{\hat{t}_1})$, REG replaces T' with $T^*_{\hat{t}_2}$, which is the best subtree of T, since

- $R(T^*_{\hat{t}_2}) = f(T^*_{\hat{t}_2}) \leq f(T') \leq f(T'')$ for any tree $T'' \in S_G(T)$ rooted in t_0 with depth greater than 0.

- $R(T^*_{\hat{t}_2}) = f(T^*_{\hat{t}_2}) \leq f(T'')$ for any tree $T'' \in S_G(T)$ not rooted in t_0 (both $T^*_{\hat{t}_2}$ and T'' have maximum depth d and the inductive hypothesis holds on $\mathcal{O}$).

Finally, if both $f(T^*_{\hat{t}_1}) > f(T')$ and $f(T^*_{\hat{t}_2}) > f(T')$ then REG does not simplify T in t_0 and the returned tree is T'. Obviously, T' is better than any tree $T'' \in S_G(T)$ rooted in t_0. Moreover, T' is better than any tree $T'' \in S_G(T)$ not rooted in t_0, since either $T'' \in S_G(T_{t_1})$ and $f(T'') \geq f(T^*_{\hat{t}_1}) > f(T')$ or $T'' \in S_G(T_{t_2})$ and $f(T'') \geq f(T^*_{\hat{t}_2}) > f(T')$.

Therefore, the returned tree T' is the smallest tree in $S_G(T)$ with the lowest error with respect to $\mathcal{O}$. ∎

The complexity of REG is $O(N_T | \log_2 N_T |)$, where $|N_T|$ is the number of nodes in T.

6   Comments on Experimental Results

The experiment aims at investigating the effect of simplification methods on the predictive accuracy of the model trees. Reduced Error Pruning and Reduced Error Grafting were implemented as a module of KDB2000 (http://www.di.uniba.it/~malerba/software/kdb2000/) and has been empirically evaluated on ten datasets, taken from either the UCI Machine Learning Repository (http://www.ics.uci.edu/~mlearn/MLRepository.html), the site of the system HTL (http://www.ncc.up.pt/~ltorgo/Regression/DataSets.html) or the site of WEKA (http://www.cs.waikato.ac.nz/ml/weka/index.html). They are listed in Table 1 and have a continuous variable to be predicted. They have been used as benchmarks in related studies on regression trees and model trees.

Table 1. Ten datasets used in the empirical evaluation of SMOTI

Dataset	No. Cases	No. Attributes	Continuous	Discrete	Goal
Abalone	4177	10	9	1	Predicting the age of abalone from physical measurements
Auto-Mpg	392	8	5	3	Predicting the city-cycle fuel consumption
Auto-Price	159	27	17	10	Predicting auto price
Bank8FM	4499	9	9	0	Predicting the fraction of bank customers who leave the bank because of full queues
Cleveland	297	14	7	7	Predicting the heart disease in a patient.
Housing	506	14	14	0	Predicting housing values in areas of Boston
Machine CPU	209	10	8	2	Predicting relative CPU performance
Pyrimidines	74	28	28	0	Predicting the activity (QSARs) from the descriptive structural attributes
Triazines	74	61	61	0	Predicting the structure (QSARs) from the descriptive structural attributes
Wisconsin Cancer	186	33	33	0	Predicting the time to recur for a breast cancer case

Each dataset is analyzed by means of a 10-fold cross-validation. For every trial, the data set is partitioned so that 90% of cases are left in the training set and 10% are put aside for the independent test set. The training set is, in turn, partitioned into growing (70%) and pruning set (30%). SMOTI is trained on the growing set, pruned on the pruning set and tested on the test set. Comparison is based on the average mean square error ($Avg.MSE$) made on the test sets:

$$Avg.MSE = \frac{\sum\limits_{i=1..k} R(T_i)}{k}$$

where k is the number of folds and $R(T_i)$ is the resubstitution error of the i-th cross-validated tree computed on the corresponding testing set.

Experimental results are listed in Table 2. The table reports the average MSE of (un-pruned/pruned) SMOTI trees built on training/growing set. For comparison purposes, results obtained on the M5', which is implemented in the public available system WEKA, are reported as well. Results show that pruning is generally beneficial since REP and REG decrease the Avg.MSE of SMOTI trees built on the growing set in nine out of ten data sets. Moreover, the pruning method implemented in M5' pruning method outperforms both REP and REG in most data sets. However, the poorer performance of REP and REG can be justified if we consider that M5' pruned a model tree, which was originally more accurate than that pruned by REP and REG because of the full use of the cases in the training set. This result is similar to that reported in [3] for decision trees. Even in that case, it was observed that methods requiring an independent pruning set are at a disadvantage. This is due to the fact that the set of pre-classified cases is limited and, if part of the set is put aside for pruning, it cannot be used to grow a more accurate tree.

A different view of results is offered in Table 3, which reports a percentage of the avg. MSE made by pruned trees on the test sets with respect to the avg. MSE made by un-pruned trees on the same testing sets. The table emphasizes the gain of the use of pruning. In particular, pruning is beneficial when the value is less than 100%, while it is not when the value is grather than 100%. Results reported confirm that pruning is beneficial for nine out of ten datasets. Moreover, the absolute difference of Avg. MSE for REP and REG is below 5% in seven datasets. Finally, it is worthwhile to notice that the gain of REP and REG is better than the corresponding gain of M5' pruning method in six datasets. This induces to hypothesize that the better absolute performances of M5' are mainly due to the fact that the tree to be pruned is more accurate because of the full use of training cases.

Table 2. Tree predictive accuracy for the pruning of two different systems: SMOTI, M5'

	SMOTI un-pruned		SMOTI pruned		M5'	
	Avg trained MSE	*Avg* grown MSE	*Avg* REP MSE	*Avg* REG MSE	*Avg* not pruned MSE	*Avg* Pruned MSE
Abalone	2,5364	6,7244	2,1851	2,1797	2,77242	2,12669
AutoMpg	3,14938	4,48666	3,56337	3,74361	3,20106	2,83555
Auto Price	2246,03	2481,74	2746,32	2890,42	2358,81	2390,12
Bank8FM	0,0383	0,0427	0,0358	0,0342	0,04099	0,03198
Cleveland	1,3160	1,5215	0,9148	0,9349	1,24963	0,90286
Housing	3,58	5,7176	4,0803	3,9120	4,27927	3,8159
Machine CPU	55,3148	71,6991	70,9533	69,1451	57,3527	58,3412
Pyrimidines	0,10566	0,18727	0,10343	0,13527	0,09279	0,08640
Triazines	0,2017	0,1820	0,1559	0,2290	0,15503	0,1318
Wisconsin Cancer	51,4138	72,3762	33,4649	37,4556	45,4064	34,3972

Table 3. Average percentage of the MSE for pruned trees w.r.t. the MSE of un-pruned trees. MSE is computed on the testing set. Best values are in bold

Data Set	REP/un-pruned SMOTI on growing set	REG/un-pruned SMOTI on growing set	Pruned M5' /un-pruned M5'
Abalone	32.49%	**32.42%**	76.71%
AutoMpg	**79.42%**	83.44%	88.58%
Auto Price	110.66%	116.47%	**101.33%**
Bank8FM	83.84%	80.09%	**78.02%**
Cleveland	**60.12%**	61.44%	72.25%
Housing	71.36%	**68.42%**	89.17%
Machine CPU	98.95%	**96.43%**	101.72%
Pyrimidines	**55.23%**	72.23%	93.11%
Triazines	85.65%	125.82%	**85.02%**
Wisconsin Cancer	**46.23%**	51.75%	75.75%

7   Conclusions

SMOTI is a TDIMT method which integrates the partitioning phase and the labeling phase. Similar to many decision tree induction algorithms, SMOTI may generate model trees that overfit training data. In this paper, the *a posteriori* simplification (or pruning) of model trees has been investigated in order to solve this problem. Specifically, we developed a unifying framework for the *a posteriori* simplification of model trees with both regression nodes and splitting nodes. Two methods, named REP and REG, have been defined on the basis of this framework, which is general enough to formulate other pruning methods. Some experimental results have been reported on the pruning methods and show that pruning is improves the average mean square error in most of datasets. Moreover, the comparison with another well-known TDIMT method, namely M5', which uses the training data both for growing and for pruning the tree, induces to hypothesize that putting aside some data for pruning can lead to worse results.

As future work, we plan to extend this comparison to other TDIMT systems (e.g. HTL and RETIS). Moreover, we intend to implement a new simplification method based on both pruning and grafting operators and to eventually extend MDL-based pruning strategies developed for regression [13] trees to the case of SMOTI trees. This extension should overcome problems we observed for small datasets since the new pruning algorithm will not require an independent pruning set.

Acknowledgments. The work presented in this paper is in partial fulfillment of the research objectives set by the MIUR COFIN-2001 project on "Methods for the extraction, validation and representation of statistical information in a decision context".

References

1. Breiman L., Friedman J., Olshen R., & Stone J. Classification and regression tree, Wadsworth & Brooks, (1984).
2. Cestnik B. and Bratko I. On estimating probabilities in tree pruning, *Proc. of the Fifth European Working Session on Learning*, Springer, (1991), 151–163.
3. Esposito F., Malerba D., Semeraro G. A comparative analysis of methods for pruning decision trees. *IEEE Trans. PAMI*, Vol. 19, Num. 5, (1997), 476–491.
4. Esposito F., Malerba D., Semeraro G. & Tamma V. The Effects of Pruning Methods on the Predictive Accuracy of Induced Decision Trees. *Applied Stochastic Models in Business and Industry*, Vol. 15, Num. 4, (1999), 277–299.
5. Karalic A. Linear regression in regression tree leaves, in *Proceedings of ISSEK '92 (International School for Synthesis of Expert Knowledge)*, Bled, Slovenia, (1992).
6. Lubinsky D. Tree Structured Interpretable Regression, in Learning from Data, Fisher D. & Lenz H.J. (Eds.), Lecture Notes in Statistics, 112, Springer, (1996), 387–398.
7. Malerba D., Appice A., Bellino A., Ceci M. & Pallotta D. Stepwise Induction of Model Trees, in F. Esposito (Ed.), *AI*IA 2001: Advances in Artificial Intelligence, Lecture Notes in Artificial Intelligence*, 2175, Springer, Germany, (2001).
8. Malerba, D., Appice A., Ceci M. & Monopoli, M. Trading-off Local versus Global Effects of Regression Nodes in Model Trees. *Proceeding of the 13th Int. Symposium on Methodologies for Intelligent Systems*, (2002).
9. Niblett, T. & Bratko, I. Learning decision rules in noisy domains. In Bramer, M. A., *Research and Development in Expert Systems III*, Cambridge University Press, Cambridge, (1986), 25–34.
10. Orkin, M. & Drogin, R. *Vital Statistics*. New York: McGraw Hill, (1990).
11. Quinlan J.R. Simplifying decision trees. *International Journal of Man-Machine Studies*; 27, (1987), 221–234.
12. Quinlan J. R. Learning with continuous classes, in *Proceedings AI'92*, Adams & Sterling (Eds.), World Scientific, (1992), 343–348.
13. Robnik-Šikonja M., Kononenko I. Pruning Regression Trees with MDL. In H. Prade (Ed.), Proceedings of the 13th European Conference on Artificial Intelligence, John Wiley & Sons, Chichester, England, (1998), 455–459.
14. Tapio Elomaa, Matti Kääriäinen (2001). An Analysis of Reduced Error Pruning. *Journal of Artificial Intelligence Research*, 15, pp. 163–187.
15. Torgo L. Kernel Regression Trees, in *Poster Papers of the 9th European Conference on Machine Learning (ECML 97)*, M. van Someren, & G. Widmer (Eds.), Prague, Czech Republic, (1997), 118–127.
16. Torgo L. Functional Models for Regression Tree Leaves, in *Proceedings of the Fourteenth International Conference (ICML '97)*, D. Fisher (Ed.), Nashville, Tennessee, (1997).
17. Wang Y. & Witten I.H. Inducing Model Trees for Continuous Classes, in *Poster Papers of the 9th European Conference on Machine Learning (ECML 97)*, M. van Someren, & G. Widmer (Eds.), Prague, Czech Republic, (1997), 128–137.
18. Weisberg S. *Applied regression analysis, 2nd edn.* New York: Wiley, 1985.

Learning Multi-label Alternating Decision Trees from Texts and Data[*]

Francesco De Comité[1], Rémi Gilleron[2], and Marc Tommasi[2]
équipe Grappa – EA 3588

[1] Lille 1 University, 59655 Villeneuve d'Ascq Cedex, France
decomite@lifl.fr
[2] Lille 3 University, 59653 Villeneuve d'Ascq Cedex, France
gilleron,tommasi@univ-lille3.fr

Abstract. Multi-label decision procedures are the target of the supervised learning algorithm we propose in this paper. Multi-label decision procedures map examples to a finite set of labels. Our learning algorithm extends Schapire and Singer's Adaboost.MH and produces sets of rules that can be viewed as trees like Alternating Decision Trees (invented by Freund and Mason). Experiments show that we take advantage of both performance and readability using boosting techniques as well as tree representations of large set of rules. Moreover, a key feature of our algorithm is the ability to handle heterogenous input data: discrete and continuous values and text data.

Keywords: boosting, alternating decision trees, text mining, multi-label problems

1 Introduction

When a patient spends more than 3 days in center X, measures of albuminuri as well as proteinuri are made. But if the patient is in center Y, then only measures of albuminuri are made.

These sentences can be viewed as a multi-label classification procedure because more than one label among {*albuminuri, proteinuri*} may be assigned to a given description of a situation. That is to say we are faced a categorization task for which the categories are not mutually exclusive. This work is originally motivated by a practical problem in medicine where each patient may be described by continuous-valued attributes (*e.g.* measures), nominal attributes (*e.g.* sex, smoker, ...) and text data (*e.g.* descriptions, comments, ...). It was important to produce rules that can be interpreted by physicians and also rules that reveal correlations between labels predictions. These requirements have lead to the realization of the algorithm presented in this paper[1].

---

[*] Partially supported by project DATADIAB: "ACI télémédecine et technologies pour la santé" and project TACT/TIC Feder & CPER Région-Nord Pas de Calais.
[1] The algorithm and a graphical user interface are available from
http://www.grappa.univ-lille3.fr/grappa/index.php3?info=logiciels

P. Perner and A. Rosenfeld (Eds.): MLDM 2003, LNAI 2734, pp. 35–49, 2003.

Multi-label classification problems are ubiquitous in real world problems. Learning algorithms that can hold multi-label problems are therefore valuable. Of course there are many strategies to apply a combination of many binary classifiers to solve multi-label problems ([ASS00]). But most of them ignore correlations between the different labels. AdaBoost.MH algorithm proposed by Schapire and Singer ([SS00]) efficiently handles multi-label problems. For a given example, it also provides a real value as an outcome for each label. For practical applications, these values are important because they can be interpreted as a confidence rate about the decision for the considered label. AdaBoost.MH implements boosting techniques that are theoretically proved to transform a weak learner – called base classifier – into a strong one. The main idea of boosting is to combine many simple and moderately inaccurate rules built by the base classifier into a single highly accurate rule. The combination is a weighted majority vote over all simple rules. Boosting has been extensively studied and many authors have shown that it performs well on standard machine learning tasks ([Bre98,FS96,FS97]). Unfortunately, as pointed by Freund and Mason an others authors, the rule ultimately produced by a boosting algorithm may be difficult to understand and to interpret.

In [FM99], Freund and Mason introduce Alternating Decision Trees (ADTrees). The motivation of Freund and Mason was to obtain intelligible classification models when applying boosting methods. ADTrees are classification models inspired by both decision trees and option trees ([KK97]). ADTrees provide a symbolic representation of a classification procedure and give together with classification a measure of confidence. Freund and Mason also propose an alternating decision tree learning algorithm called ADTBoost in [FM99]. ADTBoost algorithm originates from two ideas: first, decision tree learning algorithms may be analyzed as boosting algorithms (see [DKM96,KM96]); second, boosting algorithms could be used because ADTrees generalize both voted decision stumps and voted decision trees. Recently, the ADTree formalism has been extended to the multiclass case ([HPK+02]).

We propose in this paper to extend ADTrees formalism to handle multi-label decision procedure. Decision procedures are learned from data described by nominal, continuous and text data. Our algorithm can be understood as an extension of AdaBoost.MH that permits a better readability of the classification rule ultimately produced as well as an extension to ADTBoost in order to handle multi-label classification problems. The multi-label ADTree formalism gives an intelligible set of rules viewable as a tree. Moreover, rules allow to combine atomic tests. In our implementation, we can handle test on (continuous or discrete) tabular data as well as tests on text data. This is particularly valuable in medicine where descriptions of patients combine diagnostic analysis, comments, dosages, measures, and so on. For instance, a rule can be built on both temperature and diagnostic, *if temperature > 37.5 and diagnostic contains "Cardiovascular" then* .... This kind of combination in a unique rule is not considered by others algorithms like Boostexter which implements AdaBoost.MH. We expect the algorithm to find more concise set of rules thanks to such combinations. We are convinced that rules with several tests in their premises provide useful informations that can be interpreted by experts. In this paper, we only present results on freely available data sets. We compare our algorithm ADTBoost.MH with AdaBoost.MH on two data sets: the reuters collection and a new data set built from news articles[2].

In Sect. 2, we define multi-label problems and we recall AdaBoost.MH's functioning. Alternating Decision Trees are presented in Sect. 3. We define multi-label ADTrees which generalize ADTrees to the multi-label case in Sect. 4. An example is given in Fig. 3. A Multi-label ADTree is an easily readable representation of both different ADTrees (one ADTree per label) and of many decision stumps (one per boosting round). We propose a multi-label ADTree learning algorithm ADTboost.MH based on both ADTboost and Adaboost.MH [SS98]. Experiments are given in Sect. 5. They show that our algorithm reaches the performance of well tuned algorithms like Boostexter.

2   Boosting and Multi-label Problems

Most of supervised learning algorithms deal with binary or multiclass classification tasks. In such a case, an instance belongs to one class and the goal of learning algorithms is to find an hypothesis which minimizes the probability that an instance is misclassified by the hypothesis. Even when a learning algorithm do not apply to the multiclass case, there exist several methods that can combine binary decision procedures in order to solve multiclass problems ([DB95, ASS00]). In this paper, we consider the more general problem, called multi-label classification problem, in which an example may belong to any number of classes. Formally, let $\mathcal{X}$ be the universe and let us consider a set of labels $\mathcal{Y} = \{1, \ldots, k\}$. The goal is to find with input a sample $S = \{(x_i, Y_i) \mid x_i \in \mathcal{X}, Y_i \subseteq \mathcal{Y}, 1 \leq i \leq m\}$ an hypothesis $h : \mathcal{X} \mapsto 2^{\mathcal{Y}}$ with low error. It is unclear to define the error in the multi-label case because different definitions are possible, depending on the application we are faced with. In this paper, we only consider the Hamming error.

Hamming error: The goal is to predict the set of labels associated with an example. Therefore, one takes into account *prediction errors* (an incorrect label is predicted) and *missing errors* (a label is not predicted). Let us consider a target function $c : \mathcal{X} \mapsto 2^{\mathcal{Y}}$ and an hypothesis $h : \mathcal{X} \mapsto 2^{\mathcal{Y}}$, the *Hamming error* of h is defined by:

$$E_H(h) = \frac{1}{k} \sum_{l=1}^{k} D(\{x \in \mathcal{X} \mid (l \in h(x) \land l \notin c(x)) \lor (l \notin h(x) \land l \in c(x))\}). \quad (1)$$

---

[2] Data sets and perl scripts are available on
http://www.grappa.univ-lille3.fr/recherche/datasets.

The factor $\frac{1}{k}$ normalizes the error in the interval $[0,1]$. The training error over a sample S is:

$$E_H(h, S) = \frac{1}{km} \sum_{i,l} (\| (l \in h(x_i) \wedge l \notin Y_i \| + \| l \notin h(x_i) \wedge l \in Y_i \|) \quad (2)$$

where $\| a \|$ equals 1 if a holds and 0 otherwise.

In the rest of the paper, we will consider learning algorithms that output mappings h from $\mathcal{X} \times \mathcal{Y}$ into $\mathbb{R}$. The real value $h(x, l)$ can be viewed as a prediction value for the label l for the instance x. Given h, we define a multi-label interpretation h^m of h: h^m is a mapping $\mathcal{X} \to 2^{\mathcal{Y}}$ such that $h^m(x) = \{l \in \mathcal{Y} \mid h(x, l) > 0\}$.

AdaBoost.MH

Schapire and Singer introduce AdaBoost.MH in [SS00]. Originally, the algorithm supposes a weak learner from $\mathcal{X} \times \mathcal{Y}$ to $\mathbb{R}$. In this section we focus on boosting decision stumps. We are given a set of conditions $\mathcal{C}$. Weak hypotheses are therefore rules of the form *if c then* $(a_l)_{l \in \mathcal{Y}}$ *else* $(b_l)_{l \in \mathcal{Y}}$ where $c \in \mathcal{C}$ and a_l, b_l are real values for each label l. Weak hypotheses therefore make their predictions based on a partitioning of the domain $\mathcal{X}$.

The AdaBoost.MH learning algorithm is given in Algorithm 1. Multi-label data are firstly transformed into binary data. Given a set of labels $Y \subseteq \mathcal{Y}$, let us define $Y[l]$ to be $+1$ if $l \in Y$ and to be -1 if $l \notin Y$. Given an input sample of m examples, the main idea is to replace each training example (x_i, Y_i) by k examples $((x_i, l), Y_i[l])$ for $l \in \mathcal{Y}$. AdaBoost.MH maintains a distribution over $\mathcal{X} \times \mathcal{Y}$. It re-weights the sample at each boosting step. Basically, examples that were misclassified by the hypothesis in the previous round have an higher weight in the current round. It is proved in [SS98] that the normalization factor Z_t induced by the re-weighting realizes a bound on the empirical Hamming loss of the current hypothesis. Therefore, this bound is used to guide the choice of the weak hypothesis at each step. AdaBoost.MH tries to minimize error while minimizing the normalization factor denoted by Z_t at each step.

Let us denote $W_+^l(c)$ (resp. $W_-^l(c)$) the sum of weights of the positive (resp. negative) examples that satisfies condition c and have label l.

$$W_+^l(c) = \sum_{i=1}^{i=m} D_t(i, l) \| x_i \text{ satisfies } c \wedge Y_i[l] = +1 \|$$

$$W_-^l(c) = \sum_{i=1}^{i=m} D_t(i, l) \| x_i \text{ satisfies } c \wedge Y_i[l] = -1 \|$$

Therefore, one can prove analytically that the the best prediction values a_l and b_l which minimize Z_t at each step are:

$$a_l = \frac{1}{2} ln \frac{W_+^l(c)}{W_-^l(c)} \; ; \; b_l = \frac{1}{2} ln \frac{W_+^l(c)}{W_-^l(c)} \quad (3)$$

leading to a normalization factor Z_t :

$$Z_t(c) = 2 \sum_{l=1}^{l=k} \sqrt{W_+^l(c) W_-^l(c)} \tag{4}$$

Algorithm 1 AdaBoost.MH(T) where T is the number of boosting rounds

---

Input: a sample $S = \{(x_1, Y_1), \ldots, (x_m, Y_m) \mid x_i \in \mathcal{X}, Y_i \subseteq \mathcal{Y} = \{1, \ldots, k\}\}$; $\mathcal{C}$ is a
    set of base conditions
1: Transform S into $S^k = \{((x_i, l), Y_i[l]) \mid 1 \le i \le m, l \in \mathcal{Y}\} \subseteq (\mathcal{X} \times \mathcal{Y}) \times \{-1, +1\}$
2: Initialize the weights: $1 \le i \le m$, $l \in \mathcal{Y}$, $w_1(i, l) = 1$
3: **for** $t = 1..T$ **do**
4:     choose c which minimize $Z_t(c)$ according to Equation 4
5:     build the rule r_t : if c then $\frac{1}{2} ln \frac{W_+^l(c)}{W_-^l(c)}$ else $\frac{1}{2} ln \frac{W_+^l(c)}{W_-^l(c)}$
6:     Update weights : $w_{t+1}(i, l) = w_t(i, l) e^{-Y_i[l] r_t(x_i, l)}$
7: **end for**
Output: $f(x, l) = \blacksquare_{t=1}^{T} r_t(x, l)$.

---

3   Alternating Decision Trees

Alternating Decision Trees (ADTrees) are introduced by Freund and Mason
in [FM99]. They are similar to option trees developed by Kohavi *et al* [KK97].
An important motivation of Freund and Mason was to obtain intelligible classification models when applying boosting methods. Alternating decision trees
contain *splitter nodes* and *prediction nodes*. A splitter node is associated with a
test, a prediction node is associated with a real value. An example of ADTree
is given in Fig. 1. It is composed of four splitter nodes and nine prediction
nodes. An instance defines a set of paths in an ADTree. The classification which
is associated with an instance is the sign of the sum of the predictions along
the paths in the set defined by this instance. Consider the ADTree in Fig. 1
and the instance $x = (color = red, year = 1989, \ldots)$, the sum of predictions
is $+0.2 + 0.2 + 0.6 + 0.4 + 0.6 = +2$, thus the classification is $+1$ with high
confidence. For the instance $x = (color = red, year = 1999, \ldots)$, the sum of predictions is $+0.4$ and the classification is $+1$ with low confidence. For the instance
$x = (color = white, year = 1999, \ldots)$, the sum of predictions is -0.7 and the
classification is -1 with medium confidence.

    ADTree depicted in Fig. 1 can also be viewed as consisting of a root prediction
node and four units of three nodes each. Each unit is a decision rule and is
composed of a splitter node and two prediction nodes that are its children. It
is easy to give another description of ADTrees using sets of rules. For instance,
the ADTree in Fig. 1 is described by the set of rules:

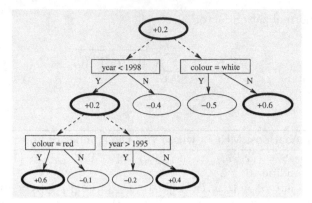

Fig. 1. an example of ADTree; bold prediction nodes define the set of nodes associated with the instance $x = (color = red, year = 1989, \dots)$

If TRUE	then (if TRUE	then +0.2 else 0	) else 0
If TRUE	then (if year < 1998	then +0.2 else -0.4	) else 0
If year < 1998	then (if colour = red	then +0.6 else -0.1	) else 0
If year < 1998	then (if year > 1995	then -0.2 else +0.4	) else 0
If TRUE	then (if colour = white	then -0.5 else +0.6	) else 0

ADTBoost

Rules in an ADTree are similar to decision stumps. Consequently, one can apply boosting methods in order to design an ADTree learning algorithm. The algorithm proposed by Freund and Mason [FM99] is based on this idea. It relies on Schapire and Singer [SS98] study of boosting methods. A rule in an ADTree defines a partition of the instance space into three blocks defined by $C_1 \wedge c_2$, $C_1 \wedge \neg c_2$ and $\neg C_1$. Following this observation, Freund and Mason apply a variant of Adaboost proposed in [SS98] for domain-partitioning weak hypotheses. Basically, the learning algorithm builds an ADTree with a top down strategy. At every boosting step, it selects and adds a new rule or equivalently a new unit consisting of a splitter node and two prediction nodes. Contrary to the case of decision trees, the reader should note that a new rule can be added below any prediction node in the current ADTree.

Freund and Mason's algorithm ADTboost is given as Algorithm 2. Similarly to Adaboost algorithm, ADTboost updates weights at each step (line 8). The quantity $Z_t(C_1, c_2)$ is a normalization coefficient. It is defined by

$$Z_t(C_1, c_2) = 2 \left(\sqrt{W_+(C_1 \wedge c_2)W_-(C_1 \wedge c_2)} + \sqrt{W_+(C_1 \wedge \neg c_2)W_+(C_1 \wedge \neg c_2)} \right) + W(\neg C_1) \quad (5)$$

where $W_+(C)$ (resp. $W_-(C)$) is the sum of the weights of the positive (resp. negative) examples that satisfy condition C. It has been shown that the product of all such coefficients gives an upper bound of the training error. Therefore, ADTboost selects a precondition C_1 and a condition c_2 that minimize $Z_t(C_1, c_2)$ (line 5) in order to minimize the training error. The prediction values a and b (line 6) are chosen according to results in [SS98].

ADTboost is competitive with boosting decision tree learning algorithms such as C5 + Boost. Moreover, the size of the ADTree generated by ADTboost is often smaller than the model generated by other methods. These two points have strongly motivated our choices although ADTboost suffers from some drawbacks *e.g.* the choice of the number of boosting rounds is difficult and overfitting occurs. We discuss these problems in the conclusion.

Algorithm 2 ADTboost(T) where T is the number of boosting rounds

---

Input: a sample $S = \{(x_1, y_1), \dots, (x_m, y_m) \mid x_i \in \mathcal{X}, y_i \in \{-1, +1\}\}$; a set of base conditions $\mathcal{C}$.

1: Initialize the weights: $1 \leq i \leq m$, $w_{i,1} = 1$
2: Initialize the ADTree: $\mathcal{R}_1 = \{r_1 : (\text{if } \boldsymbol{T} \text{ then } (\text{if } \boldsymbol{T} \text{ then } \frac{1}{2} \ln \frac{W_+(\boldsymbol{T})}{W_-(\boldsymbol{T})}) \text{ else } 0) \text{ else } 0)\}$
3: Initialize the set of preconditions: $\mathcal{P}_1 = \{\boldsymbol{T}\}$
4: **for** $t = 1..T$ **do**
5:     Choose $C_1 \in \mathcal{P}_t$ and $c_2 \in \mathcal{C}$ which minimize $Z_t(C_1, c_2)$ according to Equation 5
6:     $\mathcal{R}_{t+1} = \mathcal{R}_t \cup \{r_{t+1} : (\text{if } C_1 \text{ then } (\text{if } c_2 \text{ then } \frac{1}{2} \ln \frac{W_+(C_1 \wedge c_2)}{W_-(C_1 \wedge c_2)}) \text{ else } \frac{1}{2} \ln \frac{W_+(C_1 \wedge \neg c_2)}{W_-(C_1 \wedge \neg c_2)})$
       else 0)}
7:     $\mathcal{P}_{t+1} = \mathcal{P}_t \cup \{C_1 \wedge c_2, C_1 \wedge \neg c_2\}$
8:     update weights: $w_{i,t+1}(i) = w_{i,t}(i) e^{-y_i r_t(x_i)}$
9: **end for**
Output: ADTree $\mathcal{R}_{T+1}$

---

4   Multi-label Alternating Decision Trees

Multi-label ADTrees

We generalize ADTrees to the case of multi-label problems. A prediction node is now associated with a set of real values, one for each label. An example of such an ADTree is given in Fig. 3.

Let $\mathcal{X}$ be the universe, the conjunction is denoted by $\wedge$, the negation is denoted by $\neg$, and let $\boldsymbol{T}$ be the True condition. Let $(0)_{l \in \mathcal{Y}}$ be a vector of l zeros.

Definition 1. *Let $\mathcal{C}$ be a set of base conditions where a base condition is a boolean predicate over instances. A precondition is a conjunction of base conditions and negations of base conditions. A rule in an ADTree is defined by a precondition C_1, a condition c_2 and two vectors of real numbers $(a_l)_{l \in \mathcal{Y}}$ and $(b_l)_{l \in \mathcal{Y}}$:*

$$\text{if } C_1 \text{ then } (\text{if } c_2 \text{ then } (a_l)_{l \in \mathcal{Y}} \text{ else } (b_l)_{l \in \mathcal{Y}}) \text{ else } (0)_{l \in \mathcal{Y}},$$

A *multi-label alternating decision tree (multi-label ADTree) is a set* $\mathcal{R}$ *of such rules satisfying properties (i) and (ii):*

(i) *the set* $\mathcal{R}$ *must include an initial rule for which the precondition* C_1 *is* $\mathbf{T}$, *the condition* c_2 *is* $\mathbf{T}$, *and b equals* $(0)_{l \in \mathcal{Y}}$;
(ii) *whenever the set* $\mathcal{R}$ *contains a rule with a precondition* C_1', $\mathcal{R}$ *also contains another rule with precondition* C_1 *and there is a base condition* c_2 *such that either* $C_1' = C_1 \wedge c_2$ *or* $C_1' = C_1 \wedge \neg c_2$.

A multi-label ADTree maps each instance to a vector of real number in the following way:

Definition 2. *A rule r: if* C_1 *then (if* c_2 *then* $(a_l)_{l \in \mathcal{Y}}$ *else* $(b_l)_{l \in \mathcal{Y}}$ *) else* $(0)_{l \in \mathcal{Y}}$ *associates a real value* $r(x, l)$ *with any* $(x, l) \in \mathcal{X} \times \mathcal{Y}$. *If* (x, l) *satisfies* $C = C_1 \wedge c_2$ *then* $r(x, l)$ *equals* a_l; *if* (x, l) *satisfies* $C = C_1 \wedge \neg c_2$ *then* $r(x, l)$ *equals* b_l; *otherwise,* $r(x, l)$ *equals* 0.

An ADTree $\mathcal{R} = \{r_i\}_{i \in I}$ *associates a prediction value* $R(x, l) = \sum_{i \in I} r_i(x, l)$ *with any* $(x, l) \in \mathcal{X} \times \mathcal{Y}$. *A multi-label classification hypothesis is associated with* H *defined by* $H(x, l) = sign(R(x, l))$ *and the real number* $|R(x, l)|$ *is interpreted as the confidence assigned to* $H(x, l)$, *i.e. the confidence assigned to the label* l *for the instance* x.

ADTBoost.MH

Our multi-label alternating decision tree learning algorithm is derived from both ADTboost and AdaBoost.MH algorithms. Following [SS98], we now make precise the calculation of the prediction values and the value of the normalization factor $Z_t(C_1, c_2)$. The reader should note that we consider partitions over $\mathcal{X} \times \mathcal{Y}$.

On round t, let us denote the current distribution over $\mathcal{X} \times \mathcal{Y}$ by D_t, and let us consider $W_+^l(C)$ (resp. $W_-^l(C)$) as the sum of the weights of the positive (resp. negative) examples that satisfy condition C and have label l:

$$W_+^l(C) = \sum_{i=1}^{i=m} D_t(i, l) \parallel x_i \text{ satisfies } C \wedge Y_i[l] = +1 \parallel$$

$$W_-^l(C) = \sum_{i=1}^{i=m} D_t(i, l) \parallel x_i \text{ satisfies } C \wedge Y_i[l] = -1 \parallel$$

$$W^l(C) = \sum_{i=1}^{i=m} D_t(i, l) \parallel x_i \text{ satisfies } C \parallel$$

It is easy to prove that the normalization factor Z_t and the best prediction values a_l and b_l are:

$$a_l = \frac{1}{2}ln\frac{W_+^l(C_1 \wedge c_2)}{W_-^l(C_1 \wedge c_2)} \; ; \; b_l = \frac{1}{2}ln\frac{W_+^l(C_1 \wedge \neg c_2)}{W_-^l(C_1 \wedge \neg c_2)} \qquad (6)$$

$$Z_t(C_1, c_2) = 2\sum_{l=1}^{l=k}\left[\sqrt{W_+^l(C_1 \wedge c_2)W_-^l(C_1 \wedge c_2)}\right.$$

$$\left. + \sqrt{W_+^l(C_1 \wedge \neg c_2)W_-^l(C_1 \wedge \neg c_2)}\right]$$

$$+ W(\neg C_1) \qquad (7)$$

The algorithm ADTboost.MH is given as Algorithm 3. In order to avoid extrem values for confidence values, we use the following formulas:

$$a_l = \frac{1}{2}ln\frac{W_{+1}^l(C_1 \wedge c_2) + \epsilon}{W_{-1}^l(C_1 \wedge c_2) + \epsilon} \; ; \; b_l = \frac{1}{2}ln\frac{W_{+1}^l(C_1 \wedge \neg c_2) + \epsilon}{W_{-1}^l(C_1 \wedge \neg c_2) + \epsilon} \qquad (8)$$

with $\epsilon = \frac{1}{2mk}$.

Algorithm 3 ADTboost.MH(T) where T is the number of boosting rounds

---

Input: a sample $S = \{(x_1, Y_1), \ldots, (x_m, Y_m) \mid x_i \in \mathcal{X}, Y_i \subseteq \mathcal{Y} = \{1, \ldots, k\}\}$; $\mathcal{C}$ is a set of base conditions

1: Transform S into $S^k = \{((x_i, l), Y_i[l]) \mid 1 \leq i \leq m, l \in \mathcal{Y}\} \subseteq (\mathcal{X} \times \mathcal{Y}) \times \{-1, +1\}$
2: Initialize the weights: $1 \leq i \leq m$, $l \in \mathcal{Y}$, $w_1(i, l) = 1$
3: Initialize the multi-label ADTree:
   $\mathcal{R}_1 = \{r_1 : (\text{if } \boldsymbol{T} \text{ then } (\text{if } \boldsymbol{T} \text{ then } (a_l = \frac{1}{2}\ln\frac{W_+^l(\boldsymbol{T})}{W_-^l(\boldsymbol{T})})_{l \in \mathcal{Y}}) \text{ else } (b_l = 0)_{l \in \mathcal{Y}}) \text{ else } 0)\}.$
4: Initialize the set of preconditions: $\mathcal{P}_1 = \{\boldsymbol{T}\}$.
5: **for** $t = 1..T$ **do**
6:     choose $C_1 \in \mathcal{P}_t$ and $c_2 \in \mathcal{C}$ which minimize $Z_t(C_1, c_2)$ according to Equation 7
7:     $\mathcal{R}_{t+1} = \mathcal{R}_t \cup \{r_{t+1} : (\text{if } C_1 \text{ then } (\text{if } c_2 \text{ then } (a_l = \frac{1}{2}ln\frac{W_+^l(C_1 \wedge c_2)}{W_-^l(C_1 \wedge c_2)})_{l \in \mathcal{Y}}) \text{ else } (b_l = $
       $\frac{1}{2}ln\frac{W_+^l(C_1 \wedge \neg c_2)}{W_-^l(C_1 \wedge \neg c_2)})_{l \in \mathcal{Y}}) \text{ else } 0)\}$
8:     $\mathcal{P}_{t+1} = \mathcal{P}_t \cup \{C_1 \wedge c_2, C_1 \wedge \neg c_2\}$
9:     Update weights : $w_{t+1}(i, l) = w_t(i, l)e^{-Y_i[l]r_t(x_i, l)}$
10: **end for**
Output: multi-label ADTree $\mathcal{R}_{T+1}$

Relations with Other Formalisms

Multi-label ADTrees trivially extends several common formalisms in machine learning.

Voted decision stumps produced for instance by AdaBoost.MH presented as Algorithm 1 are obviously multi-label ADTrees where each rule has $\boldsymbol{T}$ as a precondition. These "flat" multi-label ADTrees can be the output of ADTBoost.MH if we impose a very simple control. Line 6 of Algorithm 3, we choose c_2 in $\mathcal{C}$ which minimize $Z_t(\boldsymbol{T}, c_2)$ according to Equation 7. Thus, AdaBoost.MH can be considered as a parameterization of ADTBoost.MH.

(Multi-label) decision trees: A (multi-label) decision tree is an ADTree with the following restrictions: any inner prediction node contains 0; there is at most one splitter node below every prediction node; prediction nodes at a leaf position contain values that can be interpreted as classes (using for instance the sign function in the binary case).

Weighted vote of (multi-label) decision trees: Voted decision trees $t_1, \ldots, t_k$ associated with weights $w_1, \ldots, w_k$ are also simply transformed into ADTrees. One needs to add prediction nodes containing the weight w_i at every leaf of the tree t_i and graft all trees at the root of an ADTree.

5   Experiments

In this section, we describe the experiments we conduct with ADTBoost.MH. We mainly argue that we can obtain both accurate and readable classifiers over tabular and text data using multi-label alternating decision trees.

Implementation

Our implementation of ADTBoost.MH supports items descriptions that include discrete attributes, continuous attributes and texts. In the case of a discrete attribute A whose domain is $\{v_1, \ldots, v_n\}$, the set of base conditions are binary conditions of the form $A = v_i$, $A \neq v_i$. In the case of a continuous attribute A, we consider binary conditions of the form $A < v_i$. Finally, in the case of text-valued attributes over a vocabulary V, base conditions are of the form m *occurs in* A where m belongs to V.

Missing values are handled in ADTBoost.MH as in Quinlan's C4.5 software ([Qui93]). Let us consider an ADTree R, a position p in R associated with condition c based on an attribute A and an instance for which the value of A is missing. We estimate probabilities for the assertions c to be true or false, based on the observation of the training set. The obtained values are assigned to the missing value of this instance and then propagated below p.

Data Sets

The Reuters collection is the most commonly-used collection for text classification. We use a formatted version of Reuters version 2 (also called Reuters-21450) prepared by Y. Yang and colleagues[3]. Documents are labeled to belong to at least one of the 135 possible categories. A "sub-category" relation governs categories.

---

[3] available at `http://moscow.mt.cs.cmu.edu:8081/reuters_21450/parc/`

Nine of them constitute the top level of this hierarchy. Because most of the articles in the whole Reuters data set belong to exactly one category, in the experiments we select categories and articles for which overlaps between categories are more significant.

News collection: We prepare a new data set from newsgroups archives in order to build a multilabel classification problem where cases are described by texts, continuous and nominal values. We obtain from `ftp://ftp.cs.cmu.edu/user/ai/pubs/news/comp.ai/` news articles posted in the comp.ai newsgroup in july 1997. Some articles in this forum have been cross posted in several newsgroups. The classification task consists in finding in which newsgroup a news has been cross posted.

Each news is described by seven attributes. Two of them are textual data: the subject and the text of the news. Four attributes are continuous (natural numbers): the number of lines in the text of the news, the number of references (that is the number of parents in the thread discussion), the number of capitalized words and the number of words in the text of the news. One attribute is discrete: the top level domain of sender's email address. We have droped small words, less than three letters, and non purely alphabetic words (*e.g.* R2D2)[4]. There are 524 articles and we keep only the five most frequent cross posted newsgroups as labels. The five newsgroups are: misc.writing (61 posts), sci.space.shuttle (68 posts), sci.cognitive (70 posts), rec.arts.sf.written (70 posts) and comp.ai.philosophy (73 posts). Only 171 articles were cross posted to at least one of these five newsgroups (60 in one, 51 in two, 60 in three).

Results

We first train our algorithm on the Reuters dataset in order to evaluate it against Boostexter (Available implementation of AdaBoost.MH [5]). Reuters dataset consists in a train set and a test set. But following the protocol explained in [SS00], we merge these two sets and we focused on the nine topics constituting the top hierarchy. We then select the subsets of the k classes with the largest number of articles for $k = 3 \ldots 9$. Results were computed on a 3-fold cross-validation. The number of boosting steps being set to 30. We report in table 1 one-error, coverage and average precision for Boostexter and ADTBoost.MH.

In the news classification problem, ranks of labels are less relevant. We only report the hamming error. Our algorithm ADTBoost.MH builds rules that may have large preconditions. This feature allows to partition the space in a very fine way and the training error can decrease very quickly. This can be observed on the news data set. After 30 boosting steps, the training error is 0 for the model generated by ADTBoost.MH. This is achieved by Boostexter after 230 boosting steps. On the one hand, smaller models can be generated by ADTBoost.MH. On

---

[4] Data sets and perl scripts are available on
   `http://www.grappa.univ-lille3.fr/recherche/datasets`.
[5] `http://www.cs.princeton.edu/~schapire/boostexter.html`

Table 1. Comparing Boostexter and ADTree on the Reuters data set. The number k is the number of labels in the multi-label classification problem

	ADTree			Boostexter		
k	Error	Cover	Prec	Error	Cover	Prec
3	6.01%	0.07	0.97	6.48%	0.08	0.97
4	7.03%	0.10	0.96	7.93%	0.11	0.96
5	8.31%	0.12	0.95	8.99%	0.14	0.95
6	12.70%	0.24	0.92	12.34%	0.24	0.92
7	14.72%	0.31	0.91	14.32%	0.30	0.91
8	16.01%	0.34	0.91	15.90%	0.35	0.90
9	16.77%	0.40	0.89	16.60%	0.39	0.89

Table 2. Hamming error of ADTBoost.MH and Boostexter on the cross posted news data set

Boosting steps	ADTBoost.MH	Boostexter
10	0.024	0.022
30	0.023	0.019
50	0.017	0.017
100	0.017	0.014

the other hand, both ADTBoost.MH and ADTBoost tend to overspecialize and this phenomenon seems to occur more quickly for ADTBoost.MH.

Table 2 reports the hamming error on the cross posted news data set computed with a ten-fold cross validation. Note that the hamming error of the procedure that associate the empty set of label to each case is 0.306.

Figure 2 shows an example of rules produced by ADTBoost.MH on this data set and its graphical representation is depicted in Fig. 3. Both representations allow to interpret the model generated by ADTBoost.MH. For instance, according to the weights computed in the five first rules, one may say that when an article is cross posted in sci.space.shuttle it is not in sci.cognitive. On the contrary rec.arts.sf.written seems to be correlated with sci.space.shuttle. Below is an example of a rule with conditions that mix tests over textual data and tests over continuous data.

```
If subject  (not contains  Birthday) and  (subject  not contains  Clarke)
   and (subject  not contains  Secrets)
                        Class :   misc_w  sci_sp  sci_co  comp_a  rec_ar
   If #lines >= 22.50 then        -0.37   -3.24   0.24    0.17    0.08
   If #lines < 22.50 then         -0.12   -2.88   -3.51   -0.41   -5.07
Else 0
```

6 Conclusion

We have proposed a learning algorithm ADTBoost.MH that can handle multi-label problems and produce intelligible models. It is based on boosting methods and seems

```
Rule 0
if TRUE
 Class :                  misc_w  sci_sp  sci_co  comp_a  rec_ar
    If TRUE then          -1.01   -0.95   -0.93   -0.91   -0.93
Else 0
-------------------------
Rule 1
if TRUE
                         Class :    misc_w  sci_sp  sci_co  comp_a  rec_ar
    If subject Contains  Birthday then       1.71    1.50   -6.35   -6.35   1.71
    If subject  not contains  Birthday then -7.35   -2.02   -0.86   -0.84  -1.96
Else 0
-------------------------
Rule 2
If subject  not contains  Birthday
                         Class :    misc_w  sci_sp  sci_co  comp_a  rec_ar
    If subject Contains  Emotional then     -2.93   -5.59    7.03    2.65  -5.62
    If subject  not contains  Emotional then -4.12   0.05   -0.41   -0.37   0.05
Else 0
-------------------------
Rule 3
If subject  not contains  Birthday
                         Class :    misc_w  sci_sp  sci_co  comp_a  rec_ar
    If subject Contains  Clarke then         -0.46    6.92   -5.30   -5.33   6.89
    If subject  not contains  Clarke then    -2.31   -6.92    0.01    0.01  -1.10
Else 0
-------------------------
Rule 4
If subject  not contains  Birthday
If subject  not contains  Clarke
                         Class :    misc_w  sci_sp  sci_co  comp_a  rec_ar
    If subject Contains  Secrets then        -0.17   -1.99    2.61   -5.83  -4.92
    If subject  not contains  Secrets then   -1.32   -3.59   -0.33    0.02   0.02
Else 0
```

Fig. 2. Output of ADTBoostMH on the news data set

to reach the performance of well tuned algorithms like AdaBoostMH. Further works concern a closer analysis of the overspecialization phenomenon.

The number of rules in a multi-label ADTree is related to the number of boosting rounds in boosting algorithms like AdaBoostMH. Readability of multi-label ADTree is clearly altered when the number of rules becomes large. But, this possibly large set of rules depicted as a tree comes with weights and with an ordering that permits "stratified" interpretations. Indeed, due to the algorithmic bias in the algorithm, rules that are firstly generated contribute to reduce the most the training error. Nonetheless, navigation tools and high quality user interfaces should be built to improve readability.

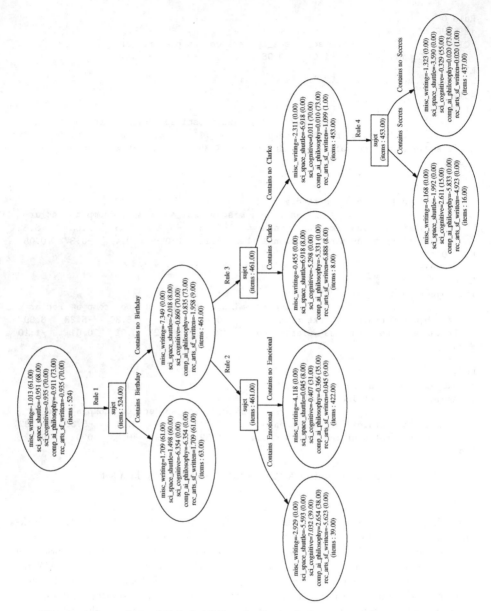

Fig. 3. A five rule multilabel ADTree built on the cross posted news data set.

References

[ASS00]   Erin L. Allwein, Robert E. Schapire, and Yoram Singer. Reducing mul-
          ticlass to binary:a unifying approach for margin classifiers. In *Proc. 17th
          International Conf. on Machine Learning*, pages 9–16, 2000.
[Bre98]   L. Breiman. Combining predictors. Technical report, Statistic Department,
          1998.
[DB95]   T.G. Dietterich and G. Bakiri. Solving multiclass learning problems via
          error-correcting output codes. *Journal of Artificial Intelligence Research*,
          2:263–286, 1995.
[DKM96]   T. Dietterich, M. Kearns, and Y. Mansour. Applying the weak learning
          framework to understand and improve C4.5. In *Proc. 13th International
          Conference on Machine Learning*, pages 96–104. Morgan Kaufmann, 1996.
[FM99]   Yoav Freund and Llew Mason. The alternating decision tree learning al-
          gorithm. In *Proc. 16th International Conf. on Machine Learning*, pages
          124–133, 1999.
[FS96]   Yoav Freund and Robert E. Schapire. Experiments with a new boosting
          algorithm. In *Proc. 13th International Conference on Machine Learning*,
          pages 148–146. Morgan Kaufmann, 1996.
[FS97]   Yoav Freund and Robert E. Schapire. A decision-theoretic generalization
          of on-line learning and an application to boosting. *Journal of Computer
          and System Sciences*, 55(1):119–139, August 1997.
[HPK+02] G. Holmes, B. Pfahringer, R. Kirkby, E. Frank, and M. Hall. Multiclass
          alternating decision trees. In *Proceedings of the European Conference on
          Machine Learning*. Springer Verlag, 2002.
[KK97]   Ron Kohavi and Clayton Kunz. Option decision trees with majority votes.
          In *Proc. 14th International Conference on Machine Learning*, pages 161–
          169. Morgan Kaufmann, 1997.
[KM96]   M. Kearns and Y. Mansour. On the boosting ability of top-down decision
          tree learning algorithms. In *Proceedings of the Twenty-Eighth Annual ACM
          Symposium on the Theory of Computing*, pages 459–468, 1996.
[Qui93]   J.R. Quinlan. *C4.5: Programs for Machine Learning*. Morgan Kaufmann,
          San Mateo, CA, 1993.
[SS98]   Robert F. Schapire and Yoram Singer. Improved boosting algorithms using
          confidence-rated predictions. In *Proceedings of the 11th Annual Conference
          on Computational Learning Theory (COLT-98)*, pages 80–91, New York,
          July 24–26 1998. ACM Press.
[SS00]   Robert E. Schapire and Yoram Singer. Boostexter: A boosting-based system
          for text categorization. *Machine Learning*, 39(2/3):135–168, 2000.

Khiops: A Discretization Method of Continuous Attributes with Guaranteed Resistance to Noise

Marc Boullé

France Telecom R&D, 2, Avenue Pierre Marzin
22300 Lannion, France
marc.boulle@francetelecom.com

Abstract. In supervised machine learning, some algorithms are restricted to discrete data and need to discretize continuous attributes. The Khiops* discretization method, based on chi-square statistics, optimizes the chi-square criterion in a global manner on the whole discretization domain. In this paper, we propose a major evolution of the Khiops algorithm, that provides guarantees against overfitting and thus significantly improve the robustness of the discretizations. This enhancement is based on a statistical modeling of the Khiops algorithm, derived from the study of the variations of the chi-square value during the discretization process. This modeling, experimentally checked, allows to modify the algorithm and to bring a true control of overfitting. Extensive experiments demonstrate the validity of the approach and show that the Khiops method builds high quality discretizations, both in terms of accuracy and of small interval number.

1 Introduction

Discretization of continuous attributes is a problem that has been studied extensively in the past [5,9,10,13]. Many induction algorithms rely on discrete attributes and need to discretize continuous attributes, i.e. to slice their domain into a finite number of intervals. For example, decision tree algorithms exploit a discretization method to handle continuous attributes. C4.5 [11] uses the information gain based on Shannon entropy. CART [4] applies the Gini criterion (a measure of the impurity of the intervals). CHAID [7] relies on a discretization method close to ChiMerge [8]. SIPINA takes advantage of the Fusinter criterion [12] based on measures of uncertainty that are sensitive to sample size. The Minimum Description Length Principle [6] is an original approach that attempts to minimize the total quantity of information both contained in the model and in the exceptions to the model.

The Khiops discretization method [2] is a bottom-up method based on the global optimization of chi-square. The Khiops method starts the discretization from the elementary single value intervals. It evaluates all merges between adjacent intervals and selects the best one according to the chi-square criterion applied to the whole set of intervals. The stopping rule is based on the confidence level computed with chi-

---

* French patents N° 01 07006 and N° 02 16733

P. Perner and A. Rosenfeld (Eds.): MLDM 2003, LNAI 2734, pp. 50–64, 2003.

square statistics. The method automatically stops merging intervals as soon as the confidence level, related to the chi-square test of independence between the discretized attribute and the class attribute, does not decrease anymore. The Khiops method optimizes a global criterion which evaluates the entire partition of the domain into intervals and not a local criterion applied to two neighboring intervals as in the ChiSplit top down method or the ChiMerge bottom-up method.

The set of intervals resulting from a discretization provides an elementary univariate classifier, which predicts the local majority class in each learned interval. A discretization method can be considered as an inductive algorithm, therefore subject to overfitting. This overfitting problem has not yet been deeply analyzed in the field of discretization. The initial Khiops discretization uses a heuristic control of overfitting by constraining the frequency of the intervals to be greater than the square root of the sample size. In this paper, we introduce a significant improvement of the Khiops algorithm which brings a true control of overfitting. The principle is to analyze the behavior of the algorithm during the discretization of an explanatory attribute independent from the class attribute. We study the statistics of the variations of the chi-square values during the merge of intervals and propose a modeling of the maximum of these variations in a complete discretization process. The algorithm is then modified in order to force any merge whose variation of chi-square value is below the maximum variation predicted by our statistical modeling. This change in the algorithm yields the interesting probabilistic guarantee that any independent attribute will be discretized within a single terminal attribute and that any attribute whose discretization consists of at least two intervals truly contains predictive information upon the class attribute.

The remainder of the document is organized as follows. Section 2 briefly introduces the initial Khiops algorithm. Section 3 presents the statistical modeling of the algorithm and its evolution. Section 4 proceeds with an extensive experimental evaluation.

2 The Initial Khiops Discretization Method

In this section, we recall the principles of the chi-square test and present the Khiops algorithm, whose detailed description and analysis can be found in [3].

2.1 The Chi-Square Test: Principles and Notations

Let us consider an explanatory attribute and a class attribute and determine whether they are independent. First, all instances are summarized in a contingency table, where the instances are counted for each value pair of explanatory and class attributes. The chi-square value is computed from the contingency table, based on Table 1 notations.

Let $e_{ij} = n_{i.}.n_{.j} / N$, stand for the expected frequency for cell (i, j) if the explanatory and class attributes are independent. The chi-square value is a measure on the whole contingency table of the difference between observed frequencies and expected frequencies. It can be interpreted as a distance to the hypothesis of independence between attributes.

Table 1. Contingency table used to compute the chi-square value

n_{ij}: Observed frequency for i^{th} explanatory value
     and j^{th} class value

$n_{i.}$: Total observed frequency for i^{th} explanatory value

$n_{.j}$: Total observed frequency for j^{th} class value

N: Total observed frequency

I: Number of explanatory attribute values

J: Number of class values

	A	B	C	Total
a	n_{11}	n_{12}	n_{13}	$n_{1.}$
b	n_{21}	n_{22}	n_{23}	$n_{2.}$
c	n_{31}	n_{32}	n_{33}	$n_{3.}$
d	n_{41}	n_{42}	n_{43}	$n_{4.}$
e	n_{51}	n_{52}	n_{53}	$n_{5.}$
Total	$n_{.1}$	$n_{.2}$	$n_{.3}$	N

$$Chi2 = \sum_i \sum_j \frac{\left(n_{ij} - e_{ij}\right)^2}{e_{ij}} \ . \tag{1}$$

Within the null hypothesis of independence, the chi-square value is subject to chi-square statistics with $(I-1).(J-1)$ degrees of freedom. This is the basis for a statistical test which allows to reject the hypothesis of independence; the higher the chi-square value, the smaller the confidence level.

2.2 Algorithm

The chi-square value depends on the local observed frequencies in each individual row and on the global observed frequencies in the whole contingency table. This is a good candidate criterion for a discretization method. The chi-square statistics is parameterized by the number of explanatory values (related to the degrees of freedom). In order to compare two discretizations with different interval numbers, we use the confidence level instead of the chi-square value.

The principle of Khiops algorithm is to minimize the confidence level between the discretized explanatory attribute and the class attribute by the means of chi-square statistics. The chi-square value is not reliable to test the hypothesis of independence if the expected frequency in any cell of the contingency table falls below some minimum value. The algorithm copes with this constraint.

The Khiops method is based on a greedy bottom-up algorithm. It starts with initial single value intervals and then searches for the best merge between adjacent intervals. Two different types of merges are encountered. First, merges with at least one interval that does not meet the constraint and second, merges with both intervals fulfilling the constraint. The best merge candidate (with the highest chi-square value) is chosen in priority among the first type of merges (in which case the merge is accepted unconditionally), and otherwise, if all minimum frequency constraints are respected, it is selected among the second type of merges (in which case the merge is accepted under the condition of improvement of the confidence level). The algorithm is reiterated until both all minimum frequency constraints are respected and no further merge can decrease the confidence level.

The computational complexity of the algorithm can be reduced to $O(N \log(N))$ with some optimizations [3].

2.3 Minimum Frequency per Interval

In order to be reliable, the chi-square test requires that every cell of the contingency table have an expected value of at least 5. This is equivalent to a minimum frequency constraint for each interval of the discretization. Furthermore, to prevent overfitting, the initial Khiops algorithm heuristically increases the minimum frequency per interval constraint up to the square root of the sample size. In this paper, we show how to replace this heuristic solution by a method with theoretical foundations to avoid overfitting.

3 Statistical Analysis of the Algorithm

The Khiops algorithm chooses the best merge among all possible merges of intervals and iterates this process until the stopping rule is met. When the explanatory attribute and the class attribute are independent, the resulting discretization should be composed of a single interval, meaning that there is no predictive information in the explanatory attribute. In the following, we study the statistical behavior of the initial Khiops algorithm.

In the case of two independent attributes, the chi-square value is subject to chi-square statistics, with known expectation and variance. We study the DeltaChi2 law (variation of the chi-square value after the merge of two intervals) in the case of two independent attributes. During a discretization process, a large number of merges are evaluated, and at each step, the Khiops algorithm chooses the merge that maximizes the chi-square value; i.e. the merge that minimizes the DeltaChi2 value since the chi-square value before the merge is fixed. The stopping rule is met when the best DeltaChi2 value is too large. However, in the case of two independent attributes, the merging process should continue until the discretization reaches a single terminal interval. The largest DeltaChi2 value encountered during the algorithm merging decision steps must then be accepted. We will try to estimate this MaxDeltaChi2 value in the case of two independent attributes and modify the algorithm in order to force the merges as long as this bound is not reached.

3.1 The DeltaChi2 Law

The expectation and the variance of chi-square statistics with k degrees of freedom and a sample of size N are:

$$E(Chi2) = k ,$$

$$Var(Chi2) = 2k + \frac{1}{N}\left(\sum_{i=1}^{k}\frac{1}{q_i} - k^2 - 4k - 1\right).$$

Let us focus on two rows r and r' of the contingency table, with frequencies n and n', and row probabilities of the class values $p_1, p_2, \ldots p_J$ and $p'_1, p'_2, \ldots p'_J$.

					Total
...	...	...	...	...	...
...	...	...	...	...	
row r	$p_1 n$	$p_2 n$	...	$p_J n$ n	
row r'	$p'_1 n'$	$p'_2 n'$	...	$p'_J n'$ n'	
...	...	...	...	...	
...	...	...	...	...	
Total	$P_1 N$	$P_2 N$	...	$P_J N$ N	

Owing to the additivity of the chi-square criterion, the variation of the chi-square value is based on the row contribution of the two rows before and after the merge.

$$Chi2_{afterMerge} - Chi2_{beforeMerge} = Chi2(r \cup r') - Chi2(r) - Chi2(r') .$$

$$Chi2_{afterMerge} - Chi2_{beforeMerge} = -\frac{nn'}{n+n'} \sum_{j=1}^{J} \frac{(p_j - p'_j)^2}{P_j} .$$

This variation of the chi-square value is always negative and is equal to zero only when the two rows hold exactly the same proportions of class values. The chi-square value of a contingency table can only decrease when two rows are merged. In the following, we define the DeltaChi2 value with the absolute value of the variation of the chi-square value for ease of use.

$$DeltaChi2 = \frac{nn'}{n+n'} \sum_{j=1}^{J} \frac{(p_j - p'_j)^2}{P_j} . \tag{2}$$

We proved in [3] that in the case of an explanatory attribute independent from a class attribute with J class values, the DeltaChi2 value resulting from the merge of two rows with the same frequencies is asymptotically distributed as the chi-square statistics with $J-1$ degrees of freedom. Under these assumptions, we can derive the following properties of the DeltaChi2 statistics.

$$p(DeltaChi2_J \geq x) \sim p(Chi2_{J-1} \geq x) .$$
$$E(DeltaChi2_J) \sim J - 1 .$$
$$V(DeltaChi2_J) \sim 2(J - 1) .$$

3.2 Statistics of the Merges of the Khiops Algorithm

During the complete discretization process toward a single terminal interval, the number of merges is equal to the sample size. A straightforward modeling of the Khiops algorithm is that all these merges are equi-distributed, independent and that they follow the theoretical DeltaChi2 statistics. This is an approximate modeling, mainly for the following reasons:
- the merges are not independent,
- the DeltaChi2 statistics is valid only asymptotically and for intervals with the same frequency,
- the Khiops algorithms uses a minimum frequency constraint that induces a hierarchy among the possible merges,
- at each step, the completed merge is the best one among all possible merges.

In order to evaluate this statistical modeling of the Khiops algorithm, we proceed with an experimental study. This experiment consists in discretizing an explanatory continuous attribute independent of a class attribute whose two class values are equi-distributed. In order to draw their repartition function, all the DeltaChi2 values associated with the completed merges are collected until one terminal interval is built. This process is applied on samples of sizes 100, 1000 and 10000. The resulting empirical repartition functions of the DeltaChi2 values are displayed on Fig. 1 and compared with the theoretical DeltaChi2 repartition function.

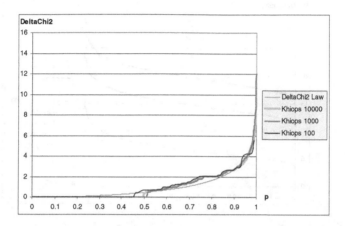

Fig. 1. Repartition functions of the DeltaChi2 values of the merges completed by the Khiops algorithm during the discretization of an explanatory attribute independent of the class attribute

The experiment shows that the DeltaChi2 empirical law is independent of the sample size and fits well the theoretical DeltaChi2 law, especially above the value p~0.85.

3.3 Statistics of the MaxDeltaChi2 Values of the Khiops Algorithm

The purpose is to settle a MaxDeltaChi2 threshold for the Khiops algorithm, so that in the case of two independent attributes, the algorithm converges toward a single terminal interval with a given probability p (p=0.95 for instance). All evaluated merges must be accepted as long as their DeltaChi2 value is below the MaxDeltaChi2 value. Based on the previous modeling where all the merges are independent, the probability that all the merges are accepted is equal to the probability that one merge is accepted, to the power N.

The MaxDeltaChi2 value is given by:

$$P(DeltaChi2_I \leq MaxDeltaChi2)^N \geq p \ .$$

Using the theoretical DeltaChi2 law:

$$P(Chi2_{J-1} \leq MaxDeltaKhi2) \geq p^{1/N} \ .$$

$$MaxDeltaChi2 = InvChi2_{J-1}(prob \geq p^{1/N}) \ . \tag{3}$$

In order to validate this modeling of the MaxDeltaChi2 statistics, we proceed with a new experiment and collect the MaxDeltaChi2 value instead of all the DeltaChi2 values encountered during the algorithm. The experiment is applied on the same two independent attributes, on samples of sizes 100, 1000, 10000 and 100000. In order to gather many MaxDeltaChi2 values, it is repeated 1000 times for each sample size. The empirical MaxDeltaChi2 repartition functions are drawn on figure 2 and compared with the theoretical repartition functions derived from equation 3.

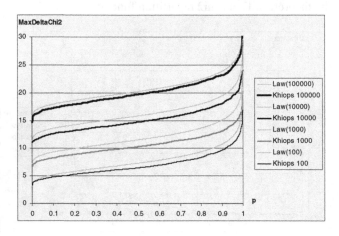

Fig. 2. Empirical and theoretical repartition function of the MaxDeltaChi2 values

The empirical and theoretical repartition functions have very similar shapes for each sample size. The theoretical values are upper bounds of the empirical values, with a moderate margin. We must keep in mind that these theoretical values result from an approximate statistical modeling of the Khiops algorithm. Their behavior as upper bounds is not proved but merely empirically observed.

3.4   The Robust Khiops Algorithm

The Khiops algorithm performs the merges of intervals as long as the confidence level of the chi-square test decreases. We keep the constraint of minimum frequency of 5 in each cell of the contingency table to ensure the reliability of the chi-square test, but we replace the former heuristic minimum frequency constraint used to prevent overfitting by a new method based on the study of the MaxDeltaChi2 statistics.

In the case of two independent attributes, the discretization should result in a single terminal interval. For a given probability p, the statistical modeling of the Khiops algorithms provides a theoretical value MaxDeltaChi2(p) that will be greater than all the DeltaChi2 values of the merges completed during the discretization, with probability p (probability higher than p according to the experimental study). The Khiops algorithm is then modified in order to force all the merges whose DeltaChi2 value is smaller than MaxDeltaChi2(p). This ensures the expected behavior of the algorithm with probability p. In the case of two attributes with unknown dependency relationship, this enhancement of the algorithm guarantees that when the discretized attribute consists of at least two intervals, the explanatory attribute truly holds information concerning the class attribute with probability higher than p. We suggest to set p=0.95, in order to ensure reliable discretization results.

Algorithm Robust Khiops
1. Initialization
1.1 Compute the MaxDeltaChi2 value with formula 3
1.2 Sort the explanatory attribute values
1.3 Create an elementary interval for each value
2. Optimization of the discretization: repeat the following steps
2.1 Evaluate all possible merges between adjacent intervals
2.2 Search for the best merge
2.3 Merge and continue as long as one of the following conditions is relevant
- At least one interval does not respect the minimum frequency constraint
- The confidence level of the discretization decreases after the merge
- The DeltaChi2 value of the best merge is below the MaxDeltaChi2 value

The impact on the initial Khiops algorithm is restricted to the evaluation of the stopping rule and keeps the supra-linear computational complexity of the optimized version of the algorithm.

3.5 Post-optimization of the Discretizations

The Khiops method is a greedy bottom-up algorithm that allows identifying fine grain structures within efficient computation time. We propose a very simple post-processing of the discretizations in order to refine the boundaries of the intervals. For each pair of adjacent intervals, the post processing searches for the best boundary between the two intervals. This local optimization step is reiterated on all the pairs of intervals of the whole discretization, until no more improvement can be found. Experiments showed that this elementary post-optimization of the discretizations repeatedly brought slight improvements.

4 Experiments

In our experimental study, we compare the Khiops method with other supervised and unsupervised discretization algorithms. In order to evaluate the intrinsic performance of the discretization methods and eliminate the bias of the choice of a specific induction algorithm, we use a protocol similar as [13], where each discretization method is considered as an elementary inductive method, that predicts the local majority class in each learned interval. The discretizations are evaluated for two criteria: accuracy and interval number.

We gathered 15 datasets from U.C. Irvine repository [1], each dataset has at least one continuous attribute and at least a few tenths of instances for each class value. Table 2 describes the datasets; the last column corresponds to the accuracy of the majority class.

Table 2. Datasets

Dataset	Continuous Attributes	Nominal Attributes	Size	Class Values	Majority Accuracy
Adult	7	8	48842	2	76.07
Australian	6	8	690	2	55.51
Breast	10	0	699	2	65.52
Crx	6	9	690	2	55.51
German	24	0	1000	2	70.00
Heart	10	3	270	2	55.56
Hepatitis	6	13	155	2	79.35
Hypothyroid	7	18	3163	2	95.23
Ionosphere	34	0	351	2	64.10
Iris	4	0	150	3	33.33
Pima	8	0	768	2	65.10
SickEuthyroid	7	18	3163	2	90.74
Vehicle	18	0	846	4	25.77
Waveform	21	0	5000	3	33.92
Wine	13	0	178	3	39.89

The discretization methods studied in the comparison are:
- Khiops: the method described in this paper,
- Initial Khiops: the previous version of the method, described in section 2,
- MDLPC: Minimum Description Length Principal Cut [6],
- ChiMerge: bottom-up method based on chi-square [8],
- ChiSplit: top-down method based on chi-square,
- Equal Width,
- Equal Frequency.

The MDLPC and initial Khiops methods have an automatic stopping rule and do not require any parameter setting. For the ChiMerge and ChiSplit methods, the significance level is set to 0.95 for chi-square threshold. For the Equal Width and Equal Frequency unsupervised discretization methods, the interval number is set to 10. We have re-implemented these alternative discretization approaches in order to eliminate any variance resulting from different cross-validation splits. The discretizations are performed on the 181 single continuous attributes of the datasets, using a stratified tenfold cross-validation. In order to determine whether the performances are significantly different between the Khiops method and the alternative methods, the t-statistics of the difference of the results is computed. Under the null hypothesis, this value has a Student's distribution with 9 degrees of freedom. The confidence level is set to 5% and a two-tailed test is performed to reject the null hypothesis.

4.1 Accuracy of Discretizations

The whole result tables are too large to be printed in this paper. The accuracy results are summarized in Table 3, which reports for each dataset the mean of the dataset attribute accuracies and the number of significant Khiops wins (+) and losses (-) of the elementary attribute classifiers for each method comparison. The results show that the supervised methods (except ChiMerge) perform clearly better than the unsupervised methods. The ChiMerge method is slightly better than the EqualWidth method, but not as good as the EqualFrequency method. The MDLPC method is clearly better than the EqualFrequency, ChiMerge and EqualWidth methods. The modified Khiops method outperforms the initial Khiops method. The Khiops and the ChiSplit methods obtain the best results of the experiment.

Table 3. Means of accuracies, number of significant wins and losses per dataset, for the elementary attribute classifiers

Dataset	Khiops	Init. Khiops	+	-	MDLPC	+	-	ChiMerge	+	-	ChiSplit	+	-	Eq. Width	+	-	Eq. Freq.	+	-
Adult	77.3	77.2	2	1	77.3	0	2	75.7	2	2	77.3	0	2	76.8	2	1	76.6	2	1
Australian	64.8	64.5	1	0	65.0	0	0	64.7	0	0	65.1	0	0	61.4	3	0	65.7	0	0
Breast	85.8	86.0	0	1	86.1	0	1	85.6	0	1	85.9	0	1	86.0	0	1	85.7	1	1
Crx	65.0	64.5	0	0	65.2	0	0	63.8	2	0	65.3	0	0	61.1	3	0	65.6	0	1
German	70.1	70.0	0	0	70.0	0	0	70.0	0	0	70.1	0	0	70.1	0	2	70.0	0	0
Heart	64.4	63.8	0	0	64.0	0	0	64.0	0	0	63.8	0	0	63.9	2	0	64.5	1	0
Hepatitis	79.6	79.4	0	0	79.3	0	0	77.8	3	0	79.3	0	0	79.8	0	0	79.9	0	0
Hypothyroid	96.1	96.0	0	1	96.1	0	1	96.0	3	0	96.1	1	0	95.4	3	1	95.2	3	1
Ionosphere	79.7	78.7	5	0	77.6	10	2	75.7	21	0	79.5	4	3	73.9	19	1	75.0	22	0
Iris	78.8	77.7	0	0	75.5	1	0	77.0	0	0	78.8	0	0	76.5	1	0	76.3	0	0
Pima	66.3	66.8	1	1	66.1	0	0	65.6	2	0	66.5	0	0	66.8	0	1	66.3	0	1
SickEuthyroid	91.3	91.4	0	0	91.3	0	0	91.3	1	0	91.3	0	0	90.7	2	0	91.0	1	0
Vehicle	41.5	40.9	3	1	40.5	4	0	41.4	2	1	42.1	0	3	40.8	3	0	40.3	3	0
Waveform	49.3	49.1	2	0	49.3	0	0	48.7	6	0	49.1	4	0	49.2	3	3	49.5	1	4
Wine	60.0	62.0	1	3	60.1	0	1	59.6	1	0	60.4	0	1	61.4	2	2	60.8	1	2
Synthesis	68.6	68.4	15	8	68.0	15	7	67.4	43	4	68.6	9	10	67.2	43	12	67.6	35	11

A close look at Table 3 indicates a special behaviour of the ionosphere dataset, where the Khiops and ChiSplit methods largely dominate the other methods. An inspection of the discretizations performed by the Khiops algorithm reveals unbalanced sets of intervals and non-monotonic distributions. The unsupervised methods cannot match the changes in the distributions since they cannot adjust the boundaries of the intervals. Furthermore, the discretizations present a frequent pattern consisting of an interesting interval nested between two regular intervals. This kind of pattern, easily detected by the Khiops bottom-up approach, is harder to discover for the MDLPC top-down algorithm since it requires two successive splits with the first one not very significant. The ChiSplit top-down method, which produces twice the interval number of the MDLPC method, manages to detect the interesting patterns at the expense of some unnecessary intervals. The ChiMerge method generates far too many intervals and over-learns the attributes.

All in all, the differences of accuracy may seem unimportant, but they are significant and must be compared to the average accuracy of the majority class classifier, which is 57.4%. Furthermore, the performances are averaged on a large variety of explanatory continuous attributes. It is interesting to analyze the differences of accuracy for the 181 attributes in more details. Figure 3 shows the repartition function of the differences of accuracy between the Khiops methods and the other discretization methods.

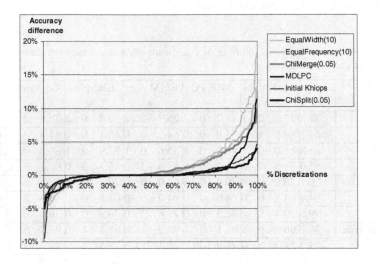

Fig. 3. Repartition function of the differences of accuracy between the Khiops method and the other discretization methods

On the left of the figure, the Khiops method is dominated by the other methods and, on the right, it outperforms the other algorithms. For about 40% of the attributes (between x-coordinates 20 and 60), all the discretization methods obtain equivalent results. Compared to the MDLPC method, the Khiops method is between 0 and 3% less accurate in about 10% of the discretizations, but is between 3 and 10% more accurate in about 10% of the discretizations. The average difference of 0.6% is thus significant and reflects potential large differences of accuracy on individual attributes.

The accuracy criterion suggests the following ranking of the tested methods:

1. Khiops, ChiSplit
2. Initial Khiops, MDLPC
3. EqualFrequency, ChiMerge
4. EqualWidth

4.2   Interval Number of Discretizations

The interval number results are summarized in Table 4. The EqualWidth and EqualFrequency methods do not always reach the 10 required intervals, for reasons of lack of distinct explanatory values. The Khiops and MDLPC methods produce small size discretizations and are not significantly different for this criterion. The modified Khiops method generates almost half the interval number of the initial Khiops method. The ChiSplit method builds discretization with more than twice the interval number of the Khiops method. The ChiMerge method generates considerable interval numbers, especially for the larger samples.

Table 4. Means of interval numbers, number of significant wins and losses per dataset, for the elementary attribute classifiers

Dataset	Khiops	Init. Khiops	+	-	MDLPC	+	-	ChiMerge	+	-	ChiSplit	+	-	Eq. Width	+	-	Eq. Freq.	+	-
Adult	8.5	20.8	2	4	8.8	2	3	1264	0	7	28.2	0	6	9.4	2	4	6.6	4	2
Australian	2.1	5.3	0	6	2.0	0	0	16.1	0	6	5.2	0	6	8.1	0	6	8.8	0	6
Breast	2.6	3.7	0	5	2.9	0	5	11.6	0	9	4.9	0	9	9.2	0	10	5.9	0	10
Crx	2.1	5.3	0	6	2.1	0	0	15.8	0	6	5.1	0	6	8.2	0	6	8.7	0	6
German	1.3	2.6	0	20	1.2	2	0	2.4	0	12	2.0	0	12	3.8	0	23	3.4	0	21
Heart	1.7	3.1	0	6	1.7	0	0	5.0	0	5	2.5	0	5	5.9	0	8	6.1	0	8
Hepatitis	1.7	2.6	1	4	1.4	1	0	6.4	0	6	2.8	0	5	8.6	0	6	9.2	0	6
Hypothyroid	3.5	4.3	3	3	3.1	3	0	15.3	0	7	6.0	0	7	9.6	0	7	8.3	0	7
Ionosphere	4.3	5.1	3	21	3.9	11	6	30.0	0	32	8.0	0	30	9.4	0	32	8.9	0	32
Iris	2.8	3.3	0	2	2.8	1	0	3.7	0	3	3.6	0	3	9.7	0	4	9.5	0	4
Pima	2.3	4.5	0	8	2.1	2	1	13.2	0	8	5.0	0	8	9.5	0	8	9.3	0	8
SickEuthyroid	3.4	7.7	0	6	3.0	3	0	17.2	0	6	5.8	0	5	9.6	0	7	8.3	0	6
Vehicle	4.0	5.8	0	16	3.9	3	3	9.7	0	18	8.0	0	18	9.6	0	18	9.6	0	18
Waveform	4.5	9.4	1	19	4.9	1	9	49.0	0	21	13.6	0	21	10.0	0	21	10.0	0	21
Wine	2.6	3.5	0	11	2.8	1	3	6.7	0	13	4.8	0	12	9.8	0	13	10.0	0	13
Synthesis	3.3	5.6	101	37	3.2	30	30	66.1	0	159	7.2	0	153	8.5	21	73	8.0	41	68

The interval number criterion suggests the following ranking of the tested supervised methods:
1. Khiops, MDLPC
2. Initial Khiops
3. ChiSplit
4. ChiMerge

4.3 Multi-criteria Analysis of the Performances

The preceding results allow the ranking of the tested discretization methods on each criterion. It is interesting to use multi-criteria methodology to better understand the relations between accuracy and interval number. Let us recall some principles of multi-criteria analysis. A solution *dominates* (or is *non-inferior* to) another one if it is better for all criteria. A solution that cannot be dominated is *Pareto optimal*: any improvement on one of the criteria causes deterioration on another criterion. The *Pareto surface* (Pareto curve for two criteria) is the set of all the Pareto optimal solutions.

In order to study the importance of the parameters, we proceed with the previous experiments, using a wide range of parameters for each method. Figure 4 summarizes all the results on a two-criteria plan with the accuracy on the x-coordinate and the interval number on the y-coordinate.

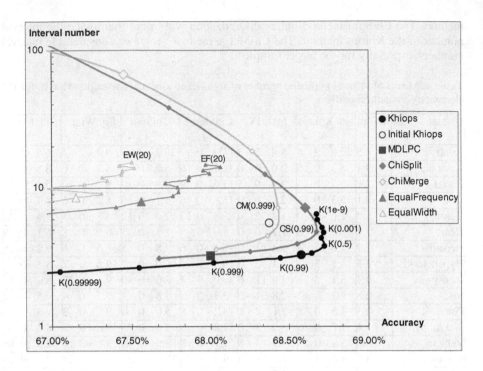

Fig. 4. Bi-criteria evaluation of the discretization methods for the accuracy and the interval number. The curves show the impact of the parameters on the performances for each method. The default parameters are located on the large size symbols

The unsupervised EqualWidth and EqualFrequency methods are largely dominated by the supervised methods. The ChiMerge method is the least performant among the supervised methods, especially for the interval number criterion. With its parameter set to 0.95, it produces 66 intervals on average. The MDLPC method builds very few intervals, but it is outperformed on accuracy by the other supervised methods, principally the Khiops and ChiSplit methods, since their parameter can be tuned. The ChiSplit method exhibits high level performances on both criteria, but it is extremely sensitive to its parameter. Its top accuracy reaches that of the Khiops method, but it always needs significantly more intervals to obtain the same level of accuracy.

The Khiops method obtains the best results for both criteria and its curve corresponds to the Pareto curve for all the tested methods. For example, with Khiops parameter set to 0.95, the MDLPC methods constructs a similar interval number but is significantly outperformed on accuracy, whereas the ChiSplit method (with best parameter 0.99) achieves the same level of accuracy with a notably greater interval number. Compared to the initial Khiops method, the changes in the robust version of the algorithm bring notable enhancements on both criteria.

The ChiMerge and ChiSplit methods display similar curves on the two-criteria plan. With very strict parameters (probability almost equal to 1), they produce few intervals at the expense of a low accuracy. The interval number and the accuracy increase when the parameter is slightly relaxed, until a maximum is reached (with parameter 0.99 for ChiSplit and 0.999 for ChiMerge). Beyond this parameter threshold, the two methods are clearly subject to overfitting and display an increasing interval number associated with a deteriorating accuracy.

The Khiops method displays a steady behavior in the range of parameters between 0.95 and 0.5. With conservative parameters (probability almost equal to 1), it produces few intervals with poor accuracy. When the parameter moves to the "reasonable" range around 0.95, the accuracy quickly improves with a marginal increase of the interval number. After a maximum around parameter 0.5, the decrease of the parameter involves an increasing interval number, but surprisingly no decay in accuracy. An analysis of this behavior shows that the new intervals correspond to small statistical fluctuations whose cumulated effect on accuracy is not meaningful.

To conclude, the Khiops method demonstrates the best trade off between accuracy and interval number and has a stable behavior concerning its parameter. On the range of parameters between 0.95 and 0.5, the Khiops method dominates all the other tested discretization methods whatever the choice of the parameter.

5 Conclusion

The principle of the Khiops discretization method is to minimize the confidence level related to the test of independence between the discretized explanatory attribute and the class attribute. During the bottom-up process of the algorithm, numerous merges between intervals are performed that produce variations of the chi-square value of the contingency table. Owing to a statistical modeling of these variations when the explanatory attribute is independent of the class attribute, we enhanced the Khiops algorithm in order to guarantee that the discretizations of independent attributes are reduced to a single interval. This attested resistance to overfitting is an interesting alternative to the classical cross-validation approach.

Extensive comparative experiments show that the Khiops method outperforms the other tested discretization methods. A multi-criteria analysis of the results in terms of accuracy and interval number is very instructive and reveals an interesting behavior of the Khiops algorithm, whose accuracy does not decrease even when the choice of its parameter might cause over-learning.

The Khiops method is an original approach that incorporates struggle against overfitting in its algorithm and exhibits both a high accuracy and small size discretizations.

Acknowledgment. I wish to thank Fabrice Clérot and Jean-Emmanuel Viallet for many insightful discussions and careful proof reading of the manuscript.

References

1. Blake, C.L., Merz, C.J.: UCI Repository of machine learning databases Web URL http://www.ics.uci.edu/~mlearn/MLRepository.html. Irvine, CA: University of California, Department of Information and Computer Science (1998)

2. Boullé, M.: Khiops: une méthode statistique de discrétisation. Extraction des connaissances et apprentissage, Vol 1-n°4. Hermes Science Publications (2001) 107–118
3. Boullé, M.: Amélioration de la robustesse de la méthode Khiops par contrôle de son comportement statistique. Note technique NT/FTR&D/7864. France Telecom R&D (2002)
4. Breiman, L., Friedman, J.H., Olshen, R.A. & Stone, C.J.: Classification and Regression Trees. California: Wadsworth International (1984)
5. Dougherty, J., Kohavi, R and Sahami, M.: Supervised and Unsupervised Discretization of Continuous Features. Proceedings of the Twelf International Conference on Machine Learning, Los Altos, CA: Morgan Kaufmann, (1995) 194–202
6. Fayyad, U., Irani, K.: On the handling of continuous-valued attributes in decision tree generation. Machine Learning, 8 (1992) 87–102
7. Kass, G.V.: An exploratory technique for investigating large quantities of categorical data. Applied Statistics, 29(2) (1980) 119–127
8. Kerber, R.: Chimerge discretization of numeric attributes. Proceedings of the 10th International Conference on Artificial Intelligence (1991) 123–128
9. Liu, H., Hussain, F., Tan, C.L. and Dash, M. Discretization: An Enabling Technique. Data Mining and Knowledge Discovery 6 (4) (2002) 393–423
10. Perner, P., Trautzsch, S.: Multi-interval Discretization Methods for Decision Tree Learning. SSPR/SPR (1998) 475–482
11. Quinlan, J.R.: C4.5: Programs for Machine Learning. Morgan Kaufmann (1993)
12. Zighed, D.A., Rabaseda, S. & Rakotomalala, R.: Fusinter: a method for discretization of continuous attributes for supervised learning. International Journal of Uncertainty, Fuzziness and Knowledge-Based Systems, 6(33) (1998) 307–326.
13. Zighed, D.A., Rakotomalala, R.: Graphes d'induction. Hermes Science Publications (2000) 327–359

On the Size of a Classification Tree

Angela Scaringella*

Facoltà di Sociologia
Università di Roma "La Sapienza"
via Salaria 113
I00198 Rome, Italy
Angela.Scaringella@uniroma2.it

Abstract. We discuss some estimates for the misclassification rate of
a classification tree in terms of the size of the learning set, following
some ideas introduced in [3]. We develop some mathematical ideas of
[3], extending the analysis to the case with an arbitrary finite number of
classes.

1   Introduction

Classification trees [3,1,2] are one of the most widely used tool in the field of
data mining (see [9] for a general introduction to the subject). Their efficiency is
largely higher than that of traditional statistical methods and it is comparable
to that of other widely used methods that have become available with the developments of powerful computers. In many applications they are chosen because
of their higher perspicuity that makes them understandable by experts in the
fields of application and give to the users the possibility of intervening in their
construction and adapting them according to their experience, even if the more
complex and effective procedures developed in [1] and [2] have the drawback of
reducing their perspicuity.

In mathematical terms we assume that we have a potentially infinite sequence of *cases* given by independent identically distributed random vectors
$(X_1, Y_1), (X_2, Y_2), \ldots$ defined on a probability space endowed with a probability
measure $\mathbb{P}$. Here the X_i's take values in the Euclidean space $\mathbb{R}^M$ whereas the
Y_i's take values in some finite set of *classes*. The goal of a classification tree is to
attribute cases to the classes on the basis of the knowledge of the X-component.
The tree performs this duty by a sequence of binary splits based on inequalities on the components of the X-vector. The tree is built by a fixed procedure
from the observation of a finite number N of cases; this set of cases is called the
learning set. We do not deal here with the details of the procedure by which a
classification tree is built. If one used the classical statistical point of view, one
would use the learning set to make inference on the distribution $\mathbb{P}$ and then
starting from this inference one would determine a classification procedure. In
building the classification tree one skips the inference part and takes a more

---

* Partly supported by a grant of the University of Rome "La Sapienza"

P. Perner and A. Rosenfeld (Eds.): MLDM 2003, LNAI 2734, pp. 65–72, 2003.

practical attitude: as what is important at last is the classification procedure, one simply chooses among a given set of procedures which one performs best on the learning set in terms of quantities like the *misclassification cost* or the *misclassification rate*. This kind of procedures have of course become feasible since powerful and fast computing instruments exist.

When a classification tree is built, two factors compete in the determination of the misclassification rate in terms of the size of the learning set. They are commonly called *bias* and *variance* and appear in all classification procedures (see [3,5,6,7,8] for a discussion of bias and variance in various classification methods). In [3] a simple model and some ideas were introduced to clarify the role played by these two factors. Here we generalize slightly the model and develop some of those ideas in order to obtain some results on the misclassification rate as a function of the size of the tree. Let S denote the set of states by which every case is classified. In general one defines a *misclassification cost* by introducings a *loss function* $l(s, s')$ defined on $S \times S$. The simplest loss function is

$$l(s, s') = \begin{cases} 0 \text{ if } s = s' \\ 1 \text{ otherwise} \end{cases}$$

If one adopts this loss function the misclassification cost is equal to the *misclassification rate*.

We consider two cases when S is finite but with an arbitrary number of elements, whereas in [3] the case where S consists of two elements. The true misclassification rate is given by $\mathbb{P}(d^*(X) \neq Y)$ where d^* is the chassification given by the tree that we are considering and X and Y are respectively the attributes and the true classification of a given case which is assumed to be extracted from the probability distribution $\mathbb{P}$.

2   Misclassification Rate

We assume that the attributes of the individuals are of the continuous type. This is crucial for the derivation of the results. However also in the discrete case, when the number of categories is large one can obtain similar results at least if the size of the learning set and of the classification tree is suitably bounded. More precisely let us assume that the attributes take values in the M-dimensional Euclidean space $\mathbb{R}^M$ and let $f_j(x)$, for $x \in \mathbb{R}^M$ be the conditional probability density for individuals in the j-th class. We assume that the probability densities have compact supports, are smooth and satisfy some genericity assumption with respect to the rectangle partition induced by the tree. We shall mostly follow the same notation used in [3].

A decision tree induces a partition of the space of attributes into a finite number of rectangles $S_1, \ldots, S_L$. The rectangle are induced by the binary splits operated at the nodes of a classification tree corresponding to inequalities with respect to single coordinates.

The true misclassification rate is given by

$$R^*(L) = \sum_{l=1}^{L} \mathbb{P}(X \in S_l, Y \neq y_l), \tag{1}$$

where y_l is the classification that the tree attributes to the rectangle S_l. This can also be expressed as

$$1 - \sum_{l=1}^{L} \mathbb{P}(X \in S_l, Y = y_l) \tag{2}$$

or also

$$1 - \sum_{l=1}^{L} \sum_{j=1}^{L} \chi(y_l = j)\mathbb{P}(Y \in S_l, Y = j). \tag{3}$$

Let $\pi(1), \pi(2), \ldots, \pi(m)$ be the probabilities for an individual taken from the probability distribution $\mathbb{P}$. These probabilities are also called *a priori* probabilities and correspond in practice to the percentages of individuals in class $1, 2, \ldots, m$ over the whole population. The Bayes optimal misclassification rate is the minimum rate that can be achieved by any classification procedure. It is given by

$$R^* = 1 - \int \max_j (\pi_j(x)f_j(x))dx. \tag{4}$$

In order to test a given classification tree one can therefore investigate how well it performs in comparison with such an optimal rate. Following [3] let y_l be the classification given by the tree to the individuals that are in the rectangle S_l. The true misclassification rate is the probability that an individual be misclassified by the tree. We can express it in the following way

$$R^*(L) = \sum_l \mathbb{P}(X \in S_l, Y \neq y_l) =$$

$$\sum_l (\mathbb{P}(X \in S_l) - \mathbb{P}(X \in S_l, Y = y_l)) =$$

$$1 - \sum_l \mathbb{P}(X \in S_l, Y = y_l) = \tag{5}$$

$$1 - \sum_l \sum_j \chi(y_l = j)\mathbb{P}(X = S_l, Y = y_j)$$

Let us define

$$y_l^* = \begin{cases} j \text{ if } \mathbb{P}(X \in S_l, Y = j) > \mathbb{P}(X \in S_l, Y = k) \text{ for } k \neq j \\ 1 \text{ if the is no index } j \text{ with the above property} \end{cases} \tag{6}$$

(the second case in the generic case has 0 probability, so it does not matter which value is attributed to y_l^* and the value 1 is just an arbitrary choice).

Then the misclassification rate can be expressed as

$$R^*(L) = 1 - \sum \max_j \mathbb{P}(X \in S_l, Y = j) + \tag{7}$$

$$\sum_l \chi(y_l \neq y_l^*)|\mathbb{P}(X \in S_l, Y = y_l) - \mathbb{P}(X \in S_l, Y = y_l^*)|.$$

In order to separate the two factors, bias and variance, following [3] one defines a rate

$$R_1^*(L) = 1 - \sum_l \max_j \mathbb{P}(X \in S_l, Y = j). \tag{8}$$

This rate can be seen as an approximation of the Bayes rate

$$R^* = 1 - \int \max_j (\pi_j(x) f_j(x)) dx$$

obtained by taking the averages of the densities over the rectangles of the partitions and taking the maximum after averaging. The part of misclassification due to bias is defined as

$$B(L) = R_1^*(L) - R^*. \tag{9}$$

The remainder term corresponds to variance: it receives contributions from those rectangles that have a majority of cases in the learning set belonging to some class different from the class that has the largest probability w. r. t. the probability measure $\mathbb{P}$.

3   Estimate for the Bias Part of the Misclassification Rate

The estimate of the bias part can be carried through as indicated in [3] with no essencial extra complication with respect to the case with only two classes. We expose it briefly using the same notation for completeness and in order to make explicit some mathematical points that were hinted at in [3].

We assume that the probability density functions $f_j(x)$ are smooth and that they satisfy some genericity conditions. Both hypotheses will be stated more explicitly in the following. The bias contribution $B(L)$ can be expressed as

$$B(L) = \sum_L \left[\int_{S_l} \max_j (\pi(j) f_j(x)) dx - \max_j \left(\int_{S_l} \pi(j) f_j(x) dx \right) \right]. \tag{10}$$

If in a rectangle S_l for some i we have that $\pi(i) f_i(x) > \pi(j) f_j(x) \ \forall x \in S_l$, we have that the term corresponding to l in the sum (10) is 0. So the only contributions to $B(L)$ come from rectangles S_l's for which there are i and j and two points $z \in S_l$, $z' \in S_l$ such that

$$\pi(i) f_i(z) > \pi(j) f_j(z)$$

$$\pi(i)f_i(z') > \pi(j)f_j(z')$$

(of course this is a necessary but not sufficient condition for a rectangle to give a contribution). Since the density are assumed to be continuous, this implies that there must be a point $x \in S_l$ such that

$$\pi(i)f_i(x) = \pi(j)f_j(x).$$

Therefore in order to estimate the bias part of the misclassification rate, one is led to consider the hypersurfaces $\mathcal{H}_{i,j}$ defined by

$$\{x \mid \pi(i)f_i(x) = \pi(j)f_j(x)\}. \tag{11}$$

for each pair of distinct classes i, j. Given that we have L rectangles and that we are in the M-dimensional Euclidean space, the sides of rectangles will decrease like $L^{-1/M}$. We assume that the densities are supported in a bounded region of $\mathbb{R}^M$. Therefore the relevant size of each of the hypersurfaces $\mathcal{H}_{i,j}$ will have a bounded $M - 1$-dimensional volume. Now we for each i, j and each rectangle we can choose a coordinate system such that the hypersurface is described in the rectangle by the points where one of the coordinates, say x_m is 0 and evaluate the corresponding integrals in (10) in such a coordinate system. The difference of the two terms appearing in (10) can be written as an integral of the form

$$\int_{S_l} ((\pi(i)f_i(x) - \pi(j)f_j(x)) \vee 0) \, dx. \tag{12}$$

In the given coordinate system the function in the integral is 0 for $x_m = 0$ and by genericity assumption we can assume that it is 0 on one side of the hypersurface and will behave as $|x_m|$ on the other side of the hypersuface. The integral on the x_m coordinate will extend on an interval of length of the order $L^{-1/M}$ which is the order of the sides of the rectangles. The integral with respect to the x_m coordinate on S_l will therefore be of the order $L^{-2/M}$. By patching together all the integral with respect to the other coordinates we get the $M - 1$-dimensional volume of the relevant part of the hypersurface $\mathcal{H}_{i,j}$ which is a bounded term. We get a bound for $B(L)$ by summing over all pairs of distinct indices i and j, i. e. a finite number of terms.

The final result is that

$$B(L) \leq CL^{-2/M}, \tag{13}$$

as stated in [3].

This part of the misclassification rate decreases with L as a power with an exponent which is sensible to the number of attributes M.

4   Estimate for the Variance Part of the Misclassification Rate

We want now to consider the behaviour of the second term. Let

$$p_l = \max_j \mathbb{P}(Y = j | X \in S_l), \quad q_l = 1 - p_l. \tag{14}$$

One observes that if the number of rectangles is large, then one can apply to the sum appearing on the r. h. s. the law of large numbers. In this way the indicator function can be replaced by its expectation and the second term can be approximated by

$$\sum_l \mathbb{P}(y_l \neq y_l^*)|\mathbb{P}(X \in S_l, Y = y_l) - \mathbb{P}(X \in S_l, Y = y_l^*)|. \tag{15}$$

Let us consider a single term of the sum corresponding to the rectangle R. For $j = 1, 2, \ldots, k$ let

$$s_j = \mathbb{P}(Y = j | X \in R). \tag{16}$$

Assume that i is such that $s_i > s_j$ for all $i \neq j$. Let n be the number of cases in the learning set with spacial coordinate in R, and let $n_1, n_2, \ldots, n_k$ with $n_1 + n_2 + \ldots + n_k = n$ be the number of cases in class $1, 2, \ldots, k$ respectively. We want to estimate the probability that $n_i > n_j$ for some $j \neq i$ or, equivalently, the probability of the complementary event.

We will use the estimate given by the following theorem that was suggested without proof in [3].

Theorem 4.1. *For every i and j with $s_i > s_j$ we have*

$$(s_i - sj)\mathbb{P}(n_j \geq n_i) \leq \frac{1}{n} \tag{17}$$

Proof. Let us fix an j, $j \neq i$. We have

$$\mathbb{P}(n_j \geq n_i) = \mathbb{P}(n_j - n_i \geq 0) \leq \tag{18}$$
$$\mathbf{E}(\exp(u(n_j - n_i))) = (1 + s_j e^{u s_j} + s_i e^{-u s_i} + 1 - s_i - s_j)^n,$$

for any $u \in \mathbb{R}, u > 0$, where we have exploited the represtation of $n_i - n_j$ as the sum of n independent variables that take the values $1, -1, 0$ with probabilities s_j, s_i, $1 - s_i - s_j$ respectively and we have applied Markov inequality (see e. g. [4]). By Taylor expanding the logarithm of $1 + s_j e^{u s_j} + s_i e^{-u s_i} + 1 - s_i - s_j$ one gets easily that

$$1 + s_j e^{u s_j} + s_i e^{-u s_i} + 1 - s_i - s_j \leq \exp(u(s_j - s_i) + e\frac{u^2}{2}). \tag{19}$$

By inserting the bound (19) into (18) we get

$$\mathbb{P}(n_j \geq n_i) \leq \exp(nu(s_j - s_i) + ne\frac{u^2}{2}). \tag{20}$$

By taking $u = \frac{s_i - s_j}{e}$ we get

$$\mathbb{P}(n_j \geq n_i) \leq \exp(-\frac{n(s_i - s_j)^2}{2e}) \leq \frac{1}{\sqrt{n}(s_i - s_j)}, \tag{21}$$

where in the last inequality we have used that $xe^{-\frac{x^2}{2}} \leq \frac{1}{\sqrt{e}}$.   □

Let us now go back to the approximate form of the variance term given by
(15). We can decompose and bound it as

$$\sum_l \sum_{j \neq i^{(l)}} \mathbb{P}(y_l = j) |\mathbb{P}(X \in S_l, Y = i^{(l)}) - \mathbb{P}(X \in S_l, Y = j)| \leq \qquad (22)$$

$$\sum_l \sum_n \sum_{j \neq i^{(l)}} \mathbb{P}(n^{(l)} = n) \mathbb{P}(n_j^{(l)} \geq n_i^{(l)} | n^{(l)} = n) |(s_i^{(l)} - s_j^{(l)})| \mathbb{P}(X \in S_l),$$

where we denoted by $n^{(l)}$ the number of cases in the learning set the fall into
the rectangle S_l, by $n_j^{(l)}$ the number of those that fall in class j and by $s_j^{(l)}$
the probability $\P(Y = j | X \in S_l)$. By the law of large numbers, assuming that
the number N of cases in the learning set is sufficiently large with respect to
the number L of rectangle, we have that with large probability $n^{(l)}$ is close to
$N\P(X \in S_l)$ and that this quantity will increase as $\frac{N}{L}$.

Therefore using (17) we obtain that the variance term in the misclassification
rate decreases as $\sqrt{\frac{L}{N}}$.

The variance part for N fixed increases as the square root of the number of
rectangles L, which is the number of nodes of the classification tree. This goes
in the opposite direction of the bias part (see (12)).

5   Final Remarks

The arguments that we have used to obtain bounds on the bias part and the
variance part of the misclassification rate are non-rigorous. The only rigorous
result is the theorem proved in the second section. Considerable extra work is
probably required for making rigorous even only some parts of the arguments in
order to show that the bounds that are shown here are indeed the true behaviour
of this important quantity.

A final point to be noted is that we have considered a partition in rectangles
corresponding to a given classification tree but we have not taken account of
the way it is obtained by means of some particular procedure starting from the
learning set. The behaviour of the misclassification rate is conjectured to have
still the stated behaviour, but this introduces some extra problems for a rigorous
derivation.

References

1. Breiman L.: Bagging Predictors. Machine Learning **26** (1996) 123–140
2. Breiman L.: Arcing Classifiers, discussion paper. Ann. Stat. **26** (1998) 801–824
3. Breiman, L., Friedman, J.H., Olshen, R.A., Stone, C.J.: Classification and Regression Trees. Chapman & Hall/CRC Boca Raton, London, New York, Washington D.
   C, (1993)
4. Feller, F.: An Introduction to Probability Theory and Its Applications. Vol. I, II.
   Wiley, New York (1971)

5. Freund, Y., Shapire, R.: Experiments with a new boosting algorithm. Machine Learning: Proceedings of the Thirteenth International Conference, July, 1996 (1996)
6. On bias, variance, 0/1 loss, and the curse of dimensionality. Journ. of Data Mining and Knowledge Discovery. (1997) 1–55
7. Geman, S., Bienestock, E., Doursat, R.: Neural networks and the bias / variance dilemma. Neural Computation 4 (1992) 1–58
8. Tibshirani, R.: Bias, Variance and Prediction Error for Classification Rules. Technical Report, Statistics Department, University of Toronto (1996).
9. Weiss, S.M., Indurkhya, N.: Predictive data mining: a practical guide. Ed. Morgan Kaufmann Publishers, San Francisco (1998)

A Comparative Analysis of Clustering Algorithms Applied to Load Profiling

Fátima Rodrigues[1], Jorge Duarte[1], Vera Figueiredo[2], Zita Vale[2], and M. Cordeiro[3]

[1] Department of Computer Engineering, Polytechnic Institute of Oporto, Portugal
GECAD – Knowledge Engineering and Decision Support Group
{fr,jduarte}@dei.isep.ipp.pt
[2] Department of Electrical Engineering, Polytechnic Institute of Oporto, Portugal
GECAD – Knowledge Engineering and Decision Support Group
{veraf,zav}@dee.isep.ipp.pt
[3] Department of Electrical Engineering, UTAD, Portugal
{cordeiro@utad.pt}

Abstract. With the electricity market liberalization, the distribution and retail companies are looking for better market strategies based on adequate information upon the consumption patterns of its electricity customers. A fair insight on the customers' behavior will permit the definition of specific contract aspects based on the different consumption patterns. In this paper, we propose a KDD project applied to electricity consumption data from a utility client's database. To form the different customers' classes, and find a set of representative consumption patterns, a comparative analysis of the performance of the K-means, Kohonen Self-Organized Maps (SOM) and a Two-Level approach is made. Each customer class will be represented by its load profile obtained with the algorithm with best performance in the data set used.

1 Introduction

The major consequence of electricity markets liberalization is the freedom that all costumers will have on the choice of their electricity supplier. This new scenario will create an unstable environment where all costumers have access to the market. The competitive environment will include the small low voltage (LV) consumers and new competitive retail companies will enter in the market. These companies will need strategies for approaching customers based on cost leadership or differentiation by additional value services. For suppliers who choose a differentiation strategy the knowledge of the needs of their costumers is very important to develop products to suit their preferences. To achieve success in the deregulated market, companies must learn to segment the market and target these segments with the most effective types of marketing methods [1]. One possible method of differentiation is the development of tailored contracts defined according to customer consumption patterns.

The consumption pattern of an electricity consumer is defined for his daily load diagram. These diagrams represent the evolution of the power consumed during the

P. Perner and A. Rosenfeld (Eds.): MLDM 2003, LNAI 2734, pp. 73–85, 2003.

period of a day. The load diagram evolution can be affected for several load factors that influence the way each consumer uses electricity. These factors can be external, like the weather condition, the day of the week or related with the type of consumer (a domestic consumer does not have the same pattern as an industrial consumer). The influence of these factors must be considered in any study related with the consumers' electrical behavior. To study the electricity consumption patterns the development of load research projects is essential.

In a load research project a sample population is defined, real time meters are installed in these clients and the data collected in these meters during the period in study is treated and analyzed to create tools to support companies. Load research projects were developed in many countries [2,3]. One of the important tools defined in these projects are the load profiles for different consumers classes. A Load Profile can be defined as a pattern of electricity demand for a consumer, or group of consumers, over a given period of time. The accurate classification of consumer classes and the association of a load profile are essential to support marketing strategies.

To move from profiling in abstract to profiling in practice a number of decisions is required and the most important and critical are the number and coverage of the profiles. Each load profile should represent a relatively homogeneous group of consumers and must be distinctly different from the others. The number of profiles should be big enough to represent the different consumption patterns but small enough to be used on the definition of market strategies.

This paper is organized as follows: in Sect. 2 we briefly resume each one of the clustering methods used: K-means, Self-Organized Maps (SOM) and a Two-Level Approach. In the next section we present our case study – a sample of low voltage consumers from a Portuguese Distribution Company, next a comparison between the different results obtained are performed, and finally, in last section, some conclusions and future work are presented.

2   Clustering Algorithms

When trying to discover knowledge from data one of the first arising tasks is to identify groups of similar objects that is to carry out cluster analysis for obtaining data partitions. There are several clustering methods that can be used for cluster analysis. Yet for a given data set, each clustering method may identify groups whose member objects are different. Thus a decision must be taken for choosing the clustering method that produces the best data partition for a given data collection. In order to support such a decision, we will use indexes for measuring the quality of the data partition. To choose the optimal clustering schema, we will follow two proposed criteria:

Compactness: members of each cluster should be as close to each other as possible;
Separation: the clusters should be widely spaced from each other.

2.1   K-Means

The K-means algorithm [4] is the most widely used clustering algorithm. The name comes from representing each of the k clusters by the mean, or weighted average, of its points, the so-called cluster center. It requires the initialization of the number of clusters and starts by assigning k cluster centers randomly selected from the pattern set. Then it proceeds by assigning each pattern from the initial set to the nearest cluster center and recomputes the center using the current cluster memberships, until the convergence criterion is met. Typically the convergence criterions are: no patterns are reassigned to a new cluster center or minimal decrease square error is reached. This algorithm has the advantage of clear geometrical and statistical meaning, but works conveniently only with numerical attributes. It is also sensible to outliers.

2.2   Kohonen Self-Organized Maps (SOM)

Kohonen Networks are a specific kind of neuronal network that performs clustering analysis of the input data. The basic units are the neurons, and these are usually organized in a two dimensional layers: the input layer, and the output layer, which is often referred to as the output map. All the input neurons are connected to all the output neurons, and these connections have "strengths" associated with them.

Input data is presented to the input layer and the values are propagated to the output layer. Each output neuron then gives a response. The output neuron with the strongest response is said to be the winner, and is the answer for that input. Initially all weights are random. In order to train, an input pattern is shown and the winner adjusts its weights in such a way that it reacts even more strongly next time it sees that (or a very similar) record. Also, its neighbors (those neurons surrounding it) adjust their weights so they also react more positively. All the input records are shown and weights updated accordingly. This process is repeated many times until the changes being made are very small.

The most attractive feature of the Kohonen Self-Organized Maps (SOM) [5] is that, once trained, the map represents the projection of the data set belonging to an N-dimensional space into a bi-dimensional one.

2.3   Two-Level Approach

If SOM is used as a clustering algorithm each map unit define a small cluster consisting of the samples in its Voronoi set. The prototype vector of each unit represents the cluster center. Because of the neighborhood relations, neighboring prototypes are pulled to the same direction, and thus prototype vectors of neighboring units resemble each other. However, the optimal situation in the SOM is not when the number of prototypes equals the number of clusters. Instead, the number of units in the output grid must be much bigger then the expected number of clusters. It is possible, according to the definition of the neighborhood function, to drawn neighboring units together, and thus neighbor units reflect the properties of the same cluster. The transition from one cluster to another on the map takes place over several map units. If a small number of clusters is desired, to avoid the reduction of the grid to a small one, the SOM units must be clustered [6]. The SOM can be used as an intermediate step and make the clustering a two level approach, improving the quality of the final results. In the first level the SOM implements an ordered dimensionality redution, mapping the data set to the output grid, reducing the computational load. The prototype units of the output layer can be clustered using either a partitive or a hierarchical method. The clustering task is now easier because is performed in a smaller number of samples. In the second level the prototypes can be directly clustered or some specific features of the SOM can be used.

3 Adequacy Measures of Clustering Outcomes

The load diagram grouping is performed using the K-means, SOM and a Two-Level Approach in a comparative analysis. To assess the efficiency of each clustering process a measure of adequacy should be employed. For this goal we use the indices proposed in [7]. These indices are based in distances computed with the multi- dimensional vectors used to represent the load diagrams of each consumer and the load profile of each class. They are adequate to perform a comparative evaluation between different algorithms used to obtain the same number of clusters.

To assist the formulation of the adequacy measures the following distances are defined:

a) Distance between two load diagrams

$$d(li,lj) = \sqrt{\frac{1}{H} \times \sum_{h=1}^{H} (li(h) - lj(h))^2} \tag{1}$$

b) Distance between a representative load diagram and the center of a set of diagrams

$$d(r^{(k)}, L^{(k)}) = \sqrt{\frac{1}{n^{(k)}} \sum_{m=1}^{n^{(k)}} d^2(r^{(k)}, l^{(m)})} \tag{2}$$

Using the distances (1) and (2) it is possible to define performance measures to evaluate the clustering tools. A good clustering tool is able to determine, well-separated classes of load diagrams and assure that the load diagrams assigned to the same class are very similar. Considering a set of X load diagrams separated in K classes with k= 1,...,K and each class is formed by a subset $C^{(k)}$ of load diagrams, where $r^{(k)}$ is a pattern assigned to cluster k, the following performance measures are defined:

Mean Index Adequacy (MIA)

The Mean Index Adequacy (MIA) directly used the Euclidian Distance Measure and depends on the average of the mean distances between each pattern assigned to the cluster and its center.

$$MIA = \sqrt{\frac{1}{K}\sum_{k=1}^{K} d^2(r^{(k)}, C^{(k)})} \tag{3}$$

Clustering Dispersion Indicator (CDI)

The Clustering Dispersion Indicator (CDI) depends on the distance between the load diagrams in the same cluster and (inversely) on the distance between the class representative load diagrams. In (4) R is the set of the class representative load diagrams.

$$CDI = \frac{\sqrt{\frac{1}{K}\sum_{k=1}^{K}\left[\frac{1}{2.n^{(k)}}\sum_{n=1}^{n^{(k)}} d^2(l^{(m)}, C^{(k)})\right]}}{\sqrt{\frac{1}{2K}\sum_{k=1}^{K} d^2(r^{(k)}, R)}} \tag{4}$$

The clustering algorithm that produces the smaller MIA and CDI values prevails over the others in terms of performance.

All experiments that will be described in the following sections were conducted using Clementine version 7.1 [8]. This is an integrated DM toolkit, which uses a visual-programming interface, and supports all KDD stages.

4   Finding Customer Load Profiles by Clustering

Broadly speaking, the KDD process consists of three phases, namely pre-processing, data mining and post-processing [9]. These phases can be overlapped and the results produced in previous iterations can be used to improve the following iterations of the process. The pre-processing phase includes three broad sub-phases, namely data selection, data cleaning and data transformation (not necessarily in this order).

4.1 Data Selection

Our case study is based on a set X = 165 LV consumers from a Portuguese utility. Information on the customer consumption has been gathered by measurement campaigns carried out by EDP Distribuição - Portuguese Distribution Company. These campaigns were based on a load research project where the previous definition of a sample population, type of consumers (MV, LV), where meters were installed, sampling cadence (15, 30 minutes...) and total duration (months, years...) of data collection were defined. The instant power consumption for each customer was collected with a cadence of 15 minutes, which gives 96 values a day for each client. The measurement campaigns were made during a period of 3 months in summer and another 3 months in winter for working days and weekends in each costumer of a sample population of LV consumers. There is also available for this population the commercial data related with the monthly energy consumption, the activity code and the hired power.

4.2 Data Pre-processing

There are always problems with data. That explains why previous to any DM process it is indispensable a data-cleaning phase to detect and correct bad data, and a data-treatment phase to derive data accordingly to DM algorithms that will be used [10]. In the data-cleaning phase we have filled missing values of measures by linear regression. There were also some values of activity type and hired power missing which were computed using logistic regression because these are categorical attributes. With this data completion the errors of the metered load curves were attenuated without making big changes in the real measures.

After this data completion we prepare data for clustering. Each customer is represented by its representative daily load curve resulting from elaborating the data from the measurement campaign. For each customer, the representative load diagram has been built by averaging the load diagrams related to each customer [11]. A different representative load diagram is created to each one of the loading conditions defined: winter, summer, working days and weekends. Each customer is now defined for a representative daily load curve for each of the loading conditions to be studied separately. We present the study performed for weekends during the winter period.

The representative daily load diagram of the mth consumer is the vector $l^{(m)} = \{l_h^{(m)}\}$ with h = 1,...,H where H = 96 representing the 15 minutes interval.

The diagrams were computed using the field-measurements values, so they need to be brought together to a similar scale for the purpose of their pattern comparison. This is achieved through normalization. For each consumer the vector $l^{(m)}$ was normalized to the [0-1] range by using the peak power of its representative load diagram. This kind of normalization permits maintaining the shape of the curve to compare the consumption patterns.

At this point each customer is represented by a group H of data consisting on values for 15 minutes intervals which gives a set of 96 values in the range [0,1].

4.3   Data Mining Operations

A clustering procedure based on Kohonen Networks (SOM) has been used to group the load patterns on the basis of their distinguishing features. If the number of clusters is unknown the clustering can be repeated for a set of different values between 2 and $\sqrt{X}$, where X is the number of patterns in the pattern set. As the goal of our clustering is finding a set of load profiles to study tariff offers, the number of clusters must be small enough to allow the definition of different tariff structures to each class. Based on information from the electricity company we fixed a minimum number of 6 and a maximum number of 9 clusters. The Kohonen network performs the projection of the H–dimensional space, containing the X vectors representing the load diagrams, into a bi-dimensional space. To each client are assigned two coordinates $KX and $KY representing the Kohonen net attributes.

To perform this clustering operation we trained a network with the following arquitecture: Input layer - 96 units and Output layer - 16 units. When applied to this set of patterns the network performs a projection of the input values in a bi-dimensional space with 9 different sets of coordinates representing 9 different clusters (Fig. 1).

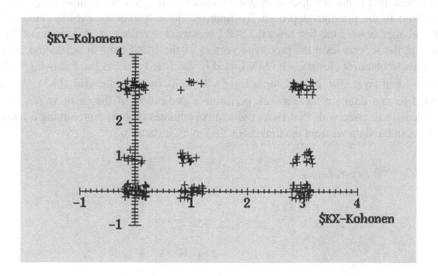

Fig. 1. Clusters formation with the Kohonen network

In order to perform a comparative analysis, to select the most suitable clustering algorithm, we perform another clustering operation using the K-means algorithm. This algorithm requires the initialization of the number of clusters that we set to 9 to keep the same number obtained with the Kohonen network. (Fig. 2).

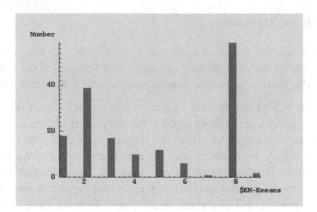

Fig. 2. Clusters obtained with K-means

From the results obtained we conclude that the K-means algorithm has a better perform-ance with this data set. This can be explained because to obtain a small number of clus-ters the dimension of the SOM's grid has a number of units close to the expected num-ber of clusters. To obtain best performances the number of units in the output layer must be much bigger then the expected number of clusters. After several experiments we conclude that is not possible to obtain 9 clusters with a number of units bigger then 16, as used in the previous approach. To improve these results we experimented a Two-Level approach. In the first level the SOM was used to reduce the dimension of the data set. In the second level the prototype vectors of the SOM units are clustered using K-means to obtain 9 clusters. The SOM used in the first level has the following architec-ture: Input layer - 96 units; Output layer - 70 units (rectangular grid 10×7). When ap-plied to this data set the network performs a projection of the input values in a bi-dimensional space with 55 different sets of coordinates (Fig. 3) representing a reduction of the initial data set from the dimension 165 to 55 instances.

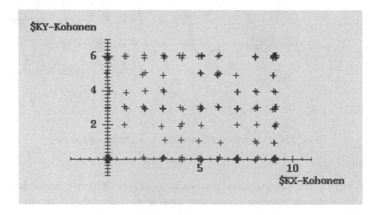

Fig. 3. Clusters formation with the Kohonen network

In the second level, the K-means algorithm is used to perform the clustering of the SOM units and obtain the expected 9 clusters (Fig. 4).

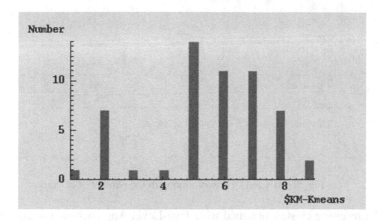

Fig. 4. Clusters formation with the Two-Level Approach

After the second level we have the initial data set grouped into 9 different clusters, which can be used to create the different load profiles.

To evaluate the different algorithms we compute the MIA and CDI indexes with the results obtained with each algorithm (Table 1). From the results obtained we conclude that the Two-Level Approach has a better performance with this data set.

Table 1. MIA AND CDI obtained for 9 clusters with K-means, SOM and Two-Level Approach

	K-means	SOM	Two-Level Approach
MIA	0,1694	0,1950	0,1622
CDI	0,5890	0,9358	0,5860

A significant improvement has been obtained using the Two-Level Approach when compared with the performance of the SOM. This can be explained by the increase of the output layer used in this approach that is much bigger than the expected number of clusters. However, when compared with K-means the better performance of this approach is not so significant because the data set used, mainly composed by numeric attributes, is adequate to K-means algorithm.

We also performed different clustering exercises using different numbers of clusters, to evaluate the evolution of the indexes with the number of clusters. As it can be seen from Fig. 5 we can conclude that, as expected, the indexes decrease as the number of clusters increases.

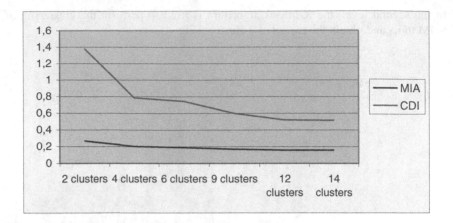

Fig. 5. MIA and CDI evolution with the number of clusters

With the resulting clusters obtained with Two-Level Approach we obtained the representative diagram for each cluster for weekends in the winter period by averaging the load diagrams of the clients assigned to the same cluster. (Fig. 6, Fig. 7). The next two figures show the representative load diagram obtained for each cluster. Each curve represents the load profile of the corresponding costumer class.

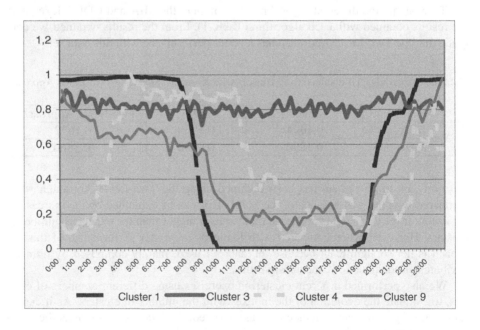

Fig. 6. Representative Load Profile for consumers with non typical behavior

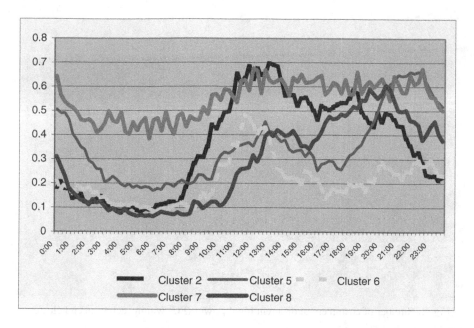

Fig. 7. Representative Load Profile for consumers with typical behavior

From the representative load diagrams obtained to each cluster it is possible to see that the clustering method used has well separated the client population, creating representative load diagrams with distinct load shapes. The method used has successfully isolated non-typical representative load diagrams what is proved by the load profiles represented in Fig. 6.

For the characterization of the customer classes a first trial was made to search for an association between the clusters and the components of the contractual data. From Figs. 8 and 9 we conclude that a poor correlation exists between the main clusters and the contractual data. These results show that the contractual data is highly ineffective from the viewpoint of the characterization of the electrical behavior of the costumers.

Further work is needed in order to produce global shape indices able to capture relevant information on the costumer's consumption behavior. To obtain more relevant information to describe the consumption patterns of each cluster population we intend to use a rule-based modeling technique (C5.0 algorithm [12]), to analyze those clusters, and to obtain their descriptions based on a set of indices derived from the daily load curves.

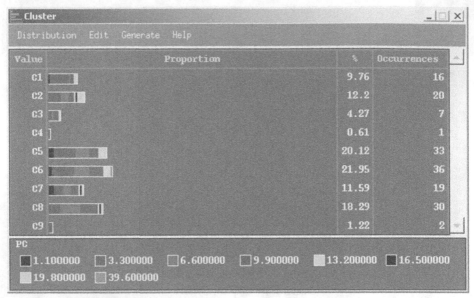

Fig. 8. Number of costumers of different hired power (PC) within each weekend cluster

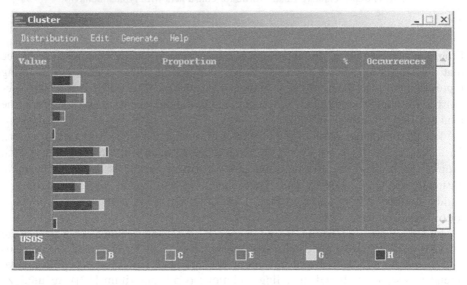

Fig. 9. Number of costumers of different activity types (USOS) within each weekend cluster

5   Conclusion and Further Work

This paper deals with the clustering of the electricity consumers based on their measured daily load curves. To obtain the clusters for the different consumer classes three algorithms were used: K-means, SOM and a Two-Level Approach. The K-means algorithm presented a better performance than the Kohonen network. However, the Two-Level Approach presents the best performance, which indicates this combination is a good practice to improve the performance of SOM as a clustering algorithm.

The results obtained so far point out that the contractual parameters are poorly connected to the load profiles, and that further work is needed in order to produce global shape indices able to capture relevant information on the costumers consuming behavior.

As further work we intend to extend the attributes space with contractual data, such as, categorical attributes in order to obtain load profiles related with contractual data.

After the division of the customers into classes, this will be achieved by the characterization of each cluster.

It is also our aim to develop a decision support system for assisting the managers in properly fixing the best tariff structure for each customer class. This one must be sufficiently flexible to follow the variations in the load patterns of the customers.

References

[1] Grønli, H., Livik, K., Pentzen, H., "Actively Influencing on Customer Actions – Important Strategic Issues for the Future., DA/DSM Europe DistribuTECH Conference, Amsterdam 14–16 October 1998, Proceedings.

[2] S.V.,Allera, A.G., Horsburgh, "Load Profiling for the Energy Trading and Settlements in the UK Electricity Markets", DA/DSM Europe DistribuTECH Conference, London 27–29 October 1996, Proceedings.

[3] C.S., Chen, J.C., Hwang, C.W., Huang, "Application of Load Survey to Proper Tariff Design", IEEE Transactions on Power Systems, Vol. 12, No. 4, November 1997, pp 1746–1751.

[4] Hartigan, J.A.,Wong, M.A. 1979. A K-*Means Clustering Algorithm*. Applied Statistics 28:100–108.

[5] Kohonen, T., "Self-Organisation and Associative Memory", 3rd Ed., Springer-Verlag, Berlin, 1989.

[6] Zhang, T., Ramakrishnon, R., and Livny M. (1996). BIRCH: An Efficient Data Clustering Method for Very Large Datebases. Proceedings of the ACM SIGMOD Conference on Management of Data, pp. 103–114, Montreal, Canada.

[7] Chicco, G., Napoli, R., Postolache, P., Troader, C.,"Electric Energy Customer Characterisation for Developing Dedicated Market Strategies", IEEE Porto Power THEC Conference, Oporto 10–13 September 2001, Proceedings.

[8] Integral Solutions Limited ISL, Clementine Data Mining System, World Wide Web page – http://www.isl.co.uk/clementine.html, 1997.

[9] Frawley, W.J., G. Piatetsky-Shapiro, C. Matheus, "Knowledge Discovery in Databases: An Overview", AI Magazine, 1992.

[10] Fayyad, U., G. Piatetsky-Shapiro, P.J. Smith, R. Uthurasamy, "From Data Mining to Knowledge Discovery: An Overview". In Advances in Knowledge Discovery and Data Mining, pp. 1–34. AAAI/MIT Press, 1996.

[11] Chicco, G, Napoli, R., Postulache, P., Scutariu, M. And Toader C., "Customer Characterization Options for Improving the Tariff Offer", IEEE Transactions on Power Systems, Vol. 18, N°1, February 2003.

[12] J. Quinlan, "C4.5: Programs for Machine Learning", Morgan Kaufmann Publishers, San Francisco, USA, 1993.

Similarity-Based Clustering of Sequences Using Hidden Markov Models

Manuele Bicego[1], Vittorio Murino[1], and Mário A.T. Figueiredo[2]

[1] Dipartimento di Informatica, Università di Verona
Ca' Vignal 2, Strada Le Grazie 15, 37134 Verona, Italy
{bicego,murino}@sci.univr.it
[2] Instituto de Telecomunicações, Instituto Superior Técnico
1049-001 Lisboa, Portugal
mtf@lx.it.pt

Abstract. Hidden Markov models constitute a widely employed tool for sequential data modelling; nevertheless, their use in the clustering context has been poorly investigated. In this paper a novel scheme for HMM-based sequential data clustering is proposed, inspired on the similarity-based paradigm recently introduced in the supervised learning context. With this approach, a new representation space is built, in which each object is described by the vector of its similarities with respect to a pre-determinate set of other objects. These similarities are determined using hidden Markov models. Clustering is then performed in such a space. By way of this, the difficult problem of clustering of sequences is thus transposed to a more manageable format, the clustering of points (vectors of features). Experimental evaluation on synthetic and real data shows that the proposed approach largely outperforms standard HMM clustering schemes.

1 Introduction

Unsupervised classification (or clustering) of data [1] is undoubtedly an interesting and challenging research area: it could be defined as the organization of a collection of patterns into groups, based on similarity. It is well known that data clustering is inherently a more difficult task if compared to supervised classification, in which classes are already identified, so that a system can be adequately trained. This intrinsic difficulty worsens if sequential data are considered: the structure of the underlying process is often difficult to infer, and typically different length sequences have to be dealt with. Clustering of sequences has assumed an increasing importance in recent years, due to its wide applicability in emergent contexts like data mining and DNA genome modelling and analysis.

Sequential data clustering methods could be generally classified into three categories: *proximity-based* methods, *feature-based* methods and *model-based* methods. In the *proximity-based* approaches, the main effort of the clustering process is in devising similarity or distance measures between sequences. With such measures, any standard distance-based method (as agglomerative clustering) can be applied. *Feature-based* methods extract a set of features from each

P. Perner and A. Rosenfeld (Eds.): MLDM 2003, LNAI 2734, pp. 86–95, 2003.

individual data sequence that captures temporal information. The problem of sequence clustering is thus reduced to a more addressable point (vector of features) clustering. Finally, *model-based* approaches assume an analytical model for each cluster, and the aim of clustering is to find a set of such models that best fit the data. Examples of models that can be employed include time series models, spectral models, and finite state automata, as *hidden Markov models* (HMM) [2]. HMMs are a widely used tool for sequence modelling, whose importance has rapidly grown in the last decade. In the context of sequence clustering, HMMs have not been extensively used, and only a few papers can be found in the literature: the corresponding state of the art is presented in Sect. 2. The proposed approaches mainly fall into the first (proximity-based) and in the third (model-based) categories. In this paper, an alternative HMM clustering scheme is proposed, classifiable as belonging to the *feature-based* class, that extends the similarity-based paradigm [3,4,5,6,7,8]. This paradigm, which has been introduced recently for supervised classification purposes, differs from typical pattern recognition approaches where objects are represented by sets (vectors) of features. In the similarity-based paradigm, objects are described using pairwise (dis)similarities, i.e., distances from other objects in the data set. The state of the art of the similarity-based paradigm is reviewed in Sect. 2.

In this paper, we propose to extend this paradigm to the problem of clustering sequences, using a new feature space, where each sequence is characterized by its similarity to all other sequences. The problem is to find a suitable metric for measuring (dis)similarities between sequences, and, as shown in [9,10], HMMs are a suitable tool for that purpose. In that space, clustering is then performed using some standard techniques: the difficult task of sequence clustering is thus transposed to a more manageable format, that of clustering points (vectors of features). Experimental evaluation on synthetic and real data shows that this approach largely outperforms standard HMM clustering schemes.

The rest of the paper is organized as follows: Sect. 2 summarizes the state of the art in HMM-based clustering of sequences and reviews the similarity-based paradigm. Section 3 reviews the fundamentals of hidden Markov models, while Sect. 4 details the proposed strategy. Experimental results are reported in Sect. 5. Finally, Sect. 6 is devoted to presenting conclusions and future work directions.

2   State of the Art

2.1   HMM-Based Sequence Clustering

HMMs have not been extensively employed for clustering sequences, with only a few papers exploring this direction. More specifically, early approaches related to speech recognition were presented in [11,12,13]. All these methods belong to the proximity-based clustering class. HMMs were employed to compute similarities between sequences, using different approaches (see for example [10,14]), and standard pairwise distance matrix-based approaches (as agglomerative hierarchical) were then used to obtain clustering. This strategy, which is considered the standard method for HMM-based clustering of sequences, is better detailed in Sect. 3.1.

The first approach not directly linked to speech was presented by Smyth [9] (see also the more general and more recent [15]). This approach consists in two steps: first, it devises a pairwise distance between observed sequences, by computing a symmetrized similarity. This similarity is obtained by training an HMM for each sequence, so that the log-likelihood (LL) of each model, given each sequence, can be computed. This information is used to build an LL matrix which is then used to cluster the sequences in K groups, using a hierarchical algorithm. In the second step, one HMM is trained for each cluster; the resulting K models are then merged into a "composite" global HMM, where each HMM is used to design a disjoint part of this "composite" model. This initial estimate is then refined using the standard Baum-Welch procedure. As a result, a global HMM modelling all the data is obtained. The number of clusters is selected using a cross-validation method. With respect to the above mentioned taxonomy, this approach can be classified as belonging to both the proximity-based class (a pairwise distance is derived to initialize the model) and the model-based class (a model for clustering data is finally obtained).

An example of an HMM-based method for sequence clustering is the one proposed in [16], where HMMs are used as cluster prototypes. The clustering is obtained by employing the *rival penalized competitive learning* (RPCL) algorithm [17] (a method originally developed for point clustering) together with a state merging strategy, aimed at finding smaller HMMs.

A relevant contribution to the model-based HMM clustering methodology was made by Li and Biswas [18,19,20,21,22]). Basically, in their approach [18], the clustering problem is addressed by focusing on the model selection issue, *i.e.* the search for the HMM topology best representing data, and the clustering structure issue, *i.e.* finding the most likely number of clusters. In [19], the former issue is addressed using the *Bayesian information criterion* [23], and extending to the continuous case the *Bayesian model merging* approach [24]. Regarding the latter issue, the sequence-to-HMM likelihood measure is used to enforce the within-group similarity criterion. The optimal number of clusters is then determined maximizing the *partition mutual information* (PMI), which is a measure of the inter-cluster distances. In [20], the same problems are addressed in terms of Bayesian model selection, using BIC [23], and the *Cheesman-Stutz* (CS) approximation [25]. A more comprehensive version of this paper has appeared in [22], where the method is also tested on real world ecological data. These clustering methodologies have been applied to specific domains, as physiology, ecology and social science, where the dynamic model structure is not readily available. Obtained results have been published in [21].

2.2   Similarity-Based Classification

The literature on similarity-based classification is not vast. Jain and Zongker [3] have obtained a dissimilarity measure, for a handwritten digit recognition problem, based on deformable templates; a multidimensional scaling approach was then used to project this dissimilarity space onto a low-dimensional space, where a 1-nearest-neighbor (1-NN) classifier was employed to classify new objects. In [4], Graepel *et al* investigate the problem of learning a classifier based on data represented in terms of their pairwise proximities, using an approach based on Vapnik's structural risk minimization [26]. Jacobs and Weinshall [5] have studied distance-based classification with non-metric distance functions (*i.e.*, that do not verify the triangle inequality). Duin and Pekalska are very active authors in this area[1] having recently produced several papers [6,7,8]. Motivation and basic features of similarity-based methods were first described in [6]; it was shown, by experiments in two real applications, that a Bayesian classifier (the RLNC - regularized linear normal density-based classifier) in the dissimilarity space outperforms the nearest neighbor rule. These aspects were more thoroughly investigated in [8], where other classifiers in the dissimilarity space were studied, namely on digit recognition and bioinformatics problems. Finally, in [7], a generalized kernel approach was introduced, dealing with classification aspects of the dissimilarity kernels.

3   Hidden Markov Models

A discrete-time hidden Markov model λ can be viewed as a Markov model whose states are not directly observed: instead, each state is characterized by a probability distribution function, modelling the observations corresponding to that state. More formally, an HMM is defined by the following entities [2]:

- $S = \{S_1, S_2, \cdots, S_N\}$ the finite set of possible (hidden) states;
- the transition matrix $\mathbf{A} = \{a_{ij}, 1 \leq j \leq N\}$ representing the probability of moving from state S_i to state S_j,

$$a_{ij} = P[q_{t+1} = S_j | q_t = S_i], \quad 1 \leq i, j \leq N,$$

  with $a_{ij} \geq 0$, $\sum_{j=1}^{N} a_{ij} = 1$, and where q_t denotes the state occupied by the model at time t.
- the emission matrix $\mathbf{B} = \{b(o|S_j)\}$, indicating the probability of emission of symbol $o \in V$ when system state is S_j; V can be a discrete alphabet or a continuous set (e.g. $V = I\!\!R$), in which case $b(o|S_j)$ is a probability density function.
- $\boldsymbol{\pi} = \{\pi_i\}$, the initial state probability distribution,

$$\pi_i = P[q_1 = S_i], \quad 1 \leq i \leq N$$

  with $\pi_i \geq 0$ and $\sum_{i=1}^{N} \pi_i = 1$.

For convenience, we represent an HMM by a triplet $\lambda = (\mathbf{A}, \mathbf{B}, \boldsymbol{\pi})$.

Learning the HMM parameters, given a set of observed sequences $\{\mathbf{O}_i\}$, is usually performed using the well-known Baum-Welch algorithm [2], which is able

---

[1] See http://www.ph.tn.tudelft.nl/Research/neural/index.html

to determine the parameters maximizing the likelihood $P(\{\mathbf{O}_i\}|\boldsymbol{\lambda})$. One of the steps of the Baum-Welch algorithm is an evaluation step, where it is required to compute $P(\mathbf{O}|\boldsymbol{\lambda})$, given a model $\boldsymbol{\lambda}$ and a sequence $\mathbf{O}$; this can be computed using the *forward-backward procedure* [2].

3.1 Standard HMM-Based Clustering of Sequences

The standard proximity-based method for clustering sequences using HMMs can be sumarized by the following algorithm. Consider a given a set of N sequences $\{\mathbf{O}_1...\mathbf{O}_N\}$ to be clustered; the algorithm performs the following steps:

1. Train one HMM $\boldsymbol{\lambda}_i$ for each sequence $\mathbf{O}_i$.
2. Compute the distance matrix $D = \{D(\mathbf{O}_i, \mathbf{O}_j)\}$, representing a similarity measure between sequences or between models; this is typically obtained from the forward probability $P(\mathbf{O}_j|\boldsymbol{\lambda}_i)$, or by devising a measure of distances between models. In the past, few authors have proposed approaches to computing these distances: early approaches were based on the Euclidean distance of the discrete observation probability, others on entropy, or on co-emission probability of two models, or, very recently, on the Bayes probability of error (see [14] and the references therein).
3. Use a pairwise distance-matrix-based method (*e.g.*, an agglomerative method) to perform the clustering.

4 Proposed Strategy

The idea at the basis of the proposed approach is conceptually simple: to build a new representation space, using the similarity values between sequences obtained via the HMMs, and to perform the clustering in that space. Similarity values allow discrimination, since this quantity is high for similar objects/sequences, i.e., belonging to the same group, and low for objects of different clusters. Therefore, we can interpret the similarity measure $\mathcal{D}(\mathbf{O}, \mathbf{O}_i)$ between a sequence $\mathbf{O}$ and another "reference" sequence $\mathbf{O}_i$ as a "feature" of the sequence $\mathbf{O}$. This fact suggests the construction of a feature vector for $\mathbf{O}$ by taking the similarities between $\mathbf{O}$ and a set of reference sequences $\mathcal{R} = \{\mathbf{O}_k\}$, so that $\mathbf{O}$ is characterized by a *pattern* (*i.e.*, a set of features) $\{\mathcal{D}(\mathbf{O}, \mathbf{O}_k), \mathbf{O}_k \in \mathcal{R}\}$.

More formally, given a set of sequences $\mathcal{T} = \{\mathbf{O}^1...\mathbf{O}^N\}$ to be clustered, the proposed approach can be briefly described as follows:

- let $\mathcal{R} = \{\mathbf{P}_1, ..., \mathbf{P}_R\}$ be a set of R "reference" or "representative" objects; these objects may belong to the set of sequences ($\mathcal{R} \subseteq \mathcal{T}$) or may be otherwise defined. In a basic case it could be $\mathcal{R} = \mathcal{T}$.
- train one HMM $\boldsymbol{\lambda}_r$ for each sequence $\mathbf{P}_r \in \mathcal{R}$;
- represent each sequence $\mathbf{O}_i$ of the data set by the set of similarities $\mathcal{D}_\mathcal{R}(\mathbf{O}_i)$ to the elements of the representative set $\mathcal{R}$, computed with the HMMs $\boldsymbol{\lambda}_1...\boldsymbol{\lambda}_R$

as:

$$
\mathcal{D}_{\mathcal{R}}(\mathbf{O}_i) = \begin{bmatrix} \mathcal{D}(\mathbf{O}_i, \mathbf{P}_1) \\ \mathcal{D}(\mathbf{O}_i, \mathbf{P}_2) \\ \vdots \\ \mathcal{D}(\mathbf{O}_i, \mathbf{P}_R) \end{bmatrix} = \frac{1}{T_i} \begin{bmatrix} \log P(\mathbf{O}_i | \boldsymbol{\lambda}_1) \\ \log P(\mathbf{O}_i | \boldsymbol{\lambda}_2) \\ \vdots \\ \log P(\mathbf{O}_i | \boldsymbol{\lambda}_R) \end{bmatrix} \tag{1}
$$

where T_i is the length of the sequence $\mathbf{O}_i$.

- perform clustering in $\mathbb{R}^{|\mathcal{R}|}$, where $|\mathcal{R}|$ denotes the cardinality of $\mathcal{R}$, using any general technique (not necessarily hierarchical) appropriate for clustering points in an Euclidean space.

In the simplest case, the representative set $\mathcal{R}$ is the whole data set $\mathcal{T}$, resulting in a similarity space of dimensionality N. Even if computationally heavy for large data sets, it is interesting to analyze the discriminative power of such a space.

5   Experimental Results

In this section, the proposed technique is compared with the standard HMM clustering scheme presented in Sect. 3. Once the likelihood similarity matrix is obtained, clustering (step 3) is performed by using three algorithms:

- two variants of the agglomerative hierarchical clustering techniques: the *complete link scheme*, and the *Ward scheme* [1].
- a non parametric, pairwise distance-based clustering technique, called *clustering by friends* [27]: this technique produces a partition of the data using only the similarity matrix. The partition is obtained by iteratively applying a two-step transformation to the proximity matrix. The first step of the transformation represents each point by its relation to all other data points, and the second step re-estimates the pairwise distances using a proximity measure on these representations. Using these transformations, the algorithm partitions the data into two clusters. To partition the data into more than two clusters, the method has to be applied several times, recursively.

Regarding the proposed approach, after obtaining the similarity representation with $\mathcal{R} = \mathcal{T}$ (*i.e.* by using all sequences as representatives), we have used three clustering algorithms:

- again the hierarchical agglomerative complete link and Ward methods, where distance is the Euclidean metrics in the similarity space: this is performed to compare the two representations with the same algorithms;
- standard K-means algorithm [1].

Clustering accuracies were measured on synthetic and real data. Regarding the synthetic case, we consider a 3-class problem, where sequences were generated from the three HMMs defined in Fig. 1. The data set is composed of 30 sequences (of length 400) from each of the three classes; the dimensionality of the similarity vectors is thus $N = 90$. Notice that this clustering task is not easy,

$$A = \begin{array}{|c|c|c|} \hline 1/3 & 1/3 & 1/3 \\ \hline 1/3 & 1/3 & 1/3 \\ \hline 1/3 & 1/3 & 1/3 \\ \hline \end{array} \quad \pi = \begin{array}{|c|} \hline 1/3 \\ \hline 1/3 \\ \hline 1/3 \\ \hline \end{array} \quad B = \begin{array}{|c|c|} \hline \mu_1 = 1 & \sigma_1^2 = 0.6 \\ \hline \mu_2 = 3 & \sigma_2^2 = 0.6 \\ \hline \mu_3 = 5 & \sigma_3^2 = 0.6 \\ \hline \end{array}$$

(a)

$$A = \begin{array}{|c|c|c|} \hline 1/3 & 1/3 & 1/3 \\ \hline 1/3 & 1/3 & 1/3 \\ \hline 1/3 & 1/3 & 1/3 \\ \hline \end{array} \quad \pi = \begin{array}{|c|} \hline 1/3 \\ \hline 1/3 \\ \hline 1/3 \\ \hline \end{array} \quad B = \begin{array}{|c|c|} \hline \mu_1 = 1 & \sigma_1^2 = 0.5 \\ \hline \mu_2 = 3 & \sigma_2^2 = 0.5 \\ \hline \mu_3 = 5 & \sigma_3^2 = 0.5 \\ \hline \end{array}$$

(b)

$$A = \begin{array}{|c|c|c|} \hline 1/3 & 1/3 & 1/3 \\ \hline 1/3 & 1/3 & 1/3 \\ \hline 1/3 & 1/3 & 1/3 \\ \hline \end{array} \quad \pi = \begin{array}{|c|} \hline 1/3 \\ \hline 1/3 \\ \hline 1/3 \\ \hline \end{array} \quad B = \begin{array}{|c|c|} \hline \mu_1 = 1 & \sigma_1^2 = 0.4 \\ \hline \mu_2 = 3 & \sigma_2^2 = 0.4 \\ \hline \mu_3 = 5 & \sigma_3^2 = 0.4 \\ \hline \end{array}$$

(c)

Fig. 1. Generative HMMs for synthetic data testing: A is the transition matrix, π is the initial state probability, and B contains the parameters of the emission density (Gaussians with the indicated means and variances)

Table 1. Clustering results on synthetic experiments

Standard classification	
ML classification	94.78%
Standard clustering	
Aggl. complete link	64.89%
Aggl. Ward	71.33%
Clus. by Friends	70.11%
Clustering on similarity space $\mathcal{S}_T$	
Aggl. complete link	95.44%
Aggl. Ward	97.89%
k-means	98.33%

as the three HMMs are very similar to each other, only differing slightly in the variances of the emission densities. The accuracy of clustering can be quantitatively assessed, by computing the number of errors: a clustering error occurs if a sequence is assigned to a cluster in which the majority of the sequences are from another class. Results are presented in Table 1, averaged over 10 repetitions. From this table it is possible to notice that the proposed methodology largely outperforms standard clustering approaches: the best performing algorithm is the partitional k-means on the similarity space, which produces an almost perfect clustering. In order to have a better insight into the discriminative power of the proposed feature space, we also computed the supervised classification results on this synthetic example. Decisions were taken using the standard *maximum likelihood* (ML) approach, where an unknown sequence is assigned to the class whose model shows the highest likelihood. Note that this classification scheme does not make use of the similarity space introduced in this paper, and repre-

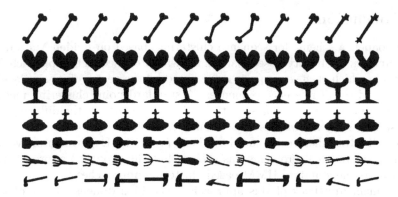

Fig. 2. Objects set used for testing

Table 2. Clustering results on real experiments

Standard classification	
ML classification	81.55%
Standard clustering	
Aggl. complete link	78.69%
Aggl. Ward	22.86%
Clus. by Friends	70.0%
Clustering on the similarity space $\mathcal{S}_\mathcal{T}$	
Aggl. complete link	63.10%
Aggl. Ward	77.62%
k-means	88.21%

sents the supervised counterpart of the standard clustering approach proposed in Sect. 3.1. The classification error is computed using the standard *leave one out* (LOO) scheme [28]. It is important to note that clustering results in the similarity space are better than the classification results, confirming the high discrimination ability of the similarity space.

The real data experiment regards 2D shape recognition, where shapes were modelled as proposed in [29]; briefly, object contours are described using curvature, and these curvature sequences are modelled using HMMs with Gaussian mixtures as emission probabilities. The object database used is the one from Sebastian *et al.* [30], and is shown in Fig. 2. In this case, only the number of clusters is known. The clustering algorithms try to group the shapes into different clusters, based on their similarity. Results, averaged over 10 repetitions, are presented in Table 2. From these tables it is evident that the proposed representation permits greater discrimination, resulting in a increasing of the clustering accuracies. Also in this case, the ML classification accuracy was computed, using the LOO scheme. From table 2 it is possible to note that the clustering results are better than the classification performances, confirming the high discriminative potentiality of the proposed similarity space.

6   Conclusions

In this paper, a scheme for sequence clustering, based on hidden Markov modelling and the similarity-based paradigm, was proposed. The approach builds features in which each sequence is represented by the vector of its similarities to a predefined set of reference sequences. A standard point clustering method is then performed on those representations. As a consequence, the difficult process of clustering sequences is cast into a simpler problem of clustering points, for which well established techniques have been proposed. Experimental evaluation on synthetic and real problems has shown that the proposed approach largely outperforms the standard HMM-based clustering approaches.

The main drawback of this approach is the high dimensionality of the resulting feature space, which is equal to the cardinality of the data set. This is obviously a problem, and represents a central topic for future investigation. We have previously addressed this issue in the context of similarity-based supervised learning [31]. In this unsupervised context, one idea could be to use some linear reduction techniques, in order to reduce the dimensionality of the space. Another idea is to directly address the problem of adequately choosing the representatives: this problem could be casted in the context of feature selection for unsupervised [32], where the prototypes to be chosen are the features to be selected.

References

1. Jain, A., Dubes, R.: Algorithms for clustering data. Prentice Hall (1988)
2. Rabiner, L.: A tutorial on Hidden Markov Models and selected applications in speech recognition. Proc. of IEEE **77** (1989) 257–286
3. Jain, A., Zongker, D.: Representation and recognition of handwritten digits using deformable templates. IEEE Trans. Pattern Analysis and Machine Intelligence **19** (1997) 1386–1391
4. Graepel, T., Herbrich, R., Bollmann-Sdorra, P., Obermayer, K.: Classification on pairwise proximity data. In M. Kearns, S. Solla, D.C., ed.: Advances in Neural Information Processing. Volume 11., MIT Press (1999)
5. Jacobs, D., Weinshall, D.: Classification with nonmetric distances: Image retrieval and class representation. IEEE Trans. Pattern Analysis and Machine Intelligence **22** (2000) 583–600
6. Pekalska, E., Duin, R.: Automatic pattern recognition by similarity representations. Electronics Letters **37** (2001) 159–160
7. Pekalska, E., Paclik, P., Duin, R.: A generalized kernel approach to dissimilarity-based classification. Journal of Machine Learning Research **2** (2002) 175–211
8. Pekalska, E., Duin, R.: Dissimilarity representations allow for building good classifiers. Pattern Recognition Letters **23** (2002) 943–956
9. Smyth, P.: Clustering sequences with hidden Markov models. In Mozer, M., Jordan, M., Petsche, T., eds.: Advances in Neural Information Processing. Volume 9., MIT Press (1997)
10. Panuccio, A., Bicego, M., Murino, V.: A Hidden Markov Model-based approach to sequential data clustering. In Caelli, T., Amin, A., Duin, R., Kamel, M., de Ridder, D., eds.: Structural, Syntactic and Statistical Pattern Recognition. LNCS 2396, Springer (2002) 734–742

11. Rabiner, L., Lee, C., Juang, B., Wilpon, J.: HMM clustering for connected word recognition. In: Proc. of IEEE ICASSP. (1989) 405–408
12. Lee, K.: Context-dependent phonetic hidden Markov models for speaker-independent continuous speech recognition. IEEE Transactions on Acoustics, Speech and Signal Processing **38** (1990) 599–609
13. Kosaka, T., Matsunaga, S., Kuraoka, M.: Speaker-independent phone modeling based on speaker-dependent hmm's composition and clustering. In: Int. Proc. on Acoustics, Speech, and Signal Processing. Volume 1. (1995) 441–444
14. Bahlmann, C., Burkhardt, H.: Measuring hmm similarity with the bayes probability of error and its application to online handwriting recognition. In: Proc. Int. Conf. Document Analysis and Recognition. (2001) 406–411
15. Cadez, I., Gaffney, S., Smyth, P.: A general probabilistic framework for clustering individuals. In: Proc. of ACM SIGKDD 2000. (2000)
16. Law, M., Kwok, J.: Rival penalized competitive learning for model-based sequence. In: Proc. Int. Conf. Pattern Recognition. Volume 2. (2000) 195–198
17. Xu, L., Krzyzak, A., Oja, E.: Rival penalized competitive learning for clustering analysis, RBF nets, and curve detection. IEEE Trans. on Neural Networks **4** (1993) 636–648
18. Li, C.: A Bayesian Approach to Temporal Data Clustering using Hidden Markov Model Methodology. PhD thesis, Vanderbilt University (2000)
19. Li, C., Biswas, G.: Clustering sequence data using hidden Markov model representation. In: Proc. of SPIE'99 Conf. on Data Mining and Knowledge Discovery: Theory, Tools, and Technology. (1999) 14–21
20. Li, C., Biswas, G.: A bayesian approach to temporal data clustering using hidden Markov models. In: Proc. Int. Conf. on Machine Learning. (2000) 543–550
21. Li, C., Biswas, G.: Applying the Hidden Markov Model methodology for unsupervised learning of temporal data. Int. Journal of Knowledge-based Intelligent Engineering Systems **6** (2002) 152–160
22. Li, C., Biswas, G., Dale, M., Dale, P.: Matryoshka: A HMM based temporal data clustering methodology for modeling system dynamics. Intelligent Data Analysis Journal **in press** (2002)
23. Schwarz, G.: Estimating the dimension of a model. The Annals of Statistics **6** (1978) 461–464
24. Stolcke, A., Omohundro, S.: Hidden Markov Model induction by Bayesian model merging. In Hanson, S., Cowan, J., Giles, C., eds.: Advances in Neural Information Processing Systems. Volume 5., Morgan Kaufmann, San Mateo, CA (1993) 11–18
25. Cheeseman, P., Stutz, J.: Bayesian classification (autoclass): Theory and results. In: Advances in Knowledge discovery and data mining. (1996) 153–180
26. Vapnik, V.: Statistical Learning Theory. John Wiley, New York (1998)
27. Dubnov, S., El-Yaniv, R., Gdalyahu, Y., Schneidman, E., Tishby, N., Yona, G.: A new nonparametric pairwise clustering algorithm based on iterative estimation of distance profiles. Machine Learning **47** (2002) 35–61
28. Theodoridis, S., Koutroumbas, K.: Pattern Recognition. Academic Press (1999)
29. Bicego, M., Murino, V.: Investigating Hidden Markov Models' capabilities in 2D shape classification. Submitted for publication (2002)
30. Sebastian, T., Klein, P., Kimia, B.: Recognition of shapes by editing Shock Graphs. In: Proc. Int Conf. Computer Vision. (2001) 755–762
31. Bicego, M., Murino, V., Figueiredo, M.: Similarity-based classification of sequences using hidden Markov models (2002) Submitted for publication.
32. Law, M., A.K. Jain, Figueiredo, M.: Feature selection in mixture-based clustering. In: Neural Information Processing Systems - NIPS'2002, Vancouver (2002)

A Fast Parallel Optimization for Training Support Vector Machine

Jian-xiong Dong[1] and Adam Krzyżak[2] and Ching Y. Suen[1]

[1] Centre for Pattern Recognition and Machine Intelligence
Concordia University
Montreal Quebec, Canada H3G 1M8
{jdong, suen}@cenparmi.concordia.ca
[2] Department of Computer Science, Concordia University
1455 de Maisonneuve Blvd. W.
Montreal Quebec, Canada H3G 1M8
krzyzak@cs.concordia.ca

Abstract. A fast SVM training algorithm for multi-classes consisting of parallel and sequential optimizations is presented. The main advantage of the parallel optimization step is to remove most non-support vectors quickly, which dramatically reduces the training time at the stage of sequential optimization. In addition, some strategies such as kernel caching, shrinking and calling BLAS functions are effectively integrated into the algorithm to speed up the training. Experiments on MNIST handwritten digit database have shown that, without sacrificing the generalization performance, the proposed algorithm has achieved a speed-up factor of 110, when compared with Keerthi et al.'s modified SMO. Moreover, for the first time ever we investigated the training performance of SVM on handwritten Chinese database ETL9B with more than 3000 categories and about 500,000 training samples. The total training time is just 5.1 hours. The raw error rate of 1.1% on ETL9B has been achieved.

1 Introduction

In the past few years, support vector machines (SVM) have performed well in a wide variety of learning problems, such as handwritten digit recognition [1,2], classification of web pages [3] and face detection [4]. However, training support vector machines with multi-classes on a large data set is still a bottle-neck [2]. Therefore, it is important to develop a fast training algorithm for SVM in order to solve some large-scale classification problems such as recognition of handwritten Chinese characters, face recognition.

Currently two important algorithms, Sequential Minimization Optimization (SMO) [5] and SVM^{light} [6], can be used to train SVM. Although both algorithms work well in a small data set, they are inefficient on a large data set due to three key problems. The computational cost of training SVM primarily depends on kernel evaluations. Kernel caching could be used to reduce kernel re-evaluations. SVM^{light} caches some rows of the total kernel matrix and uses

P. Perner and A. Rosenfeld (Eds.): MLDM 2003, LNAI 2734, pp. 96–105, 2003.

Least Recently Used (LRU) updating policy. But this caching strategy may fail because elements of kernel matrix are usually accessed irregularly. The second problem originates from access of a portion of non-contiguous memory and large data movement between CPU and memory. The first factor will result in high hardware cache and Table Lookup Buffer (TLB) missing rate. TLB miss will result in paging operations of the operating system at a very high cost. The latter leads to data traffic due to the limited memory bandwidth. Finally, although both algorithms can be used to train support vector machines with multi-classes, the computational cost is very high. For the above algorithms, the training cost for classifying n-classes is about n times as high as that for two-classes.

In this paper, we propose efficient solutions to the above problems. Two steps are designed to train support vector machines. The first step is called parallel optimization, in which the kernel matrix of support vector machines is approximated by block diagonal matrices so that the original optimization problem can be rewritten into hundreds of sub-problems which are easily solved. This step removes most non-support vectors quickly and collects training sets for the next step: sequential working set algorithm. In two steps, some effective strategies such as kernel caching and shrinking are integrated to speed up training. Further, Block Linear Algebra Subprogram (BLAS) [7], which has been optimized on Intel P4, is used to calculate kernel matrix. Those improvements make it possible to solve in practice the problem of recognizing handwritten English and Chinese. The latter problem is particularly difficult due to a large number of categories.

This paper is organized as follows. In Sect. 2 we introduce the general framework of the proposed algorithm. Then, a discussion of implementation issues is given in Sect. 3. Experimental results are presented in Sect. 5. Finally we summarize this paper and draw conclusions.

2   Parallel Optimization Framework for SVM

Given training vectors $x_i^n \in R^n$, $i = 1, \ldots, l$ and a vector $y \in R^l$ such that $y_i \in \{-1, 1\}$, training a support vector machine is to find α, which can be obtained by solving the following optimization problem:

$$\text{maximize} \quad e^T \alpha - \tfrac{1}{2}\alpha^T Q \alpha$$
$$\text{Subject to } 0 \le \alpha_i \le C, \quad i = 1, \ldots, l \tag{1}$$
$$y^T \alpha = 0$$

where $e \in R^l$ is a vector whose components are one, Q is an l by l semidefinite kernel matrix and C is a parameter chosen by the user. A larger C corresponds to a higher penalty allocated to the training errors. The training vector x_i whose corresponding α_i is non-zero is called support vector. Support vector machine maps training vectors x_i into high dimensional feature space by the function $\Phi(x)$ such that $Q_{ij} = y_i y_j K(x_i, x_j)$ and $K(x_i, x_j) = \Phi^T(x_i)\Phi(x_j)$. After the optimization problem is solved, an optimal hyperplane in high dimension feature space is obtained to separate the two-class samples. The decision function is given by

$$f(x) = \theta(\sum_{i=1}^{l} y_i \alpha_i K(x_i, x) - b).\qquad(2)$$

where

$$\theta(u) = \begin{cases} 1 & \text{if } u > 0 \\ -1 & \text{otherwise} \end{cases}\qquad(3)$$

where b is a threshold, which can be obtained by Karush-Kuhn-Tucker (KKT) conditions [8].

For the above optimization, the key problem is that the dense kernel matrix Q can not be stored into the memory when the number of training samples l is large. A good strategy is to conduct the optimization on the working set [5] [3]. But selection of the good working set becomes a problem. From the optimization (1) it can be observed that the solution does not change at all when a non support vector[1] is removed. Moreover, numerous experiments [1] [9] have shown that support vectors only consist of a small percent of the training samples. Training will speed up if we can quickly remove most non-support vectors. Since kernel matrix Q is symmetric and semidefinite, its block diagonal matrices are semidefinite, which are written as

$$Q_{\text{diag}} = \begin{bmatrix} Q_{11} & & & \\ & Q_{22} & & \\ & & \ddots & \\ & & & Q_{kk} \end{bmatrix}\qquad(4)$$

in which $Q_{ii} \in M_{l_i}{}^2$, $i = 1, \ldots, k$, and $\sum_{i=1}^{k} l_i = l$, is called block diagonal. Then we replace the kernel matrix with Q_{ii} so that we obtain k optimization subproblems. Optimization of these subproblems can be used to remove non-support vectors quickly. Further, we extend it to train support vector machine with multi-classes, where one-against-the-rest classification strategy is used. The computational diagram is depicted in Fig. 1.

The computation in Fig. 1 is efficient due to three aspects. Firstly, Kernel matrix can be effectively divided into block diagonal matrices such that each of them can fit into the memory. Secondly, for vertical computation, all classes share the same block kernel matrix, which needs to be calculated once. Finally, after we have calculated the block matrix at the first row, optimizations from the second class to the mth class are independent. Also, computation on different columns are independent. As a result, this computation diagram is suitable for parallel optimization on the architecture of multi-processors.

After the above parallel optimization, most non-support vectors for each class will be removed from the training set. Then a new training set for each class

---

[1] Its corresponding α component is zero

[2] M is the set of square matrix.

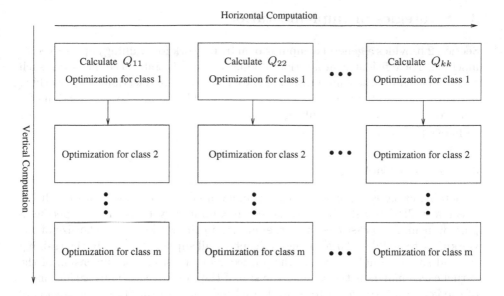

Fig. 1. Parallel optimization diagram

can be obtained by collecting support vectors from optimizations of subproblems in the same row as shown in Fig. 1. Although the size of the new training set is much smaller than that of the original one, the memory may not be large enough to store the whole kernel matrix. Therefore, a fast sequential working set algorithm for training SVM is proposed and summarized as follows:

A Fast Sequential Algorithm for Training SVM

Input: Training set is S, and the fixed size of the working set is d, where $d \leq l$ and l is the size of the training set. Also, kernel caching matrix with the dimension d is provided.

Output: Sets $\alpha_i, i = 1, \cdots, l$.

Initialization: Shuffle the training set; set α_i to zero and select a working set B such that $B \subseteq S$.

Optimization:

Repeat

    1. Apply Keerthi et al.'s SMO [10] to optimize a sub-problem in working set B, in combination with some effective techniques such as kernel caching, "digest" and shrinking strategies, then update α_i.

    2. Select a new working set with a queue technique

Until the specified stopping conditions are satisfied.

The above algorithm can also be used as the optimizer in Fig. 1, where the size of working set is the same as that of training set since each block diagonal matrix can be stored into the memory.

3   Strategies of Implementation

Section 2 provides a general computational framework for training support vector machine. For efficient computation, one needs to take into account issues such as kernel caching, the computation of kernel matrix, the selection of the working set, shrinking strategy and stopping conditions. The details about selection of a new working set, digest, shrinking strategies and stopping condition are referred to paper [11].

3.1   Kernel Caching

Generally, cache is a portion of fast memory used to overcome a mismatch between fast CPU and slow memory access in computer systems. Here it specifies a part of memory that stores the kernel matrix in the working set. The size of the working set should be large enough to contain all support vectors in the training set and small enough to satisfy the limited memory size. The dimension of the kernel cache matrix is the same as the size of the working set. Thus each element of the kernel matrix needs to be evaluated only once during the optimization of a subproblem.

3.2   Selection of a New Working Set

After optimization on the current working set is finished, a new data set will be loaded to replace the non-support vectors by queue operations. The detailed algorithm is referred to [11]. After the new working set is loaded, the kernel matrix on the new working set must be updated. It can be observed that $K(x_i, x_j)$ can be re-used if x_i, x_j are both support vectors on the last working set. For the calculation of other kernel elements, BLAS will be applied in the following subsection.

3.3   Calculation of Kernel Matrix

When a kernel can be represented as a function of $x_i^T x_j$, matrix multiplication can be used to calculate kernel elements efficiently. Obviously, three kernels such as linear, polynomial kernel and radial basic function (RBF) belong to this type. Here we describe the computational details of RBF kernel matrix, which can be easily extended to other types of kernel matrices. RBF kernel can be written as

$$K(x_i, x_j) = \exp(- \parallel x_i - x_j \parallel^2 /(2\sigma^2)) \tag{5}$$

where $\parallel . \parallel$ is Euclidean norm and

$$\parallel x_i - x_j \parallel^2 = x_i^T x_i + x_j^T x_j - 2x_i^T x_j \tag{6}$$

where $i, j = 1, \ldots, N$. $x_i^T x_i$ can be calculated by calling CBLAS function **cblas_sdot**. Let array A consist of vectors $(x_1, x_2, \ldots, x_N)$. $x_i^T x_j, i, j = 1, \ldots, N$

can be rewritten as $A^T A$. which can be easily calculated by calling CBLAS function **cblas_ssyrk**.

The kernel matrices in Fig. 1 can be calculated by the above method. To update kernel matrix in Sect. 3.2, we do not need to re-calculate the total kernel matrix since some elements can be re-used. Let the new working set be divided into two sets: support vector set represented by the array B_{sv} and non-support vector set B_{nsv}. Updating the kernel matrix requires $B_{\mathrm{sv}}^T B_{\mathrm{sv}}$, $B_{\mathrm{nsv}}^T B_{\mathrm{nsv}}$ and $B_{\mathrm{sv}}^T B_{\mathrm{nsv}}$. Since kernel elements $K(x_i, x_j)$, $x_i \in B_{\mathrm{sv}}$ and $x_j \in B_{\mathrm{sv}}$ can be re-used, $B_{\mathrm{sv}}^T B_{\mathrm{sv}}$ does not need to be re-calculated. $B_{\mathrm{nsv}}^T B_{\mathrm{nsv}}$ and $B_{\mathrm{sv}}^T B_{\mathrm{nsv}}$ can be evaluated by calling CBLAS function **cblas_ssyrk** and **cblas_sgemm**.

The rationale of the usage of BLAS package is its computational efficiency and portability. The key computational kernel of BLAS package such as matrix multiplication is implemented by assembly language, which efficiently makes use of cache, memory and speed-up instructions such as single instruction and multi-data (SIMD) on Intel Pentium series. Moreover, BLAS has been effectively implemented on multi platforms, which enables the proposed SVM algorithm to perform well in these platforms.

3.4   Inserting Positive Samples into the Working Set

In Fig. 1, it is possible that there are no positive samples[3] on some working sets when training samples for one class are insufficient. As a result, SMO will lead to an incorrect solution. In order to tackle this problem, we first randomly collect one sample from each class. During the training, if no positive sample on one working set is found, we replace the first negative sample using the positive sample from the collected set.

4   Experiments

The experimental code was written in C++ and compiled by Microsoft visual C++6.0. This algorithm ran on a 1.7 GHz P4 processor with Windows 2000 Professional operating system and 1.5 Gigabytes RAM.

Experiments are conducted on handwritten digit database MNIST[4] and handwritten Chinese character database ETL9B [12]. MNIST consists of 60,000 training samples and 10,000 testing samples. ETL9B was collected by Electrotechnical Laboratory. It contains 200 samples for each of 3036 categories, 2965 Chinese and 71 Hiragana characters. All samples are binary images of size 64(width) by 63 (height). The samples on this database are divided into 5 sets (A to E), each with 40 characters per category. In our experiment, sets (A to D) are used as training and E for testing. As a result, the sizes of training and testing set are 485760 and 121440, respectively.

For support vector machine, the one-against-the-rest method was used to construct a discriminant function for each class. That is, each discriminant function was constructed by separating one class from the rest. The finalclassification

---

[3] Their corresponding labels are 1.0

[4] http://www.research.att.com/~yann/exdb/mnist/index.html

decision was made by choosing the class with the maximal output value of its discriminant function.

In our method, the user-specified parameter C in Eq. (1) is set to 10.0.

4.1   Training Performance on MNIST

Patterns on MNIST are not truly located at the center, the preprocessing was performed by first enclosing the pattern with a rectangle, and then translating this rectangle into the center of a 28×28 box. Then patterns were smoothed using the following mask:

$$\frac{1}{16} \begin{bmatrix} 1 & 1 & 1 \\ 1 & 8 & 1 \\ 1 & 1 & 1 \end{bmatrix}. \tag{7}$$

We then used DeCoste's [2] idea to normalize each sample by its Euclidean-norm scalar value such that the dot product was always within $[-1, 1]$. The polynomial kernel was $(X_1 \cdot X_2)^7$. The dimension of input vectors was 784 (28×28). l_i in Eq. (4) and the size of the working set were set to 8000 and 4000, respectively. Figure 2 shows the average percent of support vectors in working sets of each class.

From Fig. 2 it can be seen that over 80% non-support vectors have been removed after the parallel optimization step. Also, training and IO (File read/write operations) time for this step are 390 seconds and 5 seconds, respectively. The performance measures of the proposed algorithm in the second step are depicted in Table 1, compared with Keerthi et al. SMO.

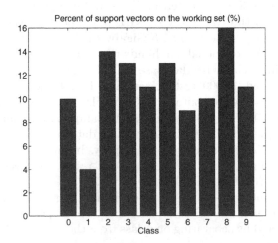

Fig. 2. Average percent of support vectors in working sets of each class

Table 1. Comparisons of performance measures

	Class	0	1	2	3	4	5	6	7	8	9
	SV	1918	891	3072	2979	2445	2907	1740	2158	3719	2657
A	hit_ratio	0.86	0.85	0.90	0.90	0.89	0.90	0.87	0.90	0.92	0.93
	CPU(s)	21	4	44	36	28	38	17	22	64	32
	Total time	306 s									
	SV	2021	973	3234	3228	2586	3092	1822	2316	4006	2939
B	CPU(s)	4469	5720	6868	8206	8336	7594	4946	8934	10541	11604
	Total time	21.44 hours									

In Table 1, A and B denote the proposed method and Keerthi et al. SMO, respectively. SV specifies the number of support vectors. The hit ratio is defined by

$$\text{hit ratio} = \frac{\text{cache hit}}{\text{cache hit} + \text{cache miss}}.$$

IO time for the second step is about 5 seconds. Then the total training and IO time are 696 (390+306) seconds and 10 (5+5) seconds. It can be seen from Table 1 that the proposed algorithm is about 110 times faster than Keerth et al.'s SMO. With respect to the generalization performance on MNIST testing set, the proposed algorithm achieved the same raw error rate without rejection as Keerthi et al.'s SMO, which was 1.1%.

4.2   Training Performance on ETL9B

In this section we present preliminary results or recognition of Chinese handwritten characters. The rationale of studying Chinese characters classification using database ETL9B is to investigate the performance of the proposed SVM training algorithm on a large data set with thousands of classes. SVM^{light} and Keerthi et al. SMO cannot be used to train SVMs on ETL9B because their computational cost is prohibitively high. Handwritten Chinese characters with large shape variations have extremely complex structure and many similar patterns exist. Original pixel values used as features do not perform well. Therefore, some preprocessing steps, including normalization and feature extraction, are required. An improved nonlinear normalization method [13] based on Yamada et al.'s [14] is applied and the resulting gray-scale normalized image of size 80 × 80 is obtained. The pixel values of normalized images range from 0 to 1.0.

After nonlinear normalization, a feature vector of size 1296 based on image gradients is extracted [13]. Its size is then reduced to 392 by means of multiple discriminant analysis [15].

In this experiment, we used RBF kernel $(\exp(-\parallel x_i - x_j \parallel^2 /(2 * 0.8)))$ in Eq. (2). Parameter l_i in Eq. (4) and the sizes of the working sets were both set to 8000 and 4000, respectively.

After training was finished, training and IO times for parallel optimization step were 15080 and 2493 seconds, respectively. We observed that about 98%

non-support vectors were removed on the working sets after this step. Consequently, the average size of training set of each class is about 3000. The sequential working set algorithm is faster, whose training and IO times are 3442 and 729 seconds, respectively. The total training and IO times of the proposed algorithm are about 5.1 hours and 0.89 hours.

The recognition rate on the training set is 100%. The substitution error rate on the test set is 1.1%, competitive with the best result 1.1% [16] on the same test set, which was achieved by Modified Quadratic Discriminant Function (MQDF). The possible reason why SVM does not outperform MQDF is that SVM with RBF kernel, a non-parametric classification method, requires sufficient training samples to achieve a higher performance while on the training set of ETL9B each class consists of only 160 ones. Further experiments on a larger handwritten Chinese character database need to be done to investigate the performance of SVM.

5   Conclusions

A fast algorithm that trains support vector machine has been proposed. The main advantage of this algorithm is to train SVM through two stages: parallel optimization and sequential working set algorithm. At the first stage, most non-support vectors of each class can be removed quickly, which dramatically reduces the training time at the second stage. Also, some strategies such as kernel caching, shrinking, calling BLAS functions are effectively integrated into the algorithm. Moreover, the proposed SVM training algorithm for multi-classes is the first version suitable for parallel computation. After it was tested on the large MNIST handwritten digit database, an overall speed-up factor of 110 was achieved by the proposed algorithm without sacrificing the generalization performance. Further, for the first time ever we trained the support vector machine on a large set (ETL9B) with more than 3000 categories. Experimental results have shown that the achieved training speed is very promising. Therefore, it paves way to apply the proposed algorithm to solve more challenging highly dimensional problems in the data mining domain.

Acknowledgments. Financial support from NSERC and FCAR is gratefully acknowledged.

References

1. Schölkopf, B., Burges, C.J.C., Vapnik, V.: Extracting support data for a given task. In: Proceedings of the First International Conference on Knowledge Discovery and Data Mining, Menlo Park, CA (1995) 252–257
2. DeCoste, D., Schölkopf, B.: Training invariant support vector machines. Machine Learning. **46(1-3)** (2002) 161–190
3. Joachims, T.: Text categorization with support vector machine: learning with many relevant features. In: Proceedings of 10th European Conference on Machine Learning (ECML) (1998) 137–142

4. Osuna, E., Freund, R., Girosi, F.: Training support vector machines: An application to face detection. In: Proceedings of the 1997 conference on Computer Vision and Pattern Recognition(CVPR'97), Puerto Rico (1997) 130–136
5. Platt, J.C.: Fast training of support vector machines using sequential minimal optimization. In: Schölkopf, B., Burges, C.J.C., Smola, A. (eds.): Advances in kernel methods: Support Vector Machines, MIT Press, Cambridge, MA (1998) 185–208
6. Joachims T.: Making large-scale support vector machine learning practical. In: Schölkopf, B., Burges, C.J.C., Smola, A. (eds.): Advances in kernel methods: Support Vector Machines, MIT Press, Cambridge, MA (1998) 169–184
7. Dongarra, J.J., Croz, J.D., Duff, I.S., Hammarling, S.: A set of level 3 basic linear algebra subprograms. ACM Trans. Math. Soft. **16** (1990) 1–17
8. Kuhn, H., Tucker, A.: Nonlinear programming. In: Proceedings of 2nd Berkeley Symposium on Mathematical Statistics and Probabilistics. University of California Press (1951) 481–492
9. Dong, J.X., Suen, C.Y., Krzyżak, A.: A fast svm training algorithm. In: Lee, S.-W., Verri, A. (eds.): Pattern Recognition with Support Vector Machines. Springer Lecture Notes in Computer Science LNCS 2388, Niagara Falls, Canada (2002) 481–492
10. Keerthi, S.S., Shevade, S.K., Bhattachayya, C., Murth K.R.K.: Improvements to Platt's SMO algorithm for SVM classifier design. Neural Computation, **13** (2001) 637–649
11. Dong, J.X., Krzyżak, A., Suen, C.Y.: A fast svm training algorithm. International Journal of Pattern Recognition and Artificial Intelligence, **17(3)** (2003) 1–18
12. Saito, T., Yamada, H., Yamamoto, K.: An analysis of handprinted character database VIII: An estimation of the database ETL9 of handprinted characters in JIS Chinese characters by directional pattern matching approach. Bul. Electrotech **49(7)** (1985) 487–525
13. Dong, J.X., Suen, C.Y., Krzyżak, A.: High accuracy handwritten Chinese character recognition using support vector machine. Tech. Rep. CENPARMI, Concordia University, Canada, (2003)
14. Yamada, H., Yamamoto, K., Saito, T.: A nonlinear normalization method for handprinted kanji character recognition-line density equalization. Pattern Recognition, **23(9)** (1990) 1023–1029
15. Duda, R.O., Hart, P.E.: Pattern Classification and Scene Analysis. John Wiley & Sons. Inc, New York (1973)
16. Kimura, F., Wakabayashi T., Tsuruoka, S., Miyake, Y.: Improvement of handwritten Japanese character recognition using weighted direction code histogram. Pattern Recognition, **30(8)** (1997) 1329–1337

A ROC-Based Reject Rule for Support Vector Machines

Francesco Tortorella

Dipartimento di Automazione, Elettromagnetismo
Ingegneria dell'Informazione e Matematica Industriale
Università degli Studi di Cassino
Cassino, Italy
tortorella@unicas.it

Abstract. This paper presents a novel reject rule for SVM classifiers, based on the *Receiver Operating Characteristic* curve. The rule minimizes the expected classification cost, defined on the basis of classification and error costs peculiar for the application at hand. Experiments performed with different kernels on several data sets publicly available confirmed the effectiveness of the proposed reject rule.

1 Introduction

Many complex classification problems involve dichotomous decisions, i.e. require to choose between two possible, alternative classes. Applications such as automated cancer diagnosis, currency verification, speaker identification, and fraud detection fall in this category. A very common point in these applications is that a classification error could have serious consequences: for this reason, the classifiers used in these situations should ensure a very high reliability to avoid erroneous decisions. Unfortunately, in real world this is rarely the case because, when working on real data, the classifiers could easily encounter samples very different from those examined during the training phase.

In this framework, the Support Vector Machines (SVMs) [1–3] are currently one of the classification systems most used because of their remarkable generalization performance motivated by the application of the *Structural Risk Minimization* principle [1]. The classification algorithm implemented by the SVMs relies on the mapping of the training samples into a high dimensional feature space where is built the *maximum margin hyperplane*, i.e. the hyperplane that maximizes the minimum distance from the hyperplane to the closest training point. The corresponding decision function evaluates the signed distance from the hyperplane of the sample to be classified and assigns it to one of the two classes on the basis of the sign obtained. However, even in the case a SVM classifier is used, there can be real situations in which the cost for a wrong classification is so high that it is convenient to reject the sample, i.e. to suspend the decision and call for a further test. Obviously, also this choice involves a not negligible cost given by the charge of employing a more powerful system or requiring the decision of a human expert. As a consequence, a rule is

P. Perner and A. Rosenfeld (Eds.): MLDM 2003, LNAI 2734, pp. 106–120, 2003.

needed to find the optimal trade-off between errors and rejects for the application at hand.

Although of practical interest, this topic has not received a great attention up to now. The unique proposal of a reject rule explicitly devised for SVM classifiers has been recently presented by Fumera and Roli in [4]. They developed a maximum margin classifier with reject option, i.e. a SVM whose rejection region is determined during the training phase. To implement such a SVM, they devised a novel formulation of the SVM training problem and developed a specific algorithm to solve it. As a result, the reject region provided by their algorithm is delimited by a pair of parallel hyperplanes whose position and orientation can change for different values of the cost of reject w_R. The drawback of this approach is that it is necessary to retrain the SVM when the reject cost changes.

A different reject method is presented in [5] with the aim of increasing the reliability of the classification of DNA microarray data. The reject is accomplished for the points near the optimal hyperplane for which the classifier may not be very confident of the class label. To this aim, the authors introduced confidence levels based on the SVM output, d, which provides the signed distance of the point from the optimal hyperplane. This allows to reject samples below a certain value of $|d|$ because they do not fall within the confidence level. These confidence levels are a function of d and are computed from the training data.

Another possible way to establish a reject option for the SVM, even though indirectly, is to evaluate an approximation of the posterior class probabilities starting from SVM output [6,7]. In this way, it could be possible to apply one of the reject rules devised for more traditional statistical classifiers. In this framework, an optimal reject rule has been proposed by Chow in [8,9]. The rationale of the Chow's approach relies on the exact knowledge of the *a posteriori* probabilities for each sample to be recognized. Under this hypothesis, the Chow's rule is optimal because it minimizes the error rate for a given reject rate (or vice versa). However, the full knowledge about the distributions of the classes is extremely difficult to obtain in real cases and thus the Chow's rule is rarely applicable "as is". An extension to the Chow's rule when the a priori knowledge about the classes is not complete is proposed in [10] and in [11], while in [12] a reject option that does not require any a priori knowledge is proposed with reference to a Multi-Layer Perceptron. Although effective, these rules are applicable only with multi-class classifiers and thus cannot help in the case of SVM classifiers.

The aim of this paper is to introduce a cost-sensitive reject rule for SVM classifiers able to minimize the expected cost of classification, defined on the basis of correct classification, reject and error costs peculiar for the application at hand. The approach proposed defines two different reject thresholds for the two classes. In this way, the reject region is delimited by two asymmetrical hyperplanes parallel to the optimal separating hyperplane, but placed at different distances. The thresholds depend on the costs defined for the application, but it is not necessary to retrain the SVM when the costs change. The method we present is based on the *Receiver Operating Characteristic* curve (ROC curve). Such curve provides a description of the performance of a two-class classifier at different operating points, independently of the *a priori* probabilities of the two classes. For this reason, it is effective for analyzing the classifier behavior under different class and cost distributions. ROC analysis is based in statistical decision theory and was first employed in signal detection problems [13]. It is now common in medical diagnosis and particularly in medical imaging [14]. Recently, it has been employed in Pattern Recognition Theory for evaluating machine learning algorithms [15] and for robust comparison of classifier performance under imprecise class distribution and misclassification costs [16].

Experiments performed with four different SVM kernels and four data sets publicly available confirmed the effectiveness of the proposed reject rule.

2   Support Vector Machine for Classification

In two-class classification problems, a sample can be assigned to one of two mutually exclusive classes that can be generically called *Positive* (*P*) class and *Negative* (*N*) class. Let us consider a data set D containing m datapoints x_i ($i = 1,...,m$) having corresponding labels $y_i = \pm 1$, where the sign of the label indicates the class to which the data point belongs. SVM classifiers [1–3], rely on preprocessing the data to represent samples in a *feature space* whose dimension is typically much higher than the original input space. With an appropriate nonlinear mapping $\Phi(.)$ to a sufficiently high dimension, samples from two classes can be discriminated by means of a separating hyperplane (w,b) which maximizes the *margin* or distance from the closest data points.

The functional form of the mapping $\Phi(.)$ does not need to be known since it is implicitly defined by the choice of a *kernel*, i.e. a function $K(x_i,x_j)$ such that $K(x_i,x_j) = \langle \Phi(x_i) \cdot \Phi(x_j) \rangle$, where $\langle x \cdot y \rangle$ denotes the inner product between the vectors x and y. In this way, the decision function $f(.)$ can be stated in terms of the kernel chosen and of the data points of D:

$$f(z) = \frac{1}{2} \sum_{i=1}^{m} \alpha_i y_i K(z, x_i) + b$$

where the bias b and the coefficients α_i are found by maximizing the Lagrangian

$$W(\alpha) = \sum_{i=1}^{m} \alpha_i - \frac{1}{2} \sum_{i,j=1}^{m} \alpha_i \alpha_j y_i y_j K(x_i, x_j)$$

subject to costraints $\alpha_i \geq 0$ and $\sum_{i=1}^{m} \alpha_i y_i = 0$. When the maximal margin hyperplane is found in feature space, only those points which lie closest to the hyperplane have $\alpha_i > 0$ and these points are the *support vectors*; all other points have $\alpha_i = 0$. The decision is based on the sign of $f(z)$ which provides the signed distance of the point z from the optimal separating hyperplane.

3 The ROC Curve for SVM Classifiers

In the previous section, we have assumed a zero threshold for the decision function. Actually, we could make a different choice, since there can be real situations in which the zero threshold is not optimal for the application at hand [6]. Operatively, a threshold t could be chosen, so as to attribute the sample to the class N if $x \leq t$ and to the class P if $x > t$. For a given threshold value t, some indices can be evaluated for measuring the performance of the SVM classifier. In particular, the set of samples whose SVM output f is greater than t contains actually-positive samples correctly classified as "positive" and actually-negative samples incorrectly classified as "positive". Hence, two appropriate performance figures are given by the *True Positive Rate TPR(t)*, i.e. the fraction of actually-positive cases correctly classified and by the *False Positive Rate FPR(t)*, given by the fraction of actually-negative cases incorrectly classified as "positive".

If $\varphi_P(f) = p(f|y = +1)$ and $\varphi_N(f) = p(f|y = -1)$ are the class-conditional densities of the SVM output, *TPR(t)* and *FPR(t)* are given by:

$$TPR(t) = \int_{t}^{+\infty} \varphi_P(f)df \qquad FPR(t) = \int_{t}^{+\infty} \varphi_N(f)df \qquad (1)$$

In a similar way it is possible to evaluate (taking into account the samples with confidence degree less than t) the *True Negative Rate TNR(t)* and the *False Negative Rate FNR(t)*, defined as:

$$TNR(t) = \int_{-\infty}^{t} \varphi_N(f)df = 1 - FPR(t) \qquad FNR(t) = \int_{-\infty}^{t} \varphi_P(f)df = 1 - TPR(t) \qquad (2)$$

As it is possible to note from eq. (2), the four indices are not independent and the pair $(FPR(t), TPR(t))$ is sufficient to completely characterize the performance of the classifier. Most importantly, they are independent of the a priori probability of the classes because they are separately evaluated on different subsets of data. Hence, it is possible to have a better insight about the performance attainable by the SVM classifier, while it is straightforward to obtain the overall accuracy of the SVM, defined as $\dfrac{p(P) \cdot TPR(t) + p(N) \cdot TNR(t)}{p(P) \cdot (TPR(t) + FNR(t)) + p(N) \cdot (TNR(t) + FPR(t))}$, where $p(P)$ and $p(N)$ are the prior probabilities of the classes. For the sake of representation, these quantities can be plotted on a plane having *FPR* on the X axis and *TPR* on the Y axis.

When the value of the threshold t varies between $-\infty$ and $+\infty$ the quantities in Eq. (1) and Eq. (2) vary accordingly, thus defining the set of the operating points, given by the pairs $(FPR(t), TPR(t))$, achievable by the SVM. The two extreme points are reached when t approaches $-\infty$ or $+\infty$; in the first case, both *TPR(t)* and *FPR(t)* approach 1 because all the negative and positive samples are classified as "positive", while the contrary happens when $t \to +\infty$; the plot obtained gives the *ROC curve* of the SVM classifier. A typical ROC curve is shown in Fig. 1 together with the class-conditional densities for the two classes.

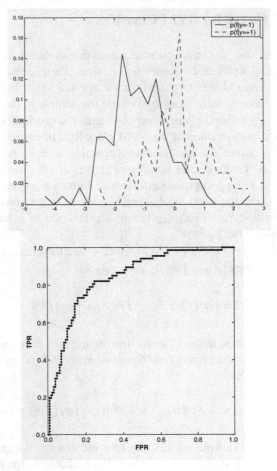

Fig. 1. The class-conditional densities produced by a linear SVM classifier on *Pima* data set (above) and the corresponding ROC curve (below)

4   The ROC-Based Reject Rule

Up to now, we have restricted our discussion to the case in which the SVM classifier can provide a choice only between the two classes *N* and *P*. However, there can be real situations in which it is desirable that the classifier refrain from making a precise choice in presence of a sample for which the corresponding outcome is considered unreliable (*reject option*). This happens when the cost of an error is so high that it is advisable to suspend the decision and to reject the sample instead of making a wrong decision possibly involving serious consequences. The reject also entails a positive cost (smaller than the error costs) which is related to the price of a new classification with another (more proficient) system. In this way, for a two-class problem which allows the reject option the cost matrix is:

Table 1. Cost matrix for a two-class problem with reject

		Predicted Class		
		N	P	Reject
True	N	CTN	CFP	CR
Class	P	CFN	CTP	

where *CFP*, *CFN* and *CR* are the costs related to a false positive error, to a false negative error and to a reject, *CTP* and *CTN* are the costs for a true positive and a true negative correct classification (these are negative costs, since they actually represent a gain). It is worth noting that $CR < CFP$ and $CR < CFN$. With these assumptions, for a SVM with reject option we can estimate an expected classification cost *EC* given by:

$$EC = p(P) \cdot CFN \cdot FNR + p(N) \cdot CTN \cdot TNR + p(P) \cdot CTP \cdot TPR + p(N) \cdot CFP \cdot FPR +$$
$$p(P) \cdot CR \cdot RP + p(N) \cdot CR \cdot RN$$

where *TPR*, *FPR*, *TNR*, *FNR* are the values obtained by the classifier for the performance parameters previously described, while *RP*, *RN* are the rejects rates on the positive and the negative class, respectively.

To accomplish the reject option on a SVM classifier, it is worth noting that, at 0-reject, the majority of errors are given by data points falling near the optimal hyperplane for which the classifier may not be very confident. This suggests to modify the decision rule introducing two thresholds instead of only one; in this way, for a generic sample with SVM output f the rule is:

$$\begin{array}{lll} \text{assign the sample to } N & \text{if } f < t_1 & \\ \\ \text{assign the sample to P} & \text{if } f > t_2 & (3) \\ \\ \text{reject the sample} & \text{if } t_1 \le f \le t_2 & \end{array}$$

where t_1 and t_2 are two decision thresholds (with $t_1 \le t_2$). As a consequence, the rates defined in eq. (1) and eq. (2) are modified in:

$$TPR(t_2) = \int_{t_2}^{+\infty} \varphi_P(f) df \qquad FPR(t_2) = \int_{t_2}^{+\infty} \varphi_N(f) df$$

$$TNR(t_1) = \int_{-\infty}^{t_1} \varphi_N(f) df \qquad FNR(t_1) = \int_{-\infty}^{t_1} \varphi_P(f) df \qquad (4)$$

while the reject rates relative to negative samples, $RN(t_1,t_2)$, and to positive samples, $RP(t_1,t_2)$, are given by:

$$RN(t_1,t_2) = \int_{t_1}^{t_2} \varphi_N(f)df = 1 - TNR(t_1) - FPR(t_2)$$

$$RP(t_1,t_2) = \int_{t_1}^{t_2} \varphi_P(f)df = 1 - TPR(t_2) - FNR(t_1) \qquad (5)$$

In Fig. 2 are shown the effects given by introducing two thresholds. The decision boundary is no longer an edge, but becomes a strip (which defines a *reject region*) including part of the area in which the two classes overlap. If the SVM output for a sample falls within the strip, the sample is rejected, otherwise it is assigned to one of the two classes: in this way, many of the errors due to the class overlap are turned into rejects. From a geometric point of view, this means to define in the feature space a reject region delimited by two hyperplanes parallel to the optimal separating hyperplane, but placed at different distances from it.

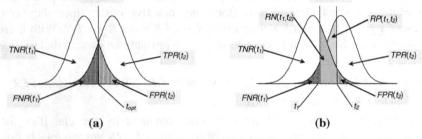

(a)   (b)

Fig. 2. (a) Even in the case the optimal threshold is chosen, a certain number of errors (hatched areas) is made by the classifier because of the overlap between the classes. (b) The effects given by the introduction of the two thresholds t_1 and t_2: note that both a part of errors and a part of correct classifications have been turned into rejects (gray areas).

It is easy to see that it is possible to enlarge the reject region to eliminate more errors, but this has the drawback of eliminating more correct classifications. To find an effective trade-off between these opposite requirements it is necessary to evaluate the consequences given by the introduction of the reject option on the expected cost. Taking into account eqs. (4) and (5), the expression for the expected cost is:

$$EC(t_1,t_2) = p(P) \cdot CFN \cdot FNR(t_1) + p(N) \cdot CTN \cdot TNR(t_1) + p(P) \cdot CTP \cdot TPR(t_2)$$
$$+ p(N) \cdot CFP \cdot FPR(t_2) + p(P) \cdot CR \cdot RP(t_1,t_2) + p(N) \cdot CR \cdot RN(t_1,t_2) \qquad (6)$$

which can be written as:

$$EC(t_1,t_2) = \varepsilon_2(t_2) - \varepsilon_1(t_1) + p(P) \cdot CFN + p(N) \cdot CTN \qquad (7)$$

where:

$$\varepsilon_1(t_1) = p(P) \cdot CFN' \cdot TPR(t_1) + p(N) \cdot CTN' \cdot FPR(t_1) \qquad (8)$$

$$\varepsilon_2(t_2) = p(P) \cdot CTP' \cdot TPR(t_2) + p(N) \cdot CFP' \cdot FPR(t_2) \qquad (9)$$

and

$$CTP' = CTP - CR \qquad CFN' = CFN - CR \qquad CTN' = CTN - CR \qquad CFP' = CFP - CR$$

In this way, the optimization problem can be simplified:

$$\min_{t_1,t_2} EC(t_1,t_2) = \min_{t_2} \varepsilon_2(t_2) - \max_{t_1} \varepsilon_1(t_1) + p(P) \cdot CFN + p(N) \cdot CTN \qquad (10)$$

and the optimal thresholds (t_{1opt}, t_{2opt}) which minimize $EC(t_1,t_2)$ can be separately evaluated:

$$t_{1opt} = \arg\max_t \varepsilon_1(t) = \arg\max_t \ p(P) \cdot CFN' \cdot TPR(t) + p(N) \cdot CTN' \cdot FPR(t) \qquad (11)$$

$$t_{2opt} = \arg\min_t \varepsilon_2(t) = \arg\min_t \ p(P) \cdot CTP' \cdot TPR(t) + p(N) \cdot CFP' \cdot FPR(t) \qquad (12)$$

To determine the optimal thresholds, it is worth noting that the objective functions in Eqs. (8) and (9) define on the ROC plane two sets of level lines with slopes, respectively:

$$m_1 = -\frac{p(N) \cdot CTN'}{p(P) \cdot CFN'} \qquad m_2 = -\frac{p(N) \cdot CFP'}{p(P) \cdot CTP'} \qquad (13)$$

Since the set of feasible points for both the objective functions is given by the ROC curve, the optimal threshold t_{1opt} can be determined by searching the point on the ROC curve belonging also to the line defined by eq. (8) which intersects the ROC and has maximum ε_1. In a similar way can be found t_{2opt}, with the only difference that we must consider the line that satisfies eq. (9), intersects the ROC curve and has minimum ε_2. It can be simply shown that, in both cases, the searched line is the level curve that intersects the ROC and has largest *TPR*-intercept. Such a line lies on the *ROC Convex Hull* [16], i.e. the convex hull of the set of points belonging to the ROC curve (see Fig. 3).

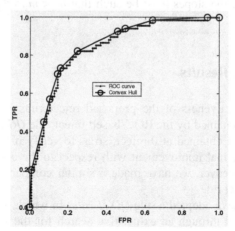

Fig. 3. The ROC curve shown in Fig. 2 and its convex hull

To give an operative method for finding the optimal thresholds, let us call $V_0, V_1, \ldots, V_n$ the vertices of the ROC convex hull, with $V_0 \equiv (0,0)$ and $V_n \equiv (1,1)$; moreover, let s_i be the slope of the edge joining the vertices V_{i-1} and V_i and assume that $s_0 = \infty$ and that $s_{n+1} = 0$.

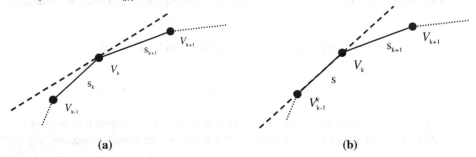

(a)   (b)

Fig. 4. Finding the optimal threshold on the convex hull: (a) a level line touching the convex hull on the point V_k; (b) a level line lying on a edge of the convex hull. In this case either the point V_{k-1} or V_k can be chosen

For each slope m_j in eq. (13), the list $\{s_i\}$ should be searched to find a value s_k such that $s_k > m_j > s_{k+1}$ or $s_k = m_j$: in the first case, the level curve touches the ROC convex hull in the vertex V_k, which provides the optimal threshold (see Fig. 4a). In the second case, the level curve and the edge are coincident and thus either of the vertices V_{k-1} and V_k can be chosen (see Fig. 4b). The only difference is that the left vertex will have lower *TPR* and *FPR*, while the right vertex will have higher *TPR* and *FPR*, thus one can refer to the requirements of the application at hand to make the most appropriate choice.

It is important to recall that t_{1opt} must be less than t_{2opt} to achieve the reject option. For this reason, the slopes must be such that $m_1 < m_2$, otherwise the reject option is not practicable.

5   Experimental Results

To evaluate the effectiveness of the proposed reject rule we have compared the classification costs obtained by the ROC-based reject rule (*RBR rule* hereafter) with the classification cost obtained at 0-reject, so as to verify if the introduction of the RBR rule gives an actual improvement with respect to the case in which the reject rule is not used. Moreover, we have made a similar comparison between the RBR rule and another reject rule.

To this aim, we have adopted a rule (*EXH rule*) in which the decision thresholds t_{1opt} and t_{2opt} are found through an exhaustive search for the values minimizing the expected cost defined in (7). In particular, let $[f_{min}, f_{max}]$ the range of the values assumed by the decision function $f(.)$ on a set of samples. Let us choose k equally spaced values F=$\{f_1, f_2, \ldots, f_k\}$ such that $f_i < f_{i+1}$ and $f_1 = f_{min}$, $f_k = f_{max}$. The expected cost

EC is evaluated on all the possible $\dfrac{k(k-1)}{2}$ pairs (t_1,t_2) where $t_1,t_2 \in F$ and $t_1 \le t_2$. The decision thresholds (t_{1opt},t_{2opt}) are given by the pair (t_1,t_2) which minimizes EC. In the experiments described below we have chosen k = 20.

To fairly estimate the results of such comparisons, we have employed various data sets and kernels; moreover, a comparison technique has been devised to assure that the outcomes obtained are statistically significant. Four data sets publicly available from the UCI Machine Learning Repository [17] have been chosen for the experiments; all of them have two output classes and numerical input features. All the features were previously rescaled so as to have zero mean and unit standard deviation. The details of the data sets are summarized in Table 2.

Four SVM's with different kernels have been employed (see Table 3). They have been implemented by means of SVM^{light} software [18], available at http://svmlight.joachims.org.

Table 2. Details of the data sets used in the experiments

Name	Number of samples	% Positive	% Negative
Pima (P)	768	34.90%	65.10%
German Credit (GC)	1000	30.00%	70.00%
Breast Cancer Wisconsin (BW)	683	34.99%	65.01%
Heart Disease - Cleveland data (HC)	297	46.13%	53.87%

Table 3. SVM classifiers used in the experiments

Name	Kernel
Linear	$\langle x_i \cdot x_j \rangle$
Polynomial	$\left(\langle x_i \cdot x_j \rangle \right)^2$
RBF	$\exp\left(-\dfrac{1}{2}\left\| x_i - x_j \right\|^2 \right)$
Sigmoid	$\tanh\left(0.1 \cdot \langle x_i \cdot x_j \rangle \right)$

To avoid any bias in the comparison, a 12-fold cross-validation has been used on all data sets. In each of the 12 runs, the data set is split in three subsets: a training set (containing 50 % of the whole data set), a validation set and a test set (each containing 25 % of the whole data set). The validation set is employed for evaluating the optimal thresholds of the RBR rule and of the EXH rule. On the test set are evaluated the three classification costs to be compared, thus obtaining, for a given data set and classifier, 12 different values for each of the costs required. To establish if the classification cost exhibited by the RBR rule is significantly better than the cost at 0-reject and the cost obtained by the EXH rule, we have used the *Wilcoxon rank-sum test* [19] to make separately the two comparisons. It is firstly verified if the mean of the RBR cost values is higher than, lower than or undistinguishable from the mean of the costs at 0-reject. The same test is then made to compare the mean of the RBR costs with the mean of the EXH costs. Both the results are provided at 0.01 level of significance.

To obtain a result unbiased with respect to the particular cost values, we apply the approach proposed in [20]: a matrix (called *cost model*) is used in which each cell contains a distribution instead of a fixed value. 1,000 different cost matrices have been generated randomly according to such distributions and, for each cost matrix, the test previously described has been repeated. In this way, we have obtained a more reliable assessment of the performance of the RBR rule. The cost models used are described in Table 4, where the notation *Unif*[a,b] denotes an uniform distribution over the interval [a,b].

Table 4. The cost models

	CTP	*CFP*	*CTN*	*CFN*	*CR*
CM1	*Unif*[-10,0]	*Unif*[0,50]	*Unif*[-10,0]	*Unif*[0,50]	1
CM2	*Unif*[-10,0]	*Unif*[0,100]	*Unif*[-10,0]	*Unif*[0,50]	1
CM3	*Unif*[-10,0]	*Unif*[0,50]	*Unif*[-10,0]	*Unif*[0,100]	1
CM4	*Unif*[-10,0]	*Unif*[0,50]	*Unif*[-10,0]	*Unif*[0,50]	*Unif*[0,30]

While the distributions of the costs for correct classifications are always the same, the error cost distributions are similar in CM1 and CM4 and very different in CM2 and CM3. The reject cost has been kept constant in all the cost models, except CM4.

Table 5. Comparison between RBR rule and 0-reject for the Linear SVM

	P	GC	BW	HC
CM1	0	0	0	0
	803	808	6	484
	197	192	994	516
CM2	0	0	0	0
	869	887	89	614
	131	113	911	386
CM3	0	0	0	0
	850	862	25	659
	150	138	975	341
CM4	0	0	0	0
	555	491	2	178
	445	509	998	822

Table 6. Comparison between RBR rule and 0-reject for the Polynomial SVM

	P	GC	BW	HC
CM1	0	0	0	0
	680	687	77	801
	320	313	923	199
CM2	0	0	0	0
	735	699	367	851
	265	301	633	149
CM3	0	0	0	0
	817	792	47	830
	183	208	953	170
CM4	0	0	0	0
	331	398	21	484
	669	602	979	516

In Tables 5–8 are presented the results of the evaluation of the RBR rule compared with the 0-reject case. Each row of the tables corresponds to a particular cost model, while the columns refer to the data sets used. Each cell of the tables contains three values which indicate the number of runs (out of 1000) for which the RBR rule classification has produced a classification cost respectively higher than, lower than or undistinguishable from the classification cost obtained at 0-reject. This last quantity contains both the cases in which the reject option is applicable and gives results quite similar to the 0-reject and the cases in which the reject option is not applicable because the condition $m_1 < m_2$ is not verified.

Table 7. Comparison between RBR rule and 0-reject for the RBF SVM

	P	GC	BW	HC
	0	0	0	0
CM1	783	792	0	837
	217	208	1000	163
	0	0	0	0
CM2	896	862	1	853
	104	138	999	147
	0	0	0	0
CM3	859	868	7	846
	141	132	993	154
	0	0	0	0
CM4	514	530	1	573
	486	470	999	427

Table 8. Comparison between RBR rule and 0-reject for the Sigmoid SVM

	P	GC	BW	HC
	0	0	0	0
CM1	803	799	4	465
	197	201	996	535
	0	0	0	0
CM2	836	849	103	492
	164	151	897	508
	0	0	0	0
CM3	813	853	2	661
	187	147	998	339
	0	0	0	0
CM4	532	553	2	180
	468	447	998	820

A first indication is that the classification cost given by the RBR rule is never higher than the classification cost at 0-reject. For almost all the experiments done with the cost models CM1-CM3, the RBR rule is definitely better than the case at 0-reject. This is less evident when the cost model CM4 is used: in this case, in fact, it is more likely that the reject cost assume high values which do not verify the condition $m_1 < m_2$.

The improvement obtained by the RBR rule is conspicuous on all the experiments, except those executed on the Breast data set, for which there is a large majority of tests in which the differences between the RBR rule and the 0-reject is quite negligible, independently of the cost model. The reason is that the Breast data set is quite separable and thus all the classifiers perform very well on it. The corresponding ROC convex hulls are consequently very near to the upper left corner of the diagram. In many cases the hulls contain few vertices and two large segments connected with an angle near 90 degrees; in these situations the RBR rule can coincide with the 0-reject because the level curves lie on the same vertex. This behavior agrees with the theoretical consideration that for a well trained classifier, where the error rate is very low, there is a less need for a reject option.

Tables 9–12 present the results of the comparison between the RBR rule and the EXH rule. The organization is the same of tables 5-8 and thus the last row of each cell reports the number of tests in which the difference between the two rules is negligible. As previously stated, this quantity includes not only the cases in which the reject is applicable and the two rules give quite similar results but also the cases in which the reject option is not applicable because of the condition $m_1 < m_2$.

Table 9. Comparison between RBR rule and EXH rule for the Linear SVM

	P	GC	BW	HC
CM1	4	13	0	0
	84	180	779	281
	912	807	221	719
CM2	8	6	0	6
	89	149	489	163
	903	845	511	831
CM3	18	17	0	0
	90	113	863	438
	892	870	137	562
CM4	2	6	0	0
	46	139	892	148
	952	855	108	852

Table 10. Comparison between RBR rule and EXH rule for the Polynomial SVM

	P	GC	BW	HC
CM1	0	0	0	0
	44	69	998	120
	956	931	2	880
CM2	0	0	0	0
	30	37	978	75
	970	963	22	925
CM3	0	0	0	0
	21	92	951	153
	979	908	49	847
CM4	0	0	0	0
	263	55	998	98
	737	945	2	902

Table 11. Comparison between RBR rule and EXH rule for the RBF SVM

	P	GC	BW	HC
CM1	0	0	0	0
	783	792	0	837
	217	208	1000	163
CM2	0	0	0	0
	896	862	1	853
	104	138	999	147
CM3	0	0	0	0
	859	868	7	846
	141	132	993	154
CM4	0	0	0	0
	514	530	1	573
	486	470	999	427

Table 12. Comparison between RBR rule and EXH rule for the Sigmoid SVM

	P	GC	BW	HC
CM1	0	0	0	0
	803	799	4	465
	197	201	996	535
CM2	0	0	0	0
	836	849	103	492
	164	151	897	508
CM3	0	0	0	0
	813	853	2	661
	187	147	998	339
CM4	0	0	0	0
	532	553	2	180
	468	447	998	820

It is worth noting that there are some few cases (187 out of 64,000) in which the RBR rule performs worse than the EXH rule. This is not surprising since this latter finds the optimal thresholds through an exhaustive search in the validation set, while the RBR rule circumscribes its search to the ROC convex hull. As a consequence, there can be situations in which the best thresholds are found only through the exhaustive search.

However, there is a much larger number of cases (16,562 out of 64,000) in which the RBR rule gives a result better than the EXH rule. This implies that, although the RBR rule considers only the operating points of the ROC convex hull, these latters are much more robust with respect to changes in costs. On the whole, the RBR rule provides a classification cost better than or equal to the cost obtained by the EXH rule in the 99.88% of the tests performed. This result clearly supports the rationale on which the RBR rule is based, i.e. that the ROC convex hull contains all the information necessary to find the reject thresholds which minimize the expected classification cost.

References

1. V. Vapnik, The nature of statistical learning theory, Springer-Verlag, New York (1995).
2. C. Cortes, V. Vapnik, Support vector networks, Machine Learning 20 (1995) 273–297.
3. N. Cristianini, J. Shawe-Taylor, An Introduction to Support Vector Machines. Cambridge University Press, Cambridge (2000).
4. G. Fumera, F. Roli, Support Vector Machines with Embedded Reject Option. In S. Lee, A. Verri, eds., *Pattern Recognition with Support Vector Machines*, Lecture Notes in Computer Science 2388, Springer-Verlag, New York (2002) 68–82.
5. S. Mukherjee, P. Tamayo, D. Slonim, A. Verri, T. Golub, J.P. Mesirov, T. Poggio, Support Vector Machine Classication of Microarray Data, AI Memo 1677, Massachusetts Institute of Technology (1998).
6. J.C. Platt, Probabilistic outputs for support vector machines and comparisons to regularized likelihood methods. In A.J. Smola, P.L. Bartlett, B. Schölkopf, and D. Schurmans, eds., *Advances in Large Margin Classifiers*, MIT Press (2000) 61–74.
7. J.T. Kwok, Moderating the outputs of support vector machine classifiers, IEEE Trans. Neur. Net. 10 (1999) 1018–1031.
8. C.K. Chow, An optimum character recognition system using decision functions, IRE Trans. Electronic Computers EC-6 (1957) 247–254.
9. C.K. Chow, On optimum recognition error and reject tradeoff, IEEE Trans. Inf. Th. IT-10 (1970) 41–46.
10. B. Dubuisson, M. Masson, A statistical decision rule with incomplete knowledge about classes, Pattern Recognition 26 (1993) 155–165.
11. R. Muzzolini, Y.-H. Yang, R. Pierson, Classifier design with incomplete knowledge, Pattern Recognition 31 (1998) 345–369.
12. L.P. Cordella, C. De Stefano, F. Tortorella, M. Vento, A method for improving classification reliability of multilayer perceptrons, IEEE Trans. Neur. Net. 6 (1995) 1140–1147.
13. J.P. Egan, Signal detection theory and ROC analysis, Series in Cognition and Perception, Academic Press, New York (1975).
14. C.E. Metz, ROC methodology in radiologic imaging, Invest. Radiol. 21 (1986) 720–733.

15. A.P. Bradley, The use of the area under the ROC curve in the evaluation of machine learning algorithms, Pattern Recognition 30 (1997) 1145–1159.
16. F. Provost, T. Fawcett, Analysis and visualization of classifier performance: comparison under imprecise class and cost distributions, Proc. 3rd Int. Conf. on Knowledge Discovery and Data Mining (1997).
17. C. Blake, E. Keogh, C.J. Merz, UCI repository of machine learning databases, [http://www.ics.uci.edu/~mlearn/MLRepository.html]. Irvine, CA: University of California, Department of Information and Computer Science (1998).
18. T. Joachims, Making large-scale SVM learning practical. In B. Schölkopf, C.J.C. Burges, A.J. Smola, eds., *Advances in Kernel Methods – Support Vector Learning*, MIT Press (1999) 169–184.
19. R.E. Walpole, R.H. Myers, S.L. Myers, Probability and Statistics for Engineers and Scientists, 6th ed., Prentice Hall Int., London (1998).
20. D.D. Margineantu, T.G. Dietterich, Bootstrap Methods for the Cost-Sensitive Evaluation of Classifiers, Proc. Int. Conf. Machine Learning ICML-2000 (2000), 582–590.

Remembering Similitude Terms in CBR

Eva Armengol and Enric Plaza

IIIA – Artificial Intelligence Research Institute
CSIC – Spanish Council for Scientific Research
Campus UAB, 08193 Bellaterra, Catalonia, Spain
{eva,enric}@iiia.csic.es

Abstract. In concept learning, inductive techniques perform a global approximation to the target concept. Instead, lazy learning techniques use local approximations to form an implicit global approximation of the target concept. In this paper we present C-LID, a lazy learning technique that uses LID for generating local approximations to the target concept. LID generates local approximations in the form of similitude terms (symbolic descriptions of what is shared by 2 or more cases). C-LID caches and reuses the similitude terms generated in past cases to improve the problem solving of future problems. The outcome of C-LID (and LID) is assessed with experiments on the Toxicology dataset.

1 Introduction

Concept learning can be achieved both using lazy learning and eager learning. Inductive concept learning is the typical eager approach, where learning is finding a description characterizing the instances of a concept (positive examples) and not the rest (negative examples). Lazy learning techniques like k-nearest neighbor and case-based reasoning define concepts extensionally, i.e. by using the extension of a concept enumerating the instances that belong to the concept (positive examples) and those that do not (negative examples). Moreover, lazy learning techniques are *problem-centered*, i.e. they take into account the new problem (sometimes called *query*) while using the information of the previous instances (*cases*). Inductive techniques are unable to do so, since by the time they observe the query they have already chosen their (global) approximation to the target function. In other words, eager techniques take a global approach to concept learning while lazy techniques (implicitly) represent the target function by combining many *local approximations* [6].

In this paper we present C-LID a lazy learning approach that reuses those *local approximations* used for solving past instances in order to improve the classification of new problems in case based-reasoning (CBR). C-LID (Caching LID) is a variant of the CBR technique LID (Lazy Induction of Descriptions) [3]. LID is a lazy concept learning technique for classification tasks in CBR based on the notion of *similitude term*. CBR approaches are based on finding the most similar (or relevant) cases for a particular problem p, and usually these degree of similarity is assessed using a distance metric. However, as explained in

P. Perner and A. Rosenfeld (Eds.): MLDM 2003, LNAI 2734, pp. 121–130, 2003.
© Springer-Verlag Berlin Heidelberg 2003

Sect. 2, LID does not use a distance. Instead, LID builds a symbolic description of the similarity D_p between p and a set of cases S_{D_p}. We call D_p a *similitude term* and contains that which is common to p and the cases in S_{D_p}. In other words, D_p is a generalization such that it covers the problem ($D_p \sqsubseteq p$) and the *retrieved cases* ($D_p \sqsubseteq c : \forall c \in S_{D_p}$). Thus, for LID, the similitude terms are the *local approximations* used for solving problems, and since they are symbolic descriptions we are able to cache them and reuse them in solving future problems. This is the approach of *Caching* LID presented in this paper. In order to define C-LID on top of LID we have only to specify two policies: a) the *caching policy* (i.e. which similitude terms are cached and which not), and b) the *reuse policy* (i.e. when and how the cached terms are used to solve a new problem) — see §3 below. Notice, however, that C-LID is still a lazy learning technique according to the definition given above. The generalizations created by LID and cached by C-LID are not global: they are local approximations.

The structure of the paper is as follows: Sect. 2 explains the Lazy Induction of Descriptions technique, then Sect. 3 introduces C-LID while Sect. 4 presents an application of C-LID to a toxicology data set and reports on the accuracy results of both LID and C-LID. The paper closes with a discussion section.

2   Lazy Induction of Descriptions

In this section we explain the LID (*Lazy Induction of Descriptions*) method. The goal of LID is to classify a problem as belonging to one of the solution classes. The main idea of LID is to determine which are the more relevant features of the problem and to search in the case base for cases sharing these relevant features. The problem is classified when LID finds a set of relevant features shared by a subset of cases belonging all of them to the same solution class. Then, the problem is classified into that solution class.

Given a case base B containing cases classified into one of the solution classes $C = \{C_1 \ldots C_m\}$ and a problem p, the goal of LID is to classify p as belonging to one of the solution classes. The problem and the cases in the case base are represented as feature terms.

Feature terms (also called *feature structures* or ψ-*terms*) are a generalization of first order terms. The intuition behind a feature term is that it can be described as a labelled graph. The edges of the graph are labelled with feature symbols and the nodes are the sorts of the feature values. Sorts have an informational order relation ($\preceq$) among them, where $\psi \preceq \psi'$ means that ψ has less information than ψ' or equivalently that ψ is more general than ψ'. The minimal element ($\bot$) is called *any* and it represents the minimum information. When a feature has unknown value it is represented as having the value *any*. All other sorts are more specific that *any*. Figure 2 shows an example of sort/subsort hierarchy.

The semantic interpretation of feature terms brings an ordering relation among feature terms that we call *subsumption*. Intuitively, a feature term ψ subsumes another feature term ψ' ($\psi \sqsubseteq \psi'$) when all the information in ψ is also contained in ψ'. In Sect. 4.1 feature terms are explained with an example. For a more formal explanation of feature terms see [1].

Function LID (S_D, p, D, C)
    if stopping-condition(S_D)
       then return $class(S_D)$
       else $f_d :=$ Select-leaf (p, S_D, C)
             $D' :=$ Add-path$(\pi(root(p), f_d), D)$
             $S_{D'} :=$ Discriminatory-set (D', S_D)
            LID $(S_{D'}, p, D', C)$
   end-if
end-function

Fig. 1. The LID algorithm. D is the similitude term, S_D is the discriminatory set of D, C is the set of solution classes, $class(S_D)$ is the class $C_i \in C$ to which all elements in S_D belong

We define the *similitude term*, s, of two cases c_1 and c_2 as a term such as $s \sqsubseteq c_1$ and $s \sqsubseteq c_2$ i.e. the similitude term of two cases subsumes both cases. In this framework, the task of similarity assessment is a search process over the space of similarity descriptions determined by the subsumption relation.

We call *discriminatory set* the set $S_D = \{b \in B | D \sqsubseteq b\}$ that contains the cases of B subsumed by the similitude term D.

The LID algorithm (Fig. 1) begins with the similitude term D initialized to the most general feature term (i.e. the feature term *any* that has no features) and the discriminatory set S_D initialized to the whole case base B (since *any* subsumes all the cases). When there is some domain knowledge, the similitude term D can be initialized to a value D^0 (where $D^0 \neq any$) as is described in [2].

Given the current similitude term D, the stopping condition of LID is that all the cases in S_D belong to one solution class $C_k \in C$. In the first call, this condition is not satisfied because the initial similitude term D subsumes the whole case base. The next step is to select a leaf for specializing D.

The specialization of a similitude term D is achieved by adding features to it. In principle, any of the features used to describe the cases could be a good candidate. Nevertheless, LID uses two biases to obtain the set F_l of features candidate to specialize D. First, of all possible features describing a case, LID will consider only those features present in the problem p to be classified. As a consequence, any feature that is not present in p will not be considered as candidate to specialize D. The second bias is to consider as candidates for specializing D only those features that are leaf features of p (i.e. to features having as values feature terms without features).

The next step of LID is the selection of a leaf feature $f_d \in F_l$ to specialize the similitude term D. Selecting the most discriminatory leaf feature in the set F_l is heuristically done using the RLM distance [5] over the features in F_l. The RLM distance assesses how similar are two partitions in the sense that the lesser the RLM distance is the more similar are the partitions. Let us suppose that the feature f_i takes as value v_i in the problem p. This feature induces a partition P_i of the case-base formed by two sets: one containing the cases that have value v_i

and the other contain those cases with value different than v_i in the feature f_i. For each feature in F_l, LID induces its associated partition.

The *correct partition* is a partition $P_c = \{C_1 \ldots C_m\}$ where all the cases contained into a set C_i belong to the same solution class. For each partition P_i induced by a feature f_i, LID computes the RLM distance to the correct partition P_c. The proximity to P_c of a partition P_i estimates the relevance of feature f_i.

Let P_i and P_j the partitions induced by features f_i and f_j respectively. We say that the feature f_i is *more discriminatory than* the feature f_j iff $RLM(P_i, P_c) < RLM(P_j, P_c)$, i.e. when the partition induced by f_i is closer to the correct partition P_c than the partition induced by f_j. Intuitively, the most discriminatory feature classifies the cases in a more similar way to the correct classification. LID uses the *more discriminatory than* relationship to estimate the features that are more relevant for the purpose of classifying a current problem.

Let us call f_d the most discriminatory feature in F_l. The feature f_d is the leaf feature of path $\pi(root(p), f_d)$ in problem p. The specialization step of LID defines a new similitude term D' by adding to the current similitude term D the sequence of features specified by $\pi(root(p), f_d)$. After this addition D' has a new path $\pi(root(D'), f_d)$ with all the features in the path taking the same value that they take in p. After adding the path π to D, the new similitude term $D' = D + \pi$ subsumes a subset of cases in S_D, namely the discriminatory set $S_{D'}$ (the subset of cases subsumed by D').

Next, LID is recursively called with the discriminatory set $S_{D'}$ and the similitude term D'. The recursive call of LID has $S_{D'}$ as first parameter (instead of S_D) because the cases that are not subsumed by D' will not be subsumed by any further specialization. The process of specialization reduces the discriminatory set $S_D^n \subseteq S_D^{n-1} \subseteq \ldots \subseteq S_D^0$ at each step.

Another stopping situation is when the current discriminatory set S_D^n contains cases belonging to several solution classes $(C_i \ldots C_j)$ but the similitude term D^n cannot be further specialized. In this situation LID uses the majority rule for propose a solution class for p, i.e. p is classified as belonging to the class C_k such that $Card(S_D^n \cap C_k) = max\{Card(S_D^n \cap C_i) \ldots Card(S_D^n \cap C_j)\}$.

Given a new problem p and a case base CB, the result of LID is the solution class and a similitude term D. The similitude term can be seen as an explanation of why p is classified as belonging to a solution class C_i. Moreover, the cases contained in the discriminatory set S_D support this classification. Notice that the stopping condition means that the similitude term is able to discriminate cases belonging to the solution class C_i with respect to the cases that does not belong to C_i. In this sense, the similitude term D can be viewed as a *partial* description of C_i. D is a partial description because, in general, it does not subsume all the cases belonging to C_i but only a subset of them (those sharing the features of D with the new problem). The similitude term D depends on the new problem, for this reason there are several partial descriptions (i.e. similitude terms) for the same solution class. In the next section we explain how the similitude term can be used as support to the LID solution.

3   Caching LID

Caching LID is implemented on top of LID by defining two policies: the caching policy and the reuse policy. C-LID considers the similitude terms built by LID as descriptions of the local approximations performed by this CBR technique. The *caching policy* determines which similitude terms are to be retained; from now one we will call *patterns* the similitude terms that are cached by C-LID. The *reuse policy* determines when and how the cached patterns are used to solve new problems.

The caching policy of C-LID states that similitude term D will be cached if it is *univocal*, i.e. when all cases covered D_p (all cases in S_{D_p}) belong to one class only. Thus, C-LID's caching policy retains only similitude terms that characterize the class of a problem p and a set or retrieved cases S_{D_p} without any uncertainty. The *reuse policy* of C-LID states that patterns will be used for solving a problem p only when LID is unable to find a similitude term D_p for p that is *univocal*. In that case all patterns that subsume p will be used together with D_p to determine the most likely class of p. Below we explain in detail how this class is determined.

C-LID can be decomposed in two steps: 1) a preprocessing of the case base in order to obtain some similitude terms to be cached; and 2) the problem solving phase that uses LID together with the cached similitude terms for clasifying new problems.

Preprocessing. During this phase the caching policy is applied. The experiments described in Sect. 4.2 are performed using the caching policy already explained. There are possible other less strict caching policies, and we briefly discuss them in Sect. 5. The preprocessing phase is done using the leave-one-out technique over the whole training set B. For each case $c \in B$, C-LID uses LID to classify it. When similitude term D_p is univocal C-LID caches it. Thus, at the end of the preprocessing phase C-LID has a set $M = \{D_1 \dots D_n\}$ of cached similitude terms (patterns).

Problem solving. In the problem solving phase the reuse policy is applied. First, a new problem p is solved using LID. If LID finds a similitude term D_p that is univocal then p is classified in the same class as the cases in S_{D_p}. Otherwise, S_{D_p} contains cases belonging to several solution classes, and the reuse policy states that relevant patterns in M are to be used to solve the problem. The relevant patterns are defined as the subset of patterns that subsume p, i.e. $M_p = \{m \in M | m \sqsubseteq p\}$. In other words, the relevant patters are those that share with p the same features that were used to classify previous problems. Let S_{m_j} be the set of cases subsumed by $m_j \in M_p$, we define S_{M_p} as the union of all cases subsumed by any relevant pattern. C-LID applies the *majority rule* to the set $S_{D_p} \cup S_{M_p}$; that is to say, C-LID classifies p as belonging to the solution class to which belong a majority of the cases in $S_{D_p} \cup S_{M_p}$.

In the next section we explain some experiments on the Toxicology dataset and we evaluate the accuracy both of LID and C-LID.

4   The Toxicology Dataset

The Toxicology dataset has been provided by the US National Toxicology Program (NTP) (http://ntp-server.niehs.nih.gov). In this dataset there are descriptions of around 500 chemical compounds that may be carcinogenic for two animal species: rats and mice. The carcinogenic activity of the compounds has proved to be different in both species and also among the sex of the same species. Therefore there are, in fact, four datasets. The chemical compounds of the dataset can be classified into eight solution classes according to the laboratory experiments: *positive, clear evidence, some evidence, equivocal, equivocal evidence, inadequate study, negative* and *negative evidence*. Nevertheless, most of the authors working on this dataset consider the classes *positive, clear evidence* and *some evidence* as the class "positive"; the classes *negative* and *negative evidence* as the class "negative"; and the compounds belonging to the other classes are removed.

The classification task in this domain is specially difficult since the predictive accuracy exhibited by the domain human experts ranges from 28% to 78% [7]. In the Predictive Toxicology Challenge 2000-2001 (PTC) [4] several authors presented different approaches for solving the classification task. Most of them try to induce rules in order to characterize both classes. The accuracy obtained by the different methods is around 63%. In fact the maximum accuracy is 65% and it is considered as the default prediction.

In the next section the representation of the chemical compounds using feature terms is explained. Then we discuss the results obtained from the experiments done using both LID and C-LID.

4.1   Representation of the Chemical Compounds

The basis of the representation we propose is the *chemical ontology* used by chemist experts and that is implicit in the chemical nomenclature of the compounds. For instance, the *benzene* is an aromatic ring composed by six carbon atoms with some well-known properties, therefore it is not necessary to describe the individual atoms in the benzene when we have the *benzene* concept in our domain ontology.

Figure 2 shows part of the chemical ontology we used for representing the compounds in the Toxicology dataset. This ontology is based on the chemical nomenclature which, in turn, is a systematic way of describing a molecule. In fact, the name of a molecule provides to a chemist all the information needed to graphically represent the structure of the molecule.

In our representation (see Fig. 3) a *compound* is a sort described by two features: main-group and p-radicals. The values of the feature main-group belong to someone of the sorts shown in Fig. 2. The value of the feature p-radicals is a set whose elements are of sort *position-radical*. The sort *position-radical* is described using two features: radicals and position. The value of the feature radicals is also of sort *compound*. This is because both, main group and radicals, are the same kind of molecules, i.e. the benzene may be the main group in one

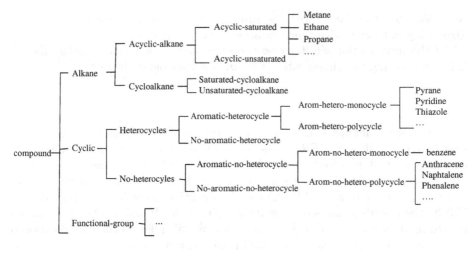

Fig. 2. Partial view of the toxicology ontology

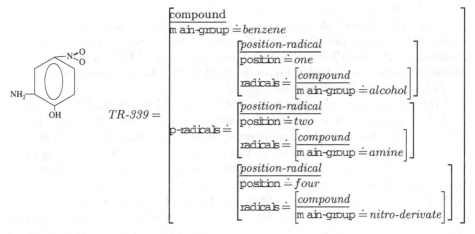

Fig. 3. Representation of the compound with identifier TR-339, the *2-amino-4-nitrophenol*, using feature terms

compound and a radical in some other compounds. The feature position of the sort *position-radical* indicates where the radical is bound to the main group.

For example, the chemical compound with identifier TR-339 in the NTP Toxicology dataset, is the *2-amino-4-nitrophenol*. This compound has a phenol as main group. The phenol, is a molecule composed of one benzene with a radical alcohol in position one. Thus, the compound TR-339 has a benzene as main group and a set of three radicals: a radical with an *alcohol* as main group in position one; a radical with an *amine* as main group in position two; and a radical with a *nitro-derivate* in position four. Notice that this information has been directly extracted from the chemical name of the compound following the nomenclature rules. We have translated, with the support of a chemist, the compounds of the Toxicology dataset to this representation based on feature terms.

In the next section we describe the experiments done using both LID and C-LID for solving the classification task in the Toxicology dataset.

4.2 Experiments

The Toxicology dataset can be seen as formed by four separate datasets: male rats (MR), female rats (FR), male mice (MM) and female mice (FM). The classification task is solved separately for each one of these datasets, i.e. solving a case means solving four classification tasks: 1) the classification of the case according to its activity in MR; 2) the classification according to its activity in FR; 3) the classification according its activity in MM; and 4) the classification according its activity in FM. From now on, we will refer to the classification of a case as the classification of the case in one dataset.

For each one of the datasets we take into account only those cases having as solution *positive* or *negative* activity, i.e. we do not considered the cases with value of activity *unknown, equivocal* or *inadequate*.

The evaluation of the predictive accuracy of the methods has been made using 10-fold cross-validation. First of all we evaluated the accuracy of LID. The column labelled as LID in Table 1 shows the accuracy of LID for each one of the datasets. Notice that LID has an accuracy of 63.09% for FR that is near to that considered as the default accuracy (65%).

Table 1 also shows the predictive accuracy of C-LID. The predictive accuracy of C-LID improves the accuracies obtained using only LID in the four datasets. These results show that the caching policy is adequate since the cached patterns allow to increase the accuracy of the LID method. Notice that the caching policy stores only the similitude terms that are univocal, i.e. those subsuming cases belonging to only one solution class. With this policy C-LID takes into account only those patterns with clear evidence of a good discrimination among classes.

In order to assess the contribution of the patterns to the accuracy improvement in C-LID we evaluated the accuracy using the set of patterns M alone. When a problem p is not subsumed by any similitude term in M, it cannot be classified. Column labeled as *Answers* in Table 1 shows the average of cases that

Table 1. Table comparing the performances of LID (column LID) and C-LID (column C-LID) on male rats (MR), female rats (FR), male mice (MM) and female mice (FM). *Answers* is the percentage of problems that can be classified using the patterns in the set M. The column M is the predictive accuracy using only the patterns generated by LID

Dataset	# cases	LID	C-LID	Answers	M
MR	297	58.27	60.54	39.96	57.67
FR	296	63.09	66.97	56.15	60.67
MM	296	52.39	53.95	32.99	53.35
FM	319	52.36	56.60	32.23	53.34

have been solved using the patterns alone. Notice that only around a third of cases can be solved. The predictive accuracy using only patterns (column M in Table 1) is greater than the accuracy of LID for mice but the accuracy for rats is lower than the LID accuracy.

The cached patterns contribute to C-LID's accuracy increase for two reasons. First, they are used only when LID is unable to yield a univocal solution. In this case C-LID wants to use patterns but not always is possible (since their applicability is about 1/3 of the cases as shown in Table 1). However, the experiments show that when they are used the accuracy of C-LID improves. The way in which patterns improve the system final decision is increasing the set of cases that C-LID take into account when the majority rule is applied. In fact, the second reason is that the cases added are really relevant to the problem C-LID is solving, as proved by the increase in accuracy that they provide.

5   Conclusions

We have presented C-LID, a lazy concept learning technique for case-based reasoning in classification tasks. C-LID is built on top of LID by caching and reusing the symbolic similitude terms generated by LID. The rationale of the C-LID is that similitude terms are the local approximations of the target function used to classify problems in CBR.

The cache policy of C-LID keeps only those similitude terms that perfectly classify the subsumed cases (i.e. those similitude terms whose cases in the discriminatory set belong all to a unique class). This policy has the rationale that it is worth caching those similitude terms that are good approximations. Clearly, there are less strict policies that are possible, e.g. caching all similitude terms that have a clear majority class among the cases in their discriminatory set. This policy retains more patterns (and thus increase their scope) but they increase the uncertainty when they are reused. We performed two experiments with less strict caching policies: similarity terms were cached when the majority class in the discriminatory set was greater that 2/3 and then greater than 3/4. The outcome was very similar to that patrons alone in Table 1. Therefore, the increase in scope is undermined by the uncertainty increase in less strict policies.

This result supports the caching policy of patterns, but why do cached patterns improve accuracy? For this we have to consider the reuse policy. First, when the "classic" approach to CBR embodied in LID works perfectly (all retrieved cases are in the same class) the patterns are not reused. That is to say, when the current local approximation is assessed to be without uncertainty no other local approximations (patterns) are reused. However, when LID's outcome involves some uncertainty we assess that this local approximation is not good enough and we search for past local approximations (patterns) that were good enough. Now, for a problem p, of all cached patterns M the reuse policy only considers as subset such that $M_p = \{m_i \in M | m \sqsubseteq p\}$—that is to say, those similitude terms whose informational content is also shared by p. Notice that each cached similitude term $m_i \in M_p$ was a good characterization of what was shared by some problem p and a subset of the case base. Since p also shares this symbolic description m_i it is likely that it would be in m_i's class. Thus, the patterns in M_p (if they exist for p) can help in reducing the uncertainty intrinsic to the "pure" CBR approach of LID.

Finally, notice that C-LID is clearly a lazy approach to concept learning. C-LID uses local approximations of the target function and not a global approximation (even if it caches generalizations of examples). The contribution of C-LID is that it uses local approximations in a new way: C-LID builds in a problem-centered way a local approximation, and then assess its goodness against the existing case base; if this local approximation is found wanting then C-LID reuses *similar* local approximations that have been cached. The similar local approximations are those that share with the problem p the content of a symbolic description of similarity among cases.

Acknowledgements. This work has been supported by the MCYT-FEDER Project SAMAP (TIC2002-04146-C05-01). The authors thank Dr. Lluis Bonamusa for his assistance in developing the representation of chemical molecules.

References

[1] E. Armengol and E. Plaza. Bottom-up induction of feature terms. *Machine Learning*, 41(1):259–294, 2000.

[2] E. Armengol and E. Plaza. Individual prognosis of diabetes long-term risks: A CBR approach. *Methods of Information in Medicine*, pages 46–51, 2001.

[3] E. Armengol and E. Plaza. Lazy induction of descriptions for relational case-based learning. In *Machine Learning: ECML-2002*, number 2167 in Lecture Notes in Artificial Intelligence, pages 13–24. Springer-Verlag, 2001.

[4] C. Helma, R. King, S. Kramer, and A. Srinivasan. The predictive toxicology challenge 2000-2001. In *ECML/PKDD 2001. Freiburg*, 2001.

[5] Ramon López de Mántaras. A distance-based attribute selection measure for decision tree induction. *Machine Learning*, 6:81–92, 1991.

[6] T.M. Mitchell. *Machine Learning*. McGraw-Hill International Editions. Computer Science Series, 1997.

[7] Bernhard Pfahringer. (the futility of) trying to predict carcinogenicity of chemical compounds. In *Proceedings of the Predictive Toxicology Challenge Workshop, Freiburg, Germany, 2001.*, 2001.

Authoring Cases from Free-Text Maintenance Data

Chunsheng Yang[1], Robert Orchard[1], Benoit Farley[1], and Maivin Zaluski[1]

[1] National Research Council, Ottawa, Ontario, Canada
{Chunsheng.Yang,Bob.Orchard,Benoit.Farley,Marvin.Zaluski}@nrc.ca

Abstract. Automatically authoring or acquiring cases in the case-based reasoning (CBR) systems is recognized as a bottleneck issue that can determine whether a CBR system will be successful or not. In order to reduce human effort required for authoring the cases, we propose a framework for authoring the case from the unstructured, free-text, historic maintenance data by applying natural language processing technology. This paper provides an overview of the proposed framework, and outlines its implementation, an automated case creation system for the Integrated Diagnostic System. Some experimental results for testing the framework are also presented.

Keywords: cased-based reasoning, case creation, case base management, natural language processing

1 Introduction

The Integrated Diagnostic System (IDS), which was developed at the National Research Council of Canada, is an applied artificial intelligent system [2] that supports the decision-making process in aircraft fleet maintenance. IDS integrates two kinds of the reasoning techniques: rule-based reasoning and case-based reasoning. The rule-based reasoner monitors the messages transmitted from the aircraft to the information monitoring system on the ground. The messages are either malfunction reports from the sensors of an aircraft (failure [FLR] or warning [WRN] messages) or digital messages typed on the keyboard by the pilot (SNAG[1] or MSG messages). IDS clusters these messages into different Fault Event Objects (FEOs), which are regarded as potential problem symptoms. These symptoms trigger the firing of rules that alert maintenance technicians to situation that could have a significant impact on the aircraft's airworthiness. IDS also helps identify the appropriate parts of troubleshooting manual that are related to the symptoms. CBR [1] is then needed to help refine these solves by retrieving similar situations from the mechanic's experiences, which have been stored in a case base.

The case bases are different from the rule bases in principle. The rules reflect the relationship between condition and consequence in real-world problems; they can be designed based on system requirements and domain knowledge, or extracted from the technical documents such as the troubleshooting manual. The cases document the

---

[1] A snag is a common term for an equipment problem in the aviition area. It is a record of the problem and the repair action.

P. Perner and A. Rosenfeld (Eds.): MLDM 2003, LNAI 2734, pp. 131–140, 2003

relation between problem symptoms and the fix applied by domain experts, and they accumulate the past experience for solving similar problems. The cases can't be created from technical documentation. They have to be authored from historic maintenance experience or by experienced domain experts.

One important piece of data is the snag message. A snag is a transcript of the hand-written notes describing a problem (reported by pilots, other crew or maintenance technicians) and the repair actions carried out to fix the problem. It is composed of well defined, fixed fields describing the date, the location, a unique snag identifier, etc. as well as unstructured free-text describing the problem symptoms, the pieces of equipment involved in the repair and the actions performed on them. It is possible for someone to create a potential case by combining the information in the snag message with information in the FEO database. To help the user to create cases from the historic snag database, we developed an off-line tool, SROV (Snag Ratification Object Validation) [1]. This tool allows the user to browse the snag database, clean up the contents of the snag message and convert the snag message into a potential case. However, it was still difficult for the user to create cases using the tool, because the problem description and repair action in the snag messages are described with unstructured free text. To extract useful information from such free-text messages requires significant human effort and domain knowledge.

In order to reduce the human effort, we propose a framework for authoring cases automatically from the unstructured free-text maintenance data by applying natural language processing (NLP) techniques [3,14]. In this paper, the proposed framework is presented in detail along with its implementation, an automated case creation system (ACCS) for IDS. Some experimental results for testing the effectiveness of the framework are also discussed.

The paper is organized as follows. Following this introduction is Sect. 2, Related Work; Sect. 3 is the proposed framework; Sect. 4 describes the technical implementation of ACCS; Sect. 5 presents some experimental results; and the final section discusses the conclusions.

2   Related Work

To date a great deal of research effort has been devoted to case base maintenance [4,5,6,7,9,10,12] in CBR systems. This research has focused on a number of crucial issues such as the case life cycle [5], the optimization of the case indices [12] and so on. Some of the earliest case base maintenance works [9,10] look at the development of maintenance strategies for deleting/adding cases from/to existing case bases. For example, in [9], a class of competence-guided deletion policies for estimating the competence of an individual case and deleting an incompetent case from a case base is presented. This technique has been further developed for adding a case to an existing case base [10]. Redundancy and inconsistency detection for case base management in CBR systems has also attracted a lot of attention from researchers [11]. In recent years, some new approaches based on automatic case base management strategies have been published. M.A. Ferrario and B. Smyth [6], introduced a distributed maintenance strategy, called collaborative maintenance, which provides an intelligent framework to support long-term case collection and authoring. To automatically maintain the case base, L. Portinale et al. [4] proposed a strategy, called LEF (Learning by Failure with Forgetting [13]), for automatic case base maintenance.

It is perhaps surprising that these works almost exclusively focus on maintaining case bases for runtime CBR systems and collecting cases from the on-line problem-solving procedures. Relatively little work has focused on automatically authoring cases at an earlier stage, using existing historic maintenance experience that can be collected from past maintenance operational data. In fact, a useful CBR system should provide the ability for a user to automatically author case bases from the recorded historic experience database at the initial stage and to automatically collect or author the cases at the on-line runtime stage. Therefore, the main contribution of this paper is to propose a useful framework for automatically authoring cases from the historic maintenance experience data by applying NLP techniques.

3   A Framework for Authomatically Authoring Cases

To describe the proposed framework, we use the following notations. Let c denote a *case* and CB denote a case base, then $CB \supseteq (c_1, c_2 \ldots \ldots, c_i, \ldots, c_n)$. A case c is defined as $c = ((p),(s),(m))$ where *(p), (s)* and *(m)* denote problem attributes (called symptoms), solution attributes to the problem and information for case base management respectively. *(m)* contains all attributes related to case base maintenance including redundancy, inconsistency, positive actions, and negative actions. *(p)* could be a single symptom or multiple symptoms, and *(s)* could be a single action or multiple actions for fixing the problem *(p)*. If SB and FB denote the historic snag maintenance database and the FEO database respectively, then $SB \supseteq (snag_1, snag_2, \ldots snag_k)$ and $FB \supseteq (f_1, f_2, \ldots f_l)$. Our task is to create CB from SB and FB. Therefore, the framework can automate this task by following five main processes:

- Preprocessing snag messages (SB),
- Identifying the symptoms(*(p)*) for the problems,
- Identifying the solution (*(s)*) for the problems,
- Creating a potential case *(c)*,
- Maintaining the case base (*(m)*).

3.1   Preprocessing Snag Messages

The task of this process is to obtain clean snag messages $snag_i \subseteq SB$ from the raw snag messages. The raw snag messages like the one shown in Table 1 are processed to give messages in italics as shown in Table 2. The parse is simple since the various fields of the raw message are in a predetermined order and of the fixed size. We extract the date, the place where the fix was done, a unique snag identifier, etc, as well as unstructured free-text describing the problem symptoms and the repair actions. The free-text contains many unnecessary symbols or words. To deal with this, we filter the unnecessary characters (such as '#', '.', '*' and so on) and using a list of "poor single" words, we remove some words as well. The list of poor single words are constructed by analyzing a large set of snag messages to see which ones were not helpful in matching the unstructured text FLR and WRN messages. For example, the free-text of the problem description obtained from the raw snag message, *RMA 27-93-2127 AVAIL. REPEAT E/W "F/CTL ELAC 1 FAULT" "ELAC 1 OR INPUT OF CAPT ROLL CTL SSTU 4CE1". R 7.* after processing, results in *RMA 27-93-2127 AVAIL REPEAT F/CTL ELAC 1 FAULT ELAC 1 INPUT CAPT ROLL CTL SSTU 4CE1,* as shown in Table 2.

Table 1. An example of the raw maintenance data record

```
ACFT_MI_SEC:UNNNNNNNNNNNNNNNNNNNNNNNYYYYYYYYYYYYYYNYNNNNNNNNYYNN
6615 437820001NM1003286 2312 2312ACA01058P28Q0CL6YUL ACA0646RT RMA 27-93-2127
AVAIL. REPEAT E/W "F/CTL ELAC 1 FAU LT"   "ELAC 1 OR INPUT OF CAPT ROLL CTL
SSTU 4CE1". R 7. I2000-09-23NNDEFN        0000000000000   0000000000000
0000000000000    00000000000000       40227AC 74577LNNS ORDER     AC74577 1998-01-
22 14:07:006650
ACFT_MI_ACTN_SEC : INNNNNNNNNNNNNNNNNNNNNNNYYYYYYNN 615437820002000
6889450001Y REPLACED CAPTAINS SIDE STICK AND TESTED AS PER AMM 27-92-41-501
42000-09-2506.36.00FIXYWG 26525AC 26525NNNNNN 000000000000           AC26525 1998-
01-30 16:00:00.898990
ACFT_PART_RMVL_SEC:NNNNNNNNNNNNNNNNNNNNNNNNNNN661543782000200068894500010
0010 001Y0000000010000NNNAC002FD 9W19XFEA 150000000042983622-9852-003
4V792      111AC26525 1998-01-30 16:00:00.89916023-80-0100        Y
ACFT_PART_INST_SEC:NNNNNNNNNNNNNNNNNYNYYNYNN6615437820002000 688945000
100010001 Y0000000010000NN AC002EA 150000000042983    1467    AC26525 1998-01-30
16:00:00.89921023-80-0100     Y
```

Table 2. A clean snag message obtained from the Table 1

Event Date & Time	*1998-01-22 14:07:00*
Report Station	*YUL*
Snag Number	*M1003286*
Problem Description	*RMA 27-93-2127 AVAIL REPEAT F/CTL ELAC 1 FAULT ELAC 1 INPUT CAPT ROLL CTL SSTU 4CE1*
Fin Number	*222*
Repar Station	*YWG*
Repair Date	*1998-01-30 16:00:00*
Repair Action	*REPLACED CAPTAINS SIDE STICK AND TESTED AS PER AMM 27-92-41-501*

3.2   Identifying the Symptoms

The task of the process, symptom identification, is to find *(P)* from the *SB and FB*. Identifying the symptoms for the problem is done using a free-text matching approach because the content of the diagnostic FLR and WRN messages is described in formal (predetermined) text while the problem description in the snag message is unstructured free text. To match such free text to the formal text of the diagnostic messages, we use an N-gram algorithm. N-gram matching refers to a fragment of N consecutive letters of a text phrase. For a given text phrase of length *L*, there are $L - N + 1$ N-grams. Such a matching algorithm helps to reduce the impact of misspelling, abbreviations and acronyms. After considering the trade-off between the algorithm performance and matching accuracy, we selected N to be 3 (tri-gram matching). For example, in the tri-gram matching algorithm, the text word "***diagnose***" could be disassembled into 6 tri-grams: $\{dia, iag, agn, gno, nos, ose\}$. If a text phrase, *"diagnose"* is matched to the misspelled one, *"diagnoes"*, the tri-gram will identify them as two similar text phases. As a result, the problem, **RMA 27-93-2127 AVAIL REPEAT F/CTL ELAC 1 FAULT ELAC 1 INPUT CAPT ROLL CTL SSTU 4CE1,** is linked to symptoms: **WRN321, FLR1188, WRN320, WRN340,** after matching the description to the **FB**.

3.3   Identifying the Solutions

Gavin a snag message, $snag_i \subseteq SB$, we also need to determine the solution *(S)*. In other words, the task of the solution identification is to extract repair action and equipment information from the snag message using NLP techniques [3, 14]. In general, the free text of the repair action description in the snag message contains one or more "sentences" with extensive use of acronyms and abbreviations, omission of certain types of words (such as the definite article), and numerous misspellings and typographic errors. Extracting the required specific information, namely the pieces of equipment involved in the repair and the actions performed on the equipment (replace, reset, repair, etc.), from the free text is a typical natural language understanding procedure as shown as Fig. 1.

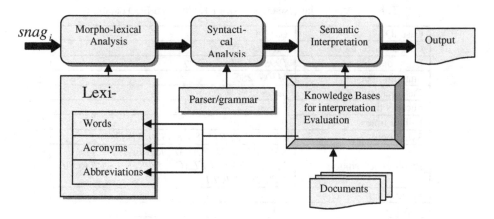

Fig. 1. Main function diagram of NLP

In the natural language understanding procedure, the unstructured free text that describes the repair action is first preprocessed to determine the nature and properties of each word and token against the lexicon which contains the words, the acronyms and the abbreviations. Then the sequence of morphologically analyzed items is syntactically analyzed with a parser and checked against a grammar that describes the patterns of valid propositions. Finally the result of the syntactic parsing is semantically interpreted to generate the class of repair action and the equipment on which the action is performed. For example, the free-text that describes the repair action in the snag message, *"#1 EIU replaced"*, is analyzed as shown as Table 3.

Table 3. The result of NLP for snag example

Attribute Name of Solution (S)	Value
Part name	EIU
Part number	3957900612
Repair action	REPLACE
Part series number	3-25-8-2-40D

3.4   Creating a Potential Case

Having *(p)* and *(S)* obtained from the previous steps, this process creates a temporary case, $C_{tmp} = ((p),(s),(m))$. We have to check this potential case to determine if the symptoms related to the problem have disappeared or not during a period of time (window size) after the repair actions were taken. The window size is set by aircraft fleet maintenance requirements. We assume that if the symptoms of the problem disappear for the specified period (window size) that the repair was successful and the case is labeled as a positive case, otherwise it is labeled as a negative one. For example, a potential case shown as Table 4 is created from Table 2 by identifying the symptoms and solutions for the problem.

Table 4. A potential case created from Table 2 and FEO database

Case ID	Case-1
Case creation date	2002-04-05
Event date time	1998-01-22 14:07:00
Snag number	M1003286
Case quality	Success
Success times	1
Failure times	0
Symptoms	WRN321 FLR1188 WRN320 WRN340
Problem description	RMA 27-93-2127 AVAIL REPEAT F/CTL ELAC 1 FAULT ELAC 1 INPUT CAPT ROLL CTL SSTU 4CE1
Fin number	222
Repair station	YWG
Repair date	1998-01-30 16:00:00
Repair actions	Remove/Install (replace)
Equipment (No)	27-92-41-501

3.5   Maintaining the Case Base

The case base maintenance process implements the basic functions for case base management to determine the attributes of (m). The first set of functionality includes detecting any redundancy or inconsistency for the potential case against the existing case base. In effect we determine whether this case is similar to cases within the existing case base or not. The second set of functionality involves adding a new case to the case base, updating an existing case in the case base, deleting a case and merging multiple cases into a new case. If a potential case is new, it will be added to the case base and the case base management information will be refreshed. If it is similar to an existing case, we have to modify the existing case by updating the case management information (m) or merge them into a new case. For example, if we detected a similar case (c_i) in the existing case base against the potential case c_{tmp}, i.e. $(p)_i \cong (p)_{tmp}{}^2$ and $(s)_i \cong (s)_{tmp}$, then $(m)_i$ will is updated to reflect the effect of the repair action applied to the problem. If c_{tmp} is a positive case, then we increase the count of successful repair actions of $(m)_i$ otherwise we increase the count of unsuccessful repair actions of $(m)_i$.

4   Implementation

The proposed framework has been applied to the IDS project for authoring the cases from the aircraft fleet maintenance historic data (snag database) and the FEO database. We developed a Java-based CBR engine, and an automated case creation system, which incorporates the CBR engine, natural language processing, free-text matching, and database technologies. The goal of the ACCS tool is to demonstrate that we can author an set of cases in an automated way that will enhance the decision making process of the maintenance technicians.

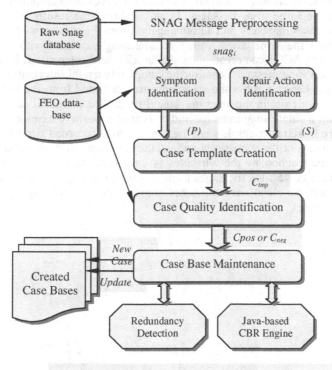

Fig. 2. ACCS system implementation

---

2 $(p)_i \cong (p)_{tmp}$ means that the problem description in case C_i is similar to one in the potential case c_{tmp}.

The ACCS, as shown in Fig. 2, identifies the five main components: snag message preprocessing, symptom identification, repair action identification, potential case creation, and case base maintenance. The potential case creation component contains two modules: case template creation and case quality identification. The repair action identification component contains three NLP modules: the lexicon, the parser/grammar, and a knowledge base for interpretation evaluation. The component of case base maintenance is supported by the Java-based CBR engine and the redundancy and inconsistency detection modules. We have used JDK2.0, JDBC, Oracle7.0, and Prolog as development environment.

5   Experimental Results

To test the effectiveness of the proposed framework, the experiments were carried out using the developed ACCS. First we asked a domain expert to manually author the cases using the SROV. The domain expert created cases from 352 historic snag messages that were generated in IDS from Jan. 1, 1998 to Jan. 31, 1998. The cases were created in several sessions in order to reduce the influence of fatigue. The times from the different sessions were summed. Then we used ACCS to automatically author the cases from the same snag messages. Figure 3 shows the results of experiments for creating the cases manually and automatically. From the results, we found that ACCS creates almost the same cases from the same snag messages with much less time, suggesting that ACCS can create the cases quickly and correctly. It is interesting that not each clean snag message contains the completely useful information for creating a potential case because either the symptoms are not found from the FEO database, or the fix does not exist in the snag message. In the 35 constructed cases, 21 cases are created from a single snag message and consist of a positive case or a negative case; 14 cases are linked to multiple snag messages, which recorded similar resolutions for similar problems or the same problem, and they contain information on the successful or failed repair action by the attributes of case base management (m). From the statistical results, 45 snag messages from 359 snag messages were linked to those 14 cases. In total, 66 clean snag messages among 359 snag messages were useful for creating the cases.

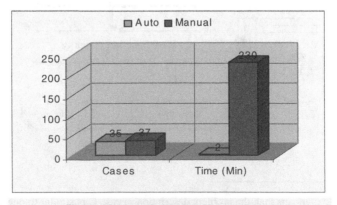

Fig. 3. The experimental result comparison

6   Conclusions

In this paper, we first presented the proposed framework for automatically authoring cases from the historic maintenance data in CBR applications, and then we described its implementation, an automated case creation system for the IDS, and discussed the experiment results. From the experimental results, it can be pointed out that the proposed framework is feasible and effective for automatically authoring cases in CBR systems and it can significantly reduce the effort required. From the experimented result, we also found that it is necessary to provide an interactive environment for the domain expert to evaluate any authored cases before they are incorporated into CBR systems such as IDS. How to evaluate the cases is a very difficult task. We will work on this issue in our future work.

Acknowledgments. Many people at NRC have been involved this project. Special thanks go to the following for their support, discussion and valuable suggestions: M. Halasz, R. Wylie, and F. Dube. We are also grateful to Air Canada for providing us the aircraft fleet maintenance data.

References

1.   Lehane, M., Dubé, F., Halasz, M., Orchard, R., Wylie, R. and Zaluski, M. (1998) *Integrated Diagnositic system (IDS) for Aircraft Fleet maintenance,* In Proceedings of the AAAI'98 Workshop: Case-Bases Reasoning Integrations, Madison, WI.
2.   Wylie, R., Orchard, R., Halasz, M. and Dubé, F. (1997) *IDS: Improving Aircraft fleet Maintenance,* In Proceeding of the 14th National Conference on Artificial Intelligence, Calif, USA, pp. 1078–1085
3.   Farley, B. (1999) *From free-text repair action messages to automated case generation,* Proceedings of AAAI 1999 Spring Symposium: AI in Equipment Maintenance Service & Support, Technical Reprot SS-99-02, Menlo Park, CA, AAAI Press, pp. 109–118
4.   Portinale, L. and Torasso, P. (2000) *Automated Case Base Management in a Multi-model Reasoning System,* In Proceedings of Advances in case-based Reasoning: 5th European Workshop, EWCBR 2000, Trento, Italy, pp. 234–246
5.   Minor, M. and Hanft, A. (2000) *The Life Cycle of Test cases in a CBR System,* In Proceedings of Advances in case-based Reasoning: 5th European Workshop, EWCBR 2000, Trento, Italy, pp. 455–466
6.   Ferrario, M. A. and Smyth, (2000) *Collaborative Maintenance – A Distributed, Interactive Case-based Maintenance Strategy,* In Proceedings of Advances in case-based Reasoning: 5th European Workshop, EWCBR 2000, Trento, Italy, pp. 393–405
7.   Shiu, S.C.K., Sun, C.H., Wang, X.Z. and Yeung, D.S. (2000) *Maintaining Case-Based Reasoning Systems Using Fuzzy Decision Trees,* In Proceedings of Advances in case-based Reasoning: 5th European Workshop, EWCBR 2000, Trento, Italy, pp. 258–296
8.   Smyth, B. (1998) *Case-Based Maintenance,* In Proceedings of the 11th Intl. Conference on Industry and Engineering Applications of AI and Expert Systems, Castellon, Spain
9.   Smyth, B. (1995) *Remembering to Forget: A Competence Persevering Deletion Policy for Case-Based Reasoning Systems,* In Proceedings of the 14th Intl. Joint Conference on AI, Morgan-Kaufmann, pp. 377–382

10. Zhu, J. and Yang, Q. (1999) *Remembering to Add: Competence Persevering Case-Addition Policy for Case-Base Maintenance*, In Proceedings of the 16th Intl. Joint Conference on AI, Stockholm, Sweden, pp. 234–239
11. Racine, K. and Yang, Q. (1996) *On the Consistency Management for Large Case Bases: The Case for Validation*, In Proceedings of AAAI-96 Workshop on Knowledge Base Validation
12. Aha, D.W. and Breslow, L.A. (1997) *Refining Conversational Case Libraies*, In Proceedings of Int'l Conference of Case-based Reasoning, RI, USA, pp. 267–278
13. Portinale, L., Torasso, P. and Tavano, P. (1999) *Speed-up, Quality and Competence in Multi-modal Case-based Reasoning,* In Proceedings of 3rd ICCBR, LNAI 1650, Springer Verlag, pp. 303–317
14. Ferlay, B. (2001), Extracting information from free-text aircraft repair notes, Artificial Intelligence for Engineering Design, Analysis and Manufacture, Cambridge University Press 0890-0604/01, pp. 295–305

Classification Boundary Approximation by Using Combination of Training Steps for Real-Time Image Segmentation

Johel Mitéran, Sebastien Bouillant, and Elbey Bourennane

Le2i – FRE CNRS 2309 Aile des Sciences de l'Ingénieur
Université de Bourgogne
BP 47870
21078 Dijon, France
miteranj@u-bourgogne.fr

Abstract. We propose a method of real-time implementation of an approximation of the support vector machine decision rule. The method uses an improvement of a supervised classification method based on hyperrectangles, which is useful for real-time image segmentation. We increase the classification and speed performances using a combination of classification methods: a support vector machine is used during a pre-processing step. We recall the principles of the classification methods and we evaluate the hardware implementation cost of each method. We present our learning step combination algorithm and results obtained using Gaussian distributions and an example of image segmentation coming from a part of an industrial inspection problem The results are evaluated regarding hardware cost as well as classification performances.

1 Introduction

In this paper, we propose a method of approximation of the decision rule of the support vector machine. This approximation allows optimised hardware implementation of the decision boundary, together with an estimation of implementation cost and classification performances. This paper focuses mainly high speed decisions (approximately 10 ns per pixel) which can be useful for image segmentation which can be solved using pixel-wise classification and specific classifiers, for detection of anomalies on manufactured parts, for example. The segmentation is usually the first step of a pattern recognition process.

Classification is a central problem of pattern recognition [4] and many approaches to the problem have been proposed, e.g. neural networks [1], Support Vector Machines (SVM) [20], k-nearest neighbours and kernel-based methods, to name the most common. The chosen classifier must either be implemented in low-cost hardware or in optimised software running in real-time.

It has been proven in the literature that the SVM method gives very good results in many practical cases [7, 14, 18]. However, this robust algorithm is not often used for pixel-wise classification because of the decision rule complexity.

P. Perner and A. Rosenfeld (Eds.): MLDM 2003, LNAI 2734, pp. 141–155, 2003.
© Springer-Verlag Berlin Heidelberg 2003

We developed a hyperrectangles-based classifier [12]: this hyperrectangle method belongs to the same family as the NGE algorithm, described by Salzberg [17].

In a previous paper [12], we have shown that it is possible to implement this classifier in a parallel component in order to obtain the required speed, and in another article [13] we indicated that the performances are sufficient for use in a face recognition algorithm. However, the performance of the training step is sometimes affected by ambiguities in the training set, and more generally, the basic hyperrectangles-based method is outperformed by the SVM algorithm.

We propose in this paper an original combination of classifiers allowing for obtaining fast and robust classification applied to image segmentation. The SVM is used during a first step, pre-processing the training set and thus rejecting any ambiguities. The hyperrectangles-based learning algorithm is applied using the SVM classified training set. We will show that the hyperrectangle method imitates the SVM method in terms of performances, for a lower cost of implementation using reconfigurable computing.

In the first part of this paper, we review the principles of the two classifiers: the Hyperrectangles-based method and the SVM. In the second part, we present our combination method and optimisation algorithm. We applied the method on Gaussian distributions, which are often used in literature for performance evaluation of classifiers [4], [2]. Finally, we present practical results obtained in image segmentation of an industrial part.

2 Classification Algorithms

2.1 Hyperrectangles-Based Method

This method divides the attribute space into a set of hyperrectangles for which simple comparators may easily satisfy the membership condition. This hyperrectangle method belongs to the same family as the NGE algorithm, described by Salzberg [17], whose performance was compared to the k-nn method by Wettschereck and Dietterich [21]. The performance of our own implementation was studied in [12].

The training step consists in collecting the set S

$$S = \left\{ \left(\mathbf{x}_1, y_1 \right), \left(\mathbf{x}_2, y_2 \right), ..., \left(\mathbf{x}_p, y_p \right) \right\}$$

of the most representative samples from the various classes and associating a local constraint (hyperrectangle) $H(\mathbf{x}_i)$. Each sample is defined by a feature vector $\mathbf{x}$ in an D dimensional space and its corresponding class $C(\mathbf{x})=y$:

$$\mathbf{x}=(x_1, x_2, ..., x_D)^T.$$

Hyperrectangle Determination: During the first step, an hyperrectangle is build for each sample $\mathbf{x}$ as follows :

Each part Q_t (see Fig. 1) defines the area where $d_\infty \left(\mathbf{x}_k, \mathbf{x}_l \right) = \left| x_t^k - x_t^l \right|$ with

$$d_\infty \left(x, y \right) = \max_{k=1,...,D} \left| x_k - y_k \right|$$

We determine **z** as the nearest neighbour belonging to a different class in each part Q_p. If d_p is the distance between **x** and **z** in a given Q_p, the limit of the hyperrectangle in the direction is computed as $d_f = d_p.R_p$.

The parameter R_p should be less or equal to 0.5. This constraint ensures that the hyperrectangle cannot contain any sample of opposite classes.

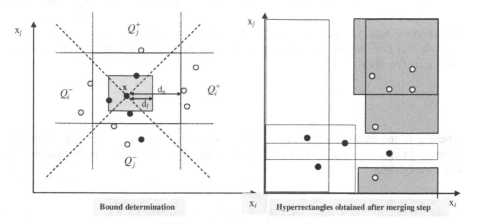

Fig. 1 Hyperrectangle computation

During the second step, hyperrectangles of a given class are merged together in order to optimise the final number of hyperrectangle.

The decision phase consists of allocating a class to a new attribute vector **x**. The membership of a new feature value x_k to a given interval I_{ik} (i^{th} hyperrectangle and k^{th} feature) is easily verified by controlling the two following conditions : $(x_k > a_{ik})$ and $(x_k < b_{ik})$, where a_{ik} and b_{ik} are respectively the lower and upper limits of each polytope or hyperrectangle. Therefore, the verification of the membership of an unknown vector **x** to a class y results in a set of comparisons done simultaneously on each feature for every hyperrectangle of class y. The resulting decision rule is:

$$C(\mathbf{x}) = y \Leftrightarrow \sum_{i=1}^{i=m_y} \prod_{k=1}^{k=d} ((x_k > a_{ik}).(x_k < b_{ik})) \text{ is true} \tag{1}$$

m_y is equal to the number of hyperrectangles of class y after a merging phase. Sum and product are logical operators. This method is easy to use, and can be implemented for real-time classification using hardware [11] or software optimisation.

We developed an algorithm allowing evaluation of the implementation cost of this method in Field Programmable Gate Array (FPGA). In recent years FPGAs have become increasingly important and have found their way into system design. FPGAs are used during development, prototyping, and initial production and are replaced by hardwired gate arrays or application specific ICs (ASICs) for highvolume production. This trend is enforced by rapid technological progress, which enables the commercial production of ever more complex devices [5]. The advantage of these components is mainly their reconfigurability [8]. It is possible to integrate the constant values (the limits of hyperrectangles) in the architecture of the decision function. We have coded a tool which automatically generates a VHDL description of a decision function given the result of a training step (i.e. given the hyperrectangles limits). We then have used a standard synthesizer tool for the final implementation in FPGA. We verified that a single comparator between a variable (feature value) and a constant (hyperrectangle limit) uses only on average a 0.5 slice (using bytes). The slice is the elementary structure of the FPGA of the Virtex family (Fig. 2), and one component can contain a few thousand of these blocks. Since the decision rule requires 2 comparators per hyperretangle and per feature, we evaluate λ_H, the hardware cost of hyperrectangles implementation (number of slices) with:

$$\lambda_H = d \sum_{y=1}^{y=z} m_y , \qquad (2)$$

where z is the number of classes. In the particular case of a 2-class problem, the summation can be computed only to $y=z-1$, since only one set of hyperrectangles defines the boundary.

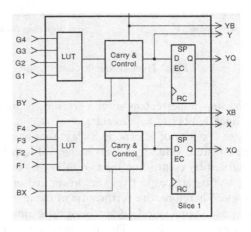

Fig. 2 Slice structure

We evaluated the performance of this method in various cases, using theoretical distributions [12] as well as real sampling [11]. We compared the performance with neural networks, the Knn method and a Parzen's kernel based method [1]. It clearly appears that the algorithm performs poorly when the inter-class distances are too small. The overlap between classes is arbitrarily classified thus introducing a classification error.

This is shown in Fig. 3, where we presented two distributions in a two-dimensional feature space. The C0 class (in red or round dots) is multimodal. The error is the dissymmetric, due to the priority given to the first class. The error rate is 18.88% for the C0 class and 24.34% for the C1 class. Moreover, an important number of hyperrectangles are created in the overlap area, slowing down the decision or increasing the implementation cost.

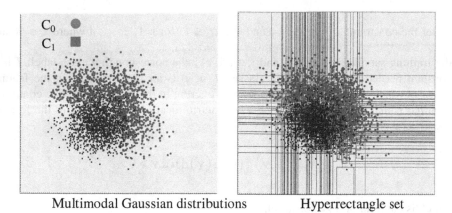

C_0 ●
C_1 ■

Multimodal Gaussian distributions   Hyperrectangle set

Fig. 3 Gaussian distributions

Many classification methods, such as neural networks, density evaluation-based method and the SVM described above are less sensitive to this overlap. It has been proven in the literature that a particular advantage of SVM over other learning algorithms is that it can be analyzed theoretically using concepts from computational learning theory. At the same time it can achieve good performance when applied to real problems [7]. We chose this method as a pre-processing step and we will show that it is possible to approximate the result of the SVM using a combination of training steps.

2.2 SVM Classification

A Support Vector Machine (SVM) is a universal learning machine developed by Vladimir Vapnik [20] in 1979. We review here the basic principles, considering here a 2-class problem (whatever the number of classes, it can be reduced, by a "one-against-others" method, to a 2-class problem).

The SVM performs a mapping of the input vectors (objects) from the input space (initial feature space) R_d into a high dimensional feature space Q; the mapping is determined by a kernel function K. It finds a linear (or non linear) decision rule in the feature space Q in the form of an optimal separating boundary, which is the one that leaves the widest margin between the decision boundary and the input vector mapped into Q. This boundary is found by solving the following constrained quadratic programming problem: maximize

$$\mathrm{W}(\alpha) = \sum_{i=1}^{n} \alpha_i - \frac{1}{2} \sum_{i=1}^{n} \sum_{j=1}^{n} \alpha_i . \alpha_j . y_i . y_j . K\left(x_i, x_j\right), \tag{3}$$

under the constraints $\sum_{i=1}^{n} \alpha_i . y_i = 0$ and $0 \le \alpha_i \le T$ for i=1, 2, ..., n where $x_i \in R_d$ are

the training sample set vectors, and $y_i \in \{-1,+1\}$ the corresponding class label. T is a constant needed for nonseparable classes. $K(u, v)$ is an inner product in the feature space Q which may be defined as a kernel function in the input space. The condition required is that the kernel $K(u, v)$ be a symmetric function which satisfies the following general positive constraint:

$$\iint_{R_d} K(u,v)g(u)g(v)\,du\,dv > 0, \qquad (4)$$

which is valid for all $g \neq 0$ for which

$\int g^2(u)\,du < \infty$ (Mercer's theorem).

The choice of the kernel $K(u, v)$ determines the structure of the feature space Q. A kernel that satisfies (4) may be presented in the form:

$$K(u,v) = \sum_{k} a_k \Phi_k(u) \Phi_k(v), \qquad (5)$$

where a_k are positive scalars and the functions Φ_k represent a basis in the space Q. Vapnik considered three types of SVM:

Polynomial SVM:

$$K(x,y) = (x.y + 1)^p, \qquad (6)$$

Radial Basis Function SVM:

$$K(x,y) = e^{\left(\frac{-\|x-y\|^2}{2\sigma^2}\right)}, \qquad (7)$$

Two-layer neural network SVM:

$$K(x,y) = Tanh\{k.(x.y) - \Theta\}. \qquad (8)$$

The kernel should be chosen a priori. Other parameters of the decision rule (9) are determined by calculating (3), i.e. the set of numerical parameters $\{\alpha_i\}_1^n$ which determines the support vectors and the scalar b.

The separating plane is constructed from those input vectors, for which $\alpha_i \neq 0$. These vectors are called *support vectors* and reside on the boundary margin. The number Ns of support vectors determines the accuracy and the speed of the SVM. Mapping the separating plane back into the input space R_d, gives a separating surface which forms the following nonlinear decision rules:

$$C(\mathbf{x}) = \mathrm{Sgn}\left(\sum_{i=1}^{N_s} y_i \alpha_i \cdot K(\mathbf{s}_i, \mathbf{x}) + b\right), \tag{9}$$

where s_i belongs to the set of Ns support vectors defined in the training step.

One can see that the decision rule is easy to compute, but the cost of parallel implementation in ASIC or FPGA is clearly more important than in the case of the hyperrectangles based method. Even if the exponential function of (7) can be stored in a particular look up table (LUT) to avoid computation, the scalar product K requires some multiplications and additions; the final decision function requires at least one multiplication and one addition per support vector. For a given model (set of support vectors), it is possible to implement operators using constant values (KCM 3), as well as we did in the hyperrectangle method. However, the cost of multiplication is significantly more important than the comparator. Chapman [3] proposes a structure using 20 slices per 8 bits multiplier. An 8 bits adder uses 4 slices. The hardware cost of a possible SVM parallel implementation or total number of necessary slices is summarized in table 1. We estimated the number of adders and multipliers needed by a fully parallel computation of K and the final sum of products, in the case of a simplified RBF kernel and a polynomial kernel. Given the number of slices needed by the computation of each elementary operator, we deduced $\lambda_{svm,}$ the hardware cost of each implementation:

Table 1. SVM hardware cost estimation

		RBF (distance L1)	Polynomial degree p
		Number of operators	Number of operators
K (per support vector)	16-bit adders (8 slices)	-	d
	8-bit adders (4 slices)	3d-1	-
	Multiplier Kx8-bit (20 slices)	-	d
	Multiplier 8x8-bit (73 slices)	-	p-1
Sum of products	Multiplier Kx16-bit (72 slices)	Ns	Ns
	16 bits adders	1	1
		Number of slices	Number of slices
Total Slices		$\lambda_{svm} = 72(3d-1)Ns + 8$	$\lambda_{svm} = (28d$ $+73(p-1)$ $+80)Ns + 8$

3   Combination

3.1   Training Method

Combining decision classifiers is a classical way used in order to increase performances of the general pattern recognition problem [9]. Three main methods are commonly used: sequential, parallel or sequential-parallel combination. These approaches allow increased performance, but the cost of hardware implementation is high since all the decision functions have to be computed in order to obtain the final classification. More generally, it is possible to combine classification methods during the training step [14]. We propose here such a combination, allowing an approximation of SVM decision boundaries using hyperrectangles (Fig. 4).

The SVM method is mainly used here in order to reject ambiguities in the learning set. The algorithm combination is as follows:

- From a training set $\mathbf{S}$

$\mathbf{S} = \left\{ (\mathbf{x}_1, y_1), (\mathbf{x}_2, y_2), ..., (\mathbf{x}_p, y_p) \right\}$, build a model M containing support vectors using SVM algorithm:

$M = \left\{ K, (\mathbf{s}_1, y_1), (\mathbf{s}_2, y_2), ..., (\mathbf{s}_{Ns}, y_{Ns}), b \right\}$

- build $\mathbf{S}$', the new training set, classifying each sample of S using M and according to eq. 8. :

$\mathbf{S}' = \left\{ (\mathbf{x}_1, y'_1), (\mathbf{x}_2, y'_2), ..., (\mathbf{x}_p, y'_p) \right\}$,

- build $\mathbf{H}$, set of hyperrectangles using $\mathbf{S}$' and the algorithm described in paragraph 0.

During the decision phase, a new test vector $\mathbf{x}$ is classified regarding $\mathbf{H}$ and the decision rule (1).

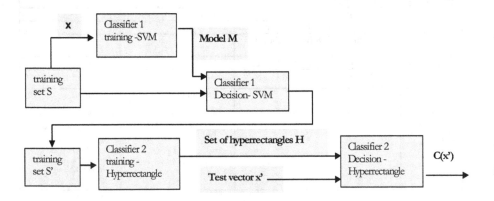

Fig. 4 Combining training steps

3.2 Application Using Gaussian Distributions

We validate the principle of the described method using Gaussian distributions. The tested configuration contains 2 classes. Results are summarised at the end of this part. We used cross-validation with $p=1000$ samples per class for the training set, and $p=10000$ samples per class for the test set. This learning set S is described in the previous paragraph. We use a RBF kernel (Eq. 6). The SVM classified set S' and the final set of hyperrectangles are depicted in Fig. 5.

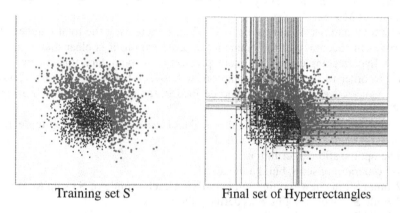

Training set S'   Final set of Hyperrectangles

Fig. 5 SVM and hyperrectangles boundaries

The results show that the hyperrectangles-based method imitates the SVM decision algorithm, giving a good approximation of boundaries. The error rate of SVM is 16.26% for the C0 class and 13.33% for the C1 class. In this case, the error obtained using final hyperrectangles (learning combination) are 15.60% and 14.20% respectively. One can see that performances are very close, and less dissymmetric than using the initial learning set.

Moreover, the number of hyperrectangles decreased, since the initial numbers were 748 (C0) and 762 (C1) before SVM classification and only 204 (C0) and 201 (C1) after SVM classification. This allows for optimizing the hardware resources in case of implementation. The cost of a direct implementation of SVM decision step is not comparable here, since the number of support vectors is 1190: the estimated hardware cost of SVM is $\lambda_{svm}= 428\ 408$ slices, whereas the hyperrectangles cost is $\lambda_H= 205$ slices.

An important improvement of performances is obtained, illustrating the good choice of the combination of training steps. However, it is still possible to optimise this result.

3.3 Optimisation

It is important to note that the final number of hyperrectangles and then the accuracy of SVM boundary approximation depend on p, the number of samples of S. We defined a method allowing to optimise the implementation minimising λ_H. This is done iterating the previous method using randomly chosen subsets of a new training set **S"**. This new training set is obtained adding pseudo-patterns or random vectors to **S**. For each sample **x** of **S'**, we generate a subset **B** of q elements:

$$B = \left\{ \left(\mathbf{x}"_1, y"_1\right), \left(\mathbf{x}"_2, y"_2\right), ..., \left(\mathbf{x}"_q, y"_q\right) \right\}$$

where $\mathbf{x}_i" = \mathbf{x}_i + \varepsilon$, and ε is a random value defined in the interval $[x_{ik}-0.1x_{ik}, x_{ik}+0.1x_{ik}]$ for each feature k. The class $y"$ of each new sample is determined using SVM decision and M Model.

The total number of sample of **S"** is p"=q.p. Increasing the total number of sample improves the accuracy of the boundary approximation: it is clear that a greater number of hyperrectangles will fit more precisely the boundary that a few number of them. In order to find the best compromise between hardware cost and classification performances, we iterate the method defined in the previous paragraph using subsets of **S"**.

The iteration can be stopped either if the classification error stop to decrease of if the maximum of slice (λ_{Hm}) is reached.

The optimisation algorithm is:
1-from training set **S**, build a model M,
2-build **S'**, the new training set, classifying each sample of **S** using M,
3-build **S"**, oversampling **S** as defined above,
4-build **T**, subsampling **S"** using q' sample,
5-build **H**, set of hyperrectangles,
6-estimate the classification error e using **H** and **S**,
7-estimate λ_H and error gradient eg from last iteration,
8-stop if $\lambda_{H>}\lambda_{Hm}$ or if eg<*Threshold*, else increase q' and go to 4,
9-use the last computed set **H** as the final hyperrectangle set.

3.4 Results

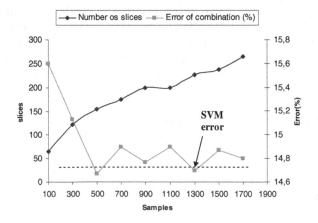

Fig. 6. Results using Gaussian distribution

The results are summarised in Fig. 6. One can see that the classification error of our method converges towards that of the SVM. The optimum number of slices $\lambda_H = 155$ is obtained for q=500.

4 Real-Time Image Segmentation for Anomalies Detection

We applied our method in a preprocessing step of an industrial project of quality control by artificial vision. The parts we have to control are made up of a spiral wire and a non-spiral part called «legs».

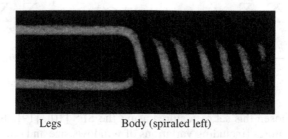

Legs   Body (spiraled left)

Fig. 7. Part to be controlled.

The anomalies existing on the whole part can be grouped into 3 categories:
- Dimensional anomalies: diameter of the wire composing the part, length of the part, length of the body (left spiraled), length of the non-spiraled part.
- Visual anomalies discoloration, stripes, cracks, flaws of surface.
All these anomalies can be found on both the legs and the body of the part.
The third category contains the various anomalies of the spiral not comprising a deterioration of the wire composing the body. We have to distinguish among thirty anomalies at the end of the project. During this preliminary work, we need to obtain a segmented image allowing extraction of high level classification features, such as distance between whorls, whorls surfaces and orientation etc.
One can note that the wire is textured: a single threshold could not be a robust operator. We extracted some simple texture features, keeping in mind real-time constraints.
The image size is 1288x1080, and the acquisition rate is 10 images/s.
A preliminary study of segmentation features led us to choose a four dimensional features space:
x_0 is the mean of luminance in 8x8 windows,
x_1 is the new value of pixel after local histogram equalisation,
x_2 is the mean of a Sobel filter in 8x8 windows,
x_3 is the mean of the local contrast in 8x8 windows.
The local contrast $V(i,j)$ in an [n x m] neighbourhood of pixel $A(i,j)$ can be expressed as follows:

$$V(i,j) = \frac{A_{max} - A_{min}}{A_{max} + A_{min}}$$

with

$$A_{max} = \max\left\{A(i+k, j+l), -\left\lfloor\frac{n-1}{2}\right\rfloor \le k \le \left\lfloor\frac{n}{2}\right\rfloor, -\left\lfloor\frac{m-1}{2}\right\rfloor \le l \le \left\lfloor\frac{m}{2}\right\rfloor\right\},$$

$$A_{min} = \min\left\{A(i+k, j+l), -\left\lfloor\frac{n-1}{2}\right\rfloor \le k \le \left\lfloor\frac{n}{2}\right\rfloor, -\left\lfloor\frac{m-1}{2}\right\rfloor \le l \le \left\lfloor\frac{m}{2}\right\rfloor\right\}$$

and $\lfloor x \rfloor$ refers to the integer part of x (floor operator).

The local mean of the Sobel gradient norm $G(i,j)$ and the local mean of luminance $S(i,j)$ in a [n x m] neighbourhood of pixels $A(i,j)$ can be written as follows:

$$S(i,j) = \frac{1}{mn}\sum_{k=p(n)}^{q(n)}\sum_{l=p(m)}^{q(m)} A(i+k, j+l) \text{ and } G(i,j) = \frac{1}{mn}\sum_{k=p(n)}^{q(n)}\sum_{l=p(m)}^{q(m)} g(i+k, j+l)$$

with $p(n) = \left\lfloor\frac{n-1}{2}\right\rfloor$, $q(n) = \left\lfloor\frac{n}{2}\right\rfloor$, and $g(i,j)$ is the Sobel gradient norm of the pixel $A(i,j)$.

We have chosen this set of features using the SFS [10], [19] algorithm from a superset of 30 features (including variations of windows size and other operators such as morphological operators, local entropy, etc).

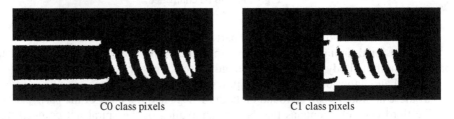

C0 class pixels   C1 class pixels

Fig. 8. Training image and areas

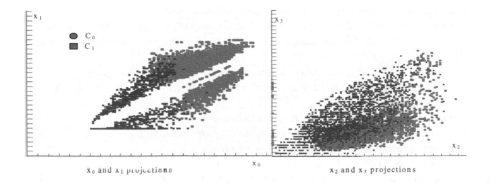

x_0 and x_1 projections x_2 and x_3 projections

Fig. 9. Training set

We defined the labels of the training set S manually, using 2 binary images which define respectively the class 0 and class 1 pixels (white pixels in Fig. 8). For each class, p=5000 pixels or samples were randomly chosen from the white areas of these pictures.

We have depicted two projections of the training set in Fig. 9. We applied our combination method described in the previous section using 10 test images. An example test image is shown in Fig. 11. The SVM kernel used in this application is RBF. The results of segmentation are depicted in Fig. 11. In order to quantify the results, we manually segmented the test images and we computed the classification error of each class for the different segmented images. We obtained the results summarized in Fig. 10.

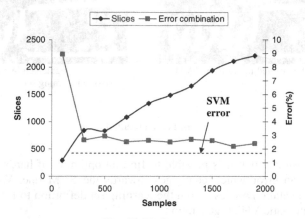

Fig. 10. Performances

This example illustrates the quality of our combination, since our classification error converges toward the SVM error. The final result of the hyperrectangles-based method is very close to the SVM result (1.94% for SVM and 2.20% for hyperrectangle), and for a lower cost of implementation.

The final implementation needs only λ_H=2110 slices (one can note that some good results (error is 2.53%) are also obtained with λ_H=2110 slices). In this particular case, the cost of implementation of SVM is very high, since a total of 475 support vectors were found during the training step. Even in the case of KCM use, the hardware cost of a full parallel decision step is here λ_{svm}=376 208 !

5   Conclusion

We have shown that it is possible to imitate the performance of the SVM classifier for a low cost of implementation combining training steps of SVM and of a particular hyperrectangles-based classifier.

We validated the performance improvement of the basic method in terms of classification as well as in terms of integration cost (or in terms of speed), since the final number of hyperrectangles is minimised.

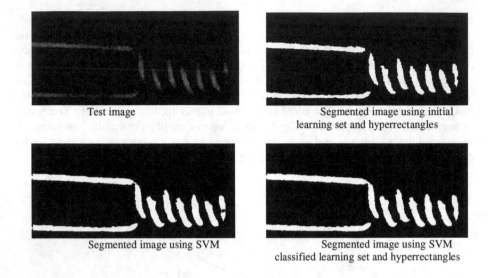

Test image	Segmented image using initial learning set and hyperrectangles
Segmented image using SVM	Segmented image using SVM classified learning set and hyperrectangles

Fig. 11. Segmented images

We demonstrated that it is possible to find an optimum of hardware implementation cost for an error which converges towards the SVM one. We developed the whole implementation process, from the learning set definition to FPGA implementation using automatic VHDL generation.

One can note that this combination well models our behaviour in front of a problem of quality control by artificial vision: the very first decision given by the expert is often modified for limit cases after observation of the results. This can be seen also as a particular application of ambiguities reject method used in many classification algorithms.

Our future work will be the improvement of the approximation method to other classification boundaries, since this principle can be applied in other case such as complex neural networks.

References

1. Bishop, C.M.: Neural networks for Pattern Recognition, Oxford University Press, (1995) 110–230.
2. Dubuisson, B.: Diagnostic et reconnaissance des formes, HERMES, Paris, (1990).
3. Chapman, K.: Constant coefficient multipliers for the XC4000E. Xilinx Application, Note XAPP054, Xilinx, Inc (1996).
4. Duda, R. O., Hart, P.E.: Pattern classification and scene analysis, Wiley, New York, (1973) 230–243.
5. Enzler, R., Jeger, T. Cottet, D., and Tröster, G.: High-Level Area and Performance Estimation of Hardware Building Blocks on FPGAs, In *Field-Programmable Logic and Applications* (Proc. FPL 00), Lecture Notes in Computer Science, Vol. 1896, Springer, (2000) 525–534

6. Hearst, M. A., Schölkopf, B., Dumais, S., Osuna, E., Platt J.: Trends and Controversies – Support Vector Machines. *IEEE Intelligent Systems*, Vol. 13(4), (1998) 18–28.
7. Jonsson, K., Kittler J., P. Li Y., Matas, J.: Support Vector Machines for Face Authentication. In T. Pridmore and D. Elliman, editors, British Machine Vision Conference, (1999) 543–553.
8. Hauck, S.: The Roles of FPGAs in Reprogrammable Systems, Proceedings of the IEEE, Vol. 86(4), (1998) 615–638.
9. Kittler, J., Hatef, M., Duin, R. P. W., Matas, J.: On combining classifiers in *IEEE transactions on pattern analysis and machine intelligence*, Vol. 20(3) (1998), 226–239.
10. Kittler, J.: Feature set search algorithms, Pattern recognition and signal processing, Sijthoff and Noordhoff, Alphen aan den Rijn, Netherlands, (1978) 41–60.
11. Miteran, J., Geveaux, P., Bailly, R. and Gorria, P.: Real-time defect detection using image segmentation *Proceedings of IEEE-ISIE 97*, Guimares, Portugal, (1997) 713–716.
12. Miteran, J., Gorria, P., Robert, M. : Classification géométrique par polytopes de contraintes. Performances et intégration , *Traitement du Signal*, Vol 11 (1994) 393–408.
13. Miteran, J., Zimmer, J. P., Yang, F. Paindavoine M. : Access control : adaptation and real-time implantation of a face recognition method, *Optical Engineering*, 40(4), (2001) 586–593.
14. Moobed, B.: Combinaison de classifieurs, une nouvelle approche, Phd. thesis, Laboratoire d'informatique de polytechnique d'Orsay ; France (1996).
15. Niyogi, P., Burges, C., Ramesh P.: Distinctive Feature Detection Using Support Vector Machines, ICASSP 99, 1, (1999) 425–428.
16. Robert, M., Gorria, P., Mitéran, J., Turgis, S.: Architectures for real-time classification processor, *Custom Integrated Circuit Conference*, San Diego CA, (1994) 197–200.
17. Salzberg S.: A nearest hyperrectangle learning method. *Machine Learning*, Vol. 6 (1991), 251–276.
18. Schölkopf, B., Smola, A., Müller, K.-R. Burges, C. J. C., Vapnik V.: Support Vector methods in learning and feature extraction, *Australian Journal of Intelligent Information Processing Systems*, Vol 1, (1998) 3–9.
19. Somol, P,. Pudil, P., Novovocova, J. Paclik, P.: Adaptative floating search methods in feature selection, *Pattern Recognition Letters*, Vol. 20, (1999) 1157–1163.
20. Vapnik, V.: The nature of statistical learning theory , Springer-Verlag New York (1995).
21. Wettschereck, D., Dietterich, T.: An Experimental Comparison of the Nearest-Neighbor and Nearest-Hyperrectangle Algorithms, *Machine Learning*, Vol. 19(1), (1995) 5–27

Simple Mimetic Classifiers*

V. Estruch, C. Ferri, J. Hernández-Orallo, and M.J. Ramírez-Quintana

DSIC, Univ. Politècnica de València, Camí de Vera s/n, 46020 Valencia, Spain
{vestruch,cferri,jorallo,mramirez}@dsic.upv.es

Abstract. The combination of classifiers is a powerful tool to improve the accuracy of classifiers, by using the prediction of multiple models and combining them. Many practical and useful combination techniques work by using the output of several classifiers as the input of a second layer classifier. The problem of this and other multi-classifier approaches is that huge amounts of memory are required to store a set of multiple classifiers and, more importantly, the comprehensibility of a single classifier is lost and no knowledge or insight can be acquired from the model. In order to overcome these limitations, in this work we analyse the idea of "mimicking" the semantics of an ensemble of classifiers. More precisely, we use the combination of classifiers for labelling an invented random dataset, and then, we use this artificially labelled dataset to re-train one single model. This model has the following advantages: it is almost similar to the highly accurate combined model, as a single solution it requires much fewer memory resources, no additional validation test must be reserved to do this procedure and, more importantly, the resulting model is expressed as a single classifier in terms of the original attributes and, hence, it can be comprehensible. First, we illustrate this methodology using a popular data-mining package, showing that it can spread into common practice, and then we use our system SMILES, which automates the process and takes advantage of its ensemble method.

Keywords: multi-classifier systems, stacking, decision trees, comprehensibility in machine learning, rule extraction

1 Introduction

Accuracy of classifiers can be improved by combining the predictions of a set (ensemble) of classifiers. These ensembles of classifiers are called multi-classifiers [9]. The effectiveness of combination is further increased the more diverse and numerous the set of hypotheses is [18] and also when several layers are arranged, known as "stacking" [29]. Many techniques for generating and combining classifier ensembles have been introduced: boosting [15,25], bagging [5,25], randomisation [10] and windowing [24], as well as several architectures, such as stacking [29] or cascading [16,17].

---

* This work has been partially supported by CICYT under grant TIC2001-2705-C03-01 and Acción Integrada Hispano-Alemana HA2001-0059.

P. Perner and A. Rosenfeld (Eds.): MLDM 2003, LNAI 2734, pp. 156–171, 2003.

Although ensemble methods significantly increase accuracy, they have some drawbacks, mainly the loss of comprehensibility of the model and the large amount of memory required to store the hypotheses [20]. Recent proposals, such as miniboosting [26], have shown that memory requirements can be considerably reduced. Nonetheless, the comprehensibility of the resulting combined hypothesis is not improved since it is still a combination of three hypotheses and not a single one. A combined hypothesis is usually a voting of many hypotheses and it is treated as a black box, giving no insight at all. In the special case of stacking, the new classifier is defined in terms of the outputs of the first-layer classifiers, and hence, it is not a model defined in terms of the original problem attributes.

Instead of this "meta-model", it would be interesting to obtain a single model, with the high accuracy the multi-classifier has, but simple and defined in terms of the original problem attributes. To do this, the main idea is to consider the combination as an "oracle" from which we label a random invented dataset, which is then used to "re-train" a decision tree and, hence, to obtain a single model that is similar to the combination. Although this idea is relatively simple, it is scarce in the literature, and usually related to the extraction of rules from neural networks (see e.g. [4,7,8]). The reason why this idea has not been spread into common practice may be that usually some restrictions are imposed on the oracle, or the decision tree learner employed to capture the semantics of the oracle is very specific, or simply because the random invented dataset has not been constructed properly. As we will see, the key point is precisely the generation of a sufficiently large invented dataset by using a proper distribution but also the reuse of the training dataset, which would permit not only a good approximation/fidelity to the oracle but a good performance in terms of accuracy, what is really aimed to. The decision tree learner need not be specific: any state-of-the-art decision tree learner, such as C5.0, can be used. Hence, the method can be easily used by any data-mining practitioner as we show with an example.

The paper is organised as follows. First, in Sect. 2, we discuss the use of ensemble methods, and how these all end up in accurate but complex, resource-inefficient and incomprehensible classifiers. We describe some previous methods in the literature for reducing the size of multi-classifiers, such as "ensemble pruning" or "mini-boosting", as well as other "black-box" approaches. Section 3 explains how multi-classifiers can be used to label a random dataset and use it for learning a new single classifier, in a way that resembles mimicking or imitating the behaviour of the combined classifier. We illustrate the process with an example using the Clementine data-mining package. In Sect. 4, we address the question of how to generate the invented dataset: uniform distribution or training distribution, appending the training dataset or not. Section 5 presents our system SMILES where the previous process is automated. A thorough experimental evaluation is illustrated in Sect. 6, which includes the analysis of the random dataset distribution, the relevance of the size of the dataset, the size of the models obtained, and the comparison with direct single classifiers (C4.5/J4.8) and other ensemble methods (bagging/boosting). Finally, the last section presents the conclusions and proposes some future work.

2   Ensemble Methods and Their Comprehensibility

Different techniques have been developed for combining the predictions obtained from multiple classifiers. According to the number of layers of classifiers, we can distinguish two different approaches:

- methods that generate a single layer of classifiers and then combine their predictions. This can be done by applying different learning algorithms to a single data set (e.g. [21] or *randomisation* [10]), or a single learning algorithm to different versions of the dataset (*bagging* [5] and *boosting* [15]).
- methods that generate multiple layer classifiers. In this case, the predictions made by the classifiers of one layer are used as input for the generation of the classifiers of the next layer (*stacking* [29] and *cascading* [16,17]).

It has been shown that accuracy is significantly improved with ensemble methods; however, the large amount of hypotheses that are generated makes the use of ensemble methods difficult due to the high resource consumption, in particular the memory required to store the set of models. A few attempts have been made in order to reduce the number of hypotheses. In [26], e.g., a new method, called *miniboosting*, has been proposed. It consists in the reduction of the ensemble to only three decision trees. Although memory requirements are considerably reduced, it obtains 40% less of the improvement that would be obtained by a 10-trial AdaBoost, and the result is still not comprehensible.

With respect to the methods based on several layers, it may seem that the last layer could be in some way comprehensible. However, let us explain in more detail how stacking and cascading work and why this is not the case.

The basic idea in stacking is to create a partition of the learning set L at layer 1, training the first-layer classifiers with one part of the partition and then using the rest for training the second-layer classifier using as attributes the outputs of each first-layer classifier and as class the original class of each example. Originally [29], the partition of L was made in a similar way as cross-validation. However, nowadays, any process of this form (with different partitions, without partition or with probability estimates) is known as *stacked generalisation*. The process as a whole can be iterated, so making up several layers (*multiple stackings*).

Cascade generalisation is a special kind of stacking algorithm which uses sequentially a set of classifiers. At each step, the original data is extended by adding new attributes which represent the probability that an example belongs to a class given by a base classifier. As in the stacked generalisation method, different learning algorithms can also be used to obtain the classifiers.

One of the main drawbacks of the above methods is that comprehensibility is lost. This is due to the use of the outputs of classifiers as input attributes for the next layer. The final layer classifier is thus defined in terms of *artificial* attributes (the outputs of the previous layer classifiers) and not exclusively in terms of the original attributes. Moreover, these "meta-classifiers" require the first layers to be preserved in order to make all the ensemble work.

Recently, a variant of stacking/cascading, known as *ensemble pruning* [22], was introduced in order to discard a subset of the available base classifiers and preserve the most relevant ones, so reducing space (this relevance is determined by using a classical "pruning" method; hence the name). A decision tree is used to "mimic" the semantics of the meta-classifier, but, again, it uses the outputs of the first layer as inputs for the second layer, and not the original attributes.

Nonetheless, it is from the area of rule extraction from neural networks where some ideas can be reused, in particular the use of the ensemble as an oracle in the same way neural networks are the "oracle" in these works, called "non-decompositional" or "black-box" rule extraction methods. For instance, the system TREPAN ([7,8]) constructs a very particular decision tree (with m-of-n expressions) from a network, using a mixture of specific splitting criteria based on fidelity to the neural network, new stopping criteria and partial queries to the network.

A more recent work [4] can be seen as a refinement of the previous work, using more traditional decision trees with a specific pruning and where the random examples are created during the construction of the decision tree. However, there is no justification why a general decision tree learner cannot be used instead, how other alternatives to the generation of random examples could work, and why the original training dataset (the training set which trained the neural network) is not reused. Moreover, the accuracy of the resulting tree is not very close to the accuracy of the neural network, maybe because they try to have high fidelity instead of high accuracy: "we concentrate on increasing fidelity more than increasing accuracy of the extracted decision tree" [4]. Finally, the empirical results are only based on four datasets, so it is very difficult to precisely evaluate the goodness of both methods.

3   Arranging Mimetic Classifiers

In the previous section we have reviewed different ensemble methods. The final model is a combined model, not a single one exclusively described in terms of the original attributes. The motivation of this work comes when we look for a new classifier that could be "semantically" similar to the accurate (and complex) combined classifier but "syntactically" or "structurally" simpler and ultimately comprehensible. In other words, we look for a new classifier that "mimics" or imitates the behaviour of the combined classifier. But how can we do this in a simple and effective manner? The method we present here is based on an additional "random dataset". This dataset can be artificially generated as large as we want, and this is possible just because we want it *unlabelled*, i.e., without class values.

The point is illustrated in Fig. 1. After a first complex multi-classifier stage, an unlabelled random dataset is "classified" or "labelled" by using the complex combined classifier (represented by a dotted circle in the figure). What we obtain now is a labelled random dataset that captures or distils (partially) the semantics of the combined classifier. And once here, the final stage is easy: we just join this labelled random dataset with the original training dataset and we train a single comprehensible model, e.g. a decision tree.

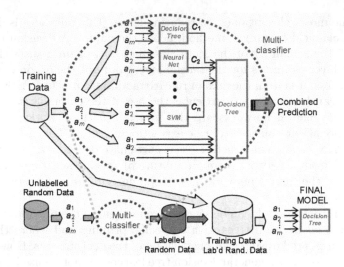

Fig. 1. Arrangement for mimicking classifiers

Note that the final model is exclusively defined in terms of the original attributes. Hence, the rest of the structure (the multiclassifier and the random data) is an auxiliar step that can be removed from memory. The outcome of the overall process is just a single model (as could be obtained by a simple decision tree learner). However, as we will justify experimentally in Sect. 6, this final model is much more accurate because it is semantically similar to the multiclassifier. An additional feature comes when we consider that the classifier used to label the random dataset can be any kind of classifier, e.g. a simple neural network. In this case, we have a methodology for giving a comprehensible representation to any other non-comprehensible (black-box) classifier.

3.1 Example

Let us illustrate the previous process on a well-known (commercial) data-mining package, SPSS Clementine 6.0.2 and a single learning problem. We selected the "balance-scale" problem from the UCI repository [2] because it is quite simple to generate random datasets for it in a handicraft way (it has 4 numeric attributes in the range 1-5 and one attribute for the class with 3 possible values). We used a partition of the original 625 examples into two datasets: training set of 325 examples and test set of 300 examples. Using the training set, we learned three different models included in Clementine: a C&R Tree, a C5.0 Tree and a Neural Network. Then, we analysed their quality by using the test set, as it is illustrated in the two topmost streams of Fig. 2.

The accuracies of each model with respect to the test set are:

```
C&R Tree: 78%          C5.0 Tree: 79.33%          NeuralNet: 88.33%
```

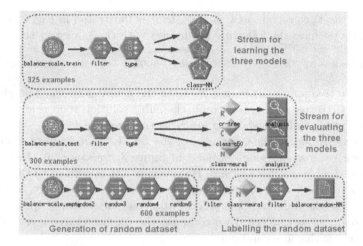

Fig. 2. First stage of mimicking using Clementine

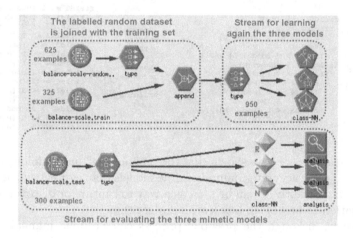

Fig. 3. Second stage of mimicking using Clementine

The neural network seems to be much better than the other two approaches for this specific problem. However, a neural network is not comprehensible.

Let us use our "mimicking" method to try to obtain a decision tree with similar accuracy to the neural network. For this, an unlabelled random dataset of size 625 examples was generated by using the uniform distribution. Since the neural network gives the best results[1], we label this dataset with it, as can be seen in the bottom part of Fig. 2. All this process (generation of random dataset and its labelling) is illustrated at the bottom of the previous Fig. 2. Finally, the second stage boils down to using this new labelled dataset (jointly with the original

---

[1] We could have made the labelling with a combination or stacking of classifiers, but we have not done it in this example for the sake of simplicity.

training dataset) to retrain new models, as it is illustrated in Fig. 3. With these new models we have the following accuracies with the same test set[2]:

$$\text{C\&R Tree: } 81.7\% \qquad \text{C5.0 Tree: } 86.0\% \qquad \text{NeuralNet: } 89.0\%$$

The decision tree solutions are now closer to the neural network. Thereby, we can choose the C5.0 tree as a better comprehensible solution than that we obtained in the first stage, quite close in accuracy to the neural network.

When we compared the structures of the first C5.0 decision tree obtained in figure 2 with the second one obtained in figure 3, we saw that the second one had almost double number of rules. However, it was overfitted to the neural net and not overfitted to the original training set. More importantly, the structure of both trees was different (the second one was not a simple specialisation of the first one), as we can see if we compare the topmost three levels of the first decision tree with the second one:

```
                    ⎧ field5 =< 1 [Mode: L]                          ⎧ field3 =< 2 [Mode: R]
                    ⎪   field2 =< 2 [Mode: L]                         ⎪   field5 =< 1 [Mode: L]
                    ⎪     field3 =< 3 [Mode: L]          SECOND       ⎪     field2 =< 3 [Mode: R]
   FIRST            ⎪     field3  > 3 [Mode: L]  -> L   DECISION      ⎪     field2  > 3 [Mode: L] -> L
  DECISION          ⎪   field2  > 2 [Mode: L]   -> L      TREE        ⎪   field5  > 1 [Mode: R]
   TREE             ⎨ field5  > 1 [Mode: R]                          ⎨     field4 =< 1 [Mode: R]
                    ⎪   field2 =< 3 [Mode: R]          labelled      ⎪     field4  > 1 [Mode: R]
  original          ⎪     field4 =< 2 [Mode: R]      random set      ⎪   field3  > 2 [Mode: L]
  training          ⎪     field4  > 2 [Mode: R]          +           ⎪     field4 =< 2 [Mode: L]
    set             ⎪   field2  > 3 [Mode: L]        training        ⎪       field2 =< 3 [Mode: L]
                    ⎪     field3 =< 2 [Mode: R]          set          ⎪       field2  > 3 [Mode: L] -> L
                    ⎩     field3  > 2 [Mode: L]                       ⎪     field4  > 2 [Mode: R]
                                                                     ⎪       field5 =< 2 [Mode: L]
                                                                     ⎩       field5  > 2 [Mode: R]
```

With this example, we have shown that the "mimicking" methodology can obtain different and more accurate comprehensible models than a direct single approach. But, more importantly, it can be seen as a way to capture or discover a symbolic representation to any black-box learning algorithm.

Obviously, although the previous process can be done manually in a few minutes using a data-mining package and can become mainstream for data-mining practitioners, it is tedious when repeated several times. Moreover, it would be impossible to scientifically evaluate this method if we do not automate the process and apply it for several datasets by using good evaluation techniques such as cross-validation. This is presented in the next three sections.

4 Random Datasets

A very important issue in the mimicking process is the generation of the random dataset in order to capture "extensionally" the semantics of the oracle. But, how should it be constructed?

Let us consider that the examples are equations of the form $f(\cdots) = c$, where f is a function symbol and c is the class of the term $f(\cdots)$. Given a function

---

[2] Note that the test set has not been used for learning in any moment.

f with a arguments/attributes, an unlabelled random example is any instance of the term $f(X_1, X_2, \cdots, X_a)$, i.e., any term of the form $f(v_1, v_2, \cdots, v_a)$ obtained by replacing every attribute X_i by values v_i from the attribute domain (attribute type). Note that an unlabelled random example is not an equation (a full example) because we include no information about the correct class.

Apparently, there are many ways to generate a random dataset. One possibility is to ignore any previous training set and just consider the types of each attribute (if known). Then we can use a uniform distribution for generating each of the attributes. One problem here arises with continuous attributes, because the *min* and *max* limits must be known. Even though it is usual that they are not known in general, the factual *min* and *max* limits can be still obtained from the training set. More precisely:

– **Uniform Distribution**: for nominal attributes, one of the seen values is randomly chosen according to a uniform distribution. For numeric attributes, one random value is generated by using a uniform distribution on the interval $\{min, max\}$, where *min* is the lowest value and *max* is the highest value observed for that attribute in the training dataset.

A second possibility is to use the training set as a reference and use the values of the attributes that appear in the training set.

– **Prior Distribution**: each attribute X_i of a new example is obtained as the value v_i in a different example $f(v_1, \ldots, v_i, \ldots, v_a)$ selected from the training set by using a uniform distribution. This procedure of generating instances assumes that all the attributes are independent. Consequently, the method just maintains the probabilities of appearance of the different values observed in each attribute of the training dataset (prior).

Both ways of obtaining the dataset are easy, although the uniform distribution can be directly implemented in any data-mining package (as shown in the previous section) or even using any spreadsheet application. Although there are more sophisticated methods (e.g. kernel density estimation methods [27]), we will just use and compare these two simple approaches.

5   Automatisation within the SMILES System

In order to evaluate the mimicking technique in general and, in particular, the best random data generation method and the best size of the random dataset, we have implemented the whole process in our SMILES system. SMILES is a multi-purpose machine learning system which includes (among many other features) the implementation of a multi-tree learner [11]. The main algorithm of SMILES is based on the usual construction of decision trees, although the rejected splits are not removed, but stored as *suspended* nodes. The further exploration of these nodes after the first solution has been built allows new models to be extracted from this structure. Since each new model is obtained by continuing the construction of the multi-tree, these models share their common parts. For this reason, a decision multi-tree can also be seen as an AND/OR tree or an option tree [6, 19], if one consider the alternative nodes as OR-nodes, and the nodes generated by an exploited OR-node as AND-nodes. The result is a multi-tree rather than a forest, with the advantage that a multi-tree shares the common parts and the forest does not. We perform a greedy search for each solution, but once the first solution is found, further trees can be obtained. The number of trees (OR-nodes) to be explored and how to select them determines the resulting multi-tree. With all these opened branches we can do two things: select one solution or combine a set of solutions. SMILES implements several criteria to combine a set of solutions given in the multi-tree. For more details on the structure and the system, we refer to [11] or the web page, http://www.dsic.upv.es/~flip/smiles/ where its user manual and several examples are freely available. SMILES has been modified in order to implement mimicking. In a first stage, the whole training set is used for training the multi-tree, obtaining a combined solution, i.e., a multi-classifier of, e.g., 100 trees. This combination, which will be used as "oracle", is usually significantly more accurate than any single classifier[11]. The next step is the generation of an unlabelled random dataset of length, e.g., 10,000 examples. This can be done automatically by SMILES in any of the two ways described in the previous section. Next, this dataset is labelled using the "oracle" (the combination). The labelled random dataset is preserved in memory and all the rest (the multi-tree structure) is freed from memory. In a second stage, we join the original training set with the labelled random dataset, so making up an even greater dataset. Finally, the last step is quite easy, we just train a *single* tree (not a multi-tree) using this final dataset. The result is, as we will see, a single tree which is approximately as accurate as the "oracle" and much more accurate than any single tree obtained by traditional means. This single tree is exclusively defined in terms of the original attributes.

In this work we have considered unpruned models for the first stage. This is because the use of models that are not 100% accurate *for the training set* could yield inconsistencies when joining the training set and the labelled random dataset. This is a limitation of the current implementation of SMILES (which does not allow inconsistencies in the class of two identical examples), but it is not a limitation of the approach (these inconsistencies could be purged or a robust decision-tree learner could be used).

6   Experiments

In this section we present an experimental evaluation of our approach by using the implementation in SMILES. For the experiments, we used GainRatio [24] as splitting criterion (for both the first stage and second stage). We chose a random method [11,12] for populating the multi-tree (after a solution is found, a suspended OR-node is woken at random) and we used the *maximum* strategy for combination [11]. Pruning is not enabled unless stated. The number of suspended OR-nodes explored in the first stage (for constructing the multi-classifier) is 100.

Table 1. Information about datasets used in the experiments

#	Dataset	Size	Classes	Nom.Attr.	Num.Attr.
1	monks1	566	2	6	0
2	monks2	601	2	6	0
3	monks3	554	2	6	0
4	tic-tac	958	2	8	0
5	house-votes	435	2	16	0
6	breast-cancer-wisc	699	2	0	9
7	chess-kr-vs-kp	3196	2	36	0
8	hepatitis	155	2	14	5
9	balance-scale	625	3	0	4
10	new-thyroid	215	3	0	5
11	tae	151	3	2	3
12	iris	150	3	0	4
13	wine	178	3	0	13
14	hayes-roth	160	3	4	0
15	cmc	1473	3	7	2
16	horse-colic-surgical	366	2	14	8

We used several datasets from the UCI dataset repository [2]. Table 1 shows the dataset name, the size in number of examples, the number of classes, and the number of nominal and numerical attributes.

Instead of fixed train-test partitions we have performed the experiments with 10-fold cross-validation. This means that the whole dataset is partitioned into 10 sub-datasets, nine are used as training set and the remainder one is reserved initially as test set, and is then used to evaluate the results in the second stage. This is done for the ten possible subdatasets. Since there are many sources of randomness, we have repeated the experiments 10 times. This makes a total of 100 runs (each one with a different first-stage multi-tree construction, random dataset construction and labelling, and second stage process) for each dataset. We show the average (in %) of these 100 runs. The last row of each table will also show the geometric mean of all the datasets.

The first thing studied is the method for generating the dataset. In Table 2 we show the accuracy of **SMILES** with different configurations. The first column ("1st") shows the results when learning a single tree (no ensemble, no mimicking). This column is similar to the results obtained by a single decision-tree learner, such as C4.5, and it is included just as a reference. The second column ("Comb") shows the accuracy of the combination of 100 trees and is, hence, the accuracy achieved by the "oracle". The next two columns ("2nd Prior" and "2nd Uniform") show the results of the mimetic classifier, i.e. the single tree obtained in the second stage, learned by using a random dataset (of size 10,000 examples) labelled by the "oracle", jointly with the training set. These two columns have used the "prior distribution" and the "uniform distribution" respectively.

The first observation from the previous table is that since we are using a good oracle (84.0 mean accuracy wrt. 81.3 original accuracy), the mimicking method

Table 2. Comparison of methods for generating the invented dataset

#	1st	Comb	2nd Prior	2nd Uniform	2nd Prior (no Train)
1	95.2	100	99.9	100	100
2	71.0	76.5	76.1	75.8	75.8
3	97.5	97.9	97.8	97.9	97.9
4	77.1	82.1	82.5	81.7	82.2
5	94.7	95.7	95.5	95.0	95.3
6	93.8	94.9	94.5	93.4	94.4
7	99.6	99.4	99.4	99.5	98.3
8	75.8	81.7	79.5	76.5	79.4
9	77.9	82.6	82.9	82.8	82.9
10	92.0	92.9	92.5	92.2	92.0
11	60.6	63.1	63.3	62.7	61.1
12	94.1	95.5	94.7	94.8	94.7
13	93.0	93.0	92.4	90.5	92.0
14	74.1	76.8	76.8	76.8	76.1
15	48.3	49.7	49.1	47.9	49.4
16	78.5	83.2	81.8	77.6	82.3
gmeans	81.3	84.0	83.6	82.7	83.3

can approach the better accuracy results of the oracle. However, it seems that the "prior distribution" is much more effective than the "uniform distribution". This was expected, because the former preserves the original distribution of the problem space. In fact, the use of 10,000 examples according to the prior distribution gets extremely close to the combination accuracy (83.6 vs. 84.0). According to these results, we will use the "prior distribution" in all the following experiments. The last column shows the effect if we do not use the training set in the second stage, i.e. we only use the labelled random dataset. Performance is slightly reduced. This may explain why related approaches that do not use the training set [4,7,8] have less improvement than that shown here (we use both datasets).

The next thing that needs to be examined is the relevance of the size of the invented dataset. The last columns in Table 3 show the results of the whole process with different random dataset sizes, from 100 to 100,000. As expected, that the greater the random dataset, the closer that the second-stage tree will be with respect to the oracle. Obviously, this has a price; the larger the random dataset, the slower the process. In practice, the optimal size of the random dataset depends on the problem; large training sets (in both number of examples and number of attributes) will require larger random datasets for good approximations. The generation and labelling of random datasets is usually a more efficient process than learning, and can be tuned to the system's resources quite comfortably. In what follows, we will use 10,000 random examples.

The previous results are remarkably positive, but a natural question arises. Are the single trees obtained in the second stage simple? Although a large decision tree can always be examined partially (top-down) and we can still extract

Table 3. Comparison of the size of the invented dataset for mimicking

#	1st	Comb	2nd 100	2nd 1000	2nd 10000	2nd 100000
1	95.2	100	97.3	99.5	99.9	99.9
2	71.0	76.5	72.3	75.4	76.1	76.0
3	97.5	97.9	97.5	97.8	97.8	97.9
4	77.1	82.1	77.8	79.1	82.5	82.1
5	94.7	95.7	94.7	95.3	95.5	95.7
6	93.8	94.9	93.7	93.8	94.5	94.9
7	99.6	99.4	99.6	99.5	99.4	99.4
8	75.8	81.7	77.6	80.4	79.5	81.4
9	77.9	82.6	78.6	81.3	82.9	82.4
10	92.0	92.9	92.6	92.3	92.5	92.7
11	60.6	63.1	62.5	62.7	63.3	62.7
12	94.1	95.5	93.9	94.5	94.7	95.3
13	93.0	93.0	90.4	91.5	92.4	92.7
14	74.1	76.8	74.8	76.8	76.8	76.8
15	48.3	49.7	48.2	48.9	49.1	49.4
16	78.5	83.2	78.3	80.2	81.8	82.1
gmeans	81.3	84.0	81.7	82.9	83.6	83.8

knowledge from it, it is quite clear that the simpler the tree the easier to be understood. In order to study this issue, the first four columns of Table 4 show the accuracy and size (number of rules) of a single tree ("1st"), as could be obtained without combination in a first stage and the accuracy and size of the second-stage tree ("2nd"). All these results are without pruning. According to these first columns, it is clear that the approximation to the oracle (the increase in accuracy) is obtained by increasing the size of the tree (from 70.9 mean number of rules to 252.9 number of rules). This is quite a pity, because although this tree is much better than the original tree, it is less comprehensible.

Nonetheless, a different portrait can be seen if we enable pruning (we have used Pessimistic Error Pruning, [23]). The next column ("1st-Pruning") shows the $best^3$ results when we enable pruning on the first-stage single tree. This is only shown for comparison, to realise that the difference with the mimetic classifier in size could even be larger (from 48.8 to 252.9) by using a traditional decision tree with pruning. The interesting thing comes, fortunately, when we use pruning on the mimetic classifier. The rightmost columns ("2nd-Pruning") show the results when pruning is enabled for the second-stage tree. In this case, and depending on the degree of pruning (0.7, 0.8 or 0.9), we see that we can obtain short trees with high accuracy, which was the motivation of this work (from 252.9 to 82.1 number of rules with similar accuracy).

Finally, in order to compare with the state of the art in ensemble methods, let us compare our results with the most successful ensemble methods: bagging and boosting. For that, we use the implementation of both included in the WEKA data mining package [28]. We have run bagging and boosting (ADA-Boost) with

---

[3] The best results for varying degrees of pruning.

Table 4. Comparison of the size of the models

#	1st Acc	1st Rules	2nd Acc	2nd Rules	1st-Pruning Acc	1st-Pruning Rules	$\frac{Acc}{(0.7)}$	$\frac{Rules}{(0.7)}$	$\frac{Acc}{(0.8)}$	$\frac{Rules}{(0.8)}$	$\frac{Acc}{(0.9)}$	$\frac{Rules}{(0.9)}$
1	95.2	87.0	99.9	55.0	95.2	86.6	100.0	60.9	100.0	60.9	100.0	60.8
2	71.0	278.5	76.1	284.1	68.2	242.6	75.8	285.6	75.8	285.6	74.8	271.8
3	97.5	37.1	97.8	38	99.1	14	97.9	20.5	98.2	19.5	98.7	14.9
4	77.1	338.7	82.5	823.5	77.6	250.0	81.3	398.1	81.3	210.3	77.5	44.5
5	94.7	48.5	95.5	316.0	95.8	17.8	95.9	61.2	95.8	30.0	95.8	7.3
6	93.8	43.2	94.5	248.7	94.0	35.6	94.7	91.4	94.5	54.4	92.9	21.8
7	99.6	47.9	99.4	113.8	99.6	46.3	99.3	52.9	99.1	39.6	97.7	23.5
8	75.8	80.7	79.5	974.7	79.6	19.3	79.7	670.4	79.7	664.4	79.2	663.7
9	77.9	139.0	82.9	142.7	78.2	126.6	82.9	142.7	82.9	142.4	82.6	119.9
10	92.0	19.1	92.5	192.6	92.3	17.2	92.4	181.6	92.4	178.9	91.9	176.3
11	60.6	63.8	63.3	483.5	61.3	57.3	61.1	325.6	59.1	267.5	55.3	195.8
12	94.1	11.2	94.7	71.0	93.8	10.6	94.8	37.1	94.7	27.1	94.5	17.0
13	93.0	14.5	92.4	453.9	92.8	14.0	92.5	175.9	92.2	85.7	90.6	27.6
14	74.1	44.0	76.8	48.8	74.3	32.7	76.8	48.6	76.8	48.6	76.6	48.4
15	48.3	929.6	49.1	2399.3	49.0	627.8	51.4	565.4	52.7	204.6	43.5	7.8
16	78.5	146.1	81.8	1310.0	82.1	64.8	83.1	42.3	82.2	8.9	76.3	2.8
gmeans	81.3	70.9	83.6	252.9	81.9	48.8	83.7	119.8	83.6	82.1	81.2	40.7

J4.8 (the Java version of C4.5) with their default parameters. Bagging was run without pruning and for boosting we enabled pruning. The results are shown in Table 5. The first two columns show the accuracy of J4.8 without pruning and with pruning. The next two columns show the results of 80 iterations of bagging[4] and 100 iterations of boosting. The final four columns show the results of SMILES with one tree (first-stage), with the combination of 100 trees (first-stage) and with the second-stage tree (mimicking with 10,000 random examples wrt. SMILES combination), without and with a slight pruning.

The results are quite encouraging. The technique presented in this paper is able to obtain single and short trees which are comparable or even excel the accuracy of the best current ensemble methods (83.7 vs. 82.4 and 83.8).

7   Conclusions

We have introduced a simple but effective method for obtaining highly accurate but still comprehensible models from evidence. The idea is based on two stages. In the first stage, we use whatever highly accurate but incomprehensible method (e.g. stacking, cascading, boosting, bagging, neural networks, support-vector machines, Bayesian methods, etc.) to learn an "oracle" that is employed for labelling a randomly generated dataset. In the second stage, this dataset (jointly with the original training dataset) is used to train a single decision tree,

---

[4] For more than 80 iterations WEKA ran out of memory.

Table 5. Comparison with state-of-the-art ensemble methods

#	J4.8 no prune	J4.8 pruning	Bagging 80	Boosting 100	SMILES 1	SMILES 100	SMILES 100-2nd	SMILES 100-2nd-0.7prune
1	95.1	98.4	100	99.5	95.2	100	99.9	100
2	62.7	64.1	67.0	82.2	71.0	76.5	76.1	75.8
3	98.7	98.9	98.9	97.9	97.5	97.9	97.8	97.9
4	79.1	80.3	83.8	82.6	77.1	82.1	82.5	81.3
5	95.5	96.5	96.6	95.1	94.7	95.7	95.5	95.9
6	94.1	94.5	96.3	96.7	93.8	94.9	94.5	94.7
7	99.4	99.4	99.4	99.6	99.6	99.4	99.4	99.3
8	79.0	79.2	82.6	84.7	75.8	81.7	79.5	79.7
9	79.4	77.7	82.9	76.0	77.9	82.6	82.9	82.9
10	93.0	93.1	94.9	95.3	92.0	92.9	92.5	92.4
11	56.5	55.7	60.7	64.8	60.6	63.1	63.3	61.1
12	94.6	94.7	94.3	94.5	94.1	95.5	94.7	94.8
13	93.5	93.4	95.9	96.9	93.0	93.0	92.4	92.5
14	72.5	74.2	56.1	65.9	74.1	76.8	76.8	76.8
15	50.0	52.0	52.7	50.4	48.3	49.7	49.1	51.4
16	83.2	81.5	83.1	81.5	78.5	83.2	81.8	83.1
gmeans	81.3	81.8	82.4	83.8	81.3	84.0	83.6	83.7

which is, as we have shown, almost as accurate as the "oracle". Pruning can be enabled to simplify the tree. No extra validation set is used during the process.

Our approach is different from stacking and cascading because we can use whatever "oracle" at the first layer to label the random dataset, which is later used to learn a single model that does not use the outputs of the previous layer as inputs of the following one and hence, it just uses the original attributes. It is also different and simpler than other "black-box" approaches [4,7,8] because any kind of classifier can be used for the first stage but also for the second stage. For instance, a rule learner or an ILP system could be used in the second stage.

Since any classifier can be used in either stage, we have shown that this idea of mimicking can be put into practice quite easily by using any data-mining package. Additionally, the technique has been automated into our system SMILES, which uses an ensemble of shared decision trees in the first stage and a simple decision tree learner in the second stage. This implementation has been used to thoroughly evaluate the method. We have shown that using the prior distribution for generating the random dataset is preferable over the uniform distribution. It has been empirically demonstrated that the size of the dataset is extremely important and that the size (in number of rules) of the second-stage classifier depends on it, but that it can be significantly reduced by using classical pruning techniques, maintaining its accuracy. We have shown that this single solution is extremely close to that of the combination (also better than other approaches, such as archetyping [14]). In comparison with other methods, the technique presented in this paper obtains, to our knowledge, the highest accuracy of existing comprehensible classifiers (decision trees and rule learners).

In this paper, we have concentrated on presenting the method and an experimental evaluation of the method. We refer to [13] for some theoretical results concerning the mimetic method. Some of these results are: first, we show that when all the arguments of the function to be learned are nominal, a sufficiently large random dataset allows a loyal mimetic classifier to capture exactly the semantics of the oracle, as expected. Secondly, and more interestingly, we show that if the function to be learned is probabilistcally pure (i.e. not fractal) and the classifier is loyal and fence-and-fill then for a sufficiently large random dataset then the error made by the the mimetic classifier will approach zero. From here, we particularise the results to decision trees, to problems with whatever combination of nominal and numerical attributes and also whatever discrete oracle (such as combined classifiers and neural networks), as the setting shown here.

As future work we would like to compare this technique (in terms of accuracy, fidelity and comprehensibility) with existing decompositional rule extraction techniques used to convert neural networks (or other incomprehensible models) into comprehensible models. On the other hand, although we have concentrated on classification, it is clear that a similar technique could also be used for regression models. The iteration of "mimicking", by using more stages or different partitions on the training dataset can also be studied in the future. Another open question is the automatic adaptation of the size of the invented dataset to the size of the problem. The generation of more refined random datasets can also be improved, especially for numerical attributes where the range of some attribute is not known a priori. In [13] we have also studied some theoretical issues on the generation of the dataset. In particular, it would be interesting that the method for generating the invented dataset is exhaustive.

Other scenarios could also be considered, such the use of existing unlabelled data. This situation is obviously better, since the given unlabelled data complements the training set prior distribution. Techniques from the field of learning from unlabelled labelled data and, especially from co-training, could be used here [3]. In fact, mimicking can be seen as an asymmetrical (i.e. one way) co-training where one of the two classifiers is considered much better than the other and where unlabelled data is generated rather than obtained from a pool. Some ideas, e.g., the notion of ranking the examples such as that more confident predictions are chosen first could also be used for the oracle-based random dataset in our mimetic framework. This is being investigated in [13].

As a more ambitious future work, we consider the use of query learning [1] directly to the oracle (in a wider sense than [7,8]), instead of using the random dataset, as a better way of "mimicking".

References

1. D. Angluin. Queries and concept learning. *Machine Learning*, 2:319, 1987.
2. C.L. Blake and C.J. Merz. UCI repository of machine learning databases, 1998.
3. A. Blum and T. Mitchell. Combining Labeled and Unlabeled Data with Co-Training. In *Proc. of the 1998 Conf. on Computational Learning Theory*, 1998.
4. O. Boz. Extracting decision trees from trained neural networks. In *8th ACM SIGKDD Intl. Conference on Knowledge Discovery and Data Mining*, 2002.
5. L. Breiman. Bagging predictors. *Machine Learning*, 24(2):123–140, 1996.
6. W. Buntine. Learning classification trees. In D.J. Hand, editor, *Artificial Intelligence frontiers in statistics*, pages 182–201. Chapman & Hall,London, 1993.
7. M.W. Craven. *Extracting Comprehensible Models from Trained Neural Networks*. PhD thesis, Dep. of Computer Sciences, University of Wisconsin-Madison, 1996.

8. M.W. Craven and J.W. Shavlik. Extracting tree-structured representations of trained networks. *Advances in Neural Information Processing*, 8, 1996.
9. T.G Dietterich. Ensemble methods in machine learning. In *First International Workshop on Multiple Classifier Systems*, pages 1–15, 2000.
10. T.G. Dietterich. An experimental comparison of three methods for constructing ensembles of decision trees: Bagging, Boosting, and Randomization. *Machine Learning*, 40(2):139–157, 2000.
11. V. Estruch, C. Ferri, J. Hernández, and M.J. Ramírez. Shared Ensembles using Multi-trees. In *8th Iberoamerican Conf. on Artificial Intelligence, Iberamia'02*, volume 2527 of *Lecture Notes in Computer Science*, pages 204–213, 2002.
12. V. Estruch, C. Ferri, J. Hernández, and M.J. Ramírez. Beam search extraction and forgetting strategies on shared ensembles. In *Fourth Workshop on Multiple Classifier Systems (MCS2003)*, volume to appear of *Lecture Notes in Computer Science*, 2003.
13. V. Estruch and J. Hernández. Theoretical Issues of Mimetic Classifiers. Technical report, Dep. Information Systems and Computation, Tech. Univ. Valencia, http://www.dsic.upv.es/~flip/, 2003.
14. C. Ferri, J. Hernández, and M.J. Ramírez. From Ensemble Methods to Comprehensible Models. In *The 5th Intl Conf on Discovery Science*, volume 2534 of *LNCS*, pages 164–177, 2002.
15. Y. Freund and R.E. Schapire. Experiments with a new boosting algorithm. In *Proc. 13th Intl Conf Machine Learning*, pages 148–146. Morgan Kaufmann, 1996.
16. J. Gama. Combining classifiers with constructive induction. In C. Nedellec and C. Rouveirol, editors, *Proc. of ECML-98*, volume 1398, pages 178–189, 1998.
17. J. Gama and P. Brazdil. Cascade Generalization. *Machine Learning*, 41(3):315–343, 2000.
18. T.K. Ho. C4.5 decision forests. In *Proc. of 14th Intl. Conf. on Pattern Recognition, Brisbane, Australia*, pages 545–549, 1998.
19. R. Kohavi and C. Kunz. Option decision trees with majority votes. In *Proc. 14th Intl. Conference on Machine Learning*, pages 161–169. Morgan Kaufmann, 1997.
20. D.D. Margineantu and T.G. Dietterich. Pruning adaptive boosting. In *14th Int. Conf. on Machine Learning*, pages 211–218. Morgan Kaufmann, 1997.
21. C.J. Merz. Using correspondence analysis to combine classifiers. *Machine Learning*, 36(1/2):33–58, 1999.
22. A.L. Prodromidis and S.J. Stolfo. Cost complexity-based pruning of ensemble classifiers. *Knowledge and Information Systems*, 3(4):449–469, 2001.
23. J.R. Quinlan. Simplifying decision trees. *International Journal of Man-Machine Studies*, 27(3):221–234, 1987.
24. J.R. Quinlan. *C4.5: Programs for Machine Learning*. Morgan Kaufmann, 1993.
25. J.R. Quinlan. Bagging, Boosting, and C4.5. In *Proc. 30th Natl. Conf. on AI and 8th Innovative Apps. of AI Conf.*, pages 725–730. AAAI Press / MIT Press, 1996.
26. J.R. Quinlan. Miniboosting decision trees. Submitted to JAIR, 1998.
27. B.W. Silverman. *Density Estimation for Statistics and Data Analysis*. Chapman and Hall, 1986.
28. I.H. Witten and E. Frank. *Data Mining: Practical Machine Learning Tools and Techniques with Java Implementations*. Morgan Kaufmann Publishers, 1999.
29. D.H. Wolpert. Stacked generalization. *Neural Networks*, 5(2):241–259, 1992.

Novel Mixtures Based on the Dirichlet Distribution: Application to Data and Image Classification

Nizar Bouguila, Djemel Ziou, and Jean Vaillancourt

DMI, Faculté des Sciences
Université de Sherbrooke
Sherbrooke, Qc, Canada J1K 2R1
{bouguila,ziou,jean.vaillancourt}@dmi.usherb.ca

Abstract. The Dirichlet distribution offers high flexibility for modeling data. This paper describes two new mixtures based on this density: the GDD (Generalized Dirichlet Distribution) and the MDD (Multinomial Dirichlet Distribution) mixtures. These mixtures will be used to model continuous and discrete data, respectively. We propose a method for estimating the parameters of these mixtures. The performance of our method is tested by contextual evaluations. In these evaluations we compare the performance of Gaussian and GDD mixtures in the classification of several pattern-recognition data sets and we apply the MDD mixture to the problem of summarizing image databases.

1 Introduction

Scientific pursuits and human activity in general generate data. These data may be incomplete, redundant or erroneous. Probabilistic methods are particularly useful in understanding the patterns present in such data. One such methods is the Bayesian approach which can be roughly described as estimating the uncertainty of a model. In fact, by the Bayesian approach we can estimate the uncertainty of a model's fit and the uncertainty of the estimated parameters themselves. The Bayesian approach can be employed with mixture models, which have been used extensively to model a wide variety of important practical situations where data can be viewed as arising from several populations mixed in varying proportions. Nowadays, this kind of statistical model is used in a variety of domains. The problem of estimating the parameters of the components of a mixture has been the subject of diverse studies [6]. The isotropic nature of Gaussian functions, along with their capability for representing the distribution compactly by a mean vector and covariance matrix, have made Gaussian Mixture Decomposition (GM) a popular technique. The Gaussian mixture is not the best choice in all applications, however, and it will fail to discover *true* structure where the partitions are clearly non-Gaussian [12]. In this paper we will show that the Dirichlet distribution can be a very good choice to overcome the disadvantages of the Gaussian. The Dirichlet distribution is the multivariate generalization of the Beta distribution, which offers considerable flexibility and ease

P. Perner and A. Rosenfeld (Eds.): MLDM 2003, LNAI 2734, pp. 172–181, 2003.

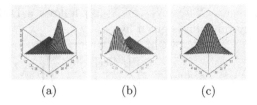

(a)   (b)   (c)

Fig. 1. The Dirichlet distribution for different parameters. (a) $\alpha_1 = 8.5$, $\alpha_2 = 7.5$, $\alpha_3 = 1.5$. (b) $\alpha_1 = 10.5$, $\alpha_2 = 3.5$, $\alpha_3 = 3.5$. (c) $\alpha_1 = 3.5$, $\alpha_2 = 3.5$, $\alpha_3 = 3.5$

of use. In contrast with other distributions such as the Gaussian, which permit only symmetric modes, the Dirichlet distribution is highly flexible and permit multiple symmetric and asymmetric modes. In fact, the Dirichlet distribution may be skewed to the right, skewed to the left or symmetric (see Fig. 1).

For all these reasons, we are interested in the Dirichlet distribution. In contrast to the vast amount of theoretical work that exists on the Dirichlet distribution, however, very little work has been done on its practical applications, such as parameter estimation. This neglect may be due to the fact that this distribution is unfamiliar to many scientists.

The paper is organized as follows. The next section describes the GDD and MDD mixtures in details. In Sect. 3, we propose a method for estimating the parameters of these mixtures. In Sect. 4, we present a way of initializing the parameters and give the complete estimation algorithm. Section 5 is devoted to experimental results. We end the paper with some concluding remarks.

2   The Generalized Dirichlet and the Multinomial Dirichlet Mixtures

Let $(X_1, \ldots, X_N)$ denote a collection of N data in a heterogenous database. Each data X_i is assumed to have *dim* different attributes, $X_i = (X_{i1}, \ldots, X_{idim})$. In general the various attributes could be either discrete or continous (variables). Generally, the goal of analysis will be to group data into homogenous classes in a probabilistic way. To accomplish this, each data X_i is assumed to be drawn from the following finite mixture model:

$$p(\boldsymbol{X}/\Theta) = \sum_{j=1}^{M} p(\boldsymbol{X}/j, \Theta_j) P(j) \tag{1}$$

where M is the number of components, the $P(j)$ ($0 < P(j) < 1$ and $\sum_{j=1}^{dim} P(j) = 1$) are the mixing proportions and $p(\boldsymbol{X}/j, \Theta_j)$ is the PDF (Probability Density Function). The symbol Θ refers to the set of parameters to be estimated: $\Theta = (\boldsymbol{\alpha_1}, \ldots, \boldsymbol{\alpha_M}, P(1), \ldots, P(M))$ where $\boldsymbol{\alpha_j}$ is the parameter vector for the jth population. In the following developments, we use the notation $\Theta_j = (\boldsymbol{\alpha_j}, P(j))$ for j = 1 ... M. In the following, we present two PDF: the GDD for continous attributes and the MDD for discrete ones.

If the random vector $\boldsymbol{X} = (X_1, \ldots, X_{dim})$ follows a Dirichlet distribution [11] the joint density function is given by:

$$p(X_1, \ldots, X_{dim}) = \frac{\Gamma(|\boldsymbol{\alpha}|)}{\prod_{i=1}^{dim+1} \Gamma(\alpha_i)} \prod_{i=1}^{dim+1} X_i^{\alpha_i - 1} \qquad (2)$$

where $\sum_{i=1}^{dim} X_i < 1$, $0 < X_i < 1$ $\forall i = 1 \ldots dim$, $X_{dim+1} = 1 - \sum_{i=1}^{dim} X_i$, $|\boldsymbol{\alpha}| = \sum_{i=1}^{dim+1} \alpha_i$ and $\alpha_i > 0$ $\forall i = 1 \ldots dim + 1$. This distribution is the multivariate extension of the 2-parameter Beta distribution. The mean and the variance of the Dirichlet distribution are given by:

$$E(X_i) = \frac{\alpha_i}{|\boldsymbol{\alpha}|} \qquad (3)$$

$$Var(X_i) = \frac{\alpha_i(|\boldsymbol{\alpha}| - \alpha_i)}{|\boldsymbol{\alpha}|^2(|\boldsymbol{\alpha}| + 1)} \qquad (4)$$

The Dirichlet distribution can be represented either as a distribution on the hyperplane $B_{dim+1} = \{(X_1, \ldots, X_{dim+1}), \sum_{i=1}^{dim+1} X_i = 1\}$ in $\mathbb{R}_+^{dim+1}$, or as a distribution inside the simplex $A_{dim} = \{(X_1, \ldots, X_{dim}), \sum_{i=1}^{dim} X_i < 1\}$ in $\mathbb{R}_+^{dim}$. This simplex represents a real handicap for us. Indeed, we can't be sure that the data we use will be inside it (between 0 and 1). Here, we propose a distribution which we call the GDD in order to overcome this problem. Thus, if the random vector $\boldsymbol{X} = (X_1, \ldots, X_{dim})$ follows a GDD with parameter vector $\boldsymbol{\alpha} = (\alpha_1, \ldots, \alpha_{dim+1})$, the joint density function is given by :

$$p(X_1, \ldots, X_{dim}) = \frac{\Gamma(|\boldsymbol{\alpha}|)}{A^{|\boldsymbol{\alpha}| - 1} \prod_{i=1}^{dim+1} \Gamma(\alpha_i)} \prod_{i=1}^{dim+1} X_i^{\alpha_i - 1} \qquad (5)$$

This density is defined in the simplex $\{(X_1, \ldots, X_{dim}), \sum_{i=1}^{dim} X_i < A\}$, and we have: $X_{dim+1} = A - \sum_{i=1}^{dim} X_i$.

Let $\boldsymbol{X} = (X_1, \ldots, X_{dim+1})$ a vector indicating the frequency of a given feature (a word for example) in a document where X_i is the number of times the feature i occurs. The vector $\boldsymbol{X}$ follows a Multinomial distribution with parameter vector $\boldsymbol{P} = (P_1, \ldots, P_{dim+1})$ given by:

$$p(\boldsymbol{X}/\boldsymbol{P}) = \prod_{k=1}^{dim+1} P_k^{X_k} \qquad (6)$$

Where: $P_k > 0$ $\forall k = 1 \ldots dim + 1$ and $\sum_{k=1}^{dim+1} P_k = 1$. The conjugate prior for $\boldsymbol{P}$ is the dirichlet distribution. Given a Dirichlet prior, the joint density is:

$$p(\boldsymbol{P}) \sim p(\boldsymbol{X}, \boldsymbol{P}/\boldsymbol{\alpha}) = p(\boldsymbol{X}/\boldsymbol{P})p(\boldsymbol{P}/\boldsymbol{\alpha}) = \frac{\Gamma(|\boldsymbol{\alpha}|)}{\prod_{k=1}^{dim+1} \Gamma(\alpha_k)} \prod_{k=1}^{dim+1} P_k^{X_k + \alpha_k - 1} \qquad (7)$$

then:

$$p(\boldsymbol{X}/\boldsymbol{\alpha}) = \int_P p(\boldsymbol{X}, \boldsymbol{P}/\boldsymbol{\alpha}) = \frac{\Gamma(|\boldsymbol{\alpha}|)}{\Gamma(\sum_{k=1}^{dim+1} X_k + |\boldsymbol{\alpha}|)} \prod_{k=1}^{dim+1} \frac{\Gamma(X_k + \alpha_k)}{\Gamma(\alpha_k)} \qquad (8)$$

We call this density the MDD.

3   Maximum Likelihood Estimation

The problem of estimating the parameters which determine a mixture has been the subject of diverse studies. During the last two decades, the method of maximum likelihood (ML) has become the most common followed approach to this problem. Of the variety of iterative methods which have been suggested as alternatives to optimize the parameters of a mixture, one most widely used is the Expectation Maximization (EM). The EM was originally proposed by Dempster et al. [4] for estimating the Maximum Likelihood Estimator (MLE) of stochastic models. This algorithm gives us an iterative procedure and the practical form is usually very simple. The EM algorithm can be viewed as an approximation of Fisher scoring method [8]. A maximum likelihood estimate associated with a sample of observations is a choice of parameters which maximizes the probability density function of the sample. Thus, with ML estimation, the problem of determining Θ becomes:

$$max_\Theta p(\boldsymbol{X}/\Theta) \qquad (9)$$

with the constraint: $\sum_{j=1}^M P(j) = 1$ and $P(j) > 0 \quad \forall j \in [1, M]$ (this constraint is satisfied). These constraints permit us to take into consideration a priori probabilities $P(j)$. Using Lagrange multipliers, we maximize the following function:

$$\Phi(\boldsymbol{X}, \Theta, \Lambda) = ln(p(\boldsymbol{X}/\Theta)) + \Lambda(1 - \sum_{i=1}^M P(i)) \qquad (10)$$

where Λ is the Lagrange multiplier. For convenience, we have replaced the function $p(\boldsymbol{X}/\Theta)$ in Eq. 9 by the function $ln(p(\boldsymbol{X}/\Theta))$. If we assume that we have N random vector $\boldsymbol{X}_i$ which are independent, we can write: $p(\boldsymbol{X}/\Theta) = \prod_{i=1}^N p(\boldsymbol{X}_i/\Theta)$ and $p(\boldsymbol{X}_i/\Theta) = \sum_{j=1}^M p(\boldsymbol{X}_i/j, \Theta_j)P(j)$. Replacing these equations, we obtain:

$$\Phi(\boldsymbol{X}, \Theta, \Lambda) = \sum_{i=1}^N ln(\sum_{j=1}^M p(\boldsymbol{X}_i/j, \Theta_j)P(j)) + \Lambda(1 - \sum_{j=1}^M P(j)) \qquad (11)$$

We will now try to resolve this optimization problem. To do this, we must determine the solution to the following equations: $\frac{\partial}{\partial \Theta}\Phi = 0$ and $\frac{\partial}{\partial \Lambda}\Phi = 0$. Calculating the derivative with respect to Θ_j, we obtain [2]:

$$\frac{\partial}{\partial \Theta_j}\Phi(\boldsymbol{X}, \Theta, \Lambda) = \sum_{i=1}^N p(j/\boldsymbol{X}_i, \Theta_j)\frac{\partial}{\partial \Theta_j}ln(p(\boldsymbol{X}_i/j, \Theta_j)) \qquad (12)$$

where $p(j/\boldsymbol{X_i}, \Theta_j)$ is the posterior probability. Since $p(\boldsymbol{X_i}/j, \boldsymbol{\alpha_j})$ is independent of $P(j)$, straight forward manipulations yield [2]:

$$P(j) = \frac{1}{N} \sum_{i=1}^{N} p(j/\boldsymbol{X_i}, \boldsymbol{\alpha_j}) \tag{13}$$

In order to estimate the $\boldsymbol{\alpha}$ parameters we will use Fisher's scoring method. This approach is a variant of the Newton-Raphson [13] method. The scoring method is based on the first, second and mixed derivatives of the log-likelihood function. Thus, we have computed these derivatives [2]. During iterations, the α_{jl} can become negative. In order to overcome this problem, we reparametrize, setting $\alpha_{jl} = e^{\beta_{jl}}$, where β_{jl} is an unconstrained real number. Given a set of initial estimates, Fisher's scoring method can now be used. The iterative scheme of the Fisher method is given by the following equation:

$$\hat{\boldsymbol{\beta}}_j^{new} = \hat{\boldsymbol{\beta}}_j^{old} + V^{old} \times \frac{\partial \phi}{\partial \hat{\beta}_j}^{old} \tag{14}$$

Where $\frac{\partial \phi}{\partial \hat{\beta}_j} = \begin{pmatrix} \frac{\partial}{\partial \hat{\beta}_{j1}} \Phi \\ \vdots \\ \frac{\partial}{\partial \hat{\beta}_{j\,dim+1}} \Phi \end{pmatrix}$ and j is the class number.

The variance-covariance matrix V is obtained as the inverse of the Fisher's information matrix $\mathbf{I} = I_{l_1 l_2} = -E[\frac{\partial^2}{\partial \beta_{jl_1} \partial \beta_{jl_2}} \Phi(\boldsymbol{X}, \Theta, \Lambda)]$. Comparing this iterative scheme based on Fisher's scoring method with a quasi-Newton method presented by the following equation [5]:

$$\beta_{jl}^{new} := \beta_{jl}^{old} - \eta \frac{\partial}{\partial \beta_{jl}} \Phi(\boldsymbol{X}, \Theta, \Lambda) \tag{15}$$

where $0 < \eta \leq 1$. we can note that the ordinary gradient $\frac{\partial \phi}{\partial \beta_l}$ is replaced by the term $V \times \frac{\partial \phi}{\partial \beta_l}$, which is called the *Natural Gradient* or *Contravariant Gradient* by Amari [1]. The relation between the natural gradient $\frac{\breve{\partial} \phi}{\partial \beta_l}$ and the ordinary gradient is given by the following equation [1]: $\frac{\breve{\partial} \phi}{\partial \beta_l} = G^{-1} \frac{\partial \phi}{\partial \beta_l}$, where G is the Fisher information matrix. The natural gradient is used where the coordinate system is nonorthonormal. In our case the parameter space is Riemmanian because of the exponential nature of the GDD and the MDD [2]. Thus, the coordinate system is nonorthonormal. Note that G is reduced to the unit matrix in the orthonormal case. This result was confirmed by experiments. Indeed, we have implemented these two methods and observed that the method given by Eq. 15 does not give good results compared with the Fisher scoring method.

4   Initialization and Convergence Test

In order to make our algorithm less sensitive to local maxima, we have used some initialization schemes including the Fuzzy C-means and the method of moments

(MM). In fact, the method of moments gives really good estimations because of the compact support of the Dirichlet distribution. From an examination of Eq. 3 and Eq. 4 we see that there are first dim first-order moments and dim second-order moments, yielding a total of $C_{dim+1}^{2(dim+1)}$ possible combinations of equations to solve for the dim parameters. According to Fieltiz and Myers [7] a symmetrical way of proceeding would be to choose the first dim first-order equations and the first second-order equation. The reason for not choosing the $(dim + 1)$-th first order equation is that the $(dim + 1)$-th equation is a linear combination of the others and together they do not form an independent set of equations. Thus we have:

$$\alpha_l = \frac{(x'_{11} - x'_{21})x'_{1l}}{x'_{21} - (x'_{11})^2} \quad l = 1, 2 \ldots, dim \text{ and } \alpha_{dim+1} = \frac{(x'_{11} - x'_{21})(1 - \sum_{l=1}^{dim} x'_{1l})}{x'_{21} - (x'_{11})^2} \text{ , where}$$

$$x'_{1l} = \frac{1}{N} \sum_{i=1}^{N} \frac{X_{il}}{\sum_{k=1}^{dim+1} X_{ik}} \quad l = 1, 2 \ldots, dim + 1 \text{ and } x'_{21} = \frac{1}{N} \sum_{i=1}^{N} \frac{X_{i1}^2}{(\sum_{k=1}^{dim+1} X_{ik})^2}$$

Thus, our initialization method can be resumed as follows (we suppose that the number of clusters M is known):

INITIALIZATION Algorithm

1. Apply the Fuzzy C-means to obtain the elements, covariance matrix and mean of each component.
2. Apply the MM for each component j to obtain the vector of parameters α_j.
3. Assign the data to clusters, assuming that the current model is correct.
4. If the current model and the new model are sufficiently close to each other, terminate, else go to 2.

We can readily note that this initialization algorithm take the distribution into account. In contrast to the *classic* initialization methods which use only algorithms such as K-means to obtain the initialization parameters, we have introduced the method of moments with an iterative scheme to refine the results. By using the method of moments, we suppose from the outset that we have a GDD or a MDD mixture. This initialization method is designed to work on large databases. When working on small data sets, applying the Fuzzy C-means and the MM only once is a feasible option. With this initialization method in hand, our algorithm for estimating of GDD or MDD mixtures can be summarized as follows:

GDD/MDD MIXTURE ESTIMATION Algorithm

1. INPUT: data X_i, $i = 1, \ldots, N$ and the number of clusters M.
2. INITIALIZATION Algorithm.
3. Update the α_j using Eq. 14, $j = 1, \ldots, M$.
4. Update the $P(j)$ using Eq. 13, $j = 1, \ldots, M$.
5. If the convergence test is passed, terminate, else go to 3.

The convergence tests could involve testing the stabilization of the β_j or the value of the maximum likelihood function.

5   Experimental Results

In this section, we validate the GDD and the MDD mixtures by pattern recognition and computer vision applications. In the pattern recognition application, our method was used to model the class-conditional densities in four standard pattern recognition data sets which differ in dimension, size and complexity. The classification was performed using the Bayes rule (X_i is assigned to class j_1 if $P(j_1)p(x_i/j_1) > P(j)p(x_i/j), \forall j \neq j_1$) after the class-conditional densities have been estimated. The goal of this application is also to compare the modeling capabilities of GDD and Gaussian mixture. We have used the EM algorithm to estimate the parameters of Gaussian mixtures. The comparison will be based essentially on errors of classification, error of fit and number of iterations in each case. We begin with two examples which are reported in [3]. The first data set describes an enzymatic activity distribution in the blood and the second one an acidity index distribution for 155 lakes. For these two data sets, a mixture of 2 distributions is identified [3]. Figures 2 and 3 show the real and the estimated histograms for the Enzyme and Acidity data sets, respectively. In both cases, it's clear that the GDD and the Gaussian fit the data. We also compared the likelihood cycle of the Gaussian and the GDD. According to this comparison our algorithm converges in a smaller number of iterations (9 for the Enzyme data set and 14 for the Acidity set) compared to the case where Gaussian mixture was considered (17 for the Enzyme data set and 20 for the Acidity set). Our algorithm was also validated with multidimensional data sets. We took two well-known examples, the Ruspini and Wisconsin Breast Cancer data sets [9]. We chose these data sets for their specific characteristics. The Ruspini data set

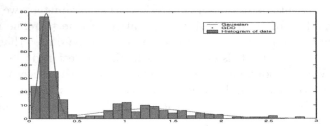

Fig. 2. Real and estimated histograms for the Enzyme data set

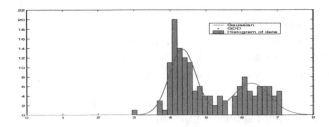

Fig. 3. Real and estimated histograms for the acidity data set

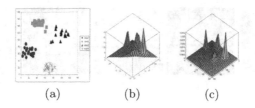

(a)   (b)   (c)

Fig. 4. (a) The Ruspini data set . (b) Representation of the Ruspini data set by a GDD mixture. (c) Representation of the Ruspini data set by a Gaussian mixture

contains two-dimensional data in four groups (see Fig. 4) and the Breast Cancer data set is characterized by its size (683 patterns) and its dimension (9). For both examples, the comparison between the GDD and the Gaussian mixtures is based on the errors of classification. By using the GDD mixture for the Ruspini data, we reached convergence in 10 iterations with an error of 1.33 percent. This is slightly better than the result found for the Gaussian mixture (an error of 2.66 percent in 11 iterations). We also plotted the results. In each case we can clearly observe the presence of 4 classes (see Fig. 4). The GDD also gave better results (an error of 1.024 percent) for the Breast Cancer data, compared with the Gaussian mixture (an error of 2.342 percent).

The second validation concerns the summarization of image databases. This application is very important especially in the case of content-based image retrieval. Summarizing the database simplifies the task of retrieval by restricting the search for similar images to a smaller domain of the database. Summarization is also very efficient for browsing. Knowing the categories of images in a given database allows the user to find the images he is looking for more quickly. Using mixture decomposition, we can find natural groupings of images and represent each group by the most representative image in the group. In other words, after appropriate features are extracted from the images, it allows us to partition the feature space into regions that are relatively homogeneous, with respect to the chosen set of features. By identifying the homogeneous regions in the feature space, the task of summarization is accomplished. We used a database containing 900 images of size 128×96, and took color as a feature for categorizing the images. In order to determine the vector of characteristics for each image, pixels were projected onto the $3D$ HSI (H = Hue, S = Saturation, and I = Intensity) space. We thus obtained a $3D$ color histogram for each image. Based on the work of Kherfi et al. [10], we obtained an $8D$ vector from this histogram. Their method consists of partitioning the space by subdividing each of the axes H, S and I into n equal intervals. This gives n^3 subspaces. The sum of the elements in each subspace is computed and the result is placed in the corresponding cell of the feature vector. In our application, we chose $n = 2$, so each image was represented by a $2^3 = 8D$ feature vector of frequency. We also asked a human subject to determine the number of groups, and he found five categories (see Fig. 5). After the feature were extracted from the images, the MDD mixture algorithm was applied to the feature vectors by specifying five classes, where each vector

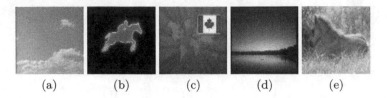

(a)   (b)   (c)   (d)   (e)

Fig. 5. Sample images from each group. (a) Class1, (b) Class2, (c) Class3, (d) Class4, (e) Class5.

Table 1. Confusion matrix for image classification by a MDD mixture

	Class1	Class2	Class3	Class4	Class5
Class1	170	0	2	0	0
Class2	0	195	0	18	7
Class3	0	0	122	0	0
Class4	0	8	0	102	4
Class5	0	3	0	6	263

represents an image. The two classifications (the one generated by the human subject and the one given by our algorithm) were compared by counting the number of misclassified images, yielding the confusion matrix (see Table 1). In this confusion matrix, the cell ($classi, classj$) represents the number of images from $classi$ which are classified as $classj$. The number of images misclassified was small: 48 images, which represents an accuracy of 94.66 percent.

6   Conclusion

In this paper, we have introduced two new mixtures, based on the Dirichlet distribution, that we call the GDD and the MDD. The GDD has the advantage that by varying its parameters, it permits multiple modes and asymmetry and can thus approximate a wide variety of shapes. The MDD is very efficient to model frequency vectors. We estimated the parameters of these mixtures using the maximum likelihood and Fisher's scoring methods. An interesting interpretation, based on the statistical geometric information, was given. Experiments involved real data classification and summarization of image databases. Other applications such as videos summarizing and text modeling can be done. Althoug the number of densities is assumed to be known in this paper, it may be estimated during the interation by using one of the traditional criteria such as Akaike, Schwarz, or the minimum description length.

Aknowledegment. The completion of this research was made possible thanks to Bell Canada's support through its Bell University Laboratories R&D program.

References

1. Amari, S. Natural Gradient Works Efficiently in Learning. *Neural Computation*, 10:251–276, 1998.
2. Bouguila, N., Ziou, D. and Vaillancourt, J. The Introduction of Dirichlet Mixture into Image Processing Applications. Submitted to. *IEEE Transactions on Image Processing*.
3. Crawford, S.L. An Application of the Laplace Method to Finite Mixture Distributions. *Journal of the American Statistical Association*, 89:259–267, 1994.
4. Dempster, A.P., Laird, N.M. and Rubin, D.B. Maximum Likelihood from Incomplete Data via the EM Algorithm. *Journal of the Royal Statistical Society, B*, 39:1–38, 1977.
5. Duda, R.O. and Hart, P.E. *Pattern Classification and Scene Analysis*. Wiley, New York, 1973.
6. Everitt, B.S. and Hand, D.J. *Finite mixture Distributions*. Chapman and Hall, London, UK, 1981.
7. Fielitz, B.D and Myers, B.L. Estimation of Parameters in the Beta Distribution. *Decision Sciences*, 6:1–13, 1975.
8. Ikeda, S. Acceleration of the EM algorithm. *Systems and Computers in Japan*, 31(2):10–18, February 2000.
9. Kaufman, L. and Rousseeuw, P.J. *Finding Groups in Data*. John Wiley, New York, 1990.
10. Kherfi, M.L., Ziou, D. and Bernardi, A. Content-Based Image Retrieval Using Positive and Negative Examples. *To appear*, 2002.
11. Kotz, S. and Ng, K.W. and Fang, K. *Symmetric Multivariate and Related Distributions*. London/New York: Chapman and Hall, 1990.
12. Raftery, A.E. and Banfield, J.D. Model-Based Gaussian and Non-Gaussian Clustering. *Biometrics*, 49:803–821, 1993.
13. Rao, C.R. *Advanced Statistical Methods in Biomedical Research*. New York: John Wiley and Sons, 1952.

Estimating a Quality of Decision Function by Empirical Risk

Victor Mikhailovich Nedel'ko

Institute of Mathematics SB RAS, Laboratory of Data Analysis
660090 Novosibirsk, Russia
nedelko@math.nsc.ru
http://math.nsc.ru/LBRT/i1/nedelko/index.html

Abstract. The work is devoted to a problem of statistical robustness of deciding functions, or risk estimation. By risk we mean some measure of decision function prediction quality, for example, an error probability. For the case of discrete "independent" variable the dependence of average risk on empirical risk for the "worst" distribution ("strategies of nature") is obtained. The result gives exact value of empirical risk bias that allows evaluating an accuracy of Vapnik–Chervonenkis risk estimations. To find a distribution providing maximum of empirical risk bias one need to solve an optimization problem on function space. The problem being very complicate in general case appears to be solvable when the "independent" feature is a space of isolated points. The space has low practical use but it allows scaling well-known estimations by Vapnik and Chervonenkis.

1 Introduction

There is well known fact that decision function quality being evaluated by the training sample appears much better than its real quality. To get true risk estimation in data mining one uses a testing sample or moving test. But these methods have some disadvantages. The first one decreases a volume of sample available for building a decision function. The second one takes extra computational resources and is unable to estimate risk dispersion.

So one needs a method that allows estimating a risk by training sample directly, i.e. by an empirical risk. This requires estimating first an empirical risk bias.

The problem was solved by Vapnik and Chervonenkis [1]. They introduced a concept of capacity (growth function) of a decision rules set. This approach is quite powerful, but provides pessimistic decision quality estimations. Obtained bias estimation is very rough, because of performed by authors replacement of a probability of a sum of compatible events by the sum of its probabilities.

The goal of this paper is to evaluate an accuracy of these estimations. We shall consider a case of discrete feature that allows obtaining an exact value of empirical risk bias.

P. Perner and A. Rosenfeld (Eds.): MLDM 2003, LNAI 2734, pp. 182–187, 2003.

2 Problem Definition

Let X be an "independent" variable values space, Y – a goal space of forecasting values and C – a set of probabilistic measures on $D = X \times Y$.

A measure $c \in C$ will be denoted as $P_c[D]$.

Hereinafter, square parentheses will hold a set on which σ-algebra of subsets the measure is assigned, but round parentheses will hold a set which measure (probability of event) is taken.

Assume also $\forall x \in X$ an existence of conditional measures $P_c[Y/x]$.

A deciding function is a correspondence $f : X \to Y$.

For the determination of deciding functions quality one need to assign a function of losses:

$$L : Y^2 \to [0, \infty).$$

By a risk we shall understand an average loss:

$$R(c, f) = \int L(y, f(x)) \; dP_c[D] = \int R_x(c, f) \; dP_c[X],$$

where $R_x(c, f) = \int L(y, f(x)) \; dP_c[Y/x]$.

To build a deciding function there is a random independent sample $v_c = \left\{ (x^i, y^i) \in D \mid i \in \overline{1, N} \right\}$ from distribution $P_c[D]$ used.

An empirical risk means sample risk estimation: $\tilde{R}(v, f) = \frac{1}{N} \sum_{i=1}^{N} L\left(y^i, f(x^i)\right)$.

For the all practically used algorithms building deciding functions an empirical risk appears to be a biased risk estimation, being always lowered, as far as algorithms minimize an empirical risk.

Consider a problem of this offset evaluation.

Let's use indications:

$$F(c, Q) = E\, R(c, f_{Q,v}), \quad \tilde{F}(c, Q) = E\, \tilde{R}(c, f_{Q,v}).$$

Here $Q : \{v\} \to \{f\}$ is an algorithm of building deciding functions, and $f_{Q,v}$ – deciding function built on the sample v by algorithm Q.

Expectation is calculated over all samples of volume N.

Define a function of the most offset:

$$S_Q\left(\tilde{F}_0\right) = \hat{F}_Q\left(\tilde{F}_0\right) - \tilde{F}_0, \tag{1}$$

where $\hat{F}_Q\left(\tilde{F}_0\right) = \sup_{c : \tilde{F}(c, Q) = \tilde{F}_0} F(c, Q)$.

The main result of the work consists in finding the dependency $S_Q\left(\tilde{F}_0\right)$ for the case of discrete X and Q that minimizes an empirical risk in each $x \in X$.

3 Discrete Case

Let X be discrete, i. e. $X = \{1,\ldots,n\}$.

Then $R(c,f) = \sum_{x=1}^{n} p_x R_x(\xi_x, f(x))$, where $R_x(\xi_x, f) = \int L(y, f(x)) \; dP_c[Y/x]$

– a conditional risk in the point x, $p_x = P_c(x)$, ξ_x – a short indication of conditional measure $P_c[Y/x]$.

Let the deciding function minimize an empirical risk:

$$f_v^*(x) = \arg\min_{y \in Y} \tilde{L}(y, v_x),$$

where $\tilde{L}(y, v_x) = \frac{1}{N_x} \sum_{v_x} L(y, y^i)$,. $N_x = |v_x|$, v_x – a subset of sample that falls to the value x.

Determine values that average risks depend on:

$$F(c,Q) = E R(c, f_v^*) = \sum_{x=1}^{n} F_x(p_x, \xi_x), \text{ where } F_x(p_x, \xi_x) = p_x \, E R_x(\xi_x, f_{v_x}^*(x)).$$

Similarly

$$\tilde{F}(c,Q) = \frac{1}{N} \, E \tilde{L}(v, f_v^*) = \sum_{x=1}^{n} \tilde{F}_x(p_x, \xi_x), \text{ where } F_x(p_x, \xi_x) = E \tilde{L}_x(v_x, f_{v_x}^*(x)).$$

Introduce the function

$$\hat{F}_x\left(p_x, \tilde{F}_x^0\right) = \sup_{\xi_x : \tilde{F}_x(p_x, \xi_x) = \tilde{F}_x^0} F_x(p_x, \xi_x).$$

Now

$$\hat{F}_Q\left(\tilde{F}_0\right) = \max \sum_{x=1}^{n} \hat{F}_x\left(p_x, \tilde{F}_x^0\right), \tag{2}$$

where maximum is taken over the all p_x and $\tilde{F}_x^0$, $x = \overline{1,n}$, with restrictions:

$$p_x \geq 0, \; \tilde{F}_x^0 \geq 0, \; \sum_{x=1}^{n} p_x = 1, \; \sum_{x=1}^{n} \tilde{F}_x^0 = \tilde{R}_0.$$

Initial extreme problem is rather simplified, being split into two stages: finding $\hat{F}_x\left(p_x, \tilde{F}_x^0\right)$ and finding the maximum of function on the simple area of Euclid space.

Function $\hat{F}_x\left(p_x, \tilde{F}_x^0\right)$ may be easily approximated by digital computation.

However it is impossible to decide a problem (2) directly by digital methods, because the dimensionality of space on which the maximization performed is $2n$ where n may be great (twenty and the more).

4   Deciding the Extreme Problem

Let's reformulate a problem (2) in abstract indications:

$$\sum_{x=1}^{n} \Phi\left(z^x\right) \rightarrow \max_{z^x},$$ (3)

$$z^x = \left(z_1^x,...,z_m^x\right), \; z_j^x \geq 0, \; \sum_{x=1}^{n} z_j^x = 1, \; j = \overline{1,m}.$$

In (2) Φ corresponds to $\hat{F}_x$, $m = 2$, $z_1^x = p_x$, $z_2^x = \dfrac{\tilde{F}_x^0}{\tilde{F}_0}$.

Suppose a space of values of vector z^x to be discrete: $z^x \in \left\{t^1,...,t^l\right\}$.

Then problem (3) now may be put in the equivalent form:

$$\sum_{i=1}^{l} \Phi\left(t^i\right) \kappa^i \rightarrow \max_{\kappa^i},$$ (4)

$$\kappa^i \geq 0, \; \sum_{i=1}^{l} t_j^i \kappa^i = 1, \; j = \overline{1,m}, \; \sum_{i=1}^{l} \kappa^i = 1, \text{ where } \kappa^i \in \left\{ \dfrac{v}{n} \;\middle|\; v = \overline{0,n} \right\}.$$

Solve a problem without the last restriction on κ^i.

This is a linear programming problem which decision is certain vertex of area of arguments values. That means that only $m+1$ of κ^i-s are to be nonzero.

Now it is easy to show that the effect of discreteness κ^i restriction has an order $\frac{m}{n}$ and one may neglect it.

As far as the conclusion on the number of nonzero κ^i-s does not depend on the step of sampling a space of values of vector z^x, the result may be spread on the initial problem.

Theorem 1. A decision of problem (3) includes (uses) not more then $m+1$ different vectors.

Thereby the dimensionality of space that maximizing is performed on decreases to $m(m+1)$. Applying to the problem (2) this comprises 6, and problem may be easily solved numerically.

5   Results

Offered method allows finding a dependency $S_Q\left(\tilde{F}_0\right)$ under any parameters n and N. However there is the most demonstrative and suitable for the comparison with other approaches the asymptotic case: $\frac{N}{n} = M = \text{const}$, $N \rightarrow \infty$, $n \rightarrow \infty$.

Considered approach is wholly acceptable already under $n = 10$, herewith it has only one input parameter M.

For an illustration consider a problem of classification (k classes).

Function of losses will be:

$$L(y,y') = \begin{cases} 0, & y = y' \\ 1, & y \neq y' \end{cases}.$$

The function $\hat{F}_x\left(p_x, \tilde{F}_x^0\right)$ was estimated digitally by generating a random ξ_x, or the conditional distribution $P_c[Y/x]$. Instead of random generating ξ_x one may use a regular grid.

Conditional distribution ξ_x is now discrete and may be assigned by k parameters (probabilities for each class). In accordance with uniform distribution on the set of parameters let's throw ξ_x, for which calculating values $F_x(p_x, \xi_x)$ and $\tilde{F}_x(p_x, \xi_x)$, received pair been drawn on graph (the left plot on fig. 1) as a spot.

In considered asymptotic case two input parameters N and p_x may be replaced by a single one: $M = Np_x$.

Results of modeling under different values of parameter M are on the left plot (values are normalized by division on $\frac{k-1}{k}$ – maximum probability of mistake).

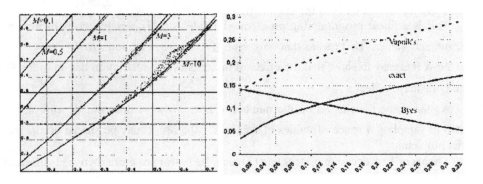

Fig. 1. The left plot contains scatter diagrams where points $\left(F_x(M,\xi_x), \tilde{F}_x(M,\xi_x)\right)$ drawn for random ξ_x and given M. The right plot shows dependences of empirical risk bias on the risk for listed methods of estimating

By $k = 2$ dots form a line. By $k > 2$ spots fill certain area by which it is also possible to approximate $\hat{F}_x\left(p_x, \tilde{F}_x^0\right)$ with sufficient accuracy.

Similarly, it is possible to perform modeling for the evaluation $\hat{F}_x\left(p_x, \tilde{F}_x^0\right)$ also in the case of the forecasting a continuous variable [4].

Now we can evaluate an accuracy of Vapnik–Chervonenkis risk estimations for the considered case of discrete X, as far as we have found an exact dependency of average risk on the empirical risk for the "worst" strategy of nature (distribution).

For $\hat{S}\left(\tilde{F}_0\right)$ in [1] there is reported estimation $\hat{S}_V'\left(\tilde{F}_0\right) = \tau$, as well as an improved

estimation: $\hat{S}_V\left(\tilde{F}_0\right) = \tau^2\left(1 + \sqrt{1 + \frac{2\tilde{R}_0}{\tau^2}}\right)$, where τ asymptotically tends to $\sqrt{\frac{\ln 2}{2M}}$.

On the right figure for $M = 5$ there are drawn dependency $\hat{S}\left(\tilde{F}_0\right)$ and its estimation $\hat{S}_V\left(\tilde{F}_0\right)$. Graph demonstrates significant greatness of the last.

The third line on the graph (straight) presents a variant of dependency obtained by Byesian approach, based on assuming uniform distribution on distributions (strategies of nature) [2,3,5].

In work [5] there is reported the result: $\hat{S}_B\left(\tilde{F}_0\right) = \frac{1 - 2\tilde{F}_0}{M + 2}$.

It may be a surprised fact that $\hat{S}\left(\tilde{F}_0\right)$ on the significant interval appears to be less than $\hat{S}_B\left(\tilde{F}_0\right)$, though Byesian approach implies an averaging by the all nature strategies of nature, but the approach suggested based on the choice of the worst c.

6 Conclusion

For the considered case of a discrete feature the exact maximum of empirical risk bias have been obtained. The comparison conducted shows that risk estimations by Vapnik and Chervonenkis may increase an expected risk up to several times from its true maximum. This means that these estimations may be essentially improved.

The work is supported by RFBR, grants 01-01-00839 and 03-01-06421.

References

1. Vapnik, V.N., Chervonenkis, A. Ja.: Theory of pattern recognition. "Nauka". Moscow (1974) 415p. (in Russian)
2. Hyghes, G. F.: On the mean accuracy of statistical pattern recognizers. IEEE Trans. Inform. Theory. V. IT-14, N 1. (1968) 55–63
3. Lbov, G.S., Startseva, N.G.: Logical deciding functions and questions of statistical stability of decisions. Institute of mathematics. Novosibirsk (1999) 211p. (in Russian).
4. Nedel'ko, V.M.: An Asymptotic Estimate of the Quality of a Decision Function Based on Empirical Risk for the Case of a Discrete Variable. Pattern Recognition and Image Analysis. Vol. 11, No. 1 (2001) 69–72
5. Berikov, V.B.: On stability of recognition algorithms in discrete statement. Artificial intelligence. Ukraine. N. 2. (2000) 5–8 (in Russian)

Efficient Locally Linear Embeddings of Imperfect Manifolds

Abdenour Hadid and Matti Pietikäinen

Machine Vision Group
Infotech Oulu, University of Oulu
P.O.Box 4500, FIN-90014, Finland
{hadid,mkp}@ee.oulu.fi

Abstract: In this paper, we explore the capabilities of a recently proposed method for non-linear dimensionality reduction and visualization called Locally Linear Embedding (LLE). LLE is proposed as an alternative to the traditional approaches. Its ability to deal with large sizes of high dimensional data and non-iterative way to find the embeddings make it more and more attractive to several researchers. All the studies which investigated and experimented this approach have concluded that LLE is a robust and efficient algorithm when the data lie on a smooth and well-sampled single manifold. None explored the behavior of the algorithm when the data include some noise (or outliers). Here, we show theoretically and empirically that LLE is significantly sensitive to the presence of a few outliers. Then we propose a robust extension to tackle this problem. Further, we investigate the behavior of the LLE algorithm in cases of disjoint manifolds, demonstrate the lack of single global coordinate system and discuss some alternatives.

1 Introduction

Recently, two techniques called Locally Linear Embedding (LLE)[1,2] and ISOmetric feature MAPping (Isomap) [3] have emerged as alternatives to both linear and non-linear methods in dimensionality reduction. Principal Component Analysis (PCA) [4] and Multidimensional Scaling (MDS) [5], as examples of linear methods, share similar properties: simplicity of implementation and failure to deal with non-linear data. However, Self-Organizing Maps (SOM)[6], Principal Curves and Surfaces [7,8] and other techniques [9,10,11,12] are able to deal with non-linear data with the cost of complex analysis involving several free parameters to be set and lack of convergence. LLE and Isomap inherit the simplicity from the linear methods and the ability to deal with complex data from the non-linear ones. Though LLE and Isomap are inspired from different intuitions, they are similar in their aims. Isomap attempts to preserve the global geometric properties of the manifold, as characterized by the geodesic distances between faraway points, while LLE attempts to preserve the local geometric properties of the manifold as characterized by the linear coefficients of local reconstructions. Our goal is not to compare these two approaches. One algorithm or the other may be most appropriate to a given application. Instead, we focus this work on

P. Perner and A. Rosenfeld (Eds.): MLDM 2003, LNAI 2734, pp. 188–201, 2003.

LLE and keep in mind that our analysis and findings might also be extended to Isomap.

LLE is an efficient approach to compute the low dimensional embeddings of high dimensional data assumed to lie on a non-linear manifold. Its ability to deal with large sizes of high dimensional data and its non-iterative way to find the embeddings make it more and more attractive. Another advantage of LLE relies on the number of free parameters which it involves: only , the number of neighbors has to be set. These virtues have attracted already several applications in visualization [1,2,13,14], classification [15] and other purposes [1,2,16]. One type of high dimensional data where LLE has shown very successful results is a set of different views of the same 3D object. When these images are well sampled and lie on a single smooth manifold, the embedding result is able to discover and represent exactly the different degrees of freedom of the data. Naturally, the range of successful applications of LLE is not limited to this single example.

However, LLE discovers a meaningful low dimensional embedding space only under certain assumptions. For example, if the data lie on a locally curved space rather than flat one (such as sphere and torus), LLE fails to handle with such manifolds. In [17], an extension of the algorithm is proposed to deal with this case. Unfortunately LLE is not only sensible to the locally curved spaces. In this work we show that the presence of a small number of deviations (outliers) is enough to destroy and affect significantly the embedding result. The result may be worse than a simple PCA projection. Thus, the generalization of LLE to deal with these problems becomes an interesting task, especially when we consider real-world measures (data), which often include outliers. Indeed, it is not unusual that data lie on disjoint manifolds or involve some samples which are far from the remaining points. Such data, that we call imperfect manifolds, make the use of LLE inappropriate. We propose here a robust extension to tackle this limitation. Our main idea consists of preprocessing the data before applying LLE. First we detect the outliers and then define a new neighborhood function to enforce these outliers to have their neighbors among the main data points. The goal of such analysis is to avoid the disconnection between the neighborhood graphs corresponding to the main data and to the outliers. Once a single connected component is obtained, we then apply successfully LLE. We show that this extension is consistent and robust.

Further, we improve our extension to deal with general cases when the main data lie on disjoint manifolds (different clusters) in addition to the presence of deviations (outliers). A simple example of disjoint manifolds is different views of different objects. In such cases, LLE fails to handle the data as a whole while it performs well on separate clusters.

2   LLE, Outliers, and Disjoint Manifolds

Since LLE has already been presented in several papers, we restrict its description just to the main steps, which facilitate the understanding of the further analysis. More details of the implementation can be found in [1,2].

Given DxN Data X (N real-valued vectors X_i each of dimensionality D), the algorithm involves a single pass trough three steps:

1. Find the k nearest neighbors of each point X_i.
2. Compute the weights W_{ij} that best reconstruct each data point from its neighbors, minimizing the cost in Eq.1.
3. Compute the vectors Y_i (of dimensionality $d \ll D$) best reconstructed by the weights W_{ij}, minimizing the quadratic form in Eq.2.

$$E(W) = \sum_i \left\| X_i - \sum_j W_{ij} X_j \right\|^2 \tag{1}$$

$$\Phi(Y) = \sum_i \left\| Y_i - \sum_j W_{ij} Y_j \right\|^2 \tag{2}$$

For a given value of d, the minimum of the function $\Phi(Y)$ is given by the $d + 1$ eigenvectors associated to the $d + 1$ smallest eigenvalues of the matrix M defined as:

$$M = (I - W)^T (I - W).$$

The final desired embeddings (Y) then correspond to the d bottom eigenvectors of M after discarding the first one. The aim of the two first steps of the algorithm is to preserve the local geometry of the data in the low dimensional space, while the last step discovers the global structure by integrating information from overlapping local neighborhoods.

The above analysis is valid only if **all** data points lie on the same connected component of the graph defined by the neighbors. This means that if different graphs of neighborhood are present, LLE fails to find the embedding.

To demonstrate this, let us assume the case when the data contain at least $k + 1$ outliers o_l (in general, $k \ll N$). We mean by 'outlier' a deviation of data point from the main data (such as noise). If we assume that those outliers are closer to each other than to the main data, thus the set of k neighbors of each point o_l contains only outliers. Consequently, the graph defined by the outlier neighborhoods is disconnected from the graph of the remaining data. As a result, two disjoint graphs are present. Let us denote $u_0, u_1, u_2, ...u_d$ the bottom eigenvectors of the matrix M associated respectively to the $d + 1$ smallest eigenvalues $\lambda_0, \lambda_1, \lambda_2,... \lambda_d$ where: $\lambda_0 < \lambda_1 < \lambda_2 < ... < \lambda_d$. The bottom eigenvector is discarded automatically because it is composed of all ones and associated to λ_0 close to 0. The remaining eigenvectors are given by LLE as the embedding result.

We can easily show that these eigenvectors, which are the result of LLE embedding, do not provide any useful representation of the data. Let us construct an N-vector v such as it has constant value α within the first connected component (within the main data points) and another constant value β within the second component (the component corresponding to the outliers). We can then verify easily that v yields a zero embedding cost in eq.2.

$$\Phi_v(Y) = \sum_{i=1}^{N} \left\| v_i - \sum_{j=1}^{N} w_{ij} v_j \right\|^2 = \sum_{i=1}^{N} \left\| v_i - \sum_{j_1 \in graph1} w_{ij_1} v_{j_1} - \sum_{j_2 \in grpah2} w_{ij_2} v_{j_2} \right\|^2$$

Where $graph1$ corresponds to set of the main data and $graph2$ corresponds to the outliers. Since the two graphs are disjoint, thus the reconstruction weights of a given data point which belong to $graph1$ (resp. $graph2$) do not involve the points in $graph2$ (resp. $graph1$). Consequently, its weights are equal to zero in $graph2$ (resp. $graph1$).

$$\sum_{j_1 \in graph1} w_{ij_1} v_{j_1} = 0 \quad or \quad \sum_{j_2 \in grpah2} w_{ij_2} v_{j_2} = 0$$

Since v has a constant value in each graph, then:

$$\Phi_v(Y) = \sum_{i=1}^{N} \left\| v_i - \sum_{j \in graph_i} w_{ij} v_j \right\|^2 = \sum_{i=1}^{N} \left\| v_i - v_i \sum_{j \in graph_i} w_{ij} \right\|^2$$

Using the fact that the weights sum to 1:, $\displaystyle\sum_{j \in graph_i} w_{ij} = 1$

$$\Phi_v(Y) = \sum_{i=1}^{N} \left\| v_i - v_i \right\|^2 = 0$$

Since LLE tries to minimize the cost function in eq.2 and v is an ideal solution, thus LLE returns v as embedding result. By construction, it is clear that this vector does not represent at all the data but codifies the presence of two manifolds. In this case, all the samples of one component are mapped into the same point. Thus, the LLE fails to find the embedding. This means that even when the LLE algorithm performed well on one connected component, $k + 1$ outliers are enough to destroy the embedding results (note that $k << N$).

Let us now consider the case when data lie on disjoint manifolds. By disjoint manifolds, we mean that the neighborhood graphs are disjoint. Here again, we can show (in the same way as above) that applying LLE on S disjoint manifolds gives at least $S - 1$ eigenvectors with same values within each component and different values in different components. This confirms the failure of LLE to deal with more than one connected component.

The failure of handling disjoint manifolds is mentioned in different papers. L. Saul and S. Roweis [1,2] stated that LLE should be applied separately to the data of each cluster. This means that the disjoint manifolds cannot be represented in one single global coordinate system of lower dimensionality. More specifically, Vlachos et al. [15] proposed an approach (based on the analysis of the eigenvalues and eigenvectors of the matrix M) to count the number of separate clusters. This provides us useful indications about the cases where LLE may fail to discover a good embedding, but the authors did not gave any explicit alternative. We think that applying LLE on every cluster separately yields to the same drawback as the mixture models for local dimensionality reduction [18,19]. These methods cluster data and perform then PCA within each cluster, which yield to a lack of single global coordinate system.

3   Robust Locally Linear Embedding

As we presented in the previous section, LLE is very sensitive even to a small number of outliers. Here, we propose a robust extension to tackle this problem. Given a set of real-world or artificial data with a potential presence of noise or (outliers), we start by defining the value of the parameter k (different alternatives may also be used here to determine the neighbors). Then, we determine the graphs corresponding to the neighborhoods. We consider the largest one as the main data and the others as outliers (This is valid under the assumption that our main data lie on one connected component and the other graphs correspond to outliers. We explore later the general case when the main data lie on disjoint components, in addition to the presence of outliers).

Our idea consists of connecting the disjoint graph corresponding to the outliers with the graph of the main data. For this purpose, we enforce the outliers to have their neighbors inside the largest component. By this way, we ensure to obtain only one connected component. Thus, we apply LLE to discover a good representation for the data in the largest connected component with an acceptable distortion of the outliers. Our proposal is valid and efficient under the assumption that the most significant data lie on a single, smooth and well-sampled manifold. While the presence of portion of non-significant data affects significantly the standard LLE approach, our robust extension is able to unfold the manifold and gives a good representation like LLE does in ideal cases.

How can we define and label the outliers? In other words, how can we distinguish between the cases when the data lie on one main component (other points are outliers) and the cases when the main data themselves lie on disjoint components? Instead of performing a complex analysis of the data, we use a simple and efficient technique. We start by constructing the neighborhood graph of the whole data. Assume that we detected different disjoint graphs. Let us note c_1 the cardinality of the largest connected component and c_r the cardinality of the set composed of the remaining points. We then define the ratio:

$$T = \frac{C_r}{C_r + C_1} \tag{3}$$

which determines whether a large amount of data is concentrated in the first component. If $T < threshold$ then the first component is considered as the main data and the remaining points as outliers. Otherwise the data is considered as lying on different manifolds. In our experiments we fixed the threshold to 0.05. This means that we admitted that if the first component contains more than 95% of the whole data, then we can consider the remaining data as outliers and their small distortion is acceptable. In contrast, if $T \geq threshold$ then we admit that the data lie on disjoint manifolds with a potential presence of outliers. In this case, we start by considering the largest component and apply LLE. Once the embedding result is obtained, we estimate the coordinates of the remaining data and the outliers in the low dimensional space. For each data point X_r which is not included in the first largest component, we find its nearest neighbors among the data points of the largest component and then determine the weights W_{rj} which best reconstruct the given data point (in the same way as in the first step of LLE algorithm). We finally use these weights to find the embedding Y_r as follows:

$$Y_r = \sum_{j \in neighbors(X_r)} W_{rj} \, Y_j \tag{4}$$

Thus we obtain a single global representation of the whole data. Here we started by considering the largest connected component as main data. This induces to a better representation of these data than the others. Depending on which cluster we focus our analysis, we can alternate and consider another connected component as main data and then find the embedding projection of the other clusters. In other words, given S disjoint clusters, we can apply LLE on each cluster separately and consider the approximation of the remaining data. Given d, we calculate thus $d * S$ eigenvectors instead of d and represent them in S different spaces for analysis.

This generalization of our extension to also deal with disjoint manifolds is not optimal. It improves the LLE embeddings but it involves S different spaces. In every space, one component is successfully represented while the others are approximated. However, in our experiment we noticed a good representation for the main cluster and acceptable one for the other data. This means that one space may be enough for analyzing different clusters together. We discuss a potential alternative to find a global coordinate space in Sect. 5. Table 1 summarizes the main steps of our extension. In the experiments, we refer to this algorithm as Robust Locally Linear Embedding (RLLE).

Table 1. Robust Locally Linear Embedding (RLLE)

Given a set of data points X, a number of nearest neighbors k, and the dimensionality d:

- Calculate the neighborhood graph corresponding to X.
- If only one connected component is present then apply LLE and go to end.
- Determine the largest component D_{c_1}.
- Calculate $T = \dfrac{C_r}{C_r + C_1}$.
- If $T < threshold$:
  - Consider the largest component (graph); let us denote X_L the data points constituting it and X_O the remaining data ($X_L \cup X_O = X$ and $X_L \cap X_O = \Phi$).
  - Find the new nearest neighbors, which belong to X_L of each point in X_O.
  - Apply LLE using the obtained neighborhood graph and go to end.
- For each disjoint cluster D_c
  - Apply LLE on the cluster D_c.
  - Find the embedding coordinates for the remaining data using eq.4.

- End.

---

4   Experiments

Due to the fact that face images are embedded in a high dimensional space and contain essential non-linear structures that are invisible to linear methods, such data are usually chosen for demonstrating the robustness of proposed algorithms of non-linear dimensionality reduction. We also considered face images to assess the consistence and validity of our analysis and findings. Thus, we took three video sequences (Sequence A, Sequence B and Sequence C) corresponding to three different persons. In every sequence, we asked the person to move his/her head once from left to right resulting 1000 frames in every sequence. We cropped the images and down-sampled them to obtain finally images of 35*45 pixels (thus $D = 1575$). Some samples from each sequence are shown in Fig. 1. During the sequence acquisitions, we controlled the position of the head instead of allowing its arbitrary movement. The goal of this constraint is to obtain smooth and well-sampled data with only one obvious degree of freedom, which is the rotation angle of the face.

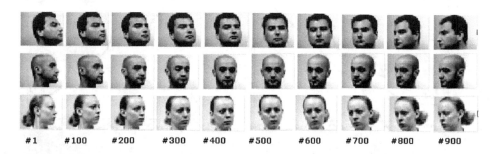

Fig. 1. Samples from the data considered in our experiments. The whole data consist of three video sequences of 1000 frames each and corresponding to three different persons. Here we show some samples from each sequence. #1 corresponds to the first frame in the sequence, #500 to the 500th frame and so on

First, we applied LLE to each video sequence separately. Figure 2 (left) shows the first component discovered by LLE with $k = 8$ neighbors per data point for the sequence A and Fig. 2 (right) shows the first component discovered by PCA. In this case, the estimation of the goodness of the embedding is based on the smoothness of the embedding and its monotony. The monotony means that 1-D space is enough to recover the different rotation angles of the face. It is clearly visible that every image has a different value in the low dimensional space discovered by LLE, while many images share the same value in the PCA representation. In other words, LLE performed well in visualizing different angles of the face in the 1-D embedding space while PCA failed to do it. In addition, we have noticed a remarkable property of LLE: the result of the embedding remains stable over a wide range of values of k (number of neighbors). This relative insensitivity demonstrates again the efficiency and robustness of LLE embedding when the data are smooth, well sampled and lie on one connected component. Note that too small or large k breaks the embedding. In the first series of experiments, we have just confirmed the efficiency of LLE since we considered data lying on one cluster without any outliers. However, our goal is to explore the behavior of LLE in cases of outliers and disjoint manifolds. This is the subject of the following experiments.

In order to check the behavior of LLE in case the data include few outliers, we considered a dataset containing a portion of the sequence A (the 700 first frames which correspond to the orientation angles in the range of $\left[-90^o, 30^o\right]$) and added few samples from the end of the same sequence (10 frames corresponding to the orientation angles in the range of $\left[70^o, 90^o\right]$).

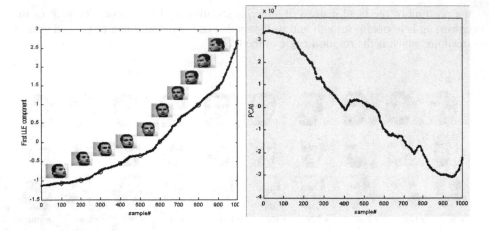

Fig. 2. Analysis of the sequence A by LLE and PCA. (Left) The first component discovered by LLE on the sequence A containing 1000 images. X-axis represents the sample number with ordered orientation angles. It shows that only one component is enough to model perfectly the degree of freedom of the data. Note that the curve is monotone. (Right) The first principal component (PCA) on the same data (sequence A). It is clear that PCA fails to discover a well representation as some samples have the same value

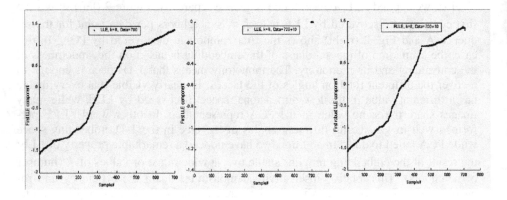

Fig. 3. Behavior of LLE when adding few outliers. (Left) LLE discovered a good representation for a data set of 700 images laying on one connected component. (Center) We added 10 outliers to the previous data set (we got a news dataset of 710 samples) and applied LLE. We can see that the first 700 samples have the same value (-1) and the outliers are projected into the same point (they have the same value equal to zero). Thus, it shows clearly that LLE failed to deal with a small number of outliers. (Right) We applied our algorithm (Robust LLE) on the same data and the embedding remained perfect even with those outliers

It is obvious that this construction yields to two disjoint components in the graph of neighbors, because the last 10 frames are different from the other frames. Therefore, we can see the whole data containing 700 samples of the main data and 10 outliers. Fig. 3 (left) shows the LLE embedding when we considered just the 700 images without outliers. The different angles of the face are well modeled. After adding just 10 samples (outliers), LLE failed to unfold the manifold. The same value was given to all the 700 samples, while a different value was assigned to the remaining 10 samples (outliers). Figure 3 (center) shows the result of this failure of visualizing data with few outliers. This was not surprising as it just confirmed our proofs in Sect. 2. In contrast, using our proposed algorithm, a good representation can be found (see Fig. 3 (right)). Adding the outliers did not affect the result of our approach. This demonstrates that our extension is efficient and robust.

The Robust LLE is able to deal with a large number of outliers even when they lie on several connected components. However, while it models well the main data, a distortion of the outliers may appear. This is due to the fact that our extension is focused on connecting the graph of neighbors rather than optimizing the reconstruction of the outliers from their neighbors.

What about if the main data lie on two or three connected components and we want to visualize well all data points? To investigate this issue, we considered a data set containing three clusters of different sizes (700 frames from the sequence A, 300 frames from the sequence B and 200 frames from the sequence C). We applied LLE and the obtained embedding in 2-D was just three points as shown in Fig. 4.

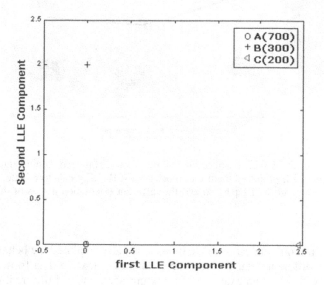

Fig. 4. The result of LLE embedding of a dataset containing three clusters: LLE projected them into three points

LLE projected the three clusters into three points. Although LLE had performed well when we considered every sequence separately, it failed to find one single global coordinate system to represent the whole data together (data partitioned into three clusters). Indeed, in the embedding discovered by LLE the lack of global representation is visible and obvious since the data are projected into three points. We applied Robust LLE, which consists in this case of applying LLE to the largest component

(700 frames from the sequence A) and then extrapolating the coordinates of the remaining data (300 frames from B and 200 frames from C). The result is shown in Fig. 5. It is very clear that different faces are represented in the same space. For the sequence A, similar representation as LLE embedding of one cluster is obtained. Also, the projections of the two other sequences gave acceptable representations.

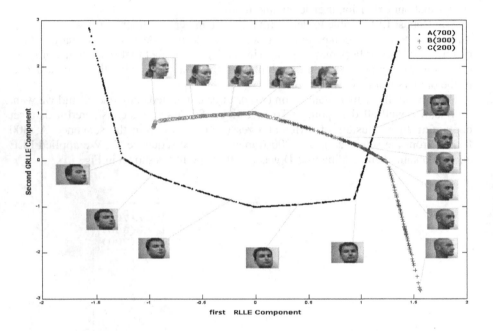

Fig. 5. The result of RLLE embedding of the same dataset containing three clusters (as in Fig. 4): While LLE projected them into three points, RLLE yields to a better representation as the three clusters are well separated and the different orientation angles of the face are visualized

To not limit our analysis on face images, we also explored the behavior of RLLE in visualizing different data. We considered different texture data from Outex database [20]. Figure 6 shows an example of a texture seen under 4 different orientations ($0°$, $30°$, $60°$ and $90°$). We considered 80 samples for each orientation and analyzed the resulting dataset (80 samples x 4 orientations = 320 images) with LLE and RLLE. Instead of using the row images, we extracted the LBP features [21] and used them as inputs to LLE and RLLE algorithms.

While LLE projected the data into three points, the RLLE embedding succeeded in representing the different orientations in the same coordinate space, as shown in Fig. 7. In this case, the RLLE algorithm consisted of finding the LLE embedding of the first class of texture (orientation $0°$) and approximating those of the other classes (orientations $30°$, $60°$ and $90°$).

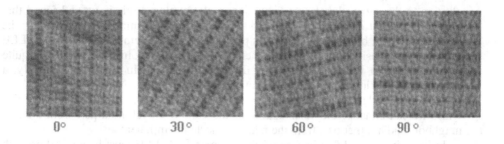

Fig. 6. Texture images from Outex database [20]: an example of a texture seen under 4 different orientations

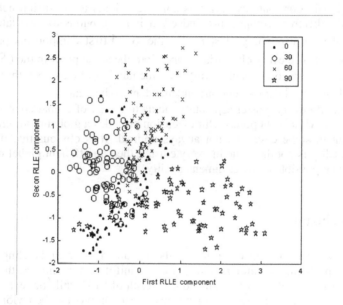

Fig. 7. The result of RLLE embedding of texture images seen under different orientations

5 Discussion

Our main idea to tackle the problems of LLE is based on either connecting the disjoint manifolds or interpolating the embeddings of some samples. In case of outliers, both approaches are   consistent. This is due to the fact that only few samples are considered as outliers and their good reconstruction is not crucial. In contrast, we found that in cases of disjoint manifolds it is preferable to apply LLE on one connected component and then map the remaining data.

In [15], an alternative to connect the graph of neighbors is proposed. It consists of using $k/2$ nearest neighbors and also $k/2$ farthest neighbors in order to gather the clusters in the same global coordinate space. We explored this issue and found that using the farthest neighbors in addition to the nearest ones improves the result of the LLE embedding, but the result remains poor since the local embedding aspect of LLE is lost when considering the farthest neighbors for every point. We adopted a quite similar approach for the outliers, but different for the main data. Consequently, a better representation is achieved using our approach.

Prior knowledge on the data can be exploited to connect the disjoint manifolds while we can enhance the visualization of the outliers by taking a part from the real neighbors and another part from the main connected component.

In [1,2], it is stated that in case of disjoint manifolds LLE must be applied on each cluster separately. More specifically, it is shown that one can extract the embeddings of every cluster just by discarding the $S - 1$ first components given by LLE instead of applying LLE to each cluster (S denotes the number of clusters). In addition to the lack of global coordinate system, this approach yields to confusion between the results of the different components. Indeed, it is not obvious to associate the embeddings to the corresponding clusters. Do the $S - 1$ first components provide useful information? Since every cluster is mapped into the same point in the $(S - 1)$ dimensional space, these components codify only the number of clusters rather than the data points. These $S - 1$ components are independent of the data.

Considering every cluster separately yields to a lack of global coordinate space to represent the whole data points. Our extension provides a global representation, which is efficient in some cases but not always optimal. It is obvious that if the intrinsic dimensionality is not the same in every cluster, then an efficient global representation might not be possible in lower dimensionality.

6   Conclusion

We proposed an efficient extension to the Locally Linear Embedding algorithm to tackle the problems of outliers and disjoint manifolds. We showed that adding few outliers affects significantly the embedding result of LLE while our extension remains insensitive. In cases of disjoint manifolds, we explored the behavior of LLE and showed the lack of a single global coordinate space to represent the different clusters. Instead of considering every cluster separately, we proposed an alternative which improves the visualization results in one global coordinate space. Though our extension improves significantly the embedding, it is still not optimal.

More investigations are needed to explore how strongly the manifold should be connected. Our aim is to get benefit of the simplicity and efficiency of LLE to cope with more general problems. However, we have to keep in mind that some data need complex analysis and others cannot be represented in a single global coordinate space.

Acknowledgements. This research was sponsored by the Academy of Finland and the Finnish Graduate School in Electronics, Telecommunications and Automation (GETA). We also thank L. Saul and M. Polito for the valuable discussions.

References

1. Roweis, S., Saul, L.: Nonlinear Dimensionality Reduction by Locally Linear Embedding. Science v. (2000) 290, No. 5500, 2323–2326.
2. Saul, L., Roweis, S.: Think Globally, Fit Locally: Unsupervised Learning of Nonlinear Manifolds. Technical Report MS CIS-02-18, University of Pennsylvania. (2002).
3. Tenenbaum, J.B., De Silva, V., Langford, J.C.: A Global Geometric Framework for Nonlinear Dimensionality Reduction. Science v. (2000) 290, No. 5500, 2319–2323.
4. Jolliffe, I.T.: Principal Component Analysis. Springer-Verlag, New York (1986).
5. Cox, T., Cox, M. :Multidimensional Scaling. Chapman & Hall, 2nd edition (2000).
6. Kohonen, T.: Self-Organizing Maps. Springer Series in Information Sciences, 3rd edition (2000).
7. Hastie, T.J., Stuetzle, W.: Principal Curves and Surfaces. Journal of the American Statistical Association (1689), 84(406), 502–516.
8. Verbeek, J.J., Vlassis, N., Kröse, B.: A K-segments Algorithm for Finding Principal Curves. Pattern Recognition Letters (2002b), 23(8), 1009–1017.
9. DeMers, D., Cottrell, G.W.: Nonlinear Dimensionality Reduction. Advances in Neural Information Processing Systems, San Mateo, CA (1993) volume 5, 580–587.
10. Bishop, C., Svensen, M., Williams, C.: GTM: The Generative Topographic Mapping. Neural Computation (1998), 10(1), 215–234 .
11. De Backer, S., Naud, A., Scheunders, P.: Non-Linear Dimensionality Reduction Techniques for Unsupervised Feature Extraction. Pattern Recognition Letters (1998) 19, 711–720.
12. Li, S., De Vel, O., Coomans, D.: Comparative Performance Analysis of Non-Linear Dimensionality Reduction Methods. Technical Report, James Cook University (1995).
13. Hadid, A., Kouropteva, O., Pietikäinen, M.: Unsupervised Learning Using Locally Linear Embedding: Experiments in Face Pose Analysis. Proc. 16th International Conference on Pattern Recognition, Quebec, Canada (2002), 1, 111–114.
14. DeCoste. D.: Visualizing Mercel Kernel Feature Spaces via Kernelized Locally Linear Embedding. 8th International Conference on Neural Information Processing. (2001).
15. Vlachos, M., Domeniconi, C., Gunopulos, D., Kollios, G., Koudas, N.: Non-Linear Dimensionality Reduction Techniques for Classification and Visualization. Knowledge Discovery and Data Mining. Edmonton, Canada(2002).
16. Perona, P., Polito, M.: Grouping and Dimensionality Reduction by Locally Linear Embedding. Neural Information Processing Systems NIPS (2001).
17. Pless, R., Simon, I.: Embedding Images in Non-Flat Spaces. Technical Report WU-CS-01-43, Washington University, December (2001).
18. Ghahramani, Z., Hinton, G.E.: The EM Algorithm for Mixtures of Factor Analyzers. Technical Report CRG-TR-96-1, Department of Computer Science, University of Toronto (May 1996).
19. Kambhatla, N., Leen, T. K.: Dimension Reduction by Local Principal Component Analysis. Neural Computation (1997) 9, 1493–1516.
20. Ojala, T., Mäenpää, T., Pietikäinen, M., Viertola, J., Kyllönen, J., Huovinen, S.: Outex – New Framework for Empirical Evaluation of Texture Analysis Algorithms. Proc. 16th International Conference on Pattern Recognition, Quebec, Canada (2002), 1, 701–706. (http://www.outex.oulu.fi/outex.php).
21. Ojala, T., Pietikäinen, M., Harwood, D.: A Comparative Study of Texture Measures with Classification Based on Feature Distributions. Pattern Recognition (1996) 29, 51–59.

Dissimilarity Representation of Images for Relevance Feedback in Content-Based Image Retrieval

Giorgio Giacinto and Fabio Roli

Dept. of Electrical and Electronic Engineering, University of Cagliari
Piazza D'Armi 09123 Cagliari, Italy
{giacinto,roli}@diee.unica.it

Abstract. Relevance feedback mechanisms are adopted to refine image-based queries by asking users to mark the set of retrieved images as being relevant or not. In this paper, a relevance feedback technique based on the "dissimilarity representation" of images is proposed. Each image is represented by a vector whose components are the similarity values between the image itself and a "representation set" made up of the images retrieved so far. A relevance score is then assigned to each image according to its distances from the sets of relevant and non-relevant images. Three techniques to compute such relevance scores are described. Reported results on three image databases show that the proposed relevance feedback mechanism allows attaining large improvements in retrieval precision after each retrieval iteration. It also outperforms other techniques proposed in the literature.

1 Introduction

The vast majority of content based image retrieval (CBIR) techniques relies on the representation of images by low-level features, e.g., color, texture, shape, etc., [2,21]. Content-based queries are often expressed by visual examples in order to retrieve from the database all images that are "similar" to the examples. It is easy to see that the effectiveness of content-based image retrieval systems (CBIR) strongly depends on the choice of the set of visual features and on the choice of the "metric" used to model the user's perception of image similarity. A number of metrics have been proposed in the literature to adequately measure (dis)similarities in a given feature space [19].

However, no matter how suitable for the task at hand the features and the similarity metric have been designed, the set of retrieved images often fits the user's needs only partly. Typically, different users may categorise images according to different semantic criteria [1]. Thus, if we allow different users to mark the images retrieved with a given query as relevant or non-relevant, different subsets of images will be marked as relevant. Accordingly, the need for mechanisms to adapt the CBIR system response based on some feedback from the user is widely recognised.

This issue has been studied thoroughly in the text retrieval field, where the relevance feedback concept has been introduced [17]. Techniques developed for text retrieval should be suitably adapted to content based image retrieval, on account of differences in both feature number and meaning, and in similarity measures [11,15].

P. Perner and A. Rosenfeld (Eds.): MLDM 2003, LNAI 2734, pp. 202–214, 2003.

Relevance feedback techniques proposed in the literature involve the optimisation of one or more CBIR components, e.g., the formulation of a new query and/or the modification of the similarity metric to take into account the relevance of each feature to the user query.

Query reformulation is motivated by the observation that the image used to query the database may be placed in a region of the feature space that is "far" from the one containing images that are relevant to the user [6,7,12,15].

Other CBIR systems employ parametric similarity metrics whose parameters are computed from relevance feedback [18,20]. Rather than modifying the similarity metric, Frederix et al. proposed a transformation of the feature space so that relevant images represented in the new feature space exhibit higher similarity values [5]. A probabilistic feature relevance scheme has been proposed in [14].

Theoretical frameworks involving both the computation of a new query and the optimisation of the parameters of similarity metric have been also proposed [8,16].

In this paper, we propose a relevance feedback mechanism based on the representation of the images in the database in terms of their (dis)similarities from a *representation set*. The use of the dissimilarity representation of objects has been recently studied in the pattern recognition field [3-4]. This representation allows building pattern classifiers characterised by low error rates, as the pair-wise (Euclidean) distances between patterns of the same class are usually smaller than those of patterns of different classes.

Analogously, in a CBIR system, images represented by dissimilarities should exhibit the same property, i.e., relevant images should be characterised by smaller pairwise distances than those between relevant and non-relevant images. In particular, the proposed technique is based on the representation of the images of the database in terms of their (dis)similarities from the set of images retrieved so far. A relevance score for each image of the dataset is then computed by taking into account the distances between the image itself and each of the relevant and non-relevant images retrieved. The relevant score is used to rank the images so that the first k are returned to the user in response of the relevance feedback.

In Sect. 2, the dissimilarity representation of images in the context of CBIR systems is proposed. The relevance feedback mechanism is described in Sect. 3, where three measures are described to rank the images according to their distances from the relevant and non-relevant images retrieved so far. Experiments with three image datasets are reported in Sect. 4. The reported results show that the proposed method outperforms other relevance feedback mechanisms recently described in the literature. Conclusions are drawn in Sect. 5.

2   Dissimilarity Representation of Images

Let us consider an image database whose images I are represented in a d-dimensional low-level feature space, e.g., color, texture, etc. Let us assume that a (dis)similarity metric $S(I_j, I_k)$ has been defined in such feature space. In the following, we will neither make any assumption about the feature space, nor about the similarity metric employed.

Let $\mathbf{Q}$ be the image used to query the image database. For each image $\mathbf{I}$ of the database, the value of $S(\mathbf{Q}, \mathbf{I})$ is computed and the first k images, with the largest similarity values, are shown to the user (the value of the k parameter is chosen by the user). The user may either stop the search if satisfied with the results, or decide to refine the query by selecting the *relevant* images among the k image returned by the system. In this case the user provides the so-called *relevance feedback*. In order to exploit such feedback, we propose to represent each image $\mathbf{I}$ of the database in terms of its similarities with each of the k images returned by the system:

$$\mathbf{I} = (S(\mathbf{I},\mathbf{I}_1), S(\mathbf{I},\mathbf{I}_2),..., S(\mathbf{I},\mathbf{I}_k)) \tag{1}$$

where $\mathbf{I}_1$, $\mathbf{I}_2$,..., $\mathbf{I}_k$ are the k images more similar to query $\mathbf{Q}$ according to the similarity measure S. It is worth noting that also the images $\mathbf{I}_1$, $\mathbf{I}_2$,..., $\mathbf{I}_k$ are represented according to equation (1). This representation allows using the Euclidean distance measure to compute the dissimilarity between pairs of images [3-4]. The image $\mathbf{I}$ will be as much as relevant as it is *near* to the relevant images and, at the same time, *far* from the non-relevant ones. The techniques proposed to exploit this property of the dissimilarity representation will be illustrated in the following section.

It is worth noting that while the query mechanisms employed by some image databases are based on the combination of a number of similarity measures (usually related to different image representations), the following discussion is limited to a single feature space where only one similarity metric is defined. The proposed method can be easily generalised to address the case where more than one similarity measure (possibly related to different image representations) is used. However, this topic is out of the scope of the present paper and will be further discussed elsewhere.

3   Relevance Feedback

The goal of this section is to compute a "relevance" score for each image of the database by exploiting the dissimilarity representation of the images.

Let us denote with R the subset of indexes $j \in \{1,...,k\}$ related to relevant images, and NR the subset of indexes $j \in (1,...,k\}$ related to non-relevant images. Let r and nr be the cardinality of the sets R and NR, respectively.

For each image $\mathbf{I}_s$ of the database, let us compute the k distances d_{js} between the image itself and the k images $\mathbf{I}_j$, $j \in \{1,...,k\}$. Since the k images $\mathbf{I}_j$, $j \in \{1,...,k\}$, have been marked as being either relevant or non-relevant, the image $\mathbf{I}_s$ is as much as relevant as the values of d_{js}, for $j \in R$, are *small* and, at the same time, the values of d_{js}, for $j \in NR$, are *large*. In other words the k distances can be subdivided into two subsets, i.e., the subset made up of the r distances related to relevant images, and the subset made up of the nr distances related to non-relevant images.

A number of functions developed in the frameworks of the fuzzy set and clustering theories can be used to "aggregate" the r relevance distances and the nr non-relevance distances, so that the two values, one related to the degree of *relevance*, and the other related to the degree of *non-relevance*, can be associated to the image $\mathbf{I}_s$ [9-10]. In this work, we propose to use the "min" function, so that the *relevance* of each image $\mathbf{I}_s$ is computed in terms of the *nearest* relevant image and in terms of the *nearest* non-relevant image:

$$distR_s = \min_{j \in R} d_{js} \tag{2}$$

$$distNR_s = \min_{j \in NR} d_{js} \tag{3}$$

Let us linearly normalise the values of $distR_s$ and $distNR_s$ for all the images of the database, so that they take values in the range $[0,1]$:

$$dR_s = \frac{distR_s - \min_s(\min(distR_s, distNR_s))}{\max_s(\max(distR_s, distNR_s)) - \min_s(\min(distR_s, distNR_s))} \tag{4}$$

$$dNR_s = \frac{distNR_s - \min_s(\min(distR_s, distNR_s))}{\max_s(\max(distR_s, distNR_s)) - \min_s(\min(distR_s, distNR_s))} \tag{5}$$

Finally, let us denote with $\mu_R(s) = (1 - dR_s)$ the degree of *relevance* of $\mathbf{I}_s$, and with $\mu_{NR}(s) = (1 - dNR_s)$ the degree of *non-relevance* of $\mathbf{I}_s$. These values can be interpreted as the degrees of "membership" of the considered image to the relevant and non-relevant sets of images respectively. As a consequence, relevant images are those with large values of $\mu_R(s)$ and large values of $1 - \mu_{NR}(s) = \mu_{\overline{NR}}(s) = dNR_s$. In other words, $\mu_{\overline{NR}}(s)$ is a measure of how much the image $\mathbf{I}_s$ should *not* be considered as non-relevant, i.e., a measure of its relevance.

In order to assign a unique value of *relevance* to each image $\mathbf{I}_s$, the two membership values, namely $\mu_R(s)$ and $\mu_{\overline{NR}}(s)$, should be aggregated. It is easy to see that such aggregation function should be: i) monotonically increasing in $\mu_R(s)$, and ii) monotonically increasing in $\mu_{\overline{NR}}(s)$. To this end, in this paper, we consider two simple functions that take values in the range $[0,1]$:

$$average: \frac{1}{2}\left(\mu_R(s) + \mu_{\overline{NR}}(s)\right) \tag{6}$$

$$ratio: \quad e^{\frac{1 - \mu_R(s)}{\mu_{\overline{NR}}(s)}} \tag{7}$$

The first function is commutative, so that the two values $\mu_R(s)$ and $\mu_{\overline{NR}}(s)$ play the same role in the final value of the degree of relevance. On the other hand, the second function is not commutative, as $\mu_{\overline{NR}}(s)$ is used to *weight* the degree of relevance measured by $\mu_R(s)$ (it is worth noting that the only purpose of the exponential is to have an aggregated value in the range $[0,1]$). In other words, the value of $\mu_{\overline{NR}}(s)$ is used to "support" the degree of relevance provided by $\mu_R(s)$, and is not considered a degree of relevance in itself.

Finally, the two aggregation functions, namely the *average* and the *ratio*, can be further aggregated to take advantage of their complementarity. As an example, the "probabilistic product" can be used [10]:

probabilistic product:

$$\frac{1}{2}\left(\mu_R(s)+\mu_{\overline{NR}}(s)\right)+e^{-\frac{1-\mu_R(s)}{\mu_{\overline{NR}}(s)}}-\frac{1}{2}\left(\mu_R(s)+\mu_{\overline{NR}}(s)\right)\cdot e^{-\frac{1-\mu_R(s)}{\mu_{\overline{NR}}(s)}} \tag{8}$$

which represents a "union" of the two functions (the "average" and the "ratio").

The relevance values computed either according to equation (6), or (7), or (8) are then used to rank the images and the first k are presented to the user.

To sum up, the proposed technique works as follows:

1. each image of the database is represented in terms of the distances between the image itself and the images retrieved so far;
2. the distances between each image of the database and the sets of relevant and non-relevant images are computed and a relevance score is obtained;
3. the images of the database are ranked according to this score and the first k are returned to the user.

4   Experimental Results

In order to test the proposed method and compare it with other methods described in the literature, three image databases have been used: the MIT database, a database contained in the UCI repository, and a subset of the Corel database. These databases are currently used for assessing and comparing relevance feedback techniques [13–16].

The MIT database (ftp://whitechapel.media.mit.edu/pub/VisTex) contains 40 texture images that have been manually classified into fifteen classes. Each of these images has been subdivided into sixteen non-overlapping images, obtaining a data set with 640 images. Sixteen Gabor filters were used to characterise these images, so that each image is represented by a 16-dimensional feature vector [14].

The database extracted from the UCI repository (ftp://ftp.ics.uci.edu/pub/machine-learning-databases/statlog/segment/) consists of 2,310 outdoor images. The images are subdivided into seven data classes. Nineteen colour and spatial features characterise each image. (Details are reported in the UCI web site).

The database extracted from the Corel collection is available at the KDD-UCI repository (http://kdd.ics.uci.edu/databases/CorelFeatures/CorelFeatures.data.html). We used a subset made up of 19513 images, manually subdivided into 43 classes. For each image, four sets of features were available at the web site. In this paper, we report the results related to the Color Moments (9 features), and the Co-occurrence Texture (16 features) feature sets [13].

For each dataset, the Euclidean distance metric was used. A linear normalisation procedure has been performed, so that each feature takes values in the range between 0 and 1.

For the MIT and UCI databases, each image is used as a query. In the case of the Corel dataset, 500 images have been randomly extracted and used as query. The top twenty nearest neighbours of each query are returned. Relevance feedback is performed by marking images belonging to the same class of the query as relevant, and all other images in the top twenty as non-relevant. This experimental set up affords an objective comparison among different methods and is currently used by many researchers [13-16].

For the sake of comparison, retrieval performances obtained with three methods recently described in the literature are also reported, namely the RFM (Relevance Feedback Method) [15], the Bayesian Query Shifting [7], and the PFRL (Probabilistic Feature Relevance Learning) [14].

RFM exploits relevance feedback by computing a new query $\mathbf{Q}_1$ according to the Rocchio formula [17]. The new query is computed as a linear combination of the original query, and the mean vectors of relevant and non-relevant images retrieved so far. The coefficients of the linear combination are usually chosen by heuristics. This query shifting formulation requires that the similarity between image vectors be measured by the cosine metric. To this end, data has been pre-processed by the so-called $tf \times idf$ normalisation, used in the information retrieval domain [15], that converts image feature vectors into weight vectors.

The Bayesian Query Shifting technique (Bayes QS) computes a new query according to the following formula derived from the Bayes decision theory:

$$\mathbf{Q}_1 = \mathbf{m}_R + \frac{\sigma}{\|\mathbf{m}_R - \mathbf{m}_N\|}\left(1 - \frac{k_R - k_N}{\max(k_R, k_N)}\right)(\mathbf{m}_R - \mathbf{m}_N) \tag{9}$$

where $\mathbf{m}_R$ and $\mathbf{m}_N$ are the mean vectors of relevant and non-relevant images respectively, σ is the standard deviation of the images belonging to the neighbourhood of the original query, and k_R and k_N are the number of relevant and non relevant images, respectively. More details on this method can be found in [7].

PFRL is a probabilistic feature relevance feedback method aimed at weighting each feature according to the information extracted from the relevant images. This method uses a weighted Euclidean metric to measure the similarity between images. The weights are computed according to the feature values of the relevant images retrieved. Two parameters chosen by experiments are used to optimise the performances. More details on this method can be found in [14].

As the performances of the RFM and PFRL techniques depend on the choice of the values of some parameters, the results reported hereafter are related to the best ones obtained in a number of experiments.

Experiments with the MIT Data Set

Figure 1 shows the average percentage retrieval precision after 10 retrievals attained by the three Dissimilarity Relevance Feedback (DRF) measures proposed in the previous section, and the three methods used for comparison purposes. After one iteration of relevance feedback (1 rf), the best performances are attained by the Bayes QS technique (91.80%), while the performances of the DRF techniques are between 89.31% (ratio) and 90.72% (probabilistic product). RFM and PFRL do not perform well, with an average precision of 84.55% and 85.47%, respectively. After two relevance feedback iterations, DRF provided the highest precision and clearly outperforms the other techniques starting from the third iteration. In addition, the proposed DRF allows further improvements, reaching the retrieval precision of 97.01% after 9 iterations with the "ratio" function. The other three techniques used for comparison does not allow to further improve the retrieval performances attained after four iterations if a larger number of iterations is performed.

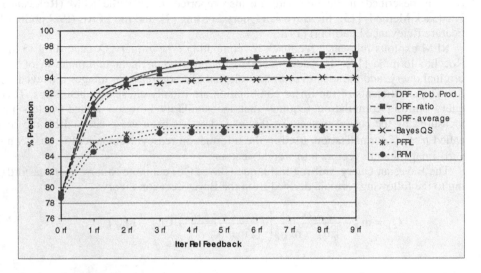

Fig. 1. Average percentage precision retrieval for the MIT data set. Nine relevance feedback iterations were performed with the considered relevance feedback techniques

The comparison of the three DRF functions shows that the "average" measure provides lower performances than those of the "ratio" and the " probabilistic product". Thus it follows that, at least for this data set, the rationale behind the "ratio" measure seems more appropriate than the one behind the "average" measure. It is worth recalling that the non-relevant membership value is used to weight the relevant membership value in the "ratio" measure, while it is used just as a relevance membership value in the "average" measure.

Experiments with the UCI Data Set

For this data set, the choices of both the similarity metric and the normalisation procedure affect the precision of the first retrieval (0 rf). The results reported in Fig. 2 show that the $tf \times idf$ normalisation is less suited than the linear normalisation, and the cosine metric (RFM) provides a lower precision (84.03%) than the Euclidean metric (90.21%) employed by all other techniques. After the first relevance feedback iteration, the best performance is attained by the Bayes QS (96.33%). The DRF with the "probabilistic product" function (96.23%) and the DRF with the "average" function (96.04%) provided similar performances, while the other techniques provided lower performances.

All the considered techniques allow improving the retrieval precision if the number of relevance feedback iteration is increased. The proposed DRF techniques attained the highest performances at each iteration. In particular, the highest values have been attained by the DRF with the "ratio" function and the DRF with the "probabilistic product" aggregation function, thus confirming the comments on the results related to the MIT data set.

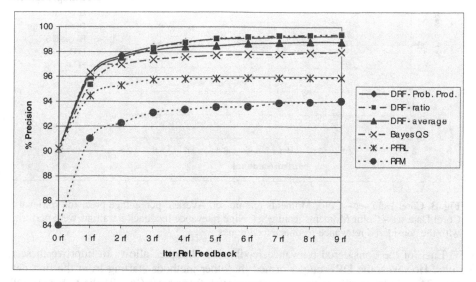

Fig. 2. Average percentage precision retrieval for UCI data set. Nine relevance feedback iterations were performed with the considered relevance feedback techniques.

Summing up, as far as the MIT and UCI data sets are concerned, the precision of the DRF after the first iteration is very close to the highest one of the Bayes QS technique. DRF clearly outperformed other techniques after two or more iterations, thus showing its validity, and the ability to exploit additional information provided by further feedbacks.

Experiments with the Corel Data Set

This data set allows a more thorough comparison among methods, as it is made up of a larger number of images. Figures 3 and 4 show the results with the color moments and co-occurrence texture feature sets, respectively. The retrieval performances related to the original query (0 rf) are quite low, thus showing that the chosen feature sets are not suited for the task at hand. In addition, different similarity metrics provided quite different results. In particular, the cosine metric provided better results than those of the Euclidean metric with both feature sets. The cosine metric attained a precision of 20.36% with the "color moments" feature set, and 17.89% with the "co-occurrence texture" feature set, while the Eulidean metric attained precisions of 17.30% and 14.13%, respectively.

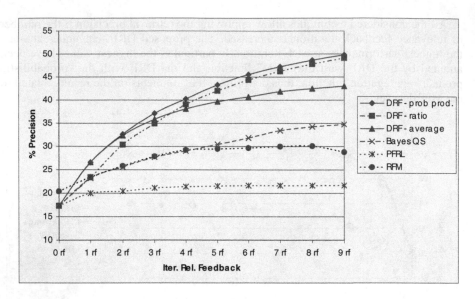

Fig. 3. Corel Data set – Color Moments feature set. Average percentage precision retrieval for Corel Data set – Color Moments feature set. Nine relevance feedback iterations were performed with the considered relevance feedback techniques.

Each of the considered relevance feedback techniques allows to improve these results. However, the DRF outperformed the other methods starting from the first iteration. The results related to the "color moments" feature set (Fig. 3) show that the DRF with the "average" function and DRF with the "probabilistic product" provide higher performances than those provided by the RFM, the DRF with the "ratio" function, the Bayes QS, and the PFRL. All the techniques but the PFRL allows increasing the retrieval precision when further iterations are performed. As an example, after three iterations the DRF with the "probabilistic product" function attains a precision of 37.12%, while the DRF with the "average function" reaches 35.83%, and the DRF with the "ratio" function attains 34.91%. The precisions of the RFM and the Bayes QS are around 28%, while the precision of the PFRL is around 21%. As noted for the results of the previous data sets, the best performances after 9 iterations are attained by the DRF with the "probabilistic product" function (49.80%) and the DRF with the "ratio" function (49.10%), the DRF with the "average" function providing much smaller performances (43%).

Similar conclusions can be drawn from the results with the "co-occurrence texture" feature set. In particular, the DRF with the "probabilistic product" function attained the best performances at each iteration, while the "average" function performed better than the "ratio" function for the first three iterations. Therefore, the "probabilistic product" allows combining the strengths of the two relevance scores.

Figures 6 and 7 show the retrieval results related to the query shown in Fig. 5. In particular, Fig. 6 shows the images retrieved from the Corel dataset when no feedback is performed. According to the overall results presented in the previous tables, the performance is quite poor: only 4 images out of 20 match the user's needs. After three feedbacks (Fig. 7) a large fraction of the images (16 out of 20) are relevant to the user's needs.

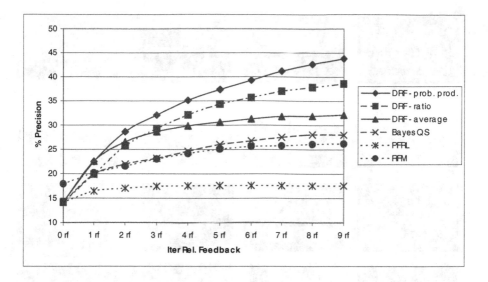

Fig. 4. Average percentage precision retrieval for Corel Data set – Co-occurrence texture feature set. Nine relevance feedback iterations were performed with the considered relevance feedback techniques.

Fig. 5. One of the query used in the experiments on the Corel dataset

5   Conclusions

In this paper, we have presented a relevance feedback technique based on a dissimilarity representation of images. The reported results on three image databases showed the superiority of the proposed method with respect to other relevance feedback techniques, especially when a number of feedbacks are performed. The superiority of DRF was more evident in the case of the Corel image dataset, where the precision without relevance feedback is quite poor.

Fig. 6. Retrieval result related to the query shown in Fig. 5 with no feedback. Relevant images have a bold border.

It is worth noting that many experiments presented in the literature on the Corel data set are based on the combination of relevance feedbacks from different feature sets, thus providing high performances. The proposed technique is also well suited for combining different feature sets, as the "dissimilarity" representation is independent on any feature-based representation. However, this topic is out of the scope of the present paper and will be discussed elsewhere.

As far as the computational complexity of the proposed technique is concerned, a large number of distances are to be computed. Nevertheless, the response time between two consecutive feedbacks was around 0.6s on the Corel dataset (made up of 19513 images), on a Celeron 450 MHz PC using the Win98 OS. This response time is far below the classic limit of 1.0s for the user's flow of thought to stay uninterrupted. Thus, despite the computational complexity of the algorithm, the response time on a not-so-fast machine can be considered acceptable for a large database. However, the response time of the implemented algorithm could be further improved by taking into account, for example, that consecutive retrievals share a number of images. As a consequence at each step only the distances related to new retrieved images should be computed, provided that distances computed in previous steps are stored.

Fig. 7. Retrieval results after three feedbacks. The number of relevant images increased significantly, and non-relevant images are ranked in

Finally, it is worth remarking that the performances of some techniques used for comparison are heavily affected by the choice of the value of a number of parameters, while the proposed technique does not rely on parameters computed by heuristics.

Acknowledgments. The authors wish to thank Dr. Jing Peng for providing the features of the MIT data set and the C-code of the PFRL algorithm used to perform some of the reported experiments. They also thank Dr. Manuel Ortega for providing the images of the Corel Data set.

References

1. Bhanu, B., Dong, D.: Concepts Learning with Fuzzy Clustering and Relevance Feedback. In: Petra, P. (Ed.): Machine Learning and Data Mining in Pattern Recognition. LNAI 2123, Springer-Verlag, Berlin (2001) 102–116
2. Del Bimbo A.: Visual Information Retrieval. Morgan Kaufmann Pub. Inc., San Francisco, CA (1999)

3. Duin R.P.W., de Ridder D., Tax D.M.J.: Experiments with object based discriminant functions: a featureless approach to pattern recognition. Pattern Recognition Letters **18**(11–13) (1997) 1159–1166
4. Duin R.P.W., Pekalska E., de Ridder D.: Relational discriminant analysis. Pattern Recognition Letters **20**(11–13) (1999) 1175–1181
5. Frederix G., Caenen G., Pauwels E.J.: PARISS: Panoramic, Adaptive and Reconfigurable Interface for Similairty Search. Proc. of ICIP 2000 Intern. Conf. on Image Processing. WA 07.04, vol. III (2000) 222–225
6. Giacinto, G., Roli, F., Fumera, G.: Content-Based Image Retrieval with Adaptive Query Shifting. In: Petra, P. (Ed.): Machine Learning and Data Mining in Pattern Recognition. LNAI 2123, Springer-Verlag, Berlin, (2001) 337–346
7. Giacinto G., Roli F.: Query shifting based on Bayesian decision theory for content-based image retrieval. Proc. of S+SSPR2002, Canada, LNCS 2396, Springer-Verlag 607–616
8. Ishikawa Y., Subramanys R., Faloutsos C.: MindReader: Querying databases through multiple examples. In Proceedings. of the 24th VLDB Conference (1998) 433–438
9. Jain A.K., Dubes R.C.: Algorithms for Clustering Data. Prentice Hall (1988)
10. Kuncheva L.I.: Fuzzy Classifier Design. Springer-Verlag (2000)
11. McG Squire D, Müller W., Müller H., Pun T.: Content-based query of image databases: inspirations from text retrieval. Pattern Recognition Letters **21**(13–14) (2000) 1193–1198
12. Nastar C., Mitschke M., Meilhac C.: Efficient query refinement for Image Retrieval. Proc. of IEEE Conf. Computer Vision and Pattern Recognition, CA (1998) 547–552
13. Ortega M., Rui Y., Chakrabarti K., Porkaew K., Mehrotra S., Huang T.S.: Supporting ranked boolean similarity queries in MARS. IEEE Trans. on KDE **10**(6) 905–925 (1998)
14. Peng J., Bhanu B., Qing S.: Probabilistic feature relevance learning for content-based image retrieval. Computer Vision and Image Understanding **75**(1–2) (1999) 150–164
15. Rui Y., Huang T.S., Mehrotra S.: Content-based image retrieval with relevance feedback: in MARS. In Proceedings of the IEEE International Conference on Image Processing, IEEE Press (1997) 815–818
16. Rui Y., Huang T.S.: Relevance Feedback Techniques in Image retrieval. In Lew M.S. (ed.): Principles of Visual Information Retrieval. Springer-Verlag, London, (2001) 219–258
17. Salton G., McGill M.J.: Introduction to modern information retrieval. McGraw-Hill, New York (1988)
18. Santini S., Jain R.: Integrated browsing and querying for image databases. IEEE Multimedia **7**(3) (2000) 26–39
19. Santini S., Jain R.: Similarity Measures. IEEE Trans. on Pattern Analysis and Machine Intelligence **21**(9) (1999) 871–883
20. Sclaroff S., La Cascia M., Sethi S., Taycher L.: Mix and Match Features in the ImageRover search engine. In Lew M.S. (ed.): Principles of Visual Information Retrieval. Springer-Verlag, London (2001) 219–258
21. Smeulders A.W.M., Worring M., Santini S., Gupta A., Jain R.: Content-based image retrieval at the end of the early years. IEEE Trans. on Pattern Analysis and Machine Intelligence **22**(12) (2000) 1349–1380

A Rule-Based Scheme for Filtering Examples from Majority Class in an Imbalanced Training Set

Jamshid Dehmeshki, Mustafa Karaköy, and Manlio Valdivieso Casique

Medicsight Plc., 46 Berkeley Square, Mayfair
London, England W1J 5AT
jamshid.dehmeshki@medicsight.co.uk

Abstract. Developing a Computer-Assisted Detection (CAD) system for automatic diagnosis of pulmonary nodules in thoracic CT is a highly challenging research area in the medical domain. It requires a successful application of quite sophisticated, state-of-the-art image processing and pattern recognition technologies. The object recognition and feature extraction phase of such a system generates a huge imbalanced training set, as is the case in many learning problems in medical domain. The performance of concept learning systems is traditionally assessed with the percentage of testing examples classified correctly, termed as accuracy. This accuracy measurement becomes inappropriate for imbalanced training sets like in this case, where the non-nodules (negative) examples outnumber nodule (positive) examples. This paper introduces the mechanism developed for filtering negative examples in the training so as to remove 'obvious' ones, and discusses alternative evaluation criteria.

1 Introduction

Early detection of lung cancer is crucial in its treatment. Conventionally, radiologists try to diagnose the disease, by examining computed tomography (CT) images of the subject's lung and then deciding if each suspicious object, i.e., region of interest (ROI) is a nodule or a normal tissue. The manual radiological analysis of CT images is a time consuming process. Therefore, developing a Computer-Assisted Detection (CAD) system for automatic diagnosis of pulmonary nodules in thoracic CT is a highly challenging research area in the medical domain [1].

Achievement of this task requires the successful application of state-of-the-art image processing and pattern recognition techniques. The image processing tasks are followed by nodule detection and feature extraction processes. This often results in large, imbalanced data sets with too many non-nodule examples, since it is important to avoid missing any nodules in the images. Constructing an accurate classification system requires a training data set that represents different aspects of nodule features. This paper assumes an object has been detected and deals with the subsequent object learning. It focuses on the problem of extremely imbalanced training sets, (i.e. the

P. Perner and A. Rosenfeld (Eds.): MLDM 2003, LNAI 2734, pp. 215–223, 2003.
© Springer-Verlag Berlin Heidelberg 2003

relatively high number of negative non-nodule results, compared to the low number of positive nodule results.)

Informally, a good performance on positive examples and negative examples is expected rather than one at the cost of the other. However, the classification performance in this kind of task cannot be expressed in terms of the average accuracy since the training set is extremely imbalanced in that the non-nodules (negative) examples heavily outnumber the nodule (positive) examples, and classifiers tend to over-fit non-nodule examples. Another problem with the training set is the training time due to the huge size of the data set. Filtering/eliminating some negative examples would help solve both problems so long as it does not deteriorate the learning performance.

2 Discovering Safe Regions in the Feature Space

Training sets for concept learning problems are denoted by pairs [x, c(x)], where x is a vector of attribute values of an example and c(x) is the corresponding concept label. In our case, c(x) is either positive or negative. Nevertheless, there is always a huge difference between the prior probabilities of the positive and negative examples. In other words, negative examples are represented by a much greater number of examples than the positive ones in the training data set, as is often the case in many learning problems of medical domain.

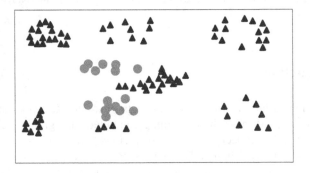

Fig. 1. An example of imbalanced training sets with two attributes

In an extremely imbalanced training data set (see Fig. 1), many sections of the feature space for x vectors, i.e., feature space, are likely to be comprised of those pairing with majority-class only and also quite far from the ones pairing with minority-class examples. Furthermore, radiologists believe that nodule cases have certain characteristics that would locate them in certain areas of feature space only. In other words, there should be many nodule free regions in the feature space. In summary, a learning model is constructed through following steps:

1. Discovering 'safe' regions in the feature space, where only negative examples exist.
2. Constructing filtering rules each of which defines the corresponding 'safe' region.
3. Eliminating training examples covered by these regions from the training data set.
4. Training a classifier or classifiers with the modified training set.

This paper focuses on reducing/filtering an imbalanced training set, which is part of our CAD system. Therefore, the last step is out of the scope of this paper.

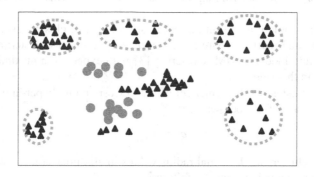

(a)
Ellipse Regions

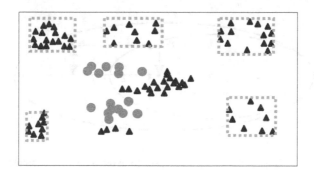

(b)
Rectangular Regions

Fig. 2. Determining safe regions

Figure 2 illustrates two examples of determining such regions for the imbalanced set with two attributes mentioned above. In a multidimensional space, those regions can be thought of as distinct hyper-ellipsoids or hyper-cuboids. Assuming the training data is a representative set of the problem it is plausible to construct rules for specification of those regions, and to label any test point satisfying any of these rules (i.e., being inside one of those regions) as non-nodule (i.e., negative). Such a rule not only diminishes the training data set for the subsequent classifier but also could be a filtering and first-level classification mechanism for 'easy' non-nodule test examples[1].

First, a clustering (unsupervised learning) algorithm is applied to the whole (imbalanced) training set, which divides the data set into a specified number of distinct groups. Then, the 'pure' negative clusters, which consist of negative examples only, are marked. For each of these pure clusters, a hyper-ellipsoid or a hyper-cuboid is specified, and all examples of these clusters are removed from the training set of the subsequent classifier.

The algorithm for determining these safe regions in terms of hyper-ellipsoids is as follows:

1. Group the whole training set into a certain number of clusters using an appropriate clustering and mark the pure negative clusters. K-means clustering [2] and Gaussian mixture model (GMM) clustering [3] with expectation maximization (EM) [4] are used in this study.
2. For each cluster, set the center (c) of the corresponding hyper-ellipsoid to its mean vector (m) as defined below:

$$c_j = m_j. \tag{1}$$

3. For each cluster, set the initial radius values in all dimensions/attributes in terms of its standard deviation vector as follows[2].

$$r_j = 3 * s_j. \tag{2}$$

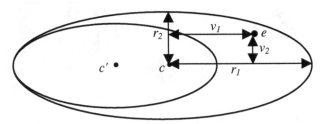

Fig. 3. Shrinking an ellipses to avoid a positive example

4. As shown in Fig. 3 on two-dimensional space for the sake of simplicity, for any positive training example (e) falling in a region, first determine the dimension (k) where the difference between example's value and the center is the biggest (v_k) as follows:

---

[1] Classifiers mostly fail on the examples close to the decision boundaries, hence these examples are difficult to classify. On the contrary, the examples far from the decision boundaries could be considered 'easy' examples.

[2] This formula makes sure that at least 99% (probably all) of the samples in the cluster are covered assuming they have a normal (i.e., Gaussian) distribution. Other heuristics could be applied instead. E.g., center and radius might be determined by minimum and maximum attribute values for the cluster.

$$v_k = \max(v_j) \qquad \text{where} \qquad v_j = |e_j - c_j| \qquad \text{for all } j. \tag{3}$$

5. Then, update (i.e., shift) the center value in that dimension and modify the radius values in all dimensions (j) as follows:

$$c'_k = (e_k + 3 * c_k + 2 * r_k)/4 \qquad \text{if } e_k < c_k \tag{4}$$
$$c'_k = (e_k + 3 * c_k - 2 * r_k)/4 \qquad \text{otherwise}$$

$$r'_k = (v_k - 2 * r_k)/4. \tag{5}$$

$$r'_j = r_j * r'_k / r_k \qquad \text{for all } j \text{ where } j \neq k. \tag{6}$$

Note the radiuses in all dimensions as well as the radius in the dimension with the maximum difference are recalculated, but also radiuses in all other dimensions are recalculated. Otherwise, the new region includes (even though relatively small but potentially not safe) areas that are outside the original region due to the shift of the center.

Similarly, the algorithm for determining these regions in terms of hyper-cuboids is as follows:

1. The first step is the same as in the previous algorithm.

2. Initially, define a hyper-cuboid for each cluster in terms of minimum and maximum values in each dimension as follows:

$$min_j = m_j - 3 * s_j. \tag{7}$$

$$max_j = m_j + 3 * s_j. \tag{8}$$

where m denotes mean vector of the cluster while s is the standard deviation vector.

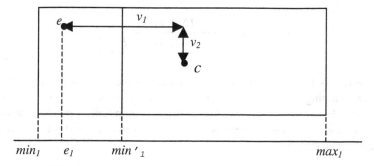

Fig. 4. Shrinking a rectangular to avoid a positive example

3. As shown in Fig. 4 on two-dimensional space for the sake of simplicity, for any positive training example (e) falling in a region, first determine the dimension (k) where the difference between example's value and the center is the biggest (v_k), and then either update the *min* value in that dimension if it is smaller than the example's value (as in Fig. 4), or update the *max* value otherwise as follows:

$$min'_k = (min_k + max_k + 2*e_k)/4 . \tag{9}$$

$$max'_k = (min_k + max_k + 2*e_k)/4 . \tag{10}$$

Once rules are constructed, the first part, i.e., the proposed filtering scheme for an overall classification system is complete. In learning phase of a two-stage classification system, this rule-based mechanism act as a filtering scheme for the training data to the classifier in the second stage, while it operates as a first-stage detection of 'easy' negative test cases in the test/classification phase.

3 Evaluation Criteria

Statisticians generally formulate the performance with a confusion matrix shown in Table 2 that characterizes the classification behavior of a concept learning system [5]. Based on this matrix, the traditional accuracy, i.e., the percentage of testing samples classified correctly, is calculated as follows:

Table 1. Confusion matrix

Real		Predicted	
		Negative	Positive
	Negative	TN	FP
	Positive	FN	TP

TN: the number of true negatives
FN: the number of false negatives
FP: the number of false positives
TP: the number of true positives

$$accuracy = \frac{TN + TP}{TN + FN + TP + FP} . \tag{11}$$

However, this bare accuracy measurement becomes inappropriate in the case of imbalanced training sets [6]. In this case, researchers choose different criteria for the performance. For instance, information retrieval community prefers to work with so called *precision* and *recall*. Below is the formulization of these measurements based on the confusion matrix:

$$precision = \frac{TP}{TP + FP}. \tag{12}$$

$$recall = \frac{TP}{FN + TP}. \tag{13}$$

These quantities are sometimes amalgamated into a single value called F-measure by giving them equivalent or different weights. When both precision and recall are considered equally important, the F-Measure (F) is computed as follows:

$$F = \frac{2 * precision * recall}{precision + recall}. \tag{14}$$

A common alternative for the combination is the geometric mean (g) of precision and recall values as given below [7]:

$$g = \sqrt{precision * recall}. \tag{15}$$

As in the F-measure formula in Equation **14**, this metric reaches high values only if both precision and recall are high and in equilibrium.

There are also other criteria such as Receiver Operating Characteristic (ROC) curve analysis[3], the one frequently used for the problems in medical domain [8]. All these measurements are more suitable than the simple accuracy value as a performance metric for the systems learning from highly imbalanced training set.

However, the scheme here is not a complete system for such a task. Rather, it will constitute part of such a system as a first-level detection of negative examples. Therefore, the criteria used for the filtering scheme consist of *error ratio* (*ER*) on the test set and *filtering ratios* (*FR*) on the test set and as well as the train set. Following are the formulae:

$$ER = \frac{FN}{FN + TP}. \tag{16}$$

$$FR = \frac{TN}{TN + FP}. \tag{17}$$

Error ratio indicates how reliable it is in terms of not missing any positive example, whereas the filtering ratio shows how useful it is with respect to detecting/eliminating as many negative examples as possible. It is aimed to get a low error ratio with as much a high filtering ratio as possible.

---

[3] Originally, ROC curve analysis was developed during World War II for the analysis of radar images as a signal detection theory. It was used to measure the ability of radar receiver operators in deciding if a blip on the screen is an enemy target, a friendly ship, or just noise. However, it was recognized as useful for interpreting medical test results after the 1970's.

4   Experiments

The whole data used in the experiments consisted of 152382 examples such that only 739 were positive examples while 151643 were negative examples with 8 attributes. The data were normalized and randomized in a pre-processing task since the attributes were in diverse ranges. In addition, the positive and negative examples were separately split into 5 groups each so as to apply 5-fold cross-validation so that the prior probabilities of the classes are the same for each fold. More precisely, for a particular fold one fifth of positive examples and one fifth of negative examples formed a validation set while the rest of the whole data was the train set.

The program written to run experiments had 3 options: the clustering method (k-means or GMM), the number of clusters and the regions shape (hyper-ellipsoid or hyper-cuboid). Table 2 reports the filtering results when training sets in folds were clustered into groups of 250 using the k-means method. There was one problem with the fourth and fifth training sets. The method failed to cluster data into 250 groups and for this reason these two were clustered into 200 groups instead. On the other hand, clustering with GMM in place of k-means did not change these results much.

Table 2. Filtering results

Fold No	Filtering Ratio		Error on Test Set
	Train Set	Test Set	
1	49.83%	49.54%	4.08%
2	52.68%	52.76%	2.72%
3	52.62%	52.48%	8.84%
4	38.44%	38.11%	2.72%
5	43.11%	43.53%	2.04%
Average	47.34%	47.28%	4.08%

5   Discussion and Conclusion

At first glance, the filtering ratios might be considered low. However, remember that this scheme alone does not offer a complete classification system. Rather, its provides a first stage appraisal of test examples by the system as well as reducing the training data set to the classifier in the second-stage. Especially considering the fact that the error ratios in all cases are below 9% (i.e., much smaller than those of the classifiers trained with the same data set where they were above 15% in all cases), this mechanism proves to be useful in reducing the learning time for model-based algorithms, and the testing time for case-based algorithms.

The specification/definition of 'safe' regions in the feature space is important. In this study, these regions are specified as hyper-cuboids or hyper-ellipsoids for the sake of simplicity of their mathematical definitions and less complexity requirements. However, distributions of examples inside clusters are not further investigated to better cover examples in the clusters based on the distribution. In this manner, some alternatives will be examined in future study.

In conclusion, this paper presented a scheme for filtering examples from the majority class in an imbalanced training set in general, and for filtering of non-nodule examples in particular, which is vital to improve the performance of our CAD system for nodule detection. As an initial evaluation of test examples in a classification process, this rule-based scheme also makes a contribution by eliminating easy negative examples, which bring about the reduction in learning time when a model-based classifier such as an Artificial Neural Network (ANN), or the reduction in decision making when an instance-based classifier such as k-nearest neighbor (kNN) is used, in addition to some improvement in performance. Hence, this mechanism also enables combination of rule-based and instance-based induction when a case-based algorithm is applied in the second stage, which differs from Domingos' RISE system that unifies these two induction strategies [9].

References

1. Lee, Y., Hara, A., Hara, T., Fujita, H., Itoh, S., Ishigaki, T.: Automated Detection of Pulmonary Nodules in Helical CT Images Based on an Improved Template-Matching Technique. In: IEEE Transactions on Medical Imaging, Vol. 20, No. 7. (2001) 595–604
2. MacQueen, J.: Some methods for classification and analysis of multivariate observations. In: Proceedings of the Fifth Berkeley Symposium on Mathematical Statistics and Probability, Vol. 1. (1967) 281–297
3. Bishop, C..: Neural Networks for Pattern Recognition. Oxford University Press, UK (1995)
4. Dempster, A., Laird, N., Rubin, D.: Maximum Likelihood from Incomplete Data via the EM Algorithm. In: Journal of the Royal Statistical Society. B39 (1) (1977) 1–38
5. Nickerson, A., Japkowicz, N., Milios, E.: Using Unsupervised Learning to Guide Resampling in Imbalanced Data Sets. In: Proceedings of the Eighth International Workshop on Artificial Intelligence and Statistics. (2001)
6. Kubat, M., Holte, R., Matwin, S.,: Learning when Negative Examples Abound. In: Proceedings of ECML-97, Vol. 1224. Springer Verlag, (1997) 146–153
7. Kubat, M., Matwin, S.,: Addressing the Curse of Imbalanced Training Sets: One-Sided Selection. In: Proceedings of 14th International Conference on Machine Learning, (1997) 179–186
8. Metz, C.: Fundamental ROC analysis. In: Beutel, J., Kundel, H., MetterHandbook, R. (eds.): Medical Imaging, Vol. 1. SPIE Press, Bellingham, WA (2000) 751–769
9. Domingos, P.: Unifying Instance-Based and Rule-Based Induction. In: Machine Learning, Vol. 24, No. 2. (1996) 141–168

Coevolutionary Feature Learning for Object Recognition

Krzysztof Krawiec* and Bir Bhanu

Center for Research in Intelligent Systems
University of California, Riverside, CA 92521-0425, USA
{kkrawiec,bhanu}@cris.ucr.edu

Abstract. In this paper, we consider the task of automatic synthesis/learning of pattern recognition systems. In particular, a method is proposed that, given exclusively training raster images, synthesizes complete feature-based recognition system. The proposed approach is general and does not require any assumptions concerning training data and application domain. Its novelty consists in procedural representation of features for recognition and utilization of coevolutionary computation for their synthesis. The paper describes the synthesis algorithm, outlines the architecture of the synthesized system, provides firm rationale for its design, and evaluates it experimentally on the real-world task of target recognition in synthetic aperture radar (SAR) imagery.

1 Introduction

Most real-world learning tasks concerning visual information processing are inherently complex. This complexity results not only from the large volume of data that one usually needs to process, but also from its spatial nature, information incompleteness, and, most of all, from the vast amount of hypotheses (concerning training data) to be considered in the learning process. Therefore, a design of recognition system that is able to learn consists in a great part in *limiting* its capabilities. To induce useful hypothesis on one hand and avoid overfitting to the training data on the other, the learning system must observe some assumptions concerning training data and hypothesis representation, known as *inductive bias* and *representation bias,* respectively. In visual learning, however, these biases have to be augmented by an extra '*visual bias*', i.e., knowledge related to the visual nature of the information being subject to the learning process. A part of that is general knowledge concerning vision (*background knowledge,* BK), for instance, basic concepts like pixel proximity, edges, regions, primitive features, etc. However, often a more specific *domain knowledge* (DK) related to particular *task/application* (e.g., fingerprint identification, face recognition, SAR target detection, etc.) is also required (e.g., the interpretation of scattering centers in SAR imagery).

Contemporarily, most recognition methods make intense use of DK to attain competitive performance level. This is however a two-edged sword, as the more DK the method uses, the more specific it becomes and the less general and transferable is the

---

* On a temporary leave from Poznań University of Technology, Poznań, Poland.

P. Perner and A. Rosenfeld (Eds.): MLDM 2003, LNAI 2734, pp. 224–238, 2003.

knowledge it acquires. The contribution of such over-specific methods to the overall body of knowledge of Machine Learning, Computer Vision, and Pattern Recognition is questionable.

Therefore, we focus on general-purpose visual learning that requires only BK. In the approach proposed here, the key characteristics of BK are (i) representation of the synthesized systems/hypotheses in the form of information processing chain that extends from the input image to the final recognition, and (ii) assumption on presence of *building blocks* (modules) in the chain. These suppositions, motivated by biological analogs, enable us to break down learning into components so as to cope with the complexity of recognition task. In particular, high-level building blocks like 'classifier' are specified explicitly; others, however, like 'features', emerge autonomously during the learning process. The success of our learning method depends on its ability to *exploit and discover the inherent modularity* of the problem at hand.

It is to be noted that the ability to identify building blocks is a necessary, but not a sufficient, precondition for successful learning/synthesis task. By analogy, arranging neurons into layers in an artificial neural network scales down the learning task by reducing the number of architectures that are considered, but does not provide explicit learning rule(s) for particular layers. To enforce learning in each identified building block, we need an *evaluation function* that spans over the space of all potential solutions and guides the learning process. Unfortunately, when no *a priori* definition of module's 'desired output' is available, this requirement is hard to meet. This is why we propose to employ cooperative coevolution [10], a variety of evolutionary algorithm, that allows breaking down the problem into subproblems without explicitly specifying objectives for each of them. This paper focuses on cooperation that takes place at feature level.

2 Related Work and Contributions

No general methodology has been developed so far that effectively automates the process of recognition system synthesis. Several methods have been reported in the literature; they include blackboard architecture, case-based reasoning, reinforcement learning, and automatic acquisition (learning) of models, to mention the most predominant. The paradigm of evolutionary computation (EC) has found applications in image processing and analysis. It has been found effective for its ability to perform effective global parallel search in high-dimensional search spaces and to resist the local optima problem. However, in most approaches the learning/adaptation is limited to parameter optimization. Relatively few results have been reported [4,8,12,13], that perform deep visual learning, i.e., with learner being able to synthesize and manipulate entire recognition system.

The major contribution of this paper is a novel method that, given exclusively training raster images, synthesizes complete feature-based recognition system. The proposed approach is general and does not require any assumptions concerning training data and application domain. Its novelty consists in (i) procedural representation of features for recognition and (ii) utilization of coevolutionary computation for their synthesis.

3 Rationale for the Synthesis Algorithm and System Design

3.1 Preliminary Assumptions

We make the following assumptions that are of methodological nature and do not affect the generality of the proposed approach.

(a)   We follow the *feature-based recognition* paradigm and split the object recognition process into two fundamental modules: feature extraction module and decision making/recognition module. The novelty of the proposed approach consists in an extensive learning process that aims at *optimizing the way the former module extracts features* from an input image, prior to the learning that takes place in the recognition module.

(b)   The synthesis of the recognition system adopts the *learning-from-examples* scheme and relies exclusively on a finite training set D of images, which is assumed to be a representative sample from the universe U. In particular, we observe the *supervised learning* setting and assume that the training data are partitioned into finite number of decision classes D_i, i.e.

$$\bigcup_i D_i = D, \forall i \neq j \; D_i \cap D_j = \varnothing .$$

(c)   Inspired to some extent by the constructive induction [7] research in machine learning, we view the feature extraction process in a *procedural* way. In particular, we assume that a single *feature extraction procedure* is a chain of n primitive, possibly parameterized, operations (building blocks), which are essentially calls to functions from predefined fixed library/collection of m such functions. A feature extraction procedure accepts an image as input and yields single scalar value as the result. A set of one or more feature extraction procedures forms a *feature vector/set S (representation)*, and is essentially equivalent with the feature extraction module introduced in (a).

3.2 Learning as Optimization Process - Complexity Issues

A well-designed representation/feature set is clearly a necessity for high recognition rate, and that is why its design is usually so demanding and resource-consuming. To automate that process and include it into the learning loop, we formulate it as a *search (optimization) problem* in the discrete space of all representations Ω, with each search state corresponding to a unique set of feature extraction procedures $S \in \Omega$. We assume also that an *evaluation function f*: $\Omega \times U \rightarrow \Re$ is given, such that, given the training data D, $f(S,D)$ is an estimate of probability of correct recognition for S for all examples U. Without loss of generality, from now on we assume that f is maximized, and that its lower bound (the worst value) is 0.

In the above setting, given the training data D, the task of synthesizing *globally optimal* feature set (representation) S^* can be formalized as:

$$S^* = \arg \max_{S \in \Omega} f(S,D) \tag{1}$$

When no assumptions are made concerning the nature of f, the task of finding S^* has exponential time complexity. To prove that, it is enough to show that the size of the search space Ω is an exponential function of representation size; this manifests itself at the following two levels:

- *Single feature* level. Let us assume for simplicity, that the primitive operations are parameter-free. Then, the number of different feature extraction procedures is m^n, where m is the size of the library of primitive operations, and n stands for the length of the feature extraction procedure.
- *Feature set* level. Given an upper bound on the representation size k (number of features), the total number of feature sets to be considered is

$$|\Omega_k| = \sum_{i=1}^{k}\binom{m^n}{i}.$$ (2)

This prohibitively large number disables the use of exhaustive search algorithm even for relatively small values of m, n, and k. Other search techniques that would possibly reduce the time complexity, like branch and bound, make some assumptions concerning the characteristic of the function f being optimized   (e.g., local upper/lower bounds, global convexity). In our learning-from-examples setting, however, f is essentially given by the training data D and no useful assumptions concerning its nature can be made.

Heuristic or metaheuristic search is, therefore, the only plausible method that can be applied to the synthesis task posed as above and that can yield reasonably good *suboptimal* solutions S_s, $f(S_s,D) < f(S^*,D)$, $f(S_s,D) \gg 0$, in polynomial time. In fact, for some problems the solutions found during the heuristic search may even be globally optimal; however, as we don't know the upper bound of recognition performance, we cannot discern it from the suboptimal ones.

3.3 Rationale for the Use of Coevolution

To search the space of representations Ω, we propose to use the cooperative coevolution (CC) [10], a variety of recognized metaheuristics of genetic algorithm. In formal terms, the choice of this particular method is irrelevant, as, according to Wolpert's 'no free lunch' theorem [16], a hunt for an universal, best-of-all metaheuristics is futile. More formally, let us define a search algorithm as an iterative process that, at each step maps its current state (a set of p points in the search space) onto a new state. Then, given any pair of search algorithms a_1 and a_2,

$$\sum_f \Pr(\vec{c}\mid f, p, a_1) = \sum_f \Pr(\vec{c}\mid f, p, a_2),$$ (3)

where f is a fitness function and $\vec{c}$ is the histogram of fitness. As a result, the average performance of any metaheuristic search over a set of all possible fitness functions is the same.

In real world, however, not all fitness functions are equally probable. Most real problems are characterized by some features that make them specific. The practical utility of a search/learning algorithm depends, therefore, on its ability to detect and benefit from those features. In particular, the *complexity* of the problem and the way it may be *decomposed* are such features.

In the last few years, coevolution has been reported as a promising approach to handle the increasing complexity of problems posed in artificial intelligence and related disciplines. In particular, its collaborative variety, the cooperative coevolutionary algorithm (CC) [10], besides being appealing from the theoretical viewpoint, has been reported to yield interesting results in some experiments [14,1]. The basic feature that makes CC different from EC is that, instead of having just single population of individuals, in CC one maintains several of them, with individuals in populations encoding only a *part* of the solution to the problem. Therefore, individuals cannot be evaluated independently; they have to be (temporarily) combined with some *representatives* from the remaining populations to form a solution, called hereafter *organism O*, that can be evaluated. This joint evaluation scheme forces the individuals from particular populations, and, as a result, the entire populations, to cooperate. In other words, it is an organism, not an individual, that corresponds to the search state S in the formalism introduced in Section 3.2 ($O \equiv S$). Except for this evaluation step, the evolution proceeds in each population independently (see Table 1).

Table 1. Comparison of EC and CC algorithms (major differences in boldface)

Evolutionary Computation (EC)	Cooperative Coevolution (CC)
solution ≡ an individual in population	solution ≡ an **organism** composed of individuals selected from different populations
initialize population	initialize **populations**
loop	*loop*
evaluate individuals	evaluate **organisms** and assign fitness to individuals in populations
store best individual	store **best organism** *for each* **population**
select mating candidates	select mating candidates
recombine parents and use their offspring as the next generation	recombine parents and use their offspring as the next generation *end for*
until stopping condition	*until* stopping condition
return best individual	*return* **best organism**

Cooperative coevolution provides the possibility of breaking up the complex problem into components *without specifying explicitly the objectives for them*. The manner in which the individuals from populations cooperate *emerges* as the evolution proceeds. In our opinion, this makes CC especially appealing to the problem of synthesis of recognition systems, where the overall target is well defined, but there is no *a priori* knowledge about what should be expected at intermediate stages of processing, or such knowledge requires an extra effort from the designer.

Recently, some advances have been made in the area of theoretical foundations of coevolution. Most work done so far focuses on attempting to prove that the behavior of coevolution is similar to that of regular evolution. For instance, it has been shown in [6], that, when some assumptions are made regarding parameters (number of populations and population size), coevolutionary algorithms exhibit the same type of dynamics as EC.

3.4 Multi-agent Approach and Decision-Level Fusion

Facing the suboptimal character of representations synthesized by the evolutionary process, we incorporate in our approach multi-agent methodology that aims to compensate for that imperfectness and allows us to boost the overall performance.

The search for performance improvement by approaching the problem with multiple algorithms/agents has a long history in AI-related disciplines. In particular, the so-called *compound-* or *meta-classifiers* became an important research issue in PR and ML during the last decade. Many results concerning stacked generalization, mixture of experts, bagging, etc. (see, e.g., [1]), indicate that employing many agents and aggregating their outcomes may significantly improve the (recognition) performance in comparison to the single-agent approach.

The basic prerequisite for the agents' fusion to become beneficial is their *diversification*. This may be ensured by using homogenous agents with different parameter setting, or homogenous agents with different training data (e.g. bagging), or heterogeneous agents, to mention only a few most popular approaches. In the approach proposed here, the diversification is naturally provided by the random nature of the genetic search. In particular, there are at least two approaches that seem to be reasonable methods for multiple-agent acquisition from genetic search:

- exploiting different well-performing systems synthesized during a *single* genetic search,
- exploiting best systems synthesized during *many* genetic searches that started from different initial states (initial populations).

Though computationally more expensive, the latter of the techniques provides better performance of particular agents and better differentiation of the resulting agents' pool, so it has been adopted in the approach described here. For the sake of simplicity, the agents differ only in the features synthesized by genetic searches; the classifiers used in particular subsystems are homogenous.

4 Technical Approach

For the sake of clarity, let us first strictly distinguish the synthesized *recognition system*, from the *synthesis algorithm* (learning algorithm) that leads to its creation. The recognition system takes an image as an input and produces recognition decision (object identity) at its output; on the contrary, synthesis algorithm takes the training data (set of images) as input and yields the recognition system. The synthesis algorithm proceeds in two *stages*, which correspond to two main *components/parts* of the synthesized system. In the following subsections we describe the recognition system and the synthesis algorithm.

4.1 Architecture of the Synthesized Recognition System

The result of synthesis is a feature-based recognition system that incorporates data fusion at different levels of processing. The top-level architecture encompasses *a set of subsystems* that work in parallel, process the input image X independently, and output recognition decisions that are further aggregated by a simple majority voting procedure into the final decision. The number of subsystems n_{sub} is a parameter set by the designer. All subsystems are homogenous as far as the structure is concerned; they only differ in the features extracted from the input image and the knowledge acquired by the classifier. Thus, for simplicity, all the following description will be concerned with a single subsystem.

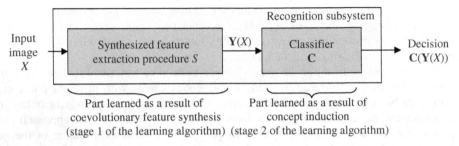

Fig. 1. The architecture of a single synthesized subsystem

Each subsystem has two major components (see Fig. 1): (i) a collection of feature extraction procedures, and (ii) a trained classifier. In each subsystem, the process of recognition starts with the input image X being fed into the set of feature extraction procedures S. The procedures from S yield feature values, which are subsequently gathered to build *representation*, i.e., a fixed-length vector of feature values $\mathbf{Y}(X)$. Finally, that feature vector is passed through the classifier $\mathbf{C}$, that yields this subsystem's vote $\mathbf{C}(\mathbf{Y}(X))$ (class probability distribution).

4.2   The Algorithm for Synthesizing Recognition System

The synthesis of recognition system consists in running independent learning process for each subsystem shown in Fig. 1. Although the synthesis algorithm used is the same for all subsystems, the results are diversified by starting the feature synthesis process from different initial populations. This is technically implemented through initializing the pseudorandom number generator with different values.

For a single subsystem, the learning encompasses two stages: (1) coevolutionary feature synthesis and (2) classifier induction. The following subsections describe both these stages in detail.

4.2.1   Coevolutionary Synthesis of Feature Extraction Procedures: The basic engine for the feature synthesis algorithm employs the search based on cooperative coevolution described in Sect. 3.3. Its result, feature set S, is implemented into the synthesized system.

The algorithm, whose overall architecture is shown in Fig. 2, maintains a collection of populations, each being a set of individuals. Each individual I encodes a single image processing/feature extraction procedure and, given an input image $X \in D$, yields a vector $\mathbf{y}(I,X)$ of scalar feature values. For clarity, this encoding and execution of feature extraction program is detailed in a separate Sect. 4.2.2.

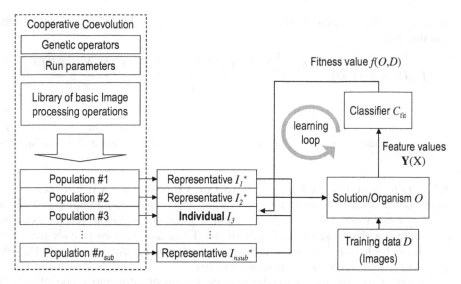

Fig. 2. The coevolutionary feature synthesis algorithm

This coevolutionary search proceeds in all populations independently, except for the evaluation phase. To evaluate an individual I_j from population j, we first provide for the remaining part of the representation. For this purpose, *representatives* I_i^* are selected from all remaining populations $i \neq j$. A representative I_i^* of ith population is defined here in a way that has been reported to work best [14]: it is the best individual w.r.t. the evaluation done in the previous generation. In the first generation of evolutionary run, however, since no prior evaluation data is given, it is a randomly chosen individual.

Then, I_j is temporarily combined with representatives of all the remaining populations to form an organism

$$O = \left\langle I_1^*, \ldots, I_{j-1}^*, I_j, I_{j+1}^*, \ldots, I_{n_{sub}}^* \right\rangle, \tag{4}$$

that corresponds to search state S (see Section 3.2). Then, the feature extraction procedures encoded by individuals from O are 'run' for all images X from the training set D. The scalar feature values $\mathbf{y}$ computed by them are grouped, building the compound feature vector $\mathbf{Y}$:

$$\mathbf{Y}(X) = \left\langle \mathbf{y}(I_1^*, X), \ldots, \mathbf{y}(I_{j-1}^*, X), \mathbf{y}(I_j, X), \mathbf{y}(I_{j+1}^*, X), \ldots, \mathbf{y}(I_{n_{sub}}^*, X) \right\rangle. \tag{5}$$

Feature vectors $\mathbf{Y}(X)$, computed for all training images $X \in D$, together with the images' decision class labels constitute the dataset:

$$\left\langle \mathbf{Y}(X), i : \forall X \in D_i, \forall D_i \right\rangle \tag{6}$$

Finally, cross-validation, i.e. multiple train-and-test procedure is carried out on these data. For the sake of speed, we use here fast classifier C_{fit} that is usually much simpler than classifier $\mathbf{C}$ used in the final synthesized system (see Fig. 1). The resulting predictive recognition ratio becomes the evaluation of the organism O, which is subsequently assigned as the fitness value to $f()$ the individual I_j, concluding its evaluation process:

$$f(I_j, D) = f(O, D) = \frac{card\left(\left\{\left\langle \mathbf{Y}(X), i \right\rangle, \forall D_i, \forall X \in D_i : C(\mathbf{Y}(X)) = i \right\}\right)}{card(D)}. \tag{7}$$

Using this evaluation procedure, the coevolutionary search proceeds until some stopping criterion (usually considering computation time) is met. The best synthesized organism/representation S becomes the part of the feature extraction module presented in Fig. 1.

4.2.2 Representation of Feature Extraction Procedures: As it has been already mentioned in Section 3, we assume that (i) basic, general-purpose building blocks are given *a priori* to the synthesis process, and (ii) that an individual feature extraction procedure is a chain/sequence of such blocks. These assumptions provide the system with basic background knowledge BK (however, not *domain* knowledge, DK) that speeds up the convergence of the search process.

Though the overall feature synthesis process relies on cooperative coevolution, for representing the feature extraction procedures as individuals in evolutionary process, we adopted a variety of Linear Genetic Programming (LGP) [1], a hybrid of genetic algorithms (GA) and genetic programming (GP), as the one that seems to meet these assumptions best. The individual's *genome*, i.e. the internal encoding of solution it represents, is a fixed-length string of numbers. The genome is interpreted as a sequential program composed of (possibly parameterized) basic operations that work on images and scalar data. This LGP-like representation combines advantages of both GP and GA, being *procedural* and at the same time more *resistant* to the destructive effect of crossover that may occur in 'regular' GP.

The above mentioned *operations* are effectively calls to image processing and feature extraction functions. They work on *registers*, i.e. working variables, and may use them both as input as well as output arguments. *Image registers* store processed images, whereas *real-number registers* keep intermediate results or scalar features. Each image register is single-channel, has the same dimensions as the input image, and maintains a single rectangular ROI that may be used by an operation as a mask. For simplicity, both the number of image registers as well as the number of real-number registers are controlled by the same parameter n_{reg}.

Technically, each individual is a fixed-length string of bytes 0..255 , with each chunk of 4 consecutive bytes encoding a single operation with the following elements:

- operation code (opcode),
- ROI flag – decides whether the operation should be global (work on the entire image) or local (limited to rectangular region of interest (ROI)),
- ROI size (ignored if ROI flag is 'off'),
- arguments – numbers (identifiers) of registers to fetch input data and store the result.

An exemplary operation is morphological opening (operation code) using rectangular ROI (ROI flag 'on') of size 14 (ROI size) on the image fetched from image register

#4 (pointed by argument #1), and storing the result in image register #5 (pointed by argument #2).

There are currently 70 operations implemented in the system. They mostly consist of calls to functions from Intel Image Processing and OpenCV libraries, encompass image processing, ROI – related operations, feature extraction, and arithmetic and logic operations.

In the above settings, the processing of a single input image (example) $X \in D$ by the LGP procedure encoded in an individual I proceeds as follows (see Fig. 3):

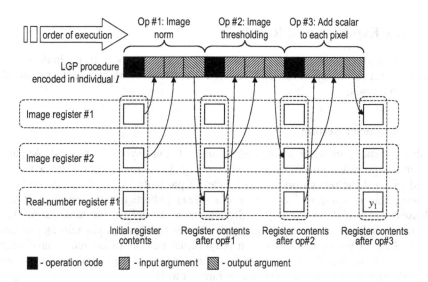

Fig. 3. Illustration of genome interpretation during procedure execution (genome length 12, one real-number register)

1. *Initialization* of register contents:
   - Each of the n_{reg} image registers is set to X. The ROIs of images are set to consecutive local features (here: bright 'blobs') found in the image, so that ROI in the ith image register encompasses i^{th} local feature.
   - Real-number registers are set to the coordinates of corresponding ROIs; in particular, real-number registers $2i$ and $2i+1$ store the coordinates of the ith image ROI.
2. *Execution*: the operations encoded by I are carried out one by one, with intermediate results passed from operation to operation by means of image and real-number registers (see example in Fig. 3).
3. *Interpretation*: the scalar values $y_j(I,X)$, $j=1,\ldots,n_{reg}$, contained in the n_{reg} real-value registers at the end of procedure's execution are interpreted as the output yielded by I for image X. There values are gathered to form an individual's output vector

$$\mathbf{y} = \left\langle y_1(I, X), \ldots, y_{n_{reg}}(I, X) \right\rangle$$

that is subject to further processing described in Sect. 4.2.1.

4.2.3 Classifier Induction: The result of the first stage of learning is the best representation S (see Fig. 1) synthesized in coevolutionary process. The second stage of learning is consists in (a) computing the compound feature vector $\mathbf{Y}(X)$ for all the training examples $X \in D$, and (b) training the classifier $\mathbf{C}$ on the resulting data set.

This process resembles the classifier induction that takes place in evaluation process described in 4.2.2. However, this time the entire set D is used for classifier training, as no more performance estimation is required. Secondly, as this learning is single-event, a more sophisticated induction algorithm $\mathbf{C}$ may be used (as compared to the classifier $\mathbf{C}_{fit}$ used in the evaluation function).

5   The Experimental Results

The primary objective of the computational experiment was to evaluate the overall performance of the approach and verify its scalability with respect to the number of decision classes.

5.1   Parameter Setting

Table 2 shows parameter settings used for the feature synthesis process. As far as the second stage of learning is concerned (see Fig. 1), a *compound* classifier $\mathbf{C}$ has been used to boost the recognition performance. In particular, $\mathbf{C}$ implements the '1-vs.-all' scheme, i.e. is composed of l *base classifiers* (where l is the number of decision classes), each of them working as discriminator between a single decision class and all the remaining classes. To aggregate their voices, a simple voting procedure is used. Support vector machines with polynomial kernels of degree 3 have been employed as base classifiers. To train them, we used fast sequential minimal optimization algorithm [9] with complexity constant set to 10.

The training time has been set to 4000 seconds to estimate the quality of results the proposed method is able to attain in a limited time. Let us stress that this demand of computational resources concerns learning only; in testing, the trained system recognizes a single object in a few dozens of milliseconds.

5.2   The Data and the Task

The proposed approach has been tested on the demanding task of target recognition in synthetic aperture radar (SAR) images. The difficulties associated with this recognition task are:
- poor visibility of objects - most of them are reflected as sets of scattering centers only (no line features are present for these man-made objects at 1 foot resolution of data),
- low persistence of features under rotation, and
- high level of noise.

Table 2. Parameter setting for feature synthesis process concerning single decision class

Parameter	Setting
Mutation operator	one-point, probability 0.1
Crossover operator	one-point, probability 1.0, cutting allowed at every point
Selection operator	tournament selection with tournament pool size = 5
Number or registers (image and numeric) n_{reg}	2
Number of populations n_{sub}	4
Genome length	40 bytes (10 operations)
Single population size	200 individuals
Classifier C_{fit} used for feature set evaluation	decision tree inducer C4.5
Time limit for evolutionary search	4000 seconds (Pentium 1.4 GHz processor)
Number of subsystems n_{sub}	10

The MSTAR public database [11] containing real images of several military targets taken at different aspects/azimuths has been used as the source of images for the experiments described in this section. The original images have the same spatial resolution of one foot, but different sizes, so they have been cropped to 48×48 pixels. Only the magnitude part of the complex images has been used. No other form of preprocessing (e.g., image enhancement) has been applied.

To investigate the scalability of the proposed approach w.r.t. to the problem size, we defined several datasets with increasing number of decision classes for 15-deg. depression angle. The smallest problem considered concerned $l=2$ decision classes: BRDM2 and ZSU. Then, the consecutive problems were created by adding the decision classes up to $l=8$ in the following order: T62, Zil131, a variant A04 of T72 (T72#A04 in short), 2S1, BMP2#9563, and BTR70#C71 (see Fig. 4).

For i^{th} decision class, its representation D_i in the training data D consists of *two* subsets of images (for cross-validation training and testing; see Section 4.2.1) sampled uniformly from the original database with respect to 6-degree azimuth step. Training set D contains therefore always $2*(360/6)=120$ images from each decision class, so its total size is $120*l$. The corresponding test set T contains all the remaining images (for given target and elevation angle) from the original MSTAR collection, i.e.

$$T = \bigcup_{i=1}^{l} \overline{D}_i \, ,$$

where $\overline{D}$ stands for complement with respect to the MSTAR database. In this way, the training and test sets are strictly disjoint.

Fig. 4. Targets and their SAR images

5.3 Results

Figure 5a presents the performance of the proposed synthesis approach on the test data as a function of the number of decision classes for the case of *forced* recognition. It may be easily observed, that, as new decision classes are added to the problem, the recognition falls down very slowly. The major drop-offs occur when T72 tank and 2S1 self-propelled gun (classes 5 and 6, respectively), are added to the training data; this is probably due to the fact that these targets are visually similar to each other (e.g., both have gun turrets, see Fig. 4) and significantly resemble the T62 tank (class 3). On the contrary, introducing consecutive targets 7 and 8 (BMP2 and BTR60) did not affect much the performance.

Figure 5b shows the receiver operating characteristic (ROC) curves obtained by modifying the confidence threshold that controls the voting procedure. Again, the presented results vote in favor of our method: the ROC curves do not drop suddenly as the false positive ratio decreases. Therefore, high probability of correct identification (PCI) may be obtained when accepting some rejection rate (e.g., for 4 decision classes, PCI=0.99 when accepting ~0.12 rejection rate).

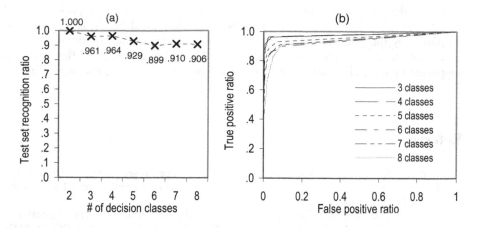

Fig. 5. (a) Test set recognition ratio as a function of number of decision classes. (b) ROC curves for different number of decision classes

6 Conclusions

In this contribution, we provided experimental evidence for the possibility of synthesizing, without or with little human intervention, a feature-based recognition system which recognizes 3D objects at the level of recognition ratio comparable to hand-crafted solutions and maintains performance as the number of objects to be recognized increases. Let us emphasize that these encouraging results have been obtained in the demanding field of SAR imagery, where the acquired images only roughly depict the underlying 3D structure of the object.

There are several major factors that contribute to the overall high performance of the approach. First of all, in the feature synthesis phase, it manipulates entire feature extraction *procedures*, as opposed to many approaches reported in the literature, which are usually limited to learning meant as parameter optimization. This allows for learning/developing sophisticated features, which are novel and sometimes very different from expert's intuition. Secondly, the paradigm of *coevolution* allows us to decompose the task of representation (feature set) synthesis into several semi-independent, cooperating subtasks. In this way, we exploit the inherent modularity of the learning process, without the need of specifying explicit objectives for each developed module. And thirdly, the *fusion at feature and decision level* helps us to aggregate, sometimes contradictory, information sources and build a recognition system that is close to perfection with a bunch of imperfect components at hand.

As no domain-specific knowledge has been used, this approach may be extended to other visual learning tasks at low expense of time and effort. This includes also *unsupervised* learning, as this is only matter of making appropriate changes to the fitness function. On the other hand, the method's background knowledge may be easily tailored to the task by modifying the library of elementary operations.

Acknowledgements. We would like to thank the authors of software packages: ECJ [5] and WEKA [15] for making their software publicly available. This research was supported by the grant F33615-99-C-1440. The contents of the information do not necessarily reflect the position or policy of the U. S. Government. The first author is supported by the Polish State Committee for Scientific Research, research grant no. 8T11F 006 19.

References

1. Banzhaf, W., Nordin, P., Keller, R., Francone F.: Genetic Programming. An Introduction. On the automatic Evolution of Computer Programs and its Application. Morgan Kaufmann, San Francisco, Calif. (1998)
2. Bhanu, B., Krawiec, K.: Coevolutionary Construction of Features for Transformation of Representation in Machine Learning. Proc. Workshop on Coevolution (GECCO 2002), AAAI Press, New York (2002) 249–254
3. Breiman, L.: Bagging predictors. Machine Learning 24 (1996) 123–140
4. Draper, B., Hanson, A., Riseman, E.: Knowledge-Directed Vision: Control, Learning and Integration. Proc. IEEE 84 (1996) 1625–1637
5. Luke, S.: ECJ Evolutionary Computation System. http://www.cs.umd.edu/projects/plus/ ec/ecj/ (2001)
6. Luke, S., Wiegand, R.P.: When Coevolutionary Algorithms Exhibit Evolutionary Dynamic. Proc. Workshop on Coevolution (GECCO 2002), AAAI Press, New York, N.Y. (2002) 236–241
7. Matheus, C.J.: A Constructive Induction Framework. Proc. 6th Int'l Workshop on Machine Learning, Ithaca, New York (1989) 474–475
8. Peng, J., Bhanu, B.: Closed-Loop Object Recognition Using Reinforcement Learning. IEEE Trans. on PAMI 20 (1998) 139–154
9. Platt, J.: Fast Training of Support Vector Machines using Sequential Minimal Optimization. Advances in Kernel Methods – Support Vector Learning, B. Schölkopf, C. Burges, and A. Smola, eds., MIT Press, Cambridge, Mass. (1998)
10. Potter, M.A., De Jong, K.A.: Cooperative Coevolution: An Architecture for Evolving Coadapted Subcomponents. Evolutionary Computation 8 (2000) 1–29
11. Ross, T., Worell, S., Velten, V., Mossing, J., Bryant, M.: Standard SAR ATR Evaluation Experiments using the MSTAR Public Release Data Set. SPIE Proc.: Algorithms for Synthetic Aperture Radar Imagery V, Vol. 3370, Orlando, FL (1998) 566–573
12. Segen, J.: GEST: A Learning Computer Vision System that Recognizes Hand Gestures. Machine Learning. A Multistrategy Approach. Volume IV, Michalski, R.S., Tecuci, G., eds., Morgan Kaufmann, San Francisco, Calif. (1994) 621–634
13. Teller, A., Veloso, M.: A Controlled Experiment: Evolution for Learning Difficult Image Classification. Proc. 7th Portuguese Conference on Artificial Intelligence, Springer Verlag, Berlin, Germany (1995) 165–176
14. Wiegand, R.P., Liles, W.C., De Jong, K.A.: An Empirical Analysis of Collaboration Methods in Cooperative Coevolutionary Algorithms. Proc. Genetic and Evolutionary Computation Conference, Morgan Kaufmann, San Francisco, Calif. (2001) 1235–1242
15. Witten, I.H., Frank, E.: Data Mining: Practical Machine Learning Tools and Techniques with Java Implementations. Morgan Kaufmann, San Francisco, Calif. (1999)
16. Wolpert, D., Macready, W.G.: No Free Lunch Theorems for Search. Tech. Report SFI-TR-95-010, The Santa Fe Institute (1995)

Generalization of Pattern-Growth Methods for Sequential Pattern Mining with Gap Constraints

Cláudia Antunes and Arlindo L. Oliveira

Department of Information Systems and Computer Science
Instituto Superior Técnico / INESC-ID
R. Alves Redol 9
1000 Lisboa, Portugal
claudia.antunes@dei.ist.utl.pt
aml@inesc-id.pt

Abstract. The problem of sequential pattern mining is one of the several that has deserved particular attention on the general area of data mining. Despite the important developments in the last years, the best algorithm in the area (Prefix-Span) does not deal with gap constraints and consequently doesn't allow for the introduction of background knowledge into the process. In this paper we present the generalization of the PrefixSpan algorithm to deal with gap constraints, using a new method to generate projected databases. Studies on performance and scalability were conducted in synthetic and real-life datasets, and the respective results are presented.

1 Introduction

With the rapid increase of stored data in digital form, the interest in the discovery of hidden information has exploded in the last decade. One approximation to the problem of discovery of hidden information is based on finding frequent associations between elements in sets, also called basket analysis. One important special case arises when this approach is applied to the treatment of sequential data. The sequential nature of the problem is relevant when the data to be mined is naturally embedded in a one dimensional space, i.e., when one of the relevant pieces of information can be viewed as one ordered set of elements. This variable can be time or some other dimension, as is common in other areas, like bioinformatics. We define sequential pattern mining as the process of discovering all sub-sequences that appear frequently on a given sequence database and have minimum support threshold. One challenge resides in performing this search in and efficient way.

In this paper, we present a generalization of the PrefixSpan algorithm to deal with gap constraints. A gap constraint imposes a limit on the separation of two consecutive elements of an identified sequence. This type of constraints is critical for the applicability of these methods to a number of problems, especially those with long sequences and small alphabets. The method we propose is based on the introduction of a new

P. Perner and A. Rosenfeld (Eds.): MLDM 2003, LNAI 2734, pp. 239–251, 2003.

method to generate projected databases that efficiently stores the subsequences of all occurrences of each frequent element.

The paper is organized as follows: Sect. 2 exposes the sequential pattern mining problem and its main application areas. Section 3 formalizes the sequential pattern mining problem and describes the specific problems addressed. Section 4 analyzes existing algorithms, paying particular attention to their behavior when dealing with gap constraints. Section 5 represents the main contribution of this work and presents a generalization of the PrefixSpan algorithm to deal with gap constraints. Section 6 describes the experimental results obtained with artificial and real-life data. Finally, Sect. 7 draws the most relevant conclusions and points out guidelines for future research.

2 Sequential Pattern Mining

The problem of sequential pattern mining has deserved particular attention inside the general area of data mining. Algorithms for this problem are relevant when the data to be mined has some sequential nature, i.e., when each piece of data is an ordered set of elements, like events in the case of temporal information, or amino-acid sequences for problems in bioinformatics.

One particularly important problem in the area of sequential pattern mining is the problem of discovering all subsequences that appear on a given sequence database and have minimum support threshold. The difficulty is in figuring out what sequences to try and then efficiently finding out which of those are frequent [7].

One of the obvious applications of these techniques is in modeling the behavior of some entity, along time. For instance, using a database with transactions performed by customers at any instant, it is desirable to predict what would be the customer's next transaction, based on his past transactions. This type of concerns is one of the main goals of temporal data mining. Examples of these tasks are easily found on a number of areas, like the prediction of financial time series, patients' health monitoring and marketing, to cite only a few. With the increase of stored data in several domains and with the advances in the data mining area, the range of sequential pattern mining applications has enlarged significantly. Today, in engineering problems and scientific research sequential data appears, for example, in data resulting from monitoring sensor networks or spatial missions [4]. In healthcare, despite this type of data being a reality for decades (for example in data originated by complex data acquisition systems like ECGs or EECs), more than ever, medical staff is interested in systems able to help on medical research and on patients monitoring [6]. In businesses and finance, applications on the analysis of product sales, client behaviors or inventory consumptions are essential for today's business planning ([1], [3]). A survey of applications and methods used in temporal data mining has been presented recently [2].

Another relevant application of sequential pattern mining is in bioinformatics, where different characteristics of proteins and other biologically significant structures are to be inferred from mapped DNA sequences. Some important applications in this domain are on molecular sequence analysis, protein structure prediction, gene mapping, modeling of biochemical pathways and drug design [8].

3 Problem Definition

Several algorithms have been proposed to deal with the problem of sequential pattern mining, but they don't always share the same set of assumptions, which makes it difficult to compare them. In order to compare the performance of the two most significant approaches proposed to date, we present the basic notions needed to clearly define the problem of sequential pattern mining.

Definition 1. A *sequence* is an ordered list of elements called *items*. A sequence is *maximal* if it is not contained in any other sequence.

The number of elements in a sequence s is called the *length* of the sequence and is denoted by $|s|$. A sequence with length k is called a *k-sequence*. The ith element in the sequence is represented by s_i. The empty sequence is denoted by <>. The result of the concatenation of two sequences x and y is a new sequence s denoted by $s=xy$.

Definition 2. A sequence $a=<a_1 a_2 ... a_n>$ is *contained in* another sequence $b=<b_1 b_2 ... b_m>$, or a is a *subsequence* of b, if there exist integers $1 \leq i_1 < i_2 < ... < i_n \leq m$ such that $a_1=b_{i_1}, a_2=b_{i_2}, ..., a_n=b_{i_n}$.

A subsequence s' of s is denoted by $s' \subseteq s$, and by $s' \subset s$ if s' is a proper subsequence of s, i.e. if s' is a subsequence of s but is not equal to s.

When considering the existence of gap constraints, such as the use of a sliding window or some time constraints (as proposed by Srikant [7]), the notion of subsequence suffers some changes. In general, we can view this relaxation as an approximation to the original measure.

Definition 3. A sequence $a=<a_1 a_2 ... a_n>$ is a *δ-distance subsequence* of $b=<b_1 b_2 ... b_m>$ if there exist integers $i_1 < i_2 < ... < i_n$ such that $a_1=b_{i_1}, a_2=b_{i_2}, ..., a_n=b_{i_n}$. and $i_k - i_{k-1} \leq \delta$. Sequence $a=<a_1 a_2 ... a_n>$ is a *contiguous subsequence* of $b=<b_1 b_2 ... b_m>$ if a is a 1-distance subsequence of b, i.e., the elements of a can be mapped to a contiguous segment of b.

Note that a contiguous subsequence is a particular case of δ-distance subsequence ($\delta=1$) and is equivalent to the original notion of subsequence. A δ-distance subsequence s' of s is denoted by $s' \subseteq_\delta s$. A contiguous subsequence s' of s is denoted by $s' \angle s$.

Definition 4. Given a database *D* of sequences and a user-specified minimum support threshold σ, a sequence is said to be *frequent* if it is *contained in* at least σ sequences in the database. A *sequential pattern* is a <u>maximal sequence that is frequent</u>.

Given a database D of sequences and a user-specified minimum support threshold σ, the problem of *mining sequential patterns* is <u>to find all of the sequential patterns</u>.

Note that beside the database and the minimum support threshold, the user may supply the δ, i.e. the maximum gap allowed between two consecutive elements in a sequence.

4 Existing Algorithms

4.1 Apriori-Based Methods

The first approach to sequential pattern mining was the AprioriAll algorithm [1]. This algorithm follows the candidate generation and test philosophy, and looks for all patterns without considering the existence of gap constraints. It considers a sequence frequent if all of its elements are present (in the given order), on a sufficient number of sequences in the database.

```
AprioriAll (DB, min_sup) {
    L₁ = { frequent 1-sequences };
    int k=2;
    while (Lₖ₋₁ ≠ ∅) {
        Cₖ = candidateGeneration(Lₖ₋₁, k);
        Cₖ = candidatePruning(Cₖ, k);
        Lₖ = supportBasedPruning(Cₖ);
        k ← k+1
    }
    return Maximal Sequences in ∪ₖ Lₖ
}
candidateGeneration (Lₖ₋₁, k){
    Cₖ = ∅;
    for each a∈Lₖ₋₁
        for each b∈Lₖ₋₁
            if (∀ n, 1≤n≤k-2: aₙ=bₙ)
                Cₖ ← Cₖ ∪ {a₁...aₖ₋₂aₖ₋₁bₖ₋₁,
                           a₁...aₖ₋₂bₖ₋₁aₖ₋₁}
    return Cₖ;
}
```

Fig. 1. AprioriAll algorithm and its candidate generation method

The candidate generation in this case works by joining two frequent k-1-sequences when their maximal prefixes are equal. Each pair of such sequences originates two k-candidates, as illustrated in Fig. 1.

The great advantage of AprioriAll resides on its iterative nature and the use of the anti-monotonicity property. Using the frequent k-1-sequences, it generates the k-candidates, thus reducing the number of sequences to be searched in the database in comparison with exhaustive search. It also performs an additional reduction on the number of candidates, by removing all the candidates that have some non-frequent k-1-subsequences, as shown in Fig. 2.

These reductions on the number of candidates are possible since the support of a sequence obeys the anti-monotonic property, which says that a k-sequence can't be frequent unless all of its k-1-subsequences are frequent.

```
candidatePruning (Lk-1, Ck, k) {
    for each s∈Ck
        if (∃ s' ⊂ s ∧ |s'|=k-1 ∧ s'∉Lk-1)
            Ck ← Ck \ {s}
    return Ck;
}
```

Fig. 2. Candidate pruning based on anti-monotonic property

Naturally, the most expensive task is the support-based pruning, since it counts the support of each candidate on the full database. AprioriAll achieves best performance when the minimum support threshold is high and there are few frequent different 1-sequences, 2-sequences and so on. This leads to maximal pruning and reduces the number of support counts.

However when gap constraints are used, the AprioriAll algorithm cannot be applied directly. To illustrate this limitation, consider for example the data in Table 1 and a minimum support threshold of 40%, which means, in this case, that a pattern has to occur at least twice in the database. Additionally, assume that the gap constraint is equal to 1, which means that only contiguous sequences are allowed.

Table 1. Database example

Database
fgfgfg
acjcde
ababa
achcde
noqrst

The first step of AprioriAll will find *a*, *c*, *d* and *e* as frequent 1-patterns and *ac*, *cd* and *de* as frequent 2-patterns. However, the process will finish without discovering *cde*, since there are no 3-candidates. This is due to limitations in the candidate-generation method, which isn't able to generate all candidates. In fact, while the candidate generation process is complete when there are no gap constraints, it becomes incomplete when gap constraints are imposed.

Although to our knowledge, this property has never been stated clearly, it eventually led to the definition of a new method for candidate generation that does not suffer from this limitation.

```
candidateGeneration (L_{k-1}, k) {
    C_k = ∅;
    for each a∈L_{k-1}
        for each b∈L_{k-1}
            if (∀1≤n≤k-2: a_{n+1}=b_n )
                C_k ← C_k ∪ {a_1...a_{k-1}b_{k-1}}
    return C_k;
}
```

Fig. 3. Candidate generation in GSP method

The GSP algorithm [7] is an evolution of AprioriAll, allowing for the incorporation of gap constraints. The key difference between these two methods resides on the candidate generation procedure. The GSP algorithm creates a new candidate whenever the prefix of a sequence is equal to the suffix of another one, as illustrated on Fig. 3.

```
candidatePruning (L_{k-1}, C_k, k, gap) {
    if (gap≠1)
        for each s∈C_k
            if (∃ s' ⊂ s ∧ |s'|=k-1 ∧ s'∉L_{k-1})
                C_k ← C_k \ {s}
    else
        for each s∈C_k
            if (∃ s' ∠ s ∧ |s'|=k-1 ∧ s'∉L_{k-1})
                C_k ← C_k \ {s}
    return C_k;
}
```

Fig. 4. Candidate pruning in GSP method

The changes in the generation method imply changes in the candidate pruning process. If gaps are not allowed only candidates with some non-frequent contiguous subsequence need to be pruned. When gaps are allowed a sequence is pruned if it contains a non-frequent subsequence. Figure 4 shows the pseudo-code for candidate pruning method.

4.2 Pattern-Growth Methods

Pattern-growth methods are a more recent approach to deal with sequential data mining problems. The key idea is to avoid the candidate generation step altogether, and to focus the search on a restricted portion of the initial database.

```
PrefixSpan (DB, min_sup) {
   return MaximalSequences in run(<>,0, DB)
}

run (α, length, DB) {
   f_list = createsFrequentItemList(DB);
   for each b∈f_list {
      α' ← αb;
      L← L ∪ α'
      L←L∪run(α',length+1,createProjectedDB (α',DB))
   }
   return L
}

createProjectedDB (α, DB) {
   for each s∈DB
      if (α ⊆ s) {
         β←s.postfix (α, 1)
         α-projDB← α-projDB ∪ {β}
      }
   return α-projDB;
}
```

Fig. 5. PrefixSpan algorithm and the creation of projected databases method

PrefixSpan [5] is the most promising of the pattern-growth methods and is based on recursively constructing the patterns, as shown in Fig. 5. Its great advantage is the use of projected databases. An α-projected database is the set of subsequences in the database, that are suffixes of the sequences that have prefix α. In each step, the algorithm looks for the frequent sequences with prefix α, in the correspondent projected database. In this way the search space is reduced in each step, allowing for better performances in the presence of small support thresholds.

Again, the PrefixSpan algorithm performs perfectly without gap constraints but is not able to deal with these restrictions. To illustrate that limitation, consider again the data in Table 1 and the conditions used before (minimum support threshold of 40% and a gap constraint equal to 1). It will find *a*, *c*, *d* and *e*, which will constitute *f_list*. Then it will call recursively the main procedure with α=*a* and an α-projected database equal to {*cjcde*, *baba*, *chcde*}. Next it will recursively proceed with α=*ac* and an α-projected database equal to {*jcde*, *hcde*}, which finishes this branch. Similarly for element *c*: *run* is called with α=*c* and an α-projected database equal to {*jcde*, *hcde*}. Since there is no frequent element at distance 1, the search stops and *cde* is not discovered. This happens because the α-projected database only maintains the suffix after the first occurrence of the last element of α.

5   Generalized PrefixSpan

In this section we show how PrefixSpan can be generalized to handle gap constraints, an important issue since gap constraints are important in many domains of application and PrefixSpan is the most efficient algorithm known for sequential pattern mining, especially in the situation of low support thresholds.

The generalization we propose for PrefixSpan (*GenPrefixSpan*) in order to be able to deal with gap constraints, is based on the redefinition of the method used to construct the projected database. Instead of looking only for the first occurrence of the element, every element's occurrence is considered. For example, in the previous example, the creation of the *c*-projected database would give as result {*jcde, de, hcde, de*} instead of {*jcde, hcde*} as before.

It is important to note that, including all suffixes after the element's occurrence changes the database and may change the number of times that each pattern appears. For instance, for the same example the *a*-projected database would be {*cjcde, baba, ba, chcde*}. In order to deal with this issue, associating an *id* to each original sequence in the database and guaranteeing that each sequence counts at most once for the support of each element is enough to keep an accurate count on the number of appearances of a given sequence.

```
initProjDB (α, DB, gap) {
   for each s∈DB {
      i←1;
      repeat {
         i←s.nextOccurrence(α, i+1);
         β←s.postfix(α, i)
         α-projDB←α-projDB ∪ {β}
      } until i + gap > |s|
   }
   return α-projDB;
}
```

Fig. 6. The new method to create projected databases

Figure 6 illustrates the new method we propose to create projected databases. This new approach is only needed in the first recursion level, since after this isolated step the database will contain all of the sequences starting with each frequent element.

So the generalized PrefixSpan will consist of two main steps: the discovery and creation of each frequent element projected database and the usual recursion, as shown in Fig. 7.

```
GenPrefixSpan (DB, min_sup, gap) {
      f_list = createsFrequentItemList(DB);
      for each b∈f_list {
        L← L ∪ b
        L← L ∪ run (b, 1,
                        initProjDB (b,DB, gap))
      }
      return MaximalSequences in L
}
```

Fig. 7. Generalized PrefixSpan main method

Note that when there is no gap constraint, the creation of projected databases is similar to the correspondent procedure defined in original PrefixSpan, since it only generates the projection relative to the first occurrence of α. In this manner, the performance of GenPrefixSpan and PrefixSpan are similar in the absence of gap constraints.

6 Comparison

In this section we present a comparative study between apriori-based and pattern-growth approaches with and without the presence of gap constraints. In order to do that, we use the AprioriAll, GSP and PrefixSpan algorithms in the absence of gap constraints, and the GSP and GenPrefixSpan algorithms in the presence of these restrictions.

All experiments were performed on a Pentium II with 300 MHz and 256MB of RAM. The sequences were generated and maintained in main memory during the algorithms processing.

All algorithms were implemented using an object-oriented approach allowing for the sharing of the basic methods used by the different algorithms and making all speed comparisons meaningful.

6.1 Experiences with Artificially Generated Data

To perform this study, we used a synthetic data set generator, based on a Zipf distribution, similar to others used on similar studies ([1, 5]). As parameters, this data generator receives the number of sequences, the average length of each sequence, the number of distinct items (or sequence elements) and a Zipf parameter that governs the probability of each item occurrence in the data set. The length of each sequence is chosen from a Poisson distribution with mean equal to the input parameter correspondent to the average length of each sequence (10 was the chosen value for the average sequence length).

The study is divided in two major sections: the scalability and the performance studies. Table 2 lists the parameters of the performed studies.

Table 2. Comparative studies performed

Study		DB size	Support	Gap	Alphabet Size
	Scalability	—	33%	0	5
Performance	Variable Support	10000	—	0	5
	Variable Gap	10000	33%	—	5
	Variable Alphabet	10000	33%	0	—

Scalability Study. As it is shown in Fig. 8, the scalability of PrefixSpan when adapted to use gap constraints suffers some degradation, having a behavior similar to that of apriori-based algorithms. This leaves open the question of whether it is possible to generalize projection based methods, such as PrefixSpan, in a way that implies minimal impact, when compared with the situation where no gap constraints are used.

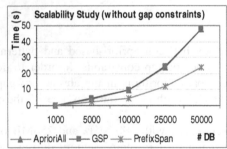 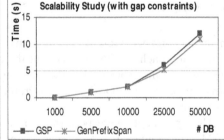

Fig. 8. Performance vs. database size

Note that the worst case to GenPrefixSpan (with gap constraints) is encountered when the database is composed of a significant number of sequences with the same element repeated several times. In this case, the projected database for each different element may be much bigger than the original database, violating the assumption that the size of projected database cannot exceed that of the original one, as is the case of the original version of PrefixSpan [5].

Performance with Variable Support. In terms of performance (Fig. 9), when the minimum support threshold varies, the behavior of PrefixSpan is similar with or without the use of gap constraints, with the same pattern of growth. This means that the advantages of PrefixSpan over apriori-based methods are still present in the situation of low value support thresholds.

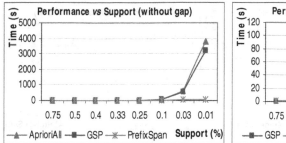
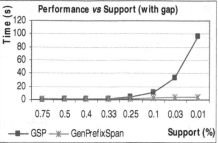

Fig. 9. Performance vs. minimum support threshold

Performance with Variable Gap Constraints. As expected (Fig. 10), when the gap constraint is relaxed, the performance decreases as in apriori-based algorithms, since the number of patterns to discover increases. Note that the difference between both methods increases with the relaxation of gap constraints. With this relaxation the probability to encounter frequent elements in the allowed gap is greater and consequently the search for the patterns is less time consuming.

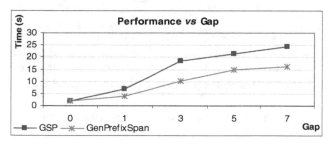

Fig. 10. Performance vs. gap value

Performance with Variable Alphabet Size. The impact of the alphabet size on the performance of the methods did not lead to any clear conclusions. The PrefixSpan method seems to be better than apriori-based methods over all ranges of the alphabet size, but the results are inconclusive and the observed evolution is not easily explainable. It is worth noting that the change in alphabet size has a significant and non-trivial impact on the type and number of patterns present in the database, as is shown in Fig. 11.

6.2 Experiences with Real-World Data

To perform this study, we used the WWW server access logs from the web site of a discussion forum. The objective was to identify common patterns of access, in order to optimize the layout of the web site and, in the future, to identify and flag abnormal behaviors. The dataset is composed of about 7000 sequences, where each sequence represents the pages visited by one user when he enters the forum.

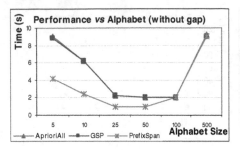
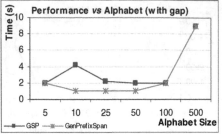

Fig. 11. Performance vs. alphabet size

In general, the results achieved with the real-life datasets (Figs. 12 and 13) confirm the results obtained with the synthetic dataset, despite the significantly different statistics of the problems. For this reason, we believe the results presented are relevant and applicable to a large range of actual problems.

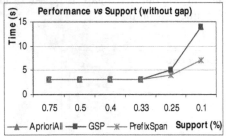
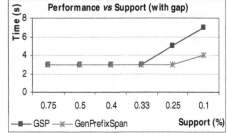

Fig. 12. Performance vs. minimum support threshold

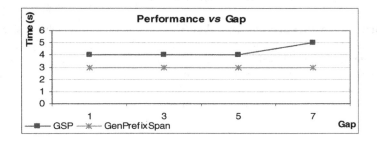

Fig. 13. Performance study with variable gap

7 Conclusions

In this paper we have presented the generalization of the PrefixSpan algorithm to deal with gap constraints. In order to achieve that goal, we have proposed a new method to generate projected databases that store the subsequences of all occurrences of each frequent element.

The modified PrefixSpan method keeps its performance advantages relatively to apriori-based algorithms in the more difficult situation of low support thresholds, although its relative advantage over these methods is reduced when compared with the high support thresholds situation.

The generalization of projection based methods to gap constrained sequential pattern problems is very important in many applications, since apriori-based methods are inapplicable in many problems where low support thresholds are used. In fact, the imposition of a gap restriction is critical for the applicability of these methods in areas like bioinformatics, which exhibit limited size alphabets and very long sequences. We are actively working in applying this methodology to the problem of motif finding in bioinformatics sequences, an area that can benefit very much from more sophisticated methods for sequential pattern analysis.

References

1. Agrawal, R. and R. Srikant, "Mining sequential patterns", in *Proc. Int'l Conf. Data Engineering* (1995), 3–14
2. Antunes, C. and A. Oliveira, "Temporal data mining: an overview" in *Proc. Workshop on Temporal Data Mining* (KDD'01) (2001), 1–13
3. Fama, E., "Efficient Capital Markets: a review of theory and empirical work". *Journal of Finance* (1970) 383–417
4. Grossman, R. and C. Kamath *et all*, *Data Mining for Scientific and Engineering Applications*. Kluwer Academic Publishers (1998)
5. Pei, J, J. Han *et all* "PrefixSpan: Mining Sequential Patterns Efficiently by Prefix-Projected Pattern Growth" in *Proc. Int'l Conf. Data Engineering* (ICDE 01) (2001)
6. Shahar, Y. and M.A. Musen, "Knowledge-Based Temporal Abstraction in Clinical Domains" in *Artificial Intelligence in Medicine* 8, (1996) 267–298
7. Srikant, R. and R. Agrawal, "Mining Sequential Patterns: Generalizations and Performance Improvements" in *Proc. Int'l Conf. Extending Database Technology* (1996) 3–17
8. Zaki, M., H.Toivonen and J. Wang, "Report on BIOKDD01: Workshop on Data Mining in Bioinformatics" in *SIGKDD Explorations*, vol. 3, nr. 2 (2001) 71–73

Discover Motifs in Multi-dimensional Time-Series Using the Principal Component Analysis and the MDL Principle

Yoshiki Tanaka and Kuniaki Uehara

Department of Computer and Systems Engineering, Kobe University
1-1 Rokko-dai, Nada, Kobe 657-8501, Japan
{yoshiki,uehara}@ai.cs.scitec.kobe-u.ac.jp

Abstract. Recently, the detection of a previously unknown, frequently occurring pattern has been regarded as a difficult problem. We call this pattern as *"motif"*. Many researchers have proposed algorithms for discovering the motif. However, if the optimal period length of the motif is not known in advance, we cannot use these algorithms for discovering the motif. In this paper, we attempt to dynamically determine the optimum period length using the MDL principle. Moreover, in order to apply this algorithm to the multi dimensional time-series, we transform the time-series into one dimensional time-series by using the Principal Component Analysis. Finally, we show experimental results and discuss the efficiency of our motif discovery algorithm.

1 Introduction

Many researchers have been studying the extraction of various features from time-series data. One of these problems, efficient extraction of previously defined patterns has been received much attention. This problem may now be essentially regarded as a solved problem. However, a more interesting problem, the detection of previously unknown, frequently occurring patterns is still regarded as a difficult challenge. We call this pattern as "motif". The term "motif" can be defined by the characteristic that it includes the subsequences with similar behavior (temporal variation) appeared frequently in the time-series. Motif extraction is useful to discover association rules from time-series data[1], or to cluster the time-series data[2], etc.

Many researchers have proposed algorithms for discovering a motif[3][4][5]. Among them, EMMA algorithm[5] has the widest application range that can discover motifs efficiently. The algorithm extracts the motifs with various period lengths. However, we need to discover the "true motifs" in the motifs. Therefore, the computation time of extracting the motifs increases. That is, if the optimal period length is not known in advance, the algorithm is not directly applicable.

We illustrate an example of different lengths of the period in Fig. 1. The motifs in Fig. 1a are considered to be valid since they are almost similar. On the other hand, if the period length is longer than that of Fig. 1a, EMMA algorithm cannot discover the motifs shown in the Fig. 1b. Similarly, the algorithm may extract too many irrelevant motifs using a shorter period length. Hence, we need to determine an optimum period of length

P. Perner and A. Rosenfeld (Eds.): MLDM 2003, LNAI 2734, pp. 252–265, 2003.

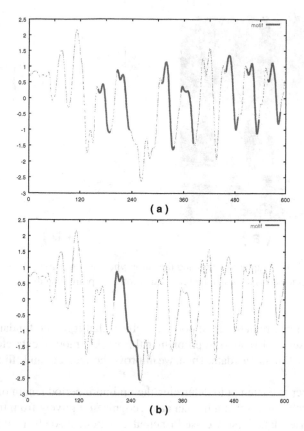

Fig. 1. Motifs discoverd from the same time-series using EMMA algorithm. Period length of motif (a) is 30 frames,(b) is 60 frames

of a motif. One idea is to solve the problem by exhaustively applying the algorithm for all possible period lengths, but, it seems to be impractical.

In our approach, we improve the algorithm that can be applied to the multi di-mensional time-series data, because, in the real world, spatial-temporal data can be represented as the multi dimensional time-series but not in the form of one dimensional time-series data.

For example, in case of motion capturing system, we can obtain 3 dimensional time series data. Here, an actor puts on 18 markers which reflect infra-red ray (Fig. 2a). He performs some actions with the markers being surrounded with 6 cameras. The cameras record the actor's action as video images and calculate 3-dimensional locations of the markers. Finally, we obtain the 3 dimensional time-series data as in Fig. 2b. The figure represents the movement of the right hand while pitching a ball.

In the work [6], Mori et al. reported the motion recognition from the 3-dimensional time series data obtained from the motion capture system. The recognition process in this study, requires temporal segmentation. The task is to divide the time series into subsequences called primitive motion at the points where velocity changes. However, in

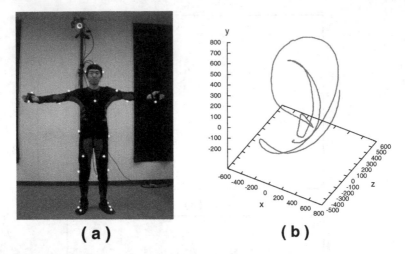

Fig. 2. (a) The motion capture system and the actor who puts on markers. (b) An example of the 3 dimensional time-series data obtained from the motion capture system

this approach, there remains an important problem that it has no fundamental basis for dividing time-series. To solve this problem in this work, a motif is extracted as a primitive motion from the time-series data. Then, we improve the accuracy and efficiency of motion recognition.

In this paper, we attempt to determine the optimum period length of motif dynamically, and discover motif that a human can recognize intuitively from the multi dimensional time-series data. First, we use Principal Component Analysis to transform multi dimensional time-series data to one dimensional time-series data. Second, based on the MDL (Minimum Description Length) principle [7] we discover optimum period lengths of motifs, that are the candidates of a motif. Finally, to discover the motif among the candidates, we employ simplified EMMA algorithm with the optimum period length. The advantage of our algorithm lies in that it can reduce the computation time for finding the motif. It can also find precise motifs than that of EMMA algorithm, from the view point of human intuition.

2   Dimensionality Reduction of Multi-dimensional Time-Series

To discover motifs from multi dimensional time-series data, we need to solve several problems. Among these problem, one significant problem is the requirement of huge amount of calculation time. Another significant problem is the complexity to discover motif directly from multi dimensional time-series. For this reason, no researcher could propose an appropriate algorithm yet.

To solve these problems, we transform multi dimensional time-series into one dimensional time-series data. We discover the motifs from the one dimensional time-series using existing motif discovery algorithm. However, in the transformation, we must minimize the loss of some information of the original multi dimensional time-series. For this purpose, we focus on the PCA (Principal Component Analysis) [8]. It is widely used in the statistical field recently.

The PCA is an effective method to find the features of the data expressed with some observed variables. For example, in a statistical field, this analysis is used to determine the data of two or more stock prices for the indexing purpose. We illustrate specific method to apply PCA to the time-series data. For example, a m dimensional time series C of length n can be represented as follows:

$$C = c_1, c_2, \cdots, c_t, \cdots, c_n \tag{1}$$
$$c_t = (x_{1t}, x_{2t}, \cdots, x_{mt})$$

In order to apply the PCA, we need to calculate a covariance matrix for the time-series by using the following equation:

$$\begin{bmatrix} \sum x_{1t}x_{1t} & \sum x_{1t}x_{2t} & \cdots & \sum x_{1t}x_{mt} \\ \sum x_{2t}x_{1t} & \sum x_{2t}x_{2t} & \cdots & \sum x_{2t}x_{mt} \\ \vdots & \vdots & \ddots & \vdots \\ \sum x_{mt}x_{1t} & \sum x_{mt}x_{2t} & \cdots & \sum x_{mt}x_{mt} \end{bmatrix} \tag{2}$$

Each eigenvalue λ_i is ordered as $\lambda_1 \geq \lambda_2 \geq \cdots \geq \lambda_m$. The eigenvector is represented as $[e_{1\lambda_i} e_{2\lambda_i} \cdots e_{m\lambda_i}]$. Then, the i-th principal component of time-series pc_{t,λ_i} is calculated by means of $x_1, x_2, \cdots, x_m$ respectively.

$$pc_{t,\lambda_i} = e_{1\lambda_i}(x_{1t} - \bar{x}_1) + e_{2\lambda_i}(x_{2t} - \bar{x}_2) +$$
$$\cdots + e_{m\lambda_i}(x_{mt} - \bar{x}_m) \tag{3}$$

Most of the variance in the data is explained by considering only the first principal component [8]. As it accounts for most of the information in the data, we use the first principal component to effectively transform the multi dimensional time series to one dimensional time-series. Finally, we obtain one dimensional time-series $\dot{C}$ as follows:

$$\dot{C} = \dot{c}_1, \dot{c}_2, \cdots, \dot{c}_t, \cdots, \dot{c}_n \tag{4}$$
$$\dot{c}_t = e_{1\lambda_1}(x_{1t} - \bar{x}_1) + e_{2\lambda_1}(x_{2t} - \bar{x}_2) +$$
$$\cdots + e_{m\lambda_1}(x_{mt} - \bar{x}_m) \tag{5}$$

In Eq. 5, the $\dot{C}$ is a linear combination of the original variables. Hence, iterational component of the significant dimensional data can be included in the first principle component. Therefore, we can assume that the discovered motif from $\dot{C}$ is same as that of the original multi dimensional time-series C.

3 Detecting an Optimum Period Length and Candidates for a Motif

To make our motif discovery algorithm useful in the various fields, it is necessary to dynamically determine a period length of a motif. In this section, we illustrate an algorithm that detects an optimum period length of motif based on the MDL principle. MDL principle is proposed by Rissanen [7]. It is used to estimate the optimality of a stochastic model. The "stochastic model" is specified to presume the "immanent structure" of the given data in various fields. The principle states that the best model to describe a set of data is that model which minimizes the description length of the entire data set. Here, for the time series data, we regard the best model as the motif. In other words, the motif minimizes the sum of the description length of a given time series data and the description length of the motif itself. Based on this idea, we introduce the algorithm to detect an optimum period length and candidates for a motif.

3.1   Transforming Time-Series into a Sequence of Symbols

We use the MDL principle for extracting an optimum pattern that is expected to be a motif. However, there is an underlying problem that the same patterns hardly appear in the time-series. In addition, we want to extract a pattern without being influenced by the "noise" of the time-series. For these reasons, we transform the time-series data into a sequence of symbols that represents the behavior excluding the noise. Then, we detect an optimum pattern of symbols in the sequence of symbols.

In order to transform time-series data into a sequence of symbols, we use dimensionality reduction algorithm based on a PAA (Piecewise Aggregate Approximation) representation [5]. Here, we show the visualization of this transformation algorithm in Fig. 3.

First, we obtain subsequences by shifting the analysis window of T_{min}, the minimum period length of motif (Fig. 3a). Second, each subsequence is transformed into a sequence of "PAA symbols" (Fig. 3b). The PAA representation is a vector expression that uses the average value in each small segment. A time series $C = c_1, \cdots, c_n$ of length n can be represented as a w-dimensional space by a vector $\bar{C} = \bar{c}_1, \cdots, \bar{c}_w$:

$$\bar{c}_i = \frac{w}{n} \sum_{j=\frac{n}{w}(i-1)+1}^{\frac{n}{w}i} c_i \tag{6}$$

In order to transform the vector of w dimension into a sequence of "PAA symbols", we need to determine "breakpoints". These breakpoints determine the range of the PAA value for assigning unique PAA symbol.

We can simply determine the breakpoints that will produce equal-sized area under Gaussian curve, because the normalized time-series has the feature that it has highly Gaussian distribution. Breakpoints are a sorted list of numbers $B = \beta_1, \cdots, \beta_{a-1}$ such that the area under a $N(0, 1)$ Gaussian curve from β_i to $\beta_{i+1} = 1/a$ (β_0 and β_a are defined as $-\infty$ and ∞, respectively). Then, all PAA coefficients that are below the smallest breakpoint are mapped to a PAA symbol "**a**". All coefficients greater than or equal to the smallest breakpoint and less than the second smallest breakpoint are mapped to the PAA symbol "**b**", etc.

Finally, "behavior symbol" is assigned for every subsequence of PAA symbols. For example, the behavior symbol "A" is assigned to the subsequence "CCBA" in Fig. 3c. Here, from a view point of our definition of the motif, we can say that discovering pattern from this sequence of behavior symbols $\tilde{C} = \tilde{c}_1, \cdots, \tilde{c}_{n_a}$ ($n_a = n - T_{min} + 1$) is same as discovering motif from original time-series.

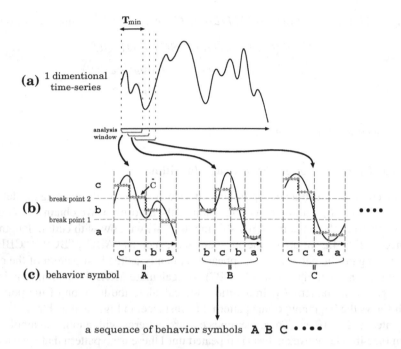

Fig. 3. Visualization of the algorithm of transforming time-series into a sequence of symbol. (a) we obtain subsequences by shifting the analysis window. (b) Each subsequence is transformed into a sequence of PAA symbols, that is based on PAA representation $\bar{C}$. (c) "behavior symbol" is assigned for every pattern in the order of PAA symbols

3.2 Estimating Extracted Motif Candidate Based on MDL Principle

To estimate the optimality of the extracted pattern from the sequence $\tilde{C}$ using the MDL principle, we need to define a description length of sequence of symbols. We assume that n_p is the length of a subsequence SC appeared in the sequence $\tilde{C}$ and s_p is the number of unique symbols used in SC. First, we need $log_2 n_p$ bits to encode the number of symbols of SC. Then, encoding the labels of all n_p symbols requires $n_p log_2 s_p$ bits. Hence, the description length of SC is defined as follows:

$$DL(SC) = log_2 n_p + n_p log_2 s_p \tag{7}$$

In addition, we need to define the description length $DL(\tilde{C}|SC)$. This is the description length of $\tilde{C}$ where a subsequence SC is replaced with one symbol. The length of such a sequence is $\acute{n}_a$ and the frequency of appearance SC in $\tilde{C}$ is q. The description length $DL(C|SC)$ is calculated as follows:

$$DL(\tilde{C}|SC) = log_2 \acute{n}_a + \acute{n}_a log_2 (s_a + q) \tag{8}$$

Where, $log_2 \acute{n}_a$ is the number of bits required to encode the number of symbols of $\tilde{C}$. $\acute{n}_a log_2 (s_a + q)$ is the number of bits required to encode the labels of all $\acute{n}_a$ symbols.

Finally, MDL estimation function $MDL(\tilde{C}|SC)$ of $\tilde{C}$ to SC is defined as follows:

$$
\begin{aligned}
MDL(\tilde{C}|SC) &= DL(\tilde{C}|SC) + DL(SC) \\
&= log_2\acute{n}_a + \acute{n}_a log_2(s_a + q) \\
&\quad + log_2 n_p + n_p log_2 s_p
\end{aligned}
\tag{9}
$$

We consider that the subsequence SC which has the minimum value of the MDL estimation function is the optimum pattern of $\tilde{C}$.

3.3 The Optimum Pattern Extracting Algorithm

In this section, we illustrate the optimum pattern detection algorithm using the definition in Sect. 3.2. Figure 4 shows the visualization of the algorithm. We obtain subsequences of symbols from the sequence $\tilde{C}$ by shifting analysis window with certain lengths. For instance, in Fig. 4a, we obtain the subsequences, such as "ABC", "BCB", "CBB" etc. Then, we regard the pattern which appears frequently as the best pattern of the current symbol sequence (in Fig. 4a, it is "BCB"). We calculate MDL estimation function M_1 and length of the pattern L_1. In addition, we calculate the location of the pointer P_1 which shows the beginning of the pattern. For instance, in Fig. 4a, the obtained pointers are located at $2, 5, 10$ etc. Then, we replace these patterns with another symbol such as "$\acute{A}$" in Fig. 4b. The above analysis is repeated until there is no pattern that appears more than twice in the sequence of symbols. (such as the sequence in Fig. 4c).

When the analysis is finished, the pattern with the smallest value of MDL estimation function is regarded as the best pattern in the sequence of $\tilde{C}$. Using the length of the pattern L_p, the optimum period length of the motif T_{opt} is calculated as follows:

$$
T_{opt} = T_{min} + L_p
\tag{10}
$$

We consider this pattern as the candidate of motif. Here, we focus on the fact that the sequence of the symbols represents the time-series data. We can guess that the sequence $\tilde{C}$ is obtained by shifting the analysis window. Hence, we can simply consider that a subsequence of original time-series which begins at the pointer P is regarded as the candidates of motif.

4   The Motif Discovery Algorithm

In this section, we describe the motif discovery algorithm from multi dimensional time-series. First, we transform multi dimensional time-series into one dimensional time series based on PCA described in Sect. 2. Then, we need to normalize one dimensional time-series. Because we need to reduce the influence of user-defined threshold of the distance of the ADM algorithm [5]. The ADM algorithm is a part of the EMMA algorithm. Second, an optimum period length is calculated based on MDL principle. Finally, we discover a motif from the candidates by simplified EMMA algorithm.

In EMMA algorithm, each subsequence of a time-series is stored in a hash table to group similar subsequence together. The address of the hash table with the largest number of subsequences is called MPC (Most Promising Candidate). Every subsequence

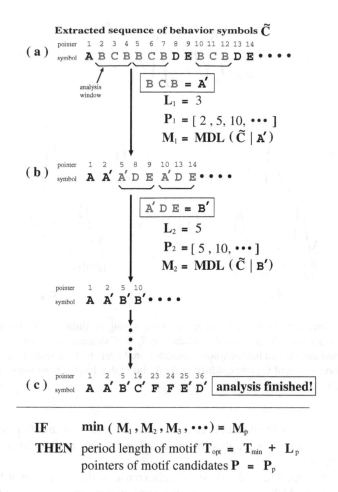

Fig. 4. Discovery of optimum motif period length and motif candidate from symbol sequence

in MPC is regarded as a candidate for a motif. However, the motifs may not be discovered from these candidates as they are shown in Fig. 1b. It is due to the invalidity of these candidates extracted only on the basis that they appear frequently in the time-series data.

On the other hand, in our algorithm, we use the candidates of motif which is extracted based on the MDL principle as the MPC. From the point of validity of the MDL principle, these subsequences are the best candidates of the motif to the time-series data. We can say that they are the optimum candidates in a broad sense, because they are extracted from a sequence of "behavior symbols". That is, these subsequences are appeared frequently in a time-series data.

On the contrast, in the EMMA algorithm, the motif is discovered from the candidates by the ADM algorithm [5]. Figure 5 shows the visualization of the algorithm. The ADM algorithm returns the best motifs from the original MPC subset. These subsequences have the feature that the distance between each two counterparts of the motifs is smaller

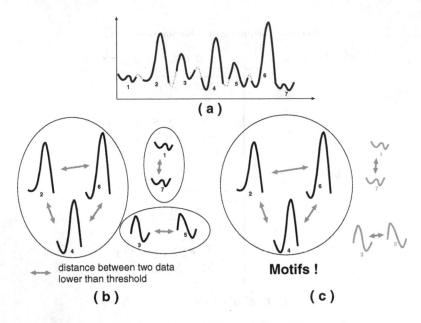

Fig. 5. Visualization of the ADM algorithm. (a) Discovering candidates of motifs using our algorithm. In this example, the number of candidates is 7. (b) Calculate distances between every two candidates and cluster candidates whose distances are lower than the user defined threshold of distance between each of the two candidates. (c) A cluster that has the most number of candidates is regarded as the best motifs

than the threshold of the distance. However, if the number of motifs is smaller than a certain value, it is considered that the extracted motif does not qualify as a "motif" as defined in Sect. 1.

Then MPC is recalculated and the algorithm retries to discover the motif with the new candidates in new MPC. This increases the computation time because of the invalidity of Lin's MPC determination method described above. On the other hand, our algorithm, needs no iteration for using the ADM algorithm. Because most subsequences of our candidates can turn into "true" motifs due to the validity of extracted candidates. Hence, we can say that our algorithm is better than the EMMA algorithm from the view point of computation time.

5   Experimental Evaluation

In this section, to show the efficiency of our motif discovery algorithm, we extract motif from multi dimensional time-series data set. We use 3 dimensional time-series data set of human motion obtained from the motion capture system.

First, we show the effects of using different T_{min} value. We assume that it is possible to discover motifs with various period length using small T_{min} value. We also assume that motifs discoverd using large T_{min} value may not satisfy the definition of motif. In Fig. 6 and Fig. 7, the examples of motifs discoverd using various T_{min} value are shown.

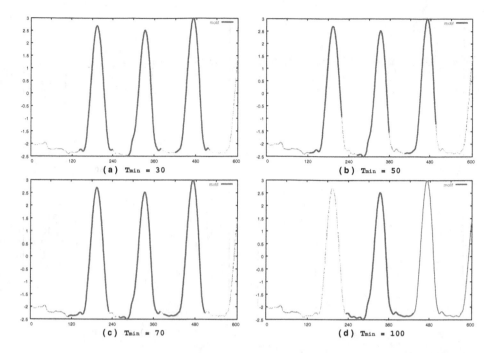

Fig. 6. Examples of discoverd motif from the time series data "Feet movement while Walking" using various value of T_{min}

We can intuitively recognize the optimum period lengths of the time series data which is about 90 in Fig. 6, and about 40 in Fig. 7. In Fig. 6a,b,c it seems that extracted motifs using the T_{min} values which are less than 90 have similar behavior and satisfy the definition of motif. On the other hand, in Fig. 7, it seems that all extracted motifs satisfy the definition of motif. However, motifs extracted using the T_{min} values which are more than 40 (Fig. 7b,c,d) are not the most frequently occuring pattern in the time series. From this result, we can prove that it is possible to extract the optimum motifs that have various optimum period lengths with small T_{min} value. So, we use $T_{min} = 30$ for the following experiments.

Figure 8 shows the motifs extracted from time series data using our motif discovery algorithm. From the result, it is observed that each motif is discovered using different period lengths. It is also observed that every extracted motif satisfies the definition of motif.

Next, we direct our attention toward considering the motif in terms of the validity of multi dimensionality. Figure 9 shows an example of each coordinate of the motif. As seen from these results, the motifs of coordinate x and y satisfy the feature of motif. Because, we can intuituvely find that these motifs have the same behavior. On the other hand, the motif of coordinate z is far from the characteristic of a motif. It occurs due to our method of dimensionality reduction. In this process, the PCA regards coordinate x and y as significant coordinates, but coodinate z as an insignificant coordinate. So, the algorithm mainly extracts information based on the former two coordinates.

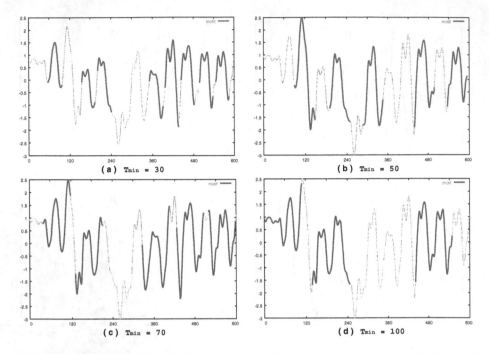

Fig. 7. Examples of discoverd motif from the time series data "Head movement while Running" using various value of T_{min}

However, it has a validity from the viewpoint of the human motion. We can recognize intuitively the feature of motion in case of walking. That is, the coodinate "y" (expressing the movement towards the upper and lower sides), the coodinate "x" (expressing the movement towards left and right), and the coodinate "z" (expressing movement towards backward and forward). For this reason, our motif discovery algorithm is useful for analysing various multi dimensional time-series data.

Besides, we estimate the efficiency of our algorithm. We can evaluate the efficiency of the proposed algorithm by simply considering the ratio of how many times the Euclidean distance function is evaluated by our algorithm, over the number of times it must be evaluated by the EMMA algorithm. So, we define the value of $efficiency$ as follows:

$$efficiency = \frac{number\ of\ times\ our\ algorithm\ calls\ Euclidean\ dist}{number\ of\ times\ EMMA\ calls\ Euclidean\ dist} \quad (11)$$

In these experiments, we extract motifs using our algorithm and EMMA algorithm for about 600 time-series data. The length of each time-series is 600. The result of our algorithm's efficiency are shown in Table 1. The result indicates a one to two order of magnitude speedup over the EMMA algorithm.

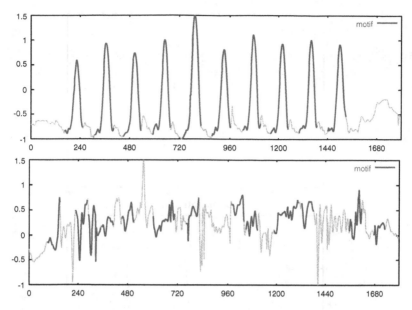

Fig. 8. The motif discoverd in various 1-dimension time series transformed from 3-dimension time series. The first figure represents "Feet movement while Walking", the second one represents "Neck movement while running"

Table 1. The efficiency of our motif discovery algorithm on verious motion datasets

Dataset	batting	kicking	pitching	running	skipping	walking
efficiency	0.0530	0.0709	0.0647	0.0842	0.0876	0.0724

6   Conclusions and Further Work

In this paper we presented an algorithm for efficiently discovering a motif from multi dimensional time-series data by dynamically detecting an optimum period length of motif. We proved our algorithm's advantage that, it can extract a motif that human can recognize intuitively. Moreover, the computation time of motif extraction is shorter than the other motif discovery algorithm such as EMMA algorithm. From the result of our experimentation, our algorithm is effective to mine the various unexpected periodicities or extracting rules from time-series, etc. There are several directions to extend this work:

- Although all data with the same behavior are transformed into sequence of symbols, it may be possible that all sequences of symbols are not necessarily be the same at all. It is due to the lack of removing "noise" from time series data completely in the process of generating the symbol sequence. For this problem, we will use the technique of pattern matching of symbol sequence that is not affected by "noise". For example, this method may be widely used in the genome analysis etc.
- A threshold of distance is used in the ADM algorithm that slightly influence the extraction of motifs. Thus, we hope to determine it dynamically.

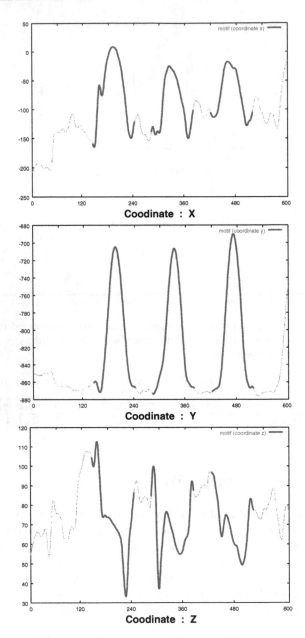

Fig. 9. An example of discoverd motif from the original 3-dimension time series, "Feet movement while Walking." The figures represent coordinate "x", "y","z", respectively

- Several researchers have suggested that the Euclidian distance may be inappropriate in some domains [9]. We hope to generalize our results to work with other distance measures. This may be more robust and more effective for multi dimensions.

References

1. Gautam, D., King-lp, L., Heikki, M., Gopal, R., Padhraic, S.: Rule Discovery from Time Series. Proc. of the 4th Int'l Conference on Knowledge Discovery and Data Mining (1998) 16–22
2. Cyril, G., Peter, T., Egill, R., Arup, N.F., Kai, H.L.: On Clustering fMRI Time Series. NeuroImage **9** (1999) 298–310
3. Yu, J.X., K.Ng, M., Huang, J.Z.: Patterns Discovery Based on Time-Series Decomposition. Proc. of PAKDD'2001 (2001) 336–347
4. Berberidis, C., Vlahavas, I., Aref, W.G., Atallah, M., Elmagarmid, A.K.: On The Discovery of Weak Periodicities in Large Time Series. Proc. of PAKDD'2002 (2002) 51–61
5. Lin, J., Keogh, E., Lonardi, S., Patel, P.: Finding Motifs in Time Series. Proc. of the 2nd Workshop on Temporal Data Mining (2002) 53–68
6. Mori, T., Uehara, K.: Extraction of Primitive Motion And Discovery of Association Rules from Human Motion. Proc. of the 10th IEEE International Workshop on Robot and Human Communication (2001) 200–206
7. Rissanen, J.: Stochastic Complexity in Statistical Inquiry. Volume 15. World Scientific (1989)
8. Heras, D.B., Cabaleiro, J.C., Perez, V.B., Costas, P., Rivera, F.F.: Principal Component Analysis on Vector Computers. Proc. of VECPAR (1996) 416–428
9. Kalpakis, K., Gada, D., Puttagunta, V.: Distance Measures for Effective Clustering of ARIMA Time-Series. Proc. of the 2001 IEEE International Conference on Data Mining (2001) 273–280

Optimizing Financial Portfolios from the Perspective of Mining Temporal Structures of Stock Returns

Kai-Chun Chiu and Lei Xu

Department of Computer Science and Engineering
The Chinese University of Hong Kong, Shatin, N.T., Hong Kong, P.R. China
{kcchiu,lxu}@cse.cuhk.edu.hk

Abstract. In the literature, return-based approaches which directly used security prices or returns to control portfolio weights were often used. Inspired by the arbitrage pricing theory (APT), some other efforts concentrate on indirect modelling using hidden factors. In this paper, we investigate how the gaussian temporal factor analysis (TFA) technique can be used for portfolio optimization. Since TFA is based on the classical APT model and has the benefit of removing rotation indeterminacy via temporal modelling, using TFA for portfolio management allows portfolio weights to be indirectly controlled by several hidden factors.

1 Introduction

Portfolio management has evolved as a core decision making activity for investors and practitioners in the financial market nowadays. Among the various machine learning methodologies suggested, the most popular one is based on maximizing the well-known Sharpe ratio [1]. In implementation, trading could be based on training a trading system on labelled data [2] or directly maximizing the expected profit via the so-called adaptive supervised learning decision networks [3,4]. In this paper, these approaches were generally referred to as return-based portfolio management because they either explicitly treated the weights as constants or to depend directly on the security price or returns.

Inspired by the arbitrage pricing theory (APT) in finance, which assumes that the cross-sectional expected returns of securities is linearly related to k hidden economic factors, typical statistical techniques such as principal component analysis (PCA), independent component analysis (ICA) [5,6], and maximum likelihood factor analysis [7] have been used. However, should we adopt either PCA or ICA for estimating the hidden factors, we have to compromise on the terms of zero noise. Likewise, we have to make a compromise on rotation indeterminacy if we use conventional factor analytic techniques.

In this paper, we aim to investigate using the technique temporal factor analysis (TFA) [8] for portfolio optimization. Since TFA is based on the classical APT model and has the benefit of removing rotation indeterminacy via temporal modelling, using TFA for portfolio management allows portfolio weights to be indirectly controlled by several hidden factors.

The rest of the paper is organized in the following way. Sections 2 and 3 briefly review the APT and the gaussian TFA models respectively. Section 4 illustrates how the APT-based adaptive portfolio management can be effected with algorithms proposed in this paper. Section 5 concludes the paper.

P. Perner and A. Rosenfeld (Eds.): MLDM 2003, LNAI 2734, pp. 266–275, 2003.

2   Review on Arbitrage Pricing Theory

The APT begins with the assumption that the $n \times 1$ vector of asset returns, R_t, is generated by a linear stochastic process with k factors [9,10,11]:

$$\mathbf{R_t} = \bar{\mathbf{R}} + \mathbf{Af_t} + \mathbf{e_t} \tag{1}$$

where f_t is the $k \times 1$ vector of realizations of k common factors, A is the $n \times k$ matrix of factor weights or loadings, and e_t is a $n \times 1$ vector of asset-specific risks. It is assumed that f_t and e_t have zero expected values so that $\bar{R}$ is the $n \times 1$ vector of mean returns.

3   Overview of Temporal Factor Analysis

Suppose the relationship between a state $\mathbf{y_t} \in \mathbb{R}^k$ and an observation $\mathbf{x_t} \in \mathbb{R}^d$ is described by the first-order state-space equations as follows [8,12]:

$$\mathbf{y_t} = \mathbf{By_{t-1}} + \varepsilon_\mathbf{t}, \tag{2}$$
$$\mathbf{x_t} = \mathbf{Ay_t} + \mathbf{e_t}, \qquad t = 1, 2, \dots, N. \tag{3}$$

where ε_t and $\mathbf{e_t}$ are mutually independent zero-mean white noises with $E(\varepsilon_i \varepsilon_j^T) = \Sigma_\varepsilon \delta_{ij}$, $E(\mathbf{e_i e_j}^T) = \Sigma_\mathbf{e} \delta_{ij}$, $E(\varepsilon_i \mathbf{e_j}^T) = 0$, Σ_ε and $\Sigma_\mathbf{e}$ are diagonal matrices, and δ_{ij} is the Kronecker delta function.

We call ε_t the driving noise upon the fact that it drives the source process over time. Similarly, e_t is called measurement noise because it happens to be there during measurement. The above model is generally referred to as the TFA model. In the context of APT analysis, (1) can be obtained from (3) by substituting $(\tilde{R}_t - \bar{R})$ for $\mathbf{x_t}$ and $\mathbf{f_t}$ for $\mathbf{y_t}$. The only difference between the APT model and the TFA model is the added (2) for modelling temporal relation of each factor. The added equation represents the factor series $\mathbf{y} = \{\mathbf{y_t}\}_{t=1}^T$ in a multi-channel auto-regressive process, driven by an i.i.d. noise series $\{\varepsilon_t\}_{t=1}^T$ that are independent of both $\mathbf{y_{t-1}}$ and $\mathbf{e_t}$. Specifically, it is assumed that ε_t is gaussian distributed. Moreover, TFA is defined such that the k sources $y_t^{(1)}, y_t^{(2)}, \dots, y_t^{(k)}$ in this state-space model are statistically independent. The objective of TFA is to estimate the sequence of y_t's with unknown model parameters $\Theta = \{\mathbf{A}, \mathbf{B}, \Sigma_\varepsilon, \Sigma_\mathbf{e}\}$ through available observations.

4   Gaussian TFA for Adaptive Portfolio Management

When the APT-based gaussian TFA model is adopted for portfolio management, portfolio weights adjustment can be made under the control of independent hidden factors that affect the portfolio. In the sequel, we illustrate how this can be achieved under the following four scenarios:

	Transaction Cost	Short Sale Permission
Scenario I	No	No
Scenario II	Yes	No
Scenario III	No	Yes
Scenario IV	Yes	Yes

4.1 Scenario I: NO Transaction Cost and Short Sale NOT Permitted

The assumptions underlying this scenario are no transaction cost and short sale not permitted. Consequently, we consider the return of a typical portfolio which is given by [12]

$$R_t = (1 - \alpha_t)r^f + \alpha_t \sum_{j=1}^{m} \beta_t^{(j)} x_t^{(j)}, \quad \text{subject to} \begin{cases} \alpha_t > 0, \\ 0 \leq \beta_t \leq 1, \\ \sum_{j=1}^{m} \beta_t^{(j)} = 1. \end{cases} \quad (4)$$

where r^f denotes the risk-free rate of return, x_t denotes returns of risky securities, α_t the proportion of total capital to be invested in risky securities and $\beta_t^{(j)}$ the proportion of α_t to be invested in the jth risky asset.

Instead of focussing on the mean-variance efficient frontier, we seek to optimize the portfolio Sharpe ratio (S_p) [4] with $S_p = M(R_T)/\sqrt{V(R_T)}$ given by [12]. In other words, the objective function to maximize is:

$$\max_{\psi, \phi} S_p = \frac{M(R_T)}{\sqrt{V(R_T)}} \quad \text{subject to} \begin{cases} \alpha_t = \exp(\zeta_t), \\ \zeta_t = g(\mathbf{y_t}, \psi), \\ \beta_t^{(j)} = \exp(\xi_t^{(j)})/\sum_{r=1}^{m} \exp(\xi_t^{(r)}), \\ \xi_t = f(\mathbf{y_t}, \phi). \end{cases} \quad (5)$$

where $M(R_T) = \frac{1}{T}\sum_{t=1}^{T} R_t$ is the conditional expected return and $V(R_T) = \frac{1}{T}\sum_{t=1}^{T} [R_t - M(R_T)]^2$ is a measure of risk or volatility, $\{\mathbf{y_t}\}_{t=1}^{N}$ is the time series of independent hidden factors that drives the observed return series $\{\mathbf{x_t}\}_{t=1}^{N}$, $g(\mathbf{y_t}, \psi)$ and $f(\mathbf{y_t}, \phi)$ are some nonlinear functions that map $\mathbf{y_t}$ to respectively ζ_t and ξ_t which in turn adjusts the portfolio weights α_t and $\beta_t^{(j)}$ respectively.

Maximizing the portfolio Sharpe ratio in effect balances the tradeoff between maximizing the expected return and at the same time minimizing the risk. In implementation, we can simply use the gradient ascent approach. The time series $\{\mathbf{y_t}\}_{t=1}^{N}$ can be estimated via the gaussian TFA algorithm in [12]. Although the functions $g(\mathbf{y_t}, \psi)$ and $f(\mathbf{y_t}, \phi)$ are not known *a priori*, it may be approximated via the adaptive extended normalized radial basis function (ENRBF) algorithm in [13].

Like radial basis function (RBF) network, ENRBF is one of the popular models adopted for function approximation. The general form of RBF is

$$f_k(\mathbf{x}) = \sum_{j=1}^{k} w_j \varphi([\mathbf{x} - \mu_\mathbf{j}]^T \Sigma_\mathbf{j}^{-1}[\mathbf{x} - \mu_\mathbf{j}]) \quad (6)$$

ENRBF is an improved modification of RBF by replacing w_j with a linear vector function $\mathbf{W_j^T x} + \mathbf{c_j}$ and dividing the term $\varphi([\mathbf{x} - \mu_j]^T \Sigma_j^{-1}[\mathbf{x} - \mu_j])$ over the aggregate of all terms to arrive at

$$f_k(\mathbf{x}) = \frac{\sum_{j=1}^{k}(\mathbf{W_j}^T\mathbf{x} + \mathbf{c_j})\varphi([\mathbf{x} - \mu_j]^T \Sigma_j^{-1}[\mathbf{x} - \mu_j])}{\sum_{j=1}^{k} \varphi([\mathbf{x} - \mu_j]^T \Sigma_j^{-1}[\mathbf{x} - \mu_j])} \tag{7}$$

where $\mathbf{W_j}$ is a parameter matrix.

Basically, each $\mathbf{W_j^T x} + \mathbf{c_j}$ represents a local linear segment. The ENRBF network approximates a globally nonlinear function by joining all piecewise linear segments weighted by probability. The set of parameters to be estimated is $\Theta = \{\mu_j, \Sigma_j, \mathbf{W_j}, \mathbf{c_j}\}_{j=1}^{k}$.

Specifically, $g(\mathbf{y_t}, \psi)$ and $f(\mathbf{y_t}, \phi)$ can be modelled by the ENRBF shown below.

$$g(\mathbf{y_t}, \psi) = \sum_{p=1}^{k}(\mathbf{W_p^T y_t} + c_p)\varphi(\mu_\mathbf{p}, \Sigma_\mathbf{p}, k) \tag{8}$$

$$f(\mathbf{y_t}, \phi) = \sum_{p=1}^{\hat{k}}(\hat{\mathbf{W}}_\mathbf{p}^T\mathbf{y_t} + \hat{\mathbf{c}}_\mathbf{p})\varphi(\hat{\mu}_\mathbf{p}, \hat{\Sigma}_\mathbf{p}, \hat{k}) \tag{9}$$

where $\varphi(\mu_\mathbf{p}, \Sigma_\mathbf{p}, k) = \frac{\exp\left(-0.5(\mathbf{y_t}-\mu_\mathbf{p})^T \Sigma_\mathbf{p}^{-1}(\mathbf{y_t}-\mu_\mathbf{p})\right)}{\sum_{r=1}^{k} \exp\left(-0.5(\mathbf{y_t}-\mu_\mathbf{r})^T \Sigma_\mathbf{p}^{-1}(\mathbf{y_t}-\mu_\mathbf{r})\right)}$.

The set of parameters in (8) and (9) to be estimated is Θ where $\Theta = \psi \cup \phi, \psi = \{\mu_\mathbf{p}, \Sigma_\mathbf{p}, \mathbf{W_p}, c_p\}_{p=1}^{k}$ and $\phi = \{\hat{\mu}_\mathbf{p}, \hat{\Sigma}_\mathbf{p}, \hat{\mathbf{W}}_\mathbf{p}, \hat{\mathbf{c}}_\mathbf{p}\}_{p=1}^{\hat{k}}$. In general, for each $\theta \in \Theta$, updating takes place adaptively in the following form:

$$\theta^{\text{new}} = \theta^{\text{old}} + \eta_0 \nabla_\theta S_p \tag{10}$$

where η_0 is the learning step size, $\nabla_\theta S_p$ denotes the gradient with respect to θ in the ascent direction of S_p. Typically, the adaptive algorithm [14] shown in Table 1 can be adopted for implementation.

4.2 Simulation

Data Considerations. All simulations in this paper are based on the past average fixed deposit interest rate, stock and index data of Hong Kong. Daily closing prices of the 1-week bank average interest rate, 3 major stock indices as well as 86 actively trading stocks covering the period from January 1, 1998 to December 31, 1999 are used. The number of trading days throughout this period is 522. The three major stock indices are respectively Hang Seng Index (HSI), Hang Seng China-Affiliated Corporations Index (HSCCI) and Hang Seng China Enterprises Index (HSCEI). Of the 86 equities, 30 of them are HSI constituents, 32 are HSCCI constituents and the remaining 24 are HSCEI constituents. The index data are directly used for adaptive portfolio management while the stock prices are used by gaussian TFA for recovering independent hidden factors y_t.

Table 1. An adaptive algorithm for implementation of the APT-based portfolio management

---

Updating rules for the parameter set ψ

$\mu_{\mathbf{p}}^{\text{new}} = \mu_{\mathbf{p}}^{\text{old}} + \eta(\nabla_{\zeta_T} S_p)\varphi(\mu_{\mathbf{p}}, \Sigma_{\mathbf{p}}, k)\tau(\mu_{\mathbf{p}}, \Sigma_{\mathbf{p}}, \mathbf{W}_{\mathbf{p}}, c_p, k)(\mathbf{y}_{\mathbf{T}} - \mu_{\mathbf{p}})$

$\Sigma_{\mathbf{p}}^{\text{new}} = \Sigma_{\mathbf{p}}^{\text{old}} + \eta(\nabla_{\zeta_T} S_p)\varphi(\mu_{\mathbf{p}}, \Sigma_{\mathbf{p}}, k)\tau(\mu_{\mathbf{p}}, \Sigma_{\mathbf{p}}, \mathbf{W}_{\mathbf{p}}, c_p, k)\kappa(\mu_{\mathbf{p}}, \Sigma_{\mathbf{p}})$

$\mathbf{W}_p^{\text{new}} = \mathbf{W}_p^{\text{old}} + \eta(\nabla_{\zeta_T} S_p)\mathbf{y}_{\mathbf{T}}\varphi(\mu_{\mathbf{p}}, \Sigma_{\mathbf{p}}, k)$

$c_p^{\text{new}} = c_p^{\text{old}} + \eta(\nabla_{\zeta_T} S_p)\varphi(\mu_{\mathbf{p}}, \Sigma_{\mathbf{p}}, k)$

Updating rules for the parameter set ϕ

$\hat{\mu}_{\mathbf{p}}^{\text{new}} = \hat{\mu}_{\mathbf{p}}^{\text{old}} + \hat{\eta}(\nabla_{\xi_T^{(j)}} S_p)(\mathbf{y}_{\mathbf{T}} - \hat{\mu}_{\mathbf{p}})\varphi(\hat{\mu}_{\mathbf{p}}, \hat{\Sigma}_{\mathbf{p}}, \hat{k})\chi(\hat{\mu}_{\mathbf{p}}, \hat{\Sigma}_{\mathbf{p}}, \hat{\mathbf{W}}_{\mathbf{p},\mathbf{q}}, \hat{c}_{p,q}, \hat{k})$

$\hat{\Sigma}_{\mathbf{p}}^{\text{new}} = \hat{\Sigma}_{\mathbf{p}}^{\text{old}} + \hat{\eta}(\nabla_{\xi_T^{(j)}} S_p)\kappa(\hat{\mu}_{\mathbf{p}}, \hat{\Sigma}_{\mathbf{p}})\varphi(\hat{\mu}_{\mathbf{p}}, \hat{\Sigma}_{\mathbf{p}}, \hat{k})\chi(\hat{\mu}_{\mathbf{p}}, \hat{\Sigma}_{\mathbf{p}}, \hat{\mathbf{W}}_{\mathbf{p},\mathbf{q}}, \hat{c}_{p,q}, \hat{k})$

$\hat{\mathbf{W}}_{\mathbf{p},\mathbf{q}}^{\text{new}} = \hat{\mathbf{W}}_{\mathbf{p},\mathbf{q}}^{\text{old}} + \hat{\eta}(\nabla_{\xi_T^{(j)}} S_p)\mathbf{y}_{\mathbf{T}}\varphi(\hat{\mu}_{\mathbf{p}}, \hat{\Sigma}_{\mathbf{p}}, \hat{k})$

$\hat{c}_{p,r}^{\text{new}} = \hat{c}_{p,r}^{\text{old}} + \hat{\eta}(\nabla_{\xi_T^{(j)}} S_p)\varphi(\hat{\mu}_{\mathbf{p}}, \hat{\Sigma}_{\mathbf{p}}, \hat{k})$

where η and $\hat{\eta}$ are learning rates,

$M(R_T) = \frac{1}{T}\sum_{t=1}^{T} R_t, \quad V(R_T) = \frac{1}{T}\sum_{t=1}^{T}[R_t - M(R_T)]^2$

$\nabla_{\zeta_T} S_p = \frac{V(R_T) - M(R_T)\frac{R_T - M(R_T) - \frac{1}{T}\sum_{t=1}^{T}(R_t - M(R_t))}{2}}{T\sqrt{[V(R_T)]^3}}\left[\frac{\sum_{r=1}^{m}\exp(\xi_T^{(r)})x_T^{(r)}}{\sum_{r=1}^{m}\exp(\xi_T^{(r)})} - r^f\right]$

$\cdot \exp(\zeta_T),$

$\nabla_{\xi_T^{(j)}} S_p = \frac{V(R_T) - M(R_T)\frac{R_T - M(R_T) - \frac{1}{T}\sum_{t=1}^{T}(R_t - M(R_t))}{2}}{T\sqrt{[V(R_T)]^3}}\frac{\exp(\zeta_T)x_T^{(j)}}{\sum_{r=1}^{m}\exp(\xi_T^{(r)})}\frac{\exp(\xi_T^{(j)})}{\sum_{r=1}^{m}\exp(\xi_T^{(r)}) - \exp(\xi_T^{(j)})} - 1,$

$\varphi(\mu_{\mathbf{p}}, \Sigma_{\mathbf{p}}, k) = \frac{\exp(-0.5(\mathbf{y}_{\mathbf{T}} - \mu_{\mathbf{p}})^T \Sigma_{\mathbf{p}}^{-1}(\mathbf{y}_{\mathbf{T}} - \mu_{\mathbf{p}}))}{\sum_{r=1}^{k}\exp(-0.5(\mathbf{y}_{\mathbf{T}} - \mu_r)^T \Sigma_r^{-1}(\mathbf{y}_{\mathbf{T}} - \mu_r))},$

$\kappa(\mu_{\mathbf{p}}, \Sigma_{\mathbf{p}}) = \Sigma_{\mathbf{p}}^{-1}(\mathbf{y}_{\mathbf{T}} - \mu_{\mathbf{p}})(\mathbf{y}_{\mathbf{T}} - \mu_{\mathbf{p}})^T \Sigma_{\mathbf{p}}^{-1}$
$\quad -0.5\text{diag}[\Sigma_{\mathbf{p}}^{-1}(\mathbf{y}_{\mathbf{T}} - \mu_{\mathbf{p}})(\mathbf{y}_{\mathbf{T}} - \mu_{\mathbf{p}})^T \Sigma_{\mathbf{p}}^{-1}],$

$\tau(\mu_{\mathbf{p}}, \Sigma_{\mathbf{p}}, \mathbf{W}_{\mathbf{p}}, c_p, k) = \frac{(\mathbf{W}_{\mathbf{p}}^T \mathbf{y}_{\mathbf{T}} + c_p) - \sum_{r=1}^{k}(\mathbf{W}_r^T \mathbf{y}_{\mathbf{T}} + c_r)\varphi(\mu_r, \Sigma_r, k)}{\sum_{r=1}^{k}\exp(-0.5(\mathbf{y}_{\mathbf{T}} - \mu_r)^T \Sigma_r^{-1}(\mathbf{y}_{\mathbf{T}} - \mu_r))},$

$\chi(\mu_{\mathbf{p}}, \Sigma_{\mathbf{p}}, \mathbf{W}_{\mathbf{p},\mathbf{q}}, c_{p,q}, k) = \frac{(\mathbf{W}_{\mathbf{p},\mathbf{q}}^T \mathbf{y}_{\mathbf{T}} + c_{p,q}) - \sum_{r=1}^{k}(\mathbf{W}_{\mathbf{p},\mathbf{r}}^T \mathbf{y}_{\mathbf{T}} + c_r)\varphi(\mu_r, \Sigma_r, k)}{\sum_{r=1}^{k}\exp(-0.5(\mathbf{y}_{\mathbf{T}} - \mu_r)^T \Sigma_r^{-1}(\mathbf{y}_{\mathbf{T}} - \mu_r))},$

$\mathbf{W}_{\mathbf{p},\mathbf{q}}$ denotes the p-th column of the q-th matrix,

$\text{diag}[M]$ denotes a diagonal matrix that takes the diagonal part of a matrix M,

$\zeta_T = g(\mathbf{y}_{\mathbf{T}}, \psi)$ as defined in (6) and $\xi_T^{(j)}$ is the j-th output of $f(\mathbf{y}_{\mathbf{T}}, \phi)$ as defined in (7).

Methodology. We consider the task of managing a portfolio which consists of four securities, the average fixed deposit interest rate and the three major stock indices in Hong Kong. The fixed deposit interest rate is used as the proxy for the risk-free rate of return r^f. The first 400 samples are used for training and the last 121 samples for testing. In the test phase, we first make prediction on $\hat{\mathbf{y}}_t$ and $\hat{x}_t$ with $\hat{\mathbf{y}}_t \approx \mathbf{B}\mathbf{y}_{t-1}$ and $\hat{x}_t \approx \mathbf{A}\hat{\mathbf{y}}_t$. Moreover, learning is carried out in an adaptive fashion such that the actual value of $\mathbf{x}_t$ at time t is used to extract $\mathbf{y}_t$ and modify the parameters once it is known (i.e., once the current time t is passed into $t+1$). The APT-based algorithm in Table 1 is adopted that uses hidden independent factors extracted by TFA for controlling portfolio weights. We refer to this approach APT-based portfolio management. For each $\mathbf{y}_t$ under test, we can adaptively get $\zeta_t = g(\mathbf{y}_t, \psi)$ and $\xi_t = f(\mathbf{y}_t, \phi_t)$ and then the portfolio weights $\alpha_t = \exp(\zeta_t)$ and $\beta_t^{(j)} = \exp(\xi_t^{(j)})/\sum_{r=1}^{m}\exp(\xi_t^{(r)})$. Finally, returns can be computed via (4). For the sake of comparison, we also implement a traditional approach

Table 2. Daily risk-return statistics of portfolio constituents

Component Name	Mean Return	Risk
Average interest rate	0.0148%	0.00%
HSI	0.18%	1.48%
HSCCI	0.03%	2.51%
HSCEI	-0.20%	2.55%

that directly uses stock returns $\mathbf{x}_t$ instead of hidden factors $\mathbf{y}_t$ [4]. Daily risk-return statistics of the portfolio constituents are given in Table 2.

Results. Graphical comparison of profit gain between the two approaches using test data is shown in Fig. 1a. Daily risk-return statistics of the portfolios are given in Table 3a.

4.3   Scenario II: HAS Transaction Cost but Short Sale NOT Permitted

Scenario II differs from Scenario I in taking into account the effect of transaction cost. Since any change on $\beta_t^{(j)}$ leads to a transaction that incurs a cost on return c_t given by

$$c_t = -\alpha_t \sum_{j=1}^{m} r_c |\beta_t^{(j)} - \beta_{t-1}^{(j)}| p_t^{(j)} / p_{t-1}^{(j)}$$

$$= -\alpha_t \sum_{j=1}^{m} r_c |\beta_t^{(j)} - \beta_{t-1}^{(j)}| (1 + x_t^{(j)}) \tag{11}$$

where r_c is a constant denoting the rate of transaction cost. Consequently, we consider the portfolio return adjusted for transaction cost given by [12]

$$R_t = (1 - \alpha_t) r^f + \alpha_t \sum_{j=1}^{m} [\beta_t^{(j)} x_t^{(j)} - r_c |\beta_t^{(j)} - \beta_{t-1}^{(j)}| (1 + x_t^{(j)})], \tag{12}$$

$$\text{subject to} \begin{cases} \alpha_t > 0, \\ 0 \leq \beta_t \leq 1, \\ \sum_{j=1}^{m} \beta_t^{(j)} = 1. \end{cases}$$

The APT-based algorithm in Table 1 could still be adopted in this case except that the two terms $\nabla_{\zeta_T} S_p$ and $\nabla_{\xi_T^{(j)}} S_p$ become respectively

$$\nabla_{\zeta_T} S_p = \frac{\left[V(R_T) - M(R_T) \left(R_T - M(R_T) - \frac{1}{T} \sum_{t=1}^{T} (R_t - M(R_t)) \right) \right]}{T \sqrt{[V(R_T)]^3}} \left(\sum_{j=1}^{m} \left[\frac{\exp(\xi_T^{(j)}) x_T^{(j)}}{\sum_{r=1}^{m} \exp(\xi_T^{(r)})} \right. \right.$$

$$\left. \left. -r_c \left| \frac{\exp(\xi_T^{(j)})}{\sum_{r=1}^{m} \exp(\xi_T^{(r)})} - \frac{\exp(\xi_{T-1}^{(j)})}{\sum_{r=1}^{m} \exp(\xi_{T-1}^{(r)})} \right| (1 + x_T^{(j)}) \right] - r^f \right) \exp(\zeta_T),$$

$$\nabla_{\xi_T^{(j)}} S_p = [V(R_T) - M(R_T)(R_T - M(R_T) - \frac{1}{T} \sum_{t=1}^{T} (R_t - M(R_t)))]$$

$$\cdot \exp(\zeta_T)[x_T^{(j)} - r_c \text{sign}(\exp(\xi_T^{(j-1)}) - \exp(\xi_T^{(j-1)}))][\sum_{r=1}^{m} \exp(\xi_T^{(r)})$$

$$- \exp(\xi_T^{(j)})] \exp(\xi_T^{(j)}) / [T \sqrt{[V(R_T)]^3} (\sum_{r=1}^{m} \exp(\xi_T^{(r)}))^2]$$

Simulation. For the purpose of simulation we fix the rate of transaction cost at $r_c = 0.1\%$. Graphical comparison of profit gain between the two approaches using test data is shown in Fig. 1b while daily risk-return statistics of the portfolios are given in Table 3b.

4.4 Scenario III: NO Transaction Cost but Short Sale IS Permitted

Scenario III differs from Scenario I in that short sale is now permitted. By removing the nonnegative constraints on α_t and β_t in (4), we get

$$R_t = (1 - \alpha_t)r^f + \alpha_t \sum_{j=1}^{m} \beta_t^{(j)} x_t^{(j)} - r_c |\beta_t^{(j)} - \beta_{t-1}^{(j)}|(1 + x_t^{(j)})$$

$$\text{subject to } \sum_{j=1}^{m} \beta_t^{(j)} = 1 \tag{13}$$

and the new objective function

$$\max_{\psi,\phi} S_p = \frac{M(R_T)}{\sqrt{V(R_T)}} \text{ subject to} \begin{cases} \alpha_t = \zeta_t = g(\mathbf{y_t}, \psi), \\ \beta_t^{(j)} = \xi_t^{(j)} / \sum_{r=1}^{m} \xi_t^{(r)}, \\ \xi_t = f(\mathbf{y_t}, \phi). \end{cases} \tag{14}$$

In implementation, the algorithm in Table 1 could be adopted except the two terms $\nabla_{\zeta_T} S_p$ and $\nabla_{\xi_T^{(j)}} S_p$ become respectively

$$\nabla_{\zeta_T} S_p = \frac{\left[V(R_T) - M(R_T)\left(R_T - M(R_T) - \frac{1}{T}\sum_{t=1}^{T}(R_t - M(R_t))\right)\right]}{T\sqrt{[V(R_T)]^3}}$$

$$\cdot \left(\sum_{j=1}^{m}\left[\frac{\xi_T^{(j)} x_T^{(j)}}{\sum_{r=1}^{m}\xi_T^{(r)}} - r_c\left|\frac{\xi_T^{(j)}}{\sum_{r=1}^{m}\xi_T^{(r)}} - \frac{\xi_{T-1}^{(j)}}{\sum_{r=1}^{m}\xi_{T-1}^{(r)}}\right|(1 + x_T^{(j)})\right] - r^f\right)$$

$$\nabla_{\xi_T^{(j)}} S_p = \frac{\left[V(R_T) - M(R_T)\left(R_T - M(R_T) - \frac{1}{T}\sum_{t=1}^{T}(R_t - M(R_t))\right)\right]\zeta_T x_T^{(j)}\left(\sum_{r=1}^{m}\xi_T^{(r)} - \xi_T^{(j)}\right)}{T\sqrt{[V(R_T)]^3}\left(\sum_{r=1}^{m}\xi_T^{(r)}\right)^2}$$

Simulation. For the purpose of simulation short selling is not applicable to the return-based approach. Graphical comparison of profit gain between the two approaches using test data is shown in Fig. 1c while daily risk-return statistics of the portfolios are given in Table 3c.

4.5 Scenario IV: HAS Transaction Cost and Short Sale IS Permitted

Scenario IV differs from Scenario I in that the effects of both transaction cost and short sale on portfolio selection have to be treated appropriately. As a result, we have

$$R_t = (1 - \alpha_t)r^f + \alpha_t \sum_{j=1}^{m}\left[\beta_t^{(j)} x_t^{(j)} - r_c|\beta_t^{(j)} - \beta_{t-1}^{(j)}|(1 + x_t^{(j)})\right], \tag{15}$$

$$\text{subject to } \sum_{j=1}^{m} \beta_t^{(j)} = 1$$

Here we have the objective function same as (14). The APT-based algorithm in Table 1 could still be adopted in this case except that the two terms $\nabla_{\zeta_T} S_p$ and $\nabla_{\xi_T^{(j)}} S_p$ become respectively

$$\nabla_{\zeta_T} S_p = \frac{\left[V(R_T) - M(R_T)\left(R_T - M(R_T) - \frac{1}{T}\sum_{t=1}^{T}(R_t - M(R_t))\right)\right]}{T\sqrt{[V(R_T)]^3}} \left(\frac{\sum_{j=1}^{m}\xi_T^{(j)} x_T^{(j)}}{\sum_{j=1}^{m}\xi_T^{(j)}} - r^f\right),$$

$$\nabla_{\xi_T^{(j)}} S_p = \left[V(R_T) - M(R_T)\left(R_T - M(R_T) - \frac{1}{T}\sum_{t=1}^{T}(R_t - M(R_t))\right)\right]$$
$$\cdot \zeta_T\left[x_T^{(j)} - r_c\mathrm{sign}\left(\xi_T^{(j)} - \xi_T^{(j-1)}\right)\right]\left[\sum_{r=1}^{m}\xi_T^{(r)} - \xi_T^{(j)}\right]$$
$$\Big/\left[T\sqrt{[V(R_T)]^3}\left(\sum_{r=1}^{m}\xi_T^{(r)}\right)^2\right]$$

Simulation. In simulation we fix the rate of transaction cost at $r_c = 0.1\%$ and short selling is not applicable to the return-based approach. Graphical comparison of profit gain between the two approaches using test data is shown in Fig. 1d while daily risk-return statistics of the portfolios are given in Table 3d.

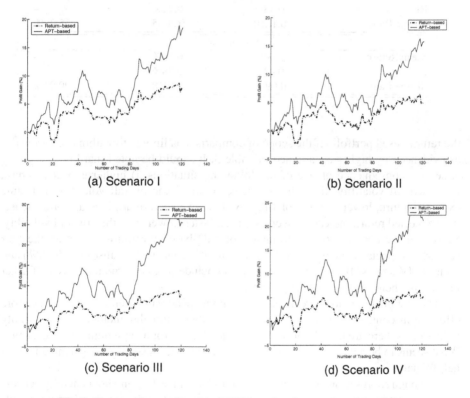

(a) Scenario I

(b) Scenario II

(c) Scenario III

(d) Scenario IV

Fig. 1. Comparative profit gain of APT-based and return-based portfolios

4.6   Performance Evaluation

To summarize the experimental results of the above four scenarios, we have noted the following two phenomena. First, the APT-based portfolio in general performs better than

Table 3. Daily risk-return statistics of the portfolio for different scenarios

	Return-based Portfolio	APT-based Portfolio	Change in Sharpe Ratio ΔS_p
Scenario I			
Mean Return	0.06%	0.14%	–
Risk	0.48%	0.81%	–
Sharpe Ratio	0.1250	0.1728	↑ 38.24%
Scenario II			
Mean Return	0.04%	0.12%	–
Risk	0.42%	0.73%	–
Sharpe Ratio	0.0952	0.1644	↑ 72.69%
Scenario III			
Mean Return	0.06%	0.19%	–
Risk	0.48%	0.92%	–
Sharpe Ratio	0.1250	0.2065	↑ 65.20%
Scenario IV			
Mean Return	0.04%	0.16%	–
Risk	0.42%	0.88%	–
Sharpe Ratio	0.0952	0.1818	↑ 90.97%

the return-based portfolio if the scope of comparison is limited to within each scenario, as evidenced by higher S_p attained in Table 3. It should be noted that higher S_p may arise as a consequence of one of the following situations: i) higher expected return, lower overall volatility; ii) higher expected return, same overall volatility; iii) same expected return, lower overall volatility; iv) both expected return increase or decrease, with expected return increases (decreases) at a faster (lower) rate than overall volatility. Second, if we compare the performance of APT-based portfolios across all the four scenarios, especially the portfolio Sharpe ratio of scenario III against I (↑ 19.50%) and scenario IV against II (↑ 10.58%), we may conclude that performance may be further improved whenever short sale is permitted.

The first phenomenon reveals the fact that independent hidden factors may be more effective in controlling portfolio weights. Possible rationales include dimensionality reduction as there are usually only a few hidden factors for a large number of securities. What seems to be a more important revelation is that the classical APT [9] model is still helpful here.

Although short selling is expensive for individual investors and not generally permissible for most institutional investors [15] in many markets, relevant experimental results reveal the hypothetical potential benefit such facility might add to the portfolio returns. The benefit mainly arises from the exploitation of downside trend in market price in addition to upward movement. This in turn reduces the chance that the fund is left idle due to declining stock prices for most stocks, which is more or less a phenomenon when the general market atmosphere is gloomy.

5   Conclusion

In this paper, we introduce how to utilize the APT-based gaussian TFA model for adaptive portfolio management. Since TFA is based on the classical APT model and has the benefit of removing rotation indeterminacy via temporal modelling, using TFA for portfolio management would allow portfolio weights to be indirectly controlled by several hidden factors. Simulation results reveal that APT-based portfolio management in general excels return-based portfolio management and portfolio returns may be somehow enhanced by short selling, especially when the general market climate is not that favorable.

Acknowledgements. The work described in this paper was fully supported by a grant from the Research Grant Council of the Hong Kong SAR (Project No: CUHK 4297/98E).

References

1. Sharpe, W.F.: Mutual fund performance. Journal of Business **39** (1966) 119–138
2. Moody, J., Wu, L., Liao, Y., Saffell, M.: Performance functions and reinforcement learning for trading systems and portfolios. Journal of Forecasting **17** (1998) 441–470
3. Xu, L., Cheung, Y.M.: Adaptive supervised learning decision networks for traders and portfolios. Journal of Computational Intelligence in Finance **5** (1997) 11–15
4. Hung, K.K., Cheung, C.C., Xu, L.: New sharpe-ratio-related methods for portfolio selection. Proc. of Computational Intelligence for Financial Engineering (CIFEr 2000) (2000) 34–37
5. Back, A.D., Weigend, A.S.: A first application of independent component analysis to extracting structure from stock returns. International Journal of Neural Systems **8** (1997) 473–484
6. Yip, F., Xu, L.: An application of independent component analysis in the arbitrage pricing theory. Proceedings of the International Joint Conference on Neural Networks (IJCNN'2000) **5** (2000) 279–284
7. Jöreskog, K.G.: A general approach to confirmatory maximum likelihood factor analysis. Psychometrika **34** (1969) 183–202
8. Xu, L.: Temporal byy learning for state space approach, hidden markov model and blind source separation. IEEE Trans. on Signal Processing **48** (2000) 2132–2144
9. Ross, S.: The arbitrage theory of capital asset pricing. Journal of Economic Theory **13** (1976) 341–360
10. Roll, R., Ross, S.: An empirical investigation of the arbitrage pricing theory. Journal of Finance **35** (1980) 1073–1103
11. Roll, R., Ross, S.: The arbitrage pricing theory approach to strategic portfolio planning. Financial Analysts Journal **40** (1984) 14–26
12. Xu, L.: Byy harmony learning, independent state space and generalized apt financial analyses. IEEE Transactions on Neural Networks **12** (2001) 822–849
13. Xu, L.: Rbf nets, mixture experts, and bayesian ying-yang learning. Neurocomputing **19** (1998) 223–257
14. Chiu, K.C., Xu, L.: Financial apt-based gaussian tfa learning for adaptive portfolio management. In: Artificial Neural Networks- ICANN'2002, LNCS 2415. (2002) 1019–1024
15. Chan, L., Karceski, J., Lakonishok, J.: On portfolio optimization: Forecasting covariances and choosing the risk model. The Review of Financial Studies **12** (1999) 937–974

Visualizing Sequences of Texts Using Collocational Networks

Camilla Magnusson[1] and Hannu Vanharanta[2]

[1]Department of General Linguistics
P.O. Box 9
00014 University of Helsinki, Finland
camilla.magnusson@helsinki.fi
[2]Pori School of Technology and Economics
Tampere University of Technology
P.O. Box 300
28101 Pori, Finland
hannu.vanharanta@pori.tut.fi

Abstract. This paper presents the collocational network, a method originating in corpus linguistics, as a tool for visualizing sequences of texts. A collocational network is a two-dimensional picture of the most central words in a text and the connections between them. When collocational networks are created out of sequences of documents, they offer the user the possibility to quickly discover the most significant differences between the documents. As a case study, a sequence of financial reports is turned into collocational networks for visual comparison.

1 Introduction

In this article collocational networks, based on a simple method originating in corpus linguistics, are used in order to visualize the textual contents of a sequence of texts. The aim is to propose this method for producing a network of the most central concepts in a text and the connections between them, thus allowing for a visual comparison to be made. A method of this kind could be useful for processing a number of different types of sequential texts, but in this article it is used for visualizing the contents of quarterly reports of a telecommunications company. Financial reports are particularly suitable for a study of this kind, as they usually have a quite uniform structure from one quarter to the next, while the textual contents may vary quite significantly.

There is also a need among shareholders and analysts for a method which visualizes series of reports while still allowing the user to spot the changes and decide what their significance is. This paper approaches this matter from a decidedly non-technical viewpoint, partly because of its origins in linguistics, but more importantly, because of its possible application to non-technical contexts such as a quick analysis of new financial data.

P. Perner and A. Rosenfeld (Eds.): MLDM 2003, LNAI 2734, pp. 276–283, 2003.

2   Collocational Networks

2.1   Background

Collocational networks are two-dimensional networks which contain interlinked collocations, i.e. words which occur together in a text. The concept of collocational networks originates in an article by Williams [1]. In his study, Williams uses the network as a corpus linguistic tool in order to create specialised dictionaries. In this article the method will be used for text visualization, but with a similar question in mind: what are the central concepts in the text, and how are they linked to each other? Instead of collecting a large corpus of specialised texts as Williams has done, here each text will be treated as a miniature corpus and turned into a collocational network.

The idea of finding the central contents of a text through linguistic methods has been explored extensively by Phillips [2]. Phillips argues that traditional linguistics cannot adequately account for the concept of subject matter, as subject matter relies on regularities in the lexical organisation of text. As an alternative, Phillips suggests what he calls a knowledge-free analysis of the terms in a text. An analysis of this kind could presumably reveal systematic textual patterning, which in turn contributes to the semantic structure of the text and functions as a basis for the emergence of the notion of content.

Williams [1], whose article is the main source for the method presented in this study, draws some of his ideas from Phillips' study. His work is slightly different, though, as his aim is to find words central to a particular sublanguage instead of words central to a particular text. This leads him to work with text corpora rather than individual texts. This study constitutes a return to Phillips' original pursuit of the contents of a text, conducted with a method used by Williams for extracting data from a corpus.

In this article, collocation will primarily be interpreted simply as "the occurrence of two or more words within a short space of each other in a text" following Sinclair [3], a central work within corpus linguistics. Another important factor in this method is the concept of significant collocation. Significant collocation takes place when two or more words occur together more frequently than would be expected by coincidence. Following Williams [1], significant collocation is measured using the Mutual Information or MI score. The MI score, an information theoretic concept introduced in linguistics by Church & Hanks [4], compares the frequency of co-occurrence of node word and collocate with the frequency of their occurrence independently of each other. The MI score is calculated as follows:

$$MI(n,c) = \log_2(f(n,c)N / f(n)f(c)) \tag{1}$$

where n stands for node, c for collocate and N for the size of the text.

2.2   Creating Networks

A starting point for the construction of a collocational network is the establishing of a nuclear node, a word which has a high concentration of collocates, and thus can be considered to represent a concept that is central to the text. The collocates of the nuclear nodes are traced, and these collocates are then treated as nodes, the collocates of which are traced. This allows for the construction of a collocational network. At some point words that have occurred earlier in the network are found. These occurrences define the outer limits of the network.

This approach gives us an opportunity to visualize the concepts that are emphasised in a particular text. These concepts are reflected through the words that constitute the nodes of the network. This approach also gives us a possibility to examine which concepts are most frequently linked to each other, by revealing which words regularly appear within a close proximity to each other.

During the drawing of the networks a number of other words with little relevance for the report as a whole were left out. Such words were prepositions, articles, conjunctions, words referring to the time span of the report (*quarter, first, second* etc.) as well as words referring to figures or currency.

The initial stage of the analysis was the calculating of the Mutual Information (MI) score for all words occurring within a span of four words from each other. A maximum span of this size is recommended by Sinclair [3] for a general study of collocations in English. The texts used in this study consisted of approximately 3000 words each, and an MI score of 2.00 was found to produce a network of a size suitable for these texts. Lowering the score would have brought in words which occur together only occasionally, whereas a higher limit would have produced a network with only the most frequent combinations, leaving out many of the interesting changes which occur among the mid-frequency words.

The construction of the networks started with the locating of the most frequent word in the text. It was given the status of central nuclear node in the network and placed on the left. Its most significant collocate (i.e. the word giving the highest MI-score) was then traced and linked onto the right side of the nuclear node. Next, the second most significant collocate was traced and linked to the nuclear node, underneath the most significant collocate. When all the collocates of the nuclear node had been linked in a similar manner, these collocates where then given the status of nuclear nodes and their collocates were then traced and linked.

This procedure was repeated until all collocates with an MI score above 2.00 had been placed on the network. In some cases the construction of the main network stopped as no more collocates to the nuclear nodes could be found, but some other pairs or chains of collocates could still be found in the text. Starting from the most frequent of these remaining words, separate networks were drawn underneath or to the right of the main network.

When reading the networks it should be kept in mind that the networks presented in this article do not take into account the order in which the words occur in the text. A collocate might occur to the left or to the right of the nuclear node in the text, but in the networks the nuclear node is always on the left and its collocates are on the right. It should also be remembered that words presented as collocates in the networks do not always occur next to each other in the text, but within a span of four words.

3   Case Study: A Visualization of a Sequence of Quarterly Reports

The material studied in this article consists of sequential quarterly reports published in 2000 and 2001 by telecommunications company Ericsson. Financial reports of this kind are of great interest to shareholders and analysts, who constantly receive numerous reports produced by listed companies. There is the need to quickly establish an opinion about the contents of these reports - where do they indicate the companies will be going? This applies to the textual contents of the reports as well as to the financial figures, although the financial ratios in particular have traditionally received more attention. There are, however, studies [5], [6] which show that the texts in these reports are of great communicative importance as well and should therefore not be overlooked.

When creating the networks, some connections can be expected as the inclusion of words in the networks is based on the statistical significance of collocation. This means that:

- a word which is very frequent in the text is likely to appear in the network.
- a word which often occurs together with a frequent word in the text is likely to appear in the network.
- pairs of words which almost exclusively occur together in the text are likely to appear in the network.

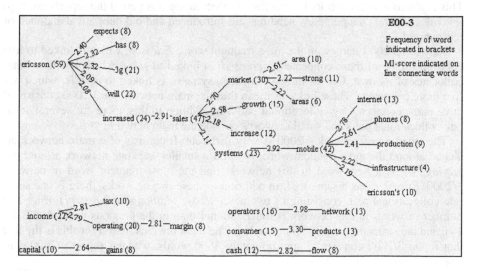

Fig. 1. Collocational network of Ericsson's report 3/2000. The network consists of 32 words

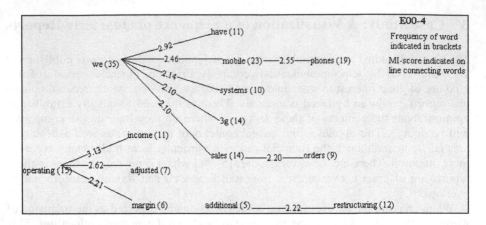

Fig. 2. Collocational network of Ericsson's report 4/2000. The network consists of 14 words

3.1   Analysis of the Networks

Figures 1 and 2 contain the collocational networks for Ericsson's quarterly reports 3/2000 and 4/2000. As can be seen, a remarkable change takes place between these networks. Structurally, they are completely different. There is also a significant difference between the lexical items used and the number of lexical items in the networks. This is also obvious when looking at the reports: during this period the reports undergo several structural changes. New headings are introduced and old ones are abandoned or reorganized.

Network 3/2000 starts with the most frequent word, *Ericsson*, which is linked to five collocates. One of these collocates, *increased*, is linked to *sales*, which has four other collocates of its own. One of these collocates, *systems*, is linked to *mobile*, which has five more collocates. These linkages mean that the main network for 3/2000 consists of three parts, connected by collocational pairs. In addition to this, there are several separate collocational pairs and small networks outside the main network.

The structure of network 4/2000 is very different. It consists of a main network attached around the most frequent word, *we*, and a smaller, separate network around *operating*. *We* is a new word in this network, and the most frequent word in network 3/2000, *Ericsson*, has disappeared. In addition to these two networks, there is one separate collocational pair, consisting of two new words, *additional* and *restructuring*. The number of words in this network is much smaller than in the previous network (33 vs. 14), and the structure is much less complex. The most obvious reason for this is the fact that report 3/2000 consists of approximately 3600 words, whereas report 4/2000 consists of approximately 2100 words.

In 3/2000, Ericsson's third quarter report for 2000, *Ericsson* is the most frequent word and thus the starting point for the network. In the text, *Ericsson* is also a very central word. It is used together with a number of different verbs, in most cases as a subject. This is clearly reflected in the network, where four out of five collocates (*expects, has, will, increased*) are verbs. The fifth collocate, *3g*, stands for third generation networks, a concept in new technology that is emphasised very strongly in the report.

Sales, the second most frequent word in the text constitutes another nuclear node. It is closely linked to the verb *increased. Ericsson, increased* and *sales* form a chain, which also occurs as such in the text three times. *Sales* is also linked to *increase* as well as to *increased.* It should be noted that no lemmatisation has been carried out in this study, which means that different word-forms occur separately. In this case, *increased* is also linked to *Ericsson,* which means that it occurs in slightly different contexts from *increase,* although these are both collocates of *sales.*

The collocates of *sales* are mainly business words. One of them is *market,* a fairly frequent word in the text. *Market* also has two collocates which can be called different word-forms of the same lemma, *area* and *areas.* These two collocates of *market* could well have been combined into a single one through lemmatisation of the text, as they occur in similar contexts. Still, lemmatisation would not have served the purposes of presenting the context of all significant collocations, as there is also a notable counter-example in the text. This is *Ericsson* and *Ericsson's,* two words which occur in very different contexts both in the text and in the network. *Ericsson's* usually occurs as an attribute whereas *Ericsson* occurs as a subject in a much more varied environment. The last part of the main network is concentrated around *mobile,* and it consists mainly of collocates which are typical for the telecommunications industry. Two of the collocates, *phones* and *infrastructure* only occur with *mobile. Internet* occurs frequently with *mobile,* but also in the complementary phrase *fixed internet* and in other, varying contexts.

Collocational pairs outside the main network are *capital* and *gains, operators* and *network, consumer* and *products* and *cash* and *flow. Capital* occurs almost exclusively in the phrase *capital gains,* twice in *return on capital* and once in *start capital. Gains* only occurs once independently of *capital,* in the phrase *gains from sale. Capital gains* usually occurs in accounting-related passages. *Operators* and *network* occur together in the phrase *network operators,* but occasionally also separately. *Network operators* is the name of one of the business segments of the company, and it is therefore quite a frequent phrase in the text. *Consumer Products* is the name of another segment, and this is why *consumer* and *products* also appear quite frequently in the text. In 4/2000, the network for the fourth quarter in 2000, *we* is the most frequent word. *Ericsson,* which was the most frequent word in the previous report, only occurs ten times in this report and therefore disappears from the network. The company has switched from referring to itself by name to using the pronoun *we* instead.

Have, the most significant collocation of *we,* occurs in the text with the subject *we* in all instances except one, where the subject is *delivery failures.* The main verb is different for every occurrence (some examples are *generated, achieved, decided, increased*), which means that none of these verbs is frequent enough to appear in the network.

The next collocate, *mobile,* also has a collocate of its own, *phones.* In the text *mobile* also occurs with words like *subscribers* and *Internet. Mobile* is often also used with *systems,* the fourth collocate of *we,* but this link does not appear in the network, as the MI score for this collocation is below 2. *3g* is also used quite frequently in this report, often in the vicinity of *we,* and thus it appears in the network as a collocate of *we.*

The fifth collocate of *we* is *sales.* This word occurs in varying contexts, telling both about increases and decreases in sales. In the network, *sales* is only linked to *orders.* The reasons for this connection might not be obvious from a linguistic point of view, but a look at the text shows that these words often occur together in lists like *orders, sales and income,* which functions as a headline, and phrases such as *sales up X%, orders up X%.*

A smaller network, not linked to the main one, consists of *operating* and its collocates *income*, *adjusted* and *margin*. In the text, *operating* usually occurs in either of the collocations *operating income* or *operating margin*. It also occurs once with *losses* and twice with *expenses*, but these collocations are too infrequent to appear in the network. *Adjusted* is a word typically used in the text in accounting contexts, and this applies to the other words in this group as well.

In order to take a look at how the texts develop Ericsson's two first reports for 2001 were also turned into collocational networks.

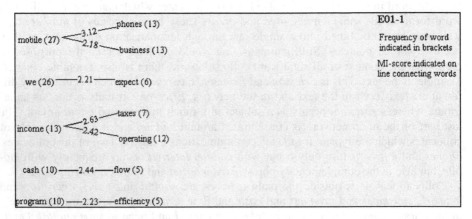

Fig. 3. Collocational network of Ericsson's report 1/2001. The network consists of 12 words

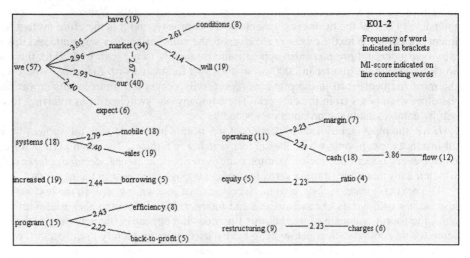

Fig. 4. Collocational network of Ericsson's report 2/2001. The network consists of 23 words

A brief look at these networks shows that the change continues. Network 1/2001 is very sparse, containing only 14 words, most of which are basic accounting terms. In contrast, the following network is much more complex as it reflects the contents of a more verbose text.

This brief analysis indicates that collocational networks definitely are a tool for visualizing changes in series of documents, more so than for visualizing single documents. As an example, from a financial analyst's point of view the change from *increased sales* (3/2000) to *additional restructuring* (4/2000) can be very thought provoking, particularly as it is followed by *efficiency program* in 1/2001.

4   Conclusion

The collocational network is a very simple method for visualizing the surface structure of texts, thus allowing for a comparison of changes that take place within a sequence of texts. A simple network can easily be created out of any document and used as a guide to the main contents of the text. The method has, however, got some limitations. The networks only reveal collocations that are frequent enough to exceed the limits of significance. This means that small changes, which may be significant to the text despite their infrequence, may go unnoticed.

Clustering the networks according to their contents and structure could easily carry this study further. In the context of financial reports, however, this has not been carried out, as it is in the readers' interest to know exactly what changes have occurred. It is not enough for them to know the degree of resemblance between the reports. The point of view of the user has been an important guideline in developing this method. These networks are proposed as a simple data mining tool which requires only some basic knowledge of statistics. In fact, the usefulness of the networks depends more on the user's knowledge of the subject matter of the texts than on her knowledge of data mining or statistics. A user-oriented, context-dependent analysis of the networks should reveal their degree of applicability in a particular situation. Such an analysis is not possible within the scope of this paper, but remains the object for further research.

Acknowledgements. Thanks to Antti Arppe and Barbro Back for their helpful comments.

References

1. Williams, G. C.: Collocational Networks: Interlocking Patterns of Lexis in a Corpus of Plant Biology Research Articles. International Journal of Corpus Linguistics 3 (1998) 151–171
2. Phillips, M.: Aspects of Text Structure. An Investigation of the Lexical Organisation of Text. North-Holland, Amsterdam (1985)
3. Sinclair, J.: Corpus, Concordance, Collocation. Oxford University Press, Oxford (1991)
4. Church, K. W., Hanks P.: Word Association Norms, Mutual Information, and Lexicography. Computational Linguistics 16 (1990) 22–29
5. Osborne, J. D, Stubbart C. I., Ramaprasad, A.: Strategic Groups and Competitive Enactment: A Study of Dynamic Relationships Between Mental Models and Performance. Strategic Management Journal 22 (2001) 435–454
6. Kohut, G. F., Segars A.H: The President's Letter To Stockholders: An Examination of Corporate Communication Strategy. The Journal of Business Communication 29 (1992) 7–21

Complexity Analysis of Depth First and FP-Growth Implementations of APRIORI

Walter A. Kosters[1], Wim Pijls[2], and Viara Popova[2]

[1] Leiden Institute of Advanced Computer Science
Universiteit Leiden
P.O. Box 9512, 2300 RA Leiden, The Netherlands
kosters@liacs.nl
[2] Department of Computer Science
Erasmus University
P.O. Box 1738, 3000 DR Rotterdam, The Netherlands
{pijls,popova}@few.eur.nl

Abstract. We examine the complexity of Depth First and FP-growth implementations of APRIORI, two of the fastest known data mining algorithms to find frequent itemsets in large databases. We describe the algorithms in a similar style, derive theoretical formulas, and provide experiments on both synthetic and real life data to illustrate the theory.

1 Introduction

We examine the theoretical and practical complexity of Depth First ($\mathcal{DF}$, see [6]) and FP-growth ($\mathcal{FP}$, see [4]) implementations of APRIORI (see [1]), two of the fastest known data mining algorithms to find frequent itemsets in large databases. There exist many implementations of APRIORI (see, e.g., [5,7]). We would like to focus on algorithms that assume that the whole database fits in main memory, this often being the state of affairs; among these, $\mathcal{DF}$ and $\mathcal{FP}$ are the fastest. In most papers so far little attention has been given to theoretical complexity. This paper is a continuation of [3].

APRIORI is an algorithm that finds all frequent itemsets in a given database of transactions; frequent sets are the necessary building blocks for association rules, i.e., if-then-rules of the form "if a customer buys products X and Y, he or she also buys product Z". So the situation is the following: we are given products and customers, where every customer buys a set of products, the so-called transaction. More general, an itemset is an arbitrary set of products; a k-itemset has k elements. The *support* of an itemset is the number of customers that buy all products from this itemset – and maybe more. An itemset is frequent if and only if its support is larger than or equal to *minsup*, a certain threshold given in advance. The APRIORI algorithm successively finds all frequent 1-itemsets, all frequent 2-itemsets, all frequent 3-itemsets, and so on. The frequent k-itemsets are used to generate candidate $(k + 1)$-itemsets, where the candidates are only known to have two frequent subsets with k elements. (In fact, the candidates are uniquely constructed out of these two subsets.) A pruning step discards those

P. Perner and A. Rosenfeld (Eds.): MLDM 2003, LNAI 2734, pp. 284–292, 2003.

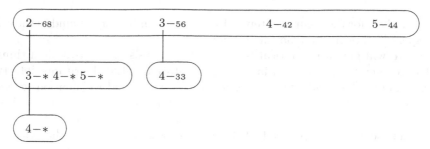

Fig. 1. Example trie

candidates for which not all subsets are frequent. This relies on the property that all subsets of frequent itemsets are frequent too. Finally the supports of the remaining candidates are computed (by means of a run through the database) in order to determine the frequent ones.

The main application of frequent itemsets is in the area of association rules. These are often used in the analysis of retail data and in medical environments. Moreover, frequent itemsets are relevant for other topics in data analysis, such as clustering and pattern recognition. The techniques can be applied in more general contexts: instead of binary data one can use data with continuous or categorical values; it is also possible to introduce hierarchies.

The crux of any implementation of APRIORI is the chosen representation for the candidates and the way to check their support. $\mathcal{DF}$ builds a *trie* of all candidate sets, and then pushes all customers through this trie – one at a time. Eventually a trie containing all frequent itemsets remains. In the example trie from Fig. 1 we have 5 items 1, 2, 3, 4 and 5, and *minsup* = 25. The small numbers indicate the supports of the itemsets, for instance the support of the itemset $\{3, 4\}$ is 33. The trie has just been augmented with 2 and its candidate subtrie. A $*$ indicates that the corresponding support is not known yet. From the picture we infer that the only frequent itemsets so far are $\{3\}$, $\{4\}$, $\{5\}$ and $\{3, 4\}$, and $\{2\}$ itself; note that every path in the trie from the root node downward identifies a unique itemset. For instance $\{3, 4, 5\}$ and $\{4, 5\}$ are not frequent here, since the corresponding paths do not occur in the trie. Since $\{3, 5\}$ is not frequent, $\{2, 3, 5\}$ is not a candidate. In the current step all customers are pushed through the part of the trie rooted at 2, in the meantime updating all counters.

$\mathcal{FP}$ proceeds differently. It makes use of a so-called FP-tree (see Sect. 4; FP means Frequent Pattern) to maintain databases of parts of transactions that matter in the future. Instead of a trie it internally has a recursion tree in which the candidates are gathered. Informally speaking, in the example trie from Fig. 1 (this being an implementation of the recursion tree), the node 2−68 would also contain all 68 transactions that have 2, restricted to the products 3, 4 and 5. An FP-tree is built that efficiently contains all these transactions, and subdatabases are derived for the recursive steps. More details can be either found in the original papers [6,4] or in the following sections.

We will give a theoretical basis for the analysis of the two algorithms. We have chosen for a somewhat informal presentation of the algorithms, intertwined with our analysis. We will present practical results, and we mention several difficulties. Indeed, $\mathcal{FP}$ is a complicated algorithm, involving recursion and serious garbage collection; the algorithm also allows several refinements that are hard to analyze. In this paper we first describe the algorithms in parallel with a theoretical analysis, we then present practical results, and finally provide conclusions and issues for further research. For some of the proofs we refer to [3].

2   Definitions

Let m denote the number of transactions (also called customers), and let n denote the number of products (also called items). Usually m is much larger than n. For a non-empty itemset $A \subseteq \{1, 2, \ldots, n\}$ we define:

- $supp(A)$ is the *support* of A: the number of customers that buy all products from A (and possibly more);
- $sm(A)$ is the smallest number in A;
- $la(A)$ is the largest number in A.

In line with this we let $supp(\emptyset) = m$. We also put $la(\emptyset) = 0$ and $sm(\emptyset) = n+1$. A set $A \subseteq \{1, 2, \ldots, n\}$ is called *frequent* if $supp(A) \geq minsup$, where the so-called *support threshold minsup* is a fixed number given in advance.

We assume every 1-itemset to be frequent; this can be effected by the first step of the algorithms we are looking at, which might be considered as preprocessing.

3   The Depth First Algorithm – Complexity

In the Depth First algorithm a trie of frequent itemsets is built. Suppose that all frequent itemsets in $\{k + 1, \ldots, n\}$ have been gathered in a trie $\mathcal{T}$. The root node is now augmented on the left side with k. Then $\mathcal{T}$ is placed in the trie under k, providing new candidate itemsets. In the example trie from Fig. 1 we have $k = 2$. Then the necessary supports (for this new subtrie) are calculated by "pushing" all customers through the trie: for every customer the paths starting at k are examined in a depth first fashion and checked against the customer, meanwhile updating the node counters denoting the supports so far. Infrequent sets are removed once all customers have been queried. The complexity of this algorithm largely depends on these queries, and we shall therefore pay special attention to them. Omitting the printing of the results, the algorithm can be described as follows:

```
procedure DF (database D)
    for k := n − 1 down to 1 do
        augment the trie in the root with k
```

attach a copy of the old trie underneath this k
for all transactions in D
update counters in the subtrie starting from this k

A "database query" is defined as a question of the form "Does customer C buy product P?" (or "Does transaction T has item I?"), posed to the original database. Note that we have mn database queries in the "preprocessing" phase in which the supports of the 1-itemsets are computed and ordered: every field of the database is inspected once. (By the way, the sorting, in which the items are assigned the numbers $1, 2, \ldots, n$, takes $O(n \log n)$ time.) The number of database queries for $\mathcal{DF}$ equals:

$$m(n-1) + \sum_{\substack{A \neq \emptyset \\ A \text{ frequent}}} \sum_{j=1}^{sm(A)-1} supp(\{j\} \cup A \setminus \{la(A)\}) \quad . \tag{1}$$

For a proof, see [3].

It makes also sense to look at the number of nodes of the trie, which is connected to the effort of maintaining and using the datastructures. Counting each trie-node with the number of items it contains, the total is computed to be:

$$n + \sum_{\substack{A \neq \emptyset \\ A \text{ frequent}}} \sum_{j=1}^{sm(A)-1} 1 = n + \sum_{\substack{A \neq \emptyset \\ A \text{ frequent}}} [sm(A) - 1] = \sum_{\substack{A \text{ frequent}}} [sm(A) - 1] \quad . \tag{2}$$

Notice that the complexity heavily depends on the sorting order of the items at the top level. It turns out that an increasing order of items is beneficial here.

4 The FP-Growth Algorithm – Complexity

The FP-growth algorithm is a clever implementation of APRIORI. The algorithm proceeds recursively. Suppose that a frequent itemset B has been found. The algorithm has saved all transactions that support B, restricted to items i with $i > la(B)$ and such that $B \cup \{i\}$ is frequent, in a "local database" D (in the form of an FP-tree; we shall return to this later). Now for these i's a recursive call (with $A = B \cup \{i\}$ as frequent itemset; note that $i = la(A)$) is made – unless for basic cases. Omitting the printing of the results, the algorithm can be described as follows:

```
procedure FP (itemset B, database D)
    for all i > la(B) with B ∪ {i} frequent do
    (i.e., for all items i occurring in D)
        set D' = the subset of transactions in D that support i
        count support for all items k from D' with k > i (%)
        remove infrequent items and items k with k ≤ i from D'
        build new FP-tree for D'
        if there is anything left (#) call FP(B ∪ {i}, D')
```

Although the title of [4] suggests otherwise, the algorithm also "generates" candidate itemsets: the recursion tree that operates underneath the surface can be viewed as doing so. In this case a node gets as its candidate children all its right siblings – but only if they are frequent. Because the child node is only a real candidate if the parent node (or rather: the entire path from the root down to the node) is frequent, we see that candidates (with t items) are now known to have at least two frequent subsets with $t - 1$ items. The local databases are handed down the recursion tree, where customers not buying a node are omitted.

Let us define a "database query" in this case as a question of the form "Does customer C buy product P?" posed to a local database D, necessary for the counting in step (%). The number of database queries (except for the "preprocessing" phase) for $\mathcal{FP}$ equals:

$$\sum_{\substack{A \neq \emptyset \\ A \text{ frequent}}} \sum_{\substack{j=la(A)+1 \\ \{j\} \cup A \setminus \{la(A)\} \text{ frequent}}}^{n} supp(A) \quad . \tag{3}$$

A consequence of Formula (1) and Formula (3) is that the contribution of the 1-itemsets is exactly the same for both $\mathcal{DF}$ and $\mathcal{FP}$. In fact, this number equals

$$\sum_{i=1}^{n} (n - i) \ supp(\{i\}) \quad , \tag{4}$$

which is minimal exactly if the 1-itemsets are sorted increasingly. The contribution for longer itemsets is more complex – and different for the two algorithms.

An FP-tree is an efficient datastructure that stores the whole local database of customers that buy (at least) some itemset A. For the current discussion it is not necessary to provide full detail on this subject, but it is good to know that every path in the FP-tree keeps track of an itemset along with its support. However, contrary to the situation in the tries above, itemsets are not uniquely represented, but may occur as subset of several itemsets. In Fig. 2 the node 2–8 tells us that there are 8 customers (out of 17 buying item 1) that buy the itemset $\{1,2\}$; however, there are $5 + 1 + 3 = 9$ customers buying the scattered itemset $\{1,4\}$.

Again we try to compute the number of nodes involved, this number being related to the effort necessary to build the FP-trees. In this case the situation is much more complex, since the recursive algorithm builds and destroys nodes on the fly, and in any FP-tree the transactions sharing the same prefix are joined into one path, thereby diminishing the number of nodes. Note that the nodes we count are no trie (or recursion tree) nodes, but the nodes necessary to maintain the FP-trees. The number of inspections necessary to create the FP-trees equals

$$mn + \sum_{\substack{A \neq \emptyset \\ A \text{ frequent}}} \sum_{\substack{j=la(A)+1 \\ A \cup \{j\} \text{ frequent}}}^{n} supp(A) = \sum_{\substack{A \text{ frequent}}} \sum_{\substack{j=la(A)+1 \\ A \cup \{j\} \text{ frequent}}}^{n} supp(A) \quad . \tag{5}$$

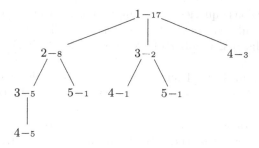

Fig. 2. Example FP-tree

And finally, let us examine the number of tree nodes for the FP-trees. Counting each node with its support (thereby establishing a rough upper bound), this is equal to the number of ones in the databases that are processed:

$$\sum_{i=1}^{n} supp(\{i\}) + \sum_{\substack{A \neq \emptyset \\ A \text{ frequent}}} \sum_{\substack{j=la(A)+1 \\ A \cup \{j\} \text{ frequent}}}^{n} supp(A \cup \{j\})$$

$$= \sum_{A \text{ frequent}} \sum_{\substack{j=la(A)+1 \\ A \cup \{j\} \text{ frequent}}}^{n} supp(A \cup \{j\}) \quad . \tag{6}$$

Note that $\mathcal{FP}$ is a real implementation of APRIORI (except for the pruning step), since every candidate itemset is known to have two frequent subsets. In case of $\mathcal{DF}$ only one subset is certainly frequent!

5   Practical Complexity

Using the well-known IBM-Almaden synthetic database (see [2]) and a real retail database (with 4,698 items and 62,797 transactions) we shall examine the "real" complexity of the two algorithms. This should be compared to the theoretical complexity from the previous sections. The parameters for generating a synthetic database are the number of transactions D (in thousands), the average transaction size T and the average length I of so-called maximal potentially large itemsets. The number of maximal frequent itemsets was set to $L = 2,000$ and the number of items was set to $N = 1,000$, following the design in [2]. The experiments were conducted at a Pentium-III machine with 256 MB memory at 733 MHz, running Windows NT. The programs were developed under the Borland C++ 5.02 environment, but are also usable with the GNU C++ compiler.

Table 1 presents the results from the experiments. The following figures are included: the number of frequent 1-itemsets (this number plays the role of n, since in previous sections we assumed all 1-itemsets to be frequent), the total number of frequent itemsets, the execution time in seconds for both algorithms (for $\mathcal{FP}$ averaged over three runs to compensate for possible garbage collection), and the number of database queries according to Formula (1) and Formula (3), respectively. Also tabulated are the number of trie nodes (for $\mathcal{DF}$; see Formula (2)), respectively the real number of tree nodes (for $\mathcal{FP}$; Formula (6) provides an upper bound).

The figures in Table 1 show some interesting phenomena. One of them is the surprising difference between the performance of the two algorithms for the retail data set at support 0.25%. This is a result of the different character of this real-life data set which turns out to be a worst-case scenario for the $\mathcal{DF}$ algorithm. Compared to the artificial data sets, the retail data contains a lot more frequent 1-itemsets but few longer frequent itemsets. For $\mathcal{DF}$ that results in a huge number of candidate 2-itemsets that have to be counted but turn out to be infrequent. That is also reflected in the difference between the small number of tree nodes for $\mathcal{FP}$ and the large number of trie nodes for $\mathcal{DF}$ for this particular case.

In fact the number of candidate 2-itemsets (influenced by n) affects the performance of $\mathcal{DF}$ in one more way through the procedure of copying. In this procedure, the current frequent itemsets are copied under the new root item to be counted. Even though the infrequent items are not copied, they are still traversed in order to find the frequent ones. Further experiments showed that this results in a high number of node-visits which explains why for D100T20I6, *minsup* 0.5%, $\mathcal{DF}$ creates more trie nodes than for the retail data at 0.25% and still for the retail data performs much worse.

A different picture can be seen in the figures for the three artificial data sets. There, due to the higher percentage of real frequent itemsets from the candidate itemsets, $\mathcal{DF}$ performs better than $\mathcal{FP}$ in most of the cases. Only for the lowest support in D100T20I6 and D100T20I4, $\mathcal{DF}$ shows slower runtime due to the rapid increase in the number of trie nodes that are generated and visited.

6   Conclusions and Further Research

We gave a theoretical analysis of Depth First and FP-growth implementations $\mathcal{DF}$ and $\mathcal{FP}$ of APRIORI. Formulas (1) and (3) capture the number of database queries for the two algorithms, whereas the number of memory cells needed for the datastructures are captured by Formulas (2) and (6).

The experiments show that the execution time is proportional to both the number of queries and the number of nodes of the datastructures. From the experiments one might conclude that $\mathcal{DF}$ outperforms $\mathcal{FP}$ for datasets with larger values of the ratio m/n. But if there are fewer transactions compared to the number of items, $\mathcal{FP}$ seems better.

$\mathcal{FP}$, as used in the experiments in Sect. 5 and as described in [4], has three refinements that improve its efficiency:

1. Identical transactions are identified in the FP-tree. From then on, the algorithm treats them as single ones, keeping track of the correct supports by means of an extra counter. This did not occur too often in our experiments.

Table 1. Experimental results

D100T20I6				
minsup	0.5%	1.0%	1.5%	2.0%
# fr. 1-itemsets	730	561	435	358
# fr. itemsets	25,040	1,090	493	361
$\mathcal{DF}$ exec. time	29	11	8	6
$\mathcal{FP}$ exec. time	22	14	11	9
# queries $\mathcal{DF}$	804,898,976	427,097,723	301,111,212	234,051,516
# queries $\mathcal{FP}$	442,562,012	329,761,608	252,044,086	198,043,844
# nodes $\mathcal{DF}$	10,558,723	401,703	116,816	65,303
# nodes-real $\mathcal{FP}$	1,961,267	1,479,935	1,322,362	1,188,134
# nodes-formula $\mathcal{FP}$	17,071,465	2,442,218	1,740,313	1,514,332

D100T20I4				
minsup	0.5%	1.0%	1.5%	2.0%
# fr. 1-itemsets	688	559	439	369
# fr. itemsets	9,438	2,046	548	382
$\mathcal{DF}$ exec. time	23	12	8	6
$\mathcal{FP}$ exec. time	19	14	12	10
# queries $\mathcal{DF}$	731,815,487	446,136,987	315,448,527	251,949,116
# queries $\mathcal{FP}$	417,996,012	338,850,828	262,917,783	213,788,927
# nodes $\mathcal{DF}$	3,912,166	676,159	134,778	72,546
# nodes-real $\mathcal{FP}$	1,908,370	1,544,726	1,389,513	1,267,268
# nodes-formula $\mathcal{FP}$	8,629,486	3,663,093	1,876,177	1,596,385

D100T20I2				
minsup	0.5%	1.0%	1.5%	2.0%
# fr. 1-itemsets	635	527	445	359
# fr. itemsets	5,435	1,415	708	441
$\mathcal{DF}$ exec. time	20	11	9	6
$\mathcal{FP}$ exec. time	20	15	14	12
# queries $\mathcal{DF}$	757,631,634	432,277,091	331,223,803	249,973,785
# queries $\mathcal{FP}$	396,861,892	321,545,022	271,150,238	210,231,042
# nodes $\mathcal{DF}$	2,512,289	456,566	174,620	83,544
# nodes-real $\mathcal{FP}$	2,265,841	1,584,755	1,476,595	1,324,171
# nodes-formula $\mathcal{FP}$	5,827,026	3,137,017	2,284,728	1,828,513

Retail data				
minsup	0.25%	0.50%	0.75%	1.00%
# fr. 1-itemsets	2,101	920	493	320
# fr. itemsets	3,058	1,086	536	330
$\mathcal{DF}$ exec. time	66	12	4	2
$\mathcal{FP}$ exec. time	7	4	3	2
# queries $\mathcal{DF}$	778,171,180	281,647,840	114,469,871	66,731,996
# queries $\mathcal{FP}$	605,209,096	213,361,480	82,454,945	46,351,860
# nodes $\mathcal{DF}$	4,148,742	571,763	142,475	54,486
# nodes-real $\mathcal{FP}$	828,336	545,504	383,085	290,001
# nodes-formula $\mathcal{FP}$	1,175,688	751,809	545,116	434,039

2. If the database "collapses", i.e., in situation (#) from the procedure in Sect. 4 all transactions turn out to be prefixes of one of them, the recursion terminates. This happens if the FP-tree is a list. Instead of giving all subsets of the current k-itemset I, the algorithm states that the $2^k - 1$ non-empty subsets of I are frequent. During experiments this hardly ever occurred: at most 100 times during one run.

3. At every step, and not only in the first one, the children are again sorted with respect to their supports.

We would like to examine the theoretical and practical behavior with respect to these refinements. Also, it can be interesting to use hash-tables instead of FP-trees.

References

1. R. Agrawal, H. Mannila, R. Srikant, H. Toivonen, and A.I. Verkamo. Fast discovery of association rules. In U.M. Fayyad, G. Piatetsky-Shapiro, P. Smyth, and R. Uthurusamy, editors, *Advances in Knowledge Discovery and Data Mining*, pages 307–328. AAAI/MIT Press, 1996.
2. R. Agrawal and R. Srikant. Fast algorithms for mining association rules. In J.B. Bocca, M. Jarke, and C. Zaniolo, editors, *Proceedings 20th International Conference on Very Large Data Bases, VLDB*, pages 487–499. Morgan Kaufmann, 1994.
3. J.M. de Graaf, W.A. Kosters, W. Pijls, and V. Popova. A theoretical and practical comparison of depth first and FP-growth implementations of Apriori. In H. Blockeel and M. Denecker, editors, *Proceedings of the Fourteenth Belgium-Netherlands Artificial Intelligence Conference (BNAIC 2002)*, pages 115–122, 2002.
4. J. Han, J. Pei, and Y. Yin. Mining frequent patterns without candidate generation. In *Proceedings 2000 ACM SIGMOD International Conference on Management of Data (SIGMOD'00)*, 2000.
5. J. Hipp, U. Günther, and G. Nakhaeizadeh. Mining association rules: Deriving a superior algorithm by analyzing today's approaches. In D.A. Zighed, J. Komorowski, and J. Żytkov, editors, *Principles of Data Mining and Knowledge Discovery, Proceedings of the 4th European Conference (PKDD 2000)*, Springer Lecture Notes in Computer Science 1910, pages 159–168. Springer Verlag, 2000.
6. W. Pijls and J.C. Bioch. Mining frequent itemsets in memory-resident databases. In E. Postma and M. Gyssens, editors, *Proceedings of the Eleventh Belgium-Netherlands Conference on Artificial Intelligence (BNAIC1999)*, pages 75–82, 1999.
7. Z. Zheng, R. Kohavi, and L. Mason. Real world performance of association rule algorithms. In F. Provost and R. Srikant, editors, *Proceedings of the Seventh ACM SIGKDD International Conference on Knowledge Discovery and Data Mining (KDD-2001)*, pages 401–406, 2001.

GO-SPADE: Mining Sequential Patterns over Datasets with Consecutive Repetitions

Marion Leleu[1,2], Christophe Rigotti[1], Jean-François Boulicaut[1], and Guillaume Euvrard[2]

[1] Laboratoire d'Ingénierie des Systèmes d'Information, Bâtiment Blaise Pascal
INSA Lyon, 69621 Villeurbanne Cedex, France
{crigotti,jfboulic}@lisisun1.insa-lyon.fr
[2] Direction de la Stratégie, Informatique CDC, 113 rue Jean-Marin Naudin
F-92220 Bagneux, France
{marion.leleu,guillaume.euvrard}@caissedesdepots.fr

Abstract. Databases of sequences can contain consecutive repetitions of items. This is the case in particular when some items represent discretized quantitative values. We show that on such databases, a typical algorithm like the SPADE algorithm tends to loose its efficiency. SPADE is based on the used of lists containing the localization of the occurrences of a pattern in the sequences and these lists are not appropriated in the case of data with repetitions. We introduce the concept of *generalized occurrences* and the corresponding primitive operators to manipulate them. We present an algorithm called GO-SPADE that extends SPADE to incorporate generalized occurrences. Finally we present experiments showing that GO-SPADE can handle sequences containing consecutive repetitions at nearly no extra cost.

Keywords: frequent sequential pattern mining, generalized occurrences, SPADE

1 Introduction

Mining sequential patterns is an active data mining domain dedicated to sequential data. For example, customer purchases, Web log access, DNA sequences, geophysical data, and so on. The objective is to find all patterns satisfying some given criterion that can be hidden within a set of event sequences. Among the selection criterion proposed in the past (e.g., syntactic properties, similarity with a consensus pattern) the minimal frequency is still one of the most commonly used. Basically, the problem can be presented as follows: Let $I = \{i_1, i_2, \ldots, i_m\}$ be a set of m distinct items. Items are ordered by a total order on I. An *event* (also called *itemset*) of size l is a non empty set of l items from $I : (i_1 i_2 \ldots i_l)$, which is sorted in increasing order. A *sequence* α of *length* L is an ordered list of L events $\alpha_1, \ldots, \alpha_L$, denoted as $\alpha_1 \rightarrow \alpha_2 \rightarrow \ldots \rightarrow \alpha_L$. A database is composed of sequences, where each sequence has a unique sequence identifier (*sid*) and each event of each sequence has a temporal event identifier (*eid*) called timestamp. In a sequence, each *eid* is unique and if an event e_i precedes event e_j in a sequence,

P. Perner and A. Rosenfeld (Eds.): MLDM 2003, LNAI 2734, pp. 293–306, 2003.

then the eid of e_j must be strictly greater than the eid of e_i. Such a database can be represented by a table like, for example, the left table of Fig. 2. A *sequential pattern* (or *pattern*) is a sequence. We are interested in the so-called frequent sequential patterns defined as follows. A sequence $s_a = \alpha_1 \rightarrow \alpha_2 \rightarrow \ldots \rightarrow \alpha_n$ is called a *subsequence* of another sequence $s_b = \beta_1 \rightarrow \beta_2 \rightarrow \ldots \rightarrow \beta_m$ if and only if there exist integers $1 \leq i_1 < i_2 < \ldots < i_n \leq m$ such that $\alpha_1 \subseteq \beta_{i_1}$, $\alpha_2 \subseteq \beta_{i_2}$, ..., $\alpha_n \subseteq \beta_{i_n}$. Let N be a positive integer called *absolute support threshold*, a pattern p is frequent in a database D if p is a subsequence of at least N sequences of D. In this paper, we also use interchangeably *relative support threshold* expressed in the percentage of the number of sequences of D. A lot of work has been done since the introduction of the frequent sequential pattern mining problem in 1995 [2]. Each presents its own interests depending on the characteristics of the database to mine (e.g., [6,10,7,4,8,11,13,12]).

In this paper we consider the problem of mining frequent patterns in sequences where same items tend to be repeated in a consecutive way. This corresponds in particular to the important practical situation where databases are built in part from quantitative time series. In this case, these time series are discretized (using for example the method proposed in [3]) and the discrete values are encoded using items. This has an impact on the form of the resulting sequences that tend to contain more consecutive occurrences of the same items. Indeed, this research is motivated by sequential pattern mining from stock market data where we observed this situation [5]. For example, if items are used to encode a discretized stock price value having slow variations, we will often find in the sequences several consecutive occurrences of the same item. As far as we know, no specific work has been done to tailored the current algorithms towards this kind of data containing repetitions. Figure 1 shows the behavior of the SPADE algorithm [11,13] (a typical sequential pattern mining algorithm) on such datasets. The results of the experiments presented in Fig. 1 correspond to extractions on two datasets: $set1\_r0$ and $set1\_r5$. $set1\_r5$ contains the same sequences that $set1\_r0$ in which a few additional consecutive repetitions of some items have been added (see Sect. 5.1 for a description of these datasets). The curves of Fig. 1 represent the costs (in term of execution time) for the extraction of different amounts of frequent patterns on each dataset, i.e., for different support thresholds. These curves show that to extract a given number of frequent patterns, SPADE execution time is much more important on the dataset containing more consecutive repetitions ($set1\_r5$).

The main contribution of this paper is to show that this extra extraction cost can be reduced drastically by using a more compact information representation. We propose such a representation and present an extension of SPADE, called GO-SPADE, that operates directly on it. We show that in practice it can be used to handle efficiently the consecutive repetitions of items in the data. This practical interest can be seen in particular the bottom right graph on Fig. 5 that presents the same experiments than Fig. 1 using both SPADE and GO-SPADE. This figure shows notably that the presence of consecutive repetitions has nearly no impact on GO-SPADE extraction time for a given amount of frequent patterns.

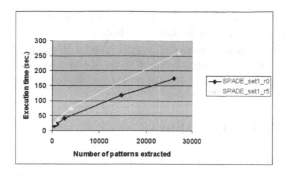

Fig. 1. Evolution of SPADE execution time on datasets with consecutive repetitions

This paper is organized as follows. Section 2 gives an overview of related work in the sequential pattern mining field. Section 3 presents in a synthetic way the SPADE algorithm before to introduce in Sect. 4 our contribution which is a novel SPADE-based algorithm. Section 5 presents experimental results that illustrate how GO-SPADE gains in efficiency compared to SPADE in the case of datasets presenting consecutive repetitions. We conclude in Sect. 6 by a summary and directions for future work.

2   Related Work

In the data mining community, the computation of the sequential patterns has been studied since 1995, e.g., [6,10,7,4,8,11,13,12]. It has lead to several algorithms that can process huge sets of sequences. These algorithms use three different types of approaches according to the way they evaluate the support of sequential pattern candidates. The first family contains algorithms that are based on the A-Priori scheme [1] and that perform a full scan of the database to evaluate the support of the current candidates, e.g., [2,10,7]. In these approaches, a particular effort is made to develop specific structures to represent the sequential patterns candidates to speed-up the support counting operations (e.g., the dedicated hash tree used in [10]). The second family (e.g., [4,8]) contains algorithms that try to reduce the size of the dataset to be scaned by performing projections of the initial database. The last family (e.g., [11,13,12]) concerns algorithms that keep in memory only the information needed for the support evaluation. These algorithms are based on the so called *occurrence lists* which contain the descriptions of the location where the pattern occur in the dataset. The projection database and occurrence list approaches seem to be more efficient than the first one in the case of low support threshold and long sequential patterns since the occurrence lists and the projected databases become more and more smaller. As far as we know, no comparative studies has been done enabling to affirm whether one approach is definitely better than the others. In the frequent itemset extraction field, these three families also exist (e.g., [9,14, 1]) and according to the experimental results of [14], it seems that techniques based on occurrence lists are more efficient at very low support thresholds (while this is not always the case for higher thresholds).

Databases containing consecutive repetitions of items present a new specific problem and, to our knowledge, has not been studied yet. We propose an algorithm based on SPADE [11,13]. It uses *generalized occurrences* lists to represent consecutive occurrences of patterns.

3   The SPADE Algorithm

In this section, we recall the principle of the SPADE algorithm [11,13]. SPADE repeats two basic operations: a generation of candidate patterns and a support counting step. Let us introduce some needed concepts. A pattern with k items is called a *k-pattern*. For example, the pattern B $\rightarrow$ ACD $\rightarrow$ CDFG is a 8-pattern. A *prefix* of a k-pattern z is a subpattern of z constituted by the $k-1$ first items of z (items in the last event of z are ordered according to the lexicographical order) and its *suffix* corresponds to its last item. For example, the *prefix* of the pattern A $\rightarrow$ BC is the subpattern A $\rightarrow$ B and its *suffix* is item C. SPADE uses two frequent k-patterns z_1 and z_2 having the same $(k-1)$-pattern as prefix to generate a $(k+1)$-pattern z. We denote this operation as $merge(z_1, z_2)$. The support counting for the newly generated pattern is not made by scanning the whole database. Instead, SPADE has stored in specific lists, called *IdLists*, the positions where z_1 and z_2 occur in the database. It then uses these two lists denoted $IdList(z_1)$ and IdList(z_2) to determine where z occurs. Then $IdList(z)$ allows to compute directly the support of z. The computation of $IdList(z)$ is a kind of *join* and is denoted $join(z_1, z_2)$. There are several different *merge* and *join* operations used depending on the form of z_1 and z_2 for *merge* and on the form of z_1, z_2 and z for *join*. Before describing in more details these operations and the structure of *IdLists* we give an abstract formulation of SPADE (algorithm 1).

To reduce the memory consumption and to enhance the efficiency, the SPADE algorithm uses various important optimizations (in particular a notion of equivalence class of patterns, dedicated breadth-first and depth-first search strategies and also a specific processing for 1-patterns and 2-patterns). These optimizations are not related to the problem tackled in this paper and we refer the reader to [11, 13] for their descriptions.

The *IdList* of a pattern z contains only the information needed to compute the support of z and the *IdLists* of the patterns that will be generated using z. $IdList(z)$ is a set of pairs $\langle sid, eid \rangle$, each pair describing an occurrence y of z in the database. *sid* is the identifier of the sequence containing y and *eid* is the timestamp of the last event of y. Examples of *IdLists* for 1-patterns are given in Fig. 2 and for the same database, the two Right-Tables of Fig. 3 present examples of *IdLists* for the 2-patterns C $\rightarrow$ D and CD.

The support of pattern z is obtained by counting the number of distinct *sids* present in $IdList(z)$. For example, in Fig. 2, the support of A and E are respectively 2 and 1.

During the *merge* operation of the generation step, SPADE distinguishes two kinds of patterns: *sequence patterns* and *event patterns*, depending on the temporal relation between the *prefix* and the *suffix* of a pattern. A pattern having

Algorithm 1 (abstract SPADE)
Input: *a database of event sequences and a support threshold.*
Output: *the frequent sequential patterns contained in the database.*

Use the database to compute:
- F_1 *the set of all frequent items*
- *IdList(z) for all element z of F_1*
let $i := 1$
while $F_i \neq \emptyset$ **do**
  let $F_{i+1} := \emptyset$
  for all $z_1 \in F_i$ **do**
    for all $z_2 \in F_i$ **do**
      if z_1 *and* z_2 *have the same prefix* **then**
        for all z *obtained by* $merge(z_1, z_2)$ **do**
          Compute IdList(z) by $join(IdList(z_1), IdList(z_2))$.
          Use IdList(z) to determine if z is frequent.
          if z *is frequent* **then**
            $F_{i+1} := F_{i+1} \cup \{z\}$
          fi
        od
      fi
    od
  od
  $i := i + 1$
od
output $\bigcup_{1 \leq j < i} F_j$

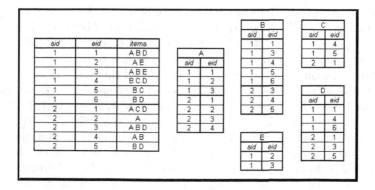

Fig. 2. A database and IdList for items A, B, C, D and E

prefix p and suffix s is called an *event pattern*, denoted ps if s occurs at the same time than the last item of p. If s occurs strictly after the last item of p, the pattern is called a *sequence pattern* and is denoted $p \to s$. For example, pattern $AB \to C \to BDF$ having pattern $AB \to C \to BD$ as *prefix* and item F as *suffix* is an *event pattern*. Pattern $AB \to C$ whose prefix is AB and suffix is C is a *sequence pattern*.

Let z_1 and z_2 be patterns having the same prefix p with respective suffix s_1 and s_2. The *merge* operation used to generate a new pattern depends on the form of z_1 and z_2 (i.e., an event pattern or a sequence pattern). The form of z determines the kind of *join* performed to compute $IdList(z)$ from $IdList(z_1)$ and $IdList(z_2)$. If z is an event pattern (resp. a sequence pattern) the *join* is made using a procedure called *EqualityJoin* (resp. *TemporalJoin*). We present these generation cases and then describe the *join* operations.

- when z_1 and z_2 are *event patterns* (generation case 1):
  z_1 and z_2 are of the forms $z_1 = ps_1$ and $z_2 = ps_2$. The pattern generated by *merge* is $z = ps_1 s_2$ and its $IdList = EqualityJoin(IdList(z_1), IdList(z_2))$.
- when z_1 is an *event pattern* and z_2 a *sequence pattern* (generation case 2):
  z_1 and z_2 are of the forms $z_1 = ps_1$ and $z_2 = p \to s_2$. The pattern generated by *merge* is $z = ps_1 \to s_2$ and we have $IdList(z) = TemporalJoin(IdList(z_1), IdList(z_2))$.
- when z_1 and z_2 are *sequence patterns*: z_1 and z_2 are of the forms $z_1 = p \to s_1$ and $z_2 = p \to s_2$. If $s_1 \neq s_2$, three patterns are generated:
  - (generation case 3) the pattern generated by *merge* is $z = p \to s_1 s_2$ and $IdList(z) = EqualityJoin(IdList(z_1), IdList(z_2))$.
  - (generation case 4) the pattern generated by *merge* is $z = p \to s_1 \to s_2$ and $IdList(z) = TemporalJoin(IdList(z_1), IdList(z_2))$.
  If $s_1 = s_2$ and $z_1 = z_2 = p \to s_1$ (generation case 5), there is only one generated pattern $z = p \to s_1 \to s_1$ and $IdList(z) = TemporalJoin(IdList(z_1), IdList(z_2))$.

The two *join* operations are defined as follows:
Computation of $IdList(z)$ using $TemporalJoin(IdList(z_1), IdList(z_2))$: For each pair $\langle s_1, e_1 \rangle$ in $IdList(z_1)$ and each pair $\langle s_2, e_2 \rangle$ in $IdList(z_2)$ check if $\langle s_1, e_1 \rangle$ represents an occurrence y_1 preceeding the occurrence y_2 represented by $\langle s_2, e_2 \rangle$ in a sequence (i.e., $s_1 = s_2$ and $e_1 < e_2$). If this is the case, it means that the events in y_1 and y_2 form an occurrence of z, then add $\langle s_1, e_2 \rangle$ to $IdList(z)$.

Computation of $IdList(z)$ using $EqualityJoin(IdList(z_1), IdList(z_2))$: For each pair $\langle s_1, e_1 \rangle$ in $IdList(z_1)$ and each pair $\langle s_2, e_2 \rangle$ in $IdList(z_2)$ check if $\langle s_1, e_1 \rangle$ represents an occurrence y_1 ending at the same time than the last event of occurrence y_2 represented by $\langle s_2, e_2 \rangle$ (i.e., $s_1 = s_2$ and $e_1 = e_2$). If this is the case, y_1 and y_2 form an occurrence of z and then add $\langle s_1, e_1 \rangle$ to $IdList(z)$.

We now describe on an example how these joins are performed. Let consider the $IdList$ of items C and D represented in Fig. 3 (from the example database of Fig. 2). The $IdList$ of pattern $C \to D$ is obtained performing a $TemporalJoin$ between $IdList(C)$ and $IdList(D)$ as follows: for a given pair (s, e_1) in $IdList(C)$, SPADE checks whether there exists a pair (s, e_2) in $IdList(D)$

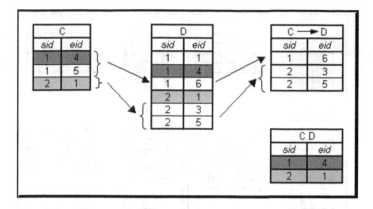

Fig. 3. Temporal and equality joins on IdList(C) and IdList(D)

with $e_2 > e_1$, which means that item D follows the item C in the sequence s. If this is true, then the pair (s, e_2) is added to the *IdList* of pattern C → D. The resulting list is represented in Fig. 3. The *IdList* of pattern CD is computed by *EqualityJoin(IdList(C),IdList(D))* and is depicted on Fig. 3. This *EqualityJoin* is performed as follows: for a given pair (s, e_1) in *IdList*(C), SPADE checks whether there exists a pair (s, e_2) in *IdList*(D) with $e_2 = e_1$, which means that item D occurs at the same time than item C in the sequence s. If this is true, then the pair (s, e_2) is added to the *IdList* of pattern CD.

4 The GO-SPADE Algorithm

4.1 Motivations

Let us revisit the example of Fig. 2 and consider the *IdList* for item A. This item occurs in a consecutive way in the sequences: at *eid* 1, 2 and 3 in the first sequence and at *eid* 1, 2, 3 and 4 in the second one. Such a situation can appear in several kind of databases in particular when the events come from some quantitative data such as time series with smooth variations. SPADE *IdList* stores one line per occurrence, that is 3 lines for the occurrences of item A in sequence 1 and 4 lines for sequence 2. We introduce the concept of *generalized occurrence* to compact all these consecutive occurrences. For example, the 3 consecutive occurrences of item A in sequence 1 can be represented by only one generalized occurrence of the form $\langle 1, [1, 3] \rangle$ containing the sequence identifier (i.e., 1) and an interval [1,3] containing all the *eids* of the consecutive occurrences. When the pattern contains several events, the interval contains all *eids* of the consecutive locations of the last event. For example, for pattern A → B, its four occurrences in sequence 1 in Fig. 4 are represented by the single generalized occurrence $\langle 1, [3, 6] \rangle$.

Using such a representation enables to reduce significantly the size of the *IdLists*, as soon as some consecutive occurrences appear in the database. This compact form of *IdList* containing generalized occurrences is termed *GoIdList*.

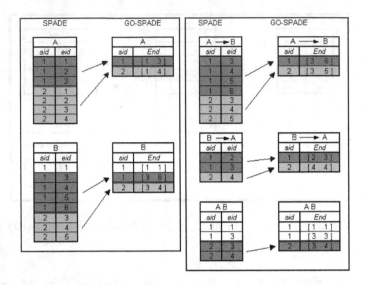

Fig. 4. *GoIdList* vs. *IdList*

Figure 4 illustrates these reductions and also shows how these reductions are propagated during the join operations. For example, *IdList*(A) contains 7 occurrences while the *GoIdList*(A) contains only 2 generalized occurrences. This figure also presents the reductions obtained for *IdList*(B) and for the *IdLists* of A → B, B → A and AB resulting from *TemporalJoin* and *EqualityJoin* operations on *IdList*(A) and *IdList*(B).

In the following, we present our new algorithm, GO-SPADE based on new join operations using *GoIdLists*.

This approach not only reduces the memory space used during an extraction process, it also reduces significantly the join cost , and thus the overall execution time. These effects (memory and time gains) will be described and analyzed in Sect. 5. For example,

4.2   GO-IdList: An IdList of Generalized Occurrences

A *generalized occurrence* represents in a compact way several occurrences of a pattern z, and contains the following informations:

- An identifier sid that corresponds to identifier of a sequence where pattern z occurs.
- An interval $[min, max]$ corresponding to consecutive occurrences of the last event of pattern z.

Such a *generalized occurrence* is denoted as a tuple $\langle sid, [min, max] \rangle$.

A *GoIdList* is a list containing all the generalized occurrences of a sequential pattern. The generalized occurrence list of the sequential pattern z is denoted by *GoIdList*(z).

4.3 GO-SPADE Algorithm

The overall principle of GO-SPADE is the same that the one of SPADE presented in Algorithm 1. The generation process remains the same as in SPADE (i.e., a new pattern z is generated from two generator patterns z_1 and z_2 sharing a same prefix p).

The difference between the two algorithms is that in GO-SPADE the occurrences of the patterns are stored in generalized occurrence lists and that the *TemporalJoin* and *EqualityJoin* computations are replaced by dedicated procedures operating on this generalized form of occurrence.

We now present the new *TemporalJoin* in Algorithm 2 and, in Algorithm 4, the new *EqualityJoin*.

Algorithms 2 and 4 generate a new *GoIdList* from the *GoIdLists* of two generator patterns z_1 and z_2. They proceed in a similar way. The nested loops of lines 1 and 2 iterate on the elements of $GoIdList(z_1)$ and $GoIdList(z_2)$. For each pair $(\langle sid_1, [min_1, max_1] \rangle, \langle sid_2, [min_2, max_2] \rangle)$, the algorithms call a function to join these two generalized occurrences using respectively *LocalTemporalJoin* (algorithm 3) and *LocalEqualityJoin* (algorithm 5). Algorithm 2 just checks before that $min_1 < max_2$ in order to verify that at least one occurrence of $\langle sid_1, [min_1, max_1] \rangle$ terminates before the end of at least one occurrence of $\langle sid_2, [min_2, max_2] \rangle$. Test in line 5 (resp. line 4) verifies that the generalized occurrence returned by *LocalTemporalJoin* (resp. *LocalEqualityJoin*) is valid. If it is the case, then it can be added to the current generated *GoIdList* (line 6, resp. line 5). These algorithms terminate after having proceeded with all couples of generalized occurrences $(\langle sid_1, [min_1, max_1] \rangle, \langle sid_2, [min_2, max_2] \rangle)$ returning the computed *GoIdList*.

Algorithm 2 (*TemporalJoin*)
Input: $GoIdList(z_1)$, $GoIdList(z_2)$
Used subprograms: *LocalTemporalJoin*
Output: *a new GoIdList*

Initialize GoIdList to the empty list.
1. for all $occ_1 \in GoIdList(z_1)$ do
2.   for all $occ_2 \in GoIdList(z_2)$ do
3.   if $(min_1 < max_2)$ then
4.   let $\langle v, add \rangle := LocalTemporalJoin$
         $(\langle sid_1, [min_1, max_1] \rangle,$
         $\langle sid_2, [min_2, max_2] \rangle)$
5.   if add then
6.   *Insert v in GoIdList*
7.   fi
8.   fi
9.   od
10. od
11. **output** *GoIdList*

Algorithm 3 (*LocalTemporalJoin*)
Input: *Two generalized occurrences*
$\langle sid_1, [min_1, max_1] \rangle$
and $\langle sid_2, [min_2, max_2] \rangle$
Output: $\langle v, add \rangle$ where:
$v = \langle sid, [min, max] \rangle$ and add, a boolean
value that is false if v cannot be created.

1. let $add := false$
2. let $v := null$
3. if $(sid_1 = sid_2)$ then
4.   find min the minimum element x
       of $[min_2, max_2]$
       such that $x > min_1$
5.   let $sid := sid_1$
6.   let $max := max_2$
7.   let $v := \langle sid, [min, max] \rangle$
8.   let $add := true$
9. fi
10. **output** $\langle v, add \rangle$

Algorithm 4 (*Equality Join*)	Algorithm 5 (*LocalEquality Join*)
Input: $GoIdList(z_1)$, $GoIdList(z_2)$	Input: *Two generalized occurrences*
Used subprograms: *LocalEqualityJoin*	$\langle sid_1, [min_1, max_1] \rangle$
(Algorithm 5)	*and* $\langle sid_2, [min_2, max_2] \rangle$)
Output: *a new GoIdList*	Output: $\langle v, add \rangle$ *where:*
	$v = \langle sid, [min, max] \rangle$ *and add, a boolean*
1.**for all** $occ_1 \in GoIdList(z_1)$ **do**	*value that is false if v cannot be created.*
2. **for all** $occ_2 \in GoIdList(z_2)$ **do**	
3. **let** $\langle v, add \rangle :=$	1.**let** $add := false$
$LocalEqualityJoin(occ_1, occ_2)$	2.**let** $v := null$
4. **if** add **then**	3.**if** $(sid_1 = sid_2)$ **then**
5. *Insert v in GoIdList*	4. **if** $(min_1 \leq max_2$ *and* $max_1 \geq min_2$) **then**
6. **fi**	5. **let** $sid := sid_1$
7. **od**	6. **let** $min := max(min_1, min_2)$
8.**od**	7. **let** $max := min(max_1, max_2)$
9.**output** $GoIdList$	8. **let** $v := \langle sid, [min, max] \rangle$
	9. **let** $add := true$
	10. **fi**
	11.**fi**
	12.**output** $\langle v, add \rangle$

Algorithm 3, *LocalTemporalJoin*, generates a new generalized occurrence from the two input ones. It first verifies that the two generalized occurrences are from a same sequence, that is $sid_1 = sid_2$ (line 3). Lines 4 to 8 generate a new generalized occurrence. Line 4 sets the *min* value of the generalized occurrence to be created with the minimum element of $[min_2, max_2]$ which is greater than min_1. This means that *min* is the first occurrence of the generalized occurrence $\langle sid_2, [min_2, max_2] \rangle$ that strictly follows the first occurrence of $\langle sid_1, [min_1, max_1] \rangle$. Secondly, Line 5 sets the *sid* value. Then, line 6 sets the *max* value of the new generalized occurrence to max_2 (the location of the last occurrence corresponding to z_2).

Algorithm 5, *LocalEqualityJoin*, first verifies that the two generalized occurrences come from the same sequence and then checks in line 4 if the intersection of the two intervals $[min_1, max_1]$ and $[min_2, max_2]$ is empty or not. If the intersection is not empty, it means that there exists occurrences of the new pattern ending at each *eid* in this intersection. Then the algorithm sets $[min,max]$ to the intersection of $[min_1, max_1]$ and $[min_2, max_2]$, and sets the value of *sid*.

4.4   Soundness and Completness

Definition 1. *(v represents y)* Let y be an occurrence of pattern z in a sequence S from a database β. Let $GoIdList(z)$ be the generalized occurrence list of this pattern and let v be one generalized occurrence from $GoIdList(z)$ denoted by the tuple $\langle sid, [min, max] \rangle$. We say that v *represents* y if $sid(v) = Id(S)$ and $min \leq end(y) \leq max$ where $end(y)$ denotes the eid of the last event of y.

Definition 2. *(soundness)* Let S be a sequence of β and z be a pattern with its generalized occurrence list $GoIdList(z)$. $GoIdList(z)$ is *sound* if for all v in

$GoIdList(z)$, where v is of the form $\langle sid, [min, max] \rangle$ with $sid(v) = \mathrm{Id}(S)$, we have: for all integer t_f in $[min, max]$, there exists an occurrence of z in S such that $end(y) = t_f$.

Theorem 1. *For all patterns z, the $GoIdList(z)$ generated by GO-SPADE is sound.*

Definition 3. *(completness)* Let z be a pattern, $GoIdList(z)$ its generalized occurrence list. $GoIdList(z)$ is *complete* if for all S in β and for all y such that y is an occurrence of z in S, then there exists v in $GoIdList(z)$ such that v *represents y*

Theorem 2. *For all patterns z, the $GoIdList(z)$ generated by GO-SPADE is complete.*

The following theorem follows directly from Theorem 1 and 2.

Theorem 3. *(correctness)* *For all patterns z, the support determined by GO-SPADE using GoIdList is the same as the support determined by SPADE using IdList.*

5 Experimental Results

We present experimental results showing that the behavior of SPADE algorithm is greatly enhanced by the use of generalized occurrences when datasets contain consecutive repetitions. Both GO-SPADE and SPADE algorithms have been implemented using Microsoft Visual C++ 6.0, with the same kind of low level optimization to allow a fair comparison. All experiments have been performed on a PC with 196 MB of memory and a 500 MHz Pentium III processor under Microsoft Windows 2000.

The experimentations have been run on synthetic datasets generated using the Dataquest generator of IBM [2]. Two datasets have been generated using the following parameters: C10-T2.5-S4-I1.25-D1K over an alphabet of 100 items (called *set1*) and C10-T2.5-S4-I1.25-D10K over an alphabet of 1000 items (called *set2*). The first one contains 1000 sequences, the second one 10000 sequences. In both cases, the average size of the sequences is 10 (see [2] for more details on the generator parameters). In these datasets, the time interval between two time stamps is 1, and there is one event per time stamp.

In order to have datasets presenting parameterized consecutive repetitions on certain items, we performed a post-processing on *set1* and *set2*. Each item founded in an event of a sequence has a probability fixed to 10% to be repeated. When an item is repeated, we simply duplicate it in the next i consecutive events. If the end of the sequence is reached during the duplication process the sequence is not extended (no new event is created) and thus, the current item is not completely duplicated. For dataset *set1* (resp. *set2*) we denote *set1_r{i}* (resp. *set2_r{i}*) the dataset obtained with a repetition parameter of value i. For the sake of uniformity, *set1* (resp. *set2*) is denoted *set1_r0* (resp.

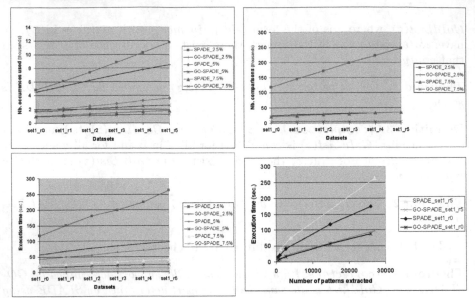

Fig. 5. Evolution of the total number of occurrences used (top left), of the total number of comparisons (top right) and of the total execution time (bottom left). Influence of consecutive repetitions on SPADE vs. Go-SPADE (bottom right)

$set2\_r0$). The post-processing on $set1\_r0$ leads to the creation of 5 new datasets $set1\_r1,\ldots, set1\_r5$. They all have been created simultaneously, to repeat the same items in all the new datasets. For example, if item A occurring in sequence 10 at timestamp 5 is chosen to be repeated, then it will be added to event at timestamp 6 in sequence 10 in $set1\_r1$, and to events at timestamps 6 and 7 in sequence 10 in $set1\_r2$, and so on.

5.1   Generalized Occurrences Impact on the List Sizes

Generalized occurrences represent in a compact way all consecutive occurrences that can be found in a sequence database. The top left graph of Fig. 5 shows the sizes of *IdLists* and *GoIdLists* (in number of elements) for extractions performed on files $set1\_r0$, $set1\_r1$, $\ldots$, $set1\_r5$ using several support thresholds (7.5%, 5% and 2.5%). The number of occurrences used by SPADE is greater than the number of generalized occurrences used by GO-SPADE. As expected, this reduction is more important when the consecutive repetition parameter increases.

5.2   Generalized Occurrences Impact on the Join Costs

As shown in the previous experiments, the size of *GoIdList* is smaller than the size of *IdList*. This reduction has a direct impact on the join costs. Indeed, let n_s and m_s be the number of occurrences of two generator patterns in a sequence s. In the worst case, and assuming that there are $nbSeq$ sequences in the database, the number of comparisons needed to perform one join between these two generator patterns is $\sum_s n_s m_s$, $s \in [1, \ldots, nbSeq]$. Suppose now that all n_s and m_s are reduced by an average factor of $\gamma \leq 1$, then the number of comparisons becomes $\sum_s \gamma^2 n_s m_s$, $s \in [1, \ldots, nbSeq]$. In this case, the number of comparisons used by GO-SPADE is reduced by γ^2 compared to SPADE.

The top right graph of Fig. 5 shows this reduction in practice during extractions performed on $set1\_r0$ to $set1\_r5$ with support thresholds 2.5% and 7.5%. For example, the cost in term of number of comparisons needed during a GO-SPADE extraction at 2.5% is significantly lower than the cost for SPADE at the same support threshold and furthermore is close to the cost for SPADE extraction at 7.5%.

5.3   Generalized Occurrences Impact on the Execution Time

The reduction of the list sizes and the reduction of the comparison number enable to greatly reduce the overall execution time of extractions. This is illustrated on the bottom left graph of Fig. 5, that presents the execution time of SPADE and GO-SPADE on datasets $set1\_r0$ to $set1\_r5$ for support thresholds 2.5%, 5% and 7.5%.

In Fig. 1 (Sect. 1), we have presented how the time needed by SPADE (to extract a given number of patterns) increases in presence of sequences containing consecutive repetitions. The bottom right graph of Fig. 5 completes these results with the corresponding times for GO-SPADE. It shows that the execution time of GO-SPADE to find a given number of patterns remains quite the same in presence of repetitions.

6   Conclusion and Future Works

We considered databases of sequences presenting some consecutive repetition of items. We showed that the SPADE algorithm [11,13], a typical sequential pattern extraction algorithm, turns out to become significantly less efficient on this kind of databases. SPADE is based on lists containing information about the localization of the patterns in the sequences. The consecutive repetitions lead to a defavorable growth of the size of these occurrence lists and thus increase the total extraction time. We defined a notion of generalized occurrences to handle in a compact way the pattern localizations. We propose an algorithm, called GO-SPADE, that extends SPADE to handle these generalized occurrences. Finally, we showed by means of experiments that GO-SPADE remains efficient when used on sequences containing consecutive repetitions. In the data mining community, the frequent sequential pattern extraction process has been enhanced by the consideration of other constraints that the minimal frequency to specify beforehand the relevancy of extracted patterns. These constraint specifications can be used to reduce both the number of extracted patterns and the search space. The c-SPADE algorithm [12], a constrained version of SPADE, is an example of such a constrained-base sequential pattern mining algorithm. A promising direction for future work is to extend c-SPADE with an appropriated form of generalized occurrences to process efficiently sequences with consecutive repetitions. Furthermore, we can now proceed with the real data about stock market analysis that has motivated this research.

References

1. R. Agrawal and R. Srikant. Fast algorithms for mining association rules. In *Proc. of the VLDB Conference*, Santiago, Chile, September 1994.
2. R. Agrawal and R. Srikant. Mining sequential patterns. In *Proc. of the 11th International Conference on Data Engineering (ICDE'95)*, pages 3–14, Taipei, Taiwan, March 1995. IEEE Computer Society.
3. G. Das, L. K.I., H. Mannila, G. Renganathan, and P. Padhraic Smyth. Rule discovery from time series. In *Proc. of the 4th International Conference on Knowledge Discovery and Data Mining (KDD'98)*, pages 16–22, New York (USA), August 1998. AAAI Press.
4. J. Han, J. Pei, B. Han Mortazavi-Asl, Q. Chen, U. Dayal, and M.-C. Hsu. Freespan: Frequent pattern-projected sequential pattern mining. In *Proc. 2000 Int. Conf. Knowledge Discovery and Data Mining (KDD'00)*, pages 355–359, August 2000.
5. M. Leleu and J. Boulicaut. Signing stock market situations by means of characteristic sequential patterns. In *Proc. of the 3rd International Conference on Data Mining (DM'02)*, Bologna, Italy, September 2002. WIT Press.
6. H. Mannila, H. Toivonen, and A. Verkamo. Discovery of frequent episodes in event sequences. *Data Mining and Knowledge Discovery*, 1(3):259–298, November 1997.
7. F. Masseglia, C. F., and P. P. The PSP approach for mining sequential patterns. In *Proc. of the 2nd European Symposium on Principles of Data Mining and Knowledge Discovery in Databases (PKDD'98)*, pages 176–184, Nantes, France, September 1998. Lecture Notes in Artificial Intelligence, Springer Verlag.
8. J. Pei, B. Han, B. Mortazavi-Asl, and H. Pinto. Prefixspan: Mining sequential patterns efficiently by prefix-projected pattern growth. In *Proc. of the 17th International Conference on Data Engineering (ICDE'01)*, 2001.
9. J. Pei, J. Han, and R. Mao. Closet: An efficient algorithm for mining frequent closed itemsets. In *ACM SIGMOD Workshop on Research Issues in Data Mining and Knowledge Discovery*, pages 21–30, May 2000.
10. R. Srikant and R. Agrawal. Mining sequential patterns: Generalizations and performance improvements. In *Proc. of the 5th International Conference on Extending Database Technology (EDBT'96)*, pages 3–17, Avignon, France, September 1996.
11. M. Zaki. Efficient enumeration of frequent sequences. In *Proc. of the 7th International Conference on Information and Knowledge Management (CIKM'98)*, pages 68–75, November 1998.
12. M. Zaki. Sequence mining in categorical domains: incorporating constraints. In *Proc. of the 9th International Conference on Information and Knowledge Management (CIKM'00)*, pages 422–429, Washington, DC, USA, November 2000.
13. M. Zaki. Spade: an efficient algorithm for mining frequent sequences. *Machine Learning, Special issue on Unsupervised Learning*, 42(1/2):31–60, Jan/Feb 2001.
14. M. Zaki and C. Hsiao. CHARM: An efficient algorithm for closed itemset mining. In *Proc. of the 2nd SIAM International Conference on Data Mining*, Arlington, Virginia , USA, April 2002.

Using Test Plans for Bayesian Modeling*

Rainer Deventer[1], Joachim Denzler[1], Heinrich Niemann[1], and Oliver Kreis[2]

[1] Chair for Pattern Recognition
[2] Chair of Manufacturing Technology
Friedrich-Alexander-Universität Erlangen–Nürnberg, 91058 Erlangen, Germany

Abstract. When modeling technical processes, the training data regularly come from test plans, to reduce the number of experiments and to save time and costs. On the other hand, this leads to unobserved combinations of the input variables. In this article it is shown, that these unobserved configurations might lead to un-trainable parameters. Afterwards a possible design criterion is introduced, which avoids this drawback. Our approach is tested to model a welding process. The results show, that hybrid Bayesian networks are able to deal with yet unobserved in- and output data.

Keywords: Bayesian network, modeling, manufacturing process, laserbeam welding

1 Introduction

Modeling of technical processes is applied in many parts of industrial everyday life, e.g. in model based control and quality management. Particularly in the domain of manufacturing, there are two, closely intertwined problems. We have to tackle with few, in most of the cases incomplete, data. The reason is the way tests are executed. Each test causes expenses for material and for the staff, carrying out the experiments. This cost pressure leads to test plans [1,10]. The main idea is to make less experiments, knowing that the used test plan is not able to reveal all possible interdependencies. Particularly interdependencies between multiple parameters are neglected. Therefore only in seldom cases all possible combinations of variables are tested.

Modeling with Bayesian networks(BN) has many advantages, e.g. the possibility of structure learning and to deal with hidden variables. But one of the drawbacks in Bayesian modeling is the sensitivity to missing combinations, if parameters, representing these combinations, are part of the network. In the training process, these parameters are trained as usual, that is depending on the frequency of the occurring cases. When the output for a yet unpresented example has to be predicted, this results in a faulty output.

---

* This work was funded by the "German Research Association" (DFG), Collaborative research center (SFB) 396, project-parts C1 and C3. Only the authors are responsible for the content of this article.

As the usage of discrete nodes causes this phenomenon, a possible solution would be the restriction to continuous nodes, with the disadvantage, that only linear functions could be modeled. Additionally it is not possible to treat each random variable as continuous random variable. The other possibility is to rely purely on a-priori knowledge. But in most of the cases it will be hard to get exact a-priori knowledge. This article shows the critical structures, to be deduced from the test plan, and discusses possible workarounds. The method is applied to the problem of modeling a welding process with 6 input parameters and one output parameter. Some of the parameters are discrete, others are continuous, thus a hybrid Bayesian network[2,7,8] is used for modeling. This enables us to model also nonlinearities. In our example two different methods are used. For one input parameter, the squared value is used as additional input. On the other side it is possible to represent a variable both as discrete and continuous random variable. Using this method also steep slopes can be modeled, e.g. the failure of the welding process. The combination of discrete and continuous nodes allows also the approximation of nonlinear functions by multiple Taylor series [3].

This article is structured as follows. Section 2 gives a brief introduction to hybrid Bayesian networks, Sect. 3 deals with modeling of manufacturing data derived from test plans. Afterwards, in Sect. 4, the data to be modeled are introduced. Section 4 is followed by the applied model and the obtained results. In comparison to other modeling methods, like neural networks and classification trees, we are able to predict both input and output signals with the same model, as the Bayesian network represents a joint distribution of all in- and output parameters, so that arbitrary variables are predicted by marginalization. The article finishes with a conclusion which contains an outlook to further research.

2   Bayesian Networks

Bayesian networks represent a multivariate distribution $P(X_1, X_2, \cdots, X_n)$ of random variables $X_1, X_2, \cdots, X_n$. In this article P denotes a distribution of discrete random variables, p is used for continuous ones. Using the Bayes rule, the probability of a configuration $x_1, \cdots, x_n$, i.e. an instantiation $X_i = x_i$ of every random variable, can be calculated as a product of conditional probabilities [15]

$$P(x_1, x_2, \cdots, x_n) = P(x_1) \prod_{i=2}^{n} P(x_i | x_{i-1}, \cdots, x_1) \ . \tag{1}$$

In many cases, X_i does not depend on all random variables $X_1, \cdots, X_{i-1}$, but only on a subset $\mathbf{Pa}(X_i) \subseteq \{X_1, \cdots, X_{i-1}\}$, called the parents $\mathbf{Pa}(X_i)$ of X_i. Using these independencies the chain rule (1) rewrites to

$$P(x_1, x_2, \cdots, x_n) = P(x_1) \prod_{i=2}^{n} P(x_i | \mathbf{pa}(X_i)) \ , \tag{2}$$

where $\mathbf{pa}(X_i)$ denotes the instantiation of $\mathbf{Pa}(X_i)$. Usually the dependencies between random variables are represented in a acyclic graph, with the random variables as nodes and directed edges from the parents $\mathbf{Pa}(X_i)$ to X_i. As an example, Fig. 1 might be used. The parents of node H are $\{X_1, X_2, X_3, X_4\}$, thus there are edges $X_i \to H$ from X_i to H. It is assumed, that H is a hidden node, which are drawn in shaded manner in this article. To distinguish discrete nodes from continuous ones, the former are drawn as circle or ellipse, the latter as square or rectangle. The next section discusses so called hybrid Bayesian networks, where discrete and continuous nodes are used at the same time.

2.1   Hybrid Bayesian Networks

At the beginning of the development of BNs, only networks with discrete nodes were used. That means that discretization is needed for all continuous variables. Additionally, a great number of parameters is required, to describe exactly a BN with discrete nodes. If only continuous nodes are regarded, it is possible to use a Gaussian network instead, where normal distributions are associated with every random variable, whose mean is calculated as linear combination of its predecessor's values. I.e. the distribution p of a random variable X with parents $\mathbf{Y}$ is

$$p(x|\mathbf{y}) = \mathcal{N}(\mu_{X_0} + \mathbf{w}_X \mathbf{y}, \sigma_X) \qquad (3)$$

with $\mathcal{N}$ as the one-dimensional normal distribution. When $\mathbf{y} = 0$ the mean of the normal distribution is μ_{X_0}, $\mathbf{w}_X$ is the weight vector between $\mathbf{Y}$ and X. Of course, it is possible to regard X also as a multidimensional random variable, but, for the purpose of the article, it is sufficient to use a one-dimensional distribution. If not only continuous variables are used, or if non-linearities are required, these needs are met by hybrid BNs as described in [7,8,11,14].

The set of nodes of a hybrid BN contains both discrete and continuous nodes. Discrete nodes, having only discrete predecessors, are handled as usual. I.e. each node X stores the conditional probabilities $P(X|\mathbf{Pa}(X))$ in a table, which is used for calculation of joint and marginal distributions. Major changes are made for continuous nodes, having both discrete and continuous predecessors. As in Gaussian networks, the values of continuous nodes are still assumed to be normal distributed, but this time a mixture of normal distribution is used with $\mathrm{P}(\mathbf{x}_p)$, the probability of the parents having configuration $\mathbf{x}_p$, as the mixing coefficients. As defined in [4], a configuration for a set of nodes is a set of states with exactly one state for each variable. Therefore, there are different means $\mu_{X_0}[\mathbf{x}_p]$, weights $\mathbf{w}_X[\mathbf{x}_p]$ and standard deviations $\sigma_X[\mathbf{x}_p]$ for every possible configuration. The distribution of node X, given that the continuous parents $\mathbf{Y}$ have value $\mathbf{y}$ and configuration $\mathbf{x}_p$ for the discrete parents, is

$$p(x|\mathbf{y}, \mathbf{x}_p) = \mathrm{P}(\mathbf{x}_p)\mathcal{N}(\mu_{X_0}[\mathbf{x}_p] + \mathbf{w}_X[\mathbf{x}_p]\,\mathbf{y}, \sigma_X[\mathbf{x}_p]) \ . \qquad (4)$$

If a continuous node has no discrete parents, there is only one possible configuration, and the equation is reduced to the pure Gaussian case. It remains the problem, whether discrete nodes are allowed to have continuous parents. Some authors, e.g. Lauritzen [7] [8] and Olesen [14] assume, that there are no such nodes allowed, which simplifies training of BNs. At the moment there are two main approaches, discussed e.g. in [12], to deal with continuous predecessors of discrete nodes. In [9] the junction tree algorithm, used for inference in BNs, is expanded for BNs with continuous nodes as predecessors of discrete nodes.

3   Modeling of Manufacturing Processes

In Sect. 2.1 an introduction to the parameterization of hybrid Bayesian networks is given. The reader should keep in mind, that for every possible configuration x_p of the parent nodes there is a set of parameters to be adapted. For a discrete node X this is usually a table with conditional probabilities $P(x|x_p)$, for continuous nodes the weights $w[x_p]$, means $\mu[x_p]$ and dispersions $\sigma[x_p]$ have to be stored. This section gives a brief overview about test plans, mainly to show that the used test plan leads to special restrictions on the used structure.

Test plans are used to save time and money for a lot of tests, which might be redundant. The reason might be, that also the influence of parameter combinations is explored, which have no effect on the output parameter, according to the engineer, executing the test. Imagine a simple, linear process with four input parameters $X_1, \cdots, X_4$, and one output Y. Suppose that combinations of three different variables have no influence on the output of the experiment. In this case, the test plan in Table 1 can be used, where the input of X_4 is calculated as the product of X_1 to X_3. The symbols '-' and '+' represent a low respectively a high instantiation of the random variables. The product $\cdot$ is defined, so that the product of two different values is negative, the product of two equal values is positive. As X_4 is the product of $X_1, \cdots, X_3$, there is no way to distinguish between the influence of X_4 and the combined influence of $X_1, \cdots, X_3$, which is no drawback, as it was supposed that $X_1 \cdot X_2 \cdot X_3$ has no influence on the outcome of the experiment. On the other hand, 50% of the experiments are saved. As test plans are applied regularly to explore the interdependencies within a process, it is necessary to discuss the effect of test plans in Bayesian modeling. Simple BNs to represent the influence of X_i on Y are depicted in Figs. 1 and 2. The hidden node H on the left hand side has as parameter a table with all conditional probabilities $P(h|x_1, x_2, x_3, x_4)$, including e.g. $P(h| - - - -)$, which represents a never tested combination.

Table 1. Example of a simple test plan

X_1	X_2	X_3	$X_4 = X_1 \cdot X_2 \cdot X_3$	Y
-	-	-	-	
-	-	+	+	
-	+	-	+	
-	+	+	-	
+	-	-	+	
+	-	+	-	
+	+	-	-	
+	+	+	+	

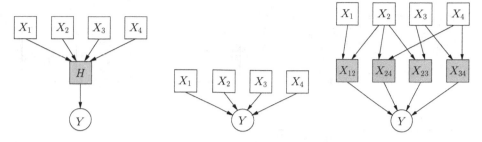

Fig. 1. Critical node H **Fig. 2.** Critical node Y **Fig. 3.** Robust model

The same problem occurs in Fig. 2, where the parameters $\mu_Y[x_1, x_2, x_3, x_4]$ and $\sigma_Y[x_1, x_2, x_3, x_4]$ can not be trained. Of course a pure continuous model will solve the problem, but in this case only linear models can be represented.

Models, as depicted in Fig. 3, might help. They show the following features:

- There is no node representing the influence of a combination of 3 variables. When designing the test plan, it is concluded, that these combinations have no influence on Y.
- For all nodes with discrete parents all configurations of the parents are observed.

Thus the preconditions for a robust modell are fulfilled. The reader should notice that this consideration provides also a criterion for structure learning, which can easily be tested. The variance analysis, usually used to evaluate tests, provides further hints for the structure of the Bayesian network.

The principles discussed in this section are applied to develop a model of the welding process discussed in Sect. 4. The resulting model, together with the result, is presented in Sect. 5.

4   Welding

The welding process is part of a shortened process chain for the manufacturing of complex, hollow bodies, that consists of the processes hydroforming, cutting, and joining by laser beam welding. Two blanks are inserted in a hydroforming tool, formed by pressing fluid between the blanks and cutted by shear cutting. The next process is the welding of the flange by a welding robot that is integrated in the forming tool. For a description of the complete process chain see [5,6].

The first input parameter of the welding process is the type of weld (Confer Fig. 4 for a complete list of the used parameters). Lap edge joint and lap seam joint were investigated. Also, the number of welds is from interest. To achieve a closed impermeable weld, the beginning of the weld has to be welded again at the end of the process. This double welding may have a negative effect on the welding quality. Furthermore, the necessary accuracy of the welding robot has to be examined by determing the influence of defocussing and of a weld offset.

Input parameters

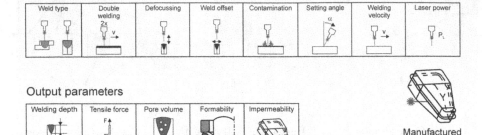

Output parameters

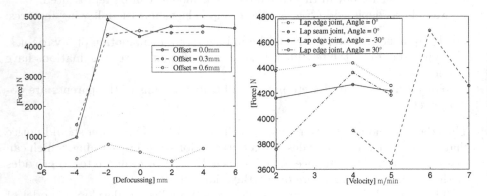

Fig. 4. In- and output parameters of welding process

Fig. 5. Tensile force F depending on the offset **Fig. 6.** Tensile force F depending on the velocity

The results of these experiments are depicted in Fig. 5. Since the welding process takes place just after the hydroforming and cutting, the blanks are contaminated with hydroforming media and lubricant. The effect of this contamination has to be determined. To ensure a constant welding velocity, a setting angle of 30° must be applicated in the corners of the flange. The last and surely most important input factor is the welding velocity. The effect of the velocity is displayed in Fig. 6. The output parameters of the welding process are welding depth, tensile force, pore volume, formability and impermeability of the weld. In this article, only the dependency of the tensile force on the input parameter is modeled.

5   Results

The principles discussed in Sect. 3 are applied to model the welding process, introduced in Sect. 4. A variance analysis shows, that the contamination has

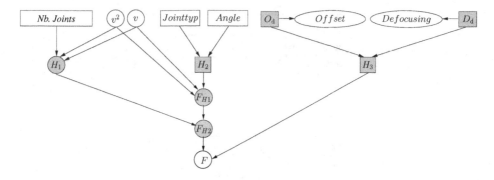

Fig. 7. Model for the tensile force

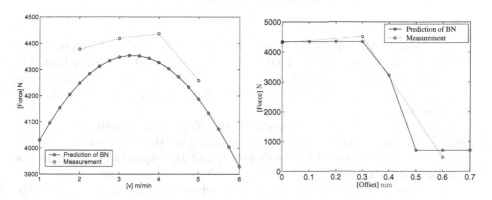

Fig. 8. Tensile force F depending on the velocity

Fig. 9. Tensile force F depending on the offset

nearly no effect on the tensile force and that both, the angle, and the type of joint, have an influence on the tensile force. Thus, there is no node for the contamination.

When developing the structure of the BN, the problem occurs, that there are no data available for the lap seam joint, together with an angle of $+/-30°$. So the problem of untrainable parameter occurs. To avoid the risk of failure, the two unobserved configurations are mapped with equal probability to neighboured configurations. E.g. the lap seam joint with an angle $= 30°$ is mapped to the lap-edge joint with an angle of $30°$, and the lap seam joint with $0°$. This mapping is done by the deterministic node H_2. This means, that the conditional probability table, which determines the behaviour of H_2 is not changed during training.

Figure 6 shows, that the tensile force depends nonlinearly on the velocity v. To enable the model to learn this nonlinearity, an additional node, representing the squared velocity, is added. The mean of node F_{H1} and the weights of the edges $v \to F_{H1}$, and $v^2 \to F_{H1}$, are initialised, so that F is approximated by a regression polynomial of second order. The used model is depicted in Fig. 7, the obtained results for an angle of $0°$ are shown in Fig. 8. The tensile force

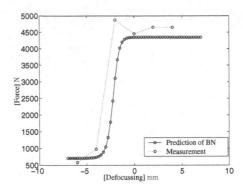

Fig. 10. Tensile force depending on defocussing

depends also on the number of joints. Node H_1 represents the difference of the tensile force for a second joint. That is $H_1 = 0$ for one joint and larger than 0 for a second joint. The results of F_{H1} and H_1 are added, i.e. both links $H_1 \rightarrow F_{H2}$ and $F_{H1} \rightarrow F_{H2}$ are initialised to 1, so that F_{H2} represents the tensile force for intact seams.

The failure of the seam is caused by the offset or defocussing being larger than a threshold. This threshold is represented by the two means of $Offset$ and $Defocusing$, triggered by the nodes O_d and D_d respectively. Again, a good initialisation is essentially.

The discrete node H_3 has two states, representing an intact or defective joint, which triggers the node F. In case of an intact joint the tensile force is determined by F_{H2}, otherwise the node F predicts approximately the mean of the tensile force of all defective joints. For a comparison of the predicted tensile force, depending on the offset and on the defocussing, see Figs. 9 and 10. The results in Fig. 10 are best for an offset of 0 mm, as the largest part of the experiments are executed with that offset.

To test our model, the Bayesian network was trained with the EM algorithm, which is already implemented in the BN-toolbox [13], which was used for the experiments described in this article.

As training data, we got 48 blocks with 6 examples each. To test, whether our model is able to make predictions also for unseen configurations, we trained our net with 47 blocks. Afterwards we compare the predictions with the measured values of the remaining block. To calculate the predictions, all the remaining, observed, variables are entered as evidence and the mean of the marginal distribution is taken as prediction. For continuous random variables (v, F), we used the relative error

$$e_r^c = \frac{|v_m - v_p|}{v_m} 100\% \qquad (5)$$

as quality criterion. In equation (5) v_m denotes the measured value, and v_p the predicted one. For discrete random variables (Number of joints, joint type, angle), the error is defined as quotient between the number of misclassifications

Table 2. Relative error

Variable	Number of joints	Velocity	Angle	Joint type	Tensile force
e_r	37.7%	22.1%	50.4%	15.5 %	17.04%

n_m and the total number of classifications n_t.

$$e_r^d = \frac{n_m}{n_t} 100\% \ . \tag{6}$$

The results are given in Table 2. For the offset and defocusing exact predictions can not be expected. Only predictions for the equivalence class, e.g. failure caused by offset or not, can be made. For the offset there are 3 misclassifications in the 48 blocks tested. For the defocusing 2 blocks are not correctly classified.

6   Conclusion

The usage of test plans is widely spread in manufacturing. Even simple test plans result in unobserved configurations, as the number of experiments grows exponentially with the number of variables.

This article has shown, that unskilful modeling might lead to a complete failure of the model. In contrary, when all configurations of discrete parents are observed, this results in a stable model. This principle is applied to the modeling of a welding process. The results show, that the discussed model is able to deal with evidences, not seen before, e.g. our model is able to predict the tensile force of yet unobserved velocities and offsets. In comparison to neural networks, a Bayesian network is also able to predict input variables, when the output is given. The price for this advantage is a higher effort for modeling, even if there are lot of structure learning algorithms available.

References

1. Larry B. Barrentine. *Introduction to Design of Experiments: A Simplified Approach.* ASQ Quality Press, Milwaukee, 1999.
2. R. Cowell. Advanced inference in bayesian networks. In M.I. Jordan, editor, *Learning in graphical models*, pages 27–49. MIT Press, Cambridge, Massachusetts, 1999.
3. R. Deventer, J. Denzler, and H. Niemann. Non-linear modeling of a production process by hybrid Bayesian Networks. In Werner Horn, editor, *ECAI 2000 (Berlin)*, pages 576–580. IOS Press, August 2000.
4. F.V. Jensen. *An introduction to Bayesian networks.* UCL Press, 1996.
5. O. Kreis and Ph. Hein. Manufacturing system for the integrated hydroforming, trimming and welding of sheet metal pairs. *Journal of Materials Processing Technology*, 115:49–54, 2001.

6. Oliver Kreis. *Integrierte Fertigung – Verfahrensintegration durch Innenhochdruck-Umformen, Trennen und Laserstrahlschweißen in einem Werkzeug sowie ihre tele- und multimediale Präsentation*. PhD thesis, Universität Erlangen-Nürnberg, Meisenbach, Bamberg, 2002. http://www.integrierte-fertigung.de.

7. S.L. Lauritzen. Propagation of probabilities, means, and variances in mixed graphical association models. *Journal of the American Statistical Association*, Vol. 87(420):1098–1108, December 1992.

8. S.L. Lauritzen and F. Jensen. Stable Local Computation with Conditional Gaussian Distributions. Technical Report R-99-2014, Aalborg University, Department of Mathematical Sciences, September 1999.

9. Uri Lerner, Eran Segal, and Daphne Koller. Exact inference in networks with discrete children of continuous parents. In *Uncertainty in Artificial Intelligence: Proceedings of the Seventeenth Conference (UAI-2001)*, pages 319–328, San Francisco, CA, 2001. Morgan Kaufmann Publishers.

10. Douglas C. Montgomery. *Design and Analysis of Experiments*. Wiley, New York, fifth edition edition, 2000.

11. Kevin P. Murphy. Inference and Learning in Hybrid Bayesian Networks. Technical Report CSD-98-990, University of California, Computer Science Division (EECS), January 1998.

12. Kevin P. Murphy. A variational approximation for bayesian networks with discrete and continuous latent variables. In Kathryn Blackmond Laskey and Henri Prade, editors, *Proceedings of the Fifteenth Conference on Uncertainty in Artificial Intelligence*, San Francisco, 1999. Morgan Kaufmann Publishers Inc.

13. Kevin P. Murphy. The Bayes Net Toolbox for Matlab. *Computing Science and Statistics*, 33, 2001.

14. K.G. Olesen. Causal probabilistic networks with both discrete and continuous variables. *IEEE Transaction on Pattern Analysis and Machine Intelligence*, 3(15):275–279, 1993.

15. J. Pearl. *Probabilistic reasoning in intelligent systems*. Morgan Kaufmann Publishers, Inc., 1988. ISBN 0-934613-73-7.

Using Bayesian Networks to Analyze Medical Data

In-Cheol Kim[1] and Yong-Gyu Jung[2]

Department of Computer Science, Kyonggi University
San 94-6 Yiui-dong, Paldal-gu, Suwon-si, Kyonggi-do, 442-760, Korea
[1]kic@kyonggi.ac.kr
[2]ygjung@shjc.ac.kr

Abstract. Due to many possible causes involved with infertility, it is often difficult for medical doctors to diagnose the exact cause of the problem and to decide the correct therapy. A Bayesian network, in general, is widely accepted as an effective graphical model for analyzing biomedical data to determine associations among variables and to make probabilistic predictions of the expected values of hidden variables. This paper presents Bayesian network-based analysis of infertility patient data, which have been collected from the IVF clinic in a general hospital for two years. Through learning Bayesian networks from the clinical data, we identify the significant factors and their dependence relationships in determining the pregnancy of an infertility patient we classify the patient data into two classes (pregnant and not-pregnant) using the learned Bayesian network classifiers. From this medical data mining, we discovered the new domain knowledge that the age of female partner and stimulants like hCG, FSH, LH, Clomiphene, Parlodel and GnRH play the key role in pregnancy of an infertility patient. Through the experiments for investigating the prediction accuracy, Bayesian network classifiers showed the higher accuracy than non-Bayesian classifiers such as the decision tree and k-NN classifier.

1 Introduction

For most prospective parents, getting pregnant takes an average of six months. Even after having frequent intercourse without birth control for one year, 10 percent to 15 percent of couples continue to have difficulty getting pregnant. When this happens, the couple is considered to have a problem with infertility. Infertility can be caused by a reproductive problem in the man, the woman, or both partners. Approximately 20 percent of couples evaluated have more than one reason for their infertility. Reproductive problems explaining infertility occur with roughly equal frequency in men and women. But in the case of female infertility, the age of a woman has a significant impact on the infertility. In general, pregnancy rates diminish progressively every five years after the age of 30. After the age of 44, pregnancy rates are exceedingly low, even when fertility medications are used [9]. In order to resolve an infertility problem, we should identify and treat the cause of the problem correctly. But such correct diagnosis and treatment require the patients to have extensive tests for ovulatory, womb, uterocervical canal, laparoscopy and others. Recently, medically assisted conception

P. Perner and A. Rosenfeld (Eds.): MLDM 2003, LNAI 2734, pp. 317–327, 2003.

methods like IVF-ET (In Vitro Fertilization) through insemination of oocyte and sperm are being widely used as treatments. The typical treatment process executed in IVF clinics is like the followings: First, oocyte and sperm are obtained separately for fertilization. To obtain as many oocytes as possible, ovulatory stimulants like hCG, FSH, LH, Clomiphene, Parlodel, GnRH are used. These stimulants make pituitary to increase the follicle stimulating hormone. Next, sperm and oocytes are fertilized in Vitro. This subprocess is called IVF (In Vitro Fertilization). If IVF fails, through the subprocess called ICSI (Intra-Cytoplasmic Sperm Injection), the sperm is injected into oocyte.

Computationally there have been attempts from medical domain to analyze various treatment factors to predict the success of therapy [1, 7, 13]. A Bayesian network is widely accepted as a graphical model, which is not only useful to illustrate the dependencies among variables under conditions of uncertainty, but also to make probabilistic predictions of the expected values of hidden variables [11]. Furthermore, in addition to observed data, prior domain knowledge can be easily incorporated in constructing and interpreting the Bayesian networks. This paper presents Bayesian network-based analysis of infertility patient data, which have been collected from the IVF clinic in a general hospital for two years. Through learning Bayesian networks from the clinical data, we identify the significant factors and their dependence relationships in determining the pregnancy of an infertility patient. And then we classify the patient data into two classes (pregnant and not-pregnant) using the learned Bayesian network classifiers.

2 Bayesian Networks

In general, a Bayesian network describes the probability distribution over a set of variables by specifying a set of conditional independence assumptions along with a set of conditional probabilities. A Bayesian network, also called Bayesian belief network, is a directed acyclic graph (DAG) with conditional probabilities for each node [8, 12]. In a Bayesian network, each node represents a problem variable and each arc between nodes represents a conditional dependency between these variables. Each node contains a conditional probability table that contains probabilities of the node being a specific value given the values of its parents. The joint probability for any desired assignment of values $<y_1, y_2, y_3, ..., y_n>$ to the tuple of network variables $<Y_1, Y_2, Y_3, ..., Y_n>$ can be computed by the formula

$$P(y_1,..., y_n) = \prod_{i=1}^{n} P(y_i \mid Parents\ (Y_i))$$

where $Parents(Y_i)$ denotes the set of immediate predecessors of Y_i in the network. The values of $P(y_i|Parents(Y_i))$ are the values noted in the conditional probability table associated with node Y_i [13].

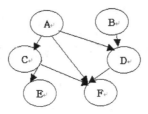

Fig. 1. A Bayesian network

Table 1. Conditional probability table

	A,B	A,~B	~A,B	~A,~B
D	0.4	0.1	0.8	0.2
~D	0.6	0.9	0.2	0

To illustrate, the Bayesian network in Fig. 1 represents the joint probability distribution over the Boolean variables A, B, C, D, E, and F. The network nodes and arcs represent the assertion that D is conditionally dependent of its immediate parents A and B, but conditionally independent of its nondescendants C and E. The Table 1 shows the conditional probability table associated with the variable D. This table provides only the conditional probabilities of D given its parent variables A and B. The top left entry in this table, for example, expresses the assertion that P(D=True | A=True, B=True)= 0.4.

We can use a Bayesian network to infer the value of some target variable given the observed values of the other variables. This inference step can be straightforward if values for all of the other variables in the network are known exactly. In the case of <A=True, B=False, C=True, E=True, F=False>, for example, consider the target value of D based on the Bayesian network in Fig. 1. Because the variable D is dependent on only its immediate parents A and B, we need to compare two conditional probabilities P(D=True | A=True, B=False) and P(D=False | A=True, B=False). Table 1 shows these posterior probabilities of D are 0.1 and 0.9 respectively. Based on these posterior probabilities of D, we may infer that the value of D must be True in this case. Hence, a Bayesian network can be used as a classifier that gives the posterior probability distribution of the classification node given the values of other attributes.

Cheng's work [2] defined several different classes of Bayesian network classifiers: (a) Naïve Bayesian Network (NBN), (b) Bayesian Network Augmented Naïve-Bayes (BAN), (c) General Bayesian Network (GBN). A Naïve Bayesian Network(NBN) is a very simple kind of Bayesian networks that assumes the attributes (or variables) are independent given the classification node.

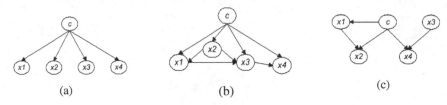

Fig. 2. (a) Naïve Bayesian Network (NBN), (b) Bayesian Network Augmented Naïve-Bayes (BAN), (c) General Bayesian Network (GBN)

A NBN has the classification node as the parent node of all other nodes (see Fig. 2a). No other connections are allowed in a NBN. Although the independence assumption is obviously problematic, NBN has surprisingly outperforms many sophisticated classifiers over a large number of datasets. As an effort to relax the problematic independence assumption, more general classes of Bayesian networks like BAN and GBN have been suggested. BAN allows attributes to form an arbitrary graph (see Fig. 2b). Unlike the other Bayesian classifiers, GBN treats the classification nodes as an ordinary node (see Fig. 2c).

In order to improve the NBN classifiers, there have been also some efforts for selecting feature subset in addition to relaxing independence assumption. In a Bayesian network, we call as the *Markov blanket* of a node *n* a subset of nodes, which is the union of *n*'s parents, *n*'s children, and the parents of *n*'s children. The *Markov blanket* of a node *n* corresponds a subset of nodes within a boundary that shields the node *n* from being affected by any node outside the boundary. If we learn an unrestricted GBN, we can get a natural feature subset by selecting only features within the *Markov blanket* around the classification node.

The two major tasks in learning a Bayesian network are learning the graphical structure, and then learning the conditional probability table entries for that structure. It is trivial to learn the conditional probabilities for a given structure from a complete dataset. But, it is known to be very hard to learn the optimal Bayesian network structure from the dataset. There are two different classes of Bayesian network structure learning methods: the scoring-based algorithms and the conditional independence(CI)-based algorithms. The CI-based learning algorithms are widely accepted to be more efficient than the scoring-based algorithms in practice.

3   Data Collection and Preprocessing

The infertility patient data used for our experiment were collected from a general hospital located in Seoul for two years. This infertility patient dataset contains about 400 treatment records of patients who had visited the IVF clinic in the hospital from Jan. 2000 to Dec. 2001. Each record consists of 39 different attributes (38 instance attributes + an additional class attribute). While each instance attribute represents one of the patient's basic information, symptoms, clinical tests, and treatment methods, the class attribute represents the final pregnancy test. 38 different instance attributes are given below: patient's name, the age of female partner, the age of male partner, the infertile period, noticeable symptoms, follicle stimulations, IVF methods, E2 level hormone, endometriosis thickness, the number of oocytes per stages (mature, inter I, inter II, immature, atretic, post), Intracytoplasmic oocytes of total, the number of embryos per state (1day, 2day, entire), ET method, assisted hatching, zona thickness, the period elapsed since embryos transfer, the number of embryos transferred(G1, G2, G3, G4, G5), PN arrested embryos, total number of embryos transferred, granular macrophage colony stimulating factor, male infertility factors (semen volume, cell count, sperm mobility of raw semen, strict morphology percentage before treatment, strict morphology of sperm treated), immune bead test, WBC cell count in raw semen, and beta hCG level.

Table 2. Discrete attributes

Attribute	Description	Value	Description	Value
Indication	Endometriosis	A	P and T	G
(IND)	Immunological	B	Tubal	H
	Ovarian	C	T and U	I
	O and T	D	Uterine	J
	O and U	E	Unexplained	U
	Peritoneal	F		
Stimulation	Long Protocol	L	Parlodel	P
	Short Protocol	S	Follicular	RF
	Ultra Short ''	U	Null	N
	HMG only	H	Clomiphene	C
	FSH	F	FSH-HMG	FSH-H
IVF	IVF-ET	C	ICSI	I
ETM	Wallace	W	Default	T
ETD	Second day	STD	Fifth day	FTD
	Third day	TTD	Sixth day	SXTD
Clin	True	1	False	0

Based on domain experts' advices, we reduced the dimension of the collected dataset by selecting 9 most relevant ones out of the total 39 attributes and removing the remaining ones. While Table 2 shows the set of 6 discrete attributes, Table 3 lists the set of 3 continuous attributes. In order to reduce the number of values for a given continuous attribute, we applied a discretization technique for dividing the range of the attribute into intervals. Among various discretization methods, the widely used ones are: Equal Width Interval Binning, Holte's 1R Discretizer [6], Recursive Minimal Entropy Partitioning [3]. In our research, Holte's 1R Discretizer was applied to discretize the continuous-value attributes. 1R Discretizer is a supervised discretization method using binning. After sorting the continuous values, 1R divides the range of continuous values into a number of disjoint intervals and adjusts the boundaries based on the class labels associated with the continuous values.

Table 3. Discretization of continuous attributes

Attribute	Description	Value	Description	Value
Female age	20 ~ 34	L	over 40	H
(FA)	35 ~ 40	M		
Total	Null	N	11 ~ 15	MH
ICT	1 ~ 5	L	16 ~ 20	H
	6 ~ 10	M	over 20	HH
Total embryos	Null	N	6~10	SHIGH
transferred(TO)	1 ~ 5	Normal	over 10	HIGH

	A	B	C	D	E	F	G	H	I
1	FA	IND	Stimulatic	IVF	ICT	ETM	ETD	TC	Clin
2	31	T	L	C	0	W	2	4	N
3	43	T	L	C	0	T	2	4	N
4	37	T	L	C	0	W	2	2	Y
5	34	T	L	C	0	T	2	6	Y
6	34	T	U	C	0	T	2	6	N
7	27	T	L	C	0	W	2	3	N
8	38	T	L	C	0	T	2	3	N
9	36	UN	L	C	0	T	2	2	N
10	37	E	L	C	0	W	2	3	Y
11	32	T	L	C	0	T	2	5	Y
12	34	T	U	C	0	W	3	7	Y
13	29	T	L	C	0	T	2	4	N
14	31	E	L	C	0	W	2	5	N
15	40	UT	L	C	2	W	3	3	N
16	36	UN	U	I	4	T	3	4	N
17	26	T	L	C	0	T	3	8	N
18	27	T	U	C	0	W	3	3	N
19	35	T	L	C	0	T	3	5	Y
20	35	T	L	C	0	W	3	6	Y

Fig. 3. A sample dataset

Unlike simple binning methods such as Equal Width Interval Binning, 1R uses the available class information to overcome the problem which forces to put two instances with the same class label in two different intervals. Figure 3 shows three attributes discretized in this way.

Additionally the required preprocessing step was data cleaning to handle incomplete, noisy, and inconsistent data. The records with either any missing data or inconsistent data were all simply eliminated from the dataset. After such data cleaning, the clean dataset containing only 269 records was obtained. Figure 3 shows a sample dataset contained in a MS Excel file.

4   Experiments

4.1   Learning Bayesian Networks

In order to analyze the feature dependencies and to make predictions of pregnancy, we learned three different types of Bayesian networks (NBN, BAN, and GBN) from the preprocessed dataset. Cheng's CBL algorithm [2], which is an efficient CI-based learning algorithm, was applied. This algorithm requires $O(N^2)$ mutual information tests. For learning both NBN and BAN from the infertility patient dataset, the classification node representing the final pregnancy test(clin) was set to be the root node. For learning GBN, on the other hand, the classification node was treated as an ordinary node. Unlike other types of Bayesian networks, NBN required no structure learning from the training data as the structure is given *a priori*. We learned the structure of BAN by allowing all attribute nodes except the root node to form an arbitrary graph. Figures 4, 5, and 6 show the learned NBN, BAN, and GBN respectively. Due to space problem, the conditional probability tables for each node are not shown.

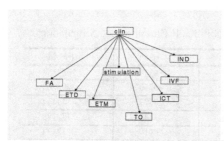

Fig. 4. Naïve Bayesian Network (NBN)

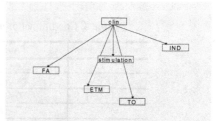

Fig. 7. Naïve Bayesian Network with Selected Features (NBNSF)

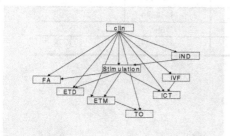

Fig. 5. Bayesian Network Augmented Naïve-Bayes (BAN)

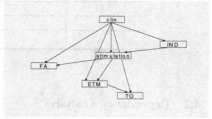

Fig. 8. Bayesian Network Augmented Naïve-Bayes with Selected Features (BANSF)

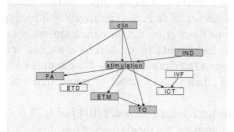

Fig. 6. General Bayesian Network (GBN)

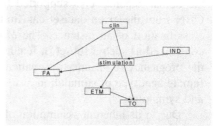

Fig. 9. General Bayesian Network with Selected Features (GBNSF)

From Fig. 6, we can see that the classification node, clin, still does not have any parents in the learned GBN, although the learner treated it as an ordinary node. The gray-colored nodes (FA, Stimulation, ETM, TO, and IND) in GBN represent the nodes within the *Markov blanket* of the classification node. The corresponding attributes are female age, type of stimulation, use of Wallace, total number of transferred embryos, and symptoms. These attributes may be considered to be the most important features directly affecting the pregnancy of infertility patients. Hence we have attempted to reduce the dimension of the dataset to the set of these six features, which contains the class attribute. Then from the reduced dataset, new NBN, BAN, and GBN have been generated. The newly learned NBN, BAN, and GBN are denoted as NBNSF, BANSF, and GBNSF respectively (see Figs. 7, 8, and 9).

Table 4. Conditional probabilities P(Clin=true | FA,Stimulation)

Stimulation	FA=H	FA=L	FA=M
C	.2083333	.5833333	.2083334
F	.2962963	.4074074	.2962963
FSH-H	.2777778	.2777778	.4444444
H	.2777778	.4444444	.2777778
L	.0574713	.6091954	.3333333
N	.3333333	.3333333	.3333334
P	.3809524	.2380952	.3809524
RF	.2777778	.4444444	.2777778
S	.1282051	.3589744	.5128205
U	.2777778	.4444444	.2777778

4.2   Dependency Analysis

Unlike NBN and BAN assuming every possible dependency between the classification node and each attribute node, GBN without such assumption tends to represent only the actual dependencies supported by the training data. In other words, learning a GBN from the given dataset can find a subset of features significantly affecting the classification of an instance. The *Markov blanket* of the classification node can be considered as such a subset of feature nodes. From Fig. 6, therefore, we can see that the pregnancy of an infertility patient depends primarily on the five features such as female age, type of stimulation, use of Wallace, total number of transferred embryos, and symptoms.

Due to its inherent assumption of attribute-independence, NBN in Fig. 4 does not have any dependency links between attributes nodes themselves. From Figs. 5 and 6, on the other hand, we can see that both BAN and GBN could find such conditional dependencies among attributes nodes themselves. Furthermore, we can also see that such inter-attribute conditional dependencies found by BAN are the same as those ones by GBN.

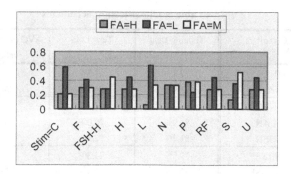

Fig. 10. Graph representing P(Clin=true | FA,Stimulation)

From Figs. 8 and 9, we can see that after feature reduction both BANSF and GBNSF still conserve the same inter-attribute dependencies as BAN and GBN. Table 4 shows the conditional probabilities P(Clin=true | FA,Stimulation) of the pregnancy of an infertility patient, given the age of female and the type of stimulation. From Table 4, we can see that if the female patient is young, stimulants of clomiphene (C) and long protocol (L) treatment can help increase the possibility of pregnancy. The most significant features in determining the pregnancy of an infertility patient and the conditional dependencies among them found through learning Bayesian networks, especially GBN, are currently accepted as an interesting discovery in the viewpoint of domain experts.

4.3 Pregnancy Prediction

For the purpose of evaluating the prediction accuracy of each Bayesian network classifier, we conducted the experiments in three different ways. The patient dataset of 269 records was split into the training dataset of 244 records and the test dataset of 25 records. Each classifier learned from the separate training dataset, and then, was tested on both the training dataset and the test dataset. In another series of experiments, each classifier was tested using 10-fold cross validation method. In order to compare Bayesian classifiers with non-Bayesian classifiers in terms of the prediction accuracy, we tested the decision-tree classifier (by C4.5 algorithm) and k-NN(k-nearest neighbors) classifier in the same ways. Additionally, In order to investigate the effect of feature reduction, we also experimented with NBNSF, BANSF, and GBNSF.

Table 5 provides the prediction accuracy of each classifier. From Table 5, we can see that all Bayesian classifiers showed the higher prediction accuracy than non-Bayesian classifiers such as the decision tree and k-NN classifier. We can also see that among the Bayesian network classifiers, GBN was proved to be the best classifier with respect to our dataset.

Table 5. Classification accuracies

Classifiers	Training Data	Test Data	AVG of 10-fold cross validation
DT(C4.5)	77.4%	64.3%	73.9%
k-NN (k=3)	78.9%	66.7%	74.8%
NBN	78.4%	67.1%	75.5%
BAN	81.9%	70.0%	78.8%
GBN	81.4%	72.9%	79.2%
NBNSF	79.9%	74.3%	78.4%
BANSF	82.4%	71.4%	79.6%
GBNSF	79.4%	65.7%	75.9%

Among the Bayesian network classifiers with selected features, BANSF showed the higher accuracy than NBNSF and GBNSF. Figure 11 shows the effect ratio by feature reduction. From Fig. 11, we can see that the prediction accuracy of NBN has been improved most drastically.

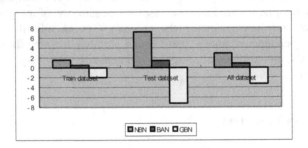

Fig. 11. Effect ratio by feature reduction

5   Conclusions

This paper presented Bayesian network-based analysis of infertility patient data, which have been collected from the IVF clinic in a general hospital for two years. Through learning Bayesian networks from the clinical data, we identified the significant factors and their dependence relationships in determining the pregnancy of an infertility patient. We classified the patient data into two classes (pregnant and not-pregnant) using the learned Bayesian network classifiers. From this medical data mining, we discovered the new domain knowledge that the age of female partner and stimulants like hCG, FSH, LH, Clomiphene, Parlodel and GnRH play the key role in pregnancy of an infertility patient. Through the experiments for investigating the prediction accuracy, Bayesian network classifiers showed the higher accuracy than non-Bayesian classifiers such as the decision tree and k-NN classifier.

References

[1] Ahmed Y. Tawfik and Krista Strickland: Mining Medical Data for Causal and Temporal Patterns, Proceedings of the 4th European Conference on the Principles and Practice of Knowledge Discovery in Databases (2000).

[2] Cheng, J. and Greiner, R. : Learning Bayesian Belief Network Classifiers – Algorithms and System, Proceedings of the 4th Canadian Conference on Artificial Intelligence (2001).

[3] Dougherty, J., Kohavi, R., and Sahami, M. : Supervised and Unsupervised Discretization of Continuous Features", Proceedings of ICML'95 (1995) 194–202.

[4] Gorrill, Marsha J., Kaplan, Paul F., Patton, Phillip E., Burry, Kenneth A.: Initial Experience with Extended Culture and Blastocyst Transfer of Cryopreserved Embryos, American Journal of Obstetric & Gynecology, vol. 180, no. 6 (1999).

[5] Hyuk Jung, Infertility: What is Problem – The Origin and Therapy, Woori Publishing (1997).

[6] Jiawei Han, Micheline Kamber, Data Mining: Concepts and Techniques, Morgan Kaufmanm (2001).

[7] Jorge C. G. Ramirez, Diane J. Cook, Lynn L. Peterson, Dolores M. Peterson: An Event Set Approach to Sequence Discovery in Medical Data, Intelligent Data Analysis, vol. 4, no.6 (2000) 513–530.

[8] Kevin Patrick Merphy: Dynamic Bayesian Networks – Representation, Inference and Learning, PhD Thesis, UC Berkeley, Computer Science Division, July (2002).

[9] Korea Society of Obsterics and Gynecology: Gynecology, Calvin Publishing (1991) 389–436.

[10] N. Friedman, M. Linial, I. Nachman, D. Pe'er: Using Bayesian Networks to Analyze Expression Data, Journal of Computational Biology (2000).

[11] Pearl, J.: Probabilistic Reasoning in Intelligent Systems, Morgan Kaufmann (1988).

[12] Tom M. Mitchell: Machine Learning, McGraw-Hill (1997).

[13] Wynne Hsu, Mong Li Lee, Bing Liu, Tok Wang Ling : Exploration Mining in Diabetic Patients Databases – Findings and Conclusions, Proceedings of KDD-2000 (2000) 430–436.

A Belief Networks-Based Generative Model for Structured Documents. An Application to the XML Categorization

Ludovic Denoyer[1] and Patrick Gallinari[1]

Laboratoire d'Informatique de Paris VI
LIP6
France
{ludovic.denoyer, patrick.gallinari}@lip6.fr
http://www-connex.lip6.fr

Abstract. We present a generative Bayesian model for the modeling of structured (e.g. XML) documents. This model allows us to simultaneously take into account structure and content information. It is used here for classifying XML documents. We adopt a machine learning approach and the model parameters are learned from a labeled training set of representative documents. We discuss the role of structural information for classification and describe experiments on a small collection of class labeled structured documents. We also present preliminary results showing how this model could classify documents with DTDs not represented in the training set.

1 Introduction

The development of large electronic document collections ands Web resources has been paralleled by the emergence of different structured format proposals, aimed at encoding content information in a suitable form, for a variety of information needs. In addition to providing standard representations, these formats allow us to enrich the document content with additional information (e.g. metadata, comments etc...) and allow to store and access this content in a more efficient way. Some proposals (e.g. RDF for Web documents) have gained some popularity. At the same time, description languages like XML have become standards and are already widely used by different communities. For text documents, these representations encode both structural and content information. Flat document collections will probably be superseded in the near future by structured collections.

There is an important need to adapt existing information access methods to these new document representations so that they take all the benefit of these richer representations and also answer new information access challenges and new user needs. Current Information Retrieval (IR) methods have mainly been developed for handling flat document representations and cannot be easily adapted to deal with structured representations. In this paper, we focus on the particular task of structured document categorization.

P. Perner and A. Rosenfeld (Eds.): MLDM 2003, LNAI 2734, pp. 328–342, 2003.

Intuitively, like for other IR tasks, structure might seem to play an important role in categorization. A word will not have the same meaning or the same significance depending on its position into the document (title, metadata, keyword, etc). Also, a large and complex document might be relevant to a specific class even when only one of its subparts is relevant to the class. This information is hardly exploited at all in classical document representations.

In this article, we examine the role of structural information for document categorization and propose methods for exploiting both the content and the structure information for categorization tasks. We describe a generative categorization model based on belief networks. This work offers a natural framezork for encoding structured representations and allows us to perform inference both on the whole document and on document subparts.

2 Previous Works

Text categorization is a classical information retrieval task which has motivated a large amount of work over the last fews years. Most categorization models have been designed for handling bag of words representations and do not consider word ordering or document structure. Generally speaking, classifiers fall into two categories: generative models which estimate class conditional densities $P(document/Class)$ and discriminant models which directly estimate the posterior probabilities $P(Class/document)$. The naive Bayes model [11] for example is a popular generative categorization model whereas among discriminative techniques support vector machines [8] have been widely used over the last few years. [19] makes a complete review of flat document categorization methods. Note that more recently, models which take into account sequence information have been proposed [4].

The expansion of the Web has motivated a series of works on Web page categorization - viz. the last two Trec competitions [20]. Web pages are built from different type of information (title, links, text, etc) which play different roles. There has been several attempts to combine these information sources in order to increase page categorization scores. There is not yet a clear conclusion on the relevance of combining these different types of information, however, this is work in progress. Many authors propose combining different classifiers each of them being trained on a specific information source. For example [17] compares three HTML page classifiers: one operates on the flat textual content of the pages, a second on page and section titles and a third on hyperlinks text. Experiments performed on one of the few available labeled HTML dataset, WebKB [2], show that indeed titles and hyperlinks information is relevant for the task and allow to increase performance compared to a purely flat textual representation. [12] maps a structured document onto a vector by encoding different structural elements (title, links, text) into different parts of the vector. For each part, he makes use of a frequential term representation (tf-idf), where the frequencies are computed on this specific type of structural element. He then uses classical classifiers on these vectors. However, this does not bring any improvement on WebKB. Dumais and Chen [6], make use of the HTML structure (tags) in order to select the more relevant document parts for the categorization problem. [21] classify hypertexts by combining 3 classifiers which operate on the different parts of the document (linked pages, HTML tags, metadata). All these approaches deal only with HTML, they propose simple schemes either for encoding the page structure or for exploiting the different types of information by combining basic classifiers. They represent an initial attempt to take into account HTML structure and do not allow us to exploit more complex structures. These models exploit a priori knowledge about the particular semantics of HTML tags, and as such cannot be extended to more complex languages like XML where tags may be defined by the user. We will see that our model does not exploit this type of semantics and is able to learn from data the importance of tag information.

The previous models use *a priori* information about the nature of the tag, i.e this model uses the information that the title of an HTML page is described between the tag called $< title >$ and $< /title >$. **We will see that our model does not use any information about the significance of the tags of an XML document.**

Some authors have proposed more principled approaches to deal with the general problem of structured document categorization. These models are not specific to HTML even when they are tested on HTML databases due to the lack of a reference XML corpus. [5] for example proposes the Hidden Tree Markov Model (HTMM) which is an extension of HMMs to a structured representation. They consider tree structured documents where in each node (structural element), terms are generated by a node specific HMM. [16] have proposed a Bayesian network for classifying structured documents. This is a discriminative model which computes directly the posterior probability corresponding to the document relevance for each class.

From a categorization model perspective, Bayesian networks (BN) have been used for information retrieval for some time, mainly for ad-hoc tasks. Inquery [1], is a well known retrieval engine based on BNs which operates on flat text. Other authors have also used BNs for the retrieval of structured documents,e.g. [14], [15]. Outside the field of information retrieval, some models have been proposed to handle structured data. The hierarchical HMM (HHMM) [7] is also a generalization of HMMs to structured data, it has been tested on handwriting recognition and on the analysis of English sentences, similar HMM extensions have been used for multi-agent modeling [13]. However, inference and learning algorithms in these models are too computationally demanding for handling large IR tasks. The inference complexity for HHMM is $O(NT^3)$ where N is the number of states in their HMM and T the length of the text in words, for comparison our model is more like $O(N + T)$ as will be seen later.

The model we propose is a generative model which has been developed for the categorization of any tree like document structure (typically XML documents). This model bears some similarities with the one in [5], however, their description being very general, we cannot further compare the models. Their model is adapted to the semantic of HTML documents and considers only the inclusion relation between two document parts. Ours is generic and can be used for any type of structured document, even when tags do not convey semantic information, it allows considering different types of relations between structured elements: inclusion, depth in the hierarchical document, etc. This model could be considered as a special case of the HHMM [7] since it is simpler and since HHMM can be represented as particular BNs [13]. It is computationally much less demanding and has been designed for handling large document collections.

[22] presents an extension of the Naive Bayes model to semi-structured documents where essentially global word frequencies estimators are replaced with local estimators computed for each path elements.

3 Document Structure

A structured document d will be represented as a Directed Acyclic Graph (DAG). Each node of the graph represents a structural entity of the document, and each edge represents a hierarchical relation between two entities (for example, a paragraph is included in a section, two paragraphs are on the same level of the hierarchy, etc). For keeping inference complexity to a reasonable level, we do not consider circular relations which might appear in some documents (e.g. Web sites), this is a simplifying assumption which is not too severe since this definition already encompasses many different types of structured documents.

Each node of the DAG is composed of:

- a **label**: for example, labels can be *section, paragraph, title* and represent the structural semantic of a document.
- a **textual information** which is the textual content associated to this node if any.

A structured document then contains three types of information:

1. the logical structure information represented by the arcs of the DAG. (the position of the tag in an XML document)
2. the label information (the name of the tag in an XML document)
3. the textual information

Figure 1 is a simple example of structured document.

4 The Generative Model

We now present our BN model which allows to handle these 3 types of information. This model can be used with any XML document without using *a priori* informations about the semantic of the structure (i.e: we do ignore the significance of the tags describe in the DTD). We first briefly introduce BNs and then describe the different elements of the model.

4.1 Belief Networks

Belief networks [9] are stochastic models for computing the joint probability distribution over a set of random variable. They are DAGs whose nodes are the

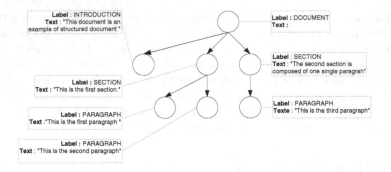

Fig. 1. An example of structured document represented as a Direct Acyclic Graph. This document is composed of an introduction and two sections. The first section has two paragraphs and the second one. Each part of the document is represented by a node with a **label** and a **textual information**

random variables and edges correspond to probabilistic dependence relations between 2 variables. The structure of the DAG reflects conditional independence properties between variables, the joint probability of a set of variables writes:

$P(x_1, ..., x_n) = \prod_{i=1..n} P(x_i/pa(x_i))$ where $(pa(x_i))$ denotes the parents of x_i in the DAG.

4.2   Model Components

Let $d = (w_d, s_d)$ denote a document, with w_d the textual content and s_d the structural organization of the document. We will construct a generative model with parameters θ for computing the probability of a document:

$$P(d|\theta) = P((w_d, s_d)|\theta) = P(s_d|\theta)P(w_d|s_d, \theta) \tag{1}$$

In the following, we will successively detail the model components for the structural $P(s_d|\theta)$ and content $P(w_d|s_d, \theta)$ terms.

The Structural Probability: $P(s_d|\theta)$

We encode the structural information of a document into a belief network. This information s_d is the realization of a set of random variables denoted $s_d = \{s_d^i\}, i \in [1..|s_d|]$ (where $|s_d|$ is the number of structured nodes for document d), with $s_d^i \in \Lambda$ where Λ is the set of all the possible labels for the nodes of the DAG representing document d. Note that Λ depends on the DTD of the training XML documents. The corresponding BN structural parameters are then the quantities $\{P(s_d^i|pa(s_d^i))\}$ which are the probabilities to observe s_d^i given its parents $pa(s_d^i)$ in the BN. In our model, we will construct one BN for each document. This BN can be thought of as a model of the structured document generation, where the generation process goes as follows: someone who wants to create a document about a specific topic will sequentially and recursively create the document organization and then fill the corresponding nodes with text. For example he first creates sections after what, for each section, he creates subsections etc... recursively. At the end, in each "terminal" node, he will create the textual information of this part as a succession of words. This is a typical generative approach which extends to structured information the classical HMM approach for modeling sequences. The corpus will then be represented as a series of BN models, 1 per document. Each will compute its structural density as:

$$P(s_d|\theta) = \prod_{i=1}^{|s_d|} P(s_d^i|pa(s_d^i)) \tag{2}$$

In order to have a robust estimation of the BN parameters, we will share sets of parameters among all the collection BNs. For the structural part, we make the hypothesis that the $\{P(s_d^i|pa(s_d^i))\}$ depend only on the labels of nodes s_d^i and $pa(s_d^i)$. i.e. two nodes in two different BNs which share the same label and whose parents also share the same labels will have the same transition probability.

Let us assume for now that our documents are XML documents which follow a specific DTD. Our "structural model" is based on the following ideas:

- Λ the set of values for the s_d^i, corresponds to the set of values for the tags in the DTD.
- We want to be able to take into account two types of structural information:
  1. The inclusion information. We want to represent the fact that a part (for example, a paragraph) is included into an other part (for example, a section).
  2. A sequential information which indicates how the different parts do appear sequentially in the document. e.g. a paragraph is followed by an other paragraph, or the first section follows the introduction, etc.
- Model complexity should remain low enough for the classification of large corpus: we will then use only first order dependencies between document parts.

Within this framework, several BN models may be associated to a document d. Figure 2 illustrates two of the models we have been working with. The DAG structure of Model 2 is copied from the tree structure of the document and reflects only the inclusion relation. The same type of relation is used in [5]. Model 1 contains both inclusion information (vertical edges) and sequence information (horizontal edges). Both models are an overly simplified representation of the real dependencies between document parts. This allows to keep the complexity of learning and inference algorithms low and to have robust inference models. Statistical models that work best are often very simple compared to the underlying phenomenon (e.g. naive Bayes in text classification or Hidden Markov Models in speech recognition), practioners of BNs have experienced the same phenomenon. In our tests on the WebKB collection, the two models behave similarly, in the experiments we show results for model 1. Note that other instances of our generic model could have also been used here.

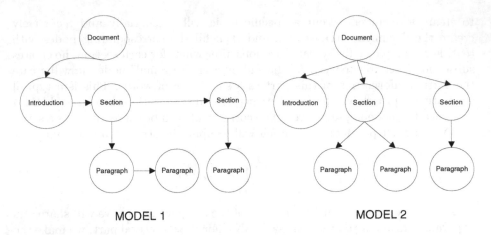

MODEL 1   MODEL 2

Fig. 2. Two possible structural belief networks constructed for the document presented in Fig. 1. For example in MODEL 1, we can compute the probability: $P(s_d) = P(intro|titre)P(sec|intro)P(sec|sec)P(par|sec)P(par|par)P(par|sec)$ with $\Lambda = \{intro, document, sec, par\}$ representing the label *document, introduction, section* or *paragraph*

Textual Probability: $P(w_d|s_d, \theta)$

Let $w_d = w_d^i, i \in [1..|w_d|]$ be the set of all word instances of the document d, $w_d^i \in V$ where V represents the space of all the possible terms (the vocabulary). We make the following hypothesis:

- **H1:** the probability of a word w_d^i depends only on the label of the node that contains this word, i.e. $P(w_i^d/s_i^d)$ only depends on the value of s_i^d and not on the place of the node in the tree.
- **H2:** in a node, words are independent (Naive Bayes assumption)

Let $sel(w_d^i) = s_d^j$ (sel = structural **el**ement) be the function which indicates that word w_d^i is in the node labeled s_d^j, we then have:

$$P(w_d|s_d, \theta) = \prod_{i=1}^{|w_d|} P(w_d^i|sel(w_d^i), \theta) \qquad (3)$$

As for the structure, both hypothesis H1 and H2 have been made to keep computation feasible. Hypothesis H1 means that word generation does not depend on the father label of the node it belongs to. For the generative model this means that the document creator generates words by considering only the local context of the part he is currently writing. We could have considered a more realistic process where word occurrence depends on the whole document path which leads to this word at the price of more complex estimation models.

The naive Bayes hypothesis H2 is not mandatory here and any other term generative model (e.g. HMM) could be used instead, however this hypothesis allows for a robust density estimation and it is not clear that more sophisticated models could lead to any performance improvement.

Final Belief Network

Combining Eqs. (2) and (3), we get:

$$P(d|\theta) = \prod_{i=1}^{|s_d|} P(s_d^i|pa(s_d^i), \theta) \prod_{i=1}^{|w_d|} P(w_d^i|sel(w_d^i), \theta) \tag{4}$$

The BN corresponding to the document in Fig. 1 is given in Fig. 3.

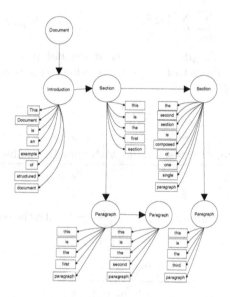

Fig. 3. The final belief network constructed to represent the document in 1. The random variables corresponding to the word variables are represented with rectangles whereas the random variables corresponding to the tags variables are represented with circles

4.3   Learning

In this model, there are two sets of parameters to learn the transition and emission probabilities respectively denoted by $P(\hat{s_i}|s_j)$ and $P(\hat{w_i}|s_j)$.

$$\theta = \{P(\hat{s_i}|s_j)\}_{s_i, s_j \in \Lambda} \bigcup \{P(\hat{w_i}|s_j)\}_{w_i \in V, s_j \in \Lambda}$$

In order to learn the θ, we use the EM algorithm. In this network, since evidence is available for any variable, this amounts to a count of each possible values of the random variables. In our case, the EM algorithm is a maximum likehood (ML) solving.

We want to maximize the log-likehood for all the BNs. Using Eq. (4), we have:

$$L = \sum_{d \in D} \sum_{i=1}^{|s_d|} \log P(s_d^i | pa(s_d^i), \theta) + \sum_{i=1}^{|w_d|} \log P(w_d^i | sel(w_d^i), \theta) \quad (5)$$

For simplification, the model parameters $P(s_d^i | pa(s_d^i))$ and $P(w_d^i | sel(w_d^i))$ are denoted $\theta_{s_d^i, pa(s_d^i)}$ and $\theta_{w_d^i, sel(w_d^i)}$. Equation 5 then writes:

$$L = \sum_{d \in D} \sum_{i=1}^{|s_d|} \log \theta_{s_d^i, pa(s_d^i)} + \sum_{i=1}^{|w_d^i|} \log \theta_{w_d^i, sel(w_d^i)} \quad (6)$$

In the following, $\theta_{n,m}$ denotes either a textual probability or a structural probability. It corresponds to $P($node with value n/his parent has the value m$)$. The derivative of L is:

$$\frac{\partial L}{\partial \theta_{n,m}} = \sum_{d \in D} \sum_{\left(s_d^i / s_d^i = n \text{ and } pa(s_d^i) = m \right)} \frac{1}{\theta_{n,m}} + \sum_{\left(w_d^i / w_d^i = n \text{ and } sel(w_d^i) = m \right)} \frac{1}{\theta_{n,m}}$$

$$= \sum_{d \in D} \frac{\text{number of times a node with value n has his parent with value m}}{\theta_{n,m}}$$

$$(7)$$

The learning algorithm then solves $\frac{\partial L}{\partial \theta_{n,m}} = 0$ with the constraint $\sum_n \theta_{n,m} = 1$. Using the Lagrange multipliers, we solve:

$$\frac{\partial (L - \lambda_m (\sum_n \theta_{n,m} - 1))}{\partial \theta_{n,m}} = 0 \quad (8)$$

Let $N_{n,m}$ the number of times a node with value n has his parent with value m for all the documents of the training set, we solve:

$$\frac{N_{n,m}}{\theta_{n,m}} = \lambda_m \quad (9)$$

So:

$$\theta_{n,m} = \frac{N_{n,m}}{\sum_i N_{i,m}} \quad (10)$$

The complexity of the algorithm is $O(\sum_{d \in D} |s_d| + |w_d|)$. In a classical structured document, the number of node of the structural network is smaller than the number of words of the document. So the complexity is quasi-equivalent to $O(\sum_{d \in D} |w_d|)$ which is the classical learning complexity of the Naive Bayes algorithm.

Remark

Let us consider what happens to the model for a classical flat document. The corresponding belief network is presented in Fig. 4. The probability of the document d derived from Eq. (4) is:

$$P(d|\theta) = \prod_{i=1}^{|w_d|} P(w_d^i|sel(w_d^i) = document, \theta) \tag{11}$$

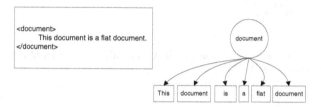

Fig. 4. A flat document (in XML format) an the associated belief network constructed using the previous hypothesis

This is the equation of a Naive Bayes model, we can conclude that **for flat documents**, our model is **strictly equivalent to Naive Bayes**.

4.4   Extending the Model to Unknown DTDs

We now show that the model could be easily extended to more complex categorization situations. As an example, we consider the categorization of XML documents with unknown DTDs (we don't know the values of the tags).

Up to now, we have made the hypothesis of a unique DTD in the corpus. This is convenient for controlled collections like e.g. an editor scientific journals. In many situations (e.g. documents gathered from the web), documents may follow different DTDs so that with our approach, one will have to learn different structures. One may also have to classify documents with DTDs not represented in the training set. We will consider here a simple instance of the latter problem where it is supposed that all the document in the training set follow the same DTD and documents in the test set do have other DTDs. We make an additional -homogeneity- hypothesis: all DTDs carry similar structural information (documents are more or less of the same type), but that tags may have different names, some may be missing and some may be added. Within this framework, we propose an extension of our model to enable the classification of documents with new DTDs.

Suppose that we have learned θ using a train set of documents with DTD1 exactly as part 4.3). We want to compute the probability of a document d which use an other unknown DTD2. We will not try to make an a priori correspondence between the two DTDs but we rather consider that the labeling information is

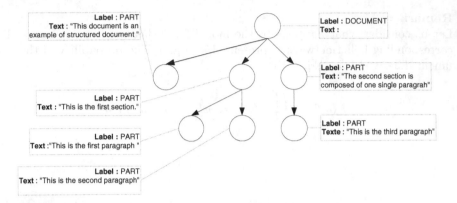

Fig. 5. The document presented in Fig. 1 with a different DTD. DTD2 corresponds to the tags $\{Document, PART\}$

missing in DTD2. This XML document contains the *textual information*, the *organization information* and no *label information* -label "'Part'" in (Fig. 5) (See part 3 for the definition of *textual information, label information* and *organization information*). We will score a document with DTD2 against the models learn with DTD1, i.e. we will try to classify this new document using the available knowledge on the document structure which is embodied in the BN models learned from DTD1. This makes sense under the homogeneity hypothesis. Alternatively, one could think of DTD1 as a reference DTD against which series of documents must be matched.

The likelihood of a document with no label information can be computed by summing over all possible labellings of the document parts into the set of allowed labels in Λ:

$$P(d|\theta) = \sum_{s_d^1, s_d^2, \dots, s_d^{|s_d|} \in \Lambda} \prod_{i=1}^{|s_d|} P(s_d^i|pa(s_d^i), \theta) \prod_{i=1}^{|w_d|} P(w_d^i|sel(w_d^i), \theta) \qquad (12)$$

This model has a higher complexity that the one presented in part 4.2. Alternatively, instead of summing over all allowed segmentations, one might compute the best segmentation of a document with unknown labels into the labels of a given DTD, i.e. compute the score of the most probable structure for this document according to the reference DTD. This can be done with a Viterbi like algorithm as for HMMs except that we deal here with structures instead of sequences. This corresponds to computing:

$$P(d|\theta) = max_{s_d^1, s_d^2, \dots, s_d^{|s_d|} \in \Lambda} \prod_{i=1}^{|s_d|} P(s_d^i|pa(s_d^i), \theta) \prod_{i=1}^{|w_d|} P(w_d^i|sel(w_d^i), \theta) \qquad (13)$$

The most probable segmentation with respect to a reference DTD could also be used for transforming a DTD2 document into a DTD1 document. This might be useful for comparing series of XML documents. However, document segmentation involves further developments and has not been tested here.

5 Experiments

We now present the experiments made with our model. Using a generative model for the task of categorization is easy. Let us consider $C = \{c_1, ..., c_{|C|}\}$ the set of all classes with probabilities $P(c_i)$. For each c_i, we will learn the model parameters denoted θ_{c_i} over all the documents of the training set within topic c_i. We consider that each document may have only one label and assume that:

$$P(d|c_i) = P(d|\theta_{c_i}) \tag{14}$$

So, the class c^d of a document d will be:

$$c^d = argmax_{c \in C} P(c) P(d|\theta_c) \tag{15}$$

5.1 The webKBXML Corpus

There are still few labeled XML corpus available for text categorization and whose documents do have a non trivial structure like in ([10,18]).

The webKB collection [2] became a reference corpus in the Machine Learning community for the classification of structured collections. It is composed of 8,282 pages which were manually classified into the categories: student, faculty, staff, department, course, project and other. For each class the data set contains pages from the four universities: Cornell, Texas, Washington, Wisconsin, and miscellaneous pages collected from other universities. In our work, we only use the 6 topics: student, faculty, staff, department, course, project.

We thus used the HTML webKB collection and transformed the pages into XML documents using a DTD with the following tags: *website, section, text, link, title, sectiontitle, highligthed*. Figure 6 represents the transformation of an HTML document to the corresponding XML document. This is more like a real XML corpus than the original WebKB, e.g., tags here do not specify the depth of a section like in HTML.

We call the constructed corpus webKBXML. This corpus is available at `http://www-connex.lip6.fr/~denoyer/corpus/wekbxml.tar.gz` The corpus has been preprocessed with Porter Stemmer, and words that do not appear in at least 5 documents are eliminated. The vocabulary size is about 8000. There are sites from 4 universities in WebKB, we used a leave one out methodology for training the models: training is performed on 3 sites and test on the 4th, this is repeated 4 times.

5.2 Results

We have used a Naive Bayes model as a baseline. Results appear in Fig. 7. The BN model achieves a mean 3% improvement with regard to Naive Bayes

```
<html> <head>
<title>CS414 Home Page</title>
</head>

<body>
<h1> The first section </h1>
   The first secion is composed of <b> two </b> paragraphes

<h2> first paragprah </h2>
 <a href="....">This is a link </a>

<h2>Second paragraph</h2>
 This is the second paragraph

<h1>This is the second section</h1>

   This thext is in <i> italic</i>
 .
 .
 .
```

```
<website>
<title>CS414 Home Page</title>

<section>
  <sectiontitle> The first section </sectiontitle>
  <text>   The first secion is composed of <text>
  <highlighted> two <highlighted>
  <text> paragraphes<text>

<section>
  <sectiontitle> first paragraph </sectiontitle>
  <link>This is a link </link>
</section>

<section>
  <sectiontitle>Second paragraph</sectiontitle>
  <text> This is the second paragraph</text>
</section>
</section>

<section>
  <sectiontitle> This is the second section</sectiontitle>
  <text>  This thext is in </text>
  <highlighted> italic</highlighted>
</section>
 .
 .
 .
```

Fig. 6. Left: The original HTML document (truncated) Right: The corresponding XML file (truncated)

for micro-average, the No Tag BN Model (the model from section 4.4) which handles a more difficult task achieves a 2% improvement. The results are very encouraging even the gain is small, it is significant and superior to that obtained on similar evaluation [5]. Note that the small size of the database penalizes the BN models compared to Naive Bayes since they have more parameters. Superior improvements should be obtained with larger databases.

The conclusion is that structure does indeed contain information, even for informal documents like those from WebKB. The proposed models allow us to take advantage of this structural information at a low increase in the complexity compared to flat classification models like Naive Bayes. The experiments show that even when the DTD tags are unknown, one can take advantage of the structure of the document in separate parts. Our generative models improve a baseline generative model (Naive Bayes) and similar ideas could be used to improve baseline discriminant models like SVM.

	course	department	staff	faculty	student	project		Micro	Macro
Naive Bayes	88.11%	100.00%	2.17%	76.32%	82.08%	66.67%		78.09%	69.22%
Model BN	89.34%	100.00%	0.00%	80.92%	86.02%	68.97%		81.12%	70.88%
Model BN No Tags	90.16%	100.00%	0.00%	76.32%	85.66%	66.67%		80.29%	69.80%

Fig. 7. The micro and macro average classification rate

6   Conclusion and Perspectives

We have presented new models for the classification of structured documents. These models are generic and can be used to classify any XML document provided they have been trained on a representative corpus. Tests have been performed on a small but representative collection and encouraging results have been obtained. Further developments are needed in order to build models able to handle the whole variety of classification tasks needed for general XML collections. We are currently working on such extensions and on the evaluation on larger databases.

References

1. Jamie P. Callan, W. Bruce Croft, and Stephen M. Harding. The INQUERY Retrieval System. In A. Min Tjoa and Isidro Ramos, editors, *Database and Expert Systems Applications, Proceedings of the International Conference*, pages 78–83, Valencia, Spain, 1992. Springer-Verlag.
2. Mark Craven, Dan DiPasquo, Dayne Freitag, Andrew K. McCallum, Tom M. Mitchell, Kamal Nigam, and Seán Slattery. Learning to extract symbolic knowledge from the World Wide Web. In *Proceedings of AAAI-98, 15th Conference of the American Association for Artificial Intelligence*, pages 509–516, Madison, US, 1998. AAAI Press, Menlo Park, US. An extended version appears as [3].
3. Mark Craven, Dan DiPasquo, Dayne Freitag, Andrew K. McCallum, Tom M. Mitchell, Kamal Nigam, and Seán Slattery. Learning to construct knowledge bases from the World Wide Web. *Artificial Intelligence*, 118(1/2):69–113, 2000.
4. Ludovic Denoyer, Hugo Zaragoza, and Patrick Gallinari. HMM-based passage models for document classification and ranking. In *Proceedings of ECIR-01, 23rd European Colloquium on Information Retrieval Research*, pages 126–135, Darmstadt, DE, 2001.
5. M. Dilegenti, M. Gori, M. Maggini, and F. Scarselli. Classification of html documents by hidden tree-markov models. In *Proceedings of the International Conference on Document Analysis and Recognition (ICDAR)*, pages 849–853, Seatle, 2001. WA (USA).
6. Susan T. Dumais and Hao Chen. Hierarchical classification of Web content. In Nicholas J. Belkin, Peter Ingwersen, and Mun-Kew Leong, editors, *Proceedings of SIGIR-00, 23rd ACM International Conference on Research and Development in Information Retrieval*, pages 256–263, Athens, GR, 2000. ACM Press, New York, US.
7. Shai Fine, Yoram Singer, and Naftali Tishby. The hierarchical hidden markov model: Analysis and applications. *Machine Learning*, 32(1):41–62, 1998.
8. Thorsten Joachims. Text categorization with support vector machines: learning with many relevant features. In Claire Nédellec and Céline Rouveirol, editors, *Proceedings of ECML-98, 10th European Conference on Machine Learning*, pages 137–142, Chemnitz, DE, 1998. Springer Verlag, Heidelberg, DE. Published in the "Lecture Notes in Computer Science" series, number 1398.
9. Jin H. Kim and Judea Pearl. A Computational Model for Causal and Diagnostic Reasoning in Inference Systems. In Alan Bundy, editor, *Proceedings of the 8th International Joint Conference on Artificial Intelligence*, Karlsruhe, Germany, August 1983. William Kaufmann.

10. David D. Lewis. *Reuters-21578 text categorization test collection*. AT&T Labs - Research, September 1997.

11. David D. Lewis. Naive (Bayes) at forty: The independence assumption in information retrieval. In Claire Nédellec and Céline Rouveirol, editors, *Proceedings of ECML-98, 10th European Conference on Machine Learning*, pages 4–15, Chemnitz, DE, 1998. Springer Verlag, Heidelberg, DE. Published in the "Lecture Notes in Computer Science" series, number 1398.

12. Cline M. Utilizing HTML structure and linked pages to improve learning for text categorization. In *Undergraduate Honors Thesis, Department of Computer Science, University of Texas.*

13. K. Murphy and M. Paskin. Linear time inference in hierarchical hmms, 2001.

14. Sung Hyon Myaeng, Dong-Hyun Jang, Mun-Seok Kim, and Zong-Cheol Zhoo. A Flexible Model for Retrieval of SGML documents. In W. Bruce Croft, Alistair Moffat, C.J. van Rijsbergen, Ross Wilkinson, and Justin Zobel, editors, *Proceedings of the 21st Annual International ACM SIGIR Conference on Research and Development in Information Retrieval*, pages 138–140, Melbourne, Australia, August 1998. ACM Press, New York.

15. Benjamin Piwowarky and Patrick Gallinari. A Bayesian Network Model for Page Retrieval in a Hierarchically Structured Collection. In *XML Workshop of the 25th ACM SIGIR Conference*, Tampere, Finland, 2002.

16. B. Piwowarski, L. Denoyer, and P. Gallinari. Un modele pour la recherche d'informations sur les documents structures. In *Proceedings of the 6emes journees Internationales d'Analyse Statistique des Donnees Textuelles (JADT2002).*

17. CH. Y. Quek. Classification of world wide web documents, 1997.

18. Reuters. The reuters corpus volume 1 english language 1996-08-20 to 1997-08-19.

19. Fabrizio Sebastiani. Machine learning in automated text categorization. *ACM Computing Surveys*, 34(1):1–47, 2002.

20. Trec. Text REtrieval Conference (trec 2001), National Institute of Standards and Technology (NIST).

21. Yiming Yang, Seán Slattery, and Rayid Ghani. A study of approaches to hypertext categorization. *Journal of Intelligent Information Systems*, 18(2/3):219–241, 2002. Special Issue on Automated Text Categorization.

22. Jeonghee Yi and Neel Sundaresan. A classifier for semi-structured documents. In *Proceedings of the sixth ACM SIGKDD international conference on Knowledge discovery and data mining*, pages 340–344. ACM Press, 2000.

Neural Self-Organization Using Graphs

Arpad Barsi

Department of Photogrammetry and Geoinformatics
Budapest University of Technology and Economics
H-1111 Budapest, Muegyetem rkp. 3, Hungary
barsi@eik.bme.hu

Abstract. The self-organizing feature map (SOFM) algorithm can be generalized, if the regular neuron grid is replaced by an undirected graph. The training rule is furthermore very simple: after a competition step, the weights of the winner neuron and its neighborhood must be updated. The update is based on the generalized adjacency of the initial graph. This feature is invariant during the training; therefore its derivation can be achieved in the preprocessing. The newly developed self-organizing neuron graph (SONG) algorithm is applied in function approximation, character fitting and satellite image analysis. The results have proven the efficiency of the algorithm.

1 Introduction

The history of the artificial neural networks begins with the famous work of W. McCulloch and W. Pitts in 1943. They described firstly the artificial neuron. F. Rosenblatt worked out the perceptron model in 1958. K. Steinbuch published his study about the learning matrix in 1961, which was the first work of the competitive learning and the "winner-takes-all" algorithm [1]. In 1969 was firstly published the "Perceptrons: An Introduction to Computational Geometry" from M. Minsky and S. Papert, which edition was revised in 1972 [2]. They introduced and used consequently the word "connectionism". Among others T. Kohonen worked at this time on linear associative memory (LAM) models. The Instar and Outstar learning methods are dated also in this year [1]. One year later Ch. von der Malsburg published his pioneering work in self-organization and a special retina model, although his study had biologic focus [3]. S. Grossberg has written an article about the short-term, long-term memories, and feature detectors in 1976 [4]; later the adaptive resonance theory (ART) models were created thereafter [1,5]. T. Kohonen published the famous "Self-Organization and Associative Memory" in 1984 [6]. D. M. Kammen compared and described the various neural network types from a biologic aspect, but the main idea of the book was the self-organization [9]. In 1991 G. A. Carpenter and S. Grossberg edited a book containing the most important documentations about the ART models. The book is a principal study collection about the self-organization [8]. The first book of T. Kohonen about the SOM was revised and updated in 1995 [7].

P. Perner and A. Rosenfeld (Eds.): MLDM 2003, LNAI 2734, pp. 343–352, 2003.

2 Self-Organizing Feature Map (SOFM)

The self-organizing feature map is an unsupervised, competitive learning algorithm for a neuron grid of regular topology.

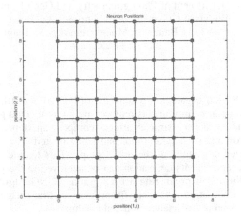

Fig. 1. Rectangular grid topology for SOFM [10]

The data (input) points are described with the following vectors:

$$\mathbf{x} = [\xi_1, \xi_2, \ldots, \xi_n]^T \in \mathbb{R}^n \tag{1}$$

The neurons, which build a regular, rectangular or hexagonal grid, have their corresponding coordinate vectors:

$$\mathbf{m}_i = [\mu_{i1}, \mu_{i2}, \ldots, \mu_{in}]^T \in \mathbb{R}^n \tag{2}$$

The algorithm, developed by T. Kohonen [6,7] has two main steps:

1. selecting the winner neuron
2. updating the weights of the winner and its neighboring neurons.

The winner selection is performed by the evaluation of the condition

$$\|\mathbf{x} - \mathbf{m}_c\| = \min_i \{\|\mathbf{x} - \mathbf{m}_i\|\} \tag{3}$$

The condition can be reformulated for better practical realization in form of

$$c = \arg\min_i \{\|\mathbf{x} - \mathbf{m}_i\|\} \tag{4}$$

In the above equation c is the identifier of the winner, $\|\cdot\|$ is a function, which gives the similarity between the neuron and the analyzed data point. In the easiest way the similarity can be defined by any geometric distance norm, e.g. Euclidean distance.

The update is achieved in two phases: in ordering and in tuning phase. Both phases use the same algorithm, but the control parameters are different. Ordering is responsible for the rough "positioning" of the neurons, while the tuning phase adjusts their final weights.

The update is formulated as follows:

$$\mathbf{m}_i(t+1) = \mathbf{m}_i(t) + h_{ci}(t)[\mathbf{x} - \mathbf{m}_i(t)] \tag{5}$$

where t and $t+1$ are discrete time steps (epochs), $h_{ci}(t)$ the time-dependent neighborhood function. The most important features of this neighborhood function are

1. $h_{ci}(t) \to 0$ if $t \to \infty$, which means: neighborhood should converge to zero during the computations
2. $h_{ci}(t) = h(\|\mathbf{r}_c - \mathbf{r}_i\|, t)$, i.e. $h_{ci}(t)$ is a function, which depends not only on the already mentioned discrete time step, but also on a distance value. In this case $\mathbf{r}_c, \mathbf{r}_i \in \mathbb{R}^n$. With the increase of $\|\mathbf{r}_c - \mathbf{r}_i\|$, $h_{ci}(t) \to 0$, which means $h_{ci}(t)$ is a distance dependent, monotonically decreasing function.

In the praxis $h_{ci}(t)$ can be realized by the use of an $\alpha(t)$ function as follows

$$h_{ci}(t) = \begin{cases} \alpha(t) & \text{if } i \in N_c(t) \\ 0 & \text{if } i \notin N_c(t) \end{cases} \tag{6}$$

where $0 \leq \alpha(t) \leq 1$ and $N_c(t)$ is the neighborhood function, e.g. as defined in Fig. 2.

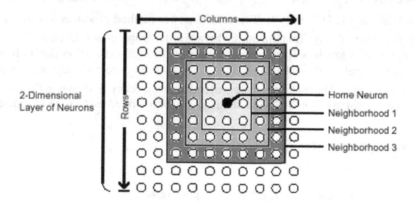

Fig. 2. A possible neighborhood function ($N_c(t)$) for SOFM [10]

3 Self-Organizing Neuron Graph (SONG)

The current development is a generalization of the SOFM method. Not only a regularly spaced neuron grid, but also other configurations can be used with the new algorithm. The basic idea is to create an undirected graph, where the neurons are in the nodes and the edges represent the connections between the neurons. The graph can be defined by a coordinate matrix of the neurons (as in Eq.2) and by an adjacency matrix (**A**). This matrix is defined as

$$\mathbf{A}_{ij} = \begin{cases} 1 & \text{if there is a connection from node } i \text{ to node } j \\ 0 & \text{otherwise} \end{cases} \tag{7}$$

The matrix is a square, symmetric matrix, where the rows mean the From nodes and the columns the To nodes. Given n neurons in the graph in two dimensions, the size of the coordinate matrix is $n \times 2$, and size of the adjacency matrix is $n \times n$. Further definitions and descriptions can be found in [11,12, 13]. Practical "recipes", hints, and applications are documented in [14, 15, 16].

The **A** matrix expresses direct connections therefore the notation $\mathbf{A}_1$ is introduced. Adjacency can be generalized, where the matrix contains values, which means the number of the minimal connections between the nodes. This general adjacency matrix is the $\mathbf{A}_n$, where the whole matrix is filled except the main diagonal (which remains zero). In our algorithm this full adjacency is not required, so an $\mathbf{A}_k$ is computed, where $k < n$.

The matrix $\mathbf{A}_k$ can be generated using efficient methods, e.g. by the use of the k-th power of the original adjacency matrix. The elements of $\mathbf{A}_k$ are calculated as follows: $\mathbf{A}^k = \mathbf{A}_{ij}^k$, where $k \in \mathbb{N}$, and $\mathbf{A}_{ij}^k = k$ if $\mathbf{A}_{ij}^k \neq 0$ and $\mathbf{A}_{ij}^s = 0$ where $s = 1, 2, \ldots, k-1$. [17, 18, 19]. This matrix power method produces a matrix containing the minimal ways (maximum k) between the graph nodes. Because the topology in the neuron graph is fixed, the adjacency and its generalization don't change (invariant), therefore the calculation of $\mathbf{A}_k$ needs to be executed only once in the preprocessing step. The meaning of the generalized adjacency is shown in Fig. 3.

The algorithm of the SONG method can be summarized using pseudo codes:

```
for t=0 to max_epochs
      alpha(t);
      d(t);
      for i=0 to number_of_points
            for j=0 to number_of_neurons
               winner_selection;
            endfor
            for j=0 to number_of_neurons
               weight_update;
            endfor
      endfor
endfor
```

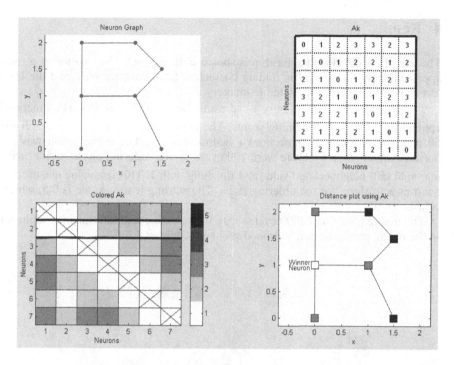

Fig. 3. The $\mathbf{A_k}$ matrix for a simple graph. The letter R is represented as a graph (*left upper picture*), for which the full adjacency matrix is calculated (*right upper picture*). Supposing the second neuron as winner, its row in the colored adjacency matrix (*left bottom picture*) is highlighted. The neuron graph can also be colored (*right bottom picture*) to show the neighborhood

The above code is a cycle, which is called twice, once in the ordering and once in the tuning phase. The algorithm of the self-organizing neuron graph has the same training rule as the Kohonen's SOFM algorithm. In the update step $h_{ci}(t)$ is modified:

$$h_{ci}(t) = \begin{cases} \alpha(t) & \text{if } \mathbf{A}_{ci}^k < d(t) \\ 0 & \text{otherwise} \end{cases} \tag{8}$$

where $d(t)$ is the time dependent, decreasing distance function. Using this modified training function for the winner's neighborhood, only the row of the winner (c) must be used in the matrix.

The selection of the winner (Eq.3, Eq.4) and the weight update (Eq.5) are the same formulas, as at SOFM.

In the realization of the SONG algorithm, $\alpha(t)$ and $d(t)$ were linear decreasing functions with given start and end parameter values.

4 Results

The use of the developed algorithm is shown in three tests. The first test is a function approximation, the second is finding characters from data samples, and the last is a test using a high-resolution satellite imagery.

The function approximation is tested using the sinc(x) function. The function was applied to generate 400 training points. The neuron graph was a linear graph having 50 neurons with direct connections ("neuron chain"). The initial graph was placed horizontally at $y = 0.5$. There were 100 cycles in the ordering phase starting with the maximal (50) neighborhood value and finishing with 1. This last value means, that the neurons act "alone" as the ordering stops. The starting learning rate is 0.5, which decreases to 0.0.

The tuning phase had 2000 cycles with 0.08 starting and 0.0 finishing alpha value. In the tuning phase the neighborhood was kept constant 1.

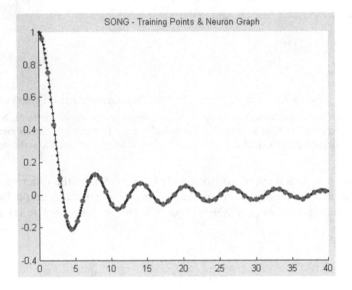

Fig. 4. SONG in approximating the function sinc(x)

The second test was character fitting. In the test three characters were applied: O, A and R. The training data set was created by sampling enlarged character images, where the black pixel coordinates were registered and used to train the neuron graph.

The main control parameters – starting learning rate ($\alpha(0)$), starting neighborhood distance ($d(0)$), number of epochs (t_{max}) – for ordering and tuning are shown in Table 1.

Table 1. Control parameters in the character fitting test

	Ordering			Tuning	
	$\alpha(0)$	$d(0)$	t_{max}	$\alpha(0)$	t_{max}
O	0.5	6	100	0.1	3000
A	0.01	3	100	0.005	5000
R	0.01	3	100	0.005	2000

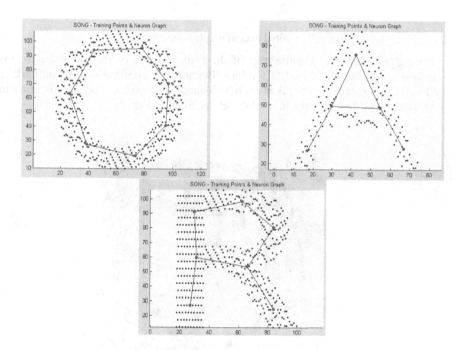

Fig. 5. The results of the character fitting for O, A and R

The last test with SONG algorithm was executed with a data set derived from satellite imagery. The image of the Pentagon building was captured by the Quickbird sensor in 02. August 2002. (The impact of the attack of 11th September can be seen on the upper part of the building.) The color image has a ground resolution of about 60 cm. SONG was applied to detect the place and orientation of the building.

Firstly the neuron graph was created. The graph is a double pentagon shape with a correct connection topology, but the graph nodes were compressed in order to achieve faster initial local coordinates (Fig. 6).

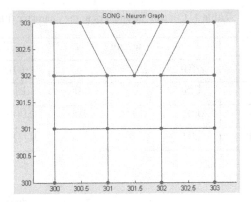

Fig. 6. The initial neuron graph for the Pentagon test

During the preprocessing the roof of the building was extracted by a maximum likelihood classifier based on RGB values. Because the roof has significant dark and light sides, 4-4 samples were taken with 3854 and 2716 pixels. The classification image was sampled to create the input data set for SONG (Fig. 7).

Fig. 7. The training data set in the Pentagon test

The neuron graph based self-organization was started with a neighborhood distance of 6 and a learning rate of 0.01. After 300 iterations the ordering phase finished with zero alpha value and with direct neighborhood. The 10000 epoch long tuning applied only direct neighborhood and started with a learning rate of 0.003. Fig. 8 shows, how the self-organization was performed after 0, 3, 10 cycles and finishing the tuning phase.

5   Conclusion

The developed self-organizing neuron graph (SONG) algorithm generalizes the Kohonen-type SOFM method. SONG requires an initial undirected graph, where the competitive neurons are in the nodes. The SONG training algorithm is based on the selection of a winner neuron, which is followed by a weight update. The generalized adjacency is an invariant feature of a graph, which is used in the update procedure.

The effectiveness of the algorithm is demonstrated in three, different test sets. The described self-organization technique is suitable for function approximation. Using the SONG algorithm, any neuron graph (or simple chain) can be fitted to the original data points. The graph can have any number of neurons; even using less neuron, a function "simplification" can be achieved.

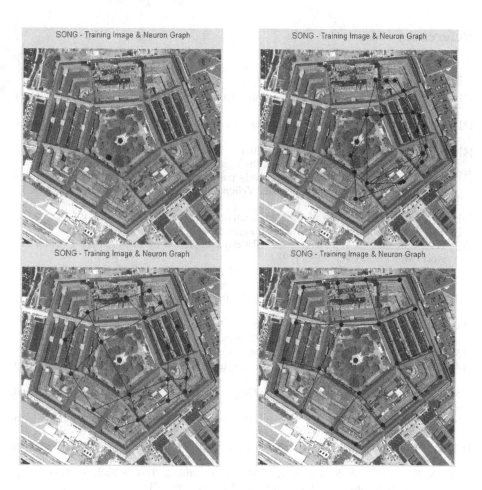

Fig. 8. The steps of the execution after 0, 3, 10 and 10300 epochs

The formerly known graph representation of the characters can also be used for the SONG method. The algorithm finds the place of the character in sampled data set, too.

In the last example the analysis of a satellite image was presented. After a sophisticated preprocessing (using image processing methods), the self-organizing neuron graph detects the place and position of the Pentagon building.

The developed algorithm can also be used with graphs representing regular grids. This means that the SONG method can be involved in all cases, where the SOFM technique: from the data clustering to the robotics. The greatest advantage of the SONG algorithm is the power to be used in tasks, where the regular grid is a drawback. The first experiments have proven that the graph based neural self-organization is a universal tool in image and pattern analysis.

References

[1] G.A. Carpenter: Neural network models for pattern recognition and associative memory, Neural Network, 1989, 2, 243–257

[2] M. Minsky, S. Papert: Perceptrons: An introduction to computational geometry, MIT Press, Cambridge, 1969 and 1972

[3] Ch. von der Malsburg: Self-organization of orientation sensitive cells in the striate cortex, Kybernetik, 1973, 14, 85–100

[4] S. Grossberg: Adaptive pattern recognition and universal recoding, Parallel development and coding of neural feature detectors, Biological Cybernetics, 1976, 23, 121–134

[5] G.A. Carpenter, S. Grossberg: A massively parallel architecture for self-organizing neural pattern recognition machine, Computer Vision, Graphics and Image Processing, 1987, 37, 54–115

[6] T. Kohonen: Self-Organization and associative memory, Springer, Berlin, 1984

[7] T. Kohonen: Self-Organizing Maps, Springer, Berlin, 1995

[8] G.A. Carpenter, S. Grossberg (Eds): Pattern recognition by self-organizing neural network, MIT Press, Cambridge, 1991

[9] D.M. Kammen: Self-organization in neural networks, Harvard University, Cambridge, 1988

[10] H. Demuth – M. Beale: Neural Network Toolbox, For Use with MATLAB, User's Guide, The MathWorks, Natick, 1998

[11] B. Bollobás: Modern Graph Theory, Springer Verlag, New York, 1998

[12] R. Balakrishnan: A Textbook of Graph Theory, Springer Verlag, New York, 2000

[13] F. Buckley, F. Harary: Distance in Graphs, Addison-Wesley, Redwood City, 1990

[14] T. Ottmann, P. Widmayer: Algorithmen und Datenstrukturen, Wissenschaftsverlag, Mannheim, 1993

[15] W.K. Chen: Applied Graph Theory, Graphs and Electrical Networks, North-Holland, Amsterdam, 1976

[16] R.G. Busacker, T.L. Saaty: Endliche Graphen und Netzwerke, Eine Einführung mit Anwendungen, Oldenbourg, München, 1968

[17] E.J. Henley, R.A. Williams: Graph Theory in Modern Engineering, Academic Press, New York, 1973

[18] I.N. Bronstein, K.A. Semendjajev, G. Musiol, H. Mühlig: Taschenbuch der Mathematik, Verlag Harri Deutsch, Frankfurt am Main, 2000, pp. 359–371

[19] M.N.S. Swamy, K. Thulasiraman: Graphs, Networks and Algorithms, Wiley, New York, 1981

Integrating Fuzziness with OLAP Association Rules Mining

Mehmet Kaya[1] and Reda Alhajj[2*]

[1] Department of Computer Engineering, Firat University, Elagi, Turkey
[2] ADSA Lab & Computer Science Dept, University of Calgary, Calgary, Alberta, Canada

Abstract. This paper handles the integration of *fuzziness* with *On-Line Analytical Processing* (OLAP)[1] association rules mining. It contributes to the ongoing research on multidimensional online data mining by proposing a general architecture that uses a *fuzzy data cube* for knowledge discovery. Three different methods are introduced to mine fuzzy association rules in the constructed fuzzy data cube, namely single dimension, multidimensional and hybrid association rules mining; the third structure integrates the other two methods. To the best of our knowledge, this is the first effort in this direction. Experimental results obtained for each of the three methods on the adult data of the United States census in 2000 show the effectiveness and applicability of the proposed mining approach.

1 Introduction

The amount of data stored in automated databases continues to grow exponentially. Intuitively, such large amount of stored data contains valuable hidden knowledge, which could be used to improve the decision-making process of the involved organizations; hence, *data mining* is necessary.

Data mining, sometimes referred to as knowledge discovery in databases, is concerned with the nontrivial extraction of implicit, previously unknown and potentially useful information from data. Discovering association rules is one of the several known data mining techniques. An association rule describes an interesting correlation among different attributes or items; it is mined out from a set of existing transactions. An example of an association rule could be stated as: "80% of the transactions that contain bread also contain butter, and 5% of all existing transactions contain these two items"; 80% is referred to as the *confidence* and 5% is the *support* of the rule. Finally, to motivate for the study presented in this paper, some approaches to association rules mining are discussed next.

---

* Contact author; Email: alhajj@cpsc.ucalgary.ca; Tel: (403) 210 9453. The research of this author is partially supported by NSERC grant and University of Calgary grant.
[1] OLAP is one of the most popular tools for on-line, fast and effective multidimensional data analysis.

P. Perner and A. Rosenfeld (Eds.): MLDM 2003, LNAI 2734, pp. 353–368, 2003.
© Springer-Verlag Berlin Heidelberg 2003

1.1 Classical Association Rules Mining: The Importance of Fuzziness

In general, association rules are classified into *boolean* and *quantitative*. The former involves binary attributes and the latter involves attributes that can take on quantitative or categorical values.

Earlier approaches for quantitative association rules mining require discretizing the domain of quantitative attributes into intervals in order to discover quantitative association rules. But, these intervals may not be concise and meaningful enough for human users to easily obtain nontrivial knowledge from the discovered rules. In other words, although current quantitative association rules mining algorithms solved some of the problems introduced by quantitative attributes, they introduced some other problems. The major problem is caused by the sharp boundary between intervals. Explicitly, existing quantitative mining algorithms either ignore or over-emphasize elements near the boundary of an interval. The use of sharp boundary intervals is also not intuitive with respect to human perception. Some work has recently been done on the use of fuzzy sets in discovering association rules among quantitative attributes in flat tables.

For instance, Hong et al [12] proposed an algorithm that integrates fuzzy set concepts with Apriori mining algorithm to find interesting fuzzy association rules from given transaction data. Gyenesei [8] presented two different methods for mining fuzzy quantitative association rules, namely *without normalization* and *with normalization*. The experiments of Gyenesei showed that the numbers of large itemsets and interesting rules found by the fuzzy method are larger than the discrete method defined by Srikant and Agrawal [24]. Chan and Au [6] utilized adjacent difference analysis and fuzziness in finding the minimum support and confidence instead of having them supplied by a user; they determine both positive and negative associations. Ishibuchi et al [15] illustrated fuzzy versions of support and confidence that can be used for evaluating each association rule; the authors employed these measures of fuzzy rules for function approximation and pattern classification problems. Finally, the approach developed by Zhang [26] extends the equi-depth partitioning with fuzzy terms. However, it assumes fuzzy terms as predefined.

1.2 OLAP Mining: The Motivation and Contributions

All of the above mentioned approaches assume a flat relational table structure. In this paper, we apply the same concepts of fuzziness to OLAP data mining, where the basic structure is a *data cube*[2]. A cube is a set of data organized similar to a multi-dimensional array of values representing measures over several dimensions. Hierarchies may be defined on dimensions to organize data on more than one level of aggregation. There are several reasons for using this structure. For instance, given a large database with a large number of attributes, users are usually interested only in a small subset of the attributes. Another reason is to help in generating association rules online by prestoring itemsets. In addition, the constructed data cube does not contain only raw data related information, but also the summarized data.

---

[2] In the OLAP framework, data are stored in data hypercubes (simply called cubes).

OLAP mining integrates online analytical processing with data mining; this substantially enhances the power and flexibility of data mining and makes mining an interesting exploratory process. So, online association rules generation is considered an important research area of data mining. In other words, OLAP is attractive in data mining because the data is organized in a way that facilitates the "preprocess once query many" concept, i.e., the mining process is improved by eliminating the need to start with the raw data each time mining is required. Some approaches have already been developed to tackle the problem. For instance, the approach described in [21] reduces the retrieval time of itemset data. On the other hand, pruning the database removes data, which is not useful [20]. Hidber [13] developed an algorithm to compute large itemsets online. Relue et al. [22] designed a specialized structure, called Pattern Repository, to provide runtime generation of association rules.

Han [10] proposed a model to perform data analysis on multidimensional data by integrating OLAP tools and data mining techniques. Then, he improved his work by integrating several data mining components to the previous architecture [11]. Later on, Han and Fu [9] introduced an Apriori based top-down progressive approach for multiple-level association rules mining from large transactional databases; their method first finds frequent data items at the top-most level and then progressively deepens the mining process into frequent descendants at lower conceptual levels. Kamber et al [16] proposed a data cube model for mining multidimensional association rules; their model combines the cube data structure with OLAP techniques, like multidimensional slicing and layered cube search. Further, efficient algorithms were developed by either using an existing data cube or constructing a data cube on the fly. Performance analysis showed that OLAP based data mining outperforms the direct extension of table-based Apriori algorithm. Finally, Agarwal and Yu [1] proposed an OLAP-style algorithm to compute association rules. They achieved this by preprocessing the data effectively into predefined itemsets with corresponding support values more suitable for repeated online queries. In other words, the general idea behind their approach is to use a traditional algorithm to pre-compute all large itemsets relative to some support threshold, say s. Then, association rules are generated online relative to an interactively specified confidence threshold and support threshold, greater than or equal to s. Although these algorithms improved the online generation of association rules in response to changing requirements, it is still an open problem.

As a result, all of the studies reported so far on OLAP mining use data cubes with binary attributes, whereas most real life databases include quantitative attributes. Motivated by this, we developed a novel approach for online association rules mining. We contribute to the ongoing research on multidimensional online data mining by proposing a general architecture that constructs and uses a fuzzy data cube for knowledge discovery. The idea behind introducing fuzzy data cubes for online mining is to allow users to query a given database for fuzzy association rules for different values of support and confidence. For this purpose, we present three different methods to mine fuzzy association rules in the constructed fuzzy data cube. The first method is dedicated to one-dimensional fuzzy association rules mining. The second method is concerned with multi-dimensional fuzzy association rules mining. The last method integrates the two previous methods into a hybrid fuzzy association rules mining method. To the best of our knowledge, this is the first attempt to utilize fuzziness in OLAP mining. Experimental results obtained for each of the three methods on the adult data of the United States census in 2000 show the effectiveness and applicability of the proposed mining approach.

The rest of this paper is organized as follows. Section 2 introduces the basic terminology used in the rest of the paper, including a brief overview of OLAP technology; introduces fuzzy data cube architecture; and describes fuzzy association rules. Section 3 presents the three proposed fuzzy data cube based mining methods, namely one-dimensional, multi-dimensional and hybrid. Experimental results for the adult data by a census of the United States in 2000 are reported in Sect. 4. Section 5 includes a summary and the conclusions.

2   OLAP Technology and Fuzzy Data Cube Construction

Data warehouses provide solutions to extract massive amounts of data from heterogeneous data sources, to clean and transform the extracted amounts of data in order to load them in large repositories that are constituted by a set of materialized views. Due to the increasing importance of data warehouses, many techniques have been developed to analyze data in large databases efficiently and effectively. Among the many available tools, OLAP is one of the most popular tools for on-line, fast and effective multidimensional data analysis [7]. It is a technology that uses a multidimensional view of aggregated data to provide fast access to strategic information for further analysis. It facilities querying large amounts of data much faster than traditional database techniques. Using OLAP techniques, raw data from large databases is organized into multiple dimensions with each dimension containing multiple levels of abstraction. Such data organization provides users with the flexibility to view data from different perspectives.

Basically, OLAP includes three stages: (1) selecting data from a data warehouse, (2) building the data cube, and (3) on-line analysis using the cube. Many data cube computation algorithms exist to materialize data cubes efficiently [7, 27]. Also, many OLAP operations exist to manipulate and analyze a data cube, including roll-up, drill-down, slice and dice, pivot, rotate, switch, push, etc [3]. In this study, we will take advantage of these widely accepted and used techniques to combine them with fuzzy association rules mining techniques.

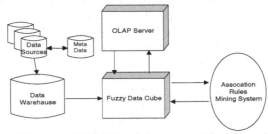

Fig. 1. The architecture of OLAP-based fuzzy association rules mining system

So, our target is to integrate fuzziness with OLAP association rules mining. To achieve this, we constructed a model that builds a fuzzy data cube first, and then utilizes the fuzzy data cube in mining fuzzy association rules. The architecture of the proposed OLAP-based fuzzy association rules mining system is shown in Fig. 1. In general, the proposed architecture consists of three main parts: (1) data warehouse, (2) fuzzy data cube and OLAP server, and (3) fuzzy association rules mining system. The major task of an OLAP server is to compute user's OLAP instructions, such as creating data cube, drilling, dicing, pivoting, etc. Finally, the fuzzy association rules mining system is responsible for the extraction of fuzzy association rules from the constructed fuzzy data cube.

The rest of this section is organized as follows. The fuzzy data cube is presented in Sect. 2.1. Fuzzy association rules are introduced in Sect. 2.2; they are recognized as a convenient tool for handling attributes with quantitative values in a human understandable manner.

2.1 Fuzzy Data Cube

Consider a quantitative attribute (interchangeably called item), say x. It is possible to define some fuzzy sets, with a membership function per fuzzy set, such that each value of x qualifies to be in one or more of the fuzzy sets specified for x. We decide on fuzzy sets by employing GAs to optimize their membership functions as described in Sect. 3. In the rest of this section we define both the degree of membership and the fuzzy data cube.

Definition 1 (Degree of Membership). Given an attribute x and let $F_x = \{f_x^1, f_x^2, ..., f_x^l\}$ be a set of l fuzzy sets associated with x. Membership function of the j-th fuzzy set in F_x, denoted $\mu_{f_x^j}$, represents a mapping from the domain of x into the interval [0,1]. Formally, $\mu_{f_x^j} : D_x - [0,1]$.

If $\mu_{f_x^j}(v) = 1$ then value v of x totally and certainly belongs to fuzzy set f_x^j. On the other hand, $\mu_{f_x^j}(v) = 0$ means that v is not a member of fuzzy set f_x^j. All other values between 0 and 1, exclusive, specify a "partial membership" degree.

According to Definition 1, given an attribute x, one of its values v, and one of its fuzzy sets, say f_x^j; the degree of membership of v in f_x^j is based directly on the evaluation of $\mu_{f_x^j}(v)$. The obtained value falls in the interval [0,1], with the lower bound strictly indicates "not a member", while the upper bound indicated "total membership". All other values specify a degree of "partial membership".

The concept described in Definition 1 is used in building a fuzzy data cube as follows.

Definition 2 (Fuzzy Data Cube). Consider a data cube with n dimensions, and given an association rules mining task involved with dimensions $d_1, d_2, ..., d_n$ of the data cube. For this purpose, the task-relevant data is pre-computed and materialized from a data warehouse into an n-dimensional fuzzy data cube. Each dimension of the cube contains $\sum_{i=1}^{k} l_i + 1$ values, where l_i is the number of membership functions (fuzzy sets) of attribute x_i in dimension X and k is the number of attributes in dimension X. The last term in the above formula, i.e., "+1" represents a special "Total" value in which each cell stores the aggregation value of the previous rows. These aggregation values show one of the essential features of the fuzzy data cube structure.

A three-dimensional fuzzy data cube that complies with Definition 2 is shown in Fig. 2; each dimension has two attributes and the number of membership functions of each attribute varies between 2 and 3.

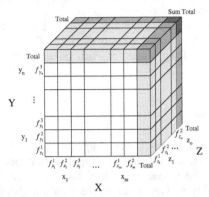

Fig. 2. An example 3-dimensional fuzzy data cube

2.2   Fuzzy Association Rules

An association rule is the correlation between data items; it is classified as either binary or quantitative. Binary association rules are defined as follows.

Definition 3 (Binary Association Rule). Let $I=\{i_1, i_2, ...,i_m\}$ be a set of binary attributes and $T=\{t_1, t_2, .., t_n\}$ be a set of transactions. Each transaction $t_i \in T$ is represented as a binary vector with

$$t_i[k] = \begin{cases} 1 & \text{if } t_i \text{ contains item } i_k \\ 0 & \text{otherwise} \end{cases}, \qquad k = 1, m$$

An association rule is defined as an implication of the form X Y where $X \subset I$, $Y \subset I$ and $X \cap Y = \phi$.

Definition 4 (Support and Confidence). An association rule X Y holds in T with support and confidence defined as $\Pr(X \cup Y)$ and $\Pr(X|Y)$, respectively.

Definition 4 simply states that the support of an association rule is the fraction of transactions that contain both X and Y, and the confidence is the fraction of transactions containing X, which also contain Y.

An association rule is interesting if and only if its support and confidence are greater than some user-supplied thresholds. Association rules that comply with Definition 3 are often referred to as boolean association rules. Boolean association rules are rather restrictive in many different aspects because they are defined over binary data and hence some recent efforts have been put into the mining of quantitative association rules.

Quantitative association rules are defined over quantitative and categorical attributes. In [24], the values of categorical attributes are mapped into a set of consecutive integers and the values of quantitative attributes are first partitioned into intervals using equi-depth partitioning, if necessary, and then mapped to consecutive integers to preserve the ordering of the values/intervals. As a result, both categorical and quantitative attributes can be handled in a uniform fashion as a set of *<attribute, integer value>* pairs. With the mappings defined in [24], a quantitative association rule is mapped into a set of boolean association rules. After the mappings, the algorithm for mining boolean association rules is then applied to the transformed data set.

However, as we have already illustrated above in Sect. 1, the interval in quantitative association rules may not be concise and meaningful enough for human experts to obtain nontrivial knowledge. Fuzzy sets provide a smooth transition between members and non-members of a set. Fuzzy association rules are also easily understandable to humans because of the linguistic terms associated with the fuzzy sets.

To elaborate on fuzzy association rules, consider again a database of transactions T, its set of attributes I, and the fuzzy sets associated with quantitative attributes in I. Notice that each transaction t_i contains values of some attributes from I and each quantitative attribute in I has at least two corresponding fuzzy sets. The target is to find out some interesting and potentially useful regularities, i.e., fuzzy association rules with enough support and high confidence. We use the following form for fuzzy association rules [18].

Definition 5 (Fuzzy Association Rules). A fuzzy association rule is defined as:
If $X=\{x_1, x_2, ..., x_p\}$ is $A=\{f_1, f_2, ..., f_p\}$ then $Y=\{y_1, y_2, ..., y_q\}$ is $B=\{g_1, g_2, ..., g_q\}$, where X, Y are itemsets, i.e., sets of attributes, which are disjoint subsets of I, and A and B contain the fuzzy sets associated with corresponding attributes in X and Y, respectively, i.e., f_i is the set of fuzzy sets related to attribute x_i and g_j is the set of fuzzy sets related to attribute y_j.

As it is the case with binary association rules, "X is A" is called the antecedent of the rule while "Y is B" is called the consequent of the rule. For a rule to be interesting, it should have enough support and high confidence.

3   OLAP-Based Mining of Fuzzy Association Rules

In this section, we describe our approach to OLAP mining of fuzzy association rules. We present three methods for fuzzy association rules mining, within a single dimension, multiple dimensions and hybrid, respectively. These methods are described next in this section, together with their corresponding algorithms.

3.1   Single Dimension Method

Single dimension association rules mining concentrates on the correlation within one dimension by grouping the other dimension. Shown in Fig. 3 is an example of such a cube with two dimensions involved in the single dimension association rules mining process. This cube has been created by the OLAP server and serves as the input fuzzy data cube for the online mining process. One of the dimensions is referred to as transaction dimension and the other dimension is the set of attributes associated with the transaction dimension.

By grouping attributes in the transaction dimension, a transaction table can be transformed into a set-based table in which items sharing the same transactional attribute are merged into one tuple. Note that there is no point in partitioning attributes in the transactional dimension into fuzzy sets because the mining process is performed in the non-transactional dimension as illustrated in Table 1.

Proposition 1: Given a tuple x_i in the relational table, if attribute y_j has membership degree $\mu^n(y_j)$ in the fuzzy set f_j^n, then the sharing rate, denoted sr, of the fuzzy set (y_j, f_j^n) to attribute x_i in the data cube is $\mu^n(y_j)$.

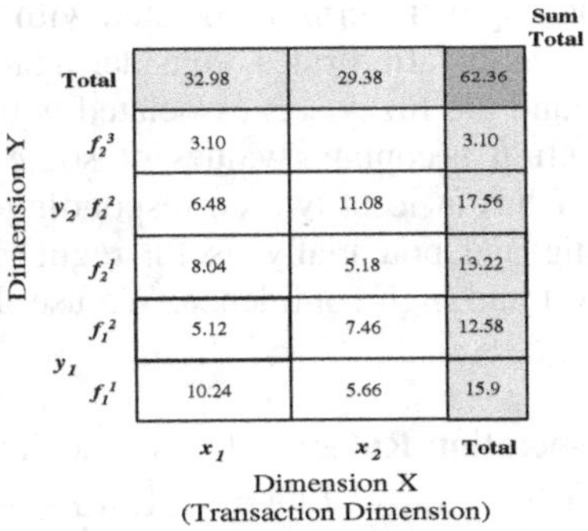

		x_1	x_2	Total (Sum Total)
	Total	32.98	29.38	62.36
y_2	f_2^3	3.10		3.10
	f_2^2	6.48	11.08	17.56
	f_2^1	8.04	5.18	13.22
y_1	f_1^2	5.12	7.46	12.58
	f_1^1	10.24	5.66	15.9

Dimension Y (vertical) · Dimension X (Transaction Dimension)

Fig. 3. An example 2-dimensional fuzzy data cube

Table 1. The transaction table generated from Fig. 3

Dimension X (Transaction Dimension)	Dimension to mine the associations among its attributes
x_1	$(y_1, f_1^1), (y_1, f_1^2), (y_2, f_2^1), (y_2, f_2^2), (y_2, f_2^3)$
x_2	$(y_1, f_1^1), (y_1, f_1^2), (y_2, f_2^1), (y_2, f_2^2)$

After the fuzzy data cube is constructed, the process of association rules mining starts by identifying large itemsets. An itemset is large if it is a combination of items that have a support over a predefined minimum support. The mining process and hence identifying large itemsets is performed based on the sum of sharing rates, denoted *SR*, and introduced in terms of the degree of membership in the fuzzy sets. If more than one membership function intersect with the real values of an attribute, then all the cells related to these functions are updated. This way, each cell in Fig. 3 stores an *SR* value.

To generate fuzzy association rules, all sets of items that have a support above a user specified threshold should be determined first. Itemsets with at least a minimum support value are called frequent or large itemsets. The following formula is used in calculating the fuzzy support value of itemset Y and its corresponding set of fuzzy sets F, denoted $FSupport(Y, F)$:

$$FSupport(Y, F) = \frac{\sum_{for\ all\ x_i\ in\ X} \prod_{y_j \in Y} SR_{(y_j, f_j^n)} (f_j^n \in F, x_i.f_j^n)}{sumTotal}$$

3.2 Multidimensional Methods

Multidimensional association rules mining deals with the correlations among dimensions of an n-dimensional fuzzy cube; an example 3-dimensional fuzzy data cube is shown in Fig. 2. In this study, we developed two different methods for mining multidimensional association rules. The first is presented in Sect. 3.2.1; it mines multidimensional rules without repetitive items within one dimension. The second is introduced in Sect. 3.2.2; it combines the method presented in Sect. 3.2.1 with the single dimension method presented in Sect. 3.1 into a hybrid method.

3.2.1 Multidimensional Rules without Repetitive Items
In this method, the correlation is among a set of dimensions, i.e., the items forming a rule come from different dimensions. Therefore, apart from one-dimension fuzzy data cube, here each dimension should be partitioned at the fuzzy set level.

Proposition 2. Given a fuzzy data cube with 3 dimensions, if attributes x_i, y_j and z_k have membership degrees $\mu^m(x_i)$, $\mu^n(y_j)$ and $\mu^o(z_k)$ in fuzzy sets f_i^m, f_j^n and f_k^o, respectively, then sr of all fuzzy sets of the corresponding cell is computed as $\mu^m(x_i) \cdot \mu^n(y_j) \cdot \mu^o(z_k)$.

Proposition 2 may be generalized for n-dimensions. This way, the frequency for each itemset can be directly obtained from one cell of the fuzzy cube. In a way similar to the single dimension case, each cell stores the product of the membership grades of different items, one item per dimension. As the example data cube shown in Fig. 2 has three dimensions, each cell stores the product of the membership grades of three items, one from each of the three dimensions. Finally, the fuzzy support value of each cell is calculated as follows: $FSupport = \dfrac{SR}{sumTotal}$

3.2.2 Hybrid Rules
This method is based on a hybrid structure, which combines single and multidimensional rules without repetitive items within one dimension. In this case, each candidate itemset can be written as $L_{hybrid} = L_{single} \cup L_{multi}$, where L_{single} and L_{multi} are the items from one dimension and multi-dimensions, respectively.

The reason for using this new method is to provide the opportunity for one dimension to dominate over others. This dominating dimension corresponds to the one referred to as non-transactional dimension in the single dimension method. The motivation is that instead of looking for all possible associations, we look for rules containing specific items in a fuzzy data cube. Then, the problem is reduced into how to efficiently identify itemsets which are relevant to our data requirements, and then construct association rules that satisfy our needs. This way, we avoid considering data and rules that do not meet the current data requirements.

To illustrate this, consider the 3-dimensional fuzzy data cube shown in Fig. 2. If the three dimensions X, Y and Z are assumed to represent the transaction, the dominating (non-transaction) and the other dimension, respectively, then we can obtain a rule including the triplet (y_1, y_2, z_1). In this case, the fuzzy support value of such a rule is calculated as: $FSupport = \dfrac{\sum_{for\ all\ x_i\ only\ in\ z_1 \in Z} \prod_{y_j \in Y} SR_{(y_j, f_j)}[f_j^n \in F, (x_i.f_i^m).(y_j.f_j^n)]}{sumTotal}$

3.3 The Employed Algorithms

Three algorithms, namely Algorithm 1, Algorithm 2 and Algorithm 3 have been developed for the above described three methods, respectively. These algorithms are given next in this section and require large itemsets in constructing one-dimension, multidimensional and hybrid fuzzy association rules, respectively. All the three algorithms invoke Function 2 when it is required to generate candidate itemsets. However, each algorithm invokes a different function to decide on intermediate frequent itemsets because fuzzy support is calculated differently for each case.

Algorithm 1 invokes Function 1 to decide on intermediate frequent itemsets. Algorithm 2 invokes Function 4, which also returns frequent k-itemsets generated from given candidate itemsets, but within the context of multidimensional fuzzy cube. Algorithm 3 performs the hybrid fuzzy association rules mining process. Finally, each of the three algorithms invokes Function 3 to construct fuzzy association rules within its own context.

Function 1. gen_frequent_one_dim(k, C_k)
$L_k = \phi$;
For each candidate $I=(Y, F) \in C_k$
$\quad FSupport(Y, F) = \dfrac{\sum_{for\ all\ x_i\ in\ X} \prod_{y_j \in Y} SR_{(y_j, f_j)}(f_j^n \in F, x_i.f_j^n)}{sumTotal}$
$\quad$ If $(FSupport(Y, F) > minsup)$ then $\quad L_k = L_k \cup \{I\}$
Return L_k;

Function 2. gen_candidate(k, L_{k-1}) //Generate candidate k-itemsets C_k from L_{k-1}
$C_k = \phi$;
For each itemset $I_1 \in L_{k-1}$
$\quad$ For each itemset $I_2 \in L_{k-1}$
$\quad\quad$ If (each of $(I_1 - I_2)$ and $(I_2 - I_1)$ contains a single element) then
$\quad\quad\quad c=Join(I_1, I_2)$;
$\quad\quad\quad$ If c has infrequent $(k-1)$ subset then $\quad$ Delete c $\quad$ else $\quad$ Add c to C_k;
Return C_k;

Function 3. gen_association_rules(L)
$R = \phi$;
For each frequent itemset L_i in L
$\quad$ For each non-empty proper subset S of L_i, that is $(L_i \neq S)$
$\quad\quad FConfidence((L_i - S) \quad S) = \dfrac{FSupport\ (L_i)}{FSupport\ (L_i - S)}$;
$\quad\quad$ If $(FConfidence \geq minconf)$
$\quad\quad\quad$ Generate an interesting rule, say $r=``(L_i - S) \quad S$'';
$\quad\quad\quad R = R \cup \{r\}$;
Return R;

Function 4. gen_frequent_multi_dim(k, C_k)

$L_k = \phi$;

For each candidate $I=(W, F) \in C_k$

$$FSupport_{(W,F)} = \frac{SR}{sumTotal};$$

If($FSupport > minsup$) then $L_k = L_k \cup \{I\}$;

Return L_k;

Algorithm 1 (One-Dimensional Fuzzy Association Rules Mining):

Input: A two dimensional fuzzy data cube $FC[X, Y]$, each cell with SR, a predefined minimum support value *minsup* and a predefined minimum confidence value *minconf*.

Output: A set of fuzzy association rules.

1. $k=1$; $L=\phi$;
2. $C_1=\{$all the distinct values in non-transaction dimension$\}$;
3. $L_1=$ gen_frequent_one_dim $(1, C_1)$;
4. While ($L_k \neq \phi$)
    $L = L \cup L_k$; $k=k+1$;
    $C_k=$gen_candidate(k, L_{k-1});
    $L_k=$ gen_frequent_one_dim (k, C_k);
5. $R=$ gen_association_rules(L);

Algorithm 2 (Multidimensional Fuzzy Association Rules Mining):

Input: A n-dimensional fuzzy data cube $FC[d_1,d_2...,d_n]$, each cell with SR, a predefined minimum support value *minsup* and a predefined minimum confidence value *minconf*.

Output: A set of fuzzy association rules.

1. $k=1$; $L=\phi$;
2. $C_{1,d_i}=\{$all the distinct values in dimension $d_i\}$;

$$C_1 = \bigcup_{i=1}^{n} C_{1,d_i} ;$$

3. $L_1=$ gen_frequent_multi_dim $(1, C_1)$;
4. While ($L_k \neq \phi$)
    $L = L \cup L_k$; $k=k+1$;
    $C_k=$gen_candidate(k, L_{k-1});
    $L_k=$ gen_frequent_multi_dim (k, C_k);
5. $R=$ gen_association_rules(L);

Algorithm 3 (Hybrid Fuzzy Association Rules Mining):

Input: A $n+2$-dimensional fuzzy data cube $FC[d_1, d_2, ..., d_{n+2}]$, each cell with SR, a predefined minimum support value *minsup* and a predefined minimum confidence value *minconf*.

Output: A set of fuzzy association rules.

1. $L = \phi$;
2. Generate all frequent itemsets L_{single} from two-dimensional cube;
3. If $(L_{single} = \phi)$ then exit;
4. $m = 1$;
5. While (1)

   $L_{multi,m} = $ gen_frequent_multi_dim (m, C_m);

   If $(L_{multi,m} = \phi)$ then exit;

   $s = 1$;

   Repeat $s = s + 1$;

   $C_{s+m} = $ Merge $L_{single,s}$ and $L_{multi,m}$;

   Generate candidate $(s+m)$-hybrid itemsets C_{s+m};

   Generate frequent itemsets L_{s+m} from C_{s+m};

   $L = L \cup L_{s+m}$;

   Prune any itemset in $L_{single,s}$ and its extensions if it is not in L_{s+m};

   Prune any itemset in $L_{multi,m}$ and its extensions if it is not in L_{s+m};

   Until $(L_{s+m} = \phi$ or $L_{single,s} = \phi)$;

   $m = m + 1$;
5. Generate association rules, $R = $ gen_association_rules(L);

4 Experimental Results

We performed some empirical tests in order to evaluate the performance of the proposed approach. All of the experiments were conducted on a Pentium III, 1.4GHz CPU with 512 MB of memory and running Windows 2000. As experimental data, we constructed the fuzzy data cube using 12 attributes and 100K transactional records from the adult data of United States census in 2000.

Three sequences of tests were carried out, one sequence for each of the three methods presented in Sect. 3. In all the experiments conducted in this study, three different cases were considered as the per attribute number of fuzzy sets (FS) is concerned, namely 2, 3, and 4 fuzzy sets, denoted FS2, FS3 and FS4, respectively. Finally, each set of experiments consists of two tests to evaluate our approach with respect to the following dimensions: 1) number of large itemsets generated for different values of minimum support, and 2) number of association rules generated for different values of minimum confidence.

The first set of experiments was carried out to test the performance of Algorithm 1 on a 2-dimensional fuzzy data cube with 8 attributes used to construct the non-transaction dimension; the results are shown in Figs. 4 and 5. Figure 4 compares the number of large itemsets obtained for different values of minimum support. A phenomenon that can be deduced from the curves plotted in Fig. 4 is that the difference between the number of frequent itemsets for different numbers of fuzzy sets is inversely proportional to the value of minimum support, i.e., when the support value is very small, the difference is very large.

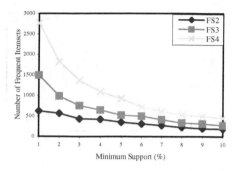
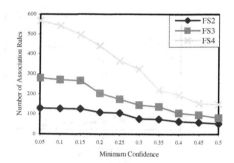

Fig. 4 Number of frequent itemsets vs minimum support on 2-dimensional fuzzy data cube

Fig. 5 Number of association rules vs minimum confidence on 2-dimensional fuzzy data cube

The curves plotted in Fig. 5 show the change in the number of association rules for different values of minimum confidence and for different numbers of fuzzy sets. In a way similar to that in Fig. 4, as the number of fuzzy sets increases, the number of association rules decreases faster until a particular confidence level (close to 0.5).

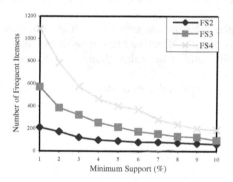
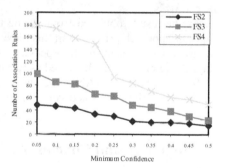

Fig. 6 Number of frequent itemsets vs minimum support on 3-dimensional fuzzy data cube

Fig. 7 Number of association rules vs minimum confidence on 3-dimensional fuzzy data cube

In the second set of experiments, we applied Algorithm 2 on a 3-dimensional fuzzy data cube; each dimension has 4 quantitative attributes. The results are shown in Figs. 6 and 7. The curves plotted in Fig. 6 show the change in the number of large itemsets, for different numbers of fuzzy sets, as the value of minimum support increases. The numbers of association rules produced for different values of minimum confidence are given in Fig. 7. In this case, each itemset of a given rule is coming from different dimensions. Here, it is worth mentioning that the same interpretation about Figs. 4 and 5 is valid for Figs. 6 and 7, respectively.

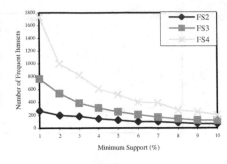
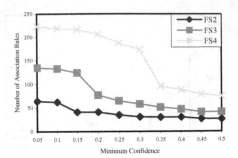

Fig. 8 Number of hybrid frequent item-sets vs minimum support on 3-dimensional fuzzy data cube

Fig. 9. Number of hybrid association rules vs minimum confidence on 3-dimensional fuzzy data cube

The last set of experiments is dedicated to the hybrid method. The results are shown in Figs. 8 and 9. Figure 8 shows the change in the number of large itemsets as the value of minimum support increases. The curves plotted in Fig. 9 reflect the decrease in the number of association rules as the minimum confidence value increases. The same statements mentioned for Figs. 4 and 5 are also valid for Figs. 8 and 9, respectively.

As the results obtained from all the three methods are consistent, it is anticipated that our approach presented in this paper is equally effective regardless of the number of fuzzy sets utilized in the process. Finally, one of the rules obtained as a result of the mining process can be stated as follows:

IF age is medium AND income is very high AND education level is medium THEN marital status is divorced is high.

5   Summary and Conclusions

OLAP is one of the most popular tools for on-line, fast and effective multidimensional data analysis. However, the research done so far on using OLAP techniques for data analysis have concentrated mainly on binary attributes, whereas, in general most databases that exist in real life include quantitative attributes. Moreover, the use of the fuzzy set theory in data mining systems enhances the understandability of the discovered knowledge when considering quantitative attributes and leads to more generalized rules. In order to tackle this bottleneck, we have proposed in this paper a general architecture that utilizes a fuzzy data cube for knowledge discovery in quantitative attributes. Also, we presented three different methods for the online mining of fuzzy association rules from the proposed architecture. One of the methods deals with the mining of fuzzy association rules in the case of 2-dimensional fuzzy data cube. The other two methods handle the mining process in multidimensional fuzzy data cube. We have already tested the last two methods on a 3-dimensional fuzzy data cube. The experiments conducted on adult data of the United States census in 2000 showed that the proposed approach produces meaningful results and has reasonable efficiency.

The results of the three methods are consistent and hence encouraging. Currently, we are investigating the possibility of combining the approach presented in this paper with the adjacency lattice developed in [1].

References

[1]   C.C. Agarwal and P.S. Yu, "A new approach to online generation of association rules," *IEEE TKDE*, Vol.13, No. 4, pp. 527–540, 2001.

[2]   S. Agarwal, et al, "On the computation of multidimensional aggregates," *Proc. of VLDB*, pp. 506–521, 1996.

[3]   R. Agrawal, A. Gupta, S. Sarawagi, "Modeling Multidimensional Databases," *Proc. of IEEE ICDE*, 1997.

[4]   R. Agrawal, T. Imielinski and A. Swami, "Mining association rules between sets of items in large databases," *Proc. of ACM SIGMOD*, pp. 207–216, 1993.

[5]   R. Agrawal and R. Srikant, "Fast algorithms for mining association rules," *Proc. of VLDB*, pp. 487–499, 1994.

[6]   K.C.C. Chan and W.H. Au, "Mining Fuzzy Association Rules," *Proc. of ACM CIKM*, pp. 209–215, 1997.

[7]   S. Chaudhuri and U. Dayal, "An overview of data warehousing and OLAP technology," *ACM SIGMOD Record*, Vol.26, pp.65–74, 1997.

[8]   A. Gyenesei, "A Fuzzy Approach for Mining Quantitative Association Rules," *TUCS Tech. Report No.336*, Mar. 2000.

[9]   J. Han and Y. Fu, "Mining multiple-level association rules in large databases," *IEEE TKDE*, Vol. 11, No. 5, pp. 798–804, 1999.

[10] J. Han, "OLAP Mining: An Integration of OLAP with Data Mining," *Proc. of IFIP International Conference on Data Semantics*, pp. 1–11, 1997.

[11] J. Han. "Towards on-line analytical mining in large databases," *Proc. of ACM SIGMOD*, 1998.

[12] T.P. Hong, C.S. Kuo and S.C. Chi, "A fuzzy data mining algorithm for quantitative values," *Proc.s of the International Conference on Knowledge-Based Intelligent Information Engineering Systems*, pp. 480–483, 1999.

[13] C. Hidber, "Online Association Rule Mining," *Proc. of ACM SIGMOD*, pp. 145–156, 1999.

[14] J. Han and M. Kamber, "Data Mining: Concepts and Techniques" *Morgan Kaufmann Publishers*, August 2000.

[15] H. Ishibuchi, T. Nakashima and T. Yamamoto, "Fuzzy Association Rules for Handling Continuous Attributes," *Proc. of IEEE International Symposium on Industrial Electronics*, pp. 118–121, 2001.

[16] M. Kamber, J. Han and J.Y. Chiang, "Meta-rule guided mining of multidimensional association rules using data cubes," *Proc. of KDD*, pp.207–210, 1997.

[17] M. Kaya, R. Alhajj, F. Polat and A. Arslan, "Efficient Automated Mining of Fuzzy Association Rules," *Proc. of DEXA*, 2002.

[18] C.M. Kuok, A.W. Fu and M.H. Wong, "Mining fuzzy association rules in databases," *SIGMOD Record*, Vol.17, No. 1, pp. 41–46, 1998.

[19] D. Margaritis, C. Faloutsos and S. Thrun, "NetCube: A Scalable Tool for Fast Data Mining and Compression," *Proc. of VLDB*, 2001.

[20] R. Ng, L. V.S. Lakshmanan, J. Han and A. Pang, "Exploratory mining and pruning optimizations of constrained associations rules," *Proc. of ACM SIGMOD*, pp. 13–24, 1998.

[21] J.S. Park, M.S. Chen and P.S. Yu, "An effective hash-based algorithm for mining association rules," *Proc. of ACM SIGMOD*, pp. 175–186, 1995.

[22] R. Relue, X. Wu and H. Huang, "Efficient Runtime Generation of Association Rules," *Proc. of ACM CIKM*, pp. 466–473, 2001.
[23] R. Srikant and R. Agrawal, "Mining generalized association rules," *Proc. of VLDB*, pp. 407–419, 1995.
[24] R. Srikant and R. Agrawal, "Mining quantitative association rules in large relational tables," *Proc. of ACM SIGMOD*, pp. 1–12, 1996.
[25] L.A. Zadeh, "Fuzzy Sets," *Information and Control*, Vol.8, pp.338–353, 1965.
[26] W. Zhang, "Mining Fuzzy Quantitative Association Rules," *Proc. of IEEE ICTAI*, pp. 99–102, 1999.
[27] Y. Zhao, P.M. Deshpande and J.F. Naughton, "An array-based algorithm for simultaneous multidimensional aggregates," *Proc. of ACM SIGMOD*, pp. 159–170, 1997.

Discovering Association Patterns Based on Mutual Information

Bon K. Sy

Queens College/CUNY
Computer Science Department
Flushing NY 11367
USA
bon@bunny.cs.qc.edu

Abstract. Identifying and expressing data patterns in form of association rules is a commonly used technique in data mining. Typically, association rules discovery is based on two criteria: support and confidence. In this paper we will briefly discuss the insufficiency on these two criteria, and argue the importance of including interestingness/dependency as a criterion for (association) pattern discovery. From the practical computational perspective, we will show how the proposed criterion grounded on interestingness could be used to improve the efficiency of pattern discovery mechanism. Furthermore, we will show a probabilistic inference mechanism that provides an alternative to pattern discovery. Example illustration and preliminary study for evaluating the proposed approach will be presented.

1 Introduction

In data mining, an association rule is typically expressed in form of A-> B. But the definition of an association rule may vary slightly among different disciplines and applications. For example, in philosophical logic [1] an association rule for two binary-valued logic variables A -> B with 80% certainty could mean 20% of the instances in its "frame of discernment" bear a relationship of (A: True B: False). In other words, the certainty factor is a measure of the "truthfulness" of a rule in the world. While in uncertain reasoning A -> B with 80% certainty means 80% chance B will happen if A happens; i.e., $Pr(B|A) = 0.8$. Yet in data mining an association rule A -> B could be associated with two measures: *support* and *confidence*; where support is a measure of significance of the presence of (A B) in the sample population of interests, while confidence is a measure of antecedence/consequence relationship much like uncertain reasoning. An example of such an association rule in data mining could be 80% of the movie goers for "The Lord of the Ring" went on to buy the book, and such a population accounts for 20% of the entire sample population.

Support and confidence are two measures widely used in data mining with the objective of detecting data patterns that exhibit antecedence/consequence relationships. However, these two measures also present conceptual and computational challenges. Let's consider the case of the above example. Let A=1 be the moviegoers watching

P. Perner and A. Rosenfeld (Eds.): MLDM 2003, LNAI 2734, pp. 369–378, 2003.
© Springer-Verlag Berlin Heidelberg 2003

"The Lord of the Ring", and B=1 be the buyers of the book. Ideally, from the perspective of the utility of an association rule, we want both $Pr(A=1 \cap B=1)$ and $Pr(B=1|A=1)$ to be high. Consider the case where $Pr(A=1) = Pr(B=1) = 0.8$, and $Pr(A=1 \cap B=1) = 0.64$, we can easily see that the antecedence/consequence relationship $Pr(B=1|A=1) = 0.8$ is quite misleading since A and B are independent of each other in the event level (because $Pr(B=1|A=1) = Pr(B=1) = 0.8$). Even subtler, an association rule A -> B manifests an antecedence/consequence relationship that suggests a time precedence relationship; i.e., B happens *after* A. But let's suppose the population is the English literature students who have an assignment on writing critiques about the story. Let's assume C=1 represents the English literature students with such an assignment. It is then no surprise to expect that the antecedence/consequence relationships are indeed C -> A and C -> B. And since watching the movie prior to reading the book could save time on getting an idea about the story, it is natural that students may watch the movie first! But from the observed data, if we do not know about C=1, we may end up concluding A -> B, thus a fallacy on the situation. This situation is referred to as spurious association [2] that has been known for a long time in the philosophy community. It is well known that a fallacy due to spurious association can only be disproved; while we may never be able to prove the truthfulness of an association rule that manifests an antecedence/consequence relationship. Nevertheless, it is possible to examine the "interestingness" of an association about whether the events in a data pattern are independent of each other or not [3], [4].

The objective of this paper is to investigate information-statistical criteria for discovering data patterns that exhibit interesting association. Our primary goal is to introduce an information-statistical measure that bears an elegant statistical convergence property for discovering association patterns. The proposed approach is more than just adding another constraint. We will show how this could lead to reduction in the computational cost based on probabilistic inference of high order patterns from low order patterns.

2   Problem Formulation and Analysis

Let $X = \{x1, x2, ..., xn\}$ be a set of n categories, and $D = \{D1, D2, ... Dn\}$ be the domain set of the corresponding categories. A domain Di is a mutually exclusive set of items of category xi, including a null value, if necessary, to indicate no item selection from the category. For the sake of discussion, we will assume each domain carries m items; i.e., $|D1| = |D2| = ... = |Dn| = m$. Note that this formulation extends beyond the Boolean values in the typical case that is based on support-confidence approach [5].

An item set transaction is represented by $Di \times Dj \times ... Dk$; where $\{Di, Dj, ... Dk\}$ is a subset of D. Let $T = \{t1 ... tn\}$ be the set of all possible transactions. An association pattern is a transaction with at least two items. Let $A = \{a1 .... av\}$ be the set of all possible association patterns. It is not difficult to find out the number of all possible association patterns $v = \sum_{k=2}^{n} m^k (n,k) = (m+1)^n - mn - 1$ where $(n,k) = n!/k!(n-k)!$. Consider a case of 11 categories (i.e., $n = 11$) and $m = 4$, the number of possible association patterns is $5^{11} - 45$. In other words, the number of association patterns grows exponentially with the number of categories [6].

A k-tuple association pattern (k > 1) is an item set of k categories. This k-tuple association pattern will also be referred to as a pattern of kth-order. For a given k-tuple association pattern, there are $\sum_{i=1}^{k-1}(k,i)$ possibilities on deriving an association rule. Since we have already mentioned the issue of spurious association, this paper will only focus on discovering significant association patterns rather than association rules. Even if our focus is to discover significant association patterns, we need to answer a fundamental question: what properties are desirable for a significant association patterns? In other words, what association patterns should be considered significant?

In this research, an association pattern *ai* consisting of items *{i1, i2, ... ip}* is considered α-significant if it satisfies the following conditions:

1. The support for *ai*, defined as *Pr(ai)*, is at least α; i.e., $Pr(ai) \geq \alpha$. *(C1)*
2. The interdependency of *{i1, i2, ... ip}* as measured by mutual information measure $MI(ai) = Log_2\, Pr(i1, i2, ... ip)/Pr(i1)Pr(i2)... Pr(ip)$ is significant. *(C2)*

As reported elsewhere [7], [8], mutual information measure asymptotically converges to χ^2. A convenient way to determine whether *MI(ai)* is significant is to compare the mutual information measure with χ^2 measure; i.e., *MI(ai)* is significant if $MI(ai) \geq \beta(\chi^2)^\gamma$; where β and γ are some scaling factors, and due to Pearson, $\chi^2 = (oi - ei)^2/ei$.

It should be noted that there were previous attempts to extend beyond support-confidence approach for data mining. For example, Brin/Motawani/Silverstein [9] proposed a concept to incorporate correlation into association rules so that the rules exhibit dependency property. The approach proposed in this research is different in the sense that our emphasis is on discovering association patterns in the event level. It can be shown that even if there is no association in the variable level, association could exist in the event level. Our approach by focusing on the event level could help to detect significant patterns that may otherwise be missed if data mining is conducted on the variable level.

In other words, to determine whether any one of the $(m+1)^n - mn - 1$ association patterns is significant or not, we test it against the above two conditions. Clearly this is computationally prohibitive if we have to test all the patterns against the two conditions above. Fortunately the famous a priori property [10], [11] allows us to prune away patterns in a lattice hierarchy that are *extensions* of a pattern, but did not survive the test against the first condition *(C1)* just mentioned.

3   State-of-the-Art: A Priori and Mutual Information Measure

An association pattern is basically a collection of items. Suppose there is a 2-tuple association pattern *a1 = {d1, d2}*; where d1 is an item element of the set *D1*, and *d2* is an item element of the set *D2*. We can consider an association pattern as an event in a probability space with random variables *x1* assuming the value *d1*, and *x2* assuming the value $d2$; i.e., $Pr(a1) = Pr(x1:d1 \cap x2:d2)$. An extension $ea1$ of a pattern $a1$ is a pattern consisting of an item set D' that is a proper superset of $\{d1, d2\}$; i.e., $\{d1, d2\} \subset D'$. It is not difficult to observe the property: $Pr(a1) \geq Pr(ea1)$ since $Pr(a1) = \sum_{D'-\{d1\ d2\}} Pr(ea1)$. Therefore, if $a1$ is not α-significant because $Pr(a1) < α$, $ea1$cannot be α-significant, thus facilitating a pruning criterion during the process of identifying significant association patterns – the essence of a priori property.

On the other hand, if the mutual information measure of $a1$ is not significant, it does not guarantee the extension of $a1$ not significant. Consider $ea1 = \{x1\ x2\ x3\}$, if $Pr(x1:d1 \cap x2:d2 \cap x3:d3)/Pr(d3) > Pr(x1:d1 \cap x2:d2)$, $Pr(x1:d1 \cap x2:d2 \cap x3:d3) > Pr(x1:d1)Pr(x2:d2)Pr(x3:d3)$, and $Pr(x1:d1 \cap x2:d2) > Pr(x1:d1)Pr(x2:d2)$, then $MI(ea1) > MI(a1)$. Furthermore, it is possible that an association pattern satisfies *(C1)*, but fails *(C2)* (mutual information measure). Therefore, *(C2)* provides a complementary pruning criterion for discovering significant association patterns.

In the process of deriving significant association patterns, we need one pass on all the transaction records to obtain the marginal probabilities required for mutual information measure. To identify second order (2-tuple) association patterns, we need to permute every pair of items in a transaction record and keep track the frequency information in the same first pass [12]. The frequency information is then used to derive the joint probability information needed for mutual information measure and for determining α-significant. At the end of the pass, we can then determine what association patterns – as well as the patterns that are the extensions – to discard, before the commencement of the next pass for identifying third-order patterns.

In each pass, the complexity is proportional to number of transaction records. In many applications such as on-line shopping, the number of transaction records tends to be very large. In such a case, the computational cost for deriving significant association patterns could be high even the complexity is linear with respect to the number of transaction records. A fundamental question is whether we could deduce high order association patterns from low order patterns without the need of repetitively scanning the transaction records. This is particularly so should the number of transaction records be large. To answer this question, we explore a novel model abstraction process that permits probabilistic inference on high order association patterns.

4   Model Abstraction for Probabilistic Inference

Let's consider a case of 11 discrete random variables (categories) $\{x1, \ldots x11\}$ and the domain of each variable consists of 4 states; i.e., xi can assume a value from a set $\{1\ 2\ 3\ 4\}$ for $i = 1 .. 11$. Let's further assume $(x1:1\ x2:1)$, $(x1:1\ x3:1)$, and $(x2:1\ x3:1)$ have been identified as significant association patterns. We want to know whether the extension $(x1:1\ x2:1\ x3:1)$ is a significant association pattern. A naïve approach is to conduct another scanning pass to obtain the frequency information for α-significant test and mutual information measure.

At the time $(x1:1\ x2:1)$, $(x1:1\ x3:1)$, and $(x2:1\ x3:1)$ are determined as significant association patterns, we would have already obtained the information of all marginal probabilities $Pr(xi)$ (where $i = 1 .. 11$), and the joint probabilities $Pr(x1:1, x2:1)$,

$Pr(x1:1\ x3:1)$, and $Pr(x2:1\ x3:1)$. Let's assume $Pr(x1:1) = 0.818$, $Pr(x2:1) = 0.909$, $Pr(x3:1) = 0.42$, $Pr(x1:1 \cap x2:1) = 0.779$, $Pr(x1:1\ x3:1) = 0.364$, and $Pr(x2:1\ x3:1) = 0.403$. $Pr(x1:1 \cap x2:1 \cap x3:1)$ is the only missing information needed for determining whether $(x1:1\ x2:1\ x3:1)$ is a significant association pattern. Suppose the value of α used for α-significant test is 0.2, if $(x1:1\ x2:1\ x3:1)$ is a significant association pattern, it must satisfy the following conditions:

$$Pr(x1:1) = 0.818 \quad \Leftrightarrow \quad \sum_{x2\ x3} Pr(x1:1 \cap x2 \cap x3) = 0.818$$
$$Pr(x2:1) = 0.909 \quad \Leftrightarrow \quad \sum_{x1\ x3} Pr(x1 \cap x2:1 \cap x3) = 0.909$$
$$Pr(x3:1) = 0.42 \quad \Leftrightarrow \quad \sum_{x2\ x3} Pr(x1 \cap x2 \cap x3:1) = 0.42$$
$$Pr(x1:1 \cap x2:1) = 0.779 \quad \Leftrightarrow \quad \sum_{x3} Pr(x1:1 \cap x2:! \cap x3) = 0.779$$
$$Pr(x1:1 \cap x3:1) = 0.364 \quad \Leftrightarrow \quad \sum_{x2} Pr(x1:1 \cap x2 \cap x3:1) = 0.364$$
$$Pr(x2:1 \cap x3:1) = 0.403 \quad \Leftrightarrow \quad \sum_{x1} Pr(x1 \cap x2:1 \cap x3:1) = 0.403$$
$$Pr(x1:1 \cap x2:1 \cap x3:1) \geq 0.2 \quad \Leftrightarrow \quad Pr(x1:1 \cap x2:1 \cap x3:1) - S = 0.2$$

where S is a non-negative slack variable
$$\sum_{x1\ x2\ 2\ x3} Pr(x1 \cap x2 \cap x3) = 1$$

Although the domain of each variable $x1$, $x2$, and $x3$ consist of 4 states, we are interested in only one particular state of the variable; namely, $x1 = 1$, $x2 = 1$, and $x3=1$. We can define a new state 0 to represent the irrelevant states $\{2, 3, 4\}$. In other words, the above example consists of only $2^3 = 8$ joint probability terms rather than $4^3 = 64$ joint terms, thus reducing the number of dimensions. In the above example, there are eight equality constraints and nine unknowns (one for each joint probability term and a slack variable). It is an underdetermined algebraic system that has multiple solutions; where a solution is a vector of size $= 9$. Among all the solutions, one corresponds to the true distribution that we are interested in. As discussed in our previous research [13], the underdetermined algebraic system provides a basis for formulating an optimization problem that aims at maximizing the likelihood estimate of the statistical distribution of the data.

Although the probabilistic inference approach just demonstrated offers an alternative to scanning the transaction records, there are three related questions about its utility. First, under what circumstances probabilistic inference approach is more attractive in comparing to a straightforward scanning? Second, how feasible and expensive is it computationally on solving the optimization problem? Third, how accurate is the estimate of the joint probability information (for example, $Pr(x1:1 \cap x2 \cap x3)$ in the above case)?

To answer the first question, we first note that probabilistic inference is applied only to the high order association patterns that we are interested in. But unless the order of association patterns is relatively low, the process of probabilistic inference has to be applied one-at-a-time to each association pattern that we are interested in. Therefore, probabilistic inference approach will have a distinct advantage over a straightforward scanning when (1) the number of transaction records is large, (2) each transaction record consists of a large number of categories, and (3) only few high order association patterns are of interests.

As we reported elsewhere [13], the problem of probabilistic inference formulated as an optimization problem under the principle of minimum biased information can be solved quite efficiently. In practice, we can solve an optimization problem with 300 some variables within a minute using a 450MMX HZ personal computer. For data mining problems, 300 some variables translates to the 8th-order association patterns (i.e., trunc($Log_2$300)). In practice, it is highly unlikely to have significant association patterns with an order of seven or above.

The third question is perhaps the most challenging one. From the perspective of computational geometry, probabilistic inference is a search process in a high dimensional probability sub-space defined by the (in)equality constraints [13]. The error percentage defined by the normalized distance between the estimated optimal joint probability and the true joint probability increases as the order of association patterns increases. This is because the joint probability (support) of the association patterns decreases as the order increases, thus increasing the error sensitivity. As a result, when the estimated joint probability of an association pattern is used in mutual information measure to determine its significance, the asymptotic convergence of mutual information measure towards chi-square distribution will need to be calibrated. As reported elsewhere [7], [8], mutual information measure of two random variables $(x1\ x2)$ has the following asymptotic convergence property: $I(x1: x2) \rightarrow \chi^2_{(K-1)(J-1)(1-\alpha)}/2N$; where K and J are the number of states of $x1$ and $x2$ respectively, N is the sample population size, and α is the significance level. The calibration for adjusting the error sensitivity of the joint probability as it is used in calculating the mutual information measure of a high order association pattern $MI(x1\ x2 .. xn)$ in the event level is shown below:

$$MI(x1, x2...xn) \rightarrow (\frac{1}{Pr(x1, x2...xn)})(\frac{\chi^2}{2N})^{(\frac{\hat{E}}{E'})^{O/2}} \qquad (1)$$

where $MI(x1,x2...xn) = Log_2 Pr(x1\ x2\ ...\ xn)/Pr(x1)Pr(x2)...Pr(xn)$
N = sample population size
χ^2 = Pearson chi-square test statistic defined as $(oi - ei)^2/ei$
    with oi = observed count = $N\ Pr(x1\ x2 .. xn)$
    ei = expected count under the assumption of independence
        = $N\ Pr(x1)Pr(x2)...Pr(xn)$
$\hat{E}$ = Expected entropy measure of estimated probability model
E' = Maximum possible entropy of estimated probability model
O = order of the association pattern (i.e., n in this case)

Referring to the previous example, the optimal solution that maximizes the likelihood estimate under the assumption of minimum biased information is $[Pr(x1:0 \cap x2:0 \cap x3:0) = 0.035, Pr(x1:0 \cap x2:0 \cap x3:1) = 0.017, Pr(x1:0 \cap x2:1 \cap x3:0) = 0.091, Pr(x1:0 \cap x2:1 \cap x3:1) = 0.039, Pr(x1:1 \cap x2:0 \cap x3:0) = 0.039, Pr(x1:0 \cap x2:0 \cap x3:1) = 0, Pr(x1:0 \cap x2:1 \cap x3:0) = 0.415, Pr(x1:1 \cap x2:1 \cap x3:1) = 0.364]$. The expected entropy measure of estimated probability model $\hat{E} = -\sum_{x1\ x2\ 2\ x3} Pr(x1 \cap x2 \cap x3)\ Log_2\ Pr(x1 \cap x2 \cap x3) = 2.006223053$. The maximum possible entropy of estimated probability model E' is the case of even distribution; i.e., $E' = -\sum_{x1\ x2\ 2\ x3} Pr(x1 \cap x2 \cap x3)\ Log_2\ Pr(x1 \cap x2 \cap x3) = 3$.

There is an interesting observation about the heuristics of the above equation. Let's consider the case of second-order association patterns; i.e., $o=2$. When the expected entropy measure of estimated probability model is identical to that of maximum likeli-hood estimate, $Pr(x1, x2) Log_2 Pr(x1, x2)/Pr(x1)Pr(x2) \rightarrow \chi^2/2N$. If we now sum up all possible association patterns defined by $(x1, x2)$ to examine the mutual information measure in the variable level (as opposed to the event level), we will obtain the as-ymptotic convergence property: $I(x1: x2) \rightarrow \chi^2/2N$ as discussed earlier.

5 Modified a Priori Algorithm

Based on the methods discussed in the previous sections, below is an algorithm that combines a priori property with mutual information measure for identifying significant association patterns:

Step 1:
Conduct a scanning pass to derive the marginal probabilities $Pr(xi = dk)$ $(i = 1..n)$ for all possible dks, and the joint probabilities $Pr(xi = dl, xj = dm)$ $(i<j, i=1..n-1, j=2..n)$ for all possible dls and dms by checking each transaction one at a time.

Remark: This can be easily achieved by creating a bin as a place holder of fre-quency count for each unique xi and $(xi\ xj)$ [14],[15], and discard the bin $(xi\ xj)$ when its frequency count at the time of $k\%$ completion of transaction record scanning is less than $N(\alpha - 1 + k/100)$ --- a condition that guarantees the frequency count to be less than the threshold α defined for α-significant.

Step 2:
Rank all w $(\leq n(n-1)/2)$ association patterns (xi, xj) survived in (i) step 1, and (ii) the test due to $(C2)$ about mutual information measure, in the descending order of the corresponding joint probabilities, and put in a collection set AS.

Step 3:
Select w' $(\leq w)$ association patterns from the top of AS, and enumerate each associa-tion pattern (referred to as a source pattern) with a new item Ij from a cate-gory/attribute variable not already in the association pattern that satisfies the following condition:

Every second-order association pattern formed by Ij and an item in its source pattern is a significant association pattern in AS. For example, suppose the source pattern is $(x1:d1, x2:d2)$, it can be enumerated to $(x1:d1, x2:d2, xj:Ij)$ if both $(x1:d1, xj:Ij)$ and $(x2:d2, xj:Ij)$ are significant association patterns.

Step 4:
Based on the number of newly enumerated patterns and the order of the patterns, de-termine according to the scenario discussed in the previous section whether the joint probabilities for the newly enumerated patterns should be derived from a new pass of transaction record scanning or probabilistic inference described earlier. In either case, proceed to derive the joint probabilities for the newly enumerated patterns and test

against the condition *(C1)* in Sect. 2. If a pattern does not pass the test, discard it from the list for further processing.

Step 5:
For each newly enumerated association pattern survived in step 4, test against the condition *(C2)* (mutual information measure) in section 2. If a pattern passes the test, insert the newly enumerated significant association pattern into a temporary bin *TB* in the descending order of joint probabilities of the patterns in *TB* is preserved.

Step 6:
Insert the items in *TB* to the top of *AS*. If the computational resources are still available, empty *TB* and go to step 3. Otherwise stop and return *AS*.

6 Preliminary Study and Result Discussion

In order to better understand the computational behavior of the proposed approach discussed in this paper, a preliminary study was conducted using a dataset about different brands of cereals. This dataset was originally published in the anonymous ftp from unix.hensa.ac.uk, and re-distributed as cereal.tar.gz/cereal.zip by [16].

This dataset is chosen because it is relatively small to allow an exhaustive data analysis to establish a "ground truth" for the purpose of evaluation. This dataset consists of 77 records. Each record consists of 11 categories/attributes. The number of possible second-order association patterns, therefore, is $4^2(11 \times 10)/2 = 880$. In this preliminary study, we set $\alpha = 0.2$ for α-significant test. 57 out of 880 association patterns survived the test due to condition *(C1)*. Among the 57 association patterns, 15 failed the test due to *(C2)* (mutual information measure).

Based on the extension of the 42 second-order significant association patterns, third-order association patterns were derived and 25 of the third-order patterns survived the test due to *(C1)*. Among the 25 association patterns, 19 passed the test due to *(C2)*. Based on the 19 third-order significant association patterns, three significant association patterns of fourth-order were found. This completes the construction of the "ground truth" for evaluation.

To evaluate how effective is the proposed algorithm presented in section 5, applying step 1 of the algorithm produced the same set of second-order association patterns. In step 2, we chose $w = 1$; i.e., only the most probable significant association pattern $(Pr(x9{:}2, x10{:}3) = 0.779)$ was used for enumeration of third-order association pattern candidates. Following the condition stipulated in step 3, eight candidates of third-order association patterns were found. Among the eight candidates, five of the 19 actual third-order significant association patterns were found. In other words, we were able to find 26% (5/19) of the third-order significant association patterns using only 2% (1/42) of the candidate set for enumeration.

To understand better the behavior of probabilistic inference, we repeated step 4 except that probabilistic inference is applied on the same eight candidates rather than scanning the dataset. The following results were found.

Table 1. Comparison between using probabilistic inference vs exhaustive scan

Case	Association pattern	Mutual information MI	Adjusted chi-square C	$MI > C$?	Ground truth
1	x1:3 x9:2 x10:3	0.315	0.208	Yes	No
2	x3:1 x9:2 x10:3	-0.005484	0.003804	No	No
3	x3:2 x9:2 x10:3	0.135	0.085	Yes	Yes
4	x4:3 x9:2 x10:3	0.221	0.135	Yes	Yes
5	x6:2 x9:2 x10:3	0.391	0.311	Yes	Yes
6	x7:2 x9:2 x10:3	0.178	0.143	Yes	No
7	x7:3 x9:2 x10:3	0.218	0.194	Yes	Yes
8	x9:2 x10:3 x11:3	0.211	0.139	Yes	Yes

When the seven cases where $MI > C$ in table 1 are used to enumerate fourth-order patterns, 11 such patterns are obtained. Among the 11 fourth-order patterns, two of the three true significant association patterns are covered.

When the probabilistic inference was applied again, only one of the two true fourth-order significant association patterns was found. This leads to a *50% false-negative* error rate. Among the nine cases that were not significant association patterns, probabilistic inference process drew the same conclusion in six cases, yielding a *33% false-positive error rate*. This results in a weighted error rate of *(2/11)0.5% + (9/11)0.333% = 36%*, or a *64% accuracy rate*.

As also noted in the study, the condition stipulated in step 3 plays an essential role in maintaining the enumeration space small. 42 second-order significant association patterns were found. An exhaustive enumeration of 42 second-order patterns will yield at least *42x(11-2)x4 – 42 = 1470* third-order association pattern candidates. In our study we used only one of the 42 patterns for an enumeration. This results in *(1x(11-2)x4)* 36 possible third-order pattern candidates while the condition stipulated in step 3 restricted the enumeration to only eight third-order pattern candidates.

7 Conclusion

This paper discussed new criteria based on mutual information measure for defining significant association patterns, and a novel probabilistic inference approach utilizing model abstraction for discovering significant association patterns. The new criteria are proposed to address the interestingness, defined by interdependency among the attributes, of an association pattern. The novel probabilistic inference approach is introduced to offer an alternative approach to deduce the essential information needed for discovering significant patterns without the need of an exhaustive scan of the entire database. The preliminary study has showed interesting results. Our follow-up study will focus on applying the proposed approach to real world data sets.

Acknowledgement. The author is grateful to the anonymous reviewers for their useful comments for improving this manuscript. This work is supported in part by PSC CUNY Research Award and NSF DUE CCLI #0088778.

References

1. Genesereth M., Nilsson N.: Logical Foundations of Artificial Intelligence. Morgan Kaufmann (1987)
2. Freedman, D.: From association to causation: Some remarks on the history of statistics. *Statistical Science* 14 Vol. 3 (1999) 243–258
3. Cover T.M., Thomas J.A.: Elements of Information Theory. New York: John Wiley & Sons (1991)
4. Rish I., Hellerstein J., Jayram T.: An Analysis of Data Characteristics that affect Naive Bayes Performance. Tec. Rep. RC21993, IBM Watson Research Center (2001)
5. Barber B., Hamilton H.J.: Extracting Share Frequent Itemsets with Infrequent Subsets. Data Mining and Knowledge Discovery. (2003) 7(2):153–168
6. Yang J., Wang W., Yu P.S., Han J.: Mining Long Sequential Patterns in a Noisy Environment. ACM SIGMOD June 4–6, Madison, Wisconsin (2002) 406–417
7. Kullback S.: Information Theory and Statistics. John Wiley & Sons Inc (1959)
8. Basharin G.: Theory of Probability and its Applications. Vol. 4 (1959) 333–336
9. Silverstein C., Brin S., Motwani R.: Beyond Market Baskets: Generalizaing Association Rules to Dependence Rules. Data Mining and Knowledge Discovery. (1998) 2(1):39–68
10. Agrawal R., Imielinski T., Swami A.: Mining Association Rules between Sets of Items in large Databases. Proc. ACM SIGMOD Conf. Washington DC, May (1993)
11. Agrawal R., Srikant R.: Fast Algorithms for Mining Association Rules. VLDDBB (1994) 487–499
12. Toivonen H.: Sampling Large Databases for Association Rules. Proc. 22nd VLDB (1996) 134–145
13. Sy B.K.: Probability Model Selection Using Information-Theoretic Optimization Criterion. J. of Statistical Computing & Simulation, Gordan & Breach. V69-3 (2001)
14. Hoeffding W.: Probability Inequalities for sums of bounded Random Variables. Journal of the American Statistical Associations. Vol. 58 (1963) 13–30
15. Zaki M.: SPADE: an efficient algorithm for Mining Frequent Sequences. Machine Learning Journal, Vol. 42–1/2 (2001) 31–60
16. http://davis.wpi.edu/~xmdv/datasets.html

Connectionist Probability Estimators in HMM Arabic Speech Recognition Using Fuzzy Logic

Lilia Lazli and Mokhtar Sellami

Research Laboratory in Computer Science – LRI
Department of Computer Science – Faculty of Engineer Science
Badji Mokhtar University, BP.12-23200, Annaba, Algeria
Tel.: (213) 38 87 29 91, Fax: (213) 38 86 22 80
l_lazli@yahoo.fr

Abstract. Hidden Markov Models (HMM) are nowadays the most successful modeling approach for speech recognition. However, standard HMM require the assumption that adjacent feature vectors are statistically independent and identically distributed. These assumptions can be relaxed by introducing neural networks in the HMM frame work. These neural networks particularly the Multi-Layer Perceptrons (MLP) estimate the posterior probabilities used by the HMM. We started in the frame work of this work, to investigate smoothing techniques combining MLP probabilities with those from others estimators with better properties for small values (e.g., a single Gaussian) in the framework of the learning of our MLP. The main goal of this paper is to compare the performance of speech recognition of an isolated speech Arabic databases obtained with (1) discrete HMM, (2) hybrid HMM/MLP approaches using a MLP to estimate the HMM emission probabilities and (3) hybrid FCM/HMM/MLP approaches using the Fuzzy C-Means (FCM) algorithm to segment the acoustic vectors.

Keywords: Arabic speech recognition, fuzzy clustering, statistical learning, artificial neural networks, MLP probability smoothing

1 Introduction

Significant advances have been made in recent years in the area of speaker independent speech recognition. Over the last few years, connectionist models, and Multi Layer-Perceptron (MLP) in particular, have been widely studied as potentially powerful approaches to speech recognition [2, 11, 17]. Hidden Markov Models (HMM) are nowadays, the most successful modeling approach for speech recognition. However, standard HMM require the assumption that adjacent feature vectors are statistically independent and identically distributed. These assumptions can be relaxed by introducing neural network in the HMM framework. These neural networks estimate the posterior probabilities used by the HMM. Among these, the hybrid approach using a MLP to estimate HMM emission probabilities has recently been shown to be particularly efficient for handwriting recognition [7], audiovisual recognition [28], it has already been successfully applied for speech recognition in American English [27] and French [6]. This is the reason why we were interested in testing the same approach on a speaker independent isolated Arabic speech recognition for small [14],

P. Perner and A. Rosenfeld (Eds.): MLDM 2003, LNAI 2734, pp. 379–388, 2003.

medium [15] and large vocabulary [16] and compared with state of the art traditional models.

In this report, we present experimental and theoretical results using a framework for training and modeling isolated Arabic speech recognition systems based on the theoretically optimal Maximum A Posteriori (MAP) criterion. This is in constrast to most state of the art systems which are trained according to a Maximum Likelihood (ML) criterion. Although the algorithm is quite general, we applied it to a particular form of hybrid system combining HMM and Artificial Neural Network (ANN) in particular, Multi Layer-Perceptron (MLP) in which MLP targets and weights are iteratively re-estimated to guarantee the increase of the posterior probabilities of the correct model, hence actually minimizing the error rate. More specifically, this training approach is applied to a transition based model that used local conditional transition probabilities (i.e., the posterior probability of the current state given the current acoustic vector and the previous state) to estimate the posterior probabilities of sequences.

We develop also, a method based on concepts of fuzzy logic for clustering and classification of acoustic vectors: Fuzzy C-Means (FCM) algorithm, and demonstrate its effectiveness with regard to K-Means traditional algorithm [18, 20].

When the MLP are trained to least mean square or entropy criteria, it can be shown that large values of probabilities will be better estimated that small values [1]. As a consequence, we started in the framework of this work, to investigate smoothing techniques combining MLP probabilities with those from others estimators with better properties for small values (e.g., a single Gaussian) [18].

2   Databases

Two speech databases have been used in this work:

1) The first one, referred to as DB1 contained about 30 speakers saying their last name, first name, the city of birth and the city of residence. Each word should be marked 10 times. The used training set in the following experiments consists of 1200 sounds (1000 sounds for training and 200 for cross validation used to adapt the learning rate of the MLP [6]).

2) The second database, referred to as DB2, contained the 13 control words (i.e. View/new, save/save as/ save all) so that each speaker pronounces each control word 10 times. The used training set in the following experiments consists of 3900 sounds (3000 sounds for training and 900 for cross validation) saying by 30 speakers.

The data test set by 8 speakers (4 men and 4 women) pronounce the sequence "last name – first name – city of birth – city of residence", 5 times for the first set and pronounce 5 times, the control words selected with hazards.

3   Acoustic Features

Speech recordings were sampled over the microphone at 11 kHz. After pre-emphasis (factor 0.95) and application of a Hamming windows, two sets of acoustic features have been used: The log RASTA-PLP (RelActive SpecTrAl processing – Perceptral Linear Predictive) features [8] and the MFCC (Mel-scale Frequency Cepstral Coefficients) [5]. These parameters were computed every 10 ms on analysis windows of 30 ms.

Each frame is represented by 12 components plus energy (MFCC \ log RASTAPLP + E). The values of the 13 coefficients are standardized by their standard deviation measured on the frames of training. The feature set for our hybrid HMMMLP system was based on a 26 dimensional vector composed of the cepstral parameters (log RASTA-PLP or MFCC parameters), the cepstral parameters, the energy and the energy. Nine frames of contextual information were used at the input of the MLP (9 frames of context being known as yielding usually the best recognition performance) [1].

4 Clustering Algorithm

In general, a purely acoustic segmentation of the speech cannot suitably detect the basic units of the vocal signal. One of the causes is that the borders between these units are not acoustically defined. For this reason, we were interested to use the automatic classification methods which based on fuzzy logic in order to segment the acoustic vectors. Among the adapted algorithms, we have chooses the Fuzzy C-means (FCM) algorithm which already successfully used in various fields and practically in the image processing [9, 25, 29].

FCM algorithm is a method of clustering which allows one piece of data to belong to two or more clusters. The use of the measurement data is used in order to notice the speech data by considering in spectral domain only. However, this method is applied for searching some general regularity in the collocation of patterns focused on finding a certain class of geometrical shapes favored by the particular objective function. The FCM method [4] is frequently used in pattern recognition. It is based on minimization of the following objective function, with respect to U, a fuzzy c-partition of the data set, and to V, a set of K prototypes:

$$J_m(U,V) = \sum_{j=1}^{m} \sum_{i=1}^{c} u_{ij}^m \left\| X_j - V_i \right\|^2 \tag{1}$$

$$1 \le 1 \prec \infty$$

where m is any real number greater than 1, u_{ij} is the degree of membership of x_j in the cluster i, X_j is the j th of d-dimensional measured data, V_i is the d-dimension center of the cluster, and $\|*\|$ is the any norm expressed the similarity between any measured data and the center.

Fuzzy partition is carried out through an iterative optimization of (1) with the update of membership u and the cluster centers V by :

$$u_{ij} = \frac{1}{\sum_{k=1}^{c} \left(\dfrac{d_{ij}}{d_{ik}} \right)^{2/m-1}} \tag{2}$$

$$V_i = \frac{\sum\limits_{j=1}^{n} u_{ij}^m X_j}{\sum\limits_{j=1}^{n} u_{ij}^m} \tag{3}$$

The criteria in this iteration will stop when $\max\limits_{ij} \left| u_{ij} - \hat{u}_{ij} \right| \prec \varepsilon$ where ε is a termination criterion between 0 and 1.

5 Hybrid HMM-MLP Models

Our discussion of neural networks for speech will be focused on MLP, which are the most common ANN (Artificial Neural Networks) architecture used for speech recognition. However, all of the basic conclusions about the utility of these structures for estimating probabilities or local costs for an HMM will also hold for order structures such as a Recurrent Neural Network (RNN) [26], or a Time-Delay Neural Network (TDNN) [13]. The diagram of the training and recognition processes of our hybrid HMM-MLP system is shown in Fig. 1.

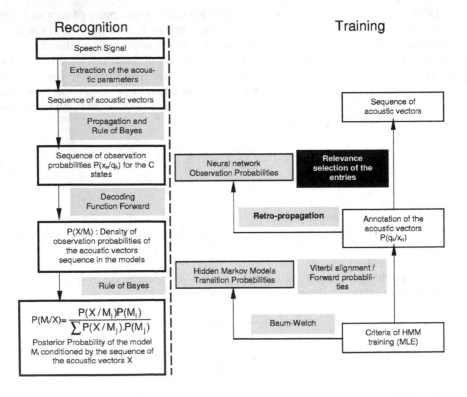

Fig. 1. Diagram of the training and recognition processes of the hybrid HMM-MLP system

5.1 MLP as Statistical Estimators

For statistical recognition systems, the role of the local estimator must be to approximate probabilities. In particular, given the basic HMM equations, we would like to estimate something like the probability $p(x_n/q_k)$, that is, the probability of the observed data vector given the hypothesized HMM state. However, HMM are based on a very strict formalism that is difficult to modify without losing the theoretical foundations or the efficiency of the training and recognition algorithms. Fortunately, ANN can estimate probabilities, and so can be fairly easily integrated into an HMM – based approach. In particular, ANN can be trained to produce the posterior probability $p(q_k/x_n)$, that is, the posteriori probability of the HMM state given the acoustic data, if each MLP output is associated with a specific HMM state. This can be converted to emission probabilities using Bayes' rule (cf. figure 2).

It has been experimentally observed that, for systems trained on a large amount of speech, the outputs of a properly trained MLP do in fact approximate posterior probabilities, even for error values that are not precisely the global minimum. Thus, emission probabilities can be estimated by applying Bayes' rule to the MLP outputs. In practical system, we actually compute:

$$p(q_k \setminus x_n) = \frac{p(x_n \setminus q_k)p(q_k)}{p(x_n)} \tag{4}$$

That is, we divide the posterior estimates from MLP outputs by estimates of class priors, namely the relative frequencies of each class as determined from the class labels that are produced by a forced Viterbi alignment of the training data. The scaled likelihood of the left hard side can be used as an emission probability for the HMM, since, during recognition, the scaling factor $p(x_n)$, is a constant for all classes and will not change the classification.

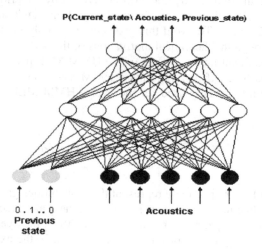

Fig. 2. Structure of hybrid HMM-MLP model

5.2 Disadvantages of HMM and Motivations of MLP

Among the numerous advantages of the MLP and the disadvantages of HMM, we can mention: [1, 14, 18, 20]

Disadvantages of HMM	Advantages of MLP
☹ Ignore correlation between acoustic vectors.	☺ MLP can extract local and high-level correlations between the successive acoustic vectors.
☹ Requirements for distributional assumptions (e.g., uncorrelated features within an acoustic vector).	☺ Highly parallel structures.
☹ Poor discrimination.	☺ Discriminant learning.
☹ 1st order Markov model assumption for phone or subphone states.	☺ No assumptions about the underlying statistical distribution of the input data.

5.3 MLP Probability Smoothing

When the MLP are trained to least mean square or entropy criteria, it can be shown that large values of probabilities will be better estimated that small values [1]. As a consequence, we started in the framework of this work, to investigate smoothing techniques combining MLP probabilities with those from others estimators with better properties for small values (e.g., a single Gaussian).

Theoretically, this should be done through a weighted sum of the different likelihood's or posteriori probabilities. This however, can lead to problems when trying to combine the scaled likelihood's obtained (after division by the priors) at the output of the MLP with (unscaled) likelihood's obtained (e.g., from standard Gaussian or standard discrete likelihood's). To avoid this problem, we simply multiplied these different estimates. Although the theoretical motivations of this are still not clear. This consistently led to significant improvements of the HMM-MLP performance (at least for the task considered here). If q_k represents a HMM state and x_n the current acoustic vectors, the probability actually used for the hybrid HMM-MLP approach was given by:

$$P(x_n/q_k) = \frac{P_{MLP}(q_k/x_n)}{P(q_k)}.P_d(x_n/q_k) \tag{5}$$

Where $P_{MLP}(.)$ and $P_d(.)$ respectively represent the probabilities given by the MLP and a standard discrete likelihood estimator. In this case, the scaling factor $P(x_n)$ remains a multiplicative factor (independent of q_k and does not affect the dynamic programming (when using minus log probabilities as local distances). In the experiments reported here, this consistently leads to an (absolute) improvement of about 2 % at the word level.

6 Recognition Results

6.1 Discrete HMM

In this case, the acoustic features were quantified into 4 independent codebooks according to the k-means algorithm:

- 128 clusters for the MFCC / log RASTA-PLP coefficients,
- 128 clusters for the first time derivative of cepstral vectors,
- 32 clusters for the first time derivative of energy,
- 32 clusters for the second time derivative of energy.

The models of words in 10 states, strictly left-to-right were used to model each basic unit (words). Note that only the choice of 10 states per model was selected in an empirical manner.

6.2 Discrete MLP with Entries Provided by the K-Means Algorithm

10-states, strictly left-to-right, word HMM with emission probabilities computed from an MLP with 9 frames of quantified acoustic vectors at the input, i.e., the current acoustic vector preceded by the 4 acoustic vectors on the left context and followed by the 4 acoustic vectors on the right context. Each acoustic vector was represented by a binary vector composed of 4 fields (representing the 4 acoustic features – see discrete HMM) respectively containing 128, 128, 32, and 32 bits. In each field, only one bit was "on" to represent the current associated cluster. Since 9 frames of acoustic vectors were used at the input of the MLP, this resulted in a (very sparse) binary MLP input layer of dimension 2.880 with only 36 bits "on" (we do not have to compute the 0's during the forward calculation of the MLP). In the experiments reported below, we restricted ourselves to MLP with binary inputs only since it was not possible to train MLP with continuous inputs given the excessive CPU time required for training on standard computers. A hidden layer of variable size, an output layer made up of as many neurons than there are HMM states. The number of neurons of the hidden layer was chooses so as to satisfy the following heuristic rule [12]:

Number of hidden neurons = (a number of entry neurons * number of output neurons)$^{1/2}$

6.3 Discrete MLP with Entries Provided by the FCM Algorithm

For this last case, we compare the performance of the basis hybrid model with that of an hybrid HMM-MLP model using in entry of the network an acoustic vector composed of real values which were obtained by applying the FCM algorithm. We presented each cepstral parameter (log RASTA-PLP/MFCC, log RASTAPLP/ MFCC, E, E) by a real vector which the components definite the membership degrees of the parameter to the various classes of the "code-book". The topology of the MLP is similar to model 2, nevertheless that the entry layer is made up of a real vector with 2880 real components corresponding to the various membership degrees of the acoustic vectors to the classes of the "code-book ".

These three types of models were compared within the framework of an isolated words recognition. Figure 3 summarizes the various results obtained of the models using only the acoustic parameters provided by a log RASRA-PLP analysis owing to the fact that MFCC coefficients did not give good results for the considered task. All the tests of the three models were carried out on the DB1 in first then on the DB2 and finally on DB1 + DB2 set.

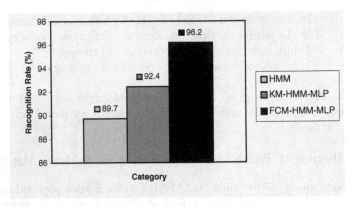

Fig. 3. Recognition rates for the three types of models.

7   Conclusion & Perspectives

These preliminary experiments have set a baseline performance for our hybrid FCM/HMM/MLP system. Better recognition rates were observed for speakers not having taken part in the training for an isolated words recognition. From the effectiveness view point of the models, it seems obvious that the hybrid models are more powerful than discrete HMM.

However, the recognition rates obtained are at least good that we do not hope for it. We thus envisage:

- To improve the performance of the suggested system, it would be important to use other techniques of parameters extraction and to compare the recognition rate of the system with that using the log RASTA-PLP analysis. We think of using the LDA (Linear Discriminate Analysis) and CMS (Cepstral Mean Substraction) owing to the fact that these representations are currently considered among most powerful in ASR.

- Although the FCM algorithm improved the performance of the suggested system nevertheless, this algorithm suffers from some defects also raised by the traditional classification methods (k-means, dynamic clouds, etc.) who are the need for knowing a priori, the number of clusters, the sensitivity to the choice of the initial configuration as well as convergence towards local minima. We tried in a former work to apply a new method of the speech segmentation and which a makes it possible to mitigate the principal raised defects. A comparison of performance was already carried out with that of the FCM algorithm and which gave very promising results [19, 21, 22]. We think of integrating this method in the proposed ASR system.

- It appears also interesting to use the continuous HMM with a multi-Gaussian distribution and to compare the performance of the system with that of the discrete HMM.

- In addition, for an extended vocabulary, it is interesting to use the phonemes models instead of words, which facilitates the training with relatively small bases.

References

1. J.-M. Boite, H. Bourlard, B. D'Hoore, S. Accaino, J. Vantieghem. "Task independent and dependent training: performance comparison of HMM and hybrid HMM/MLP approaches". *IEEE 1994, vol. I, pp. 617–620, (1994).*

2. H. Bourland, S. Dupont. "Sub-band-based speech recognition". *In Proc, IEEE International, Conf, Acoustic, Speech and Signal Process, Munich, pp. 1251–1254, (1997).*

3. F. Berthommier, H. Glotin. "A new snr-feature mapping for robust multi-stream speech recognition". *In Berkeley University of California, editor, Proceeding. International. Congress on Phonetic Sciences (ICPhS), Vol1 of XIV, pp. 711–715, Sanfrancisco, (1999).*

4. Bezdek, J.C., J. Keller, R. Krishnapwam, and N.R. Pal. "Fuzzy models and algorithms for pattern recognition and image processing". *Kluwer, Boston, London, (1999).*

5. S.B. Davis, P. Mermelstein. "Comparison of parametric representations for monosyllabic word recognition in continuously spoken sentences". *Proceedings of the International Conference on Acoustics, Speech and Signal processing, pp. 357–366, (1980).*

6. O. Deroo, C. Riis, F. Malfrere, H. Leich, S. Dupont, V. Fontiine, J.-M. Boite. "Hybrid HMM/ANN System for speaker independent continuous speech recognition in French". *Faculté Polytechnique de Mons – TCTS, Belgium, (1997).*

7. N. Gorsky, V. Anisimov, E. Augustin, S. Mystro, J.-C. Simon. "A new A2iA Bank-cheek Recognition System". *Third European Workshop on Handwriting Analysis and Recognition. IEE 1998, pp ?, (1998).*

8. H. Hermansky, N. Morgan. "RASTA Processing of speech". *IEEE Trans. On Speech and Audio Processing, vol. 2, no. 4, pp. 578–589, (1994).*

9. F. Höppner, F. Klawonn, R. Kruse, T. Runkler. "Fuzzy Cluster Analysis". *Methods for Classification, Data Analysis and Image Recognition, John Wiley & Sons, Ltd, (1999).*

10. Hagen, A. Morris. "Comparison of HMM experts with MLP experts in the full combination multi-band approach to robust asr". *To appear in International Conference on Spoken Language Processing, Beijing (2000).*

11. A. Hagen, A. Morris. "From multi-band full combination to multi-stream full combination processing in robust asr" *to appear in ISCA Tutorial Research Workshop ASR2000, Paris, France, (2000).*

12. J.-F. Jodouin. "Les réseaux de neurones : Principes & définitions". *Edition Hermes, Paris, France, (1994).*

13. K.-J. Lang, A.-H. Waibel. "A time-delay neural network architecture for isolated word recognition". *Neural Networks, vol. 3, pp. 23–43, (1990).*

14. L. Lazli, M. Sellami. "Proposition d'une Architecture d'un Système Hybride HMM-PMC pour la Reconnaissance de la Parole Arabe". *Proceedings of the Seventh Magrebian Conference on Computer Sciences, 7th MCSEAI'02, 6–8th May, vol. I, pp. 101–109, Annaba, Algeria, (2002).*

15. L. Lazli, M. Sellami. "Reconnaissance de la parole arabe par système hybride HMM/MLP". *Proceeding of the second national conference on automatic and signals, SNAS'02, pp. 13, Oct 27–28, Department of Electronics, Annaba, Algeria, (2002).*

16. L. Lazli, M. Sellami. "Reconnaissance de la parole arabe par système hybride HMM/MLP". Proceeding of the second national conference on *electric genius, CGE'02 pp. ? December 17–18, EMP. Polytechnic military academy, Algiers, Algeria, (2002).*

17. L. Lazli, H. Bahi, M. Sellami. "Modèle Neuro-symbolique pour la Reconnaissance de la Parole Arabe". Proceeding of the second national conference on *electric genius, CGE'02 pp. 64, December 17–18, EMP. Polytechnic military academy, Algiers, Algeria, (2002).*

18. L. Lazli, M. Sellami. " Modèle hybride HMM – MLP basé flou: Appliqué à la reconnaissance de la parole arabe". *Proceeding of SETIT2003, international conference : "Sciences Electroniques, Technologies de l'Information et des Télécommunications", pp. 104, March 17–21 , Suza, Tunisia, (2003).*

19. L. Lazli, M. Sellami. "A new method for unsupervised classification: Application for the speech clustering". *Proceeding of SETIT2003, international conference: "Sciences Electroniques, Technologies de l'Information et des Télécommunications", pp. 97, March 17–21 , Suza, Tunisia, (2003).*

20. L. Lazli, M. Sellami. "Hybrid HMM-MLP system based on fuzzy logic for arabic speech recognition". *PRIS2003, The third international workshop on Pattern Recognition in Information Systems, pp. 150–155, April 22–23, Angers, France, (2003).*

21. L. Lazli, M. Sellami. "Arabic Speech Segmentation using a New Unsupervised Approach". *Proceeding of ISPS`2003: tne International Symposium on Programming and Systems, pp. ? May 5–7, Algiers, Algeria, (2003).*

22. L. Lazli, M. Sellami. "Arabic Speech clustering using a new Algorithm". *Accepted in AICCSA`2003: tne ACS/IEEE International Conference on Computer Systems and Applications, pp. ? July 14–18, Tunis,Tunisia, (2003).*

23. A. Morris, A. Hagem, H. Glotin, H. Bourlard. "Multi-stream adaptative evidence combination for noise robust asr". *Accepted for publication in Speech Communication, 2000.*

24. A. Morris, A. Hagen, H. Bourlard. "MAP combination of multi-stream HMM or HMM/ANN experts". *Accepted for publication in Euro-speech 2001, Special Event Noise Robust Recognition, Aalborg, Denmark, (2001).*

25. D.-L. Pham, J.-L. Prince. "An Adaptive Fuzzy C-means algorithm for Image Segmentation in the presence of Intensity In homogeneities". *Pattern Recognition Letters. 20(1), pp. 57–68, (1999).*

26. A.-J. Robinson. "An application of recurrent nets to phone probability estimation". *Proceedings of the IEEE Transactions on Neural Network, vol.5, pp. 298–305, (1994).*

27. S.-K. Riis, A. Krogh . "Hidden Neural Networks: A framework for HMM-NN hybrids". *IEEE 1997, to appear in Proc. ICASSP-97, Apr 21–24, Munich, Germany, (1997).*

28. P.-J. Robert-Ribes, J.-L. Schwartz, A. Guerin-Dugue. "Comparing models for audiovisual fusion in noisy-vowel recognition task". *IEEE Trans. Speech Audio Processing 7, pp. 629–642, (1999).*

29. H. Timm . "Fuzzy Cluster Analysis of Classified Data". *IFSA/Nafips 2001, Vancouver, (2001).*

30. Y. Yan, M. Fanty, R. Cole. "Speech Recognition Using Neural Networks with Forward-Backward Probability Generated Targets", *ICASSP, vol. 4, pp. 32–41, (1997).*

Shape Recovery from an Unorganized Image Sequence

Kazuhiko Kawamoto[1], Atsushi Imiya[2,3], and Kaoru Hirota[1]

[1] Interdisciplinary Graduate School of Science and Engineering, Tokyo Institute of
Technology, 4259 Nagatsuta, Midori-ku, Yokohama 226-8502, Japan
[2] Institute of Media and Information Technology, Chiba University
1-33 Yayoi-cho, Inage-ku 263-8522, Chiba, Japan
[3] Software Research Division, National Institute of Informatics
2-1-2 Hitotsubashi, Chiyoda-ku, Tokyo 101-8430, Japan
kawa@hrt.dis.titech.ac.jp

Abstract. We propose a method for recovering a 3D object from an
unorganized image sequence, in which the order of the images and
the corresponding points among the images are unknown, using a
random sampling and voting process. Least squares methods such that
the factorization method and the 8-point algorithm are not directly
applicable to an unorganized image sequence, because the corresponding
points are a priori unknown. The proposed method repeatedly generates
relevant shape parameters from randomly sampled data as a series of
hypotheses, and finally produces the solutions supported by a large
number of the hypotheses. The method is demonstrated on synthetic
and real data.

Keywords: shape recovery, unorganized image sequence, hough
transform, random sampling, voting

1 Introduction

We propose a method for recovering 3D objects from an unorganized image
sequence, in which the order of the images is not organized and the corresponding points among the images are not determined, using a random sampling and
voting process. This process is based on the concept underlying the Hough transform [1,2,3], which clusters sample points that lie on straight lines and estimates
the parameters of the straight lines. In shape recovery, the clustering of sample
points and the estimation of parameters correspond to the detection of point
trajectories in the spatiotemporal space and the recovery of 3D objects. If a
sequence of images is organized, least squares methods such as the factorization
method [10] and the 8-point algorithm [11] is suitable. However, these methods
are not directly applicable to an unorganized image sequence. In shape recovery
from a cloud of unorganized sample points in a space, the neighborhood relation is used to describe the topology in a local region on the sample points [4].
and the combinatorial methods [5] yield an organized structure using Voronoi

P. Perner and A. Rosenfeld (Eds.): MLDM 2003, LNAI 2734, pp. 389–399, 2003.

tessellation, Delauney triangulation, and Gabriel graph. In classical variational methods, sample points are pre-organized before model fitting. Recently, Osher's group proposed a method to reconstruct surfaces from unorganized points [6].

For the organization of sample points, we employ algebraic constraints which describe geometrical configurations between cameras and 3D objects [7,8]. In this paper, the algebraic constraints, called the epipolar constraint and the trifocal tensor [9], are used to organize sample points. We also show that the searching of the nullspaces of matrices which are derived from unorganized sample points to recover 3D objects from an unorganized image sequence. This property is based on the algebraic property that points in a space are described by systems of homogeneous equations. The Hough transform estimates the parameters of straight lines by detecting the nullspaces of the subspaces spanned by sample data.

2   Hough Transform and Nullspace Search

We review the Hough transform as a technique for organizing a point set, and show that this technique achieves the detection of the nullspaces spanned by sample points. Setting $\boldsymbol{\xi}$ to be the homogeneous coordinates of point $\boldsymbol{x}$ on the two-dimensional plane, a set of points $\{\boldsymbol{x}_i\}_{i=1}^n$ on a straight line satisfies $\boldsymbol{a}^\top \boldsymbol{\xi}_i = 0$, where $\boldsymbol{a}$ is a given vector on the unit semisphere. This expression shows that vector $\boldsymbol{a}$ lies in the nullspace spanned by $\{\boldsymbol{\xi}_i\}_{i=1}^n$. If sample points $\{\boldsymbol{\xi}_i\}_{i=1}^n$ are given, estimation of $\boldsymbol{a}$ is achieved by solving an overdetermined system of homogeneous equations $\boldsymbol{\Xi}\boldsymbol{a} = \boldsymbol{0}$, for $\boldsymbol{\Xi} = [\boldsymbol{\xi}_1, \boldsymbol{\xi}_2, \dots, \boldsymbol{\xi}_n]^\top$, that is, vector $\boldsymbol{a}$ lies in the nullspace of matrix $\boldsymbol{\Xi}$.

The Hough transform classifies sample points $\{\boldsymbol{\xi}_i\}_{i=1}^n$ into $\{\boldsymbol{\xi}_{ij}\}_{i=1 j=1}^{m\ n(i)}$, and estimates a collection of the parameters $\{\boldsymbol{a}_i\}_{i=1}^m$. The classified sample points and estimated parameters satisfy the relations $\|\boldsymbol{a}_i^\top \boldsymbol{\xi}_{ij}\|^2 \leq \epsilon, i = 1, 2, \dots, m, j = 1, 2, \dots, n(i)$, for a small positive constant ϵ. From these relations, setting

$$\boldsymbol{\Xi}_i = [\boldsymbol{\xi}_{i1}\boldsymbol{\xi}_{i2}, \dots, \boldsymbol{\xi}_{in(i)}]^\top, \tag{1}$$

each $\boldsymbol{a}_i$ lies in the nullspace of matrix $\boldsymbol{\Xi}_i$. Therefore, the Hough transform determines the nullspaces spanned by sample points by clustering sample points. This fact enables us to search a collection of nullspaces for unorganized sample points.

3   Points, Lines, and Perspective Projection

We summarize the geometry between 3D points and their perspective projections as well as 3D lines, and derive the linear equations for the geometry. The expressions derived in this section are used in formulating the shape recovery problem in Sect. 4. Let $\boldsymbol{v} = (X, Y, Z, W)^\top$ be a 3D point and $\boldsymbol{\xi} = (x, y, z)^\top$ be a perspective projection of $\boldsymbol{v}$ onto an image in homogeneous coordinates. The relationship between a 3D point $\boldsymbol{v}$ and its perspective projection $\boldsymbol{\xi}$ can be written as $\lambda \boldsymbol{\xi} = \boldsymbol{P}\boldsymbol{v}$, where λ is an arbitrary nonzero scalar and $\boldsymbol{P}$ is a 3×4 matrix called the perspective projection matrix [8]. Eliminating the scale factor λ, we obtain a pair of linear equations

$$(x\boldsymbol{p}_3 - z\boldsymbol{p}_1)^\top \boldsymbol{v} = 0, \qquad (y\boldsymbol{p}_3 - z\boldsymbol{p}_2)^\top \boldsymbol{v} = 0, \tag{2}$$

where $\boldsymbol{p}_i^\top, i = 1, 2, 3$, are rows of the matrix $\boldsymbol{P}$. Since a 3D point provides two linear equations in eq. (2), we can uniquely solve the system of equations in $\boldsymbol{v}$, if we observe at least two projections of the same 3D point.

Let us turn our attention to the perspective projection of lines. Setting $\boldsymbol{\xi}_1$ and $\boldsymbol{\xi}_2$ to be two distinct points on an image plane, the 2D line passing through these two points is computed by $\lambda\boldsymbol{\psi} = \boldsymbol{\xi}_1 \times \boldsymbol{\xi}_2$ up to a scale factor. Then we obtain the following relation:

$$\lambda\boldsymbol{\psi} = \boldsymbol{P}\boldsymbol{v}_1 \times \boldsymbol{P}\boldsymbol{v}_2 = \begin{bmatrix} (\boldsymbol{p}_2 \wedge \boldsymbol{p}_3)^\top \\ (\boldsymbol{p}_3 \wedge \boldsymbol{p}_1)^\top \\ (\boldsymbol{p}_1 \wedge \boldsymbol{p}_2)^\top \end{bmatrix} \left[\boldsymbol{v}_1 \wedge \boldsymbol{v}_2 \right], \tag{3}$$

where $\wedge$ is the exterior product In eq. (3), a 6×1 vector $\boldsymbol{\rho} = \boldsymbol{v}_1 \wedge \boldsymbol{v}_2$ expresses the 3D line passing through the two 3D points $\boldsymbol{v}_1$ and $\boldsymbol{v}_2$ [12]. The coordinates of $\boldsymbol{\rho}$ are called the *plücker coordinates* of the 3D line. Equation (3) is rewritten as $\lambda\boldsymbol{\psi} = \boldsymbol{P}_l\boldsymbol{\rho}$, where $\boldsymbol{P}_l$ is the 3×6 matrix defined by $\boldsymbol{P}_l^\top = [\boldsymbol{p}_2 \wedge \boldsymbol{p}_3 \ \boldsymbol{p}_3 \wedge \boldsymbol{p}_1 \ \boldsymbol{p}_1 \wedge \boldsymbol{p}_2]$. Therefore, $\boldsymbol{P}_l$ models perspective projection of lines. Eliminating the scale factor λ, we obtain a pair of linear equations

$$(a\,\boldsymbol{p}_1 \wedge \boldsymbol{p}_2 - c\,\boldsymbol{p}_2 \wedge \boldsymbol{p}_3)^\top \boldsymbol{\rho} = 0, \qquad (b\,\boldsymbol{p}_1 \wedge \boldsymbol{p}_2 - c\,\boldsymbol{p}_3 \wedge \boldsymbol{p}_1)^\top \boldsymbol{\rho} = 0, \tag{4}$$

where $\boldsymbol{\psi} = (a, b, c)^\top$ expresses a straight line on an image plane. Since a 3D line provides two linear equations in eq. (4), we can uniquely solve the system of equations in $\boldsymbol{\rho}$, if we observe at least three projections of the same 3D point.

4   Problem Formulation

In this section, we formulate the recovery of a 3D object from an image sequence as the *nullspace search*, using linear algebra. For the achievement of 3D recovery, we must perform both of the determination of the correspondences among images and the estimation of 3D positions. For solving the two problems, we search nullspaces [1] of given data points, and then we call the formulation the nullspace search. From this formulation, the relationship between the 3D recovery and the nullspace search becomes clear.

4.1   Estimation of 3D Positions

Each perspective projection of a 3D point $\boldsymbol{v}$ provides a pair of linear equations. Such pairs of linear equations in $\boldsymbol{v}$ derive a set of homogeneous linear equations

---

[1] Precisely, the basic vector spanning a nullspace should be used instead of the term "nullspace".

$\boldsymbol{\Xi v} = \boldsymbol{0}$, where $\boldsymbol{\Xi}$ is a matrix containing the entries of perspective projection matrices and the coordinates of perspective projections of the same 3D point. If we observe m 3D points $\{\boldsymbol{v}_i\}_{i=1}^m$ from n pinhole cameras represented by $\{\boldsymbol{P}^j\}_{j=1}^n$, we have m sets of homogeneous linear equations

$$\boldsymbol{\Xi}_i \boldsymbol{v}_i = \boldsymbol{0}, \quad i = 1, \ldots, m. \tag{5}$$

A set of perspective projections of the same 3D line also gives a set of homogeneous linear equations $\boldsymbol{\Psi \rho} = \boldsymbol{0}$, where $\boldsymbol{\Psi}$ is a matrix containing the entries of perspective projection matrices and the coordinates of perspective projections of the same 3D line. If we observe m 3D lines $\{\boldsymbol{\rho}_i\}_{i=1}^m$ from n pinhole cameras represented by $\{\boldsymbol{P}_l^j\}_{j=1}^n$, we have m sets of homogeneous linear equations

$$\boldsymbol{\Psi}_i \boldsymbol{\rho}_i = \boldsymbol{0}, \quad i = 1, \ldots, m. \tag{6}$$

Solutions of eqs. (5) and (6) yield the 3D positions of spatial points and lines of a 3D object, respectively. To avoid the trivial solutions $\boldsymbol{v}_i = \boldsymbol{0}$ and $\boldsymbol{\rho}_i = \boldsymbol{0}$, the coefficient matrices $\boldsymbol{\Xi}_i$ and $\boldsymbol{\Psi}_i$ are rank-deficient, i.e., the ranks of $\boldsymbol{\Xi}_i$ and $\boldsymbol{\Psi}_i$ are at most 3 and 5, respectively. This means that each solution is in the nullspace of each coefficient matrix, and then $\boldsymbol{v}_i \in \mathcal{N}(\boldsymbol{\Xi}_i)$ and $\boldsymbol{\rho}_i \in \mathcal{N}(\boldsymbol{\Psi}_i)$ hold, where $\mathcal{N}(\boldsymbol{A}) = \{\boldsymbol{x} : \boldsymbol{Ax} = \boldsymbol{0}\}$.

Therefore, we generally formulate the estimation of 3D positions as follows.

Problem 1.   *Setting $\boldsymbol{A}_i$ to be a $M \times N$ matrix such that $M > N$, solve the overdetermined set of homogeneous equations*

$$\boldsymbol{A}_i \boldsymbol{x}_i = \boldsymbol{0}, \quad i = 1, \ldots, m. \tag{7}$$

This problem is solved by searching the solution $\boldsymbol{x}_i$ in the nullspace of the matrix $\boldsymbol{A}_i$. Since the vector spanning the nullspace is defined up to a scale factor, the normalization of the length of the vector is required, that is, $\|\boldsymbol{x}_j\| = 1$. From this normalization, the vectors to be estimated are distributed on the $(N - 1)$-dimensional unit sphere.

4.2   Determination of Correspondences

Since we do not predetermine the correspondences among the images, we do not know the entries of the coefficient matrices $\boldsymbol{\Xi}_i$ and $\boldsymbol{\Psi}_i$. Therefore we need to determine the entries of $\boldsymbol{\Xi}_i$ and $\boldsymbol{\Psi}_i$ for solving Problem 1.

The ranks of $\boldsymbol{\Xi}_i$ and $\boldsymbol{\Psi}_i$ are at most 3 and 5, respectively. Except for some degenerate configurations, each solution is in the one-dimensional nullspace, and then $\dim(\mathcal{N}(\boldsymbol{\Xi}_i)) = 1$ and $\dim(\mathcal{N}(\boldsymbol{\Psi}_i)) = 1$ hold. These geometrical properties of $\boldsymbol{\Xi}_i$ and $\boldsymbol{\Psi}_i$ lead to the following problem for the determination of correspondences.

Problem 2.   *Let $\boldsymbol{a}_i$ be a N-dimensional homogeneous vector. From given data $\{\boldsymbol{a}_i\}_{i=1}^k$, find $M \times N$ matrices $\{\boldsymbol{A}_j\}_{j=1}^m$, $M > N$ such that*

$$\boldsymbol{A}_j^\top = [\boldsymbol{a}_{1(j)} \boldsymbol{a}_{2(j)} \ldots \boldsymbol{a}_{M(j)}], \quad \text{s.t. } \dim(\mathcal{N}(\boldsymbol{A}_j)) = 1. \tag{8}$$

Since the resultant rows of A_j correspond to each other, the construction of the matrices A_j in Problem 2 is equal to the determination of the correspondences among images.

The formulation includes many model detection problems in computer vision, e.g., line detection in an image since a subset of sample points which lies on one line has the same form as eqs. (5) and (6).

5 Nullspace Search by Voting

In the formulation in Sect. 4, Problem 1 is an inverse problem, since it is solved by fitting a model to given data points. This problem can be solved by the LSMs, and then its solution can be uniquely obtained. Problem 2 is also an inverse problem. The difference between Problems 1 and 2 is that the solution of Problem 2 is not uniquely determined. Indeed there are many combinations for the selection of the vectors $\{a_i\}$ in Problem 2. This corresponds to the fact that the correspondences among images are not determined without the help of other information such as pixel intensity. For solving the 3D recovery problem, we adopt a voting process which is the main concept underlying the Hough transform [1,2]. The Hough transform can detect multiple lines on an image from given data points using voting. Since line detection is an inverse problem, the Hough transform is capable of solving an inverse problem. Furthermore, since line detection can be formulated in the form of Problems 1 and 2, the idea of the Hough transform for line detection can be applied to the 3D recovery task from a sequence of images.

Using the idea of the Hough transform for line detection, we develop a voting scheme for 3D recovery. As mentioned above, the nullspaces to be estimated are distributed on the $(N-1)$-dimensional unit sphere. For searching the nullspaces, our voting scheme repeatedly generates hypotheses onto the $(N-1)$-dimensional unit sphere, and then the solution is accepted by selecting the hypothesis supported by a number of given data. This hypothesis generation is based on the following proposition.

Proposition 1.   *Let A be a $M \times N$ matrix with $M > N$ and B be any $N \times N$ matrix which is obtained by selecting N rows from A. If $\mathrm{rank}(A) = N - 1$, then*

$$\mathrm{rank}(B) = N - 1, \tag{9}$$

or equivalently

$$\dim(\mathcal{N}(B)) = 1, \tag{10}$$

and the matrices A and B share a one-dimensional nullspace.

Proposition 1 enables us to generate hypotheses onto a nullspace on the $(N-1)$-dimensional unit sphere from sampled data points as follows:

Procedure: Nullspace Search
1. Randomly select N homogeneous vectors $\{a_{i(1)}, a_{i(2)}, \ldots, a_{i(N)}\}$ from $\{a_i\}_{i=1}^{k}$.
2. If the matrix B such that $B^\top = [a_{i(1)}, a_{i(2)}, \ldots, a_{i(N)}]$ has a one-dimensional nullspace, vote 1 to the nullspace of B.

If this hypothesis generation is iterated until an appropriate number, the nullspaces are estimated by detecting peaks of the vote on the $(N-1)$-dimensional unit sphere. Therefore, the estimation of 3D positions can be solved by this iteration.

In Procedure Nullspace Search, the computation of the nullspaces of given matrices is required. In our implementation, we adopted the singular value decomposition (SVD) for this purpose. If matrix A has only a zero singular value, then the nullspace of A is spanned by the right singular vector associated with the zero singular value. Therefore, setting $\sigma_1 \geq \ldots \geq \sigma_N$ to be the singular values of the sampled $N \times N$ matrix B and $v_1, \ldots, v_N$ to be the corresponding right singular vectors, if the relationship $\sigma_1 \geq \ldots > \sigma_N = 0$ holds, the nullspace to be generated is the vector v_N.

These properties of matrices derive the following algorithm for nullspace search.

Algorithm
1. Repeat the following steps from Step **2** to Step **6** until a predefined number.
2. Randomly select N homogeneous vectors $\{a_{i(1)}, a_{i(2)}, \ldots, a_{i(N)}\}$ from $\{a_i\}_{i=1}^{k}$.
3. Construct the $N \times N$ matrix B such that $B^\top = [a_{i(1)}, a_{i(2)}, \ldots, a_{i(N)}]$.
4. Compute the SVD of B and let $\sigma_1 \geq \ldots \geq \sigma_N$ be its singular values and $v_1, \ldots, v_N$ be the corresponding right singular vectors.
5. If the smallest singular value is not equal to 0, that is, $\sigma_1 \geq \ldots \geq \sigma_N > 0$, then go to Step **2**.
6. Add 1 to the accumulator of the right singular vector v_N associated with the smallest singular value σ_N.
7. Detect the vectors whose values of the accumulators are larger than a predefined constant.

6   Multilinear Constraints for Searching Correspondences

In this section, we consider the 3D recovery problem. We use multilinear constraints [9] among images for searching correspondences. Using the multilinear constraints, we can reduce the computational cost of the algorithm. We use the bilinear constraint for points and the trilinear constraint for lines.

6.1   Bilinear Constraint

Two perspective projections of the same 3D point derive the 4×4 matrix containing the entries of perspective projection matrices and the coordinates of the projections as described in Sect. 2. Setting $\boldsymbol{\varXi}_i$ to be the 4×4 matrix and $\boldsymbol{\xi}_i^j$ and $\boldsymbol{\xi}_{i'}^{j'}$ to be the two perspective projections of the same 3D point, if the 4×4 matrix $\boldsymbol{\varXi}_i$ is a singular matrix, the singular condition is written in the following bilinear form

$$\boldsymbol{\xi}_i^{j\top} \boldsymbol{F} \boldsymbol{\xi}_{i'}^{j'} = 0, \tag{11}$$

where $\boldsymbol{F}$ is a fundamental matrix containing only the entries of perspective projection matrices [8]. This means $\mathrm{rank}(\boldsymbol{\varXi}_i) \leq 3$ iff $\boldsymbol{\xi}_i^{j\top} \boldsymbol{F} \boldsymbol{\xi}_{i'}^{j'} = 0$. Therefore, if we determine whether eq. (11) holds for a selected pair of points before the SVD computation, we omit the SVD computation for a meaningless pair of points, i.e., if a selected pair of points does not satisfy eq. (11), we continue to select another pair of points.

6.2   Trilinear Constraint

In the case of lines, there are no constraints for perspective projections between two images. Three perspective projections of the same 3D line are required. Setting $\boldsymbol{\varPsi}_i$ to be a 6×6 matrix containing a selected triplet of lines on three different images and $\boldsymbol{\psi}_i^j$, $\boldsymbol{\psi}_{i'}^{j'}$ and $\boldsymbol{\psi}_{i''}^{j''}$ to be the selected lines, if the 6×6 matrix $\boldsymbol{\varPsi}_i$ is a singular matrix, the singular condition is written in the following trilinear form

$$\boldsymbol{\psi}_i^j \times \begin{bmatrix} \boldsymbol{\psi}_{i'}^{j'\top} \boldsymbol{T}_1^1 \boldsymbol{\psi}_{i''}^{j''} \\ \boldsymbol{\psi}_{i'}^{j'\top} \boldsymbol{T}_1^2 \boldsymbol{\psi}_{i''}^{j''} \\ \boldsymbol{\psi}_{i'}^{j'\top} \boldsymbol{T}_1^3 \boldsymbol{\psi}_{i''}^{j''} \end{bmatrix} = 0, \tag{12}$$

where $\boldsymbol{T}_1^1$, $\boldsymbol{T}_1^2$ and $\boldsymbol{T}_1^3$ are trifocal tensors containing only the entries of perspective projection matrices. Determining whether eq. (12) holds, we omit the SVD computation for a meaningless triplet of lines.

7   Experiments

7.1   Synthetic Data

We evaluated the performance of our algorithm, using two synthetic data "Sphere Object" and "Grid-Object", shown in Figs. 1 and 2, both of which are digitized in 256×256 pixels. We measured 30 views of the spherical object and 20 views of the grid-object, respectively. Spatial configurations between each 3D object and the cameras we used are shown in Figs. 1b and 2b, respectively.

Sphere Object: We predetected grid points on the spherical object on the image sequence and inputted the homogeneous coordinates of the grid points into our algorithms. Figure 1c shows the reconstructed result of our algorithm. In this experiment, the number of iterations was 10^6 times and the threshold for detecting peaks in the accumulator space was 10. The result shows our algorithm works well, and works for synthetic data. Since the spherical 3D object

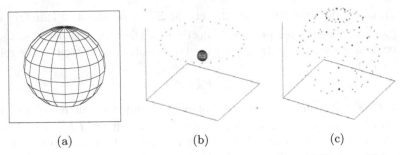

Fig. 1. Figures (a) and (b) show an example of input images of "Sphere Object" and 3D positions of both of the spherical object and the cameras, respectively. Figure (c) shows the reconstructed result of our algorithm

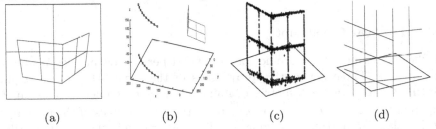

Fig. 2. Figures (a) and (b) show an example of input images of "Grid-Object" and 3D positions of both the grid-object and the cameras, respectively. Figures (c) and (d) show the reconstructed results of our algorithm for 3D points and 3D lines, respectively

produces a similar pattern over an image sequence, it is difficult to determine correspondences among the images. Our algorithm also works well in this case.

For the evaluation of the efficiency of the algorithm, which uses the multilinear constraint, two algorithms were tested for the same spherical object. One algorithm did not use the multilinear constraint, as described in Sect. 5, and the other algorithm used the constraint, as explained in Sect. 6. The following table shows the execution time of the two algorithms. In the table, Algorithms 1

Type	Time (s)
Algorithm 1	60.06
Algorithm 2	5.62

and 2 indicate the former and latter algorithms, respectively. In the experiment, the tests were executed on an UltraSPARC-II 297MHz processor. For both the algorithms, the number of iterations and thresholds for peak detection are the same as in the above experiment. As observed in the table, Algorithm 2 is about eleven times as fast as Algorithm 1. This experimental result shows that the multilinear constraint efficiently works in our algorithm.

Grid-Object: In the previous experiment, we recovered sparse feature points on the 3D spherical object. In this experiment, we used edge points on the images of the 3D grid-object as the inputted data, that is, we carried out our algorithm for dense data. Figure 2c shows the reconstructed result of our algorithm. The result shows our algorithm works well for dense edge points. Therefore, it is possible to apply our algorithm to a 3D object on which curve segments appear.

Next, we predetected straight lines on the images of the 3D grid-object, and then inputted the parameters of the straight lines to our algorithm. Figure 2d shows the reconstructed result of our algorithm. Unlike the recovery of 3D points, the nullspaces to be estimated are distributed on the five-dimensional unit sphere, since a 3D line is expressed by the six-dimensional homogeneous coordinates. In the previous and these experiments, we showed that our algorithm described in Sect. 5 was applied to both the 3- and 6-dimensional cases. The results reveal that our algorithm works well in any dimension.

7.2   Real Data

We also evaluated the performance of our algorithm, using real data "Model House", shown in Fig. 3, which are digitized in 768×576 pixels. This image sequence was created at Visual Geometry Group, University of Oxford. In the experiment, we first predetected corner points on the images using SUSAN corner detector [13], and second, manually selected a part of the detected points because of the removal of the points which do not correspond to actual corners on the images.

In the experiment, in order to confirm the ability to organize image data, we assumed that the consecutive images in the sequence were not known. Thus, we inputted the images at random, as shown in Fig. 3. Figure 4 shows the reconstructed result of our algorithm for the image sequence "Model House". In this experiment, the number of iterations was 10^7 and the threshold for detecting peaks in the accumulator space was 55. In Fig. 4b, we connected the reconstructed corner points with straight lines to show the relationship between the reconstructed points and the 3D house object. The algorithm recovered the spatial points on the 3D house object. The result shows our algorithm works well and also works for real data. Furthermore, since we assumed that the order of images was unknown, the result shows that the algorithm organizes image data.

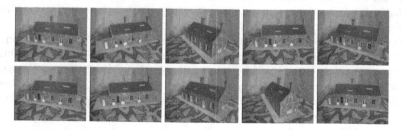

Fig. 3. The figures show the image sequence "Model House". This image sequence is arranged at random. We inputted the images in this order in the experiment in order to confirm the ability to organize image data, that is, we assumed that the consecutive images in the sequence were not known

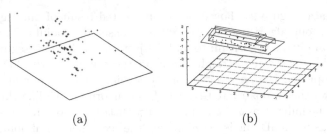

(a)   (b)

Fig. 4. Figure (a) shows the reconstructed result for the image sequence "Model House". In Figure (b), the wireframe model of the house object is superimposed on the result

8   Conclusions

In this study, we first formulated the recovery of a 3D object from an image sequence without predetecting correspondences among images as the nullspace search. The formulation includes many model detection problems in computer vision, e.g., line detection and conic detection in an image. For the achievement of the nullspace search, we developed the algorithm based on the random sampling and voting process, which is the main concept underlying the randomized Hough transform. Furthermore, using bilinear and trilinear constraints, we developed an efficient algorithm for the 3D recovery task.

References

1. J. Illingworth and J. Kittler. A Survey of the Hough Transform. *Computer Vision, Graphics, and Image Processing*, **44**-1, 87–116, 1988.
2. V.F. Leavers. Which Hough Transform? *Computer Vision, Graphics, and Image Processing: Image Understanding*, **58**-2, 250–264, 1993.
3. L. Xu and E. Oja. Randomized Hough Transform: Basic Mechanisms, Algorithms, and Computational Complexities. *Computer Vision, Graphics, and Image Processing: Image Understanding*, **57**-2, 131–154, 1993.
4. H. Edelsbrunner. Shape Reconstruction With Delaunay Complex. *Proc. of the 3rd Latin American Symposium on Theoretical Informatics, Lecture Notes in Computer Science*, **1380**, 119–132, 1998.
5. D. Attali and A. Montanvert. Computing and Simplifying 2D and 3D Continuous Skeletons. *Computer Vision and Image Understanding*, **67**-3, 261–273, 1997.
6. H.-K. Zhao, S. Osher, B. Merriman and M. Kang. Implicit and Nonparametric Shape Reconstruction from Unorganized Data Using a Variational Level Set Method. *Computer Vision and Image Understanding*, **80**-3, 285–319, 2000.
7. K. Kanatani. *Geometric Computation for Machine Vision*. Oxford Univ. Press, Oxford, U.K., 1993.
8. O.D. Faugeras. *Three-Dimensional Computer Vision: A Geometric Viewpoint*. MIT Press, Cambridge, MA, 1993.
9. R.I. Hartley and A. Zisserman, *Multiple View Geometry in Computer Vision*. Cambridge University Press, 2000.

10. C. Tomasi and T. Kanade. Shape and Motion from Image Streams under Orthography: A Factorization Method. *Int. J. of Computer Vision*, **9**-2, 137–154, 1992.
11. H.C. Longuet-Higgins. A Computer Algorithm for Reconstructing a Scene from Two Projections. *Nature*, **293**, 133–135, 1981.
12. S. Carlsson. Multiple Image Invariance using the Double Algebra. *Proc. of the 2nd Joint European–US Workshop on Application of Invariance in Computer Vision, Lecture Notes in Computer Science*, **825**, 145–164, 1994.
13. S.M. Smith and J.M. Brady. SUSAN – A New Approach to Low Level Image Processing. *Int. J. of Computer Vision*, **23**-1, 45–78, 1997.

A Learning Autonomous Driver System on the Basis of Image Classification and Evolutional Learning

Klaus-Dieter Kuhnert and Michael Krödel

University of Siegen, Institute for Real-Time-Systems, Hölderlinstrasse 3
D-57068 Siegen / Germany

Abstract. Driver Systems for autonomous vehicles are the nucleus of many studies done so far. In this light, they mainly consist of two major parts: the recognition of the environment (usually based on image processing) as well as any learning aspects for the driving behaviour. The latter is the nucleus of this research whereby learning aspects are understood that way that the driving behaviour should be optimised over time, therefore the most appropriate actions for each possible situation should be self-created and lastly offered for selection. The current research bases the learning aspects on means of Reinforcement Learning which is in sharp contrast to other research studies done before being mainly based on explicit modelling or neural nets.

1 Introduction

The research presented in this paper deals with the concept and the implementation of a system which, based on experience over time, is able to autonomously learn to steer different vehicles and to optimise itself to various possible road courses. This shall be done a different way than researched in many other works before as described further below.

Basically, this research extracts significant situation information out of the video images from a connected video camera and firstly clusters the images according to their situations they describe. Any new incoming image is then being classified into such situation cluster. Such situation clustering and image classification is being done by means of pattern matching leading to the ability to recognize the situation a vehicle is in, respectively determine a similar situation a vehicle has been in before.

Next to the determination of previous similar situations a vehicle has been in, the corresponding steering command set (for steering wheel, brake and accelerator), therefore the corresponding action, is being stored and is accessible as well. Based on such available information, an evolutional learning algorithm is being built on top. In specific, any issued action is being memorized and rated at a later time triggered by an explicit reward or punishment. After a series of such ratings, any action can be classified into a more or less appropriate action for corresponding situation. Since such evolutional learning algorithm also handles several possible actions for a situation it can therefore pick the best action from many possible. Lastly the evolutional learning algorithm also permanently enhances the set of possible actions by issuing randomly modified ones also allowing their evaluation. Such way it automatically

P. Perner and A. Rosenfeld (Eds.): MLDM 2003, LNAI 2734, pp. 400–412, 2003.

enhances it's situation-action state-space and - over a series of valuations - facilitates it's convergence.

All in all, the main targets of this research are:

- Self-tuning of the system to any combination of environment and vehicle, therefore true learning of driving skills
- Autonomous exploration of new actions for situations, therefore autonomous optimisation
- Transparency of the relationship between situations and actions for analysis and further optimisation

In order to achieve such goals a system is being build based on Pattern Matching and Reinforcement Learning. The Pattern Matching part is responsible for identifying the situation the vehicle is currently in and for retrieving a list of possible actions for this situation. The Reinforcement Learning part is responsible for judging the appropriateness of issued actions. An initial image processing part is responsible for extracting situation descriptions out of incoming images from a connected video camera.

2 General Structure

The general structure is being show in Figure 1 and consists of then two main parts: Pattern Matching and Reinforcement Learning, enhanced by an auxiliary part called Intelligent Image Processing which extracts situation descriptions out of the incoming video stream.

As displayed, the system gathers all input purely out of the video information coming from a connected camera. The camera digitises the current scene and permanently renders Single Images to the system. Consequently, no ultrasonic sensors, no information from a speedometer or a compass system, no stereo cameras or no information from a GPS system are being required.

2.1 Intelligent Image Processing

The first part of this research converts the video information from the Single Images into patterns, respectively Abstract Complete Situation Descriptions (ACSD's). Such conversion process is a reduction process and in addition to the requirement of the reduction to the relevant value-containing information, the calculation of such ACSD's has to be very quick. Therefore, this part combines traditional edge finding operators [14] with a new technique of Bayes prediction for each part of the video image. Such way, the algorithm of this part is able to build itself a knowledge base of what to look for and optimise processing time for such task.

Consequently, this first part is referred to as Intelligent Image Processing (IIP).

2.2 Pattern Matching

A second part performs the actual Pattern Matching. The ACSD's from the Intelligent Image Processing are being permanently stored for further reference by a pattern-recognition algorithm. The algorithm used in this project is an advanced variant of the well known nearest neighbour algorithm which allows searching within approximate 10.000 Patterns in several milliseconds. In the end, the pattern recognition algorithm is utilized such way, that based on the current situation, vehicle behaviours of previous similar situations are being retrieved and appropriate steering commands are being calculated.

As mentioned above, other researches successfully implemented such capabilities by using neural networks as well but are therefore limited to implicit knowledge being build between the neural elements. Our approach stores the knowledge explicitly in a database which allows detailed analysis of behaviour and, most important, the further implementation of a learning system on top in order to further improve any behaviour. These parts of the research are implemented now and a video may be shown of running the system on a driving simulator.

2.3 Reinforcement Learning

A third part deals with the implementation of learning by interaction. Instead of choosing a fixed model based approach the system will improve its behaviour itself over time simply based on rewards and punishments (respectively rewards only since punishments can be issued as negative rewards). Those rewards, however, will only be received after some time since it is usually not possible to instantly judge the appropriateness of every single issued action.

Therefore, one major task of this third part is to cope with such delayed rewards and to distribute them over previous issued actions, usually with decreasing impact since the earlier an action has been the smaller the influence on any current situation usually was.

A second major task of this part is to weigh between exploration and exploitation. Once a certain behaviour has been learned the system could use the existing knowledge (therefore exploit the learned behaviour) but would then be deprived of any further optimisation. If the system, on the other hand, always tries to find new actions in every situation (therefore explore new behaviour) it receives additional important rewards for further optimisation, however risks that too much optimisation will worsen the behaviour of the overall system, respectively endanger the convergence of the learning system.

Therefore this part has to deal with the trade-off between exploration and exploitation. Those requirements span the area of Reinforcement Learning which combine the classical ways of dynamic programming and supervised learning [1,2].

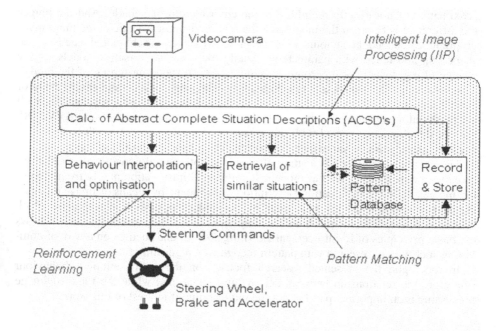

Fig. 1. Structure of the system

3   Related Work

Up to now the visual control of systems for autonomous vehicle driving with learning components have been implemented in several ways. [3] describes a short direct connection between image processing and one soft computing learning method using a neural network. This approach provides good results but only as long as input pictures of the scene are similar to the training pattern. In [4] this approach got enhanced by a multiple neural network but could not completely solve the dependency problem of the taught training patterns. Further developments then included a GPS system [5] to support orientation or enhanced the approach with object-oriented vision in order to distinguish between road following and obstacle detection [6]. In all those variations, however, neural networks with their inherent dependency on training patterns are embedded. Also, as a major difference to the presented research, the established knowledge on vehicle driving is stored within the neural net but not explicitly available, e.g. for optimisation or further evolutional learning processes.

A completely different approach is being followed by using explicit modelling, therefore trying to rebuild a model of both environment as well the vehicle and deriving proper actions from it. The basic idea of such a model is to try to understand interaction between vehicle and environment and to predict consequences of any behaviour thus allowing vice-versa to determine a suitable behaviour in a given situation. The major problem lies in the fact that any model is only a model and can only approximate, but not exactly rebuild, the true environment or vehicle. And the bigger the difference is between the model and the real environment/vehicle, the more inappropriate calculated behaviours may become. Also, any such model needs to be shaped up and tuned with parameters. Usually there are no versatile models so any change of e.g. vehicle or environment requires a corresponding tuning of the model. This means in other words, any tuned model is valid only for a certain environment or vehicle and invariant to any changes of those. [7] describes an early success with international attention of a vehicle system using a real-time vision system BVV2 [8]. Further developments stayed with the aspect of modelling (e.g. [9]), thus always in need for loading the system with many parameters for the modelling process.

The presented approach is a study of avoiding both neural networks or similar approximation methods as well as models. It gathers all information purely from incoming images. It derives a Situation Description of the scene by means of Image processing and develops a driving behaviour by a standard optimisation technique. With reference to the need for machine learning capabilities the current research follows the basic principles of Reinforcement Learning e.g. [2] and focuses on a way of combining such area of research with pattern recognition algorithms.

In this light, the presented research focuses on the optimisation of behaviour (therefore the relationship between actions and situations) while the topic of image processing is an important part but not the major point of interest of this work.

4   Concept of Subsystem Intelligent Image Processing

The needed output from the Subsystem Intelligent Image Processing is a parametric description of the road course visible in the incoming Single Image which further will be referred to as the Abstract Complete Situation Description (ACSD). The course of a road is best described by the extraction of the road marks, respectively its edges (the Road Mark Edges). In order to find those, a typical initial approach would be to scan any Single Image horizontally for big contrast or colour differences since the road marks are supposed to be in sharp optical contrast to the tar of the road. However, even if Road Mark Edges are being indicated by contrast differences in a Single Image, it cannot be necessarily concluded that vice versa all contrast differences in any Single Image do represent Road Mark Edges. Consequently, pure scanning for contrast differences is not good enough.

The Subsystem Intelligent Image Processing therefore includes a possibility to use pre-build knowledge on some characteristics of road marks and therefore can weigh the probability on whether a contrast difference might result out of a Road Mark Edge or not. This is being achieved by once analysing road courses and their possible orientations depending on their position within the Single Image and storing the results in a statistics database. Such analysis and building up of the statistics database is being done prior to the runtime of the System.

During the runtime of the System, a first pass then scans for horizontal contrast differences and memorises all locations where the colour values of two neighbouring pixels from the Single Image with some specific filtering exceed a certain threshold and therefore represent a possible candidate of a Road Mark Edge. In a second pass, all those candidates are tried to be connected to a chain with each other – according to information out of the statistics database which indicate the expected orientation of the road course in this location within the Single Image. If a chain can be established and fulfils minimum requirements on length and number of interconnection points in between (nodes), the whole chain is being stored as a confirmed representation of a Road Mark Edges. Otherwise, the considered candidates of Road Mark Edges are being rejected.

Therefore, the basic idea is to discretely approximate the probability –density function $f(P_{x,y} \mid P_{x+\Delta x, y+\Delta y})$ where $P_{x,y}$ is the event that the pixel at (x , y) is on a Road Mark Edge and $P_{x+\Delta x, y+\Delta y}$ is the event that the pixel at (x +Δ x , y + Δ y) is also on a Road Mark Edge. This function is quite smooth in the near region of the road image but depends obviously on (x, y). Therefore, the Single Image is separated into Tiles and a separate function $f_{x,y}$ is estimated for each Tile. One connection between $P_{x,y}$ and $P_{x+\Delta x, y+\Delta y}$ is called a Chaining Vector. So, this function can not only be utilised for describing the statistical properties of Road Mark Edges but also for defining a search strategy, i.e. all the Chaining vectors belonging to the position (x, y) can be searched in the order of their probability thus optimising the search speed.

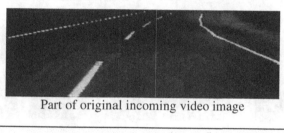

Part of original incoming video image

Road Mark Edges build without Chaining Vectors (vertically compressed)

Road Mark Edges build with Chaining Vectors (vertically compressed)

Fig. 2. Rebuilding the road mark edges with/without chaining vectors

More details on concept, implementation as well as experimental results are being described in [10] and [11].

5 Concept of Subsystem Pattern Matching

Main task for this subsystem is, as described before, to locate similar situations. Therefore, any Abstract Complete Situation Description (ACSD) ever experienced is stored in a database. The more ACSD's have been calculated based on the Single Images the larger this database gets. At the same time, any calculated ACSD is also forwarded to a module called Pattern Matching / Situation Recall. This module scans the database for similar ACSD's experienced before using an Approximate Nearest Neighbour (ANN) algorithm [15]. As a result the most similar ACSD's are being identified.

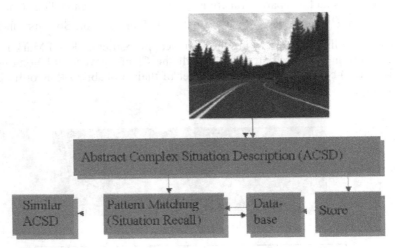

Fig. 3. Retrieval of similar situations via pattern matching

Such way, the system locates several similar situations in comparison to the actual situation. Along with every stored situation description (ACSD) the steering commands (actions) issued at any such situation have been recorded as well (acceleration a; steering wheel angle φ). Therefore, any situation recall results in a list of several similar experienced situations, each with many different possible actions. All those actions together are further treated as possible actions for the current situation.

At this time, however, it is not clear which of those actions is the best one for the current situation. Therefore it has to be decided which of the possible actions shall be performed: the most similar, the most similar (weighed), the best? Ideally the latter is the case (therefore the "best") but this prerequisites a criterion on how to determine the best and a possibility to establish optimisation of this criterion. This is being done by the subsystem Reinforcement Learning being described further below. The Reinforcement Learning sections also deals with the questions, whether the best possible action retrieved is good enough, therefore whether new (better) actions need to be build and offered for selection.

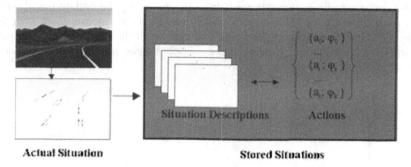

Fig. 4. Retrieval of actions for the actual situation

6 Concept of Subsystem Reinforcement Learning

This subsection is responsible for providing learning capabilities, respectively permanently updates a quality criterion on which action is the best for a situation. Also, it permanently probes for new actions and tests them regarding appropriateness.

Therefore, every situation, respectively ACSD from the subsystem Pattern Matching is now being enhanced with a quality value $q(a, \varphi)$ for each action (acceleration a and Steering Wheel angle φ).

A Situation Recall in the subsection Pattern Matching therefore results in similar situations (ACSD's) and for each of those ACSD's different possible actions; each of those possessing a quality value $q(ACSD, a, \varphi)$.

$$
\begin{pmatrix} \{a_0; \varphi_0\} \\ \dots \\ \{a_i; \varphi_i\} \\ \dots \\ \{a_n; \varphi_n\} \end{pmatrix} \rightarrow \begin{pmatrix} \{a_0; \varphi_0; q(a_0, \varphi_0)\} \\ \dots \\ \{a_i; \varphi_i; q(a_i, \varphi_i)\} \\ \dots \\ \{a_n; \varphi_n; q(a_n, \varphi_n)\} \end{pmatrix} \rightarrow \begin{pmatrix} \{ACSD_0; a_0; \varphi_0; q(ACSD_0, a_0, \varphi_0)\} \\ \dots \\ \{ACSD_j; a_i; \varphi_i; q(ACSD_j, a_i, \varphi_i)\} \\ \dots \\ \{ACSD_m; a_n; \varphi_n; q(ACSD_m, a_n, \varphi_n)\} \end{pmatrix}
$$

per ACSD   per ACSD   *with i={0;n} for every j; j={0;m}*

Fig. 5. Enhancement of every possible action with a cumulated rating q

Those quality values $q(ACSD, a, \varphi)$ are now being updated based on rewards and punishments according to the future success of their actions. Such update is being done in retro-perspective by the implementation of a Reinforcement Learning algorithm ([1],[2]) according to the following formula

$$Q(ACSD_t, a_t, \varphi t) = r(ACSD_t - \gamma \cdot q(ACSD_t + 1, a_{t+1} \varphi_{t+1}) \quad (1)$$

with r as the reward and γ as the discount factor.

The rewards and punishments are being self-created by the system based on deviations from the centre of the lane, respectively based on time measurements for driving along certain road sections. After a series of updates of the q-values of many possible actions for a situation, a 2 dimensional curve converges which allows to choose the best action for a situation.

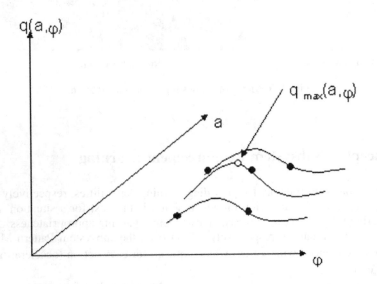

Fig. 6. Exploration modes selects (a, φ with highes q-value

In order to ensure convergence many actions have to be chosen as the basis for the q-value update. That means it is necessary, that the system autonomously explores new actions, therefore optimises itself on it's own.

This is being achieved by randomly changing from exploitation mode (location of best action, therefore action with highest q-value as described so far) to exploration mode in which random actions are being created and issued. Such new actions are also being rated according to Reinforcement Learning and lead this way to a continuous exploration of new actions for each situation.

Further details to the actual concept are being described in [12] and [13].

7   Experimental Results

7.1   Results Intelligent Image Processing

Results of the subsystem Intelligent Image Processing are discussed in [10] and [11] and Fig. 2 gives an impression of the rebuilding of the road mark edges. Since the topic of image processing is an important part but not the major point of interest of this work further discussion are not being included at this point.

7.2 Results Pattern Matching

The quality of the subsystem Pattern Matching can be shown twofold. Firstly, the following image shows a series of images where the first image on the top is the incoming Single Image coming from the attached video camera. All remaining images are the ones classified by the Pattern Matching algorithm as similar ones. If considered that those classified images are only some out of a pattern database with several thousand record entries which contain all various types of images it can be seen that all images classified as similar are truly similar to the first image.

Incoming Singe Image

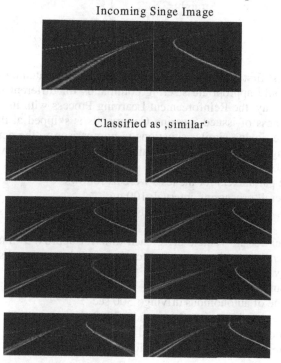

Classified as ‚similar'

Fig. 7. Retrieval of similar situations based on pattern matching

From a pure image comparison point of view this might not be astonishing but in our case it needs to be noted that this has been achieved in addition to speed optimisation (search time for finding those 8 similar images out of a database of around 5.000 images can be done in less than 5 ms on any ordinary PC) and adaptation to road situations (the further course of the road to the left or right has higher priority on the classification of similarity than any objects on or next to the road which would distract ordinary algorithms on image retrieval).

The second way to demonstrate the results of the Subsystem Pattern Matching is the display of the confusion matrix. The Table below displays such matrix indicating the statistics of finding the proper course type (e.g. a left curve). It can be seen that in average 61,0 % of all classifications were correct and even the hit-rates for curves are up to 45.3%, respectively 50.5%. At a first glance this result looks not very impressing but is has to be considered that almost all errors stem from quantization e.g. confusing a very slight left curve with a straight road etc.

Table 1. Confusion matrix for retrieval of similar situations

		True Road Type			
		Left	Straight	Right	
	Left	235	324	71	37,3%
Classified as:	Straight	220	1335	185	75,7%
	Right	64	305	261	41,4%
		45,3%	68,0%	50,5%	61,0%

In order to test first driving skills based on the pattern matching algorithm a pattern database with only appropriate steering commands for different situations has been build up. Such way, the Reinforcement Learning Process with its challenge to weigh the appropriateness of issued Steering Commands is skipped at the moment but the difficulties of retrieving similar situations in comparison to the actual one and therefore first driving by pattern matching can be tested. Such way several test runs have been performed.

In Detail the parameters for the tests were as follows:
-    Overall processing interval: 100 ms
-    No. of entries in Pattern database: approx. 5.400

The tests then let the vehicle drive each time for approx. 5 minutes along a curvy and partial unknown road course. The results of such tests are listed below and can also be shown via video.

Average results of tests:
-    Time of autonomous driving : 300 sec
-    Calculated Steering Commands: 3000 (10 per second)
-    Number of major errors (road course left completely): 1
-    Number of errors (crash barrier scratched): 4

If it is assumed that at each conducted error is the result of around 10 steering commands (the actual one and the previous 9 ones) the failure rate amounts to $(5 \cdot 10)$ / 3000 equals 1.6 %. Noting that the autonomous driving is purely done on pattern matching since both Reinforcement Learning as well as intelligent calculation of Steering Commands are still outstanding the results shown above are promising.

7.3   Results Reinforcement Learning

As described before the Reinforcement Learning system builds itself a database of different situations, each situation itself referring to several different possible actions. Every such action indicates, by means of a quality value q, the appropriateness of this action at the corresponding situation. The algorithm for selection an appropriate action for a certain situation therefore locates the action with the highest q-values and issues the associated action. This mode is referred to as the exploitation mode. In exploration mode the algorithm also locates the action with the highest q-value but deviates in some situations (triggered by random generator) the action to some extend and also issues this 'new' action.

Every action being issued, never mind whether determined/calculated in exploitation mode or in exploration mode, is then being rated according to the reinforcement learning update procedure.

The result of our experiments can be best displayed with two short videos of 30 seconds duration each.

In both videos, the Reinforcement Learning System classified 1.543 situations and in total 3.196 actions. The actions stored are partially proper actions for the corresponding situation but partially wrong ones (e.g. steering to the right in left curve).

Video 1 shows a driving sequence when the q-values have not converged yet, and many 'wrong' actions are chosen. The driving behaviour is quite bumpy and on a straight road section the driving system stopped one time. After the recording of Video1 a phase of autonomous driving has been performed in which the system receives it's rewards and punishments thus allowing the q-values to converge. Video 2 shows a driving sequence with such converged q-values based on which the driving behaviour is much smoother than in Video 1.

8   Summary

Pattern Matching allows autonomous driving with knowledge being directly accessible (for further optimisation). Reinforcement Learning allows autonomous optimisation of behaviours based on self-created rewards and punishments, even if delayed. Combining both techniques allow learning and optimising of the visual steering of an autonomous vehicle.

References

[1]   Mance E. Harmon, Stephanie S. Harmon, Reinforcement Learning – A Tutorial, Wright Laboratory, Centerville (USA)

[2]   Richard Sutton, A.G. Barto, Reinforcement Learning: An introduction, MIT-Press, 2000, Cambridge (USA)

[3]   D. A. Pommerleau, Efficient Training of Artificial Neural Networks for Autonomous Navigation, Neural Computation 3, 1991

[4]   T.M. Jochem, D.A. Pomerleau, C.E. Thorpe. MANIAC: A Next Generation Neurally Based Autonomous Road Follower, IAS-3, Int. Conference on Intelligent autonomous Systems, February 15–18, 1993, Pittsburgh/PA, USA, F.C.A. Groen, S. Hirose, C.E. Thorpe (eds), IOS Press, Washington, Oxford, Amsterdam, Tokyo, 1993

[5]   T.M. Jochem, D.A. Pomerleau, C.E. Thorpe, Vision Guided Lane Transition, Intelligent Vehicles '95 Symposium, September 25–26, 1995, Detroit/MI, USA

[6]   Expectation-based selective attention for visual monitoring and control of a robot vehicle, S. Baluja, D.A. Pomerleau, Robotics and Autonomous System, Vol.22, No.3–4, December, 1997

[7]   E.D. Dickmanns, A. Zapp, Autonomous High Speed Road Vehicle Guidance by Computer Vision, Preprints of the 10th World Congress on Automatic Control, Vol.4, International Federation of Automatic Control, Munich, Germany, July 27–31, 1987

[8]   K.-D. Kuhnert, A Vision System for Real Time Road and Object Recognition for Vehicle Guidance, Proc. Mobile Robots, Oct 30–31, 1986, Cambridge, Massachusetts, Society of Photo-Optical Instrumentation Engineers, SPIE Volume 727

[9]   E.D. Dickmanns, R. Behringer, D. Dickmanns, T. Hildebrandt, M. Maurer, F. Thomanek, J. Schiehlen, The Seeing Passenger Car 'VaMoRs-P', Intelligent Vehicles '94 Symposium, October 24–26, 1994, Paris, France

[10]   M. Krödel, K.-D. Kuhnert, Towards a Learning Autonomous Driver System, IEEE International Conference on Industrial Electronics, Control and Instrumentation, October 22–28, 2000, Nagoya, Japan

[11]   M. Krödel, K.-D. Kuhnert, Pattern Matching as the Nucleus for either Autonomous Driving or Drive Assistance Systems, IEEE Intelligent Vehicle Symposium, June 17–21, 2002, Versailles, France

[12]   K.-D. Kuhnert, M. Krödel, Reinforcement Learning to drive a car by pattern matching, Anual symposium of Pattern recognition of DAGM, September 16–18, 2002, Zurich (Switzerland)

[13]   K.-D. Kuhnert, M. Krödel, Autonomous Driving by Pattern Matching and Reinforcement Learning, International Colloquium on Autonomous and Mobile Systems, June 25–26, 2002, Magdeburg, Germany

[14]   Jähne, Bernd. Digital Image Processing, Springer Verlag 1997

[15]   David M. Mount, ANN Programming Manual, Department of Computer Science and Institute for Advance Computer Studies, University of Maryland, 1998

Detecting the Boundary Curve of Planar Random Point Set

A. Imiya[1,2], K. Tatara[3], H. Ootani[3], and V. Hlaváč[4]

[1] National Institute of Informatics, Japan
[2] Institute of Media and Information Technology, Chiba University, Japan
[3] School of Science and Technology, Chiba University, Japan
[4] Center for Machine Perception, Czech Technical University, Czech Republic

Abstract. In this paper, we develop an algorithm for the learning of the boundary and the medial axis of random point sets, employing the principal curve analysis. The principal curve analysis is a generalization of principal axis analysis, which is a standard method for data analysis in pattern recognition.

1 Introduction

In this paper, we develop an algorithm for the learning of the boundary of random point sets, employing the principal curve analysis. The principal curve analysis is a generalization of principal axis analysis, which is a standard method for data analysis in pattern recognition.

For the vector space method of data mining, each datum is expressed as a point in the higher dimensional Euclidean space. Symbolic expressions of these point sets are required for the visual interface for the data mining systems. Furthermore, these data are sometimes transformed as a point distribution in lower dimensional vector spaces, usually tow or three dimensional spaces, for the visualization of data distribution on CRT. Therefore, the extraction of the symbolic features of random point sets in two and three dimensional is a basic process for the visual interpretation of random point sets for the visualization of the data space.

For the tele-surgery by robots, we are required to detect the geometric information of deformable organs in the human body while surgery. If we measure deformable objects using multi-directional camera systems, we obtain a noisy cloud of sample points which distribute around the surface of the deformable object. For the tracking and computation of geometric parameters of deformable objects from the cloud of sample points, we are required to estimate the boundary of object which lies in the cloud of sample points.

Computational geometry provides combinatorial methods for the recovery of boundary curves as polygonal curves. These algorithms are based on Voronoi tessellation, Delaunay triangulation, Gabriel graphs, crust, α-shape, and β-skeleton [1–3]. The reconstructed curves by these methods are piecewise linear. Furthermore, the solutions are sensitive against noise and outlayers, since these methods construct polygons and polyhedrons using all sample points.

P. Perner and A. Rosenfeld (Eds.): MLDM 2003, LNAI 2734, pp. 413–424, 2003.

In this paper, we introduce method for the estimation of the boundary of a random point set. we first develop an algorithm for the detection of a closed curve from a planar random point set. Furthermore, we also develop a procedure for the estimation of the boundary curve of a random point set using Delaunay triangulation and mathematical morphology for random point sets.

2   Mathematical Preliminary

Setting $\mathbf{A}$ to be a finite closed set in the n-dimensional Euclidean space $\mathbf{R}^2$, the Minkowski addition and subtraction of sets are defined as

$$\mathbf{A} \oplus \mathbf{B} = \bigcup_{\boldsymbol{x} \in \mathbf{B}, \boldsymbol{y} \in \mathbf{B}} (\boldsymbol{x} + \boldsymbol{y}), \ \mathbf{A} \ominus \mathbf{B} = \overline{\overline{\mathbf{A}} \oplus \overline{\mathbf{B}}}. \tag{1}$$

The inner and outer boundary of point set $\mathbf{A}$ with respect to radius λ are defined as

$$\Delta_\lambda^+ \mathbf{A} = (\mathbf{A} \oplus \lambda \mathbf{B}) \setminus \mathbf{A}, \ \Delta_\lambda^- \mathbf{A} = \mathbf{A} \setminus (\mathbf{A} \ominus \lambda \mathbf{B}) \tag{2}$$

for the unit desk such that $\mathbf{B} = \{\boldsymbol{x} | \boldsymbol{x} \leq 1\}$, where $\lambda \mathbf{A} = \{\lambda \boldsymbol{x} | \boldsymbol{x} \in \mathbf{A}\}$ for $\lambda > 0$. We call $\mathbf{A}_\lambda = \Delta_\lambda^+ \mathbf{A} \bigcup \Delta_\lambda^- \mathbf{A}$ the boundary belt of $\mathbf{A}$ with respect to λ. Geometrically, we have the relation

$$\lim_{\lambda \to +0} \mathbf{A}_\lambda = \partial \mathbf{A}, \tag{3}$$

where $\partial \mathbf{A}$ is the boundary curve of set $\mathbf{A}$.

Setting $\{\boldsymbol{p}_i\}_{i=1}^n$ to be a point set in $\mathbf{R}^n$, the region

$$\mathbf{V}_i = \{\boldsymbol{x} | |\boldsymbol{x} - \boldsymbol{p}_i| \leq |\boldsymbol{x} - \boldsymbol{p}_j|, i \neq j\} \tag{4}$$

is called Voronoi region with respect to the generator $\boldsymbol{p}_i$. The hyperplane

$$F_i = \{\boldsymbol{x} | |\boldsymbol{x} - \boldsymbol{p}_i| = |\boldsymbol{x} - \boldsymbol{p}_j|\} \tag{5}$$

is the Voronoi face. Setting $\boldsymbol{p}_i$ and $\boldsymbol{p}_j$ to be the generators of Voronoi regions sharing a face, a geometric graph which connect all pairs of generators in the face-sharing region is called Dalaunay triangulation. The Voronoi tessellation and the Dalaunary triangulation are dual figures each other.

Regression model fitting for planar sample points $\{(x_i, y_i)^\top\}_{i=1}^n$ for $x_1 < x_2 < \cdots < x_n$ is achieved, for example [9], by minimizing the criterion

$$J(f) = \sum_{i=1}^n \rho(|y_i - f(x_i)|) + \lambda \sum_{i=1}^{n-1} \int_{x_i}^{x_{i+1}} \left| \frac{d^2 f(\tau)}{d\tau^2} \right|_{\tau = x} dx, \tag{6}$$

where $\rho(\tau)$ is a positive symmetry function.

3   Principal Axes and Curves

Let $\mathbf{X}$ be a mean-zero point distribution in $\mathbf{R}^2$. The major principal component $\boldsymbol{w}$ maximizes the criterion

$$J(\boldsymbol{w}) = E_{\boldsymbol{x} \in \mathbf{X}} |\boldsymbol{x}^\top \boldsymbol{w}|^2 \qquad (7)$$

with respect to $|\boldsymbol{w}| = 1$, where $E_{\boldsymbol{x} \in \mathbf{X}}$ expresses the expectation over set $\mathbf{X}$. Line $\boldsymbol{x} = t\boldsymbol{w}$ is a one-dimensional linear subspace which approximates $\mathbf{X}$. A maximization criterion

$$J(\boldsymbol{P}) = E_{\boldsymbol{x} \in \mathbf{X}} |\boldsymbol{P}\boldsymbol{x}|^2 \qquad (8)$$

with respect to $rank\,\boldsymbol{P} = 1$, determines a one dimensional linear subspace which approximates $\mathbf{X}$. If $\mathbf{X}$ is not a mean-zero point distribution in $\mathbf{R}^2$ and the centroid of $\mathbf{X}$ is not predetermined, the maximization criterion

$$J(\boldsymbol{P}, \boldsymbol{g}) = E_{\boldsymbol{x} \in \mathbf{X}} |\boldsymbol{P}(\boldsymbol{x} - \boldsymbol{g})|^2 \qquad (9)$$

with respect to $rank\,\boldsymbol{P} = 1$, determines a one-dimensional linear manifold which approximates point distribution $\mathbf{X}$. If $\boldsymbol{g} = 0$, $\boldsymbol{P}$ is computed using PCA [6]. In the previous papers [7, 8], we extend the idea of PCA for $\boldsymbol{g} \neq 0$. This mechanism automatically estimates $\boldsymbol{g}$ and $\boldsymbol{P}$, even if many clusters exist in a space [7, 8].

For the partition of $\mathbf{X}$ into $\{\mathbf{X}_i\}_{i=1}^N$ such that $\mathbf{X} = \cup_{i=1}^N \mathbf{X}_i$, vectors $\boldsymbol{g}_i$ and $\boldsymbol{w}_i$ which maximize the criterion

$$J(\boldsymbol{w}_1, \cdots, \boldsymbol{w}_N, \boldsymbol{g}_1, \cdots, \boldsymbol{g}_N) = \sum_{i=1}^N E_{\boldsymbol{x} \in \mathbf{X}_i} |(\boldsymbol{x} - \boldsymbol{g}_i)^\top \boldsymbol{w}_i|^2 \qquad (10)$$

determine a polygonal curve [4], $\boldsymbol{l} = \boldsymbol{g}_i + t\boldsymbol{w}_i$. Furthermore, for an appropriate partition of $\mathbf{X}$ into $\{\mathbf{X}\}_{i=1}^N$, such that $\mathbf{X} = \cup_{i=1}^N \mathbf{X}_i$, vector $\boldsymbol{g}_i$ and orthogonal projector $\boldsymbol{P}_i$, which maximize the criterion

$$J(\boldsymbol{P}_1, \cdots, \boldsymbol{P}_N, \boldsymbol{g}_1, \cdots, \boldsymbol{g}_N) = \sum_{i=1}^N E_{\boldsymbol{x} \in \mathbf{X}_i} |\boldsymbol{P}_i(\boldsymbol{x} - \boldsymbol{g}_i)|^2 \qquad (11)$$

with respect to $rank\,\boldsymbol{P}_i = 1$, determine a piecewise linear curve, $\mathbf{C}_i = \{\boldsymbol{x} + \boldsymbol{g}_i | \boldsymbol{P}_i\boldsymbol{x} = \boldsymbol{x}\}$. This piecewise linear is called the principal curve [4].

4   Curve Detection

Set $\mathbf{D}$ and $\mathbf{S}$ to be a random point set and the vertices of polygonal curve, respectively, and the distance between point $\boldsymbol{x} \in \mathbf{S}$ and $\boldsymbol{y} \in \mathbf{D}$ is defined as $d(\boldsymbol{x}, \mathbf{D}) = \min_{\boldsymbol{y} \in \mathbf{D}} d(\boldsymbol{x}, \boldsymbol{y})$ for the Euclidean distance in a plane.

The initial shapes $\mathbf{S}$ and $\mathbf{C}$ are a line segment whose direction is equivalent to the major component $\boldsymbol{w}_1$ of a random point set and a regular triangle whose vertices are determined from the principal components $\boldsymbol{w}_1$ and $\boldsymbol{w}_2$. For a sequence of vertices $\langle \boldsymbol{v}_1, \boldsymbol{v}_2, \cdots \boldsymbol{v}_n \rangle$ of a polygonal curve, we define the tesselation as

$$V_\alpha = \{\boldsymbol{x} | d(\boldsymbol{x}, \boldsymbol{v}_\alpha) < d(\boldsymbol{x}, \boldsymbol{v}_i), d(\boldsymbol{x}, \boldsymbol{v}_\alpha) < d(\boldsymbol{x}, \boldsymbol{e}_{ij}), \alpha \neq i\},$$
$$E_{\alpha\alpha+1} = \{\boldsymbol{x} | d(\boldsymbol{x}, \boldsymbol{e}_{\alpha\alpha+1}) < d(\boldsymbol{x}, \boldsymbol{v}_i), d(\boldsymbol{x}, \boldsymbol{e}_{\alpha\alpha+1}) < d(\boldsymbol{x}, \boldsymbol{e}_{ii+1}), \alpha \neq i\},$$

where $\boldsymbol{e}_{ii+1}$ is the edge which connects $\boldsymbol{v}_i$ and $\boldsymbol{v}_{i+1}$. The minimization criterion of reference [5] is expressed as

$$I = \sum_{\boldsymbol{v}_k \in \mathbf{C}} F(\boldsymbol{v}_k, \mathbf{D}) + \lambda \sum_{\boldsymbol{v}_k \in \mathbf{P}} \sum_{i=-1}^{1} \frac{\boldsymbol{v}_{i-1i}^\top \boldsymbol{v}_{ii+1}}{|\boldsymbol{v}_{i-1i}||\boldsymbol{v}_{ii+1}|} \qquad (12)$$

for

$$F(\boldsymbol{v}_k, \mathbf{D}) = \sum_{\boldsymbol{x} \in E_{k-1k}} d(\boldsymbol{x}, \boldsymbol{v}_k) + \sum_{\boldsymbol{x} \in V_k} d(\boldsymbol{x}, \boldsymbol{v}_k) + \sum_{\boldsymbol{x} \in E_{kk+1}} d(\boldsymbol{x}, \boldsymbol{v}_k).$$

Using this criterion, we obtain an algorithm for the detection of the principal curve [5] where I_K is the value of I with K vertices.

1. Set the vertices of the initial curve as $\mathbf{S}$.
2. Move all vertices $\boldsymbol{v}_i$ $i = 1, 2, \cdots, K$, to minimize I_K.
3. Generate the new vertex $\boldsymbol{v}_{K+1}$ on the curve $\mathbf{S}$.
4. If $|I_K - I_{K-1}| \leq \varepsilon$ for a positive constant ε, then stop, else set $\mathbf{S} := \mathbf{S} \cup \{\boldsymbol{v}_{K+1}\}$ and go to 2.

This incremental algorithm preserves the topology of the initial curve, since the algorithm generates new vertices on the curve. This geometrical property leads to the conclusion that this algorithm reconstructs closed or open curves, if the initial curve is closed or open, respectively. As the initial curves for closed curves, we adopt a triangle using the direction of principal axes of point distribution.

5   The Boundary Curve of Random Point Set

The principal curve and principal surface enable us to extract the medial manifold of a random point set. This mathematical property implies that it is possible to extract the principal boundary using our method, if we have the boundary cloud of a random point set. In the following, we develop an algorithm for the extraction of the principal boundary of a random point set by introducing some definitions for the distribution of a random point set.

Definition 1. *For a point $\boldsymbol{p}$ in a random point set* $\mathbf{V}$, *we call* $\boldsymbol{p}_\delta = \{\boldsymbol{x} | |\boldsymbol{p} - \boldsymbol{x}| < \delta, \boldsymbol{p} \in \mathbf{V}, \forall \boldsymbol{x} \in \mathbf{R}^2\}$ *the effective region of point $\boldsymbol{p}$ with respect to radius δ.*

As the union of the effective region of each point, we define the effective region of a random point set.

Definition 2. *For a random point set* **V**, *we call* $\overline{\mathbf{V}} = \bigcup_{\boldsymbol{p} \in \mathbf{V}} \boldsymbol{p}_\delta$ *the effective region of point set* **V** *with respect to radius* δ.

If points in **V** are sampled from a connected region in $\mathbf{R}^2$, $\overline{\mathbf{V}}$ becomes a connected region in $\mathbf{R}^2$, selecting an appropriate δ. Therefore, we introduce a method for the selection of a suitable radius for the estimation of the connected region from a random point set. Using this estimated connected region, we develop an algorithm for the construction of the boundary of a random point set.

Setting E to be the set of edges of the Delaunay triangulation D constructed from the points in random point set **V**, we set $\delta = \mathrm{median}_{e \in E}|e|$, if points distribute uniformly in a region. Then, we define the boundary set as

$$\mathbf{V}_\gamma = \overline{\mathbf{V}}_\gamma \bigcap \mathbf{V}, \quad \overline{\mathbf{V}}_\gamma = \overline{\mathbf{V}} \setminus \{\overline{\mathbf{V}} \ominus \gamma D(\delta)\}, \tag{13}$$

where $\gamma > 1$ is a constant and $D = \{\boldsymbol{x} | |\boldsymbol{x}| \leq \delta\}$ is the set of all points in the circle with radius δ. We call $\mathbf{V}_\gamma$ the γ-boundary of random point set **V**. We extract the principal manifold from the γ-boundary.

Definition 3. *The principal boundary of a random point set is the principal manifold of the point in the γ-boundary of a random point set.*

We also call this principal manifold extracted from random point set **V** the γ-surface of **V**.

Using these definitions, we have the following algorithm for the construction of the principal boundary of a random point set.

1. Construct Delaunay triangulation D from random point set **V**.
2. For the collection of all edges E of D, detect the median length, and set it as δ.
3. Compute the effective region of random point set **V**.
4. Compute γ-boundary of random point set **V**.
5. Compute γ-surface of random point set **V**.

The construction of the Delaunay triangulation using all points in **V** is in practice an time-consuming process for a large number of points even if we use an optimal algorithm. Furthermore, we only need the lengths of the Delaunay triangles for the construction of the effective region of the neighborhood of a random point set. Therefore, we replace steps 1 and 2 of the algorithm to the following random sampling process.

1. Select a finite closed subset **S** of $\mathbf{R}^2$.
2. Compute Delaunay triangulation for points in $\mathbf{S} \bigcap \mathbf{V}$.
3. Compute the median of length of edges of Delaunay triangles with respect to subset **S**.
4. Repeat steps 1 to 3 until the predetermined number of times.
5. Select the maximum length.

6   Topology of Planar Point Set

The algorithm proposed in the previous section reconstructs closed or open curves, if the initial curve is closed or open, respectively. Therefore, if we evaluate the number of data points in the tessellations yielded by the algorithm, we can also detect the topology of point clouds on a plane. If the distribution of sample points in a region E_{ii+1} is space, we can conclude that the principal curve of a random point set is open. Then, we obtain an extension of the algorithm derived in reference [5].

Algorithm C

1. First phase:
    (a) Set the vertices of the initial curve as a closed curve such that $\mathbf{C} := \{v_1, v_2, v_3\}$.
    (b) Move all vertices v_i $i = 1, 2, \cdots, K$ to minimize I_K.
    (c) Generate the new vertex v_{K+1} on the curve $\mathbf{C}$.
    (d) If $|I_K - I_{K-1}| \leq \varepsilon$ for a positive constant ε, then stop, else set $\mathbf{C} := \mathbf{C} \cup \{v_{K+1}\}$ and go to 1(b).
2. Condition evaluation:
    After an appropriate number of iterations, evaluate the topological condition of the curve. If the topology of the initial shape derives a contradiction of the tessellations, then go to 3, else go to 1 (b).
3. Second phase:
    (a) Select the new initial point set as an open curve such that $\mathbf{S} := \{v_1, v_2\}$.
    (b) Move all vertices v_i $i = 1, 2, \cdots, K$ to minimize I_K.
    (c) Compute v_{K+1}.
    (d) If $|I_K - I_{K-1}| \leq \varepsilon$ for a positive constant ε, then stop, else set $\mathbf{S} := \mathbf{S} \cup \{v_{k+1}\}$ and go to 3(b).

The criterion defined by eq. (12) does not depend on the dimensions of a space. Therefore, the method extracts the principal curve of a random point set in a 3-space. **Algorithm C** detects the medial set of a random point set as the principal curve. This geometrical property yields the definition of the curve skeleton of a random point set, following the definition of the curve skeleton in the discrete 2-space.

Definition 4. *A polygonal curve derived by* **Algorithm C** *is the curve skeleton of a random point set on a plane and in a space.*

7   Numerical Examples

In Fig. 1, we show in (a) and (b) synthetic random point sets and in b (c) and (d) γ-boundaries extracted by the algorithm. Furthermore, (e) and (f) show the boundary curves of the generator figures estimated by extracting the principal curves from γ-boundaries of the point sets. We can conclude that the extract

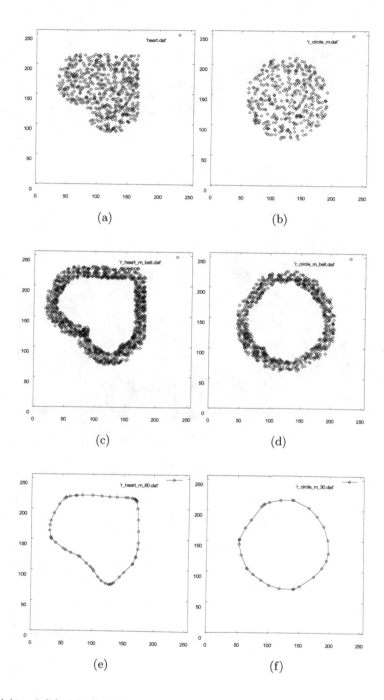

Fig. 1. (a) and (b) are synthetic random point sets. (c) and (d) are their γ-boundary. And (e) and (f) are boundary curves of random point sets detected as the principal curves of the γ-boundary

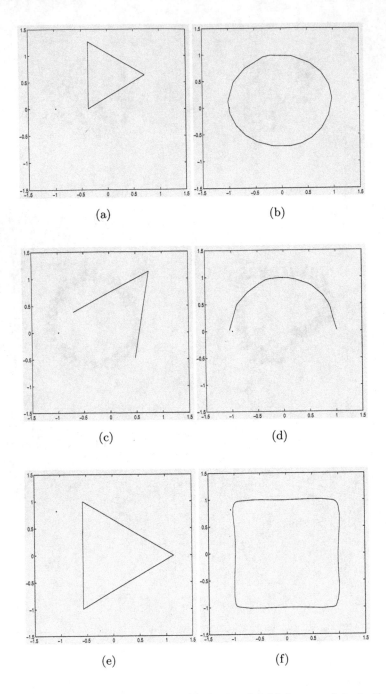

Fig. 2. Initial curves and final curves. (a) A closed initial curve detects the closed principal curve (b). (c) An open initial curve detects the open principal curve (d). (e) A closed initial curve detects the closed principal curve (f). The initial point distributions of (a) and (c) are the same

the boundary curve of a random point by our algorithm is a similar boundary curve of a random point set which human beings extract.

Figure 2 shows the two-dimensional version of topology detection of random point sets. (a), (c), and (e) show the original random point sets and the initial curves superimposed on them. As shown in (b) and (d), starting from a closed curve, if a segment of a polygonal curve appears in the region in which the point distribution is sparse, we conclude the principal curve of random point set is open.

8   Conclusions

We have defined the boundary curve of a random point set and developed an algorithm for the detection the boundary curve using the Delaunay triangulation and the principal curve analysis. Numerical examples promised our definition and extraction algorithms of the boundary curve of a random point set. The method might be used for the extraction of the symbolic data from random point set in a plane.

For the data compression of time varying point sets, we are required to detect the time dependent principal curves of the sequence of time varying point sets. Setting $\mathbf{V}(t_n)$ to be the point set at time $t_n = \Delta n$ for $n = 0, 1, 2, \cdots$, the algorithm developed in the previous sections permits us to compute the principal curve $\mathbf{C}(t_n)$ from point set $\mathbf{V}(t_n)$.

If both principal curves $\mathbf{C}(t_n)$ and $\mathbf{C}(t_{n+1})$ exist in a finite region, that is all $\mathbf{V}(t_n)$ for $n = 1, 3, \cdots$ remaine in a finite rigion, it is possible to adopt $\mathbf{C}(t_n)$ as the initial curve for the computation of $\mathbf{C}(t_{n+1})$. This variation of the algorithm saves the time for the computation of the principal curves for a sequence of point sets. In Figs. 3 and 4, we illustrate sequences of the closed and opne principal curves, respectively of sequences of point sets. The principal curve in each frame is sequentially computed from the principal curve of the previous frame.

Furthermore, once the polygonal boundary of a random point set is estimated, it is possible to compute the linear skeleton of the polygonal boundary [10, 11]. Therefore, we adopt the linear skeleton of the polygonal boundary of a random point set as the linear skeleton of the random point set.

Acknowledgment. We express thanks to Mr. H. Yamagishi for the computation of principal corves for a time sequence of a random point set as a part of his undergraduate project at Chiba University in 2002/2003.

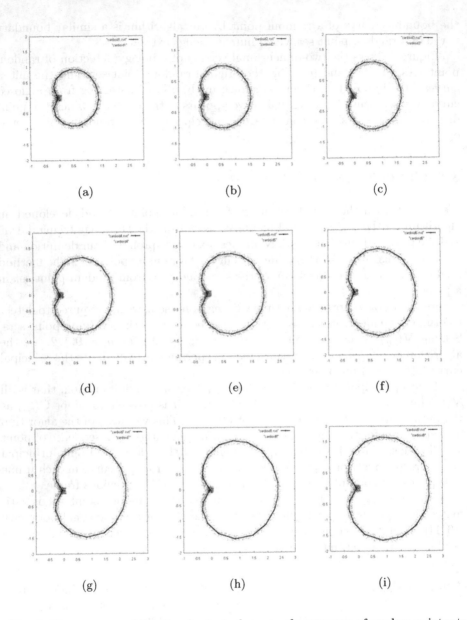

Fig. 3. The sequence of the closed principal curves of a sequence of random point sets. The principal curve in each frame is sequentially computed from the principal curve of the previous frame

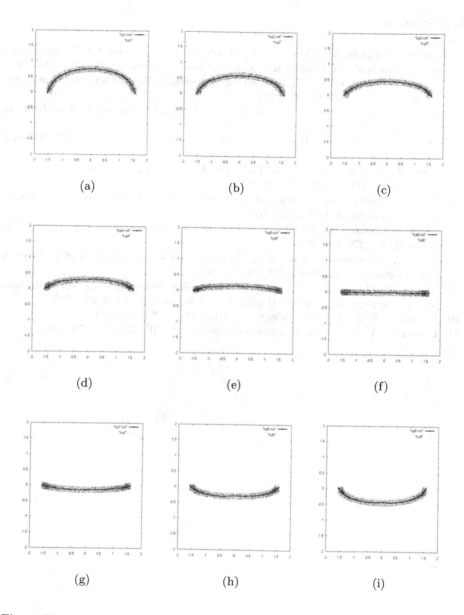

(a)   (b)   (c)

(d)   (e)   (f)

(g)   (h)   (i)

Fig. 4. The sequence of the open principal curves of a sequence of random point sets. The principal curve in each frame is sequentially computed from the principal curve of the previous frame

References

1. Amenta, N., Bern, M., Eppstein, D., The crust and the β-skeleton:Combinatorial curve reconstruction, Graphical Models and Image Processing, **60**, 125–135, 1998.
2. Attali, D., Montanvert, A., Computing and simplifying 2D and 3D continuous skeletons, CVIU, **67**, 261–273, 1997.
3. Edelsbrunner, H., Shape reconstruction with Delaunay complex, Lecture Notes in Computer Science, **1380**, 119–132, 1998.
4. Hasite, T., Stuetzle, T., Principal curves, J. Am. Statistical Assoc., **84**, 502–516, 1989.
5. Kégl, B., Krzyzak, A., Linder, T., Zeger, K., Learning and design of principal curves, IEEE PAMI, **22**, 281–297, 2000.
6. Oja, E., Principal components, minor components, and linear neural networks, Neural Networks, **5**, 927–935, 1992.
7. Imiya, A., Ootani, H., PCA-based model selection and fitting for linear manifolds, LNAI, **2123**, 278–292, 2001.
8. Imiya, A., Kawamoto, K., Learning dimensionality and orientations of 3D objects, Pattern Recognition Letters, **22**, 75–83, 2001.
9. Silverman, B. W., Some aspects of the spline smoothing approach to non-parametric regression curve fitting, J. R. Statist. Soc, B. **47**, 1–52, 1985.
10. Bookstein, F. L., The line-skeleton, CVGIP, **11**, 1233–137, 1979
11. Rosenfeld, A., Axial representations of shapes, CVGIP, **33**, 156–173, 1986.

A Machine Learning Model for Information Retrieval with Structured Documents

Benjamin Piwowarski and Patrick Gallinari

LIP6 – Université Paris 6, 8, rue du capitaine Scott, 75015 Paris, France
{bpiwowar,gallinar}@poleia.lip6.fr

Abstract. Most recent document standards rely on structured representations. On the other hand, current information retrieval systems have been developed for flat document representations and cannot be easily extended to cope with more complex document types. Only a few models have been proposed for handling structured documents, and the design of such systems is still an open problem. We present here a new model for structured document retrieval which allows to compute and to combine the scores of document parts. It is based on bayesian networks and allows for learning the model parameters in the presence of incomplete data. We present an application of this model for ad-hoc retrieval and evaluate its performances on a small structured collection. The model can also be extended to cope with other tasks such as interactive navigation in structured documents or corpus.

1 Introduction

With the expansion of the Web and of large textual resources like e.g. electronic libraries, appeared the need for new textual representations allowing interoperability and providing rich document descriptions. Several structured document representations and formats were then proposed during the last few years together with description languages like e.g. XML. For electronic libraries, Web documents, and other textual resources[1], structured representations are now becoming a standard. This allows for richer descriptions with the incorporation of metadata, annotations, multimedia information, etc. Document structure is an important source of evidence, and in the IR community some authors have argued that it should be considered together with textual content for information access tasks [1]. This is a natural intuitive idea since human understanding of documents heavily relies on their structure. Structured representations allow capturing relations between document parts as it is the case for books or scientific papers. Information retrieval engines should be able to cope with the complexity of new document standards so as to fully exploit the potential of these representations and to provide new functionalities for information access. For example, users may need to access some specific document part, navigate through complex documents or structured collections; queries may address both metadata and textual content. On the other side, most current information retrieval systems still rely on

---

[1] See for example the DocBook standard [18]

P. Perner and A. Rosenfeld (Eds.): MLDM 2003, LNAI 2734, pp. 425–438, 2003.

simple document representations like e.g. bag of words and completely ignore the richer information allowed by structured representations.

Extending information retrieval systems so that they can handle structured documents is not trivial. Many questions for designing such systems are still open, e.g. there is no consensus on how to index these documents, nor on the design of efficient algorithms or models for performing information access tasks. Furthermore, this need being quite recent there is a lack of textual resources for testing and comparing existing systems and prototypes. The goal of this paper is to propose a new generic system for performing different IR tasks on collections of structured documents. Our model is based on bayesian networks (BN), probabilistic inference is used for performing IR tasks, BN parameters are learned so that the model may adapt to different corpora. In the paper, we consider ad-hoc retrieval and focus on the BN model. For simplification, we will only consider the case of hierarchical document structures, i.e. we make the hypothesis that documents may be represented as trees. This encompasses many different types of structured documents. For all other cases (e.g. Web sites), this will be an approximation of the reality which allows to keep inference model complexity down to a reasonable level.

The paper is organized as follows: Sect. 2 makes a review of the literature on structured documents and IR, Sect. 3 describes a general BN model for information retrieval and a particular instance of this model we have developed for document part retrieval in a web site, the last section discusses experiments on a test collection which has been built using the Hermitage museum web site.

2 State of the Art

One of the pioneer work on document structure and IR, is that of Wilkinson [24] who attempted to use the document division into sections of different types (abstract, purpose, title, misc., ...) in order to improve the performances of IR engines. For that he proposed several heuristic for weighting the relative importance of document parts and aggregating their contributions in the computation of the similarity score between a query and a document. Doing this way, he was then able to improve a baseline IR system.

A more recent and more principled approach is the one followed by Lalmas and co-workers [10]–[13]. Their work is based on the theory of evidence which provides a formal framework for handling uncertain information and aggregating scores from different sources. In this approach, when retrieving documents for a given query, evidence about documents is computed by aggregating evidence of sub-document elements. Paragraph evidence is aggregated to compute section evidence which in turn will allow computing the document relevance. They also make use of confidence measures which come with the evidence framework in order to weight the importance of document part score in the global aggregated score. The more confident the system is in a document element, the more important this element will be in the global score. In [12], tests were performed on a small home made collection.

Another important contribution is the HySpirit system developed by Fuhr et al. [5]. There model is based on a probabilistic version of datalog. When complex objects like structured documents are to be retrieved, they use rules modeling how a document part is accessible from another part. The more accessible this part is, the more will it will influence the relevance of the other part.

A series of papers describing on-going research on different aspects of structured document storage and access, ranging from database problems to query languages and IR algorithms is available in the special issue of JASIST [1] and in two SIGIR XML-IR workshops[2]. There is also the recent INEX initiative for the development and the evaluation of XML IR systems. The first meeting of INEX was held in December 2002 and proceedings are available on line[3].

Since Inquery [2],[22], bayesian networks have been shown to be a theoretically sounded IR model, which allows to reach state of the art performances and encompasses different classical IR models. The simple network presented by Croft, Callan and Turtle computes the probability that a query is satisfied by a document[4]. This model has been derived and used for flat documents. Ribeiro and Muntz [20] and Indrawan et al. [6] proposed slightly different approaches also based on belief networks, with flat documents in minds. An extension of the Inquery model, designed for incorporating structural and textual information has been recently proposed by Myaeng et al. [16]. In this approach, a document is represented by a tree. Each node of the tree represents a structural entity of this document (a chapter, a section, a paragraph and so on). This network is thus a tree representation of the internal structure of the document with the whole document as the root and the terms as leaves. The relevance information goes from the document node down to the term nodes. When a new query is processed by this model, the probability that each query term represents the document is computed. In order to obtain this probability, one has to compute the probability that a section represents well the document, then the probability that a term represents well this section and finally the probability that a query represents well this term. In order to keep computations feasible, the authors make several simplifying assumptions. Other approaches consider the use of structural queries (*i.e.* queries that specifies constraints on the document structure). Textual information in those models is boolean (term presence or absence). Such a well known approach is the Proximal Nodes model [17]. The main purpose of these models is to cope with structure in databases. Results here are boolean: a document match or doesn't match the query.

Corpus structure has also been used for categorization, mainly for improving performance when dealing with small quantities of positive examples in the training sets. Some authors make use of specialized classifiers for each category [3],[8], others introduce constraints between different sets of parameters [14]. These investigations have shown that taking into account some type of structure present in the dataset may prove beneficial for the retrieval performances.

Our work is an attempt to develop a formal modeling of documents and of inferences for structured IR. In this sense, our goal is similar to that of Lalmas et al. [10]. Our formal modeling relies on bayesian networks instead of evidence theory in [10] and thus provides an alternative approach to the problem. We believe that this approach allows casting different access information tasks into a unique formalism, and that these models allow performing sophisticated inferences, e.g. they allow to compute the relevance of different document parts in the presence of missing or uncertain information. Compared to other approaches based on BN, we propose a general framework which should allow adapting to different types of structured documents or collections. Another original aspect of our work is that model parameters are learned from data, whereas none of the other approaches relies on machine learning. This allows adapting the model to different document collections and IR tasks.

3   A Model for Structured Information Retrieval

We first describe below (Sect. 3.1) how Bayesian networks can be used to model and retrieve documents or document parts, we then present the general lines of our model (Sect. 3.2) and describe in details the particular implementation we have been using for our experiments (section 3.3).

3.1 Bayesian Networks for Structured Documents Retrieval

Bayesian networks [7],[9],[15],[19] are a *probabilistic framework* where conditional independence relationships between random variables are exploited, in order to simplify or/and to model decision problems. They have been used in different contexts, with many real world applications with an emphasis on diagnosis problems. For textual data, the seminal work of Turtle & Croft [22] raised interest in this framework, and since that, simple BN have been used for IR tasks (see Sect. 2). Bayesian networks provide a formal framework which allows representing the relations between document parts as conditional dependence (or independence). They also allow performing sophisticated inferences on the relevance of document parts for a given query and allowing to model different combinations of evidence. Note that strong simplifying assumptions are needed with textual data, since documents are represented in very large characteristic spaces.

Let us now present using a simple illustrative case how BN could be used to model and perform inference on structured documents. We will suppose that for retrieving documents, $P(d/q)$ is used as the relevance score of document d with respect to query q.

Consider the simple document of Fig. 1a, composed of two sections and three paragraphs. A simple way to take into account the structure of d is to decompose the score $P(d/q)$ as follows:

$$P(d/q) = \sum_{s_1,s_2,p_1,p_2,p_3} P(d,s_1,s_2,p_1,p_2,p_3/q)$$

Where s and p are random variables associated respectively to sections and paragraphs. Suppose now that each random variable (node) in this network can take two values (R = relevant/ $\neg$R = irrelevant with respect to a given query). To compute the joint probability values $P(d,s_1,s_2,p_1,p_2,p_3)$. We need 2^6-1 values for this simple document, and summations with up to 2^5 terms in order to compute $P(d/q)$, $P(s_1/q)$, ... This is clearly infeasible with documents with many structural entities.

BN make use of conditional independence assumptions in order to simplify these computations. Let us proceed with our example.

In our model, BN are used to represent documents, one specific BN being associated to each document. Each node of a BN document model is a boolean variable which indicates whether or not the information associated to this node is relevant to the query. The structure of the BN is directly derived from the document structure. Different BN may be considered for modeling a document. Figures 1b,c show two different models for the simple document of Fig. 1a.

Let us first focus on the d, s and p nodes. Figure 1b represents a model where the relevance of a part is conditioned on the relevance of its subparts, section relevance is computed from the relevance of its paragraphs and document relevance from its sections. Figure 1c represents a model where the dependences are in the reverse order, section relevance depends on document relevance and paragraph relevance depends on section relevance. Both models are valid, but have different semantics.

Variables t_i represent relevance information on textual data, i.e. this is where the text comes into the model. They can be connected different nodes in the BN, examples are given in Figs. 1b,c. In Fig. 1b, textual evidence has been inserted at the paragraph level, whereas in Fig. 1c, it has been considered that textual information is present at any node in the BN. The choice of a particular model depends on the targeted task and on practical considerations (e.g. the complexity of the computation)[5].

The relevance of a document or document part is computed using the conditional independence assumptions encoded in the BN. As an example, the probability of relevance of Sect. 1 with the model 1c is given by:

$$P(s_1) = \sum_{d,t_1,t_2} P(d|t_1)P(t_1)P(s_1|d,t_2)P(t_2),$$

where $P(t_i)$s are prior probabilities and the summation is over the R, ¬R values of the d and t_i variables. With such a model, complexity drops from $O(2^N)$ where N is the number of random variables to $O(N2^{Nmax})$ where N_{max} is the maximal number of parents for a given random variable in the Bayesian network.

3.2 General Model

We will now describe our BN model and in the next section, detail the particular implementation we have used for our experiments. In our bayesian network, there are two different kinds of variables, those associated with the relevance of a structural part and those associated with the relevance of textual data. Both are binary and take values from the set {R = Relevant to the query, ¬R = Irrelevant to the query }. The former are computed using inference in the bayesian network, and the latter may be computed by any probabilistic model as described below and are *a priori* probabilities for our BN. The BN thus propagates relevance probabilities from one node to its descendants. Although the binary scale may appear restrictive, it is used in most information retrieval models since it allows for a limited computational cost.

---

[5] The model in Fig. 1c can be used for passage retrieval or page retrieval in a web site as it will be shown in our experiments, whereas the other one (b) is more directed towards document retrieval where information about relevance of paragraphs is used to compute the document relevance

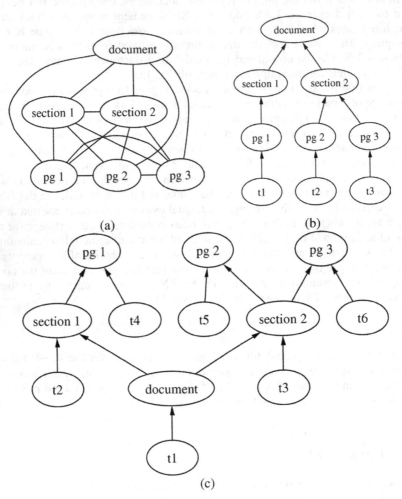

Fig. 1. Three different models of the same document. (a) All parts are dependent, (b) and (c) are two different models for conditional independences in the document network

Let T be a variable associated with textual data. In our experiments, text relevance *prior* probabilities are computed by the Okapi model [23] as follows:

$$P(T) = cosine(T,q)$$

Okapi gives scores between 0 and 1 which are used here *as* probabilities. Okapi has been used for simplicity since it is also our baseline model in the experiments, but other models could be used as well for computing priors. Note that the same BN framework could also be used for multimedia documents provided the relevance probability of content elements is computed by a model adapted to the media type of this element.

For random variables associated with structural parts, we do not use *prior* probabilities but conditional probabilities such as:

$$P(A \text{ relevance} | B_1, ..., B_n \text{ relevance}),$$

where the B_i are the parents of A in the bayesian network (Fig. 2). In the model used in our experiments, these conditional probabilities are stored in a simple table for each node. They are learned from data and the probability estimates are the parameters of our BN model, they will be denoted Θ in the following.

This model operates in two modes, training and retrieval, which we now describe.

Training

In order to fit a specific corpus, parameters are learnt from observations using the Estimation Maximization (EM) algorithm. An observation $O^{(i)}$ is a query with its associated relevance assessments (document/part is relevant or not relevant to the query). EM [4] optimizes the model parameters Θ with respect to the likelihood L of the observed data $L(O, \Theta) = \log P(O / \Theta)$ where $O = (O^{(1)}, ... , O^{(N)})$ are the N observations.

Observations may or may not be *complete*, *i.e.* relevance assessments need not to be known for each document part in the BN in order to learn the parameters. Each observation $O^{(i)}$ can be decomposed in two sets of variables $O^{(i)} = (E^{(i)}, H^{(i)})$ where

- $E^{(i)}$ corresponds to structural entities for which we know whether they are relevant or not, *i.e.* structural parts for which we have a relevance assessment. $E^{(i)}$ is called the evidence and is a vector of 0/1 in our model.

- $H^{(i)}$ corresponds to hidden observations, i.e. all other nodes of the BN. Note that variables T associated with textual relevance (Okapi *a priori*) are in this set.

Instead of optimizing directly L, EM optimizes the auxiliary function

$$L' = \sum_{i=1}^{N} \sum_{H^{(i)}} Q(H^{(i)}) \log P(E^{(i)}, H^{(i)} / \Theta)$$

with

$$Q(H^{(i)}) = P(H^{(i)} / E^{(i)}, \Theta)$$

EM attempts to find the parameters maximizing the probability to observe the relevance judgments given in the training set. Optimizing L' is performed in two steps. The first one is the *Expectation* step in which we optimize L' with respect to Q -i.e. Q is estimated while Θ is kept fixed. This corresponds to a simple inference step in our bayesian network. The second one is the *Maximization* step where L' is optimized with respect to Θ. This step is performed by constraint optimization. In the first section, we gave the update formula used for our specific application.

Retrieval

For retrieval, when a new query Q has to be answered, *a priori* probabilities are first computed. For textual variables T, this is done using baseline models as described above; for non textual variables, ad-hoc priors will be used. After that, joint probabilities needed for scoring the document can be computed using the learned conditional probabilities and the priors. This is done using an inference algorithm suited to our bayesian network. Documents with highest scores are then presented to the user. If we are interested into retrieving document parts which correspond to BN nodes, instead of whole documents, we can proceed in the same way.

1. Prehistoric art
    a. Paleolithic art
        i. Female figurine
        ii. Anthropomorhpic figurine
        iii. ...
    b. Neolithic art
    c. ...
2. Antiquity
    a. Ancient Italy
    b. ...
3. ...

Fig. 2. A Web site viewed as a structured document

3.3   Instantiating the Model for Document Part Retrieval

We used an instance of this general model for retrieval on a hierarchically organized Web site: a part of the Hermitage museum web site in St Petersburg. This test collection was kindly given to us by M. Lalmas [12] and is one of the very few structured collection of documents where queries and corresponding relevance assessments are provided. This is a single Web site structured in 441 pages. Our goal here, similar to that of [12] is to retrieve pages relevant to a query, such pages are supposed to provide good entry points to relevant material on the site. For this particular application, we consider the Web site as a single document, hierarchically structured as shown in Fig. 3.

The structure of our network is directly inspired from the structure of the Web site. The relevance of each page depends on the relevance of its text and the relevance of the page that has a link to it. For example, on figure 4, "P_2 relevance" given "P_1 relevance" and "P_2 text relevance" (T_2) is independent of other variables. In other words, "P_2 relevance" is *determined* by its "text relevance" and "P_1 relevance"

As for the conditional probability tables associated to the nodes of this model, we will distinguish 2 cases.

For all nodes except the root P_1 the $P(P/T_i, P_i$ parent) are learned from the data via EM as described below.

For the main page P_1 there is no other source of information than text to assess a relevance judgment for the main page. P_1 relevance is then:

$$P(P1) = P(P/T_1 = R) \, P(T_1 = R) + P(P/T_1 = \neg R) \, P(T_1 = \neg R)$$

With the conditional probabilities set as follows:

$$P(P/T_1 = R) = 1 \text{ and } P(P/T_1 = \neg R) = 0$$

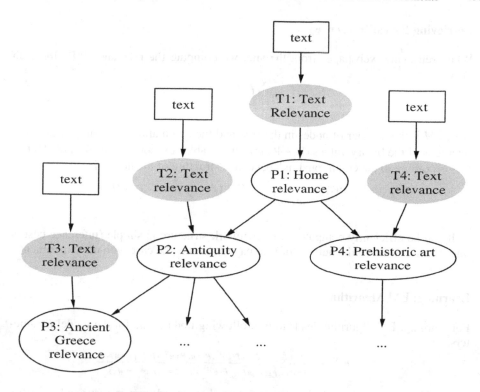

Fig. 3. A part of the network used for the Hermitage Web site. In this example, four different pages in three different levels are shown (home page, antiquity, ancient Greece, prehistoric art). The Hermitage Web site contains 441 pages.

In order to reduce the number of parameters to be learned, different nodes in the BN do share their parameters. For this application, all nodes within one layer do share the same conditional probability table. Let $\theta_{a,b,c}^{(l)}$ denote the conditional probability parameters for layer l.

Under the above shared parameters assumption, we have for the network of Fig. 4:

$$\theta_{a,b,c}^{(2)} = P(P_2=a|T_2=b,P_1=c) = P(P_4=a|T_4=b,P_1=c)$$

Where a, b and c may take the values R or ¬R respectively for the current node P_2 or P_4, the text node T_2 or T_4 and the parent node P_1. Note that except for $l = 1$, $\theta^{(l)}$ is an array with 2^3 real values. Besides providing more robust estimators, parameter sharing allows to learn general relationships between structural entities of the Web site. We will then learn *how* the relevance of the homepage influences the relevance of department pages, and *how* relevance of department pages influences the relevance of a specific collection, and so on. Additional constraints may be imposed as described in the experiments below (Sect. 4).

Retrieving Pages: Inference

When retrieving web pages from the site, we compute the relevance $P(P_i)$ for each page:

$$P(P_i) = \sum_{\{p_k, t_k\}_{k \neq i}} P(P_1, ..., P_M, T_1..., T_M)$$

where M is the number of nodes in the BN, and the summation is taken over all combinations of the binary values $(R, \neg R)$ for all variables except P_i. This formula factorizes according to the conditional independence structure of the network:

$$P(P_i) = \sum_{\{p_k, t_k\}_{k \neq i}} \prod_{j=1..M} P(P_j / P_j \text{ parent}, T_j) P(T_j)$$

It can be efficiently computed if the network structure is simple (inference cost is linear with respect to the number of web pages), as it is the case with our experiments.

Learning: EM Algorithm

For learning, EM algorithm leads to the following update rule for the model parameters:

$$\theta^{(l)}_{a,b,c} \leftarrow \frac{1}{K_{i,b,c}} \sum_{i=1}^{N} \sum_{P \text{ in level } l} \frac{P(E^{(i)}, P = a, P \text{ text} = b, P \text{ parent} = c)}{P(E^{(i)}, P \text{ text} = b, P \text{ parent} = c)}$$

where N is the number of observations, and the second sum is restricted to pages where $P(E^{(i)}, P \text{ text}= b, P \text{ parent}=c) \neq 0$. K is a normalizing constant that insures that probabilities sum to 1:

$$K_{l,b,c} = \theta^{(i)}_{\text{relevant},b,c} + \theta^{(i)}_{\text{not relevant},b,c}$$

4   Experiments

The test collection contains 441 documents and 15 queries that were randomly split into a training and a test set. For comparison, we used as a baseline model Okapi [23] to compute the relevance of the web pages. Okapi is one of the best known, top ranking, IR model for ad-hoc retrieval on flat documents, with this model, corpus structure is ignored. We also used the model proposed by Lalmas and Moutogianni as described in [12], this model takes into account the corpus structure.

Each document is a single page of the Hermitage web site. The maximum depth (largest distance between the main page and any other page) of this site is 6 and there is an average number of children of 1 (ranging from 0 to 16).

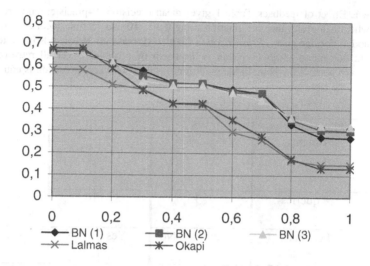

Fig. 4. Precision-recall curve with Okapi, Lalmas & Moutogianni model and our model (BN).

Different experiments were performed with different settings for the model parameters. Our model is denoted "BN (*depth*)" where d*epth* corresponds to the maximum number of different conditional probabilities tables we learn. For example, with depth 1, we constrain $\theta^{ij}=\theta^{ij} \; \forall \; i, j$. (*i.e.* only one set of parameters is learned for the whole network), with a depth of 2 we constrain $\theta^{ij}=\theta^{ij}$ .for $i, j \geq 2$ and so on.

In our experiments, we performed 9 EM steps in order to learn the parameters: since our database is small, the EM algorithm converged very fast.

The first experiment () compares three different models: Okapi, Lalmas' and ours. We performed cross-validation on the dataset. The query set was divided into 5 equal parts (3 queries each), we performed 5 different runs, each time using 3 queries for testing and 12 for training. Results were averaged over all runs. This allows our bayesian model to optimize its parameters with a sufficient number of queries while using all the queries for the evaluation.

In Fig. 4, *recall* is the ratio between the number of retrieved relevant documents and the total number of relevant documents. *Precision* is the ratio between the number of retrieved relevant documents and the number of retrieved documents.

All experiments show that for this dataset, the BN model does improve the baseline Okapi. This is a nice result since Okapi is a very efficient IR system which has been tuned over years. It also performed better than Lalmas & Moutogianni model in our experiments. The increase is significant as can be seen on the figure. For all experiments, the three BN variants do offer similar performances, the BN with a depth of 3 being slightly better. Overfitting was not observed even when using more parameters and performing more EM steps.

Table 1. Effect of feedback Table 1 gives mean precision, R-precision and break-even measures when using relevance information using the 5, 10 and 15 first documents returned by our BN model. For one query, *R-precision* is the precision at rank R where R is the total number of relevant document. *Mean Precision* is the mean of precisions over all retrieved documents. *Break-even point* is the point in the precision/recall curve where precision is equal to recall. All values in the table are averages over all test queries.

# Relevance assessments	5		10		15	
# queries	13		10		9	
Feedback	Yes	No	Yes	No	Yes	No
Mean precision	0.46	0.32	0.38	0.17	0.39	0.16
R-precision	0.43	0.25	0.37	0.10	0.36	0.13
Break-even point	0.47	0.34	0.39	0.19	0.40	0.16

In a second series of experiments, we introduced feedback in the BN model. We first use the BN model to rank documents with respect to a query q. We use the known relevance assessments for the top n retrieved documents as evidence for the BN. In a practical situation, this feedback will be provided by the user. Let $d'_1,...,d'_n$ denote the top n ranked documents.

We then compute for any document not in the top n its relevance for q, knowing the relevance of the d's. Stated otherwise, with feedback, we compute for any document d not in the top n $P(d/q, d'_1,...,d'_n)$ instead of $P(d/q)$ without feedback. In the BN, this means that inference is performed with a known value (R or I) for the variables corresponding to $d'_1,...,d'_n$. We then perform an evaluation[7] using cross-validation as above. $P(d/q, d'_1,...,d'_n)$ represents the distribution of the probabilities of relevance *knowing that the user found d' relevant to his/her need.*

This experiment measures the potential of the model for incorporating evidence (feedback) during a session. It also measures in some way the ability of the system to help interactive navigation through the site: when the user provides feedback on some documents, the system takes this information into account and outputs a list of new documents.

---

[7] Note that we removed the query from the evaluation set when all relevant documents were in the top n documents, since looking for other documents had no sense. We thus indicate in Table 1 how many queries were used for each evaluation.

When we increase the value of n, fewer documents remain in the test set and he performance measures decrease. The values above should be compared for a given value of n. It shows a clear improvement when using feedback. This demonstrates the ability of the model to incorporate feedback in a natural way and to perform tasks such as interactive navigation in a structured corpus.

5 Conclusion

We have described a new model for performing IR on structured documents. It is based on BN whose conditional probability tables are learned from the data via EM. Experiments on a small structured document collection have shown that this model can significantly improve performance compared to a state of the art "flat" information retrieval system like Okapi. These results show that even simple structures like the one we have been dealing with are a valuable source of information for retrieving documents. Of course, further experiments are needed in order to assess this improvement on different types of corpora and on larger collections. The only corpus we are aware of for XML-IR is the one being built for the INEX initiative. We are currently participating to this task using a slightly different model than the one described here, but our results are still too preliminary to be presented here.

The model has still to be improved and developed in order to obtain an operational structured information retrieval system. Nevertheless results are already encouraging and findings are interesting enough to continue investigating this model. Bayesian networks can handle different sources of information and allows training which proves to be important for many IR applications.

Acknowledgement. Many thanks to M. Lalmas who gave us the structured collection we have been using in our experiments.

References

[1] ACM SIGIR 2000 Workshop on XML and Information Retrieval. Athens, Greece. July 28, 2000 – also published in JASIST, Vol 53, n° 6, 2002, special topic issue : XML.

[2] Jamie P. Callan, W. Bruce Croft, and Stephen M. Harding. The INQUERY Retrieval System. In A. Min Tjoa and Isidro Ramos, editors, *Database and Expert Systems Applications, Proceedings of the International Conference*, pages 78–83, Valencia, Spain, 1992. Springer-Verlag.

[3] Soumen Chakrabarti, Byron Dom, Rakesh Agrawal, and Prabhakar Raghavan. Using taxonomy, discriminants, and signatures for navigating in text databases. In *23rd International Conference on Very Large Data Bases*, Athens, Greece, 1997.

[4] A.P. Dempster, N.M. Laird, and D.B. Rubin. Maximum Likelihood from incomplete data via de EM algorithm. *The Journal of Royal Statistical Society*, 39:1–37, 1977.

[5] Fuhr, N. and Rölleke, T. HySpirit – a Probabilistic Inference Engine for Hypermedia Retrieval in Large Databases. In: Schek, H.-J.; Saltor, F.;Ramos, I.; Alonso, G. (eds.). *Proceedings of the 6th International Conference on Extending Database Technology (EDBT)*, Valencia, Spain, pages 24–38. Springer, Berlin, 1998.

[6] Maria Indrawan, Desra Ghazfan, and Bala Srinivasan. Using Bayesian Networks as Retrieval Engines. In *ACIS 5th Australasian Conference on Information Systems*, pages 259–271, Melbourne, Australia, 1994.

[7] Finn Verner Jensen. *An introduction to Bayesian Networks*. UCL Press, London, England, 1996.

[8] Daphne Koller and Mehran Sahami. Hierarchically Classifying Documents Using Very Few Words. In *ICML-97: Proceedings of the Fourteenth International Conference on Machine Learning*, pages 435–443, San Francisco, CA, USA, 1997. Morgan Kaufmann.

[9] Paul Krause. Learning Probabilistic Networks. 1998.

[10] Mounia Lalmas. Dempster-Shafer's Theory of Evidence Applied to Structured Documents: Modelling Uncertainty. In *Proceedings of the 20th Annual International ACM SIGIR*, pages 110–118, Philadelphia, PA, USA, July 1997. ACM.

[11] Mounia Lalmas. Uniform representation of content and structure for structured document retrieval. Technical report, Queen Mary & Westfield College, University of London, London, England, 2000.

[12] Mounia Lalmas and Ekaterini Moutogianni. A Dempster-Shafer indexing for the focussed retrieval of a hierarchically structured document space: Implementation and experiments on a web museum collection. In *6th RIAO Conference, Content-Based Multimedia Information Access*, Paris, France, April 2000.

[13] Mounia Lalmas, I. Ruthven, and M. Theophylactou. Structured document retrieval using Dempster-Shafer's Theory of Evidence: Implementation and evaluation. Technical report, University of Glasgow, UK, August 1997.

[14] Andrew McCallum, Ronald Rosenfeld, Tom Mitchell, and Andrew Y. Ng. Improving Text Classification by Shrinkage in a Hierarchy of Classes. In Ivan Brasko and Saso Dzeroski, editors, *International Conference on Machine Learning (ICML 98)*, pages 359–367. Morgan Kaufmann, 1998.

[15] Kevin Patrick Murphy. A Brief Introduction to Graphical Models and Bayesian Networks. web: http://www.cs.berkeley.edu/~murphyk/Bayes/bayes.html, October 2000.

[16] Sung Hyon Myaeng, Dong-Hyun Jang, Mun-Seok Kim, and Zong-Cheol Zhoo. A Flexible Model for Retrieval of SGML documents. In W. Bruce Croft, Alistair Moffat, C.J. van Rijsbergen, Ross Wilkinson, and Justin Zobel, editors, *Proceedings of the 21st Annual International ACM SIGIR Conference on Research and Development in Information Retrieval*, pages 138–140, Melbourne, Australia, August 1998. ACM Press, New York.

[17] Gonzalo Navarro and Ricardo Baeza-Yates. Proximal Nodes: A Model to Query Document Databases by Content and Structure. *ACM TOIS*, 15(4):401–435, October 1997.

[18] OASIS. Docbook standard. http://www.oasis-open.org/specs/docbook.shtml

Author Index

Lecture Notes in Artificial Intelligence (LNAI)

Lecture Notes in Computer Science